HADID

Philip Jodidio

HADID

Zaha Hadid
Complete Works 1979–today

TASCHEN

CONTENTS

CONTENTS

THE EXPLOSION REFORMING SPACE

In a time of fluid uncertainty that envelops health and security, the economy, environment, and politics, it would seem natural that contemporary architecture should reflect the state of flux, and most probably take no discernable direction, wavering between ascetic minimalism, green proselytism, and neo-baroque decoration. Some, though, are courageous enough to make a wholehearted grasp at continuity, to dare say that there can be, indeed is, a new paradigm worthy of interest, even emulation. Few may have been more qualified to issue this rallying call than Zaha Hadid, winner of the 2004 Pritzker Prize. Her untimely death in March of 2016 was universally mourned. It is Patrik Schumacher, Hadid's longtime collaborator, who signed a text in the 2008 catalog of the Venice Architecture Biennale that reads in part: "There is an unmistakable new style manifest within avant-garde architecture today. Its most striking characteristic is its complex and dynamic curvelinearity. Beyond this obvious surface feature one can identify a series of new concepts and methods that are so different from the repertoire of both traditional and modern architecture that one might speak of the emergence of a new paradigm for architecture. The shared concepts, formal repertoires, tectonic logics, and computational techniques that characterize this work are engendering the formation of a new hegemonic style: *Parametricism*. Parametricism is the great new style after Modernism. Postmodernism and Deconstructivism were transitional episodes that ushered in this new, long wave of research and innovation. Modernism was founded on the concept of space. Parametricism differentiates fields. *Fields* are full, as if filled with a fluid medium. From compositions of parts we proceed to dynamic fields of particles.[1] This sensibility has been both radicalized *and* refined over the course of 30 years of work. New modes of representation played a crucial part in making this possible."[2]

Whether the name "parametricism" sticks and, indeed, becomes that of a style or a recognized school of contemporary architecture or not remains to be seen, but it is clear that Zaha Hadid Architects has called attention to a method and an approach to architecture that has challenged many of its fundamental assumptions, beginning just over 30 years ago. Aside from her willingness to question geometry, or more precisely the very organization and spatial disposition of architecture, Hadid showed a remarkable consistency and continuity in her thought over the entire period of her professional activity. Nor is this continuity tied to the kind of grid-driven style that animated Richard Meier or Tadao Ando, for example. Her built work and projects do resemble each other in terms of the fluidity of their plans and the movement of space and surface that she generated, but from the angular Vitra Fire Station (Weil am Rhein, Germany, 1991–93; see page 116) to the more recent *Dune Formations* series of objects (David Gill Galleries, 2007; see page 562), there is a spirit that casts doubt onto the architecture and furniture of the past. What if the many assumptions of architecture and design, from rectilinear form to the ways that buildings and furniture function, were all subject to question and indeed to profound renewal? If nature is capable of generating an endless variety of objects that have a fundamental legitimacy beyond any conceivable question, might architecture, the art of creating the built environment, not also be able to attain a similar legitimacy by reading context and function in new ways, by willfully creating voids as well as solids, by doubting the primacy of the right angle, itself very rare in nature? Would this be the artificial nature that many architects and thinkers have imagined?

HYBRIDIZE, MORPH, DE-TERRITORIALIZE

Schumacher describes parametricism in formal terms that may seem less revolutionary than fundamentals of Hadid's architecture that clearly go beyond the formalist debate. "The program/style consists," says Schumacher, "of methodological rules: some tell us what paths of research to avoid (negative heuristics), and others what paths to pursue (positive heuristics). The defining heuristics of *parametricism* are fully reflected in the taboos and dogmas of our design culture. Negative heuristics: avoid familiar typologies, avoid platonic/hermetic objects, avoid clear-cut zones/territories, avoid repetition, avoid straight lines, avoid right angles, avoid corners [...] Positive heuristics: hybridize, morph, de-territorialize, deform, iterate, use splines, nurbs, generative components, script rather than model [...]"[3]

Just as Zaha Hadid formed a remarkably coherent and consistent oeuvre over a period of 30 years, often returning to ideas first mooted early in her career, so, too, any description of her work may logically be made up of strands that, when brought together, describe her accomplishment not as a linear progression, but as an interwoven complex of idea, line, and form. It is thus by no means incongruous to leap back from the 2008 Venice Architecture Biennale and the manifesto "Experimentation within a Long Wave of Innovation" to a moment almost 30 years ago, when Zaha Hadid first came to the attention of the general public.

The Oxford English Dictionary defines deconstruction as "a strategy of critical analysis [...] directed toward exposing unquestioned metaphysical assumptions and internal contradictions in philosophical and literary language." Rendered popular by the French philosopher Jacques Derrida (1930–2004), deconstruction was used in the philosophical sense to explain some architecture. Derrida himself applied his thinking to architecture in a 1986 text about Bernard Tschumi's "Follies" in the Parc de la Villette in Paris, "Point de folie: Maintenant l'architecture." He spoke of "programmatic deconstruction," or a "general dislocation of the follies that seems to question everything that gave meaning to architecture until now. More precisely, that which related the order of architecture to meaning. The follies deconstruct, but not only, the semantics of architecture."[4]

The radical program implied in literary deconstruction was indeed not that far from the surprising forms that first emerged in public discourse with the 1988 exhibition curated by Philip Johnson and Mark Wigley at New York's Museum of Modern Art (MoMA) *Deconstructivist Architecture*. Seven architects were selected for that show: Frank Gehry, Daniel Libeskind, Rem Koolhaas, Peter Eisenman, Zaha Hadid, Coop Himmelb(l)au, and Bernard Tschumi with his structures for the Parc de la Villette. The premise of the exhibition confirmed the idea of a radical about-face in contemporary architecture. "Architecture has always been a central cultural institution valued above all for its provision of stability and order. These qualities are seen to arise from the geometric purity of its formal composition," wrote Mark Wigley. "The projects in this exhibition," he went on to write, "mark a different sensibility, one in which the dream of pure form has been disturbed. Form has thus become contaminated. The dream has become a kind of nightmare."[5]

If not otherwise indicated, all quotes come from the interview with Zaha Hadid and Patrik Schumacher by the author, London, April 10, 2008.

[1] "We might think of liquids in motion, structured by radiating waves, laminal flows, and spiraling eddies," says Patrik Schumacher.

[2] Patrik Schumacher, "Zaha Hadid Architects – Experimentation within a Long Wave of Innovation," in *Out There: Architecture Beyond Building*, Marsilio Editori, Venice, 2008, vol. 3, pp. 91–92.

[3] Ibid., pp. 94–95.

[4] Jacques Derrida, "Point de folie: Maintenant l'architecture," in *La Case Vide*, La Villette, 1985. "Une 'déconstruction programmatique,' une dislocation générale (dans laquelle les folies) entraînent tout ce qui semble avoir, jusqu'à maintenant, donné sens à l'architecture. Plus précisément ce qui semble avoir ordonné l'architecture au sens. Elles déconstruisent d'abord, mais non seulement, la sémantique architecturale."

[5] Mark Wigley, in *Deconstructivist Architecture*, The Museum of Modern Art, New York, 1988.

THE TWISTED CENTER
OF MODERNIST PURITY

While the word "deconstruction" implied an act of destruction to many, Mark Wigley and the architects involved were pursuing a different agenda. "A deconstructive architect is not one who dismantles buildings, but one who locates the inherent dilemmas within buildings. The deconstructive architect puts the pure forms of the architectural tradition on the couch and identifies the symptoms of a repressed impurity. The impurity is drawn to the surface by a combination of gentle coaxing and violent torture: the form is interrogated," said Wigley.[6] Wigley and others related the work of the seven selected architects to the artistic revolution embraced by the Russian Constructivist and Suprematist movements shortly after the more political upheavals of 1917. "The Russian avant-garde posed a threat to tradition by breaking the classical rules of composition, in which the balanced, hierarchical relationship between forms creates a unified whole. Pure forms were now used to produce 'impure,' skewed geometric compositions."[7] It is a fact that drawings by Vladimir Krinskii reproduced in the exhibition catalog, or the Suprematist paintings of Kasimir Malevich, immediately bring to mind the work of Frank Gehry, or of the sole female participant, Zaha Hadid. It was Hadid's winning entry for the Hong Kong Peak International Competition (1982–83; see page 50) that Johnson and Wigley chose to show at MoMA. Wigley wrote of this design for a health resort: "The club is stretched between the emptiness of the void and the density of the underground solids, domains normally excluded from modern architecture but found within it by pushing modernism to its limits, forcing it apart. In this way, the pleasure palace, the hedonist resort, is located in the twisted center of modernist purity."[8]

Twenty years later, Zaha Hadid and her partner Patrik Schumacher still referred to the MoMA exhibition. "The MoMA show concerned the contraction of two words," said Hadid, "deconstruction in the sense of thought and Constructivism, the Russian movement. Using those two words made it a hybrid thing. I believe that show was very important because it was the first time that people began to look at non-normative architecture. Unfortunately, in that period there was not great deconstructivist work done. None of us were building, which I think is a pity." Hadid's attachment to the work of the Suprematists was evident in such very early works as a meticulous painting executed for her thesis (*Horizontal Tektonik, Malevich's Tektonik, London*, acrylic on cartridge, 128 x 89 cm, 1976–77, San Francisco Museum of Modern Art; see page 32). More than 10 years after her thesis, by the time of the MoMA exhibition, Hadid had gone on to apply the lessons of Suprematism to architecture in a way that took real structure into account. As an architect, and one formed in the circle of Koolhaas, she had had the intuition to realize that the time to change the art of building had come. Others involved in the MoMA exhibition, like Frank Gehry, left a strong mark on contemporary architecture, but in Gehry's case it might seem that the art is all, a dancing symphony of forms that do indeed free buildings from their geometric constraints but may not address the deeper questions of the very logic of architecture to which Zaha Hadid was always attached.

BREAKING ALL THE RULES
BUT DRAWING IT RIGHT

Although Wigley had affirmed that these architects were not engaged in dismantling, Patrik Schumacher has a slightly different take on the time: "You could

[6]   Mark Wigley, in *Deconstructivist Architecture*, The Museum of Modern Art, New York, 1988.

[7]   Ibid.

[8]   Ibid.

[9]   "Zaha Hadid Becomes the First Woman to Receive the Pritzker Architecture Prize," The Pritzker Architecture Prize, accessed on July 1, 2013, http://www.pritzkerprize.com/2004/announcement.

see deconstructivism as a transitional style. It was a kind of creative destruction that set the scene for a positive agenda." Perhaps Wigley's own definition of the movement was too modest when it came to a figure like Zaha Hadid, who went on to redefine architecture in ways that defy the description of "skewed geometric compositions" employed in 1988. "The MoMA show was interesting," said Hadid recently, "because it broke rules and went away from ideas of typology. The most critical thing was the breaking up of plan organization and section. Contrary to what some people thought, we were very precise. Our work was very precise in terms of geometry, it was not a cartoon. Breaking up typology, breaking the rules, these were very important steps because it was the first time that people became aware of these possibilities."

From the first, contrary to what some critics might have once suggested, Zaha Hadid's work was based not only on a full understanding of architecture but also of draftsmanship and of the profound relationships between the two. This fact of course immediately distanced her somewhat from the Russian revolutionaries of another era who were often engaged more in geometric speculations and aesthetic questioning than in any real desire to build. Hadid combined their challenge to accept spatial alignments with a real knowledge of architecture and that is what made her more than "deconstructivist." The combination of a cerebral revolution in architecture with the facts of construction and its possibilities has animated the work of Zaha Hadid Architects throughout the existence of the firm. When asked about her relationship to structural engineers, Zaha Hadid responded: "We always work with the same ones, although with different firms. We have established a system. That also allowed us to think of space in a different way and I think it has been a very exciting collaboration. Engineers don't come in at the end, they come in right from the beginning. They have to be involved in these enormous landscape structures that also hold the floor or support the roof." Rather than mistrusting engineers as any innovative architect might, Hadid embraced their assistance, but in the process created a method that integrates their input into a completed whole. This process began even before she really built much, another proof of a constancy and drive that have today earned her a justifiable reputation as one of the most important creative architects in the world.

THE POWER OF
INNOVATION REVEALED

Zaha Hadid was born in Baghdad in 1950 and studied at the Architectural Association (AA) in London, where she won the Diploma prize in 1977. She became a partner in the Office for Metropolitan Architecture (OMA) and taught with OMA founder Rem Koolhaas at the AA, where she led her own studio until 1987. She held the Kenzo Tange Chair at the Harvard University Graduate School of Design; the Sullivan Chair at the University of Illinois, School of Architecture (Chicago); and guest professorships at the Hochschule für bildende Künste (Hamburg, Germany), and the University of Applied Arts (Vienna, Austria), and was the Eero Saarinen Visiting Professor of Architectural Design at Yale University (New Haven, Connecticut, 2004). Few architects have had such a considerable impact through graphic works (paintings and drawings) and teaching as Hadid. Indeed, until a recent date, her built work might have been considered decidedly scarce by the standards of world-class architects. The first patron for one of her built works was Rolf Fehlbaum, chief executive officer of the furniture company Vitra. The Vitra Fire Station (Weil am Rhein, Germany, 1991–93; see page 116) entered magazines and books on contemporary architecture even before it was completed—its sharp, angular concrete design challenging the aesthetics of almost every known building. Fehlbaum was a member of the 2004 Pritzker Prize jury that gave its prestigious award to a woman for the first time with Hadid. "Without ever building," said Fehlbaum on that occasion, "Zaha Hadid would have radically expanded architecture's repertoire of spatial articulation. Now that the implementation in complex buildings is happening, the power of her innovation is fully revealed."[9]

WHAT IF THE MANY ASSUMPTIONS OF ARCHITECTURE AND DESIGN FROM RECTILINEAR FORM TO THE WAYS THAT BUILDINGS AND FURNITURE FUNCTION WERE ALL SUBJECT TO PROFOUND RENEWAL?

The Vitra project was followed by Landscape Formation One (LF One, Weil am Rhein, Germany, 1996–99; see page 130); the first museum built by a woman in the United States, the Lois & Richard Rosenthal Center for Contemporary Art (Cincinnati, Ohio, USA, 1997–2003; see page 164); Terminus Hoenheim-Nord (Strasbourg, France, 1998–2001; see page 148); and the Bergisel Ski Jump (Innsbruck, Austria, 1999–2002; see page 156). Aside from a pavilion under the Millennium Dome in Greenwich (London, UK, 2000, see page 142), these were the completed works of Hadid when she won the Pritzker Prize. Lord Jacob Rothschild, Pritzker Jury Chairman, commented: "For the first time, a woman—and a very remarkable one—has been awarded the Pritzker Prize. Zaha Hadid, born in Iraq, has worked throughout her life in London—but such are the forces of conservatism that sadly one cannot find one single building of hers in the capital city where she has made her home. For more than a decade she was admired for her genius in envisioning spaces which lesser imaginations believed could not be built. For those who were prepared to take the risk from Vitra's Fire Station to a ski jump on a mountainside in Austria, to a tram station in France, and more recently to a museum building in a town in the deep midwest of the United States, the impact has been transforming. At the same time as her theoretical and academic work, as a practicing architect she has been unswerving in her commitment to modernism. Always inventive, she's moved away from existing typology, from high tech, and has shifted the geometry of buildings. No project of hers is like the one before, but the defining characteristics remain consistent."[10]

LIKE A CHTHONIC CREATURE

At this defining stage in her career, when Hadid was 54 years old, quite young by the standards of world-renowned architects, she had just begun to leave her mark in the area of actual completed buildings, but one might ask if Lord Rothschild and others were right in putting the emphasis on her "unswerving commitment to modernism" or, indeed, in defining her work in terms of "shifted" geometry. In an essay about the LF One pavilion, the German architecture critic Michael Mönninger wrote: "The gardening pavilion rises from the ground like a chthonic creature whose direction of movement is linear through adaptation to the underground. The streamlined bends of the architectural path bundle are, if seen strictly, not space-creating but rather space-avoiding elements in between which the ancillary rooms, the café, the exhibition hall and the environmental center literally unfold in passing."[11] The words, 11 years earlier, of Mark Wigley immediately return with a new relevance: "... the emptiness of the void and the density of the underground solids, domains normally excluded from modern architecture but found within it by pushing modernism to its limits, forcing it apart." The Greek term employed by Mönninger, "a chthonic creature" (deities or spirits of the Underworld in ancient Greek mythology), might seem to be at the very opposite end of the spectrum when compared to a seminal work like Le Corbusier's Villa Savoye (Poissy, France, 1929), which sits on the ground so lightly, its pristine forms unrelated to anything so dark and unpredictable as the Underworld. Other architects, like Peter Eisenman, have experimented actively with forms related to the earth, such as plate tectonics, but even as Zaha Hadid was winning the Pritzker Prize in 2004, it had long since become evident that, rather than an "unswerving commitment to modernism," she had embarked on a full-fledged questioning of that which is modern, of architecture itself. It may be that the comment of Bill Lacy, the Executive Director of the Pritzker Prize, was more to the point when he wrote: "Only rarely does an architect emerge with a philosophy and approach to the art form that influences the direction of the entire field. Such

an architect is Zaha Hadid, who has patiently created and refined a vocabulary that sets new boundaries for the art of architecture."[12]

In fact, what the German critic identified as a relation to worlds beneath the surface in the LF One pavilion is quite literally a deep current in the work of Zaha Hadid. "This whole idea of the ground and ground manipulation starts from the very early projects," she explained. "I would say it goes back to the Residence for the Irish Prime Minister [Phoenix Park, Dublin, Ireland, 1979–80; see page 46] because this project already involved the related idea of the artificial landscape, and also the studies for Vitra's extended fields, and then when we did the V&A [finalist competition entry for the Boilerhouse Gallery, Victoria and Albert Museum, London, UK, 1995], where this idea develops into an interior complex terracing as if a pastoral landscape began to be really sucked into the interior."[13]

THE DREAM OF PURE FORM DISTURBED

Conceived as a winning competition entry just after the LF One pavilion was completed, the Phaeno Science Center (Wolfsburg, Germany, 2001–05; see page 186) was described by the architect as a "covered artificial landscape" constituted of "craters, caverns, terraces, and plateaus." Its construction made use of individually fabricated formwork elements and special cast-in-place "self-compacting concrete" (SCC) that made its unusual shapes—some of them very sharp—possible. Though it does not sit as much in the earth as the LF One project, there is something of the great chthonic creature here, too, only one that has fully emerged onto the surface. "The Phaeno is the most ambitious and complete statement of our quest for complex, dynamic and fluid spaces," said Zaha Hadid. "The visitor is faced with a degree of complexity and strangeness, ruled by a very specific system based on an unusual volumetric structural logic. The floors are neither piled above each other nor could they be seen as a single volume. The Phaeno's mass is supported and also structured by funnel-shaped cones protruding into it and extending from it. Through some of these funnels, the interior of the box is accessible: others are used to lighten the space inside, while some of them house necessary functions. This project combines formal and geometric complexity with structural audacity and material authenticity. A lot of time and energy was concentrated on achieving this result."[14] Mark Wigley's words—"the dream of pure form has been disturbed"—take on their full meaning here, though deconstruction itself seems far away. The concept of artificial nature is more to the point, creating an entity that might be imagined as a living creature, surely not formed like any animal of this earth, but put together with a driving logic that courses through its plan and section.

In describing two other projects, both for museums of contemporary art, conceived at about the same time, the Lois & Richard Rosenthal Center for Contemporary Art (Cincinnati, Ohio, USA, 1999–2003; see page 164) and the MAXXI, The National Museum of XXI Century Arts (Rome, Italy, 1998–2009; see page 262), Zaha Hadid unveils more of her process and thought and also suggests why her buildings pursue the same ideas but look so different. "What is [...] similar between them is that both commissions are modernized sites which drew the insertion of a cultural program. In both cases, the urban context is expected to change in time and our respective projects are seen as agents of transformation [...] The internal geometric complexity in the Rome project is a condensation of the different orientations of the surrounding contexts. One might say that the project discovers urban routes, which lie dormant within the neighboring context. Every shift in the field relates to a neighboring contextual condition. The Cincinnati project is equally contextual, although the way it is translated in each case feels very different. So the formal thing is not really decided in advance, it is just that these different formal systems emerge in the engagement with rather different conditions. One is much more imploded into the interior, the other has much more to do with perpetually negotiating between the interior and the exterior."

---

10 http://www.pritzkerprize.com/laureates/2004/index.html, accessed on January 9, 2009.

11 Michael Mönninger, in *LF One*, Birkhäuser Publishers, Basel, 1999.

12 "Zaha Hadid Becomes the First Woman to Receive the Pritzker Architecture Prize," cit.

13 Zaha Hadid interviewed at El Croquis, 103, Madrid, 2001.

14 Zaha Hadid quoted in the press release, Zaha Hadid Architects, November 23, 2005.

IT MAY BE SUGGESTED THAT THE EARLY GRAPHIC WORK OF ZAHA HADID MAY WELL HAVE ANTICIPATED THE COMPUTER REVOLUTION THAT HAS ALLOWED HER OFFICE TO NOW DESIGN VERY COMPLEX STRUCTURES.

LOOKING FOR NATURAL LINES

A dense urban site or even a campus design like Hadid's proposal for the new campus center for IIT (Illinois Institute of Technology, Chicago, USA, 1998) are well suited to her complex patterns of interweaving lines and forms related to the location. However, in some instances, the site yields much less fundamental information. This is the case of her work in Dubai, for example the very large Signature Towers (Business Bay, Dubai, UAE, 2006; see page 462). What about context in an area that is literally rising from the sand? "In that case, you invent it," said Hadid. "The geometry of the context has an important impact. If you look at the IIT project in Chicago, there were lines that connected the project to certain schools. Views and vistas are not always important though. The Rome Museum doesn't look like anything there, but it is influenced by the context. Every shift in that building relates to existing geometry." "Sometimes the project is so large that it creates its own context," added Patrik Schumacher. "This is the case in Business Bay in Dubai, where the project exceeds half a million square meters. It is a highly integrated composition. It is one of the largest projects anywhere to have such a total coherence as a single integrated building." It would appear, then, that at a certain scale Hadid's projects become self-referential in terms of their coherence and internal logic, but the architect underlined that even where very large areas were concerned—such as in her Kartal-Pendik Master Plan (Istanbul, Turkey, 2006–; see page 438), a scheme for an entire new city center in a former industrial area—fundamental connections were made to the place and to what might be called its natural energy. "If you look at a project like the master plan for Istanbul," she said, "each segment is very different, but it is recognizable as one place. We have looked for natural lines and addressed the water. We looked at the topography of Istanbul to create another topography on the other side."

Hadid's 70 000-square-meter Guangzhou Opera House (Guangzhou, China, 2003–08; see page 278) offers other clues to her approach as viewed in the setting of a major Chinese city, currently in the throes of rapid expansion and modernization. Her "Conceptual Interpretation" of the site and the building combines references to geology ("twin boulders") and the layout of the city, including its river front: "Overlooking the Pearl River, the Guangzhou Opera House is at the heart of Guangzhou's cultural sites development. Adopting state-of-the-art technology in its design and construction, it will be a lasting monument to the new millennium, confirming Guangzhou as one of Asia's cultural centers. Its unique twin-boulder design will enhance urban function by opening access to the riverside and dock areas and creating a new dialogue with the emerging new town." This description highlights a decided strength of Hadid's approach in that she makes reference to the reality of the city and at the same time to high technology, a source of pride in China, but in any case a link to the present and future. The past, as inevitable as two boulders and a river, here meets the future, where culture in the form of opera and architecture have their place. Her "Urban Strategy/Landscape" for the Guangzhou project makes it clear that the city itself and the new building is the landscape that she is forming and integrating: "The structure rises and falls at the foot of Zhujiang Boulevard, bringing together the two adjacent sites for the proposed Museum and Metropolitan Activities. As an adjunct to the Haixinsha Tourist Park Island, the Opera House presents a contoured profile to provide a large riverside focus to visitors. When viewed from the park at the center of the Zhujiang Boulevard, the Opera House creates a visual prelude to the Tourist Park Island beyond. When viewed from the river, the towers of Zhujiang New Town provide a dramatic backdrop to the Opera House and give a unified vision of civic and cultural buildings on a riverside setting. An internal street, an approach promenade, is cut into the landscape, beginning at the proposed Museum site at the opposite side of the central boulevard, leading to the

Opera House. Café, bar, restaurant, and retail facilities, which are embedded shell-like into these landforms, are located to one side of the approach promenade."[15]

The key words in this description would appear to be "landforms" and "unified vision"—which in this instance clearly takes in not only the existing urban environment, but also a future museum near the site. As surprising as Zaha Hadid's forms may seem to some, they derive their legitimacy from their "seamless" integration into a site, or in the case of cities like Dubai, from an indisputable and continuous internal logic. Just as her furniture can be accumulated and disposed to define a continuous interior space, so her architecture may rise up out of the earth in its layered density, challenging assumptions about rectilinear "order" to create an artificial nature not unlike its real inspiration.

WAITING FOR FORMZ

The paintings and drawings of Zaha Hadid for such earlier projects as The Peak have relevance not only for her celebrity, but also for the very nature of her design. Her creative process is one that she described herself as being made up of layering and of multiple approaches to the same problem, accumulated and intertwined until a result emerges which has the legitimacy of a place and function. "It is important to emphasize that the line drawings have had an impact on the work," said Zaha Hadid. "There are things that resurface 10 or 20 years later. In the early years, I used a very layered system of sketching. All of the graphic techniques—layering in the drawing became layering in the project. The complexity in the drawing became complexity in the architecture." In this sense, it may be suggested that the early graphic work of Zaha Hadid may well have anticipated the computer revolution that has allowed her office to now design very complex structures. "I think the design method can be considered the precursor to computing," affirmed Hadid. "The computer software called formZ, for example, is very similar to the drawing technique. The drawings remain more complex than computer drawings I think, though. Even when you have a kind of wild project, it is actually quite resolved and the drawings show that. The process has a kind of inherent logic to it. There was a correlation between the way the drawings were done and the architecture. The computer side lead to research that made it possible to create complex buildings, but, fundamentally, the method has not changed. The system of doing it has changed but the ideas are still the same. If I look at some of my own sketches they look exactly like computer drawings. Now we know through a computer that you can actually do things that I sketch." Because she had already been involved in the highest levels of architecture for going on 30 years, Zaha Hadid has worked astride the period in which computers came to dominate design. Her own realization that her process and drawings closely resembled computer-assisted design might be a kind of self-fulfilling prophecy in which her own influence helped to shape the very direction of software and the architecture it generates. More likely, because her creative process anticipated the computer, its emergence served only to vindicate and strengthen her resolve. While others were left trying to adapt Euclidean geometry and modernist form to the new world, Zaha Hadid began her quest in the realm of complex surfaces and multilayered architecture.

When asked if she still sketched, Hadid responded: "Sometimes I do. I think that the reference is to one's own repertoire. You can reference back and there is a kind of knowledge. It is not so much about the power of the hand as it is the power of the idea. All that work was not about how to do a nice sketch; it was really about how to develop an idea. After many takes and layers, the idea began to be developed, and it allows you to make these complex forms and to organize the interiors." Patrik Schumacher draws this line of reasoning further into the current work of the office when he says: "We are interested in nature as well, branching systems, rivers, and so on. We use these ideas to develop architectural space. Before, that was indicated through sketching and now it is done on a computer. The new tools have a great capacity to simulate environments and complex surfaces."

15 Zaha Hadid Architects, "ZHA-Guangzhou Opera House – China – Conceptual Interpretation," January 24, 2008.

**THE WAY VEGETATION RUNS UP
A MOUNTAIN MAKES SENSE.
WE ARE TRYING TO BRING THIS KIND OF
LOGIC INTO ARCHITECTURE.**

In the work of Zaha Hadid, there is surely a "reference to one's own repertoire," as she put it, but there is also a radical, new approach to the relationship between architecture and nature, some of which has developed out of the increasing use of computer-assisted design. As Patrik Schumacher makes clear: "The nature reference is an old trope. It's not only the modernists; Renaissance and Classical architecture also reflected back and wanted to set its constructs within cosmology and an understanding of nature. In terms of the digital world, we see a proliferation of natural morphologies that are exciting and can be made to work and enrich the compositional and organizational repertoire—not just in terms of appearance, but also as organization patterns. For us [these morphologies] are navigation and orientation issues that can give more order to a complex environment."[16]

INHERENTLY LAWFUL
AND COHERENT

To the question of just how "natural morphologies" as manipulated through the use of the computer can improve architecture—a fundamental question where the work of Zaha Hadid is concerned—Patrik Schumacher responds: "The kinds of morphologies which come out of it are inherently lawful and coherent. There were prior attempts to establish this kind of coherency and law, either through talent and composing, where architects attempted to intuitively mimic the dynamic equilibrium, for instance, that you find in nature or to just restrict themselves to platonic geometries and symmetries—very basic orders. To have a more complex order, rather than some kind of ugly disorder, is possible with these new tools and, of course, there is a whole world of tools that exists for all sorts of purposes outside of architecture that can be harnessed, like RealFlow, etc. And their whole sensibility, in a sense, relates back to the perception of natural systems."[17]

It may indeed be that Zaha Hadid, whose extensive training in draftsmanship is evident in her careful drawings and paintings, did to some extent regret the days before computers took over. "I think that the work before analyzed and understood the context better than now. There was much more study and analysis of the site. Certain shifts were made because of site analysis. I don't think that there is any site analysis now. Context and site analysis are no longer part of the topic. There is no longer a discussion of context; they are mostly just objects that land there. The issue is not so much about computing or not computing. The problem with computing is that it isolates the object. It is inward-looking as opposed to outward-looking. It is an object. The nature of the piece is like that." Asked if she was resigned to that reality, Zaha Hadid responded: "I am actually quite critical of it. We used to distinguish between the object and the field and I think it is because of technique that we don't anymore. There is no longer plan analysis." Patrik Schumacher for his part argues for what he calls "elegance" in contemporary architecture and specifically in the work of Zaha Hadid Architects. This elegance is found in an extensive search for a solution involving many studies and an incremental extrusion of the appropriate forms. "Each element is highly related to what is coming next and to its place within the overall scheme. That means that there is a lot of information embedded in these morphologies. It is a bit like a symphony. You cannot destroy a core of the melody, whereas in a cacophony you can take anything out and put it somewhere else. We now have the tools to do that in some of our projects. Everything means something, nothing is arbitrary." The cacophony Schumacher refers to is that which exists in a city such as Tokyo, a layered and embedded city if ever there was one, and yet not a system in which the "elegance" and new order sought by Zaha Hadid is at all apparent.

A FORM OF NATURAL COMPUTING

It is here that Zaha Hadid's quest, expressed in a multitude of different objects, buildings, drawings, or even exhibition designs, reveals its ultimate continuity and the strong binding agent that held together a career that is like no other in contemporary architecture. Though Hadid spoke of topography willingly, she did not often express her search in terms of the creation of an artificial nature. "We moved away from the idea of creating large objects and we looked at topography and the ground. We looked at the many layers of public space and how to interpret what is above ground and what is below. From there the natural move was to look at [...] nature," said Hadid. Patrik Schumacher again makes the connection between the fundamental thinking of Hadid and its newly built forms. "There are millions of natural objects and each has its own coherency," he says. "It is open-ended. If you have geological layers shifted against each other, there are always continuities. This is a form of natural computing if you want. The incident sits within a field of incidents where it makes sense. The way vegetation runs up a mountain makes sense. We are trying to bring this kind of logic into architecture. There is a sense of eloquent beauty and intuitive understanding that enters into the matter."

I WOULDN'T CALL IT SCULPTURE

Zaha Hadid was unusual in that she created furnishings or, more precisely, objects that are meant to form interior space. Her work for David Gill Galleries and Established & Sons took on the sort of numbered and signed originality usually reserved for works of art, but there is clearly no such distinction to be made, even if Zaha Hadid rejected the word "sculpture" to describe her pieces. She responded quite clearly to the question of how she came to design objects. "Of course we didn't really do architectural projects for a long time, and the question came up about how one could deal with furnishings in spaces that are not conventional. They also become part of the interior world, they become space dividers. When we did the Sawaya & Moroni things it was about having this kind of landscape or topography [Z-Scape Furniture, 2000; see page 533]. The idea was to make a piece of furniture that is part of an ensemble which could be squished into a very small room like an environment, or you can spread it out." In fact, the discussion of what precisely linked Hadid's object designs to her architecture is quite revealing in terms of the conception of both. "The transition between parts certainly applies to the design as well as the architecture," according to Patrik Schumacher. "The transition is smooth and not like bolting a tabletop onto four legs for example. It has to do with the spirit of the style—the total environment. In the hotel, we look at furniture as a space-making substance." The hotel referred to here is the Puerta América (Madrid, Spain, 2003–05; see page 214) where Hadid created a seamlessly integrated floor and rooms made with thermoformed LG HI-MACS acrylics. In this astonishing environment, visitors are greeted by Hadid's edgeless surfaces as soon as they exit the elevator. Rooms have ceilings that become walls, desks that protrude directly from those walls, or even bathtubs that blend into their setting without any apparent edges. The visitor who does not have an acute sense of design may be forgiven for asking just why a desk needs to flare out from a wall only to turn into a bed. Practicality may be less important here than challenging the established order of right angles that has so long dominated design and architecture.

THE DIAGONAL WAS
THE BEGINNING OF ALL THIS

"I always think about how we can put the objects together," continued Zaha Hadid. "For the Seamless Collection [Established & Sons, 2006], I think of them as multiples so you can have a number of them, a tower of cabinets. They can always be seen as an isolated object or as many pieces together." The functionali-

---

16 Patrik Schumacher, in *MAD Dinner*, Actar, Barcelona, 2007.

17 Ibid.

**THE DIAGONAL BECOMES A METAPHOR
FOR THE ACT OF EXPLODING SPACE, OF QUESTIONING
THE MOST FUNDAMENTAL AND "OBVIOUS"
ASSUMPTIONS OF ARCHITECTURE.**

ty described here, no matter how beautifully the objects flow together, is what surely made Hadid react to the question of whether she would call this work sculptural. "No, I wouldn't use that word," she said bluntly. "Sculptural as opposed to what, flatware? Much mass-produced furniture was conceived as being flat. But the car— that was a whole idea about assembly that was never flat. For furniture now you can have pieces that are customized. You don't have to do flat shelves. These are definitely not minimalist—those are two worlds apart. It is about no 90° corners. The diagonal was the beginning of all this. The diagonal created the idea of the explosion reforming space. That was an important discovery."

The "explosion reforming space" that Zaha Hadid referred to here is amply visible in her drawings and paintings for The Peak in 1983. Where the straight lines and 90° angles of modernism had been the rule, in part for reasons of productivity, she actively pursued the diagonal, in her architecture as well as in her objects. Beyond the hard-edged tectonics of her earlier work on to the seamless smoothness of the Puerta América Hotel, the diagonal becomes a metaphor for the act of exploding space, of questioning the most fundamental and "obvious" assumptions of architecture. A table has a flat top and four legs bolted on to it, a building is made up of an accumulation of Euclidian solids with hardly a worrisome void in sight. As complex as Zaha Hadid's work may sometimes seem, her real originality can be touched on in the questions she has asked about such obvious affirmations, the very framework of an architecture reproduced by rote for generations. Hers was, indeed, an explosion that reforms space.

When Hadid showed her *Dune Formations* (David Gill Galleries, 2007; see page 562) at the Scuola dei Mercanti in Venice during the 2007 Biennale, she proved another most interesting point. Her burnt-orange aluminum and resin objects appeared to glide from one state or function to another within the confines of a very traditional Venetian building. Most of all, there was no inherent contradiction between the past and the future represented by the high-ceilinged rectilinearity of an old building and her flowing, curving shapes. Somewhat like natural objects that cannot be contested in their ultimate formal legitimacy, so, too, the *Dune Formations,* inspired surely, as their name suggests, by the shifting sands of the desert, in no way seemed out of place in Venice. The viewer who senses this legitimacy may be coming close to understanding why Zaha Hadid was an important architect and designer. Her forms are like no other objects or buildings seen until now, notwithstanding any early connections to Russian Suprematism, for example, and yet their physical existence seems to be rooted in the earth as much as in computer-assisted design. Her layered complexity may not always have achieved this kind of intuitive legitimacy, but when it did, as in the case of the *Dune Formations*, it opened new vistas for the future of art, architecture, and design.

YOU HAVE TO SEE IT
AS TEAMWORK

An obvious transition occurred in the career of Zaha Hadid, perhaps after she completed the Rosenthal Center in 2003. With 300 architects working under her orders, and projects underway from the UK to China, Zaha Hadid was very much in demand. She remarked candidly: "I think it is interesting to work that way, but I am taking advantage of the current situation. I don't think it could happen in one's lifetime many times, with the clients actually wanting this kind of work all over the world. I don't put any geographic limits on my work, but there are some countries where you have to be on the ground—it doesn't work with e-mails." Did the 2004 Pritzker Prize have anything to do with this explosion in demand for her designs? "I think so," she replied. "Of course we were doing things before, but the level of interest multiplied. Also, I think that people are interested in this kind of work. I have no idea if the same kind of thing happened to other Pritzker architects at the same level as it happened to us." Asked how she deals with the quantity of new work, Hadid responded: "There is Patrik, of course, but we have lots of people who have been here for a long time.

Many of the people were students of mine or of Patrik. We do things over many times to get them right. Our organizational structure is surely not a pyramid where I come up with an idea and hand things down. I think you have to see it as teamwork. Within the office we are involved in research that everybody understands."

The transition from a personal quest, whose first evidence might be the 1976–77 painting *Horizontal Tektonik, Malevich's Tektonik, London*, to the path of a globe-straddling architect was managed by Zaha Hadid with an aplomb that obviously escapes many of her colleagues in the profession. Rem Koolhaas, who is six years older than Hadid, has also moved from a justifiable reputation as a theorist to running an office capable of building as astonishing a building as the CCTV Tower in Beijing, yet even OMA cannot boast the kind of project list that Zaha Hadid Architects was recently engaged in.

The list of projects "on site" published in this book, some of which will be finished by the time readers have the volume in hand, shows a remarkable geographic spread but also a continuous effort to redefine the very typology of buildings that will leave a mark, even for those who may question the style and dynamics of the Hadid office. With the MAXXI, the National Museum of XXI Century Arts in Rome, Hadid aimed "to confront the material and conceptual dissonance evoked by art practice since the late 1960s," redefining not only the form but also the reactivity of museums to the art of today. Her 842-meter-long Sheikh Zayed Bridge was more than 13 years in the making (Abu Dhabi, UAE, 1997–2010; see page 272) and weaves structural strands together, assuming a "sinusoidal waveform" over the channel between Abu Dhabi and the mainland. It questions and redefines the form of the bridge, usually the pure province of engineers, but surely a most "practical" object, here rendered dynamic enough to become "a destination in itself and potential catalyst in the future urban growth of Abu Dhabi." The London Aquatics Centre (London, UK, 2005–11; see page 292) was a noted element of the 2012 Olympic Games in the English capital, the first major structure in the city where Zaha Hadid elected residence for so long. Its double-curvature parabolic roof and design "inspired by the fluid geometry of water in motion" extend the range and nature of Hadid's references to nature, or perhaps more precisely to objects born of an artificial nature as legitimate as the sand dunes or flowing water she evokes. The Centre includes two areas, respectively with seating for 17 500 people for the main competition pool and diving, and 5000 seats for water polo. Further afield, the Heydar Aliyev Cultural Center (Baku, Azerbaijan, 2007–12; see page 354) makes a clear reference to topography, as the "building itself merges into the landscape [...] blurring the boundary between the building and the ground." In the midst of designing so many large, complex buildings, Hadid also took the time to design a remarkable private house, the Capital Hill Residence (Moscow, Russia, 2006–; see page 378). With its lower volume partly embedded in a hillside in a "strategy that extends the exterior topography to the interior of the building," the house features a 22-meter-high tower that allows residents to look over the neighboring 20-meter-high trees.

In recent years Zaha Hadid completed two significant projects in southern France. The first of these, the CMA CGM Tower (Marseille, 2006–11; see page 302), invests a commercial port site that is 100 meters from the water, and surrounded by roads. The 94 000-square-meter complex imposes itself on the surroundings but its graceful upward sweep gives it an elegance that is a hallmark of the architect. The second project is a 28 500-square-meter administrative building for the Hérault region of France. Hadid called Pierresvives (Montpellier, 2002–12; see page 322) "one of the most ambitious and comprehensive assertions of our will to create dynamic and fluid spaces. It blends formal geometric complexity with bold structures and an innovative use of materials. Architectural creation," she concluded, "involves pushing the boundaries—and I believe that Pierresvives is an excellent demonstration of that."

THE NATURE REFERENCE
IS AN OLD TROPE

Zaha Hadid was by no means the first architect to link her designs to nature. "The nature reference is an old trope," as Schumacher says. Significant figures, from Frank Lloyd Wright to Toyo Ito, have anchored their work in natural settings, but perhaps in a more literal way than Hadid. Did Fallingwater by Frank Lloyd Wright (Edgar J. Kaufmann House, Mill Run, Pennsylvania, USA, 1934–37) seem as futuristic to visitors in the late 1930s as the Capital Hill Residence will in the forest near Moscow? The seamless designs of Hadid, today given reality by cutting-edge technology and materials, never seem to descend into any mimicry of nature. The goal was elsewhere and that is why Hadid was no follower of Wright. This nature indeed rises up from the ground or the cityscape "like a chthonic creature" not born of any common experience, but somehow as unquestionable as an ancient myth. Geometry is here, but made up of the complex curves and overlaid patterns that sprang up from Zaha Hadid's mind only to be given form by the revolution in computer-assisted design and manufacturing that render the unique possible. The newness of modernism was pristine in its delicate avoidance of the world below in almost every sense. Architecturally speaking, modernist buildings only rarely venture in any visible way below grade. A basement is meant to be hidden, and above ground the reign of the sharply defined Euclidean solid is absolute. Elegant pilotis even kept the white virginity of the newly modern from being sullied by the earth. Ludwig Mies van der Rohe communed with a natural setting in a masterpiece such as his Farnsworth House (1945–50, Plano, Illinois, USA). For all its crystalline purity, the Farnsworth House was mocked at the time by the magazine *House Beautiful* as "a glass cage on stilts." With Hadid, nature may be artificial, but it is nature, with all its dark surprises intact.

AN ARCHITECTURAL LANGUAGE
OF FLUIDITY AND NATURE

Two recent ephemeral projects by Zaha Hadid serve to demonstrate the breadth of her interests and accomplishments, but also the voracity she displayed in proving that her methods were applicable in the most diverse circumstances. Her Mobile Art, Chanel Contemporary Art Container (various locations, 2007–08; see page 244) could hardly have a relation to a specific context since it was intended to move at the whim of the original client, Karl Lagerfeld. Using sophisticated computer design, this exhibition pavilion employed what Hadid called "an architectural language of fluidity and nature," or again, "an artificial landscape." Significantly, Lagerfeld, an aesthete with an intuitive understanding of design, says of Hadid: "She is the first architect to find a way to part with the all-dominating post-Bauhaus aesthetic." Today, the work has found a permanent location near Jean Nouvel's Institut du Monde Arabe in Paris.

A second ephemeral work (*Lilas*, Temporary Installation, Serpentine Gallery, Kensington Gardens, London, UK, 2007; see page 570) consisted in a series of three 5.5-meter-high parasols arrayed on a 310-square-meter platform. Clad in heat-welded PVC fabric, these parasols took their inspiration "from complex natural geometries such as flower petals and leaves," but above all seemed sculptural in their presence when they were erected on an extremely tight schedule for the Serpentine Gallery's Summer Party. The American sculptor Richard Serra has said

that the difference between art and architecture is that architecture serves a purpose. The *Lilas* installation clearly served a purpose, but its presence and nature surely link it to the world of art, at least the art that remains connected to the world, to nature and to beauty. Nicolai Ouroussoff, the architecture critic of *The New York Times,* wrote of Hadid: "By collecting such disparate strands into one vision, she defiantly embraces a cosmopolitanism that is hard put to assert itself in our dark age. It is as close to a manifesto for the future as we have."[18]

Patrik Schumacher's theory of "elegance" with respect to the work of Zaha Hadid responds to the underlying question of just what the innovations brought forth by the firm mean, and how useful they are. "Why should we bother to strive for this increasingly difficult elegance? Does this elegance serve a purpose beyond itself?" he asks. And his response bears reading: "Contemporary architectural briefs are marked by a demand for evermore complex and simultaneous programmatic provisions to be organized within evermore complex urban contexts. Elegance allows for an increased programmatic complexity to coincide with a relative reduction of visual complication by means of integrating multiple elements into a coherent and continuous formal and spatial system. The general challenge is to find modes of composition that can articulate complex arrangements and relationships without losing legibility and the capacity to orient users. Elegance, as defined here, signifies this capacity to articulate complex life processes in a way that can maintain overall comprehension, legibility, and continuous orientation within the composition."[19]

ARCHITECTURE SET FREE

Where others ventured with gusto into the realm of the largely meaningless computer-generated "blob," Zaha Hadid emerged from the pre-computer era with ideas that the new technology rendered possible. Her precise, layered drawings were always meant to give rise to real buildings; she was never interested in pure aesthetics, even when she looked to the Suprematists for inspiration. It should be said that the Constructivists and Suprematists, unlike the Soviet-era masters of Russia's political destiny, really did imagine a brave new world. Hadid broke not only the post-Bauhaus aesthetic, but more significantly the grid and the Euclid-ean solid. Her space ebbs and flows like the natural systems of branching evoked by Patrik Schumacher. Her work is at the juncture between architecture, art, and design, not always necessarily fully resolved because hers is an ongoing, formative process. "Avant-garde architecture produces manifestos: paradigmatic expositions of a new style's unique potential, not buildings that are balanced to function in all respects," says Schumacher with some bravado.[20] Significantly, as a number of the built projects in this book demonstrate, Hadid successfully made the transition from theory and image to real buildings. This progress was only moderately slowed by the world economic crisis after 2008. Today she is renowned as being one of the most emblematic architects of the time.

The adventure of Zaha Hadid was a remarkable one. Her success was formed by a constancy and commitment to the belief that architecture and design need not be as they always were. Indeed, Bauhaus-inspired architecture did relate to industrial methods and the need for repetition to generate economies of scale. Hadid's concept of architecture, born of rigorous logic and design, yet freed of its Euclidean constraints, was rendered possible by another industrial revolution driven by computer-assisted design and CNC milling. Desks sprang from walls and bridges danced in sinusoidal undulations. Zaha Hadid set architecture free, and it will never be the same again.

Philip Jodidio, Grimentz, Switzerland

[18] Nicolai Ouroussoff, "Zaha Hadid: A Diva for the Digital Age," in *The New York Times*, June 2, 2006.

[19] Patrik Schumacher, "Arguing for Elegance," *AD* (Architectural Design), London, January/February 2007.

[20] Patrik Schumacher, "Zaha Hadid Architects – Experimentation within a Long Wave of Innovation," cit, pp. 93–94.

DIE RAUMERNEUERNDE EXPLOSION

In Zeiten, in denen Gesundheit und Sicherheit, Wirtschaft, Klima und Politik zusehends im Fluss sind, ist nachvollziehbar, dass Architektur diesen Zustand reflektiert, tendenziell keiner erkennbaren Richtung folgt und zwischen asketischem Minimalismus, grünem Missionseifer und neobarocker Ornamentierung oszilliert. Dennoch gibt es einige, die so mutig sind, nach Kontinuität zu streben und zu postulieren, dass es durchaus Vorbilder gibt, denen es nachzueifern lohnt. Nur wenige waren so prädestiniert, diese Parole auszurufen, wie Zaha Hadid, die 2004 den Pritzker-Preis erhielt. Ihr viel zu früher Tod im März 2016 wurde weltweit betrauert. Patrik Schumacher, seit Langem Hadids engster Mitarbeiter, schreibt im Katalog der Architekturbiennale 2008 in Venedig: „In der heutigen Avantgardearchitektur manifestiert sich ein unverwechselbarer neuer Stil. Sein markantes Merkmal ist seine komplexe, dynamisch geschwungene Linienführung. Abgesehen von dieser offensichtlichen Oberfläche sind hier verschiedene neue Konzepte und Methoden auszumachen, die sich so stark vom Repertoire traditioneller und moderner Architektur unterscheiden, dass man vom Entstehen eines neuen Paradigmas in der Architektur sprechen könnte. Die Konzepte, das formale Repertoire, die tektonische Logik und die Computertechniken, die diesen Arbeiten gemein sind, zeugen von der Herausbildung eines neuen vorherrschenden Stils: des *Parametrismus*. Der Parametrismus ist der große Nachfolger der Moderne. Postmoderne und Dekonstruktivismus waren Übergangsphasen, die diese neue, sich langfristig durchsetzende Ära der Forschung und Innovation eingeläutet haben. Konzeptuell fußte die Moderne auf dem Raumbegriff. Der Parametrismus hingegen differenziert Felder. Und *Felder* sind gefüllt wie mit einem flüssigen Medium. Wir verabschieden uns von Kompositionen aus einzelnen Teilen und wenden uns dynamischen Feldern aus Teilchen zu.[1] Dieses Gespür für diese Zusammenhänge wurde im Lauf einer 30-jährigen Tätigkeit radikalisiert *und* verfeinert. Um dies überhaupt zu ermöglichen, waren die neuen technischen Darstellungsformen von entscheidender Bedeutung."[2]

Ob sich die Bezeichnung „Parametrismus" durchsetzen und womöglich zu einer Schule werden wird, bleibt abzuwarten. Dennoch hat das Büro Zaha Hadid die Aufmerksamkeit auf neue Methoden und Ansätze gelenkt, mit denen die verschiedensten grundlegenden Prämissen hinterfragt werden. Hadid war bereit, die Geometrie auf den Prüfstand zu stellen, die fundamentale Organisation und den Raumbegriff der Architektur als solche, und bewies in ihrer Laufbahn erstaunliche theoretische Konsequenz und Kontinuität. Diese Kontinuität hat jedoch nichts mit einem rasterorientierten Stil zu tun, wie er beispielsweise Richard Meier oder Tadao Ando motiviert. Hadids gebaute Projekte und Entwürfe ähneln einander im Hinblick auf den Fluss ihrer Grundrisse und die Dynamik von Raum und Oberfläche. Ihre Arbeiten, von der spitzwinkligen Feuerwache für Vitra (Weil am Rhein, 1991–93; Seite 116) bis zu ihrer Objektserie *Dune Formations* (David Gill Galleries, 2007; Seite 562), stellen zur Debatte, wie Architektur und Mobiliar zu verstehen sind. Was, wenn die vielfältigen Prämissen in Architektur und Design – von geradliniger Formgebung

bis hin zum Funktionsverständnis von Bauten und Möbeln – allesamt fraglich wären, ja von Grund auf der Erneuerung bedürften? Die Natur ist fähig, eine schier endlose Vielfalt von Objekten hervorzubringen. Könnte die Architektur – die Kunst, das gebaute Umfeld schöpferisch zu gestalten – dies nicht ebenso legitim für sich beanspruchen, indem sie Kontext und Funktion neu deutet, bewusst nicht nur Volumina, sondern auch Leerräume schafft und das Primat des rechten Winkels hinterfragt, den es in der Natur so selten gibt? Wäre dies jene künstliche Natur, von der so viele Architekten und Denker träumen?

HYBRIDISIEREN, VERWANDELN, ENTTERRITORIALISIEREN

Schumacher umreißt den Parametrismus mit formalen Begriffen, die weniger revolutionär scheinen als die eigentliche Architektur Hadids, die weit über jede formalistische Debatte hinausgeht: „Das Programm/der Stil besteht aus methodologischen Gesetzmäßigkeiten: Manche zeigen an, was nicht weiterzuverfolgen ist (negative Heuristik), andere, welchen Pfaden wir folgen sollten (positive Heuristik). Die entscheidende Heuristik des Parametrismus lässt sich an den Tabus und Dogmen der Designkultur ablesen. Negative Heuristik: Vermeide altbekannte Typologien, meide platonische/hermetische Körper, meide klar umrissene Zonen/Territorien, meide Wiederholung, meide gerade Linien, meide rechte Winkel, meide Ecken [...] Positive Heuristik: hybridisiere, verwandele, entterritorialisiere, deformiere, wiederhole, arbeite mit Splines, NURBS und generativen Komponenten, schreibe statt zu modellieren [...]"[3]

Gerade so, wie Zaha Hadid im Verlauf von 30 Jahren ein bemerkenswert kohärentes und konsequentes Œuvre schuf und dabei oft auf Ideen zurückgriff, die zu Beginn ihrer Laufbahn noch umstritten waren, setzt sich auch die Beschreibung ihres Werks aus verschiedenen Strängen zusammen. Würde man diese zusammenfügen, zeigte sich das Erreichte nicht als lineare Entwicklung, sondern als komplexes Gewebe aus Ideen, Linie und Form. Insofern ist es keineswegs abwegig, den Bogen von der Architekturbiennale in Venedig 2008 und dem dazugehörigen Manifest „Experimentation within a Long Wave of Innovation" zu einem Zeitpunkt 20 Jahre zuvor zu schlagen, als Zaha Hadid der Öffentlichkeit bekannt wurde.

Das Oxford English Dictionary definiert Dekonstruktion als „Strategie kritischer Auseinandersetzung [...], die darauf zielt, unhinterfragte metaphysische Prämissen und immanente Widersprüche im philosophischen und literarischen Sprachgebrauch aufzudecken". Bekannt wurde der Dekonstruktivismus durch den französischen Philosophen Jacques Derrida (1930–2004). 1986 wandte er seinen Ansatz erstmals explizit auf die Architektur an, in einem Text über Bernard Tschumis „follies" (Verrücktheiten) im Parc de la Villette in Paris: „Am Nullpunkt der Verrücktheit: Jetzt die Architektur". Derrida sprach von einer „programmatischen Dekonstruktion": „Die Verrücktheiten bewerkstelligen einen allgemeinen Zerfall, sie reißen alles mit hinein, was bis jetzt der Architektur Sinn gegeben zu haben scheint. Genauer das, was die Architektur dem Sinn zugeordnet zu haben scheint. Sie dekonstruieren zunächst, aber nicht allein, die zur Architektur gehörende Semantik."[4]

Das radikale Programm des literaturwissenschaftlichen Dekonstruktivismus unterschied sich letztendlich kaum von den erstaunlichen Formen, die 1988 mit der von Philip Johnson und Mark Wigley kuratierten Ausstellung *Deconstructivist Architecture* im New Yorker Museum of Modern Art (MoMA) erstmals den Weg in den öffentlichen Diskurs fanden. Präsentiert wurden sieben Architekten: Frank Gehry, Daniel Libeskind, Rem Koolhaas, Peter Eisenman, Zaha Hadid, Coop Himmelb(l)au und Bernard Tschumi mit seinen „follies" für den Parc de la Villette. Die Ausstellung legte nahe, dass es in der zeitgenössischen Architektur zu einer radikalen Kehrtwende gekommen war. Der Kurator Mark Wigley schrieb: „Architektur ist immer eine zentrale kulturelle Einrichtung gewesen und wird vor allem geschätzt, weil sie für Stabilität und Ordnung sorgt. Diese Qualitäten, so meint man, resultieren aus der geometrischen Klarheit ihrer formalen Komposition. Die hier vorgestellten

---

Sofern nicht anders angegeben, stammen alle Zitate aus einem Interview des Autors mit Zaha Hadid und Patrik Schumacher in London vom 10. April 2008.

[1] „Wir können auch an bewegte Flüssigkeiten denken, mit Strudeln, Wellen und Interferenzen", sagt Patrik Schumacher.

[2] Patrik Schumacher, „Zaha Hadid Architects – Experimentation within a Long Wave of Innovation", in: Out There. Architecture Beyond Building, Marsilio Editori, Venedig, 2008, Bd. 3, S. 91–92.

[3] Ebd., S. 94–95.

[4] Jacques Derrida, „Am Nullpunkt der Verrücktheit – Jetzt die Architektur", in: Wolfgang Welsch (Hg.), Wege aus der Moderne. Schlüsseltexte der Postmoderne-Diskussion, Akademie Verlag, Berlin, 1994, S. 215–232. Im französischen Original: „Une ,déconstruction programmatique', une dislocation générale (dans laquelle les folies) entraînent tout ce qui semble avoir, jusqu'à maintenant, donné sens à l'architecture. Plus précisément ce qui semble avoir ordonné l'architecture au sens. Elles déconstruisent d'abord, mais non seulement, la sémantique architecturale."

Projekte sind durch eine andere Art von Sensibilität gekennzeichnet, durch eine Sensibilität, bei welcher der Traum von der reinen Form gestört worden ist. Die Form ist verunreinigt worden. Der Traum wurde zu einer Art Albtraum."[5]

DAS VERZERRTE ZENTRUM MODERNISTISCHER REINHEIT

Auch wenn der Begriff „Dekonstruktion" für viele einen Akt der Zerstörung zu implizieren scheint, hatten Mark Wigley und die Architekten ein völlig anderes Anliegen. Wigley schrieb: „Ein dekonstruktiver Architekt ist deshalb nicht jemand, der Gebäude demontiert, sondern jemand, der den Gebäuden inhärente Probleme lokalisiert. Der dekonstruktive Architekt behandelt die reinen Formen der architektonischen Tradition wie ein Psychiater seine Patienten – er stellt die Symptome einer verdrängten Unreinheit fest. Diese Unreinheit wird durch eine Kombination von sanfter Schmeichelei und gewalttätiger Folter an die Oberfläche geholt: Die Form wird verhört."[6] Wigley und andere assoziierten die sieben Architekten mit dem russischen Konstruktivismus und Suprematismus, die kurz nach den politischen Umwälzungen von 1917 aufkamen. „Die russische Avantgarde stellte für die Tradition eine Bedrohung dar, weil sie die klassischen Regeln jener Kompositionsweise brach, bei der die ausgewogene, hierarchische Beziehung zwischen den Formen ein einheitliches Ganzes erzeugt. Reine Formen wurden nunmehr dazu benützt, ‚unreine', schiefe geometrische Kompositionen zu schaffen."[7] Tatsächlich wecken die Zeichnungen von Wladimir Krinski, die im Ausstellungskatalog reproduziert waren, oder die suprematistischen Gemälde von Kasimir Malewitsch unmittelbar Assoziationen an Arbeiten Frank Gehrys oder Entwürfe der einzigen weiblichen Protagonistin der Ausstellung, Zaha Hadid. Für die MoMA-Ausstellung hatten Johnson und Wigley Hadids Siegerbeitrag im internationalen Wettbewerb für den Fitnessklub The Peak in Hongkong (1982–83; Seite 50) ausgewählt. Wigley schrieb: „Der Klub erstreckt sich zwischen der Leere des Luftraums und der Dichte des Baugrunds, Bereichen, die gewöhnlich von der modernen Architektur ausgeschlossen werden, aber in ihr auftauchen, wenn die Moderne an ihre Grenzen gezwungen und verdrängt wird. So gesehen liegt das hedonistische Refugium im verzerrten Zentrum modernistischer Reinheit."[8]

Auch 20 Jahre später nahmen Zaha Hadid und Patrik Schumacher noch Bezug auf die MoMA-Ausstellung. „Die MoMA-Schau beschäftigte sich mit zwei Begriffen, die dort miteinander verschmolzen wurden", sagte Hadid, „der Dekonstruktion im Sinne eines Denkansatzes und der russischen Bewegung des Konstruktivismus. Der Bezug auf diese beiden Begriffe ließ die Schau zum Hybrid werden. Ich glaube, die Ausstellung war sehr wichtig, weil die Menschen zum ersten Mal begannen, nichtnormative Architektur wahrzunehmen. Leider wurden damals kaum bedeutende dekonstruktivistische Projekte realisiert. Keiner von uns baute tatsächlich." Hadids Interesse an den Suprematisten zeigte sich schon in frühen Arbeiten, etwa einem Bild für ihre Abschlussarbeit *(Horizontal Tektonik, Malevich's Tektonik, London,* Acryl auf Zeichenkarton, 128 x 89 cm, 1976–77, San Francisco Museum of Modern Art). Über zehn Jahre nach ihrem Abschluss, zum Zeitpunkt der MoMA-Ausstellung, hatte Hadid die Lehren des Suprematismus auf eine Art und Weise auf die Architektur übertragen, die realen konstruktiven Bedingungen gerecht wurde. Als Architektin, geprägt vom Koolhaas-Umfeld, erkannte sie intuitiv, dass die Baukunst damals kurz vor einer Veränderung stand. Auch andere Beteiligte der Ausstellung, etwa Frank Gehry, hinterließen deutliche Spuren in der Architektur. Doch vielleicht ist die Kunst als solche bei Gehry schon alles: die tanzende Sinfonie der

Formen, die tiefer greifende Fragen jedoch außer Acht lässt, etwa die Frage nach der Logik der Architektur, die Zaha Hadid immer am Herzen lag.

ABSOLUTER REGELBRUCH, AKKURAT GEZEICHNET

Obwohl Wigley bekräftigte, es ginge den ausgestellten Architekten nicht darum, etwas zu demontieren, fällt Patrik Schumachers Einschätzung der damaligen Zeit etwas anders aus: „Man könnte den Dekonstruktivismus als Übergangsstil verstehen. Er war eine Art kreative Zerstörung, die den Weg für neue Ziele ebnete." Vielleicht ist Wigleys Definition zu bescheiden, wenn es um eine Persönlichkeit wie Zaha Hadid geht. Schließlich definierte sie die Architektur auf eine Weise neu, die der 1988 formulierten Beschreibung „schiefe geometrische Kompositionen" spottet. „Die MoMA-Ausstellung war interessant", sagte Hadid, „weil sie Regeln brach und sich von typologischen Vorstellungen löste. Das Entscheidendste war, die Organisation der Grundrisse und Schnitte aufzubrechen. Anders als manche glaubten, waren wir sehr präzise. Unsere Arbeiten waren geometrisch höchst akkurat. Typologien aufzubrechen, Regeln zu brechen, das waren überaus wichtige Schritte, weil es das erste Mal war, dass man sich dieser Möglichkeiten überhaupt bewusst wurde."

Von Anfang an, anders als manche Kritiker unterstellten, gründete Zaha Hadids Werk auf einem umfassenden Verständnis von Architektur, handwerklichem Können und der fundamentalen Wechselbeziehung zwischen beiden. Natürlich trennt sie dieser Umstand in gewisser Weise von den russischen Avantgardisten, die sich oft eher mit geometrischen Spekulationen und ästhetischen Fragestellungen befassten, als eine reale Leidenschaft für das Bauen zu haben. Bei Hadid verband sich das Aufbegehren gegen überkommene räumliche Ordnungen mit realem architektonischem Sachverstand – und genau das machte sie zu mehr als nur zur „Dekonstruktivistin". Seit Gründung des Büros waren die Projekte von Zaha Hadid immer geprägt vom Zusammenspiel einer intellektuellen Revolution in der Architektur mit konkreten baulichen Realitäten und umsetzbaren Möglichkeiten. Auf die Frage nach ihrem Verhältnis zu Statikern antwortete Hadid: „Wir arbeiten immer mit denselben [Statikern], wenn auch mit verschiedenen Firmen. Wir haben ein System eingeführt. Das erlaubt uns unter anderem, den Raum anders zu verstehen, was ich als spannende Zusammenarbeit empfinde. Ingenieure stoßen bei uns nicht zum Schluss dazu, sondern direkt zu Anfang. Bei solch enormen konstruktiven Landschaften, die noch dazu Böden oder Dach tragen, müssen wir sie einfach einbinden." Statt den Ingenieuren mit Misstrauen zu begegnen, wie manche innovative Architekten das mitunter tun, begrüßte Hadid ihre Unterstützung, hatte jedoch in ihrem Arbeitsablauf eine Methode entwickelt, der ihren Beitrag ins Gesamtbild integrierte. Diese Methode gab es schon, bevor sie viel baute, und sie ist ein weiterer Beweis für die Kontinuität und Dynamik, die ihr den verdienten Ruf eingebracht haben, die bedeutendste kreative Architektin weltweit zu sein.

DIE MACHT DER INNOVATION KOMMT ANS TAGESLICHT

Zaha Hadid, 1950 in Bagdad geboren, studierte an der Architectural Association (AA) in London, wo sie 1977 den Diploma-Preis gewann. Sie wurde Partnerin im Office for Metropolitan Architecture (OMA) und lehrte mit OMA-Gründer Rem Koolhaas an der AA, wo sie bis 1987 ein eigenes Büro leitete. Sie hatte den Kenzo-Tange-Lehrstuhl an der Graduate School of Design der Harvard University inne, den Sullivan-Lehrstuhl an der Architekturfakultät der Universität von Illinois (Chicago) sowie Gastprofessuren an der Hochschule für bildende Künste (Hamburg) und der Universität für angewandte Kunst (Wien). Darüber hinaus war sie Eero-Saarinen-Gastprofessorin für architektonisches Entwerfen an der Yale University (New Haven, Connecticut, 2004). Nur wenige Architekten haben sowohl durch ihr

---

5   Mark Wigley, Dekonstruktivistische Architektur, Verlag Gerd Hatje, Stuttgart, 1988, S. 10, 11.

6   Ebd., S. 11.

7   Ebd., S. 12.

8   Ebd., S. 68.

grafisches Werk (Malerei und Zeichnung) als auch durch die Lehre so großen Einfluss wie Hadid. Doch ihre gebauten Projekte waren bis vor Kurzem im Vergleich zu anderen international bedeutenden Architekten dünn gesät. Ein erster Förderer war Rolf Fehlbaum, Leiter des Möbelunternehmens Vitra. Die Feuerwache für Vitra (Weil am Rhein, 1991–93; Seite 116) wurde noch vor ihrer Fertigstellung in Zeitschriften und Büchern publiziert. Der kantige Entwurf in Beton stellte die Ästhetik so gut wie aller bis dato bekannter Bauten infrage. Fehlbaum war 2004 zudem Mitglied der Pritzker-Preis-Jury, die Hadid als erste Frau auszeichnete. „Auch ohne jemals zu bauen", sagte Fehlbaum zu diesem Anlass, „wäre es Zaha Hadid gelungen, das architektonische Repertoire räumlicher Ausdrucksformen radikal zu erweitern. Doch wo nun die Umsetzung in Form komplexer Bauten erfolgt, wird die Macht dieser Innovation umfassend deutlich."[9]

Es folgten die Landscape Formation One (Weil am Rhein, 1996–99; Seite 130), das erste von einer Frau erbaute Museum der USA, das Lois & Richard Rosenthal Zentrum für zeitgenössische Kunst (Cincinnati, Ohio, 1997–2003; Seite 164), die Straßenbahnendhaltestelle Hoenheim-Nord (Straßburg, 1998–2001; Seite 148) sowie die Bergisel-Schanze (Innsbruck, 1999–2002; Seite 156). Abgesehen von einem Pavillon im Millennium Dome im Londoner Stadtteil Greenwich waren dies die einzigen realisierten Bauten Hadids, als sie den Pritzker-Preis erhielt. Lord Jacob Rothschild, Vorsitzender der Pritzker-Preis-Jury, merkte an: „Zum ersten Mal wurde eine Frau – und noch dazu eine sehr bemerkenswerte – mit dem Pritzker-Preis ausgezeichnet. Zaha Hadid, geboren im Irak, hat ihr Leben lang in London gearbeitet – dennoch haben sich die konservativen Kräfte bedauerlicherweise als so stark erwiesen, dass in der Hauptstadt, die zu ihrer Wahlheimat wurde, nicht ein einziges Bauwerk von ihr zu finden ist. Über ein Jahrzehnt lang wurde sie für ihr Genie bewundert, mit dem sie Räume erdachte, von denen weniger kreative Geister glaubten, man könne sie nicht bauen. Für diejenigen, die bereit waren, das Risiko einzugehen – von der Vitra-Feuerwache über eine Skischanze in den österreichischen Bergen bis hin zu einer Straßenbahnhaltestelle in Frankreich sowie in jüngster Zeit einem Museumsbau in einer Stadt im tiefsten Mittleren Westen der USA – waren die Folgen von transformierender Kraft. Zugleich blieb Hadid neben ihrem theoretischen und akademischen Werk als praktizierende Architektin immer der Moderne verpflichtet. Stets schöpferisch, löste sie sich von überkommenen Typologien, vom Hightech und verschob die Geometrie ihrer Bauten. Keines ihrer Projekte gleicht dem vorigen, dennoch sind die entscheidenden Merkmale überall zu finden."[10]

WIE EIN CHTHONISCHES URWESEN

In dieser entscheidenden Phase ihrer Laufbahn, Hadid war 54 Jahre alt und relativ jung im Vergleich zu anderen weltbekannten Architekten, hatte sie gerade begonnen, Bauten zu realisieren. Dennoch darf man sich fragen, ob Lord Rothschild und andere tatsächlich Recht haben, wenn sie Hadids „stete Verpflichtung gegenüber der Moderne" betonten oder ihr Werk unter anderem als „verschobene Geometrien" interpretierten. In einem Essay zur LF One schrieb der Architekturkritiker Michael Mönninger: „Der Gartenschaupavillon [erhebt sich] wie ein chthonisches Urwesen aus dem Boden, dem die Anverwandlung an den Untergrund die lineare Bewegungsrichtung vorgibt. Die stromlinienförmigen Windungen des architektonischen Wegebündels sind streng genommen keine raumbildenden, sondern raumaussparende Elemente, zwischen denen sich die Nutzräume des Cafés, Ausstellungssaals und Umweltzentrums im buchstäblichen Sinne beiläufig entfalten."[11] In diesem Zusammenhang gewinnt die elf Jahre zuvor formulierte Einschätzung von Mark Wigley von der „Leere des Luftraums und der Dichte des Baugrunds, Bereichen, die gewöhnlich von der modernen Architektur ausgeschlossen werden, aber

in ihr auftauchen, wenn die Moderne an ihre Grenzen gezwungen und verdrängt wird" neue Relevanz. Der von Mönninger gewählte griechische Begriff „chthonisches Urwesen" (Götter oder Geister der Unterwelt in der griechischen Mythologie) bezeichnet einen deutlichen Gegenpol zu einem so exemplarischen Schlüsselwerk der Moderne wie der Villa Savoye von Le Corbusier (Poissy, Frankreich, 1929), die mit großer Leichtigkeit über dem Boden schwebt und deren makellose Formen weit entfernt von etwas so Dunklem und Unberechenbarem wie der Unterwelt sind. Andere Architekten, etwa Peter Eisenman, haben durchaus bewusst mit erdverbundenen Formen experimentiert, etwa mit der Plattentektonik. Dennoch, nachdem Zaha Hadid 2004 den Pritzker-Preis gewonnen hatte, wurde deutlich, dass sie sich durchaus nicht „immer der Moderne verpflichtet" fühlte, sondern vielmehr begonnen hatte, das Moderne und sogar die Architektur selbst radikal zu hinterfragen. Vielleicht ist der Kommentar von Bill Lacy, Direktor des Pritzker-Preises, zutreffender: „Nur selten gibt es Architekten, deren Philosophie und Herangehensweise an diese Kunstform die Ausrichtung des gesamten Fachs beeinflusst. So eine Architektin ist Zaha Hadid. Geduldig schuf und verfeinerte sie eine Formensprache, die die Grenzen der Baukunst neu definiert."[12]

Tatsächlich ist die Beziehung zu Welten unterhalb der Erdoberfläche, die der Kritiker beim Pavillon LF One ausmacht, eine Unterströmung im Werk von Hadid. „Diese Idee vom Boden und der Manipulation des Bodens beginnt mit den allerfrühesten Projekten", sagte sie selbst. „Ich würde sagen, sie geht zurück bis zur Residenz des irischen Premierministers (Phoenix Park, Dublin, 1979–80; Seite 46), denn dieses Projekt bezieht die verwandte Vorstellung von der künstlichen Landschaft schon mit ein; dann sind da die Studien für die Erweiterungen von Vitra. Als wir mit dem V&A beschäftigt waren [Wettbewerbsbeitrag der Finalisten für die Galerie im Kesselhaus des Victoria & Albert Museums, London, 1995], entwickelte sich die Idee schließlich zur komplexen Terrassenbildung im Innern, als wäre die pastorale Landschaft gewissermaßen in den Innenraum gesogen worden."[13]

DER GESTÖRTE TRAUM VON DER REINEN FORM

Unmittelbar nach Fertigstellung des LF-One-Pavillons konnte sich das Wissenschaftszentrum Phaeno (Wolfsburg, 2000–05; Seite 186) in einem Wettbewerb durchsetzen. Die Architektin beschreibt den Komplex als „überdachte künstliche Landschaft aus Kratern, Höhlen, Terrassen und Plateaus". Der Bau besteht aus zahlreichen individuell gefertigten Schalungselementen und Self-Compacting Concrete (SCC), einem speziellen, selbstverdichtenden Ortbeton, was die ungewöhnlichen – in einigen Fällen äußerst scharfkantigen – Formen realisierbar machte. Obwohl der Bau nicht so tief im Erdreich sitzt wie LF One, ist auch hier etwas vom großen chthonischen Urwesen zu spüren, das diesmal allerdings vollständig an die Oberfläche getreten ist. „Das Phaeno ist die bisher ehrgeizigste, umfassendste Manifestation unserer Suche nach komplexen, dynamischen und fließenden Räumen", sagt Hadid. „Der Besucher sieht sich einer Komplexität und Fremdheit gegenüber, die von einem sehr speziellen System gesteuert wird, das auf einer außergewöhnlichen volumetrischen strukturellen Logik gründet. Die Etagen sind weder übereinandergestapelt noch lassen sie sich als einheitliches Volumen betrachten. Die Masse des Phaenos wird von trichterartigen Kegeln, die in es eindringen und aus ihm herausragen, gestützt und gegliedert. Durch einige Trichter wird das Innere erschlossen, andere dienen dazu, den Innenraum zu belichten, wieder andere beherbergen die notwendige Haustechnik. Hier verbinden sich formale und geometrische Komplexität mit konstruktiver Kühnheit und materieller Authentizität. Um dieses Ziel zu erreichen, wurden viel Zeit und Energie investiert."[14] Mark Wigleys Formulierung, „der Traum von der reinen Form [sei] gestört" worden, gewinnt hier eine ganz neue Bedeutung, obgleich man vom Dekonstruktivismus weit entfernt ist. Das Konzept „künstliche Natur" scheint es vielleicht eher zu treffen; hier entstand ein Gebilde, das wie ein Lebewesen, doch keineswegs wie ein Tier von dieser Welt

9   „Zaha Hadid Becomes the First Woman to Receive the Pritzker Architecture Prize", The Pritzker Architecture Prize, http://www.pritzkerprize.com/2004/announcement (aufgerufen am 1. Juli 2013).

10   Ebd.

WAS, WENN DIE VIELFÄLTIGEN PRÄMISSEN IN ARCHITEKTUR UND DESIGN – VON GERADLINIGER FORMGEBUNG BIS HIN ZUM FUNKTIONSVERSTÄNDNIS VON BAUTEN UND MÖBELN – ALLESAMT DER ERNEUERUNG BEDÜRFTEN?

wirkt, sondern von einer gestalterischen Logik bestimmt wird, die in Grundriss und Querschnitt deutlich spürbar ist.

In Beschreibungen zweier weiterer Projekte gab Hadid zusätzlichen Einblick in ihren Arbeitsprozess sowie ihre Denkweise und deutete an, warum ihre Bauten dieselben Ideen verfolgen und dennoch so verschieden aussehen. Beide Bauten sind Museen für zeitgenössische Kunst, deren Erstentwürfe etwa in dieselbe Zeit fallen: das Lois & Richard Rosenthal Zentrum für zeitgenössische Kunst (Cincinnati, Ohio, 1997–2003; Seite 164) und das MAXXI, Nationalmuseum für Kunst des XXI. Jahrhunderts (Rom, 1998–2009; Seite 262). Hadid führte aus: „Worin sich beide [Bauten] ähneln, ist die Tatsache, dass beide in Sanierungsgebieten liegen und die Eingliederung eines kulturellen Programms gewünscht war. In beiden Fällen geht man davon aus, dass sich der urbane Kontext verändern wird, unsere Projekte sind Kräfte des Wandels [...] Die geometrische Komplexität der Innenräume des Projekts in Rom ist eine Verdichtung der verschiedenen Achsen seines Kontexts. Das Projekt entdeckt urbane Routen, die in der Nachbarschaft schlummern. Jede Verschiebung innerhalb des Felds entspricht einer Situation in der Umgebung. Auch das Projekt in Cincinnati ist kontextuell angelegt, obwohl die Umsetzung von Fall zu Fall höchst unterschiedlich empfunden wird. Die formale Frage wird nicht im Vorfeld entschieden, die verschiedenen formalen Systeme ergeben sich aus den äußerst unterschiedlichen Bedingungen. Eines [der beiden Museen] implodiert stärker nach innen, während das andere permanent zwischen Innen- und Außenraum vermittelt."

AUF DER SUCHE NACH NATÜRLICHEN LINIEN

Ein dichtes urbanes Umfeld oder gar ein Campusentwurf, wie Hadids Vorschlag für das neue Campuscenter am IIT (Illinois Institute of Technology, Chicago, 1998), eignen sich bestens für die komplexen Muster, die sie aus Linien und Formen webte und in Bezug zum Umfeld setzte. Doch mitunter bietet der Standort weniger Anhaltspunkte. Dies gilt beispielsweise für Projekte in Dubai wie die monumentalen Signature Towers (Business Bay, Dubai, VAE, seit 2006; Seite 462). Wie sieht es in einer Umgebung, die buchstäblich aus dem Sand entsteht, mit einem Kontext aus? „In einem solchen Fall erfindet man ihn", sagte Hadid. „Die Geometrie des Kontexts hat entscheidende Auswirkungen. Beim IIT-Projekt in Chicago gab es Linien, die das Projekt mit anderen Instituten verknüpften. Doch Ausblicke und Sichtachsen sind nicht immer entscheidend. Das Museum in Rom ähnelt seinem Standort überhaupt nicht, und doch wurde es von seinem Kontext beeinflusst. Jede Verschiebung im Bau bezieht sich auf eine bereits existierende Geometrie." Patrik Schumacher fügte hinzu: „Manchmal ist das Projekt so groß, dass es seinen eigenen Kontext schafft. Dies gilt etwa für die Business Bay in Dubai, ein Projekt, das über eine halbe Million Quadratmeter groß ist. Es handelt sich um eine ausgesprochen integrierte Komposition. Es ist eines der größten Projekte überhaupt mit einer so umfassenden Kohärenz wie ein einzelnes integriertes Bauwerk." Es scheint, als wären Hadids Projekte ab einer gewissen Größe selbstreferenziell. Dennoch betonte die Architektin, dass selbst bei ungewöhnlich großen Flächen – etwa beim Kartal-Pendik-Masterplan (Istanbul, seit 2006; Seite 438), einem Entwurf für ein völlig neues Stadtzentrum in einem ehemaligen Industriegebiet – fundamentale Bezüge zum Standort und zu etwas, das man vielleicht als dessen natürliche Energie bezeichnen könnte, hergestellt wurden. „Betrachtet man ein Projekt wie den Masterplan für Istanbul", sagte Hadid, „dann ist jedes Segment anders, und dennoch ist das Ganze

11 Michael Mönninger in: LF One, Birkhäuser, Basel, 1999, S. 81.

12 „Zaha Hadid Becomes the First Woman to Receive the Pritzker Architecture Prize", a.a. O.

13 Interview mit Zaha Hadid in: El Croquis, 103, Madrid, 2001.

14 Zaha Hadid laut Presseerklärung des Büros vom 23. November 2005.

15 Zaha Hadid Architects, ZHA-Guangzhou Opera House – China – Conceptual Interpretation, 24. Januar 2008.

als Ort erkennbar. Wir haben nach natürlichen Linien gesucht und das Wasser mit einbezogen. Wir haben uns die Topografie Istanbuls angesehen, um am gegenüberliegenden Ufer eine eigene Topografie zu gestalten."

Hadids 70 000 m² großes Opernhaus in Guangzhou (China, 2003–10; Seite 278) veranschaulicht ihren Ansatz in einer der wichtigsten Städte Chinas, einer Stadt, die derzeit rapides Wachstum und eine Phase der Modernisierung erlebt. In ihrer „konzeptuellen Interpretation" von Standort und Gebäude verknüpfte Hadid Bezüge zur Geologie („Zwillingsfelsen") und zur Stadtanlage einschließlich der Uferbereiche: „Mit seinem Blick auf den Perlfluss zählt das Opernhaus zu den Herzstücken der kulturellen Erschließung Guangzhous. Dank hochmoderner Technologie bei Entwurf und Bau wird das Gebäude zweifellos ein bleibendes Monument des neuen Jahrtausends werden und den Rang Guangzhous als eines der kulturellen Zentren Asiens bekräftigen. Seine einzigartige Gestaltung in Form von Zwillingsfelsen wird seine urbane Funktion untermauern, indem es den Zugang zum Fluss und zu den Hafengegenden erschließt und einen Dialog mit der entstehenden Stadt initiiert." Die Beschreibung veranschaulicht eine ausgeprägte Stärke von Hadids Ansatz: Sie nahm nicht nur Bezug auf die Realität der Stadt, sondern auch auf die Hochtechnologie, Chinas ganzen Stolz –, ein Brückenschlag zwischen Gegenwart und Zukunft. Die Vergangenheit, so unverrückbar wie zwei Felsen und der Fluss, begegnet hier der Zukunft, in der die Kultur in Form von Oper und Architektur ihren Platz einnimmt. Hadids „urbane Strategie/Landschaft" für das Guangzhou-Projekt macht deutlich, dass sie Stadt und Neubau insgesamt als Landschaft verstand, die sie formte und integrierte: „Der Bau erhebt und senkt sich unter dem Zhujiang Boulevard und verbindet zugleich die zwei angrenzenden Grundstücke, auf denen ein Museumsbau und städtische Einrichtungen geplant sind. Als Erweiterung der Haixinsha Tourist Park Island präsentiert sich das Opernhaus mit seinem klar konturierten Profil als monumentaler Brennpunkt am Fluss, der die Aufmerksamkeit der Besucher auf sich ziehen wird. Vom Park in der Mitte des Zhujiang Boulevard wirkt die Oper wie ein visuelles Vorspiel zu der dahinter gelegenen Insel. Vom Fluss aus präsentieren sich die Hochhäuser des Neubauviertels Zhujiang als dramatische Kulisse für das Opernhaus, und so entsteht ein einheitliches Gesamtbild aus städtischen und kulturellen Einrichtungen am Flussufer. Eine Promenade führt zum Opernhaus. Sie durchschneidet die Landschaft und beginnt am geplanten Museumsbau am anderen Ende des zentralen Boulevards. Café, Bar, Restaurant und Einkaufsmöglichkeiten sind wie Muscheln in die landschaftsartigen Formationen integriert."[15]

Die Schlüsselbegriffe dieser Beschreibung sind sicherlich „landschaftsartige Formationen" und „einheitliches Gesamtbild" – das in diesem Fall nicht nur das bestehende urbane Umfeld einschließt, sondern auch einen geplanten Museumsbau unweit des Grundstücks. So überraschend Zaha Hadids Formen auch scheinen mögen, beziehen sie ihre Legitimität doch aus ihrer „nahtlosen" Integration in den jeweiligen Standort oder, wie in Dubai, aus ihrer folgerichtigen inneren Logik. So wie sich Hadids Möbelentwürfe zu einem geschlossenen Ganzen anordnen lassen, erhebt sich ihre Architektur in all ihrer geschichteten Dichte aus dem Erdboden und hinterfragt überkommene geradlinige „Ordnungs"-Begriffe. Diese Architektur lässt eine künstliche Natur entstehen, die ihrem Vorbild durchaus nicht unähnlich ist.

WARTEN AUF FORMZ

Die Malereien und Zeichnungen Zaha Hadids, etwa für frühe Projekte wie The Peak, haben die Architektin nicht nur berühmt gemacht, sondern auch Einfluss auf ihre Entwürfe gehabt. Hadid beschrieb ihren kreativen Prozess als Schichtung vielfältiger Herangehensweisen an eine Fragestellung, die akkumuliert und miteinander verwoben werden, bis sich ein Ergebnis abzeichnet, das sich als Raum und Funktion legitimieren kann. „Die Strichzeichnungen hatten definitiv Einfluss auf mein Werk", so Zaha Hadid. „Es gibt Dinge, die tauchen 10 oder 20 Jahre später wieder auf. In den ersten Jahren habe ich zeichnerisch stark mit Schichten gearbeitet.

MAN KÖNNTE SAGEN, DASS DAS FRÜHE GRAFISCHE WERK HADIDS DURCHAUS DIE COMPUTERREVOLUTION VORWEGNAHM, DIE ES IHREM BÜRO HEUTE ERMÖGLICHT, HÖCHST KOMPLEXE KONSTRUKTIONEN ZU ENTWERFEN.

All diese grafischen Techniken wurden zu Schichtungen im Projekt. Die Komplexität der Zeichnung wurde zu Komplexität in der Architektur." Man könnte also sagen, dass das frühe grafische Werk Hadids durchaus die Computerrevolution vorwegnahm, die es ihrem Büro heute ermöglicht, komplexe Konstruktionen zu entwerfen. „Man kann diesen Entwurfsansatz als Vorläufer der digitalen Technik begreifen", bestätigte Hadid. „Die Computersoftware formZ etwa ist der Zeichentechnik sehr ähnlich. Dennoch glaube ich, dass Handzeichnungen komplexer sind als Computerzeichnungen. Selbst ein vergleichsweise unkonventionelles Projekt hat eine gewisse Konsequenz, und die Zeichnungen zeigen das. Der Prozess hat eine gewisse innere Logik. Es gibt eine Korrelation zwischen dem zeichnerischen Vorgang und der Architektur. Der Computer hat Erfindungen ermöglicht, die es erlauben, komplexe Bauten zu gestalten. Dennoch hat sich die Methode im Kern nicht verändert. Die Arbeitsweise hat sich geändert, die Ideen sind noch immer dieselben. Wenn ich mir manche meiner Skizzen anschaue, sehen sie wie Computerzeichnungen aus. Inzwischen wissen wir dank des Computers, dass man das, was ich zeichne, tatsächlich realisieren kann." Hadid war nahezu 30 Jahre auf anspruchsvollem Niveau architektonisch tätig und erlebte mit, wie die Computer begannen, den Entwurfsprozess zu dominieren. Vielleicht hatte sie Einfluss darauf, in welche Richtung sich die Software und mit ihr die Architektur entwickelte. Doch da ihr kreativer Prozess lange vor der Vorherrschaft des Computers begann, ist es wahrscheinlicher, dass er ihre Konsequenz im Grunde nur bestätigte und stärkte. Während andere noch damit beschäftigt waren, die euklidische Geometrie und die Formensprache der Moderne einer neuen Welt anzupassen, hatte Zaha Hadid ihre Suche nach komplexen Oberflächen und einer vielschichtigen Architektur schon längst begonnen.

Auf die Frage, ob sie nach wie vor zeichne, antwortete Hadid: „Manchmal. Ich glaube, dass man auf sein eigenes Repertoire Bezug nimmt. Man kann auf ein gewisses Wissen zurückgreifen. Es geht nicht so sehr um die Hand, als vielmehr um die Idee. Es geht nicht darum, eine gefällige Zeichnung anzufertigen, sondern darum, wie man eine Idee entwickelt. Nach zahlreichen Ansätzen und Schichten beginnt die Idee, Gestalt anzunehmen. Sie macht es möglich, komplexe Formen zu gestalten und Räume zu organisieren." Patrik Schumacher überträgt diese Argumentation auf die Arbeit des Büros: „Wir interessieren uns für die Natur, für sich verzweigende Systeme, Flüsse und so weiter. Wir nutzen diese Vorstellungen, um architektonische Räume zu entwickeln. Früher wurde das durch Zeichnungen angedeutet, heute wird es am Computer gemacht. Die neuen Hilfsmittel haben ein großartiges Potenzial, Umfelder und komplexe Oberflächen zu simulieren."

Hadid nahm zweifellos „auf [ihr] eigenes Repertoire Bezug". Doch es gibt auch eine radikale neue Herangehensweise an das Verhältnis von Architektur und Mensch, die unter anderem eine Folge des zunehmenden Einsatzes von CAD-Systemen ist. Patrik Schumacher führt aus: „Der Bezug zur Natur ist ein alter Tropus. Es waren nicht nur die Modernen, schon die Architektur der Renaissance und des Klassizismus besann sich zurück und wollte ihre Bauten kosmologisch und mit einer bestimmten Naturauffassung verstanden wissen. In der digitalen Welt ist eine Verbreitung natürlicher Morphologien zu beobachten, die dazu beitragen können, neue Organisationsmuster zu entwickeln. Für uns sind [diese Morphologien] eine Navigations- und Orientierungshilfe, die einem komplexen Umfeld größere Ordnung verleihen kann."[16]

VON NATUR AUS GESETZMÄSSIG UND KOHÄRENT

Fragt man Patrik Schumacher, wie digital manipulierte „natürliche Morphologien" die Architektur konkret optimieren können – eine fundamentale Frage im Hinblick auf Hadids Werk – antwortet er: „Morphologien, die auf diese Weise entstehen, sind oft von Natur aus gesetzmäßig und kohärent. Schon vorher gab es Versuche, mittels Talent oder Komposition eine solche Kohärenz und Gesetzmäßigkeit zu erzielen. Architekten versuchten etwa, intuitiv jene Art von dynamischem Gleichgewicht zu imitieren, die man in der Natur findet, oder beschränkten sich ganz einfach auf platonische Geometrien und Symmetrien – ausgesprochen einfache Ordnungen. Mit den neuen digitalen Hilfsmitteln ist es nun möglich, eine komplexere Ordnung statt einer hässlichen Unordnung zu gestalten, und natürlich gibt es eine Palette verschiedener Werkzeuge, die für verschiedenste Zwecke jenseits der Architektur gedacht sind, die sich aber nutzen lassen, wie RealFlow etc. Ihre Sensibilität greift in gewisser Weise auf die Wahrnehmung natürlicher Systeme zurück."[17]

Vielleicht trauerte Zaha Hadid, deren fundierte grafische Ausbildung an ihren sorgsamen Zeichnungen und Malereien deutlich wird, sogar jenen Tagen nach, bevor der Computer die Herrschaft übernahm. „Ich glaube, dass man den Kontext damals besser analysiert und verstanden hat als heute. Es gab eine wesentlich stärkere Untersuchung und Analyse des Standorts. Manche Modifikationen ergaben sich aus der Standortanalyse. Ich glaube, dass es heute keine Standortanalyse mehr gibt. Kontext- und Standortanalyse sind kein Thema mehr. Meistens sind es nur noch Objekte, die irgendwo landen. Die Frage ist nicht so sehr, ob man Computer nutzt oder nicht. Das Problem des Computers ist, dass er Objekte isoliert. Er richtet den Blick nach innen statt nach außen." Auf die Frage, ob sie sich mit dieser Realität abgefunden habe, antwortete Zaha Hadid: „Ich stehe dem Ganzen sehr kritisch gegenüber. Früher haben wir zwischen Objekt und Feld unterschieden, und ich glaube, dass es an der Technik liegt, dass wir damit aufgehört haben. Es gibt keine Plananalyse mehr." Patrik Schumacher wiederum plädiert für etwas, das er „Eleganz" nennt – in der zeitgenössischen Architektur und besonders im Werk von Zaha Hadid Architects. Diese Eleganz liegt in der intensiven Suche nach einer Lösung, die zahlreiche Studien und ein schrittweises Hervorbringen geeigneter Formen umfasst. „Jedes Element ist eng verknüpft mit dem, was ihm folgt, ebenso wie mit seinem Platz im Gesamtbild. Das bedeutet, dass in diesen Morphologien erhebliche Information eingebettet ist. Es ist ein bisschen wie mit einer Sinfonie. Man kann das Herzstück einer Melodie nicht zerschlagen; bei einer Kakofonie jedoch lässt sich alles herausgreifen und an anderer beliebiger Stelle einfügen. Inzwischen verfügen wir über die nötigen digitalen Hilfsmittel, um dies in einigen unserer Projekte zu realisieren. Alles bedeutet etwas, nichts ist zufällig." Die Kakofonie, von der Schumacher spricht, gibt es etwa in Städten wie Tokio, einer Stadt, die so geschichtet und verschachtelt ist wie kaum eine andere. Sie ist kein System, in dem eine „Eleganz" und Ordnung, wie man sie bei Hadid findet, auch nur ansatzweise erkennbar wäre.

EINE ART NATÜRLICHER COMPUTERANWENDUNG

Hier zeigte Zaha Hadids Suche, die sich in den verschiedensten Objekten, Bauten, Zeichnungen und Ausstellungsarchitekturen manifestierte, ihre ultimative Kontinuität, die in der zeitgenössischen Architektur ihresgleichen sucht. Obwohl Hadid gern von Topografie sprach, definierte sie ihre Suche eher selten als Schaffung einer künstlichen Natur: „Wir haben uns von der Vorstellung gelöst, monumentale Objekte zu schaffen, und begonnen, uns mit der Topografie und dem Boden zu befassen. Wir haben uns mit den zahlreichen Schichten des öffentlichen Raums auseinandergesetzt und damit, wie sich Oberirdisches und Unterirdisches interpretieren lassen könnte. Danach war es der naheliegendste Schritt, sich mit […] der Natur zu befassen", sagte Hadid. Und wieder stellt Patrik Schumacher die Verbindung zwischen dem Kerngedanken Hadids und neuartigen baulichen Formen her. „Es gibt Millionen von natürlichen Objekten, und jedes hat seine eigene Kohärenz", sagt er. „Das Ende bleibt offen. Wo sich geologische Schichten gegeneinander verschieben, gibt es immer Kontinuitäten. Es ist eine Art natürlicher Compu-

---

[16] Patrik Schumacher in: MAD Dinner, Actar, Barcelona, 2007.

[17] Ebd.

DIE ART UND WEISE, WIE VEGETATION AN EINEM BERG EMPORWÄCHST, ERGIBT EINEN SINN. WIR VERSUCHEN, DIESE ART VON LOGIK AUF DIE ARCHITEKTUR ZU ÜBERTRAGEN.

teranwendung, wenn Sie so wollen. Das Ereignis wird inmitten eines Ereignisfelds positioniert, genau dort, wo es sinnvoll ist. Die Art und Weise, wie Vegetation an einem Berg emporwächst, ergibt einen Sinn. Wir versuchen, diese Art von Logik auf die Architektur zu übertragen. Auf diese Weise fließen ausdrucksstarke Schönheit und intuitives Verstehen in die Dinge ein."

ICH WÜRDE ES NICHT ALS SKULPTUR BEZEICHNEN

Ungewöhnlich an Zaha Hadid war auch, dass sie Möbel gestaltete, oder besser gesagt, Objekte, die einen Innenraum definieren. In den letzten Jahren präsentierte Hadid ihre Arbeiten für David Gill Galleries oder Established & Sons als nummerierte und signierte Originale, eine Präsentationsform, die üblicherweise Kunstwerken vorbehalten ist. Natürlich lässt sich diese Trennung nicht scharf ziehen, wenngleich Zaha Hadid den Begriff „Skulptur" für ihre Objekte zurückwies. Sie nahm Stellung zu der Frage, wie sie dazu kam, Designobjekte zu gestalten. „Natürlich haben wir unsere architektonischen Projekte lange Zeit nicht realisieren können, und so kam die Frage auf, wie man sich mit Möbeln in unkonventionellen Räumen beschäftigen könnte. Sie werden Teil einer Innenraumwelt, werden zu Raumteilern. Als wir Objekte für Sawaya & Moroni gestalteten, ging es darum, eine Art von Landschaft oder Topografie zu schaffen [Z-Scape Furniture, 2000; Seite 533]. Der Gedanke war, ein Möbelstück zu gestalten, das Teil eines Ensembles ist und sich wie ein ‚Environment' in einen beengten Raum zwängt, sich aber auch ausdehnen lässt." Tatsächlich gibt die Diskussion, was genau Hadids Designobjekte und ihre Architektur verband, Aufschluss über die Konzeption beider. „Der Übergang zwischen einzelnen Teilen ist im Design ebenso relevant wie in der Architektur", so Patrik Schumacher. „Der Übergang ist fließend und nicht etwa so scharf abgrenzbar, als würde man eine Tischplatte auf vier Beine schrauben. Es ist so etwas wie der Geist des jeweiligen Stils – die totale Umgebung. Im Hotel verstehen wir das Mobiliar als raumschaffende Substanz." Das hier erwähnte Hotel ist das Hotel Puerta América in Madrid (2003–05; Seite 214), für das Hadid nahtlos integrierte Böden und Räume aus thermisch geformtem LG-HI-MACS-Acryl gestaltete. In diesen erstaunlichen Räumen werden die Besucher von Hadids kantenfreien Oberflächen begrüßt, sobald sie den Aufzug verlassen. In den Zimmern werden Decken zu Wänden, Schreibtische wachsen unvermittelt aus der Wand heraus, und sogar die Badewannen fügen sich nahtlos ohne erkennbaren Ansatz in ihr Umfeld ein. Besuchern ohne ausgeprägtem Sinn für Design mag man nachsehen, wenn sie fragen, warum ein Schreibtisch organisch aus der Wand herauswachsen muss, um schließlich zum Bett zu werden. Hier geht es sicherlich weniger um Praktikabilität, als darum, das überkommene Ordnungsprinzip des rechten Winkels zu hinterfragen, das in Design und Architektur so lange geherrscht hat.

MIT DER DIAGONALE FING ALLES AN

„Ich denke ständig darüber nach, wie wir Objekte zusammenfügen könnten", erklärte Zaha Hadid. „Für die Seamless Collection [Established & Sons, 2006] sehe ich die Objekte als multiple Module, von denen man mehrere besitzen kann, etwa einen ganzen Turm aus Schrankmöbeln. Sie lassen sich stets als isolierte Solitäre oder mehrteilige Objekte verstehen." Zweifellos ist es die hier beschriebene Funktionalität – ganz gleich, wie ästhetisch die Objekte auch ineinanderfließen mögen – die erklärt, warum Zaha Hadid diese Arbeiten nicht als skulptural bezeichnete. „Nein, den Begriff würde ich nicht wählen", sagte sie unumwunden. „Skulptural als Gegensatz wozu, zur Flächigkeit? Viele in Serie produzierte Möbel gelten als ‚flach'. Das Auto hingegen – das war ein Montageprinzip, bei dem nichts flach ist. Bei Möbeln kann man inzwischen auch Sonderanfertigungen bekommen. Regale müssen nicht flach sein. Diese [Objekte] hier sind ganz bestimmt nicht minimalistisch – da-

zwischen liegen Welten. Es geht um den Verzicht auf 90°-Winkel. Mit der Diagonale fing alles an. An der Diagonale entzündete sich die Idee von der raumerneuernden Explosion. Das war eine entscheidende Entdeckung."

Die „raumerneuernde Explosion", die Zaha Hadid erwähnte, zeigt sich nur allzu deutlich in ihren Zeichnungen und Gemälden, die 1983 für The Peak entstanden. Waren gerade Linien und 90°-Winkel in der Moderne noch die Regel, etwa aus Gründen der Produktivität, orientierte sich Hadid bewusst an der Diagonalen, in ihrer Architektur ebenso wie in ihren Objekten. Von der scharfkantigen Tektonik ihrer frühen Arbeiten bis hin zur nahtlosen Glätte des Hotels Puerta América wurde die Diagonale zur Metapher für eine bewusst provozierte Explosion des Raums. Sie stellte die grundlegendsten und „offensichtlichsten" Prämissen der Architektur infrage: „Ein Tisch hat eine flache Oberfläche mit vier daran befestigten Beinen"; „Ein Gebäude besteht aus einer Kombination euklidischer Körper ohne lästige Lücken". So komplex Zaha Hadids Werk oft auch scheinen mag, ihre wahre Originalität ist zu ahnen, wo sie selbstverständliche Prämissen und damit das Fundament einer über Generationen tradierten Architektur infrage stellte. Ihre Architektur war tatsächlich eine raumerneuernde Explosion.

Als Hadid ihre *Dune Formations* (David Gill Galleries, 2007) in der Scuola dei Mercanti in Venedig auf der Biennale 2007 präsentierte, lenkte sie den Blick auf einen weiteren höchst interessanten Aspekt: Ihre aus Aluminium und Kunstharz gefertigten Objekte in einem gebrochenen Goldton schienen im geschlossenen Raum des venezianischen Palazzos gleitend von einem Zustand in den nächsten und einer Funktion zur nächsten überzugehen. Entscheidender war jedoch, dass kein Widerspruch zwischen Vergangenheit und Zukunft zu spüren war, zwischen der Geradlinigkeit und den hohen Decken des Altbaus einerseits und Hadids fließenden, geschwungenen Formen andererseits. Wie natürliche Objekte, die in ihrer ultimativen formalen Legitimität nicht anfechtbar sind, so schienen auch die *Dune Formations* – vom wandernden Wüstensand inspiriert – in Venedig keineswegs deplatziert. Wer diese Legitimität spürt, versteht vielleicht ansatzweise, warum Hadid eine bedeutende Architektin und Designerin war. Trotz ihrer frühen Nähe zum russischen Suprematismus gleichen ihre Objekte und Bauten im Grunde nichts, was wir kennen. Dabei scheinen sie ebenso sehr in der Erde zu wurzeln, wie sie von digitalen Entwurfswerkzeugen herrühren. Nicht immer erreichte die geschichtete Komplexität intuitive Legitimität, doch wenn dies tatsächlich gelang, wie bei den *Dune Formations,* schufen sie neue Perspektiven für die Zukunft von Kunst, Architektur und Design.

MAN MUSS ES ALS TEAMWORK VERSTEHEN

Nach der Fertigstellung des Rosenthal-Zentrums 2003 erlebte Hadids Laufbahn einen merklichen Wandel. 300 Architekten arbeiteten nach ihren Vorgaben, Projekte von Großbritannien bis China wurden realisiert – Zaha Hadid war ausgesprochen gefragt. Mit ungewöhnlicher Offenheit merkte sie an: „Ich finde es interessant, so zu arbeiten, aber ich nutze die gegenwärtige Situation auch aus. Ich glaube, es passiert nicht oft im Leben, dass Auftraggeber diese Art von Projekten tatsächlich auf der ganzen Welt wollen. Ich setze meiner Arbeit keine geografischen Grenzen, doch es gibt einige Länder, in denen man vor Ort sein muss – da funktioniert es nicht per E-Mail." Hatte der 2004 verliehene Pritzker-Preis etwas mit der sprunghaft angestiegenen Nachfrage nach ihren Entwürfen zu tun? „Ich denke schon", antwortete Hadid. „Natürlich waren wir auch vorher schon tätig, aber das Ausmaß des Interesses hat sich vervielfacht. Außerdem glaube ich, dass die Leute an dieser Art von Arbeit interessiert sind. Ich habe keine Ahnung, ob es anderen Pritzker-Architekten in ähnlichem Ausmaß so ergangen ist wie uns." Auf die Frage, wie sie mit der Menge an neuen Projekten umgehe, antwortete Hadid: „Da ist natürlich Patrik, aber wir haben auch viele andere Leute, die schon seit Langem hier sind. Viele von ihnen haben bei mir oder Patrik studiert. Bei vielen Dingen fangen wir

DIE DIAGONALE [WURDE] ZUR METAPHER FÜR EINE BEWUSST PROVOZIERTE EXPLOSION DES RAUMS. SIE STELLTE DIE GRUNDLEGENDSTEN UND „OFFENSICHTLICHSTEN" PRÄMISSEN DER ARCHITEKTUR INFRAGE.

immer wieder von vorne an, bis das Ergebnis stimmt. Unsere Organisationsstruktur ist keine Pyramide, bei der ich mit einer Idee ankomme und Dinge nach unten delegiere. Ich glaube, man muss es als Teamwork verstehen. Im Büro forschen wir an Dingen, in die jeder hier Einblick hat."

Den Übergang von einer persönlichen Suche, die sich erstmals in ihrem Gemälde *Horizontal Tektonik, Malevich's Tektonik, London* von 1976/77 zeigte, zu einer global tätigen Architektin meisterte Zaha Hadid mit einer Bravour, die vielen Kollegen in ihrer Branche zu fehlen scheint. Rem Koolhaas, sechs Jahre älter als Hadid, hat sich ebenfalls vom renommierten Theoretiker zum Leiter eines Büros entwickelt, das in der Lage ist, ein so erstaunliches Bauwerk wie die Zentrale des chinesischen Fernsehsenders CCTV in Peking zu realisieren. Doch selbst die Projektliste von OMA lässt sich nicht mit dem vergleichen, woran das Büro Zaha Hadid arbeitet. Die Liste der „im Bau" befindlichen Projekte in diesem Band, von denen einige fertiggestellt sein werden, bis die Leser das Buch schließlich in Händen halten, hat eine beachtliche geografische Bandbreite. Zugleich zeugt sie vom kontinuierlichen Bemühen, Bauten, die Spuren hinterlassen werden, typologisch grundlegend neu zu definieren, selbst wenn sie den Stil und die Dynamik des Büros Hadid infrage stellen könnten.

Mit dem MAXXI, dem Staatsmuseum für Kunst des XXI. Jahrhunderts in Rom (Seite 262), beabsichtigte Hadid, „der materiellen und konzeptuellen Dissonanz, die von der Kunstpraxis seit den 1960er-Jahren vermittelt wird, die Stirn zu bieten". Dabei geht es nicht nur darum, die Form des Museums neu zu definieren, sondern auch die heute übliche Haltung der Museen, auf Kunst ausschließlich zu reagieren. Hadids 842 m lange Sheikh Zayed Bridge wiederum hatte eine Planungszeit von über 13 Jahren (Abu Dhabi, VAE, 1997–2010; Seite 272): Sie verknüpft strukturelle Stränge und überspannt den Kanal zwischen Abu Dhabi und dem Festland mit einer „sinusförmigen Welle". Zugleich stellt Hadid die Brücke (üblicherweise das Terrain von Ingenieuren) formal zur Debatte und definiert sie neu. Dabei bleibt die Konstruktion ein überaus „praktikables" Objekt, das dynamisch genug ist, um „zum Wahrzeichen und potenziellen Katalysator für die zukünftige Entwicklung Abu Dhabis zu werden". Das London Aquatics Centre (London, 2005–11; Seite 292) war zweifellos ein bemerkenswerter Austragungsort der Olympischen Sommerspiele 2012 und zugleich der erste große Bau in einer Stadt, die seit Langem Hadids Wahlheimat war. Das parabolische, zweifach geschwungene Dach und die gesamte Gestaltung der Schwimmhalle, „inspiriert von der fließenden Geometrie bewegten Wassers", ist auch formal eine neue Dimension für Hadids Naturbezüge oder genauer gesagt ihre Bezugnahme auf Objekte, die einer künstlichen Natur entsprungen sind und dabei doch so legitim wirken wie die Dünen oder das fließende Wasser, das sie heraufbeschwören. Das Centre umfasst zwei Bereiche mit Plätzen für 17 500 Zuschauer im zentralen Wettkampf- und Sprungbereich und 5000 Zuschauer bei Wasserpolospielen. Ein entlegeneres Projekt, das Heydar-Aliyev-Kulturzentrum (Baku, Aserbaidschan, 2007–12; Seite 354), nimmt deutlichen Bezug auf die Topografie vor Ort, denn der „Bau verschmilzt mit der Landschaft [...] und verwischt die Grenzen zwischen Bau und Baugrund". Hadid fand außerdem Zeit, eine bemerkenswerte Privatresidenz zu entwerfen, die Capital Hill Residence (Moskau, 2006–14; Seite 378). Das untere Volumen des Hauses wurde teilweise in den Hügel hineingebaut, Teil einer „Strategie, die die Topografie des Außenraums in das Innere des Baus ausdehnt". Darüber hinaus hat es einen 22 m hohen Turm, von dem aus die Bewohner über die 20 m hohen Bäume in der Umgebung blicken können.

In den letzten Jahren konnte Zaha Hadid zwei bedeutende Projekte in Südfrankreich fertigstellen. Einerseits den CMA CGM Tower (Marseille, 2006–11; Seite 302) auf einem Industriehafengelände, umgeben von Straßen und keine 100 m vom Wasser entfernt. Der 94 000 m² große Komplex dominiert seine Umgebung, doch dank des Schwungs seiner aufwärtsstrebenden Formen ist er von einer Eleganz, die längst zum Erkennungszeichen der Architektin geworden ist. Zum anderen das 28 500 m² große Verwaltungsgebäude für das französische Département Hérault. Hadid beschrieb Pierresvives (Montpellier, 2002–12; Seite 322) als „eine

der bisher ambitioniertesten und konsequentesten Umsetzungen unserer Vision von dynamischen, fließenden Räumen. Hier verschmelzen formal-geometrische Komplexität und gewagte Formen mit einer innovativen Nutzung baulicher Materialien. Kreative Architektur geht immer über Grenzen hinaus – ich bin überzeugt, dass Pierresvives der beste Beweis hierfür ist."

DER BEZUG ZUR NATUR IST EIN ALTER TROPUS

Zaha Hadid war keineswegs die erste Architektin, die mit ihren Entwürfen an die Natur anknüpfte. Wie Schumacher bemerkt, ist „der Bezug zur Natur ein alter Tropus". Bedeutende Persönlichkeiten von Frank Lloyd Wright bis Toyo Ito haben ihr Werk im natürlichen Umfeld verankert, wenn auch buchstäblicher als Hadid. Wirkte Frank Lloyd Wrights Fallingwater (Edgar J. Kaufmann House, Mill Run, Pennsylvania, 1934–37) in den späten 1930er-Jahren auf die Besucher ebenso futuristisch wie es die Capital Hill Residence in den Wäldern um Moskau zweifellos tut? Die nahtlos glatten Entwürfe Hadids, die dank neuester Technologien und Materialien realisiert werden konnten, lassen sich nie auf reine Naturnachahmung reduzieren. Ihr Ziel war etwas anderes, und deshalb war Hadid auch keine Wright-Schülerin. Ihre Art von Natur erwächst aus dem Boden oder der Stadtlandschaft wie ein „chthonisches Urwesen", das nicht etwa aus einer gemeinsamen Erfahrung geboren wird, sondern so selbstverständlich wirkt wie ein uralter Mythos. Hier herrscht Geometrie, die jedoch aus komplexen Kurven und einander überlagernden Mustern besteht. Sie sind dem Geist Zaha Hadids entsprungen, um nun dank der digitalen Revolution in Entwurf und Fertigung, die das Einzigartige möglich macht, Gestalt anzunehmen. Die Neuartigkeit der Moderne lag unter anderem in ihrer Makellosigkeit, sie mied die Unterwelt aufs Peinlichste. Nur selten haben moderne Bauten sichtbar den Schritt unter die Erde gewagt. Keller galt es zu verbergen, über der Erde herrschte der scharf umrissene euklidische Körper absolut. Elegante Stützen schützten die weiße Unschuld der neuen Moderne vor der Beschmutzung durch die Erde. Mit einem Meisterwerk wie dem Farnsworth House (1945–50, Plano, Illinois) strebte Ludwig Mies van der Rohe nach der Verschmelzung mit der Natur. Dennoch wurde sein Bau damals trotz seiner kristallinen Klarheit von der Zeitschrift „House Beautiful" abfällig als „Glaskäfig auf Stelzen" abgetan. Bei Hadid hingegen mag die Natur vielleicht künstlich sein – trotzdem ist sie Natur, mit all ihren dunklen Geheimnissen.

EINE FLIESSENDE UND NATÜRLICHE ARCHITEKTURSPRACHE

Zwei jüngere, temporäre Projekte von Zaha Hadid illustrieren die Bandbreite ihrer Interessen und ihres Schaffens. Zugleich veranschaulichen sie auch die Unersättlichkeit, mit der sie unter Beweis stellte, dass ihre Methoden unter den verschiedensten Bedingungen umsetzbar waren. Ihr mobiler Ausstellungspavillon für Chanel (verschiedene Standorte, 2007–08; Seite 244) konnte keinen Bezug auf spezifische Kontexte nehmen, da er auf Wunsch des ursprünglichen Auftraggebers Karl Lagerfeld auch an anderen Standorten einsetzbar sein sollte. Erstellt mithilfe modernster digitaler Entwurfstechniken, bediente sich der Pavillon einer, wie Hadid formulierte, „fließenden und natürlichen Architektursprache" oder auch „einer künstlichen Landschaft". Bemerkenswerterweise sagt Lagerfeld, Ästhet mit intuitivem Gespür für Design, über Hadid: „Sie ist die erste Architektin, die einen Weg gefunden hat, sich von der alles beherrschenden Post-Bauhaus-Ästhetik zu lösen." Heute hat der Pavillon eine dauerhafte Heimat in Paris gefunden, unweit von Jean Nouvels Institut du Monde Arabe.

Ein zweites temporäres Projekt (*Lilas*, temporäre Installation, Serpentine Gallery, Kensington Gardens, London, 2007; Seite 570) bestand aus drei 5,5 m hohen Schirmen, die auf einer 310 m² großen Plattform angeordnet waren. Die mit heiß verschweißtem PVC-Gewebe ummantelten Schirme waren von „komplexen natürlichen Formen wie Blütenblättern und Blättern inspiriert", wirkten jedoch in erster Linie skulptural, als man sie für die Sommerparty der Serpentine Gallery mit extrem knappem Zeitplan installiert hatte. Der amerikanische Bildhauer Richard Serra sagte einmal, der Unterschied zwischen Kunst und Architektur bestehe darin, dass Architektur einen Zweck habe. Die *Lilas*-Installation diente zweifellos einem Zweck, doch besonders durch ihre Präsenz knüpfte sie ohne Frage an die Kunstwelt an, zumindest an eine Form von Kunst, die sich der Welt, Natur und Schönheit nach wie vor verpflichtet fühlt. Nicolai Ouroussoff, Architekturkritiker der *New York Times*, schrieb über Hadid: „Indem sie so disparate Stränge zu einer Vision verknüpft, bejaht sie trotzig einen Kosmopolitismus, der sich in unserem dunklen Zeitalter nur schwer behaupten kann. Das kommt einem Manifest für die Zukunft so nahe wie nur möglich."[18]

Patrik Schumachers Theorie der „Eleganz" im Werk Zaha Hadids ist im Grunde auch eine Antwort auf die unterschwellige Frage, was genau die Innovationen des Büros ausmacht und von welchem Nutzen sie sind. „Warum sollten wir uns die Mühe machen, nach dieser immer schwerer zu findenden Eleganz zu streben? Hat sie einen Nutzen, der über den reinen Selbstzweck hinausgeht?", fragt er. Es lohnt, seine Antwort genau zu lesen: „Heute sind die Anforderungen an die Architektur von einer Forderung nach immer komplexeren und zugleich programmatischen Vorgaben gekennzeichnet, die in immer komplexeren urbanen Kontexten organisiert werden müssen. Eleganz erlaubt, zunehmende programmatische Komplexität mit einem Minimum an visueller Kompliziertheit zu realisieren, indem sie heterogene Elemente in ein kohärentes und kontinuierliches, formales und räumliches System integriert. Die Herausforderung besteht im Grunde darin, kompositionelle Lösungen zu finden, um komplexe Arrangements und Beziehungen gestalten zu können, ohne dabei Lesbarkeit und Orientierung für die Nutzer zur Disposition zu stellen. Eine solchermaßen definierte Eleganz steht für das Vermögen, komplexe Lebensprozesse so zu artikulieren, dass Verständlichkeit, Lesbarkeit und nahtlose Orientierung innerhalb der Komposition gewährleistet sind."[19]

ENTFESSELTE ARCHITEKTUR

Während sich andere vorzugsweise dem zumeist bedeutungsfreien computergenerierten „Blob" verschrieben haben, hat Zaha Hadid aus der Vorcomputerzeit Ideen hinübergerettet, die nun mithilfe neuer Technologien realisierbar sind. Ihre präzisen, schichtartig aufgebauten Zeichnungen waren schon immer darauf angelegt, reale Bauten hervorzubringen. Hadid war nie an bloßer Ästhetik interessiert, obwohl sie sich von den Suprematisten inspirieren ließ. Allerdings sollte gesagt werden, dass die Konstruktivisten und Suprematisten, anders als die Meister der Sowjetzeit, die Russlands Schicksal werden sollten, tatsächlich eine Vision von einer schönen neuen Welt vor Augen hatten. Hadid hat nicht nur die Post-Bauhaus-Ästhetik aufgebrochen, sondern – was wesentlich wichtiger ist – das Primat des Rasters und der euklidischen Körper. Ihr Raum wogt hin und her wie die Systeme der natürlichen Verzweigungen, auf die Patrik Schumacher verweist. Ihr Werk steht an der Schnittstelle zwischen Architektur, Kunst und Design, eine Verbindung, die nicht immer vollständig gelingt, da sich ihr Gestaltungsprozess unablässig entwickelt. „Die Architektur der Avantgarde schafft Manifeste: paradigmatische Demonstrationen des einzigartigen Potenzials eines neuen Stils und nicht etwa Bauten, die ausgewogen sind und in jeder Hinsicht funktionieren",[20] postuliert Schumacher mit einiger Kühnheit. Entscheidend ist jedoch – wie zahlreiche Projekte in diesem Band

belegen – dass Hadid erfolgreich der Sprung von Theorie und bildlicher Darstellung zu realen Bauten gelang. Diese Entwicklung wurde durch die Wirtschaftskrise nach 2008 nur geringfügig gebremst. Als sie starb, war sie eine der gefragtesten und unverwechselbarsten Architektinnen unserer Zeit.

Zaha Hadids abenteuerliche Reise war bemerkenswert. Ihren Erfolg verdankte sie ihrer Unbeirrtheit und der Überzeugung, dass Architektur und Design nicht zwangsläufig so sein müssen, wie sie schon immer waren. Die vom Bauhaus inspirierte Architektur war im Grunde an industrielle Fertigungsmethoden gebunden und notgedrungen repetitiv, um kosteneffizient sein zu können. Hadids Architekturkonzept hingegen, geboren aus einer rigorosen Logik und einem Designverständnis, das die euklidischen Grenzen sprengt, wurde erst durch eine neuerliche industrielle Revolution möglich, die von digitalen Entwurfs- und Fertigungsmethoden vorangetrieben wurde. Schreibtische konnten aus Wänden hervorspringen und Brücken begannen, in sinusförmigen Wellen zu tanzen. Zaha Hadid entfesselte die Architektur – und nichts wird sein wie zuvor.

Philip Jodidio, Grimentz, Schweiz

---

[18] Nicolai Ouroussoff, „Zaha Hadid: A Diva for the Digital Age", in: The New York Times, 2. Juni 2006.

[19] Patrik Schumacher, „Arguing for Elegance", in: AD (Architectural Design), London, Januar/Februar 2007.

[20] Patrik Schumacher, „Zaha Hadid Architects – Experimentation within a Long Wave of Innovation", a. a. O., S. 93–94.

FAIRE EXPLOSER L'ESPACE
POUR LE REMETTRE EN FORME

Dans cette période d'incertitude envahissante qui touche aussi bien à la santé, à la sécurité, à l'économie et à l'environnement qu'à la politique, il pourrait sembler naturel que l'architecture contemporaine reflète cet état de flux et se montre incapable de choisir une direction déterminée. On la voit ainsi se disperser entre minimalisme ascétique, prosélytisme écologique et décoration néobaroque. Néanmoins, certains praticiens sont suffisamment courageux pour s'attaquer au problème de la continuité, et oser dire que se dessine peut-être un nouveau paradigme digne d'intérêt et même d'émulation. Peu ont été aussi qualifiés pour animer ce mouvement que Zaha Hadid, Prix Pritzker 2004, dont la disparition prématurée en mars 2016 est universellement pleurée. Patrik Schumacher, son collaborateur de longue date, a signé en 2008 un texte publié dans le catalogue de la Biennale d'architecture de Venise qui disait : « Un style indéniablement nouveau se manifeste aujourd'hui dans l'architecture d'avant-garde. Sa caractéristique la plus frappante est sa linéarité faite de courbes complexes et dynamiques. Au-delà de cette spécificité d'apparence, il est possible d'identifier une série de nouveaux concepts et méthodes, si différents du répertoire de l'architecture moderne ou traditionnelle que l'on pourrait parler d'émergence d'un nouveau paradigme en architecture. Les concepts, les répertoires formels, les logiques tectoniques et les techniques informatiques qui caractérisent ce travail donnent naissance à un nouveau style à vocation dominante, le « paramétricisme ». Le paramétricisme est ce style nouveau qui succède au modernisme. Le postmodernisme et le déconstructivisme ont été des épisodes de transition qui annonçaient cette nouvelle et profonde vague de recherche et d'innovation. Le modernisme se fondait sur le concept d'espace. Le paramétricisme différencie les champs. Les champs sont remplis, comme occupés par un médium fluide. De la composition des parties, nous nous orientons vers des champs de particules dynamiques [1]. Cette sensibilité s'est radicalisée et raffinée au cours de trente années de travail. Les nouveaux modes de représentation ont joué un rôle crucial pour rendre ces avancées possibles [2]. »

Que le terme de paramétricisme convienne et devienne celui d'un style ou d'une école d'architecture contemporaine reconnue reste à voir, mais il est clair que l'agence Zaha Hadid Architects, depuis ses débuts, il y a un peu plus de trente ans, a mis le projecteur sur une méthode et une approche de l'architecture qui interpellent bon nombre de ses hypothèses fondamentales. En dehors de sa volonté de remettre en question la géométrie ou plus précisément l'organisation même et la disposition spatiale utilisées en architecture, Hadid a fait preuve d'une remarquable consistance et continuité de pensée tout au long de sa carrière professionnelle. Cette continuité n'est pas liée à un style reposant sur une trame comme chez Richard Meier ou Tadao Ando, par exemple. Son œuvre construite et ses projets se ressemblent en termes de fluidité de plans et de mouvement des volumes et des surfaces, mais de l'anguleux poste d'incendie pour Vitra (Weil am Rhein, Allemagne, 1991–93, page 116) à sa plus récente installation d'objets mobiliers *Dune Formations* (David Gill Galleries, 2007, page 562), se retrouve un esprit identique qui fait regarder d'un œil différent l'architecture et les meubles du passé. Que se passerait-il si les nombreuses hypothèses sur lesquelles reposent l'architecture et le design – de la forme rectiligne aux modes de fonctionnement d'une construction ou d'un meuble – étaient remises en questions et soumises à un profond renouvellement ?

Si la nature est capable de générer une infinie variété d'objets dotés d'une légitimité fondamentale, l'architecture, qui est l'art de construire notre environnement bâti, ne pourrait-elle atteindre à une légitimité semblable par une lecture nouvelle du contexte et de la fonction, par la création volontaire de vides au même titre que de pleins, par la remise en question de la primauté de cet angle droit si rare dans la nature ? Serait-ce là cette nature artificielle à laquelle tant d'architectes et de penseurs ont rêvé ?

HYBRIDISATION, MORPHISME, DÉTERRITORIALISATION

Schumacher décrit le paramétricisme en termes formels pouvant paraître moins révolutionnaires que les fondamentaux de l'architecture de Hadid qui dépassent à l'évidence le débat formaliste. « Ce programme/style consiste en règles méthodologiques : certaines nous indiquent quelles voies de recherche éviter (heuristique négative) et d'autres quelles voies poursuivre (heuristique positive). L'heuristique qui définit le paramétricisme se reflète pleinement dans les tabous et les dogmes de notre culture du projet. L'heuristique négative : éviter les typologies familières, éviter les objets platoniciens/hermétiques, éviter les zones/territoires nettement délimités, éviter la répétition, éviter les lignes droites, éviter les angles droits, éviter les coins [...]. Heuristique positive : hybrider, morpher, déterritorialiser, déformer, réitérer, utiliser des rainures, des nœuds, des composants générateurs, le scénario plutôt que la maquette [3] [...] ».

De même que Zaha Hadid a constitué une œuvre remarquablement cohérente et consistante sur une période de plus de trente ans, revenant souvent sur des idées dont l'ancrage apparaît très tôt dans sa carrière, toute description de son travail pourrait évoquer des torons qui, une fois réunis, décriraient sa réussite non comme une progression linéaire, mais comme un tissage complexe d'idées, de lignes et de formes. Il n'est donc pas incongru de sauter de la Biennale d'architecture de Venise 2008 et du manifeste « Expérimentation dans une longue vague d'innovation », au moment, vingt ans plus tôt, qui a vu Zaha Hadid attirer pour la première fois l'attention du grand public.

L'Oxford English Dictionary définit la déconstruction comme « une stratégie d'analyse critique [...] qui a pour but la mise en évidence de présupposés métaphysiques et de contradictions internes, non remis en cause dans le langage philosophique et littéraire ». Popularisée par le philosophe français Jacques Derrida (1930–2004), la déconstruction a été utilisée au sens philosophique pour expliquer en partie l'architecture. Derrida lui-même a appliqué sa pensée à l'architecture dans un texte sur les « folies » de Bernard Tschumi pour le Parc de la Villette à Paris, « Point de folie : maintenant l'architecture ». Il y parlait de « déconstruction programmatique », ou « d'une dislocation générale des folies qui semble remettre en question tout ce qui a, jusqu'à aujourd'hui, donné du sens à l'architecture. Plus précisément, ce qui semble avoir ordonné l'architecture dans son rapport au sens. Les folies déconstruisent d'abord, mais non seulement, la sémantique architecturale [4]. »

Le programme radical qu'impliquait la déconstruction littéraire n'était en fait pas si éloigné des formes surprenantes qui avaient fait leur apparition publique lors de l'exposition intitulée « Deconstructivist Architecture », organisée au Museum of Modern Art de New York (MoMA) en 1988, et dont Philip Johnson et Marc Wigley étaient les commissaires. Sept architectes avaient été sélectionnés : Frank Gehry, Daniel Libeskind, Rem Koolhaas, Peter Eisenman, Zaha Hadid, Coop Himmelb(l)au et Bernard Tschumi pour son intervention sur le Parc de la Villette. Les attendus des commissaires confirmaient l'idée d'un changement radical dans l'architecture contemporaine. « L'architecture a toujours été une institution culturelle centrale appréciée par-dessus tout parce qu'elle apportait stabilité et ordre. On peut considérer que ces qualités étaient issues de la pureté géométrique de ses compositions formelles », écrivait Marc Wigley, qui poursuivait : « ... Les projets présentés dans cette exposition annoncent une sensibilité différente, dans laquelle

[1] Sauf indication contraire, toutes les citations proviennent d'un entretien entre Zaha Hadid, Patrik Schumacher et l'auteur, qui s'est tenu à Londres le 10 avril 2008.

« On pourrait penser à des liquides en mouvement, structurés par des vagues irradiantes, des flux laminaires et des tourbillons en spirale », dit Patrik Schumacher.

[2] Patrik Schumacher, « Zaha Hadid Architects – Experimentation within a Long Wave of Innovation », dans : *Out There, Architecture Beyond Building*, Marsilio Editori, Venise, 2008, vol. 3, p. 91–92.

[3] Ibid., p. 94–95.

[4] Jacques Derrida, « Point de folie : maintenant l'architecture », in *La Case Vide*, La Villette, 1985.

[5] Mark Wigley in *Deconstructivist Architecture*, The Museum of Modern Art, New York, 1988.

le rêve de la forme pure a été brouillé. La forme a ainsi été contaminée. Le rêve est devenu une sorte de cauchemar [5]. »

AU CŒUR COMPLEXE
DE LA PURETÉ MODERNISTE

Si le mot « déconstruction » impliquait pour beaucoup un acte de destruction, Mark Wigley et les architectes adeptes de ce mouvement poursuivaient des buts différents. « Un architecte déconstructiviste n'est pas celui qui démantèle des bâtiments, mais celui qui repère les dilemmes inhérents à ces bâtiments. L'architecte déconstructiviste place les formes pures de la tradition architecturale sur le divan et identifie les symptômes d'une impureté refoulée. L'impureté est attirée à la surface par une combinaison de douces cajoleries pleines de douceur et de violentes tortures : la forme est soumise à un interrogatoire [6] », explique Wigley. Lui et d'autres avaient repéré un lien entre le travail des sept architectes sélectionnés et la révolution artistique des mouvements constructivistes et suprématistes russes peu après la révolution beaucoup plus politique de 1917. « L'avant-garde russe a menacé la tradition en rompant avec les règles classiques de composition par lesquelles une relation équilibrée et hiérarchique entre les formes créait un tout unifié. Les formes pures servaient maintenant à produire des compositions géométriques "impures" biaisées [7]. » Il est un fait que les dessins de Wladimir Krinsky reproduits dans le catalogue de l'exposition, ou les peintures suprématistes de Kasimir Malevitch, font directement penser à l'œuvre de Frank Gehry ou à celle de la seule femme participante, Zaha Hadid. Le projet qui lui avait permis de remporter le concours international pour le Peak de Hongkong (1982–83, page 50) que Johnson et Wigley choisirent de présenter au MoMA. Sur ce projet de club privé Wigley écrivait : « Le club s'étire entre les creux du vide et la densité de masses pleines souterraines, domaines normalement exclus de l'architecture moderne mais que l'on retrouve en poussant de force le modernisme dans ses limites. Ainsi, ce palais des plaisirs, ce club hédoniste trouve sa place au cœur complexe de la pureté moderniste [8]. »

Vingt ans plus tard, Zaha Hadid et son associé Patrik Schumacher se référaient encore à cette exposition du MoMA. « [Elle] portait sur la contraction de deux mondes, disait-elle, la déconstruction au sens de pensée et le constructivisme, ce mouvement russe. Utiliser ces deux mots en faisait quelque chose d'hybride. Je crois que cette exposition a été très importante parce que c'était la première fois que des gens commençaient à regarder une architecture non normative. Malheureusement, il n'y avait guère alors de réalisation déconstructiviste d'importance à montrer. Aucun d'entre nous ne construisait, ce qui était dommage, à mon avis. » L'intérêt de l'architecte pour les suprématistes était évident dans ses tout premiers travaux comme dans cette peinture méticuleusement exécutée pour sa thèse (*Horizontal Tektonic, Malevich's Tektonik, London*, acrylique sur papier cartouche, 128 x 89 cm, 1976–77, San Francisco Museum of Modern Art, page 32). Plus de dix ans après cette thèse, au moment de l'exposition du MoMA, Hadid était prête à appliquer à l'architecture les leçons du suprématisme et à prendre la structure en compte. En tant qu'architecte formée dans le cercle de Koolhaas, elle avait eu l'intuition que le moment de faire évoluer l'art de construire était venu. D'autres participants à cette fameuse exposition, comme Frank Gehry, laissèrent une forte marque sur l'architecture contemporaine, mais, dans le cas de ce dernier, on peut voir que l'art prime chez lui dans une symphonie de formes dansantes qui libère certes les bâtiments de leurs contraintes géométriques, mais ne répond sans doute pas aux questions profondes de la logique même de l'architecture auxquelles Zaha Hadid avait toujours été attachée.

---

[6] Ibid.
[7] Ibid.
[8] Ibid.

BRISER TOUTES LES RÈGLES,
MAIS TOUJOURS BIEN DESSINER

Bien que Wigley ait affirmé que ces architectes ne voulaient rien démanteler, Patrik Schumacher exprime une vision légèrement différente : « Vous pouvez voir le déconstructivisme comme un style de transition. C'était une sorte de destruction créative qui installait le cadre d'objectifs positifs. » La définition de Wigley du mouvement était peut-être trop modeste pour s'appliquer à une personnalité comme Zaha Hadid qui continua à redéfinir l'architecture en défiant la description de « compositions géométriques en biais » utilisée en 1988. « L'exposition du MoMA était intéressante, disait récemment Hadid, car elle brisait des règles et s'écartait des idées de typologie. L'élément le plus important était la rupture entre le plan d'organisation et de la coupe. Contrairement à ce que certaines personnes pensaient alors, nous étions très précis. Notre travail était très affiné en termes de géométrie, ce n'était pas de la bande dessinée. Rompre avec la typologie, rompre les règles, représentaient des démarches très importantes parce que c'était la première fois que l'on prenait conscience de ces possibilités. »

Dès le départ, contrairement à ce que certains critiques ont pu jadis suggérer, le travail de Zaha Hadid reposait non seulement sur une authentique compréhension de l'architecture, mais aussi sur un réel talent de dessin et une relation profonde entre les deux. Ceci la séparait à première vue et d'une certaine façon des révolutionnaires russes d'une autre époque souvent plus engagés dans les spéculations géométriques et le questionnement esthétique que dans un désir réel de construire. Hadid combinait le défi qu'ils lançaient aux alignements spatiaux alors de mise avec une connaissance concrète de l'architecture et c'est ce qui lui donne une dimension autre que celle de simple « déconstructiviste ». La combinaison d'une révolution intellectuelle en architecture et des réalités pratiques de la construction anime le travail de Zaha Hadid Architects depuis les débuts de l'agence. Lorsqu'on l'interrogeait sur ses relations avec les ingénieurs structurels, elle répondait : « Nous travaillons toujours avec les mêmes, bien qu'appartenant à des bureaux d'études différents. Nous avons mis au point un système, ce qui nous a permis de penser l'espace de façon différente et je pense que ça a été une collaboration très stimulante. Les ingénieurs n'interviennent pas à la fin, mais dès le départ. Ils doivent être impliqués dans ces énormes structures-paysages qui supportent les sols ou soutiennent la toiture. » Plutôt que de se défier des ingénieurs comme beaucoup d'architectes novateurs, Hadid avait recherché leur aide, mais à l'intérieur d'un processus méthodologique qui intégrait leur apport dans le tout. Ce processus avait même débuté avant qu'elle ne construise vraiment beaucoup, autre preuve de sa constance et de son énergie qui lui ont valu la réputation justifiée de compter parmi les architectes les plus créatifs au monde.

LA PUISSANCE DE
L'INNOVATION RÉVÉLÉE

Née à Bagdad en 1950, Zaha Hadid a étudié l'architecture à l'Architectural Association (AA) de Londres, où elle a obtenu le prix du Diplôme en 1977. Elle est ensuite devenue partenaire de l'Office for Metropolitan Architecture (OMA) et a enseigné avec le fondateur de l'OMA, Rem Koolhaas à l'AA où elle a dirigé son propre atelier jusqu'en 1987. Elle a été titulaire de la chaire Kenzo Tange à la Harvard University Graduate School of Design, de la chaire Sullivan de l'École d'architecture de l'université de l'Illinois (Chicago) et professeure invitée à la Hochschule für bildende Künste à Hambourg (Allemagne) ainsi qu'à l'Université des Arts appliqués de Vienne (Autriche), et professeure invitée Eero Saarinen de conception architecturale à l'université Yale (New Haven, Connecticut, 2004). Peu d'architectes ont eu un impact aussi considérable que celui de Hadid par ses travaux graphiques (peintures et dessins) et par leur enseignement. En fait, jusqu'à une date relativement récente, son œuvre construite aurait pu être considérée comme très réduite selon les standards habituels des grands architectes internationaux. L'un de ses premiers clients a été Rolf Fehlbaum, président-directeur général de la société de mobilier allemande Vitra. Le poste d'incendie de l'usine Vitra figurait dans les livres et les magazines d'architecture contemporaine, avant même d'être construit. Ses formes vives et anguleuses en béton défiaient l'esthétique de quasiment toute construction connue. Fehlbaum fut également membre du jury du prix Pritzker qui, en 2004, conféra cette prestigieuse distinction pour la première fois à une femme, Zaha Hadid. « Sans avoir jamais construit, déclara-t-il à cette occasion, Zaha Hadid avait déjà radicalement enrichi le répertoire d'articulations spatiales de l'architecture. Maintenant que cette avancée s'incarne dans ses constructions complexes, la puissance de son innovation est pleinement reconnue [9]. »

Le projet pour Vitra fut suivi par Landscape Formation One (LF One, Weil am Rhein, Allemagne, 1996–99, page 130), par le Centre d'Art contemporain Lois & Richard Rosenthal (Cincinnati, Ohio, 1999–2003, page 164) – premier musée construit par une femme aux États-Unis – par le Terminal intermodal d'Hoenheim-Nord (Strasbourg, France, 1998–2001, page 148) et par le tremplin de ski de Bergisel (Innsbruck, Autriche, 1999–2002, page 156). En dehors d'un pavillon monté sous le Millennium Dome à Greenwich (Londres, 2000, page 142), c'étaient alors ses seules réalisations achevées lorsqu'elle remporta le prix Pritzker. Lord Jacob Rothschild, président du jury déclara : « Pour la première fois, une femme – et une femme très remarquable – reçoit le prix Pritzker. Zaha Hadid, née en Irak, a travaillé toute sa vie à Londres, mais telles sont les forces du conservatisme que l'on doit regretter de ne pas trouver un seul bâtiment construit par elle dans la ville dont elle a fait sa résidence. Depuis plus d'une décennie, elle a été admirée pour son génie de la vision d'espaces que des esprits moins imaginatifs auraient pu penser irréalisables. Pour ceux qui furent prêts à prendre le risque, du poste d'incendie de Vitra à un tremplin de saut à ski en Autriche, d'une gare de trams en France à, plus récemment, un musée dans une ville du Midwest américain profond, l'impact a été radical. Tant dans son travail théorique que dans son enseignement et sa pratique, elle s'est montrée inébranlable dans son engagement au service de la modernité. Toujours inventive, elle s'est écartée des typologies existantes, du *high-tech* et a fait évoluer la géométrie architecturale. Aucun de ses projets ne ressemble à celui qui précède, mais les caractéristiques qui les définissent restent cohérentes [10]. »

COMME UNE CRÉATURE CHTONIENNE

À ce stade important de sa carrière, à 54 ans, donc assez jeune selon les standards des grands architectes, elle commence seulement à imposer sa marque, mais on peut se demander si Lord Rothschild et les autres membres du jury ont eu raison d'insister sur son « engagement inébranlable en faveur du modernisme », ou même de définir son travail en termes de géométrie « évoluée ». Dans un essai sur le Pavillon LF One, le critique d'architecture allemand Michael Mönninger a écrit : « Ce pavillon de jardin s'extrait du sol comme une créature chtonienne dont le mouvement linéaire s'extrairait du sous-sol. Les courbes épurées de ce cheminement architectural, si on les regarde bien, ne sont pas des éléments qui créent le volume, mais plutôt l'évitent, et les pièces de service, le café, la salle d'expositions et le centre sur l'environnement se déploient littéralement entre elles, comme en passant [11]. » Le commentaire de Mark Wigley, prononcé onze années plus tôt, revient à l'esprit avec une nouvelle pertinence : « Entre les creux du vide et la densité des masses solides souterraines, domaines normalement exclus de l'architecture moderne, mais que l'on retrouve dans son essence en poussant le modernisme à ses limites. » Le terme grec utilisé par Mönninger de « créature chto-

nienne » (divinités ou esprits du monde souterrain dans les croyances grecques) pour décrire cette réalisation, la situe radicalement à l'opposé d'une œuvre fondamentale du modernisme, comme la Villa Savoye de Le Corbusier (Poissy, France, 1929) qui repose avec légèreté sur le sol, et dont les formes épurées n'entretiennent pas la moindre relation avec un monde souterrain imprévisible et obscur. D'autres architectes comme Peter Eisenman ont activement travaillé sur des formes liées au sol, ou à la tectonique des plaques, mais même lorsque Hadid a remporté son prix Pritzker en 2004, il était depuis longtemps évident que plutôt que dans une « engagement inébranlable envers le modernisme », elle s'était lancée dans une remise en question intégrale de ce qui est moderne et de l'architecture elle-même. Il se peut que le commentaire de Bill Lacy, directeur exécutif du prix Pritzker, ait été plus pertinent lorsqu'il écrivait : « Il est rare qu'apparaisse un architecte possédant une philosophie et une approche de l'art qui influencent les orientations de toute une profession. Zaha Hadid en fait partie, qui a patiemment créé et mis au point un vocabulaire qui modifie les limites imposées à l'art de l'architecture [12]. »

En fait, ce que le critique allemand percevait comme une relation avec le monde souterrain dans le Pavillon LF One est, assez littéralement, l'un des courants profonds qui animaient le travail de Zaha Hadid. « Cette idée de sol et de manipulation du sol part de mes tout premiers projets, expliquait-elle. Je dirais qu'elle remonte à la résidence conçue pour le Premier ministre d'Irlande (Phoenix Park, Dublin, 1979–80, page 46) parce que ce projet traitait déjà de l'idée de paysage artificiel et également des études pour les extensions de Vitra. Puis nous avons fait le V&A (finaliste au concours pour la Boilerhouse Gallery, Victoria and Albert Museum, Londres, 1995) dans laquelle cette idée se matérialise sous forme d'un terrassement complexe du volume intérieur, comme si un paysage pastoral était en voie d'être aspiré par l'intérieur [13]. »

LE RÊVE DE LA FORME PURE PERTURBÉ

Projet lauréat d'un concours remporté juste après l'achèvement du Pavillon LF One, le Centre des Sciences Phaeno (Wolfsburg, Allemagne, 2000–05, page 186) est présenté par l'architecte comme « un paysage artificiel couvert » constitué de « cratères, cavernes, terrasses et plateaux ». La réalisation de ces formes inhabituelles, dont certaines très aigues, a nécessité des coffrages spéciaux et un « béton autocompactant » (SCC) coulé en place. Même s'il ne s'appuie pas autant sur le sol que le projet LF One, on y retrouve un peu d'une gigantesque créature chtonienne qui aurait fait surface. « Le Phaeno est le plus ambitieuse et la plus complète manifestation de notre recherche sur les espaces complexes, dynamiques et fluides », a déclaré Zaha Hadid. Le visiteur est confronté à un degré élevé de complexité et d'étrangeté régies par un système très spécifique reposant sur une logique structurale volumétrique originale. Les sols ne sont ni empilés les uns sur les autres, ni ne peuvent être considérés comme formant un volume unique. Le Phaeno est soutenu et structuré par des cônes en forme d'entonnoir qui se projettent de sa masse ou la pénètrent. Certains permettent d'accéder à l'intérieur, tandis que d'autres servent à alléger l'espace intérieur ou à abriter des fonctions de service nécessaires. Ce projet associe la complexité formelle et géométrique à l'audace structurelle et l'authenticité matérielle. Il a fallu beaucoup d'énergie et de temps pour atteindre ce but [14]. » Les mots de Mark Wigley, « Le rêve de la forme pure a été perturbé », prennent ici tout leur sens, bien que l'esprit déconstructiviste soit très éloigné. Le concept de nature artificielle semble plus pertinent, qui crée une entité visible comme une créature vivante, certainement pas un quelconque animal vivant sur cette planète, mais animée par une logique qui court à travers son plan et ses coupes.

Dans sa description de deux autres projets, tous deux réalisés pour des musées d'art contemporain et conçus à peu près au même moment, le Lois & Richard Rosenthal Center for Contemporary Art et MAXXI, le Musée national des arts du XXIe siècle (Rome, 1998–2009, page 262), Zaha Hadid dévoile encore un peu plus son processus de pensée, et éclaire une raison pour laquelle des projets qui poursuivent les mêmes buts semblent si différents. « La similarité entre eux est que

---

[9] « Zaha Hadid, première femme à recevoir le prix Pritzker d'architecture », www.pritzkerprize.com/2004/announcment., consulté le 1er juillet 2013.

[10] Ibid.

[11] Michael Mönninger in LF One, Birkhäuser Verlag, Bâle, 1999.

[12] « Zaha Hadid, première femme à recevoir... », cit.

[13] Zaha Hadid interrogée par *El Croquis*, 103, Madrid, 2001.

QUE SE PASSERAIT-IL SI LES NOMBREUSES HYPOTHÈSES SUR LESQUELLES REPOSENT L'ARCHITECTURE ET LE DESIGN – DE LA FORME RECTILIGNE AUX MODES DE FONCTIONNEMENT D'UNE CONSTRUCTION OU D'UN MEUBLE – ÉTAIENT SOUMISES À UN PROFOND RENOUVELLEMENT ?

ces deux commandes portent sur des sites rénovés se prêtant à l'insertion d'un programme culturel. Dans les deux cas, le contexte urbain devrait changer avec le temps, et nos projets sont perçus comme des agents de cette transformation. [...] La complexité géométrique interne du projet romain condense les différentes orientations des contextes environnants. On pourrait dire qu'il révèle des cheminements urbains qui existaient sans le savoir dans le contexte du voisinage. Chaque mouvement dans son champ est lié à une condition contextuelle de voisinage. Le projet de Cincinnati est tout aussi contextuel bien que la manière dont il s'exprime soit très différente. Ainsi l'aspect formel n'est pas vraiment décidé par avance. Ces différents systèmes formels émergent dans des conditions assez différentes. L'un est plus imposé, l'autre davantage soumis à une négociation permanente entre intérieur et extérieur. »

À LA RECHERCHE DE LIGNES NATURELLES

Un site urbain dense ou même un projet de campus comme la proposition de Zaha Hadid pour le nouveau centre de l'IIT (Illinois Institute of Technology, Chicago, 1998) sont des sujets particulièrement adaptés à ses compositions complexes de lignes et de formes entrelacées qui entretiennent des liaisons directes avec le lieu. Cependant, dans certains cas, le site ne fournit guère d'informations sur lesquelles s'appuyer, par exemple dans ses interventions à Dubaï, dont les très impressionnantes Signature Towers (Business Bay, Dubaï, EAU, 2006, page 462). Que dire du contexte dans cette zone littéralement récupérée sur les sables ? « Dans ce cas, vous l'inventez, expliquait Hadid. La géométrie du contexte exerce un impact important. Si vous considérez le projet IIT à Chicago, vous trouverez certains axes qui relient le projet à certaines écoles. Néanmoins, les vues et les perspectives ne sont pas toujours importantes. Le musée de Rome n'a rien qui ressemble à ce que l'on voit dans son quartier, mais il est néanmoins influencé par le contexte. Tout mouvement dans le bâtiment est lié à la géométrie existante. » Patrik Schumacher ajoutait : « Parfois le projet est si vaste qu'il crée son propre contexte. C'est le cas pour la Business Bay à Dubaï, qui dépasse les 500 000 mètres carrés. Composition extrêmement intégrée, c'est l'un de plus vastes projets au monde à présenter une telle cohérence globale dans un bâtiment unique et intégré. » Il pourrait sembler, qu'à une certaine échelle, les projets de Zaha Hadid soient autoréférents en termes de cohérence et de logique interne, mais l'architecte soulignait que même lorsqu'il s'agit de très grandes surfaces, comme dans le plan directeur de Kartal-Pendik (Istanbul, 2006 ; page 438) proposé pour un nouveau centre urbain créé dans un ancien quartier industriel, les connexions fondamentales se font par rapport au lieu et à ce que l'on pourrait appeler son énergie naturelle. « Si vous regardez un projet comme le plan directeur d'Istanbul, disait-elle, chaque segment est très différent, mais on reconnaît qu'il appartient à un même lieu. Nous avons cherché des axes naturels et tenu compte de l'eau. Nous avons étudié la topographie d'Istanbul pour créer une autre topographie de l'autre côté. »

L'Opéra de Guangzhou de 70 000 mètres carrés (Guangzhou, Chine, 2003–10, page 278) offre d'autres clés de son approche dans le cadre d'une très grande ville chinoise qui connaît une expansion et une modernisation rapides. Son « interprétation conceptuelle » du site et du bâtiment associe des références à la géologie (rochers jumeaux) et au plan de la ville, y compris des rives du fleuve : « Dominant la rivière des Perles, l'Opéra de Guangzhou est au cœur du développement des sites culturels de la cité. Bénéficiant de technologies de pointe aussi bien dans la phase de conception que sur le chantier, ce sera l'un des monuments majeurs de ce nouveau millénaire, confirmant le rôle de cette ville qui devrait être un des grands centres culturels d'Asie. Son concept de rochers jumeaux améliorera les fonctionnalités urbaines en ouvrant l'accès aux rives du fleuve et aux zones portuaires, et créera un nouveau dialogue avec la ville nouvelle en construction. »

Cette description met en valeur l'une des grandes forces de l'approche de Zaha Hadid qui fait référence dans le même temps à la réalité de la ville et à la haute technologie, source de fierté en Chine, ainsi qu'à un lien entre le présent et le futur. Le passé, aussi incontestable que la présence des deux rochers et un fleuve, vient ici à la rencontre d'un futur où la culture, sous la forme de l'opéra et de l'architecture, trouve sa place. Sa « stratégie urbaine/paysage » fait comprendre clairement que la ville elle-même et le nouveau bâtiment sont un paysage qu'elle forme et intègre : « La structure s'élève et redescend sur le boulevard Zhujiang, réunissant les deux sites adjacents prévus pour un musée et diverses activités urbaines. Adjonction au parc touristique de l'île d'Haixinsha, l'Opéra présente un profil complexe qui offre aux visiteurs une ample vision sur les rives. Vu du parc, au centre du boulevard Zhujiang, il vient en prélude visuel au parc touristique situé en contrebas. Vues du fleuve, les tours de la ville nouvelle de Zhujiang constituent plan de fond spectaculaire et donnent une vision unifiée des bâtiments culturels et municipaux implantés dans le site du fleuve. Une rue intérieure, promenade d'approche qui débutant au niveau du futur musée, du côté opposé du boulevard central, a été découpée dans le paysage, et conduit à l'Opéra. Un café, un bar, un restaurant et des commerces de détail, incrustés comme des coquillages dans ces formes de relief, sont implantés sur l'un des côtés de ce parcours d'approche [15]. »

Les mots-clés de cette description sont « formes de relief » et « vision unifiée » ce qui prend à l'évidence en compte non seulement l'environnement urbain existant, mais aussi le futur musée prévu à proximité du site. Aussi surprenantes que puissent paraître, aux yeux de certains, les formes de Zaha Hadid, elles tirent leur légitimité de leur intégration « sans rupture » au site, ou, dans le cas de villes comme Dubaï, d'une logique interne continue et indiscutable. De même que ses meubles peuvent être accumulés et disposés pour créer un espace intérieur continu, son architecture peut s'élever du sol dans sa densité stratifiée et défier les présupposés de l'ordre orthogonal pour créer une nature artificielle proche de son inspiration réelle.

EN ATTENDANT FORMZ

Les peintures et dessins réalisés par Zaha Hadid pour des projets antérieurs, comme The Peak par exemple, expliquent non seulement sa célébrité, mais aussi la nature intime de sa création. Elle parlait de son processus créatif comme d'une accumulation de strates et d'approches multiples du problème, accumulées et entrelacées jusqu'à ce qu'émerge un résultat qui ait la légitimité du lieu et de la fonction. « Il est important de souligner que les dessins ont eu un impact sur mon travail, expliquait-elle. Il y a des choses qui refont surface dix ou vingt ans plus tard. Au début, j'utilisais un système de croquis très stratifié. Les techniques graphiques, les strates du dessin devenaient celles du projet. La complexité du dessin se transformait en complexité de l'architecture. » En ce sens, on pourrait même suggérer que les travaux graphiques initiaux de Zaha Hadid aient pu anticiper la révolution de l'informatique qui allait permettre à son agence de concevoir les plans de ces structures très complexes. « Je pense que ma méthode de conception peut être considérée comme précurseur de l'informatique », affirmait Hadid. « Le logiciel formZ, par exemple, fonctionne de manière très similaire aux techniques de dessin. Je crois cependant que les dessins restent plus complexes que ce que l'on obtient par ordinateur. Même si vous vous lancez dans un projet extravagant, il est en fait très calculé, et les dessins le montrent. Le processus possède une sorte de logique inhérente en soi. Il y avait une corrélation entre la façon dont les dessins étaient réalisés et l'architecture. L'informatique a conduit à des recherches qui ont permis de créer des bâtiments complexes, mais fondamentalement la méthode n'a pas changé. Si le système utilisé pour les faire a évolué, les idées restent les mêmes. Si je regarde certains de mes dessins, ils présentent exactement l'aspect de dessins par ordinateur. Aujourd'hui, nous savons que, grâce à l'ordinateur, on peut vraiment réaliser ce que j'ai imaginé en dessin. » Au plus haut niveau de la recherche architecturale depuis plus de trente ans, Zaha Hadid a connu l'apparition et la révolution de l'informatique. Qu'elle ait réalisé que son processus de travail et ses dessins ressemblaient étroitement à des images créées par ordina-

14 Zaha Hadid, citée dans le communiqué de presse de Zaha Hadid Architects, 23 novembre 2005.

15 Zaha Hadid Architects, « ZHA-Guangzhou Opera House – China – Conceptual Interpretation », 24 janvier 2008.

ON POURRAIT SUGGÉRER QUE LES TRAVAUX GRAPHIQUES INITIAUX DE ZAHA HADID AIENT PU ANTICIPER LA RÉVOLUTION DE L'INFORMATIQUE QUI ALLAIT PERMETTRE À SON AGENCE DE CONCEVOIR LES PLANS DE CES STRUCTURES TRÈS COMPLEXES.

teur pourrait être une sorte de prophétie autoréalisatrice dans laquelle son influence a contribué à mettre en forme l'orientation même des logiciels et de l'architecture qu'elle génère. Plus probablement, son émergence a surtout servi à défendre et renforcer sa résolution. Tandis que d'autres essayaient encore d'adapter la géométrie euclidienne et la forme moderniste à ce monde nouveau, Zaha Hadid entamait la quête d'un nouvel univers de surfaces complexes et d'architecture stratifiée.

À la question de savoir si elle dessinait toujours, Zaha Hadid répondait : « Parfois. Je pense que la référence se fait d'abord par rapport à son propre répertoire. Vous pouvez vous référer au passé et y voir une sorte de connaissance. Il ne s'agit pas tant du pouvoir de la main que de celui de l'idée. Le sens de tout ce travail ne touchait pas à la manière de faire un beau dessin. Il s'agissait vraiment de la mise au point d'une idée. Après de multiples essais et niveaux d'analyse, l'idée commence à prendre son ampleur, ce qui permet de faire ces formes complexes et d'organiser les volumes intérieurs. » Patrik Schumacher pousse ce raisonnement encore plus loin quand il parle du travail actuel de l'agence : « Nous nous intéressons aussi à la nature, aux systèmes de branchement, aux rivières, etc. Nous nous servons de ces idées pour mettre au point des espaces architecturaux. Avant, tout ce travail passait par le dessin et aujourd'hui, il est mis au point sur ordinateur. Les nouveaux outils ont une grande capacité de simulation des environnements et des surfaces complexes. »

On trouve certainement dans le travail de Zaha Hadid une « référence à son propre répertoire », comme elle le dit, mais aussi une approche radicale et nouvelle de la relation entre l'architecture et la nature, qui s'est en partie amplifiée dans son recours grandissant à la conception assistée par ordinateur. Comme Patrik Schumacher l'explique : « La référence à la nature est un trope ancien. Elle ne concerne pas que les modernistes. Les architectures de l'âge classique et de la Renaissance en faisaient également état et imaginaient leurs projets dans le cadre d'une cosmologie et d'une compréhension de la nature. En termes d'informatique, nous voyons la prolifération de morphologies naturelles qui sont stimulantes, peuvent être mises en œuvre et enrichissent le répertoire de composition et d'organisation – non seulement en termes d'aspect, mais également de modèles d'organisations. Pour nous, [ces morphologies] sont des enjeux de navigation et d'orientation qui apportent davantage d'ordre dans un environnement complexe [16]. »

LÉGITIME ET COHÉRENT PAR HÉRITAGE

À la question posée sur comment « les morphologies naturelles » manipulées par le biais de l'ordinateur peuvent améliorer l'architecture – question fondamentale qui concerne directement l'œuvre de Zaha Hadid –, Patrik Schumacher répond : « Le type de morphologies qui en sort est légitime et cohérent par héritage. On a pu observer des tentatives antérieures d'établir ce type de cohérence et de lois, que ce soit par le talent et la composition, lorsque des architectes essayèrent, par exemple, de reproduire instinctivement l'équilibre dynamique trouvé dans la nature, ou se limitaient d'eux-mêmes aux géométries et symétries platoniques très basiques. Accéder à un ordre plus complexe, plutôt qu'à une sorte d'affreux désordre, est possible grâce à ces outils nouveaux et, bien sûr, il existe de multiples outils adaptés à toutes sortes d'objectifs, hors de l'architecture, qui peuvent être récupérés, comme RealFlow, etc. Et leur sensibilité, en un sens, revient à la perception des systèmes naturels [17]. »

Peut-être que Zaha Hadid, dont la formation approfondie en dessin est évidente dans ses études et peintures, regrettait, dans une certaine mesure, la période d'avant la prise de pouvoir de l'ordinateur. « Je pense que dans le monde d'avant, on analysait et comprenait mieux le contexte que maintenant. Il y avait

beaucoup de recherches et d'analyse sur le site. Certaines évolutions se sont produites du fait de l'analyse du site. Je ne pense pas qu'il y ait d'analyse du site aujourd'hui. Le contexte et l'analyse de celui-ci ne font plus partie du sujet. Il n'y a plus de discussion autour du contexte. Il y a juste, la plupart du temps, des objets qui atterrissent. L'enjeu n'est pas tant sur l'usage ou non de l'ordinateur. Et le problème de l'ordinateur est qu'il isole l'objet. Il est tourné vers l'intérieur, comme opposé à l'ouverture sur l'extérieur. C'est un objet. La nature de la pièce est ainsi. » Quand on demandait à Zaha Hadid si elle se résignait devant cette réalité, elle répondait : « Je suis en fait assez critique par rapport à cette situation. On avait l'habitude de faire une distinction entre l'objet et le fond et je pense que c'est à cause de la technique que nous ne le faisons plus. Il n'y plus d'analyse du plan. » Patrik Schumacher, pour sa part, défend ce qu'il appelle « l'élégance » de l'architecture contemporaine, en particulier dans le travail de Zaha Hadid Architects. Cette élégance se trouve dans une recherche extensive d'une solution à partir de nombreuses études et dans la mise au point incrémentielle de formes appropriées. « Chaque élément est fortement relié à celui qui suit et à sa place dans le projet d'ensemble. Ceci veut dire qu'il y a beaucoup d'informations enfouies dans ces morphologies. C'est un peu comme une symphonie. Vous ne pouvez pas supprimer un accord dans une mélodie, alors que dans une cacophonie vous pouvez retirer n'importe quoi et le placer ailleurs. Nous disposons maintenant des outils qui peuvent le faire dans certains de nos projets. Tout signifie quelque chose. Rien n'est arbitraire. » La cacophonie à laquelle se réfère Schumacher est celle d'une ville comme Tokyo, cité stratifiée s'il y en eut jamais, et qui n'est pourtant pas un système dans lequel « l'élégance » et le nouvel ordre recherché par Zaha Hadid apparaissent.

UNE FORME DE CALCUL NATUREL

C'est ici que la quête de Zaha Hadid, qui s'exprimait dans une multitude d'objets, de bâtiments, de dessins, et même d'expositions, révélait sa continuité fondamentale et les liens puissants qui structurèrent une carrière unique dans l'architecture contemporaine. Bien qu'elle parlât volontiers de topographie, elle n'exprimait pas très souvent sa recherche en termes de création de nature artificielle. « Nous nous sommes éloignés de l'idée de créer de grands objets et nous nous sommes intéressés à la topographie et au sol. Nous avons observé les multiples strates de l'espace public et réfléchi à l'interprétation de ce qui se trouve au-dessus du sol et en dessous. À partir de là, l'évolution normale était d'étudier [...] la nature », disait-elle. Patrik Schumacher, une fois encore, fait le lien entre la réflexion fondamentale de Hadid et son bâti récent. « Il existe des millions d'objets naturels et chacun possède sa propre cohérence, dit-il. La situation est ouverte. Si vous vous trouvez face à des strates géologiques qui se déplacent les unes contre les autres, vous trouvez toujours des continuités. C'est une forme de calcul naturel si vous voulez. L'incident se produit à l'intérieur d'un champ d'incidents où il prend son sens. La façon dont la végétation recouvre une montagne fait sens. Nous essayons d'insuffler ce type de logique en architecture. Il existe dans la matière un sens de beauté éloquente et de compréhension intuitive. »

JE NE PARLERAIS PAS DE SCULPTURE

Zaha Hadid était aussi un personnage à part, en ce sens qu'elle travaillait activement sur des projets de meubles, ou, plus précisément, sur des objets supposés mettre en forme l'espace intérieur. Récemment, ses projets pour les David Gill Galleries et Established & Sons avaient été édités en exemplaires signés à tirage limité, une formule habituellement réservée à des œuvres d'art. Cette distinction n'a d'ailleurs pas lieu d'être, même si Zaha Hadid rejetait le mot de « sculpture » pour définir ses créations. À la question du comment en était-elle venue à dessiner activement des objets, Hadid donnait une réponse tout à fait claire : « Bien sûr, nous

[16] Patrik Schumacher, dans : Ma Yanson, *MAD Dinner*, Actar, Barcelone, 2007.

[17] Ibid.

LA FAÇON DONT LA VÉGÉTATION RECOUVRE UNE MONTAGNE FAIT SENS. NOUS ESSAYONS D'INSUFFLER CE TYPE DE LOGIQUE EN ARCHITECTURE.

n'avons pas eu de projets architecturaux à réaliser pendant longtemps, et nous nous sommes naturellement posé la question du mobilier dans des espaces non conventionnels. Il fait partie de l'univers intérieur, les meubles sont des séparateurs ou des diviseurs d'espace. Lorsque que nous avons réalisé ces projets pour Sawaya & Moroni, nous recherchions un type de paysage ou de topographie [Z-Scape Furniture, 2000, page 533]. L'idée était de créer un meuble qui fasse partie d'un ensemble et puisse se glisser dans une très petite pièce comme un environnement ou au contraire s'étaler. » En fait, le débat sur ce qui reliait précisément le design de Zaha Hadid à son architecture est assez révélateur en termes de conception aussi bien de l'un que de l'autre. Pour Patrik Schumacher, « l'idée de transition entre les parties s'applique certainement au design et à l'architecture. La transition est douce et n'a rien à voir avec l'idée de visser un plateau de table sur quatre pieds, par exemple. Elle relève de l'esprit du style, de l'environnement total. Dans l'hôtel, nous avons considéré le mobilier comme une substance génératrice d'espace ». Cet hôtel est le Puerta América (Madrid, 2003–05, page 214) pour lequel Hadid a créé un plateau intégré sans la moindre rupture, et des chambres en acrylique thermoformé LG HI-MACS. Dans cet environnement étonnant, les visiteurs, dès qu'ils quittent l'ascenseur, découvrent les surfaces sans rebords de Zaha Hadid. Les plafonds des chambres se transforment en murs, les bureaux se projettent de ces murs, et même les baignoires se fondent dans ce cadre sans la moindre limite apparente. Le visiteur qui n'aurait pas un sens très développé du design pourrait se demander pourquoi un bureau doit jaillir d'un mur pour se transformer en lit, mais l'aspect pratique est ici moins important que la remise en question de l'ordre de l'angle droit, qui a si longtemps dominé le design et l'architecture.

AU COMMENCEMENT ÉTAIT LA DIAGONALE

« Je réfléchis toujours à la façon de faire vivre ensemble ces objets », poursuivait Zaha Hadid. « Pour la collection Seamless [Established & Sons, 2006], je les ai pensés comme des multiples et donc vous pouvez en avoir un certain nombre, et faire une tour avec ces meubles. » Cette fonctionnalité, sans parler de la beauté du jeu de ces objets entre eux, est certainement ce qui la faisait réagir à la question de savoir si elle les considérait comme des sculptures. « Non je n'utiliserais pas ce mot », disait-elle sèchement. « Sculptural par opposition à quoi ? Plat ? Beaucoup de meubles de série sont conçus à plat. Mais la voiture était une idée d'assemblage de quelque chose qui n'était jamais plat. Aujourd'hui, pour le mobilier, vous pouvez avoir des pièces personnalisées. Vous n'êtes pas forcé de faire des étagères plates. Celles-ci ne sont pas du tout minimalistes, ce sont deux mondes séparés. L'idée est de ne pas avoir d'angles à 90°. Au commencement était la diagonale. La diagonale vient de l'idée de l'explosion qui "reforme" l'espace. Ce fut une découverte importante. »

« L'explosion "re-formant" l'espace » à laquelle se référait Zaha Hadid est largement visible dans ses dessins et peintures pour The Peak (1983). Alors que la ligne droite et l'angle droit modernistes régnaient encore, en partie pour des raisons de productivité, elle explorait déjà activement son idée de diagonale, aussi bien dans son architecture que dans ses objets. Au-delà de la tectonique dure de ses premiers travaux jusqu'au caractère lisse du projet pour l'hôtel Puerta América, la diagonale est devenue une métaphore de l'acte consistant à faire exploser l'espace, dans le questionnement des présupposés les plus fondamentaux et les plus « évidents » de l'architecture : une table est faite d'un plan horizontal vissé sur quatre pieds, un bâtiment se compose d'une accumulation de formes euclidiennes qui laisse à peine place à un vide qui gênerait… Aussi complexe l'œuvre de Zaha Hadid puisse-t-elle parfois paraître, son originalité réelle s'impose dans les questions qu'elle pose sur les affirmations évidentes qui limitent une architecture reproduite par routine au cours des générations. Son approche était bien celle d'une explosion qui « reforme » l'espace.

Lorsque Zaha Hadid exposa ses *Dune Formations* (David Gill Galleries, 2007, page 562) à la Scuola dei Mercanti à Venise au cours de la Biennale 2007, elle apporta une preuve supplémentaire des plus intéressantes. Ses objets en aluminium et résine orange brûlée semblaient glisser d'un état ou d'une fonction à un autre dans le cadre de ce bâtiment vénitien très traditionnel. Mais surtout, on n'observait aucune contradiction intrinsèque entre le passé et le futur, entre les volumes orthogonaux à grande hauteur plafonds de ce bâtiment ancien et ces formes aux courbes fuyantes. Un peu comme des objets naturels dont la légitimité formelle serait incontestable, les *Dune Formations*, certainement inspirées comme leur nom le suggère des sables du désert, ne paraissaient en rien déplacées à Venise. Le spectateur sensible à cette légitimité peut arriver à comprendre pourquoi Zaha Hadid était une architecte et designer aussi importante. Ses formes ne ressemblent à rien de ce que l'on a pu voir jusqu'à présent, à l'exception de quelques connexions anciennes avec le suprématisme russe, par exemple, et cependant leur existence physique semble enracinée autant dans le sol que dans les contingences de la CAO (conception assistée par ordinateur). Cette complexité stratifiée n'a peut-être pas toujours atteint à cette sorte de légitimité intuitive, mais lorsqu'elle y parvenait, comme dans le cas des *Dune Formations*, elle ouvrait de nouvelles perspectives sur le futur de l'art, de l'architecture et du design.

VOYEZ-LE COMME UN TRAVAIL D'ÉQUIPE

L'achèvement du Rosenthal Center, en 2003, marqua une transition assez nette dans la carrière de Zaha Hadid. Dirigeant une équipe de trois cents collaborateurs, multipliant les projets de la Grande-Bretagne à la Chine, elle était très demandée. Elle faisait remarquer avec candeur : « Je pense qu'il est intéressant de travailler de cette façon, mais je profite de la situation actuelle. Dans le monde entier, des clients ont envie de ce type de travail et je ne pense pas que cette chance puisse se reproduire plusieurs fois dans une vie. Je ne fixe aucune limite géographique à mon travail, mais dans certains pays, vous devez vraiment être sur place, on ne peut pas travailler par e-mail. » Le prix Pritzker 2004 aurait-il eu une influence sur l'explosion de cette demande ? « Je le crois, répondait-elle. Bien évidemment, nous travaillions avant, mais le niveau d'intérêt s'est fortement accru. Je pense aussi que davantage de gens s'intéressent maintenant à ce type de travail. Je ne sais pas si le même phénomène s'est produit pour d'autres titulaires du Pritzker. » Comment pouvait-elle faire front à un tel afflux de commandes ? « Il y a Patrik, c'est sûr, affirmait-elle, mais nous avons de nombreux collaborateurs qui sont avec nous depuis longtemps. Beaucoup ont été mes étudiants ou ceux de Patrik. Nous revenons sans cesse sur les projets pour qu'ils soient au point. Notre structure organisationnelle ne ressemble certainement pas à une pyramide où j'arriverais avec une idée que je transmettrais pour réalisation. Je pense qu'il faut voir ce que nous produisons comme un travail d'équipe. À l'agence, nous nous consacrons à des recherches compréhensibles par tout le monde. »

La transition entre une recherche personnelle, dont les premières manifestations remontent à la peinture *Horizontal Tektonik, Malevich's Tektonik, London*, et la position d'une architecte sillonnant le monde a été gérée par Zaha Hadid avec un aplomb que beaucoup de ses confrères n'ont pas su avoir. Rem Koolhaas, de six ans plus âgé, est également passé du stade de théoricien reconnu à la direction d'une agence capable d'édifier une tour aussi étonnante que le siège de CCTV à Pékin, et pourtant OMA ne peut prétendre rivaliser avec la liste de chantiers sur laquelle travaillait récemment Zaha Hadid Architects.

Les projets publiés dans cet ouvrage, dont certains seront achevés à la date de sa publication, témoignent d'une remarquable diversité géographique mais également d'un effort continu de redéfinition de la typologie même de bâtiments qui imposent leur marque, même auprès de ceux qui s'interrogent sur le style et la dynamique de l'agence Hadid. Avec le MAXXI, le Musée national des arts du XXIe siècle à Rome, Hadid a voulu « confronter le matériau et la dissonance conceptuelle de la pratique artistique depuis la fin des années 1960 », redéfinissant non seulement la forme, mais aussi la réactivité des musées à l'art d'aujourd'hui. La conception et la réalisation du pont Cheikh Zayed, de 842 mètres de long (Abu Dhabi, EAU, 1997–2010, page 272) ont nécessité plus de treize années de travail. Il tisse littéralement des « fils » structurels pour prendre une « forme de vague sinusoïdale » déployée au-dessus du chenal entre Abu Dhabi et le continent. Il remet en question et interroge la forme du pont, objet utilitaire par excellence et habituellement chasse gardée des ingénieurs, dynamisé ici pour devenir « une destination en soi et un catalyseur potentiel de la croissance future d'Abu Dhabi ». Le London Aquatics Centre (Londres, 2005–11, page 292) a été une réalisation majeure des Jeux olympiques 2012 qui se sont déroulés dans la capitale britannique, mais aussi la première grande réalisation de Zaha Hadid dans la ville où elle habitait depuis si longtemps. Sa toiture à double incurvation parabolique, et son dessin « inspiré de la géométrie fluide de l'eau en mouvement » accroît la gamme et la nature des références de l'architecte à la nature, ou peut-être plus précisément aux objets nés d'une nature artificielle aussi légitime que les dunes de sable ou les flux aquatiques qu'elle évoque. Ce Centre comprend deux grandes sections, l'une qui offre 17 500 places aux spectateurs des principales compétitions de natation et l'autre 5000 places pour les matches de water-polo. Plus loin, le Centre culturel Heydar Aliyev (Bakou, Azerbaïdjan, 2007–12, page 354) fait clairement référence à la topographie, le « bâtiment fusionne avec le paysage… brouille les frontières entre le bâtiment et le sol. » Au milieu de tant de projets importants, Hadid avait également trouvé le temps de concevoir une remarquable résidence privée, Capital Hill Residence (Moscou, 2006–page 378). Composée d'un volume surbaissé en partie enterré dans le flanc d'une colline, fruit d'une « stratégie qui étend la topographie extérieure à l'intérieur du bâtiment », cette maison se signale par une tour de 22 mètres qui offre à ses occupants une vue au-delà des arbres environnants de 20 mètres de haut.

Au cours de ces dernières années, Zaha Hadid avait réalisé deux importants projets dans le Sud de la France. Le premier, la tour CMA CGM (Marseille, 2006–11, page 302) occupe en bordure du port un terrain cerné de voies de circulation. Ce complexe de 94 000 mètres carrés s'impose dans son environnement mais l'élégance de sa forme élancée exprime aussi le style caractéristique de Zaha Hadid. Le second projet est un bâtiment administratif de 28 500 mètres carrés construit pour le département de l'Hérault. Pour Hadid ces « Pierresvives » (Montpellier, 2002–12, page 322) était « une des affirmations les plus ambitieuses et les plus complètes de notre volonté de créer des espaces fluides et dynamiques. Le bâtiment fusionne complexité géométrique formelle, structure audacieuse et utilisation novatrice de certains matériaux. La création architecturale signifie aussi repousser les frontières, et je crois que les Pierresvives en sont une excellente démonstration ».

LA NATURE, UNE INSPIRATION DE LONGUE DATE

Zaha Hadid n'était certainement pas la première architecte à s'inspirer de la nature dans son travail de conception. Et comme le précisait Patrik Schumacher : « La référence à la nature est un trope ancien. » De Frank Lloyd Wright à Toyo Ito, des créateurs importants ont ancré leurs projets dans des cadres naturels,

---

18 Nicolai Ouroussoff, « Zaha Hadid : A Diva for the Digital Age », dans : *The New York Times*, 2 juin 2006.

19 Patrik Schumacher, « Arguing for Elegance », dans : *AD, Architectural Design*, Londres, janvier/février 2007.

20 Patrik Schumacher, « Zaha Hadid Architects – Experimentation within a Long Wave of Innovation », dans : *Out There. Architecture Beyond Building*, Marsilio Editori, Venise, 2008, vol. 3, pp. 93–94.

mais de façon peut-être plus littérale que Zaha Hadid. Est-ce que la résidence de Fallingwater par Wright (Maison Edgar J. Kaufmann, Mill Run, Pennsylvanie, 1934–37) a paru aussi futuriste aux visiteurs de la fin des années 1930 que la Capital Hill Residence édifiée dans une forêt de la région de Moscou à ceux d'aujourd'hui ? Les dessins épurés d'Hadid, qui ont pu se matérialiser grâce à des technologies et des matériaux d'avant-garde, ne semblent jamais tomber dans l'imitation de la nature. Son objectif était ailleurs, et c'est pourquoi elle n'était pas une suiveuse de Wright. Sa « nature » sort du sol ou du paysage urbain « comme une créature chtonienne » qui n'est pas née du quotidien mais s'impose, indiscutable, à la manière d'un mythe ancien. La géométrie est certes présente, mais s'exprime dans des courbes complexes et des motifs superposés sortis de l'esprit de l'architecte pour prendre une forme concrète grâce à la révolution de la conception et de la fabrication assistées par ordinateur qui permettent de réaliser des objets uniques. La nouveauté du modernisme puisait sa pureté dans un délicat évitement du monde terrestre. Architecturalement parlant, ses réalisations ne se sont que rarement aventurées en sous-sol. La cave doit être cachée, tandis que règne au-dessus du sol des objets euclidiens aux définitions précises et absolues. Les élégants pilotis empêchent même toute souillure de la terre. Si Ludwig Mies van der Rohe a su communier avec le cadre naturel dans ce chef-d'œuvre qu'est la maison Farnsworth (1945–50, Plano, Illinois), le magazine *House Beautiful* se moquait à l'époque de cette pureté cristalline, la qualifiant de « cage de verre sur pilotis ». Chez Hadid, la nature peut être artificielle, mais elle conserve intact son obscur pouvoir de surprise.

UN LANGAGE ARCHITECTURAL FAIT DE FLUIDITÉ ET DE NATUREL

Deux récents projets éphémères de Zaha Hadid illustrent l'ampleur de ses intérêts et de sa réussite, mais également l'ardeur qu'elle affichait dans sa volonté de prouver que ses méthodes étaient applicables aux circonstances les plus diverses. Son « Mobile Art, Chanel Contemporary Art Container » (divers lieux, 2007–08, page 244) n'est pas en relation avec un contexte spécifique, puisqu'il se déplace en fonction des envies de son client original, Karl Lagerfeld. À partir de logiciels sophistiqués, ce pavillon d'expositions employait ce que Hadid appelait « un langage architectural de fluidité et de nature », ou, une fois encore, un principe de « paysage artificiel ». Lagerfeld, personnalité esthète qui comprend instinctivement la problématique de la conception, a dit d'elle : « Elle est le premier architecte à trouver une façon de rompre avec l'esthétique post-Bauhaus dominante. » Aujourd'hui, cette petite structure a trouvé son emplacement permanent au pied de l'Institut du monde arabe, de Jean Nouvel, à Paris.

Autre réalisation à caractère éphémère (*Lilas*, Installation temporaire, Serpentine Gallery, Kensington Gardens, Londres, 2007, page 570) consistait en trois parasols de 5,5 mètres de haut disposés sur une plate-forme de 310 mètres carrés. Tendus d'un tissu de PVC soudé à chaud, ils tiraient leur inspiration « de géométries naturelles complexes comme celles des pétales de fleurs ou des feuilles », mais surtout possédaient une réelle présence sculpturale. Ils furent montés pour la réception d'été de la Serpentine Gallery dans des délais extrêmement courts. Le sculpteur américain Richard Serra a dit que la différence entre l'art et l'architecture est que l'architecture obéit à une fonction. L'installation *Lilas* remplissait bien un objectif fonctionnel, mais sa présence et sa nature la reliaient à l'univers de l'art, du moins d'un art connecté au monde, à la nature et à la beauté. Nicolai Ouroussoff, le critique d'architecture du *New York Times*, avait écrit d'Hadid : « En réunissant des inspirations aussi variées en une seule vision, elle embrasse avec provocation un cosmopolitisme qui a du mal à s'exprimer dans ces périodes sombres. C'est le plus proche que nous ayons d'un manifeste en faveur du futur [18]. »

La théorie de « l'élégance » que développe Patrik Schumacher en parlant du travail de Zaha Hadid répond à la question sous-jacente du sens et de l'utilité des innovations apportées par l'agence. « Pourquoi devrions-nous nous battre

LA DIAGONALE EST DEVENUE UNE MÉTAPHORE DE L'ACTE DE FAIRE EXPLOSER L'ESPACE, UN QUESTIONNEMENT DES PRÉSUPPOSÉS LES PLUS FONDAMENTAUX ET LES PLUS « ÉVIDENTS » DE L'ARCHITECTURE.

pour cette élégance de plus en plus difficile à atteindre ? Possède-t-elle un objectif au-delà d'elle-même ? » demande-t-il. Sa réponse : « Les cahiers des charges architecturaux contemporains sont marqués par une demande de provisions programmatiques simultanées de plus en plus perfectionnées, organisées dans des contextes urbains de plus en plus sophistiqués. L'élégance fait qu'une complexité programmatique accrue peut coïncider avec une diminution relative de la complication visuelle, en intégrant de multiples éléments dans un système spatial et formel cohérent et continu. Le défi général est de trouver des modes de composition qui peuvent articuler des arrangements et des relations difficiles à appréhender, sans perdre de leur lisibilité et de leur pouvoir d'orienter les utilisateurs. L'élégance, telle que nous la définissons, signifie une capacité à articuler des processus de vie complexes d'une façon qui peut préserver une compréhension, une lisibilité et une orientation d'ensemble continues à l'intérieur de la composition [19]. »

L'ARCHITECTURE LIBÉRÉE

Tandis que d'autres se sont joyeusement aventurés dans un univers de « blobs » tout droit sortis de l'ordinateur, mais sans grand sens, Zaha Hadid est venue de l'ère d'avant l'informatique avec des idées que les nouvelles technologies rendaient possibles. Ses dessins fouillés ont toujours eu pour but de créer des constructions bien réelles et elle ne s'est jamais intéressée à l'esthétique pure, même lorsqu'elle cherchait son inspiration du côté des suprématistes. À cet égard, il faut se rappeler que les constructivistes et les suprématistes, à la différence des maîtres de l'URSS, voulaient vraiment imaginer le meilleur des mondes. Hadid a rompu non seulement avec l'esthétique post-Bauhaus, mais de façon plus significative avec la trame et les solides euclidiens. Ses espaces flottent et s'incurvent comme ces systèmes naturels de branches évoqués par Patrik Schumacher. Son œuvre est à la jonction de l'architecture, de l'art et du design, selon des problématiques qui ne sont peut-être pas toujours entièrement résolues, mais sa recherche est permanente et en devenir. « L'architecture d'avant-garde produit des manifestes, des expositions paradigmatiques du potentiel original d'un style nouveau, et non des constructions offrant l'équilibre attendu pour fonctionner comme on le voudrait [20] », affirme Schumacher non sans quelque provocation. Comme un certain nombre de projets présentés ici le montrent, Hadid a réussi la transition entre théorie, image et bâti. Cette avancée n'a guère été freinée par la crise économique globale survenue après 2008. Aujourd'hui, elle est une des architectes les plus emblématiques et les plus recherchées du moment.

L'aventure de Zaha Hadid fut remarquable. Sa réussite s'est nourrie de sa constance et de sa conviction que l'architecture et le design doivent pouvoir évoluer. L'architecture inspirée du Bauhaus était liée aux méthodes industrielles de production et au besoin de répétition pour générer des économies d'échelle. Son concept d'architecture, né d'un processus de conception et d'une logique rigoureuses, mais libérés des contraintes euclidiennes, a été rendu possible par une autre révolution industrielle, celle de la conception et de la production assistées par ordinateur. Les bureaux ont jailli des murs et les ponts ont entamé une danse sinusoïdale. Zaha Hadid a libéré l'architecture qui, après elle, ne sera plus jamais la même.

Philip Jodidio, Grimentz, Suisse

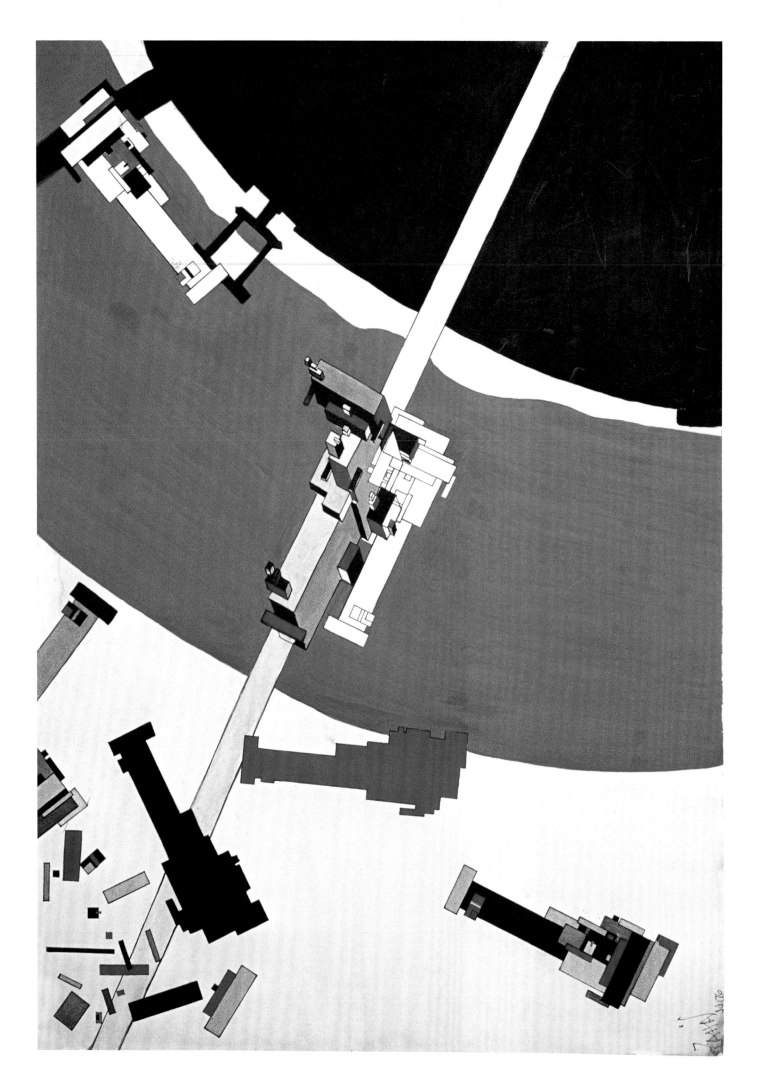

EARLY WORK

Early projects
PAINTING ARCHITECTURE

Pages 34–35:
JEWELS (DETAIL)
CARDIFF BAY OPERA HOUSE
Acrylic on black cartridge, 100 x 70 cm
Cardiff, Wales, UK, 1994–1996

Pages 36:
THE WORLD (89 DEGREES)
Acrylic on canvas,189 x 220 cm
1983

Again set at an angle that questions the rapport between horizontality and verticality, this work sums by expanding or compressing projects generated in the seven-year period that began with Hadid's work as a student at London's Architectural Association (AA).

Auch dieses Werk, ebenfalls aus einer Perspektive präsentiert, die das Verhältnis von horizontal und vertikal infrage stellt, versammelt verschiedene Projekte, die hier komprimiert oder maßstäblich gestreckt dargestellt sind und einer siebenjährigen Phase entstammen, die mit Hadids Studienzeit an der Londoner Architectural Association (AA) begann.

Là encore, sous un angle qui remet en cause le rapport entre horizontalité et verticalité, cette œuvre reprend en compression ou expansion certains projets étudiés au cours des sept années suivant l'entrée de Zaha Hadid comme étudiante à la London Architectural Association.

Pages 38–39:
TRAFALGAR SQUARE
GRAND BUILDINGS,
TRAFALGAR SQUARE
Acrylic on canvas, 250 x 140 cm
London, UK, 1985

Seen on the previous double page, this work presented a radical solution for one of the most famous London squares—allowing for an extension of the public realm into office space. The vertiginous angles of the painting and, indeed, of the proposed structures impart a dynamism to the location that also challenges the more traditional view of the English capital.

Die auf der vorigen Doppelseite abgebildete Arbeit präsentierte ein radikales Konzept für einen der bekanntesten Plätze Londons – mit Ausdehnung des öffentlichen Raums bis in die Bürobauten. Die schwindelerregende Perspektivführung des Gemäldes und die vorgesehenen Bauten geben dem Ort eine Dynamik, die das eher traditionelle Verständnis der englischen Hauptstadt infrage stellt.

Double-page précédente : Cette œuvre illustre une solution radicale proposée pour l'une des plus fameuses places de Londres et l'extension du domaine public dans celui des bureaux. Les angles de vue vertigineux de la peinture et des constructions imaginées génèrent une dynamique qui remet en question les vues traditionnelles de la capitale britannique.

From the time of her earliest work, and in particular *Horizontal Tektonik, Malevich's Tektonik, London* (acrylic on cartridge, 128 x 89 cm, 1976–77, San Francisco Museum of Modern Art), Zaha Hadid expressed her ideas in large-format paintings that came to define her presence on the international scene with events such as the presentation of her Hong Kong Peak project in the 1988 exhibition *Deconstructivist Architecture* at New York's Museum of Modern Art. Shown again recently at the 2008 Venice Architecture Biennale, many of these works continue to have both an artistic presence and also stand out as the seminal pieces defining the style and surprising break with orthogonal or modernist architecture that Zaha Hadid has come to exemplify. In part because her thoughts and forms were so radical that some found it difficult to imagine building them, her reputation and influence grew to a large extent in the first instance through these paintings. Sometimes related to specific projects and sometimes not, the early paintings of Zaha Hadid are more than the aesthetic musings of a talented artist; they are the blueprints for her revolutionary approach to architecture.

Seit ihren frühesten Arbeiten, insbesondere seit *Horizontal Tektonik, Malevich's Tektonik, London* (Acryl auf Zeichenkarton, 128 x 89 cm, 1976–77, San Francisco Museum of Modern Art), hat Zaha Hadid ihre Ideen in großformatigen Gemälden zum Ausdruck gebracht, die auch ihre internationalen Auftritte prägten, wie etwa die Präsentation ihres Hongkong-Peak-Projekts bei der Ausstellung *Deconstructivist Architecture* (1988) am New Yorker Museum of Modern Art. Viele dieser Arbeiten, die kürzlich wieder auf der Architekturbiennale 2008 in Venedig zu sehen waren, sind nach wie vor von starker künstlerischer Präsenz und stechen zudem als bahnbrechende Arbeiten hervor, die jenen Stil und jenen Bruch mit einer rechtwinklig geprägten, modernen Architektur verkörpern, für die Zaha

Hadid so bekannt wurde. Auch weil ihre Überlegungen und ihre Formensprache so radikal waren und manche sich nur schwer vorstellen konnten, sie baulich zu realisieren, gründete sich ihr Ruf und Einfluss zunächst in erster Linie auf diese Gemälde. Diese frühen Werke Hadids – mitunter auf spezifische Projekte bezogen, mitunter nicht – sind durchaus mehr als die ästhetischen Fingerübungen einer talentierten Künstlerin; vielmehr sind sie die Blaupause für ihr revolutionäres Architekturverständnis.

Dès ses premiers travaux, et en particulier dès *Horizontal Tektonik, Malevich's Tektonik, London* (acrylique sur papier cartouche, 128 x 89 cm, 1976–77, San Francisco Museum of Modern Art), Zaha Hadid a cherché à exprimer ses idées sur des toiles de grandes dimensions. C'est sous cette forme que sa présence a d'abord été remarquée sur la scène internationale lors de manifestations comme l'exposition de 1988 au Museum of Modern Art de New York « Deconstructivist Architecture » où figurait son projet du Hong Kong Peak. Présentées de nouveau récemment à la Biennale d'architecture de Venise en 2008, beaucoup de ces œuvres continuent à exercer un impact artistique et sont par ailleurs devenues des pièces fondamentales qui définissent le style personnel de l'architecte et illustrent sa rupture surprenante avec l'orthogonalité architecturale moderniste. Même si sa réflexion et ses explorations formelles paraissaient tellement radicales que certains ne pouvaient imaginer leur réalisation concrète, sa réputation et son influence se sont accrues en grande partie au départ grâce à ces peintures. Liées à des projets spécifiques ou non, les premières toiles d'Hadid sont plus que les recherches artistiques d'une artiste de talent. Elles sont les premières épures de son approche révolutionnaire de l'architecture.

**AERIAL PERSPECTIVE
VICTORIA CITY AERIAL**
Acrylic on cartridge, 254 x 90 cm
Berlin, Germany, 1988

Seen on the right, this work involves a competition project for a site in the center of West Berlin just before the end of the Cold War period, when the Berlin Wall was still in place. Although Zaha Hadid's work appears to approach the abstract, she in fact is carefully studying a very real situation, making use of existing buildings, while proposing a new architectural order.

Die Arbeit rechts entstand in Zusammenhang mit einem Wettbewerb für ein Projekt im Herzen West-Berlins, kurz vor Ende des Kalten Krieges, als die Berliner Mauer noch stand. Obwohl Hadids Arbeit nahezu abstrakt wirkt, analysiert sie die reale Raumsituation tatsächlich sehr genau, integriert existierende Bauten und schlägt zugleich eine architektonische Neuordnung vor.

À droite, cette œuvre porte sur un projet de concours pour un site du centre de Berlin-Ouest, juste avant la fin de la Guerre froide, lorsque le mur était encore debout. Bien que son style semble se rapprocher ici de l'abstraction, Zaha Hadid étudie en fait soigneusement une situation très concrète qui utilise les constructions existantes tout en proposant une nouvelle organisation architecturale.

**BLUE BEAM
VICTORIA CITY AERIAL**
Acrylic on cartridge, 253 x 100 cm
Berlin, Germany, 1989

The work below, *Victoria Blue Beam*, represents a dense overlapping of office "beams" and shopping facilities. Major thoroughfares—including street, rail, and pedestrian paths—run through the space, emphasizing its eminently urban and fundamentally new concept of space.

Die unten zu sehende Arbeit *Victoria Blue Beam* lässt ein dichtes Geflecht von einander überschneidenden Büro-„Riegeln" und Einkaufszentren erkennen. Hauptadern des Verkehrs – Straßen, Bahngleise und Fußgängerwege – kreuzen den Raum und unterstreichen das ausgesprochen urbane und fundamental neuartige Raumkonzept.

L'œuvre ci-dessous, *Victoria Blue Beam*, représente une superposition à haute densité de « faisceaux » de bureaux et de commerces. De grands axes – rues, voies ferrées et voies piétonnières – sillonnent l'espace et mettent en valeur un concept d'espace éminemment urbain et fondamentalement nouveau.

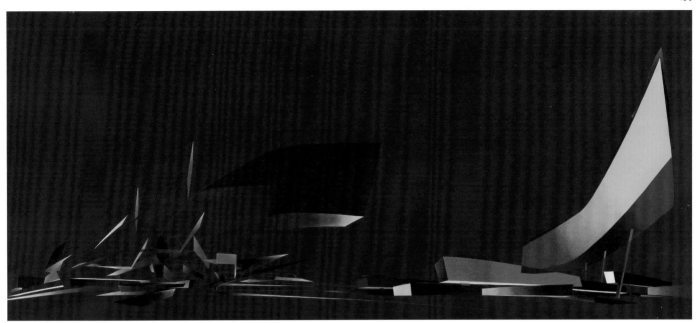

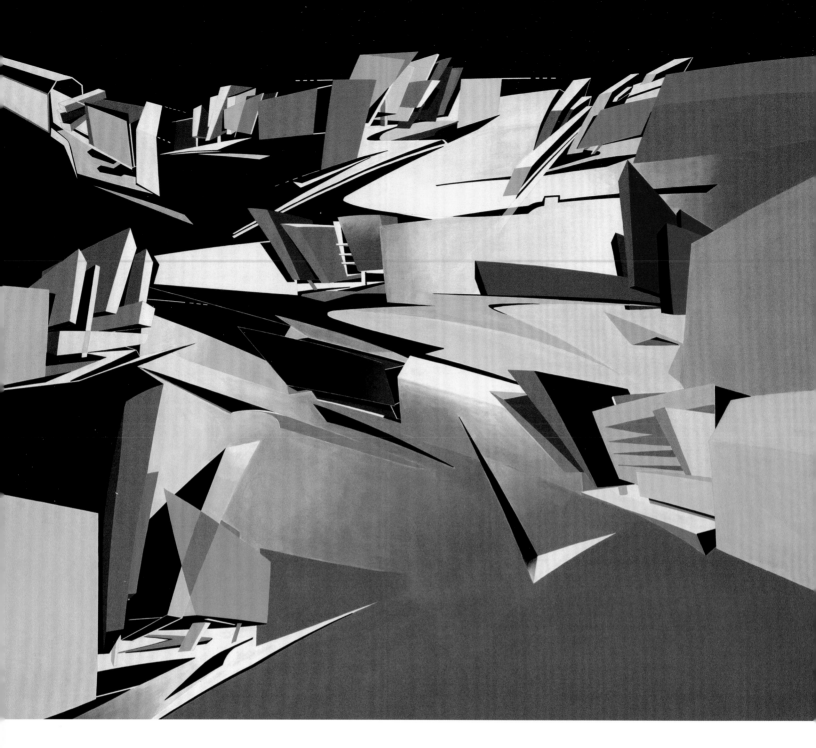

ELEVATION STUDIES
HAFENSTRASSE DEVELOPMENT

Acrylic on cartridge, 100 x 120 cm
Hamburg, Germany, 1990

Zaha Hadid's idea of an "explosion reforming space" is most readily apparent in this painting, where an embankment area of Hamburg is transformed into a recreation area with links running through an old harbor street.

Anhand dieses Gemäldes wird Zaha Hadids Vorstellung von einer „raumerneuernden Explosion" unmittelbar anschaulich. In der Hamburger Hafengegend, die in ein Naherholungsgebiet umgestaltet werden sollte, kreuzen Verbindungsrouten eine alte Straße am Hafen.

L'idée de Zaha Hadid d'une « explosion reformant l'espace » apparaît plus directement encore dans cette œuvre, où un quai de Hambourg se transforme en zone de loisirs d'où partent des liaisons reprenant une ancienne rue du port.

BLUE AND GREEN SCRAPERS
LEICESTER SQUARE

Acrylic on black cartridge, 230 x 110 cm
London, UK, 1990

Both in aesthetic and in architectural terms, this painting represents an apparently abstract rethinking of a major London square—suggesting that it should be considered as a "public room, habitable and submerged beneath the surface, a heart that beats with the city." Rather than adding fountains, for example, the architect proposes to sink them into the earth upside down.

Dieses Gemälde illustriert die ästhetische und architektonische Umgestaltung eines zentralen Londoner Platzes. Der Entwurf sah vor, den Platz als öffentlichen Raum zu begreifen, der „wohnliche Qualitäten hat und zugleich unter der Oberfläche liegt; als pochendes Herz der Stadt". Anstatt beispielsweise Brunnen zu errichten, sieht die Architektin vor, diese kopfüber im Erdboden zu versenken.

En termes aussi bien esthétiques qu'architecturaux, cette peinture est la redéfinition apparemment abstraite d'une grande place londonienne considérée comme « une grande salle publique, habitable, sous la surface, un cœur qui bat en accord avec la ville ». Plutôt que d'ajouter des fontaines à l'extérieur, par exemple, l'architecte propose de les enfoncer à l'envers dans le sol.

BERLIN 2000
Acrylic on paper mounted on gatorfoam,
composition, 2 parts (222 x 96 cm each)
Berlin, Germany, 1988

Working again before the fall of the Berlin Wall, the
architect here made proposals intended to regen-
erate the city, taking into account the physical reality of the Wall itself, imagining it as a "linear park…
decorated with buildings."

Travaillant là encore avant la chute du mur de Berlin,
l'architecte fait des propositions de rénovation de
la ville qui prennent en compte la réalité physique
du mur lui-même, l'imaginant comme « un parc
linéaire… décoré de constructions ».

Auch für dieses Projekt, das ebenfalls vor der Öffnung der Berliner Mauer ausgearbeitet wurde,
plante die Architektin eine Umgestaltung der Stadt,
in diesem Fall durch eine direkte Bezugnahme
auf die Realität der Mauer, die in ihrer Vision zu
einem „linearen Parkstreifen …" wurde, der „mit
Bauwerken ausgestaltet" werden sollte.

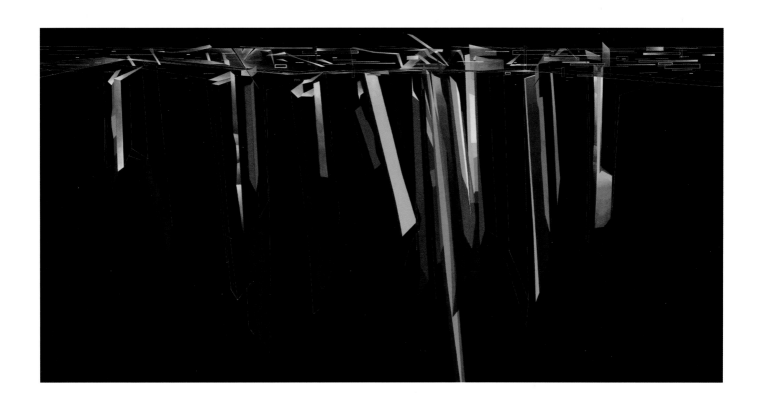

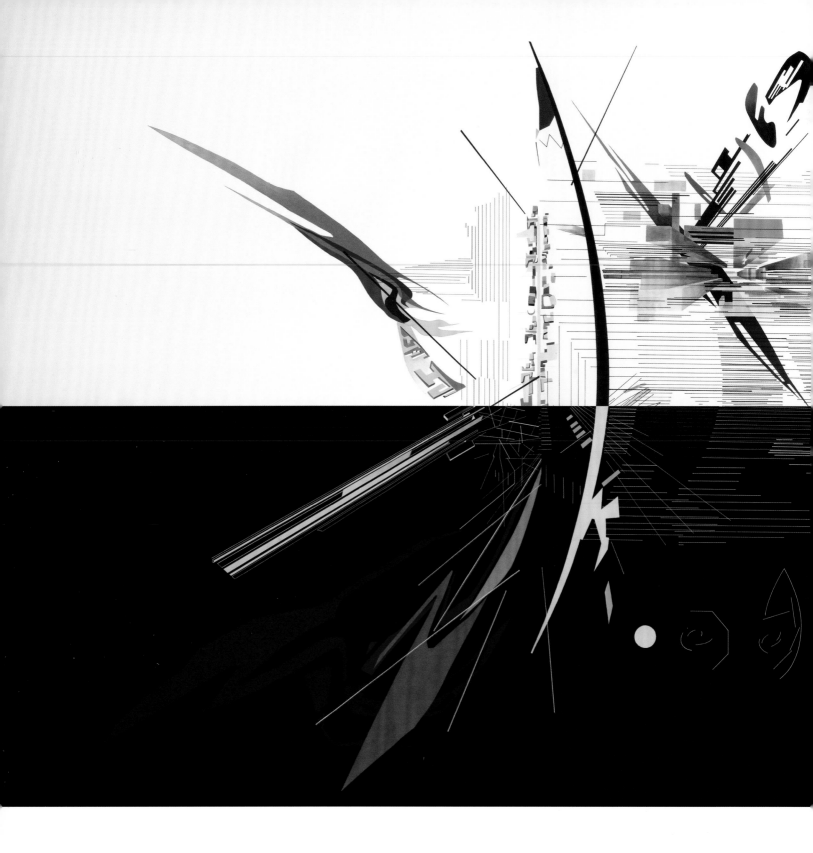

**MULTI COLOUR ON WHITE
VISION FOR MADRID**

Acrylic on cartridge, composition of 4 paintings
(two: 241 x 85 cm and two: 120 x 85 cm)
Madrid, Spain, 1992

The apparently abstract design of this work represents the Spanish capital as a "successive bursting of shells"—from the circular medieval city to linear 20th-century development that threatens it with "formlessness"—a conclusion that Hadid sought to avoid by directing future development and regeneration in four specified directions.

Der scheinbar abstrakte Entwurf begreift die spanische Hauptstadt als „aufeinander folgende Reihe von Explosionen" – von der mittelalterlichen, runden Stadtanlage bis hin zur linearen Entwicklung im 20. Jahrhundert. Diese wird wegen ihrer „Formlosigkeit" zur Bedrohung für die Stadt – eine Konsequenz, die Hadid zu vermeiden sucht, indem sie künftige Entwicklungen und Erneuerungen in vier klar definierte Richtungen lenkt.

Le style apparemment abstrait de cette œuvre fait de la capitale espagnole une « succession d'explosion de coquilles », de celle de la cité médiévale concentrique aux développements linéaires du XXᵉ siècle qui la menacent d'une « absence de formes », conclusion qu'Hadid cherche à éviter en réorientant les futures extensions et zones de rénovation dans quatre directions précises.

IRISH PRIME MINISTER'S RESIDENCE

Dublin, Ireland. 1979–80

IRISH PRIME MINISTER'S RESIDENCE

Location
DUBLIN, IRELAND

Pages 46–47:
OVERALL PLAN
Ink and Acrylic on Mylar, 84 x 136 cm
1980

Page 48:
OVERALL ISOMETRIC PLAN
Acrylic, watercolor and ink on paper, 101 x 181 cm
1980

Zaha Hadid's presentation of this project presages her slightly more familiar style for The Peak. A painterly evocation of the project in its spatial reality rather than a traditional plan or perspective, Hadid's vision of architecture is already laid out in this early work.

Hadids Projektpräsentation nimmt den schon bekannteren Stil von The Peak vorweg. Bereits in dieser malerischen Darstellung des Frühwerks, in der räumliche Qualitäten eher angedeutet werden, als sie mit einem traditionellen Grundriss oder Perspektivzeichnungen darzustellen, klingt Hadids architektonische Vision an.

La manière de présenter ce projet annonce le style un peu plus familier que Zaha Hadid développera pour The Peak. C'est une évocation picturale du projet dans sa réalité spatiale plutôt qu'un plan ou une perspective traditionnels. Une vision personnelle de l'architecture est déjà présente dans les premiers travaux d'Hadid.

To be located in Phoenix Park, Dublin, the largest enclosed urban public park in Europe, this project, Hadid's first major design, a competition entry, was intended to create a feeling of "weightlessness and freedom from the stress of public life." The residence was to be attached to a state function room via a road and walkway. A guesthouse was proposed for a site in an existing enclosed garden. As Hadid's early drawings for this project show, a sense of connection between the volumes was of primary importance, as was the idea of "floating" in space. Somewhat less stylized than her later paintings or drawings, the work for the Irish Prime Minister's Residence shows a keen knowledge of architectural form and the unexpected, abstract association of volumes in space.

Hadids erster großer Entwurf, ein Wettbewerbsbeitrag, sollte im Phoenix Park in Dublin realisiert werden, dem größten innerstädtischen Park Europas, und „Schwerelosigkeit und Freiheit vom Stress des öffentlichen Lebens" vermitteln. Geplant war, die Residenz durch eine Straße und einen Verbindungsgang an repräsentative Empfangsräumlichkeiten anzuschließen. Auf einem bereits vorhandenen privaten Gartengrundstück hätte ein Gästehaus entstehen sollen. Wie Hadids frühe Zeichnungen für das Projekt illustrieren, ging es in erster Linie darum, das Zusammenspiel der einzelnen Volumina und ein „Schweben" im Raum zu vermitteln. Der Entwurf für die Residenz des irischen Premierministers wirkt weniger stilisiert als spätere Gemälde und Zeichnungen und zeugt von Hadids ausgeprägtem Verständnis für architektonische Formen und unerwartete, abstrakte Verknüpfungen von Baukörpern im Raum.

Ce projet de concours pour Phoenix Park à Dublin, plus vaste parc public clos d'Europe, est la première création importante de Zaha Hadid. Elle voulait susciter un sentiment « d'impondérabilité et de libération des tensions de la vie publique ». La résidence aurait été rattachée à un bâtiment officiel de bureaux par une voie et un passage. Une maison pour invités était également prévue dans un jardin clos situé à proximité. Comme le montrent les premiers dessins d'Hadid réalisés pour ce projet, l'impression d'interconnexion des volumes était d'importance primordiale, de même que l'idée de « flottement » dans l'espace. Légèrement moins stylisé que ses dessins et peintures ultérieurs, ce travail témoigne d'une connaissance aiguë de la forme architecturale et montre une surprenante association de volumes abstraits dans l'espace.

THE PEAK

Hong Kong, China. 1982–83

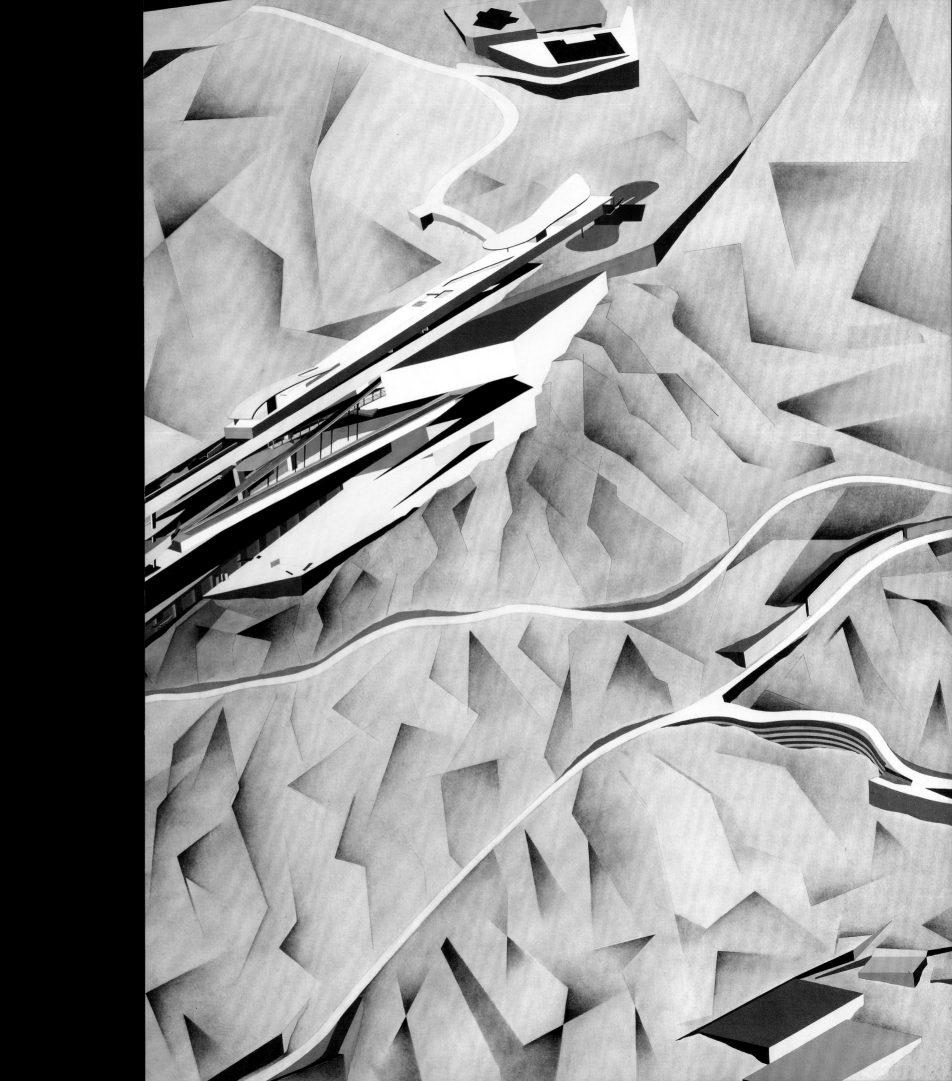

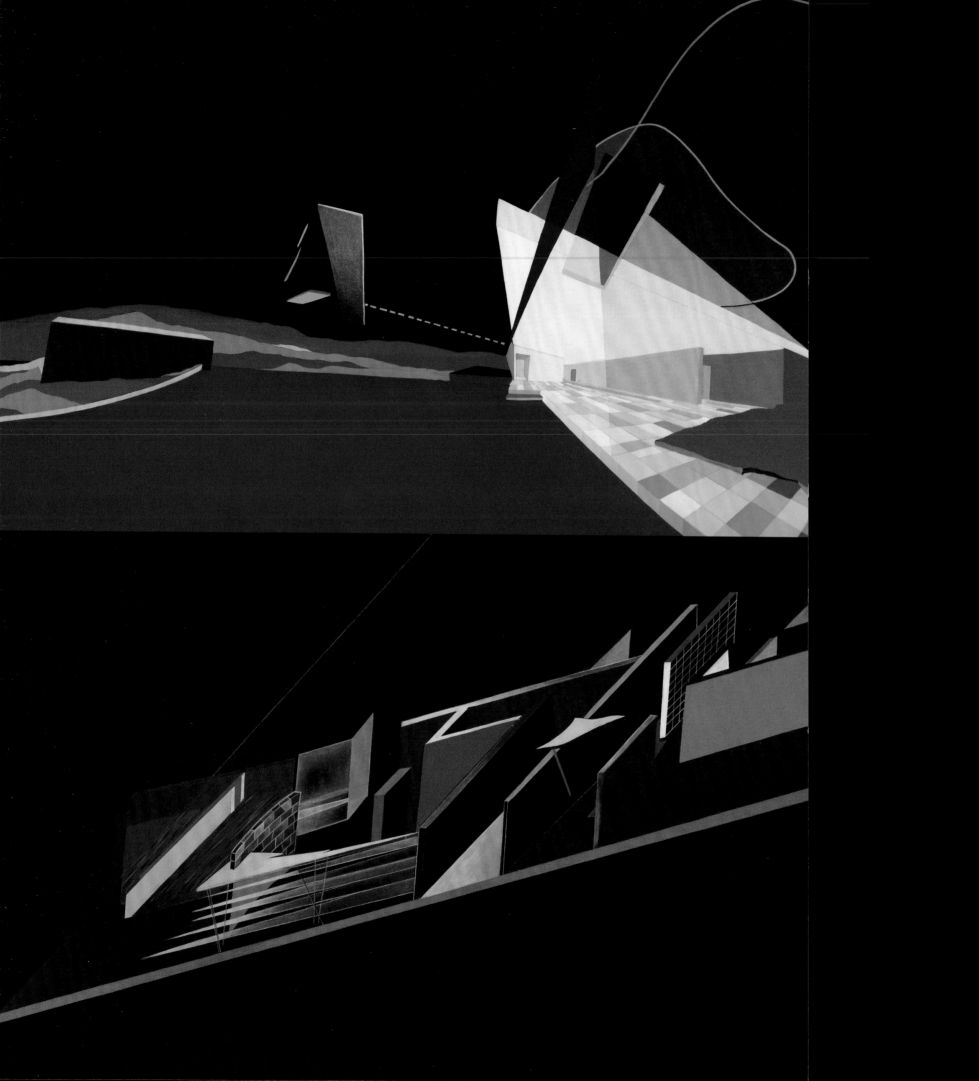

Project
THE PEAK

Location
HONG KONG, CHINA

Pages 50–51:
**OVERALL ISOMETRIC
(PART 2 OF 2, DETAIL)**
Acrylic on cartridge, 184 x 132 cm
1983

Page 52 top:
**PERSPECTIVE OF FRONT
WITH DIVING BOARD**
Acrylic on cartridge, 87 x 62.3 cm
1983

Page 52 bottom:
LOWER PENTHOUSE APARTMENTS
Acrylic and ink on paper, 87 x 62.3 cm
1983

This international competition entry (first prize) for a leisure club for wealthy clients, the first internationally celebrated project of Zaha Hadid, was included in the landmark 1988 Museum of Modern Art exhibition *Deconstructivist Architecture,* curated by Philip Johnson and Mark Wigley. Though the reference to early modern Russian art contained in the exhibition title may not have been fully accurate for all those concerned, Zaha Hadid did refer to "Suprematist geology" in describing The Peak. She also said that "the architecture is like a knife cutting through the site. It cuts through traditional principles of organization and reconstitutes new ones, defies nature and resists destroying it." Hadid's approach consisted in excavating the site and then making artificial cliffs with the excavated rock. This blurring of the lines between nature and architecture, between site and building, are significant even today in her work, thus The Peak remains a seminal project in Zaha Hadid's career. Four great beams constitute another important element of the project, symbolically related to the skyscrapers in the city below. Breaking with almost any preexisting orthogonal system of design, Hadid here creates a surprising 13-meter-wide void in the gap between the upper and lower beams in which decks, a swimming pool, and a snack bar are suspended. Fifteen double-height studio apartments were designed for the lower layer of beams, with a further 20 apartments above. The roof of this second layer becomes the podium of the actual club, located further above. An enclosed pedestrian ramp leads from a lobby deck into what Hadid called "the man-made mountain," where restaurants and indoor club facilities are located. Still higher than the club, a fourth and fifth level contain penthouse apartments. Hadid refers to a "gentle seismic shift" in referring to this project and, indeed, her project, and the drawings and paintings associated with it, did create just such a shift in architecture, extending the realm of the possible well before sophisticated computer-assisted design made the end of the strict modernist grid inevitable.

Dieser luxuriöse Freizeitklub war ein Beitrag für einen internationalen Wettbewerb (erster Preis). Es war zudem der erste Entwurf Zaha Hadids, der international bekannt wurde und in der wegweisenden Ausstellung *Deconstructivist Architecture* zu sehen war, die Philip Johnson und Mark Wigley 1988 für das Museum of Modern Art kuratiert hatten. Obwohl die im Ausstellungstitel anklingende Anspielung auf die russische Avantgarde sicherlich nicht auf alle beteiligten Architekten zutraf, sprach Zaha Hadid in ihrer Beschreibung von The Peak tatsächlich explizit von „suprematistischen geologischen Schichten". Sie erklärte darüber hinaus: „Wie ein Messer schneidet die Architektur durch das Terrain. Sie durchbricht traditionelle Organisationsprinzipien und definiert neue, sie grenzt sich von der Natur ab und vermeidet dennoch, sie zu zerstören." Hadids Ansatz sieht vor, das Terrain ausschachten zu lassen und mit den ausgegrabenen Felsbrocken künstliche Klippen errichten zu lassen. Auch heute spielt dieses Verwischen der Grenzen von Natur und Architektur, von Terrain und Bauwerk eine entscheidende Rolle in Hadids Œuvre; The Peak darf als Schlüsselwerk ihrer Laufbahn gelten. Ein weiteres wichtiges Element sind vier monumentale Riegel, die symbolisch die Wolkenkratzer der im Tal liegenden Stadt aufgreifen. Hadid bricht hier mit so gut wie allen gängigen rechtwinkligen Gestaltungssystemen und definiert einen erstaunlichen 13 m breiten Leerraum zwischen den oberen und unteren Gebäuderiegeln, in dem Terrassen, ein Pool und eine Snackbar zu hängen scheinen. In der unteren Ebene der „Riegel"-Struktur sind 15 Studioapartments mit doppelter Raumhöhe geplant, weitere 20 in der oberen Ebene. Das Dach der zweiten Ebene bildet zugleich den Sockel für den darüberliegenden, eigentlichen Klub. Eine umbaute Fußgängerrampe führt von der Eingangsebene in den, Hadid zufolge, „künstlichen Berg" hinein, zu Restaurants und Klubräumen. Über dem Klub liegen eine vierte und fünfte Ebene mit Penthouseapartments. Hadid beschreibt das Projekt als „sanfte seismische Verschiebung", und tatsächlich löste der Entwurf mit den dazugehörigen Zeichnungen und Gemälden ein Erdbeben in der Architektur aus. Er erweiterte das Spektrum des Möglichen, lange bevor digitale Entwurfswerkzeuge zum unausweichlichen Ende des strengen modernistischen Rasters führten.

Ce projet, premier prix d'un concours international, portait sur un club de loisirs destiné à une clientèle aisée. Pour la première fois, l'attention du monde de l'architecture était attirée sur Zaha Hadid. The Peak figura d'ailleurs dans l'exposition historique organisée par Philip Johnson et Mark Wigley en 1988 au Museum of Modern Art, sous le titre de « Architecture déconstructiviste ». Bien que la référence à l'art moderne russe évoquée par le titre de cette manifestation ne convenait pas forcément à chacun de ses participants, Zaha Hadid se référait à la « géologie suprématiste » dans sa description du projet. Elle y expliquait également : « L'architecture est comme un couteau qui tranche dans le site. Elle découpe les principes traditionnels d'organisation et en reconstruit de nouveaux, défie la nature et résiste à la détruire. » Hadid creusait le site et dressait des falaises artificielles à l'aide de la roche excavée. Le flou des frontières entre la nature et l'architecture, entre le site et le bâti, reste encore aujourd'hui caractéristique de son œuvre, et The Peak est l'un des projets fondateurs de sa carrière. Quatre énormes poutres constituent un second élément important, symboliquement lié aux gratte-ciel de la ville situés en contrebas. Rompant avec pratiquement tous les systèmes de plans orthogonaux préexistants, Hadid crée un surprenant vide de 13 m de haut entre la poutre inférieure et la poutre supérieure, entre lequelles des terrasses, une piscine et un *snack-bar* viennent se suspendre. Quinze appartements-studios double hauteur étaient logés contre la trame des poutres inférieures et vingt appartements au-dessus. La couverture de cette seconde strate devenait un podium pour le club lui-même, situé au sommet. Une rampe piétonnière fermée partait de la terrasse d'accueil, vers ce que Hadid appelait « la montagne faite à la main de l'homme » où se trouvaient des restaurants et des installations sportives. Plus haut encore, un quatrième et un cinquième niveau contenaient des appartements en penthouses. Hadid parle de ce projet comme d'un « glissement sismique en douceur », et c'est bien ce que provoquèrent ses dessins et peintures dans le monde de l'architecture, car ils ouvraient de nouvelles voies dans le domaine du possible, bien avant que les logiciels sophistiqués de CAO n'annoncent la fin de la rigoureuse trame moderniste.

Page 54:
The divers
Acrylic on cartridge, 97 x 178 cm
1983

An unusual, rather figurative view of the swimming pool imagined by Zaha Hadid for The Peak. Here, as is always the case, the future appearance of an architectural space is imagined in a specific style, which is informed by the very complete and accurate vision of the architect, even if more aesthetic matters also play a role in the composition.

Eine ungewöhnliche, eher figurative Visualisierung des Pools, den Zaha Hadid für The Peak vorgesehen hatte. Das Erscheinungsbild des geplanten architektonischen Raums wird hier wie üblich in einem spezifischen Stil umrissen. Dieser Stil entsteht aus der umfassenden und höchst präzisen Vision der Architektin, obwohl bei der Gestaltung der Komposition auch ästhetische Aspekte eine Rolle spielen.

Vue étonnante, assez figurative, de la piscine proposée par Zaha Hadid pour The Peak. Comme d'habitude l'aspect futur de l'espace architectural est imaginé dans un style spécifique nourri de la vision très complète et précise de l'architecte, même si des préoccupations esthétiques ont également joué un rôle dans la composition.

Page 55:
CONFETTI:
SUPREMATIST SNOWSTORM
Acrylic on cartridge, 91 x 275 cm
1983

Confetti is part of the development work done by Zaha Hadid on The Peak project. In this instance, she is concerned with the scales and colors of the architecture. As the title of the work indicates, the architect establishes a connection with the work of the Russian Suprematists.

Confetti entstand im Zuge von Hadids Entwurfsarbeiten für ihr Projekt The Peak. Hier geht es ihr um Größenverhältnisse und Farbgebung der Architektur. Wie schon der Titel nahelegt, knüpft die Architektin mit dieser Arbeit an das Werk der russischen Suprematisten an.

Confetti fait partie du travail de mise au point du projet du Peak par Zaha Hadid. Ici, se voit son intérêt pour les échelles et les couleurs. Comme l'indique le titre complet de l'œuvre, l'architecte établissait une connexion avec les suprématistes russes.

Hadid's objects gain from being seen from different angles because their design is by no means regular or rectilinear. Rather than being a succession of planes or Euclidean solids assembled according to convention, they inevitably imply the continuity of space.

Hadids Objekte gewinnen aus verschiedenen Blickwinkeln, schließlich ist ihr Design alles andere als regelmäßig oder geradlinig. Statt konventionell aus Flächen oder euklidischen Körpern zusammengesetzt zu sein, schaffen sie aus sich heraus ein räumliches Kontinuum.

Les objets d'Hadid gagnent à être vus sous des angles différents puisque leur design n'est ni régulier ni rectiligne. Ils ne sont pas une succession de plans ou de solides euclidiens assemblés selon des normes conventionnelles. Implacablement, ils génèrent une continuité de l'espace.

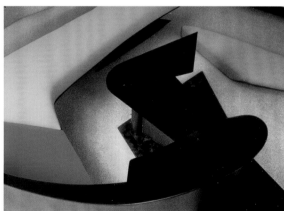

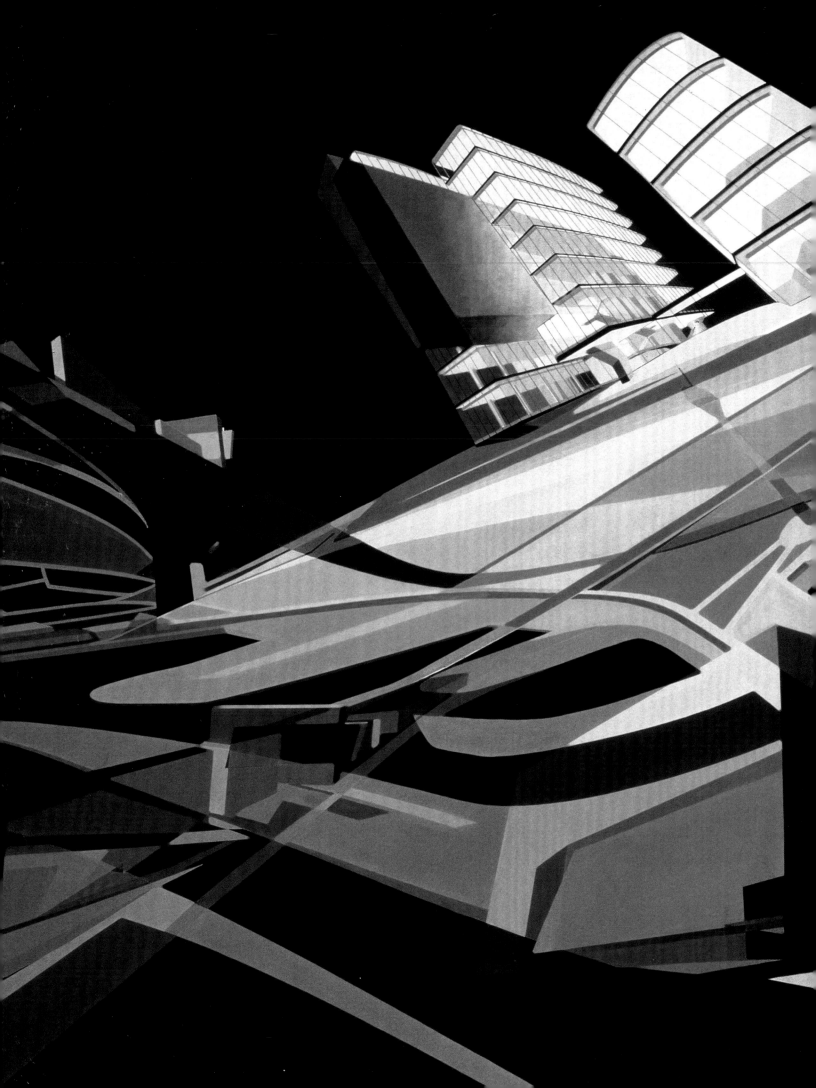

ZOLLHOF 3 MEDIA PARK

Düsseldorf, Germany. 1989–93

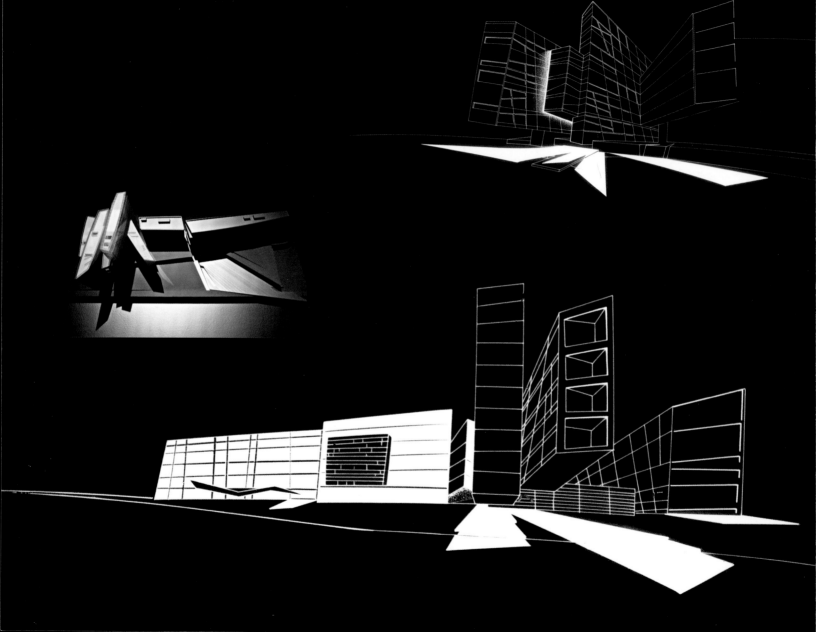

Project

ZOLLHOF 3 MEDIA PARK

Location

DÜSSELDORF, GERMANY

Client

KUNST- UND MEDIENZENTRUM
RHEINHAFEN GMBH

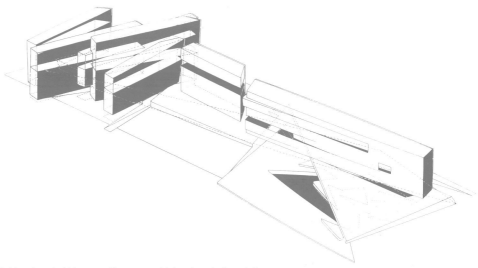

Pages 70–71:
**LANDSCAPE PERSPECTIVE
ROTATION PAINTING**
Acrylic on cartridge, 220 x 106 cm
1989

Though this project is based on straight lines, the unexpected alignments and jagged compositions create a new form. Lines extending into the site tie the complex together.

Zwar basiert dieses Projekt auf geraden Linien, doch durch die überraschende Anordnung und zerklüftete Komposition entsteht eine neue Formensprache. Linien, die das Grundstück zerschneiden, halten den Komplex zusammen.

Bien que ce projet s'appuie sur des lignes droites, les alignements inattendus et la composition en zigzag créent une forme nouvelle. La projection des lignes dans le site assure au complexe sa cohésion.

Though it may not be as well known as The Peak project, this design exploits a similar break with orthogonal traditions in architecture. The ambition of the Düsseldorf design was to help to develop the former harbor of the city into an enterprise zone in communication or related creative professions. Offices were to be mixed with retail and leisure facilities in the same zones. Zaha Hadid proposed a 90-meter-long "wall" of offices, shielding an "artificially modeled landscape" near the Rhine River, where sport and leisure activities are located. A metallic triangle breaks the office wall to offer an entrance ramp access to the street. Linear incisions and cantilevered floors create a variety in the office structure or "wall" that clearly announce the non-standardized nature of the architecture. A 320-seat movie theater is inscribed in a curve in the wall. Advertising-agency space is located in "an even more fragmented series of slabs, set perpendicular to the street." A void between floor slabs with a "grand curved stair" offers space for conference rooms and exhibition areas, while lift and service cores are presented as detached elements. With this project, Hadid further defines the unexpected, fragmented nature of her drawings and paintings, creating a style that is informed by a sound knowledge of architecture while reaching deep into the realm of contemporary art.

Wenn auch nicht so bekannt wie The Peak, so stellt dieser Entwurf doch auf ähnliche Weise einen Bruch mit den rechtwinkligen Gestaltungsmustern der Architektur dar. Ziel des Düsseldorfer Entwurfs war es, den ehemaligen Stadthafen als Gewerbegebiet für Unternehmen aus der Werbe- und Medienbranche und ähnliche kreative Berufe zu erschließen. Es sollten gemischte Zonen aus Büroflächen, Geschäften und Freizeiteinrichtungen entstehen. Zaha Hadid entwarf einen 90 m langen Riegel aus Bürobauten, hinter dem unweit des Rheins eine „künstlich modellierte Landschaft" mit Sport- und Freizeiteinrichtungen liegt. Ein monumentales metallisches Dreieck zerschneidet den Büroriegel und bildet eine Rampe, die den Bau an die Straße anbindet. Lineare Einschnitte und auskragende Geschosse lockern den Büroriegel strukturell auf, der nach außen deutlich signalisiert, dass diese Architektur alles andere als standardisiert ist. Ein Kino mit 320 Plätzen ist in einen geschwungenen Abschnitt des Riegels einge-

schrieben. In „noch stärker fragmentierten, lotrecht zur Straße stehenden Gebäudescheiben" sind Räumlichkeiten für Werbeagenturen untergebracht. Zwischen den Grundplatten liegt ein Leerraum mit einer „imposanten geschwungenen Treppe", in dem sich Konferenz- und Ausstellungsräume befinden. Aufzugs- und Haustechnikbereiche werden als separate Elemente artikuliert. Mit diesem Projekt werden Hadids erstaunliche, zersplitterte Zeichnungen und Gemälde noch detaillierter ausgearbeitet. Die Architektin definiert einen Stil, der von fundierter architektonischer Kenntnis zeugt und zugleich stark in das Terrain der zeitgenössischen Kunst vorzudringen scheint.

Bien qu'ils ne soient pas aussi célèbres que ceux du projet du Peak, ces plans illustrent une rupture du même ordre avec la tradition orthogonale en architecture. L'ambition de cette proposition pour Düsseldorf se plaçait dans le cadre de la transformation des anciennes zones portuaires de la ville en une zone d'activité consacrée à la communication et aux professions créatives liées. Les bureaux devaient être mélangés à des commerces et à des installations de loisirs. Zaha Hadid avait proposé un « mur » de 90 m de long, abritant un « paysage artificiellement modelé » au bord du Rhin où se trouvaient des activités sportives et de loisirs. Un triangle métallique transperçait le mur des bureaux pour permettre le passage d'une rampe d'accès à la rue. Des incisions linéaires et des plateaux en porte-à-faux créaient une diversité visuelle dans le « mur » de bureaux qui annonçait clairement la nature non standard de cette nouvelle architecture. Un cinéma de 320 places s'inscrivait dans une courbe du « mur ». Un espace pour agences de publicité était logé « dans une série de dalles encore plus fragmentées, perpendiculaires à la rue ». Le vide entre les dalles et un « grand escalier incurvé » était occupé par des salles de conférences et des lieux d'expositions, les ascenseurs et les noyaux techniques étant traités comme des éléments séparés. À travers ce projet, Hadid approfondissait la définition du caractère inhabituel et fragmenté de ses dessins et peintures pour créer un style nourri de sa connaissance concrète de l'architecture, mais qui soit dans le même temps en profonde résonance avec l'art contemporain.

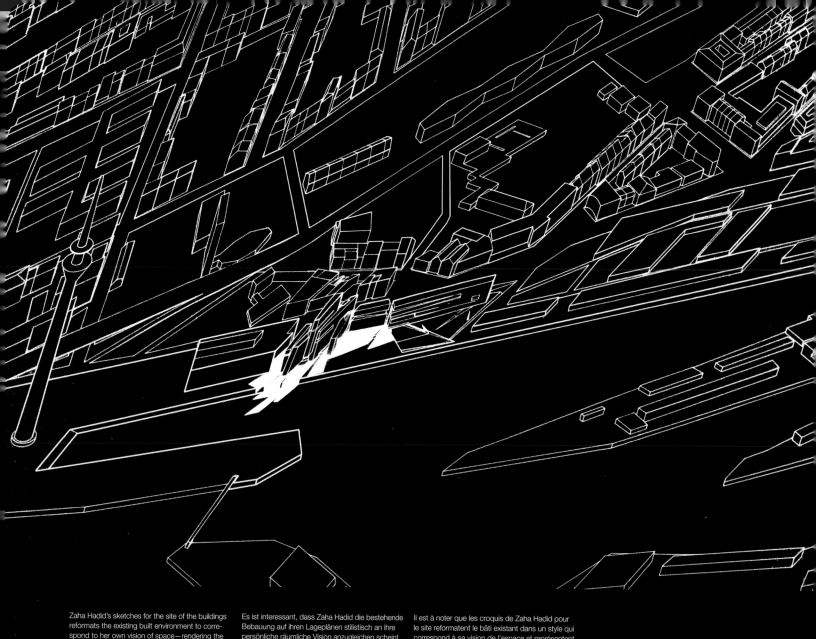

Zaha Hadid's sketches for the site of the buildings reformats the existing built environment to correspond to her own vision of space—rendering the surroundings somewhat more fractured and angular than they might be in reality, thus more fully explaining her own proposal for the new project.

Es ist interessant, dass Zaha Hadid die bestehende Bebauung auf ihren Lageplänen stilistisch an ihre persönliche räumliche Vision anzugleichen scheint. So wirkt die Umgebung zersplitterter und winkliger als sie in Wirklichkeit sein dürfte, liefert jedoch auch eine schlüssige Erklärung für ihren Projektvorschlag.

Il est à noter que les croquis de Zaha Hadid pour le site reformatent le bâti existant dans un style qui correspond à sa vision de l'espace et représentent l'environnement plus fracturé et anguleux qu'il n'est en réalité. Cette approche explique encore mieux sa proposition.

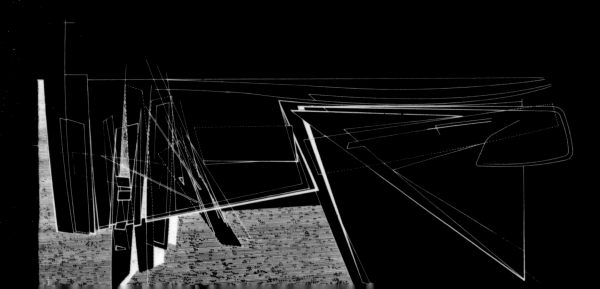

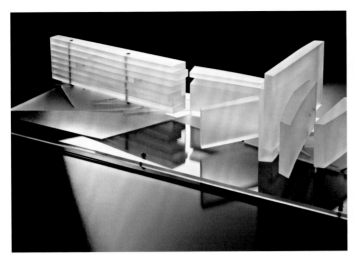

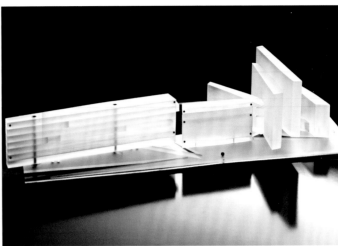

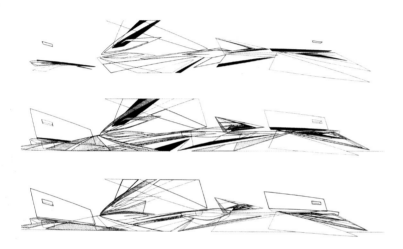

Models or drawings make the link between the original drawings and the reality of the built designs, which are, of course, completely practical despite their cantilevers or unusual plans. Sketches (above) render the dynamic impression usually given by the work of Zaha Hadid, a dynamism that is harder to interpret in models, for example.

Modelle und Zeichnungen sind stets Bindeglieder zwischen ersten Entwürfen und gebauter Realität, die hier trotz der Auskragungen und ungewöhnlichen Grundrisse absolut praxisorientiert ist. Skizzen (oben) vermitteln die Dynamik, die Hadids Arbeiten in der Regel ausstrahlen – eine Dynamik, die im Modell schwerer zu interpretieren ist.

Les maquettes et dessins font le lien entre les croquis originaux et la réalité de projets de construction parfaitement réalisables quel que soit l'aspect inhabituel de leurs plans et leurs porte-à-faux. Les croquis (ci-dessus) apportent ce sentiment de dynamique habituel chez Zaha Hadid, plus difficile à interpréter dans les maquettes.

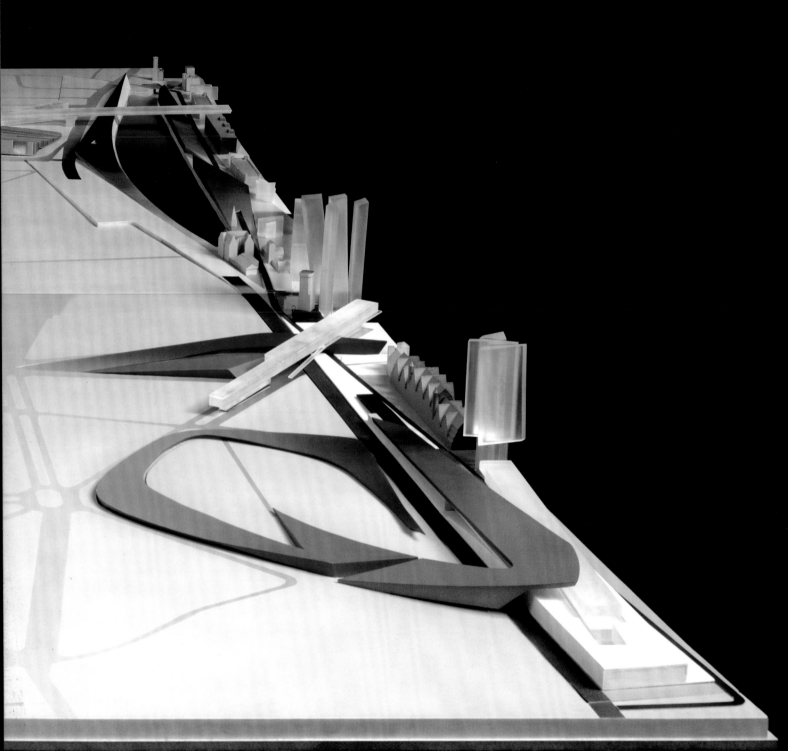

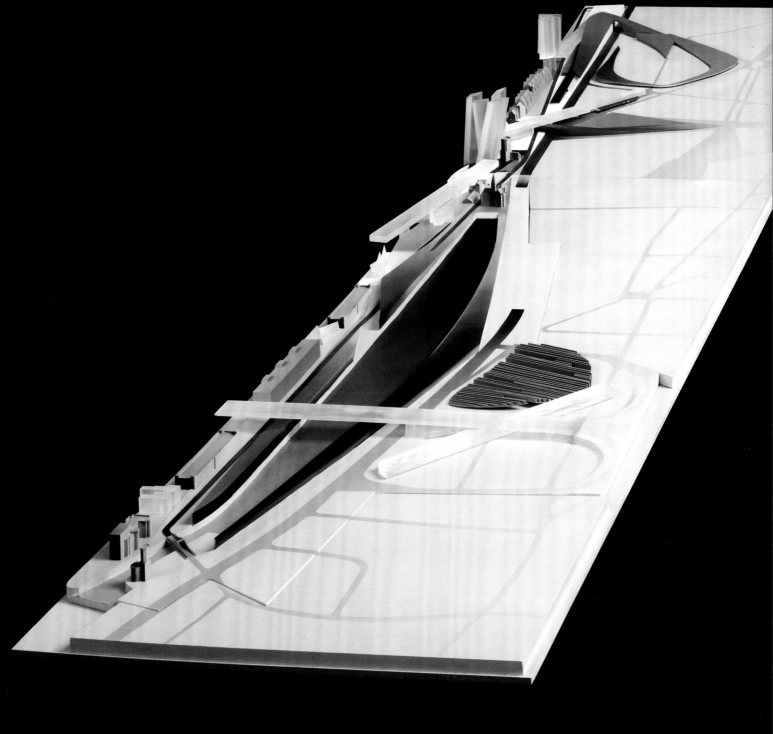

RHEINAUHAFEN REDEVELOPMENT

Cologne, Germany. 1993

Project
RHEINAUHAFEN REDEVELOPMENT
Location
COLOGNE, GERMANY

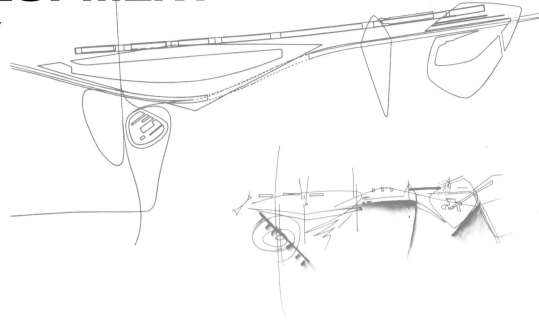

Here Hadid experiments with tying together a large area with different forms and the fluidity of her style becomes a natural asset in the process.

Hier experimentiert Hadid damit, ein größeres Gelände durch unterschiedliche Formen zu einem Gesamtbild zu fügen. Ihr flüssiger Stil erweist sich hierbei als natürlicher Vorteil.

Ici, Zaha Hadid expérimente la définition d'un vaste espace à travers différentes formes. La fluidité de son style s'impose au cours de ce processus.

The redevelopment of Rheinau Harbor, located between the Rhine and the city center of Cologne, was one of the largest urban projects in Germany, covering an area of 15 hectares. Zaha Hadid's 1993 competition entry for the urban plan called for three territories, respectively called the Trapezoid, the Wedge-like section, and the Spiral, to the south. Hadid uses her sharp-edged forms to stitch the zone together, using the trapezoid to combine both sides of the harbor into a single entity, or two long buildings on the quay sides starting at a height of eight meters and running down to ground level, allowing visitors to enter the yachting facilities and check-in areas for river shuttle service from the roofs, which serve as ramps. Three warehouses, listed as historic monuments and intended as facilities for culture, are located on the harbor peninsula, linked to the northern conference center and parking zone via a footbridge. Hadid proposed placing these three structures on a 1.5-meter-high platform to link them together and to act as a flood barrier. Housing, massed to resemble the former warehouses, is arranged in blocks raised 10 meters above the ground on stilts. As is often the case, Hadid here analyzes the specific topography and architecture of the site and weaves her proposal into the existing elements, creating new relationships and paths, essentially resolving difficult urban problems with a cohesive and aesthetically continuous solution.

Mit einer Gesamtfläche von 15 ha war die bauliche Umgestaltung des Kölner Rheinauhafens zwischen Rhein und Stadtmitte eines der größten Stadtentwicklungsprojekte Deutschlands. Zaha Hadids Beitrag für den 1993 ausgeschriebenen Wettbewerb sah die Schaffung von drei Bereichen vor, einem Trapez, einem Keil und einer Spirale im Süden. Hadid bedient sich der spitzwinkligen Formen, um das Gebiet zusammenzuführen. Das Trapez verbindet beide Seiten des Hafens zu einer Einheit, zwei Großbauten an den Kaimauern senken sich von 8 m Höhe bis auf Bodenniveau ab, sodass Besucher über die rampenförmigen Dächer zum Jachthafen und den Anlegestellen der Rheinfähren gelangen können. Drei denkmalgeschützte Lagerhäuser auf der Halbinsel im Hafen sind für kulturelle Einrichtungen vorgesehen und können vom Kongresszentrum am nördlichen

Ende des Geländes sowie vom Parkplatz aus über eine Fußgängerbrücke erreicht werden. Hadids Entwurf sieht vor, die drei Bereiche zum Schutz vor Hochwasser auf 1,5 m hohe, miteinander verbundene Plattformen zu setzen. Wohnflächen werden gebündelt und knüpfen optisch an die ehemaligen Lagerhäuser an. Diese Wohnblocks sind 10 m über dem Boden aufgeständert. Wie so oft analysiert Hadid auch hier die vorhandene Topografie und Architektur des Standorts und integriert ihren Entwurf in die existierenden Elemente. So entstehen neue Wechselbeziehungen und Wegenetze, zugleich werden komplexe urbane Problemstellungen dank eines schlüssigen und ästhetisch durchkomponierten Konzepts gelöst.

La rénovation du port de Rheinau, entre le Rhin et le centre-ville de Cologne, est l'un des plus vastes projets urbains d'Allemagne. Il couvre une surface de 15 ha. La proposition présentée par Zaha Hadid lors du concours pour un plan d'urbanisme en 1993 suggérait la création de trois territoires respectivement appelés le Trapézoïde, la Section en coin et la Spirale (au sud). Hadid a repris son principe de formes anguleuses pour « coudre » ensemble ces zones, en se servant d'un trapézoïde pour réunir les deux côtés du port en une seule entité, soit deux longs bâtiments érigés le long des quais qui débutent à une hauteur de 8 m et descendant vers le niveau du sol, ce qui permet aux visiteurs d'accéder aux installations du port de plaisance et à la navette fluviale à partir de leurs toits servant de rampes. Trois entrepôts, classés monument historiques et dédiés à des installations culturelles, ont été conservés sur la péninsule portuaire, reliés au centre de conférences et aux parkings nord par une passerelle. Hadid avait proposé de placer ces trois structures sur une plate-forme de 1,5 m de haut qui les aurait réunis, tout en servant de digue contre les inondations éventuelles. Des logements, traités en plan masse de façon à rappeler les entrepôts, étaient disposés en blocs posés sur des pilotis de 10 m de haut. Comme souvent, Hadid a analysé ici la topographie et l'architecture des lieux et imaginé ses propositions par rapport aux éléments existant, créant de nouvelles relations et de nouveaux cheminements en résolvant de délicats problèmes d'urbanisme grâce à une solution esthétiquement cohérente et continue.

CARDIFF BAY OPERA HOUSE

Cardiff, Wales, UK. 1994–96

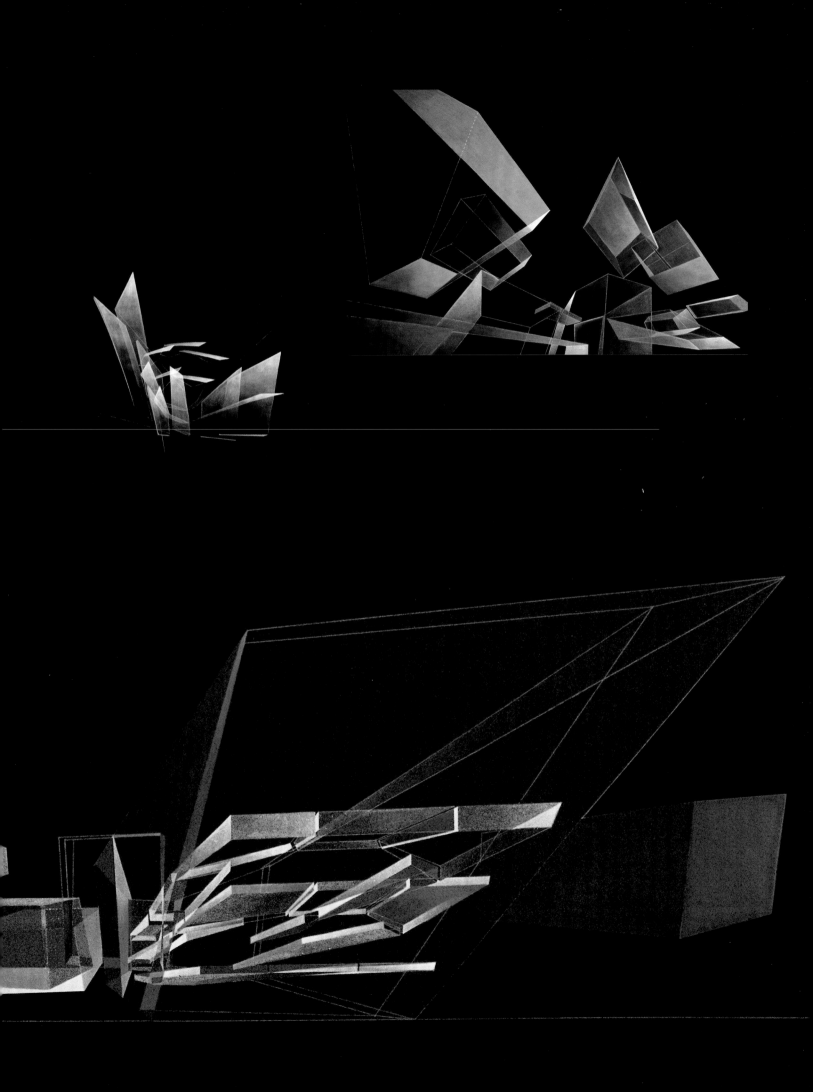

Project
CARDIFF BAY OPERA HOUSE

Location
CARDIFF, WALES, UK

Client
CARDIFF BAY OPERA HOUSE TRUST

Area/Size
25 000 m²

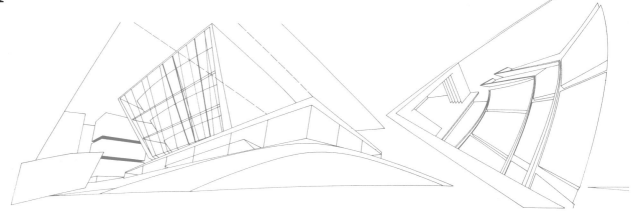

Pages 80–81:
JEWELS
Acrylic on black cartridge,
100 x 70 cm
1994

**2 VIEWS FROM THE OVAL
BASIN PIAZZA**
Acrylic on black cartridge, 100 x 35.5 cm
(painting divided here in two parts)
1995

Skewed angles and strong cantilevers are the most prominent features in the images to the left. The drawings above suggest how the different forms might have fit together.

Schiefe Winkel und starke auskragende Volumina prägen die Ansichten links. Die Zeichnungen oben illustrieren, wie alternative Anordnungen der einzelnen Segmente hätten aussehen können.

Des angles aigus et d'importants porte-à-faux sont les caractéristiques les plus évidentes de ces images (à gauche). Les dessins ci-dessus suggèrent la manière dont des formes différentes peuvent s'adapter ensemble.

Zaha Hadid won the competition to give the Welsh National Opera Company a new home, but unfortunately this project was never built. This 25 000-square-meter building presents itself as a folded continuum of varied spaces opening onto the Oval Basin Piazza. Hadid's models for the project in fact show the volumes at first arrayed along a straight line and then progressively folded in a composition of angled forms that create a nautilus-like enclosure with a raised perimeter—but with an open heart that is accessible from the exterior and yet enclosed by the architecture. The architect also describes this presentation as being related to that of an inverted necklace with a series of jewels that correspond to "serviced and servicing spaces"—when the necklace is closed, or almost so, the real correspondence between the volumes and their functions becomes apparent, creating a coherent that has a decidedly non-orthogonal plan. Though straight lines are the rule here, the disposition of the architecture is skewed and angled in such a way that different perspectives appear from each possible position of a visitor. Two main axes that correspond to the main pedestrian entrance form the Oval Basin Piazza and the concourse entrance and nonetheless order the volumes. The raised perimeter is broadly pierced where its corner faces the pier head—creating the opening in which the auditorium itself is the main volume. The Opera House is described as projecting a "strong landmark figure against the waterfront," and yet its raised internal plaza with views to the bay and harbor, and space for outdoor performances, makes it largely accessible.

Zaha Hadid gewann den Wettbewerb für ein neues Gebäude für die walisische Nationaloper, das Projekt konnte jedoch leider nie realisiert werden. Das 25 000 m² große Gebäude präsentiert sich als gefaltetes Kontinuum aus verschiedenen Volumina und öffnet sich zur Oval Basin Piazza, dem Platz am ovalen Hafenbecken. Hadids Modelle zeigen, wie die Baukörper zunächst längs aufgereiht und schließlich nach und nach zu einer kantigen Nautilusmuschel gefaltet wurden. Trotz der ringförmigen Umbauung bleibt das Herzstück des Baus offen, wird von der Architektur eingefasst und bleibt dennoch von außen zugänglich. Die Architektin vergleicht den Entwurf mit einer Halskette, wobei die verschiedenen „Versorgungs- und Nutzungsbereiche" einzelnen Juwelen entsprechen. Wird die Kette geschlossen – oder beinahe geschlossen – wird das Wechselspiel von

Baukörpern und Funktion deutlich. Es entsteht ein schlüssiges Gesamtbild mit eindeutig nicht rechtwinkligem Grundriss. Obwohl eine gerade Linienführung hier die Regel ist, wirkt die Architektur verzerrt und schiefwinklig, sodass sich dem Besucher von jedem Standpunkt aus unterschiedliche Ansichten bieten. Nichtsdestotrotz werden die Volumina durch zwei Hauptachsen gegliedert, die den Zugängen von der Oval Basin Piazza und durchs Hauptfoyer entsprechen. Die Umbauung öffnet sich an der zur Mole weisenden Ecke. Durch die Öffnung taucht der Konzertsaal als zentraler Baukörper auf. Das Opernhaus wird zum „eindrucksvollen Wahrzeichen am Ufer". Dennoch wirkt der Komplex durch die erhöhte Piazza mit Blick auf Bucht und Hafen und einen Platz für Freiluftkonzerte offen.

Zaha Hadid avait remporté le concours pour le nouveau siège de la Welsh National Opera Company, projet qui n'a malheureusement jamais abouti. Ce bâtiment de 25 000 m² formait un *continuum* de divers espaces ouvrant sur la « place du Bassin ovale ». Les maquettes réalisées montrent les premiers volumes disposés le long d'un axe rectiligne, qui se replient progressivement en une composition de formes inclinées créant une sorte de périmètre surélevé, évoquant un nautile, mais dont le cœur resterait accessible de l'extérieur tout en étant intégré à l'architecture. L'architecte parle d'un collier inversé, fait d'une série de pierres précieuses, qui correspondent aux « volumes serveurs et servants » lorsque le collier est fermé ou presque, ce qui fait apparaître une correspondance pratique entre ces volumes et leur fonction en dessinant un plan cohérent, mais certainement pas orthogonal. Bien que les lignes droites soient de règle dans ce projet, la disposition des divers éléments est traitée en biais et en inclinaisons, de telle façon qu'en se déplaçant le visiteur perçoive différentes perspectives. Les deux axes principaux, qui correspondent à l'entrée principale des piétons, donnent forme à la « place du Bassin ovale » et à l'atrium de l'entrée, tout en ordonnant les volumes. Le périmètre surélevé est largement ouvert vers le départ de la jetée, dégageant un espace pour le volume principal, celui de l'auditorium. Cet opéra est décrit comme projetant une « forte présence monumentale vers le front de mer », et sa place intérieure surélevée, avec ses vues sur la baie et le port, ses espaces pour spectacles de plein air, le rendent largement accessible.

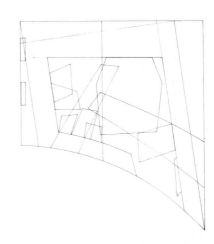

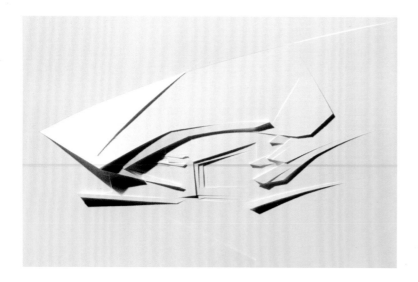

Drawings and models allow an overview of the project, whose complexity and coherence becomes most apparent through this kind of accumulation of documents.

Zeichnungen und Modelle vermitteln einen Überblick über das Projekt, dessen Komplexität und Kohärenz durch das Zusammenspiel dieser verschiedenen Dokumente am deutlichsten wird.

Ces dessins et maquettes donnent une vue globale du projet dont la complexité et la cohérence s'éclairent particulièrement à travers cette accumulation de documents.

Page 85 middle:
CARDIFF INTERNAL COURTYARD
Acrylic on black cartridge, 100 x 70 cm
1994

Page 85 bottom:
VIEW FROM EAST BUTE STREET
Acrylic on black cartridge, 100 x 70 cm
1994

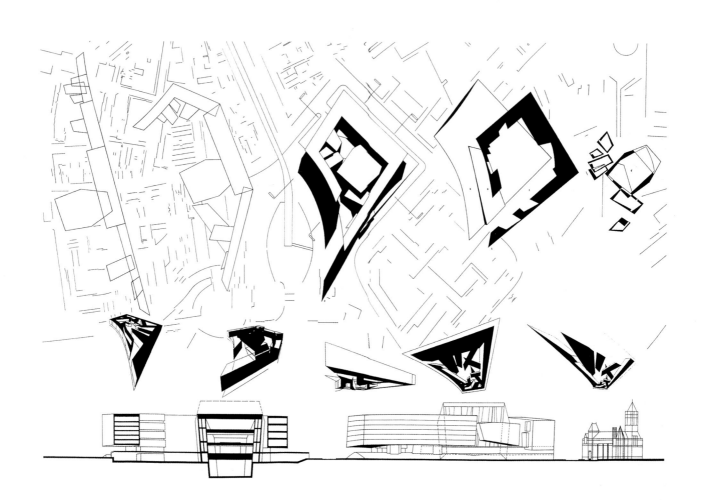

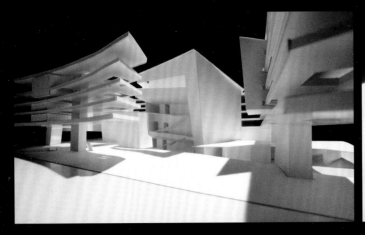
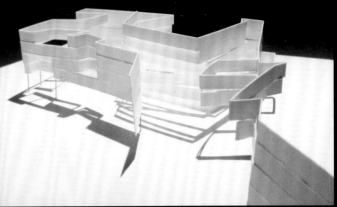

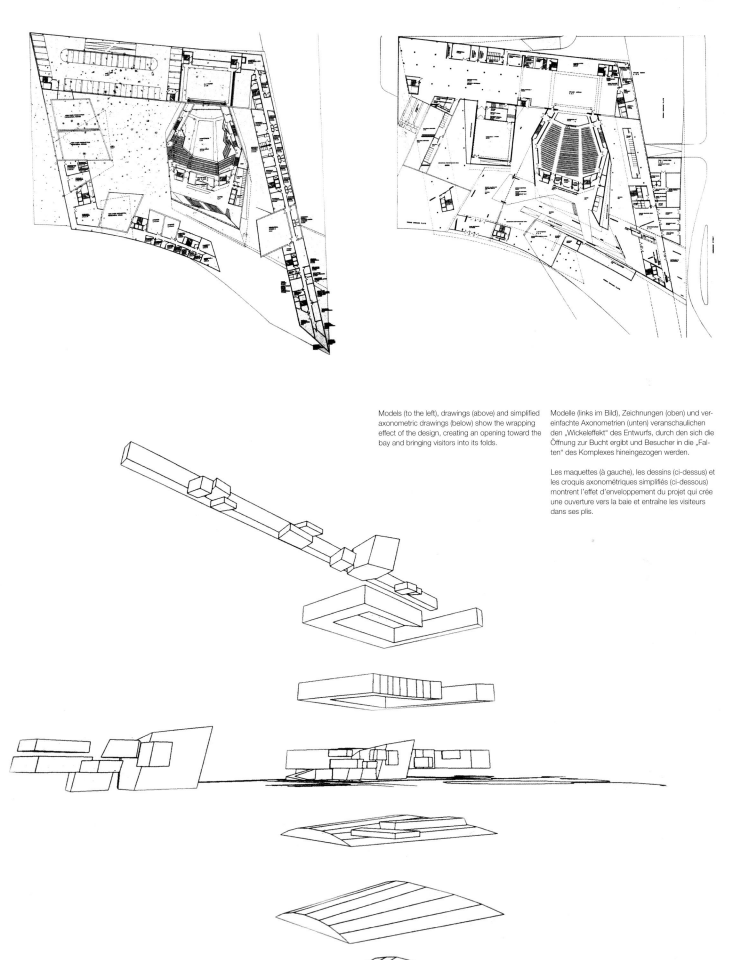

Models (to the left), drawings (above) and simplified axonometric drawings (below) show the wrapping effect of the design, creating an opening toward the bay and bringing visitors into its folds.

Modelle (links im Bild), Zeichnungen (oben) und vereinfachte Axonometrien (unten) veranschaulichen den „Wickeleffekt" des Entwurfs, durch den sich die Öffnung zur Bucht ergibt und Besucher in die „Falten" des Komplexes hineingezogen werden.

Les maquettes (à gauche), les dessins (ci-dessus) et les croquis axonométriques simplifiés (ci-dessous) montrent l'effet d'enveloppement du projet qui crée une ouverture vers la baie et entraîne les visiteurs dans ses plis.

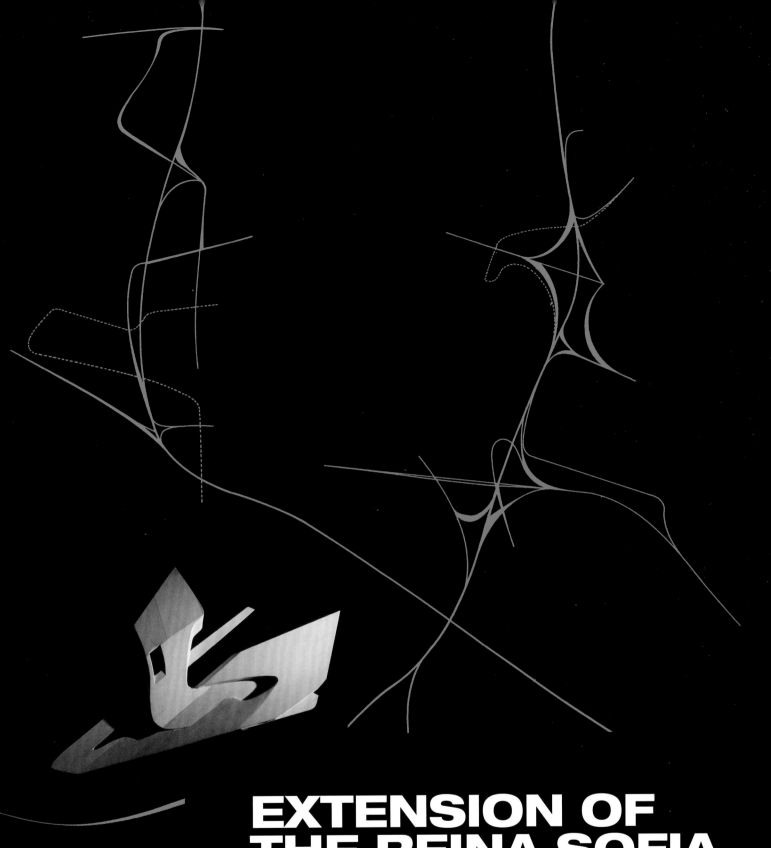

EXTENSION OF THE REINA SOFIA MUSEUM

Madrid, Spain. 1999

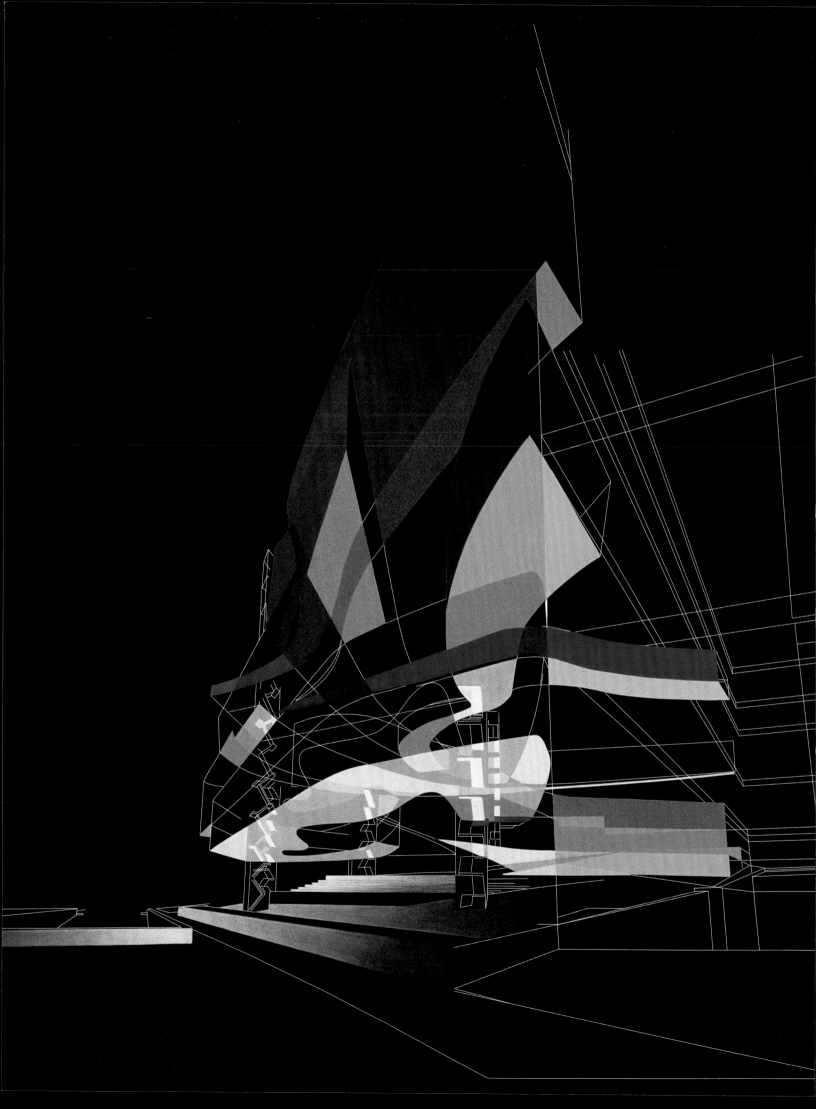

Project
EXTENSION OF THE REINA SOFIA MUSEUM

Location
MADRID, SPAIN

Client
REINA SOFIA MUSEUM

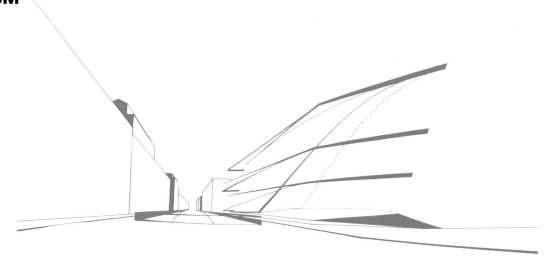

EXTERIOR PERSPECTIVE
Acrylic on black cartridge, 84 x 118 cm
1999

Described by Zaha Hadid as "splayed and split," her design provides an obvious counterpoint to the existing building used for the Reina Sofia center in Madrid.

Zaha Hadids Entwurf, den sie selbst als „gespreizt und zersplittert" beschrieben hat, bildet einen auffälligen Kontrast zum Altbau des Museums Reina Sofia in Madrid.

Décrit par Zaha Hadid comme « dispersé et divisé », ce projet vient en contrepoint au bâtiment existant du Centre Reina Sofia à Madrid.

Inaugurated in 1992 in a former 18th-century hospital building in central Madrid, the Museo Nacional Centro de Arte Reina Sofía is dedicated to contemporary art. The architect Jean Nouvel won the 1999 competition to create an extension to the museum and his building was inaugurated in 2005. Zaha Hadid's proposal was to provide a "vividly different [...] dynamic counterpoint to the serene Sabatini Building." Her presentation for the project insists on the idea of "constructive pluralism" in gallery design. "There is no one way to exhibit an object, there are many ways; spacing, lighting, etc. The same object can be shown in many ways without any of them being 'the' right way," she says. Her design aims to create a clear path through the structure, a task rendered somewhat complicated by the rather dense and sober façades of the existing building and its status as a revered landmark. Her solution for the galleries introduces a series of "splayed and split" paths that allow for a maximum amount of overhead natural light. Intended in part for temporary exhibitions, the extension also includes spaces for education and the interpretation of works. The galleries were a priority for the architect, though Hadid also addressed such specific problems as the existing delivery zone, which conflicted with car parking.

Das Museo Nacional Centro de Arte Reina Sofía wurde 1992 in einem ehemaligen Hospital, einem Bau aus dem 18. Jahrhundert, eröffnet und widmet sich zeitgenössischer Kunst. 1999 konnte sich Jean Nouvel in einem Wettbewerb für einen Erweiterungsbau durchsetzen. Sein Anbau wurde 2005 eingeweiht. Zaha Hadids Entwurf wollte ein „lebendiger, andersartiger, [...] dynamischer Kontrapunkt zum strengen Sabatini-Bau" sein. Ihre Projektpräsentation legte besonderen Wert auf einen „konstruktiven Pluralismus" bei der Gestaltung der Ausstellungsräume. „Es gibt nicht nur eine einzige Art, Objekte auszustellen, es gibt viele verschiedene – Raumgestaltung, Beleuchtung etc. Ein und dasselbe Objekt kann auf verschiedenste Weisen ausgestellt werden, ohne dass eine die ‚richtige' wäre." Ihr Entwurf will eine klare Wegeführung durch den Bau er-

möglichen, eine Aufgabe, die wegen der vergleichsweise massiven und strengen Fassade des Altbaus und seines Status als geschätztes Wahrzeichen schwierig ist. Ihre Lösung für die Galerieräume war eine Reihe „gespreizter, zersplitterter" Gänge, die von oben maximal belichtet werden. Im z. T. für Sonderausstellungen vorgesehenen Anbau waren zudem Räume für Bildungsangebote des Museums geplant. Zwar hatten die eigentlichen Ausstellungsräume für die Architektin Priorität, doch sie setzte sich auch mit anderen Problemen auseinander, etwa mit einer bestehenden Lieferzone, die mit Plänen für Parkplätze kollidierte.

Inauguré en 1992, le Museo Nacional Centro de Arte Reina Sofía, installé dans un ancien hôpital datant du XVIIIe siècle, se consacre à l'art contemporain. L'architecte Jean Nouvel a remporté le concours organisé en 1999 pour l'extension de ce musée, projet réalisé et inauguré en 2005. La proposition de Zaha Hadid visait à offrir un « contrepoint tonique différent [...] dynamique au bâtiment serein de Sabatini ». Sa présentation du projet insistait sur l'idée d'un « pluralisme constructif » dans la conception des musées. « Il n'existe pas qu'une seule façon de présenter des objets, mais plusieurs : espace, éclairage, etc. Le même objet peut être présenté de diverses façons sans qu'aucune ne soit forcément la "bonne" . » Son projet avait pour objectif de créer un cheminement clair à travers la structure, tâche compliquée par les façades assez massives et fermées du bâtiment existant et son statut de monument historique intouchable. La solution qu'elle proposait pour les galeries introduisait une série de cheminements « s'écartant qui divergent », pour permettre de bénéficier au maximum de l'éclairage zénithal. Prévue en partie pour des expositions temporaires, cette extension comprenait également des espaces réservés à l'éducation et à l'interprétation des œuvres. Les galeries étaient une priorité, bien que Zaha Hadid se soit aussi intéressée à des problèmes aussi spécifiques que la zone de livraison existante venant en conflit avec les parkings.

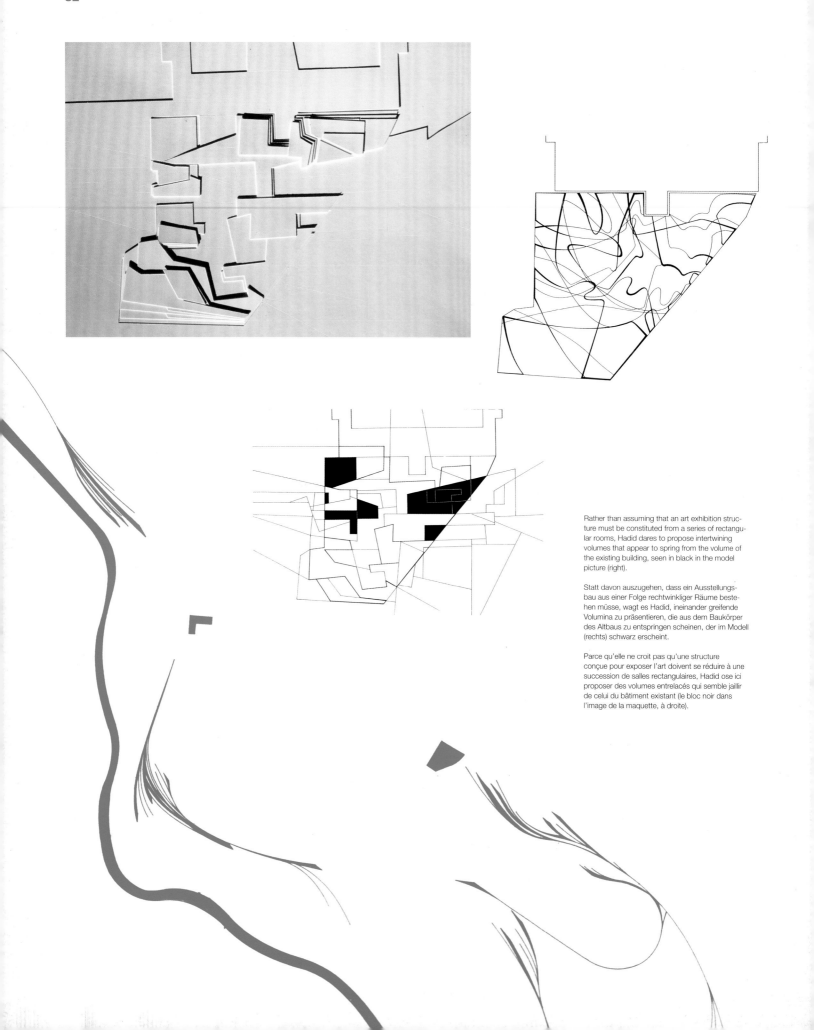

Rather than assuming that an art exhibition structure must be constituted from a series of rectangular rooms, Hadid dares to propose intertwining volumes that appear to spring from the volume of the existing building, seen in black in the model picture (right).

Statt davon auszugehen, dass ein Ausstellungsbau aus einer Folge rechtwinkliger Räume bestehen müsse, wagt es Hadid, ineinander greifende Volumina zu präsentieren, die aus dem Baukörper des Altbaus zu entspringen scheinen, der im Modell (rechts) schwarz erscheint.

Parce qu'elle ne croit pas qu'une structure conçue pour exposer l'art doivent se réduire à une succession de salles rectangulaires, Hadid ose ici proposer des volumes entrelacés qui semble jaillir de celui du bâtiment existant (le bloc noir dans l'image de la maquette, à droite).

Drawings and a model view render explicit the layering and the juxtaposition of Hadid's new building vis-à-vis the old one. Visitor circulation and discovery take on as much, or more, importance than any predetermined style.

Zeichnungen und Modell veranschaulichen die Schichtungen und den Kontrast des Neubauentwurfs gegenüber dem alten Gebäude. Der Verkehrsfluss der Besucher und ihre Entdeckungsreise durch den Bau ist mindestens ebenso wichtig, wenn nicht gar wichtiger als ein spezifischer Stil.

Des dessins et une maquette expliquent la stratification et la juxtaposition du nouveau bâtiment et de l'ancien. La circulation des visiteurs et le circuit de découverte prennent autant, voire plus, d'importance qu'un style qui aurait été prédéterminé.

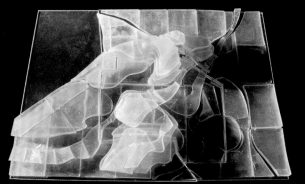

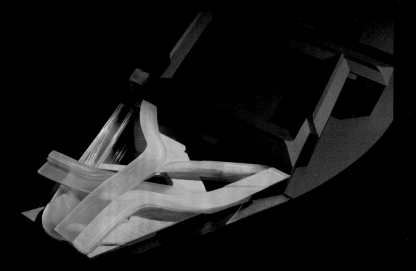

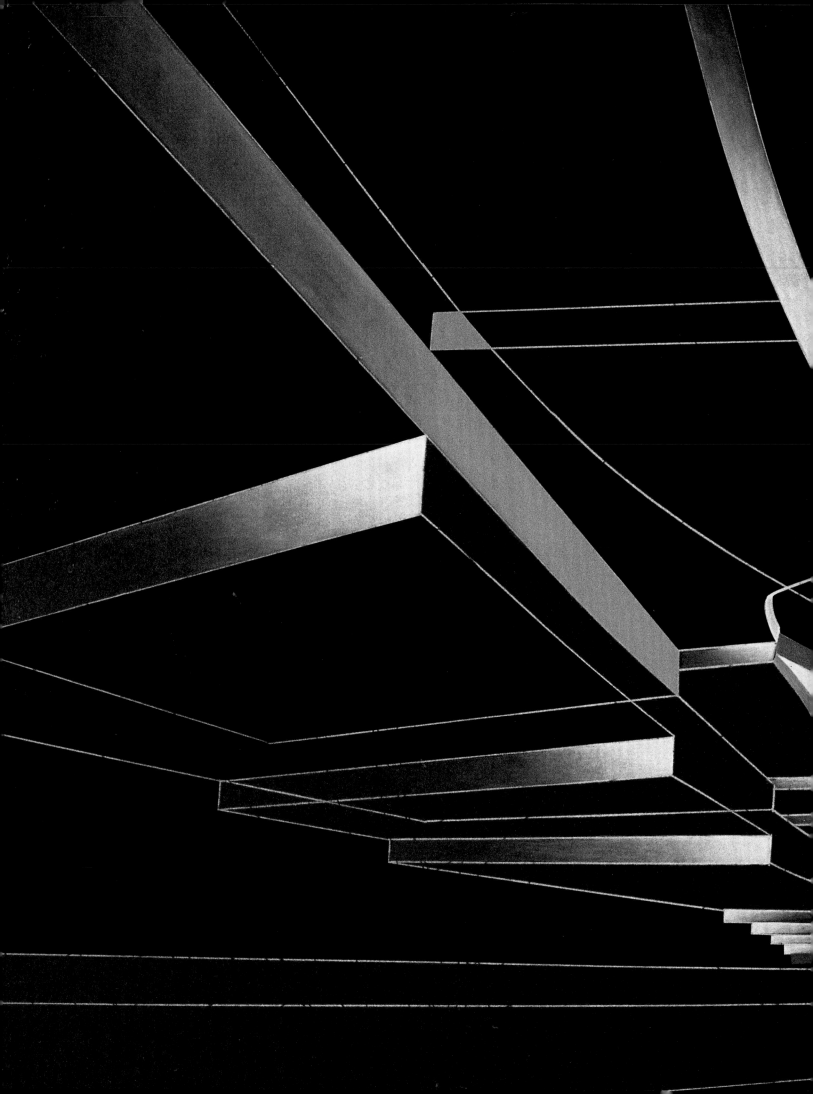

MUSEUM FOR THE ROYAL COLLECTION

Madrid, Spain. 1999

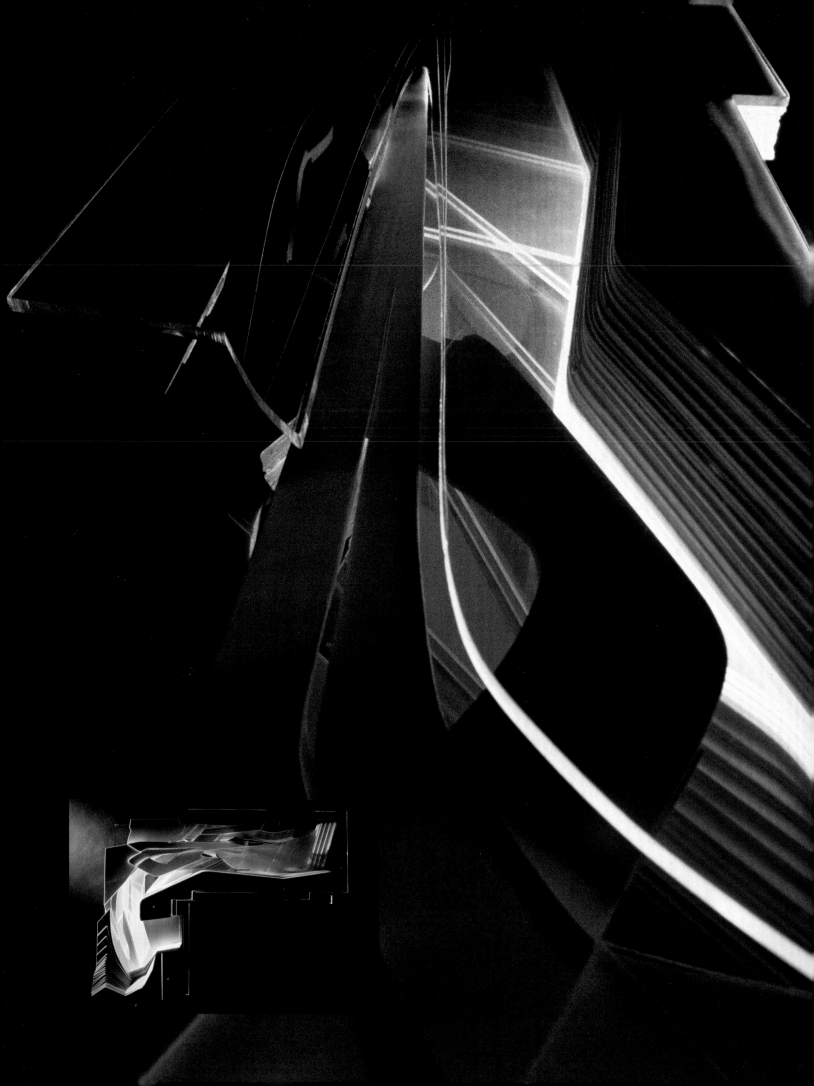

Project
MUSEUM FOR THE ROYAL COLLECTION

Location
MADRID, SPAIN

Client
ROYAL COLLECTION

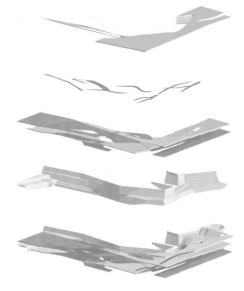

Pages 94–95:
INTERIOR PERSPECTIVE
Acrylic on black cartridge, 60 x 84 cm
1999

In this instance, the architect pursues her interest in largely nonorthogonal, flowing spaces, but here below grade, which makes the design more unexpected.

Auch hier lässt sich die Architektin von ihrem Interesse an zumeist nicht rechtwinkligen, fließenden Räumen leiten, die hier unterirdisch liegen, was den Entwurf umso überraschender macht.

Ici, l'architecte poursuit son exploration d'espaces essentiellement non-orthogonaux traités comme des flux, mais cette fois en sous-sol, ce qui rend le projet encore plus surprenant.

In this 1999 competition entry, Zaha Hadid proposed a structure to be located below the space between the Royal Palace (Palacio Real) and the Almudena Cathedral. Her design provided for a slight bowing of the ground-level plaza with incisions revealing the volumes below. One of these incisions is the main access ramp, and the rest of the plaza, forming the roof of the new museum, remains accessible to the public. The architect refers to a "cliff-edge condition" in describing the incisions and the design itself. The whole new structure snakes its way into the space, adding irregular forms to the largely orthogonal layout of the surrounding area. The interior spaces include public galleries and "back-of-the-house" spaces, including reserves, workshops, and offices. A dividing wall slicing through the volume affirms this division clearly. To simplify or enrich visitor orientation, the design provides either for a direct route that allows an overview of the collections, or alternative shortcuts. The entire sequence is wheelchair accessible, perhaps not a simple achievement in an underground gallery. Views through the space permit visitors to see where they have been and where they may next be headed. The idea of weaving architectural volumes into an existing space (here of course hollowed out of the ground) and creating a continuous path of circulation from the access ramp that slices into the ground, and into the galleries, is typical of Zaha Hadid. She creates a kind of artificial nature that is a topography combining the existing site with function and a sense for breaking through orthogonal strictures.

Bei diesem Wettbewerbsbeitrag von 1999 entwarf Zaha Hadid einen Bau, der unterirdisch zwischen dem Palacio Real und der Almudena-Kathedrale liegen sollte. Der Entwurf sieht eine leichte Absenkung des ebenerdigen Platzes vor sowie Bodeneinschnitte, durch die Einblicke in die darunterliegenden Räumlichkeiten möglich sind. Einer dieser Einschnitte führt als Rampe zum Haupteingang, während der übrige Platz – zugleich das Dach des neuen Museums – der Öffentlichkeit zugänglich bleibt. Die Architektin versteht die Einschnitte und den Entwurf insgesamt als „klippenähnliche Landschaft". Der Neubau windet sich wie eine Schlange in den Raum und behauptet sich mit seiner unregelmäßigen Form als Pendant zur überwiegend orthogonalen Anlage der Umgebung. Im Inneren befinden sich öffentlich zugängliche Museumsräume sowie solche für die Arbeit „hinter den Kulissen", wie etwa Magazine, Werkstätten und Büros. Eine Wand, die das gesamte Volumen durchschneidet, unterstreicht diese Trennung. Um den

Besuchern die Orientierung zu erleichtern, ermöglicht der Entwurf sowohl eine direkte Wegeführung, die einen Überblick über die gesamte Sammlung bietet, als auch Abkürzungen. Alle Galerieräume sind barrierefrei gestaltet, was bei einem unterirdischen Museum unter Umständen keine leichte Aufgabe ist. Blickachsen durch den Raum lassen die Besucher erfassen, wo sie bereits waren und wohin sie gehen. Typisch für Zaha Hadid ist der Gedanke, mehrere Baukörper in ein bestehendes räumliches Umfeld zu integrieren (hier, indem sie in den Boden gegraben werden), sowie die Entwicklung eines räumlichen Kontinuums für den Rundweg, der hier von einer in den Boden und die Museumsräume schneidenden Rampe ausgeht. Hadid definiert eine Art künstlicher Natur, die zugleich Topografie ist. Darüber hinaus bereichert sie das bestehende Umfeld um eine neue Funktion und durchbricht restriktive orthogonale Raummuster.

Pour ce concours organisé en 1999, Zaha Hadid avait proposé de construire sous l'espace libre situé entre le Palais royal (Palacio Real) et la cathédrale d'Almudena. Son plan présentait une légère incurvation de la place dans laquelle des incisions auraient révélé les volumes souterrains. L'une d'entre elles constituait la rampe d'accès principale et le reste de la place formait donc la couverture du nouveau musée, tout en restant accessible au public. L'architecte évoque « une arête de falaise » pour décrire le projet et ces incisions. La nouvelle structure se glisse en serpentant sous le sol, enrichissant de formes irrégulières le plan en grande partie orthogonal du bâti environnant. Les volumes intérieurs comprennent des galeries ouvertes au public et des espaces de service comprenant des réserves, des ateliers et des bureaux. Un mur de partition élevé à travers le volume affirme clairement son rôle de division entre ces deux grandes fonctions. Pour simplifier ou enrichir le parcours des visiteurs, le plan propose soit une voie directe qui permet une vue d'ensemble des collections, soit des raccourcis. Le parcours est entièrement accessible aux handicapés, ce qui n'est pas un mince exploit dans une galerie souterraine. Des perspectives traversantes permettent au visiteur de voir d'où il vient et où il va. L'idée d'entrelacer des volumes architecturaux dans un espace existant (ici creusé dans le sol) et de créer une circulation continue de la rampe d'accès aux galeries est typique de Zaha Hadid. Elle crée là une sorte de nature artificielle, une topographie combinant le site existant avec sa nouvelle fonction, et donnant un sentiment de rupture avec le dogme de l'orthogonalité.

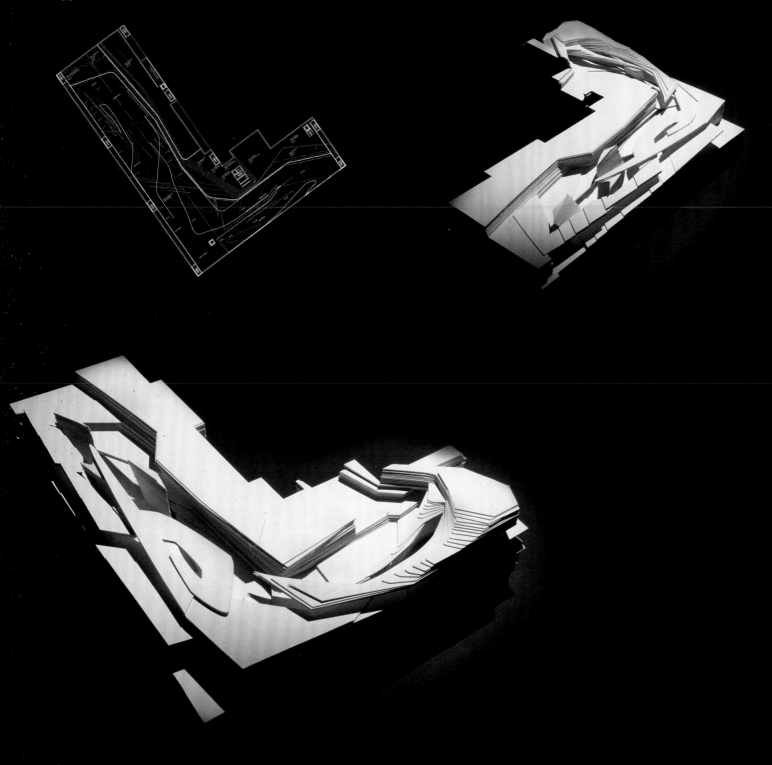

In models in particular, it becomes clear that floor levels do not have the same sense here as they might in a traditional building. The entire design is about shifts and changes in level that are not operated as whole numbers (i. e. first floor, second floor), but as a continuous process of movement.

Insbesondere an den Modellen wird deutlich, dass die Geschossebenen nicht auf dieselbe Weise funktionieren wie bei einem traditionellen Gebäude. Im gesamten Entwurf geht es um Verschiebungen und den Wechsel zwischen den Ebenen, die nicht aufeinander folgend organisiert sind (erster Stock, zweiter Stock etc.), sondern als kontinuierlicher Bewegungsfluss.

Ces maquettes permettent de comprendre en particulier que les niveaux représentent les sols n'ont pas le même sens que dans une construction traditionnelle. Le projet tout entier joue avec des glissements et des changements de niveaux qui ne correspondent plus à une numérotation précise (1er étage, 2e étage par exemple) mais à un processus continu de déplacement.

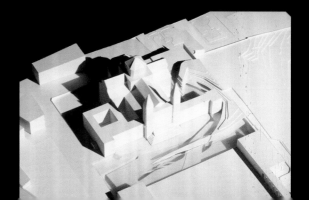

Models or section drawings (below) make clear not only the complexity of the design, but the fact that it is the result of a deliberate layering of different elements related to site, function, and, finally, a coherent vision of what architecture should be.

Modelle und Aufrisse (unten) veranschaulichen nicht nur die Komplexität des Entwurfs, sondern auch, dass er aus dem bewussten Übereinanderlagern verschiedener orts- und funktionsspezifischer Aspekte entsteht und letztendlich eine schlüssige Vision dessen ist, was Architektur sein sollte.

Les maquettes et les coupes (ci-dessous) font comprendre non seulement la complexité du projet mais aussi qu'il est en fait la résultante d'une stratification voulue de différents éléments liés au site et à la fonction et, finalement, une vision cohérente de ce que l'architecture devrait être.

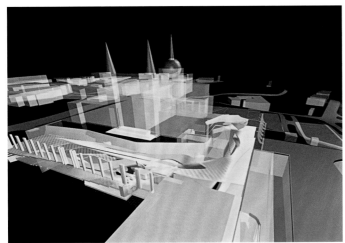

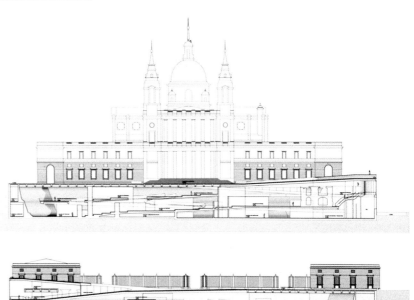

ART MUSEUM
IN GRAZ

Graz, Austria. 1999

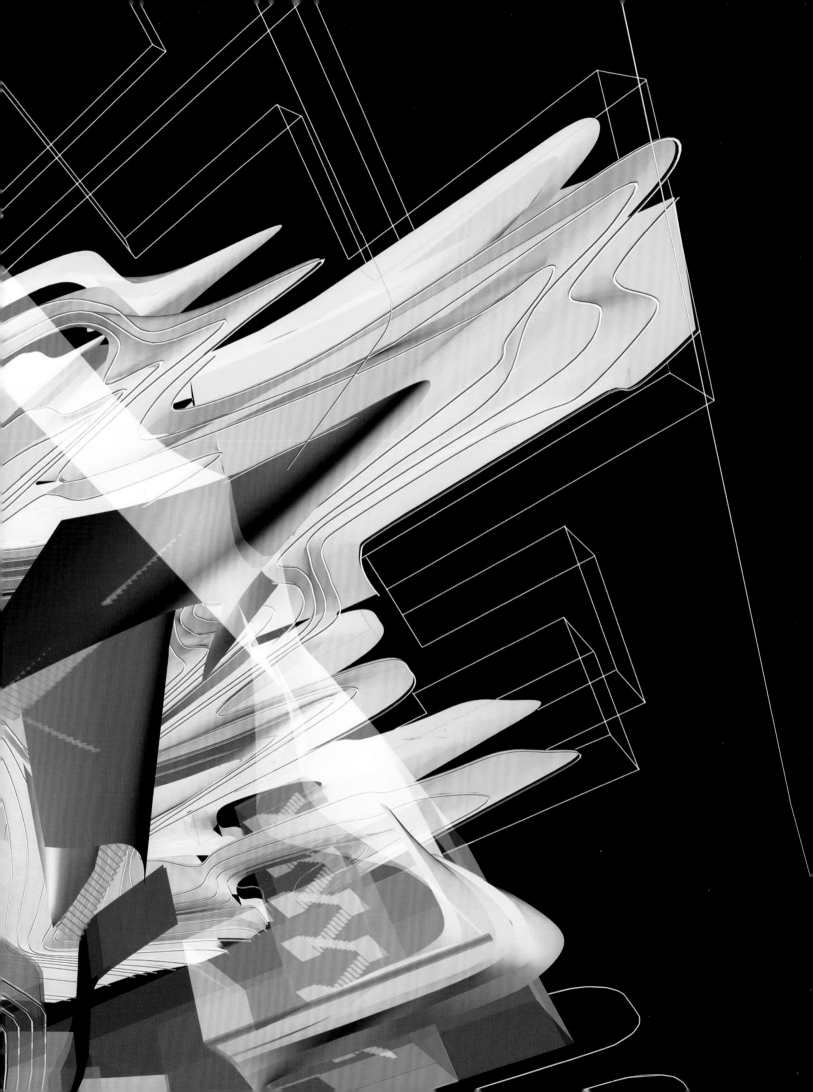

Project
ART MUSEUM IN GRAZ

Location
GRAZ, AUSTRIA

Client
CITY OF GRAZ AND KUNSTHAUS GRAZ

The layered planes of the project as seen in the images to the left allow for a renewal of the function of the Kunsthaus at the same time as they impose a new and different aesthetic response to construction in a historic city.

Die übereinander geschichteten Ebenen des Projekts (links) erlauben, die Funktion des Kunsthauses neu zu definieren und sind zugleich eine neuartige ästhetische Alternative zur Baupraxis in einer historischen Stadt.

Comme le montrent les images de gauche, la stratification des plans permet de renouveler la fonction de la Kunsthaus tout en imposant une esthétique nouvelle et différente qui répond à la difficulté de construire dans une cité historique.

Peter Cook and Colin Fournier won this 2000 competition, and their unusual "alien" project was completed in 2003. Zaha Hadid proposed to cantilever the building over and across the Lend Quay toward the Mur River, creating a kind of large canopy 12 meters off the ground. As Hadid's description has it: "Like a forest of mushrooms the canopy has a depth (height) varying between three to six meters. Its morphology is, on the one hand, derived from the urban context—as it was projecting forward the profile of existing fabric on the back of the site—and, on the other, it has developed from the structural logic of the tapering mushroom columns. The art center is entered below the strongest cantilever." Hadid refers to "inverted trumpet forms" made of reinforced concrete in describing the support cores of the structure. The lobby, commercial spaces, and a ground-floor exhibition area are situated on the ground floor below this canopy. A media center and photography forum are enclosed within the canopy. The canopy structure would step over the existing Eisernes Haus that would contain a restaurant, exhibition spaces, and administrative offices. The cantilever of the primary structure over the Eisernes Haus is permitted by a "three dimensional 'vierendeel' structure formed by the interconnection of the walls and upper floors."

In diesem 2000 ausgeschriebenen Wettbewerb konnten sich letztlich Peter Cook und Colin Fournier durchsetzen, deren ungewöhnliches, futuristisches Projekt 2003 fertiggestellt wurde. Zaha Hadid hatte vorgeschlagen, den Bau über den Lendkai zur Mur hin auskragen zu lassen und so eine Art monumen-

tales Baldachindach, 12 m über dem Boden, zu schaffen. Hadids Beschreibung liest sich wie folgt: „Das Baldachindach ähnelt einer Pilzbesiedlung und hat eine Tiefe (Höhe) von 3 bis 6 m. Die Morphologie leitet sich auf der einen Seite aus dem urbanen Kontext ab – indem sie das Profil des bestehenden Gefüges auf seiner Rückseite nach vorn projiziert – und entwickelt sich andererseits logisch-strukturell aus dem Motiv sich verjüngender, pilzähnlicher Stützen. Das Kunstzentrum selbst wird unterhalb des tiefsten Auslegers betreten." Hadid bezeichnet die zentralen Stützen des Baus aus Stahlbeton als „auf dem Kopf stehende Trompetenformen". Lobby, Geschäfte und Ausstellungsflächen im Erdgeschoss liegen unter dem Baldachindach. Ein Medienzentrum und ein Fotoforum werden von der Dachkonstruktion umschlossen. Diese sollte zudem über das bestehende Eiserne Haus auskragen, in dem ein Restaurant, weitere Ausstellungsräume und Büros geplant waren. Der Ausleger des Hauptbaus über dem Eisernen Haus wird durch eine spezielle Konstruktion ermöglicht, eine „dreidimensionale Vierendeel-Konstruktion, die aus den Wänden und oberen Geschossplatten gebildet wird".

Ce sont Peter Cook et Colin Fournier qui ont remporté ce concours organisé en 2000. Leur très surprenant projet « extraterrestre » a été achevé en 2003. Zaha Hadid avait proposé de placer son bâtiment en porte-à-faux au-dessus du quai Lend orienté vers la rivière Mur, pour créer une sorte de vaste auvent à 12 m du sol. Selon son descriptif : « Traité comme une sorte de forêt de champignons, l'auvent présente une profondeur (hauteur) de 3 à 6 m. Sa morphologie dérive d'un côté du contexte urbain – en se projetant hors du profil du tissu urbain existant sur la partie arrière du site – et de l'autre se développant à partir de la logique structurelle de colonnes-champignons évasées vers le haut. L'accès au Centre d'art se fait en dessous de la partie la plus épaisse du porte-à-faux. » Hadid se réfère à « des formes de trompettes inversées » en béton armé pour décrire le supports de la structure. Le hall d'accueil, les espaces commerciaux et une aire d'expositions au rez-de-chaussée se trouvent sous l'auvent qui contient un centre médias et un forum pour la photographie. La structure de cet auvent aurait absorbé la Eisernes Haus existante, transformée en restaurant, espaces d'expositions et bureaux administratifs. Le porte-à-faux de la structure au-dessus de ce bâtiment ancien était rendu possible grâce à « une construction tridimensionnelle de type Vierendeel formée par l'interconnexion des murs et des niveaux supérieurs ».

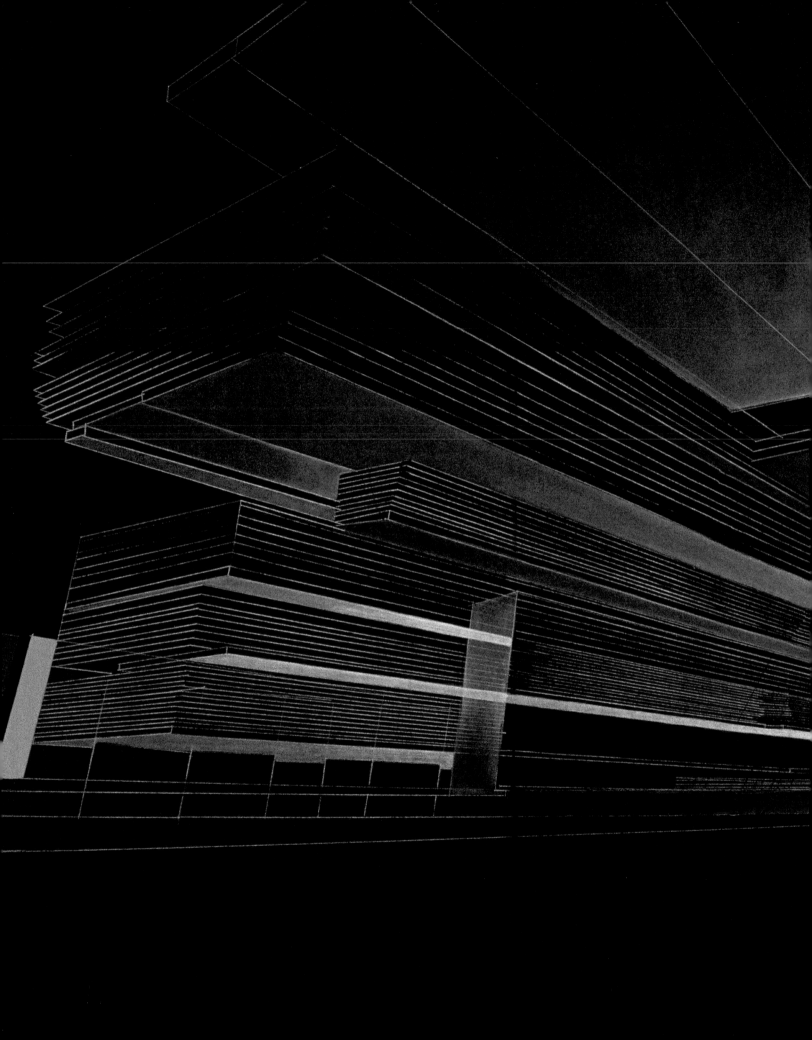

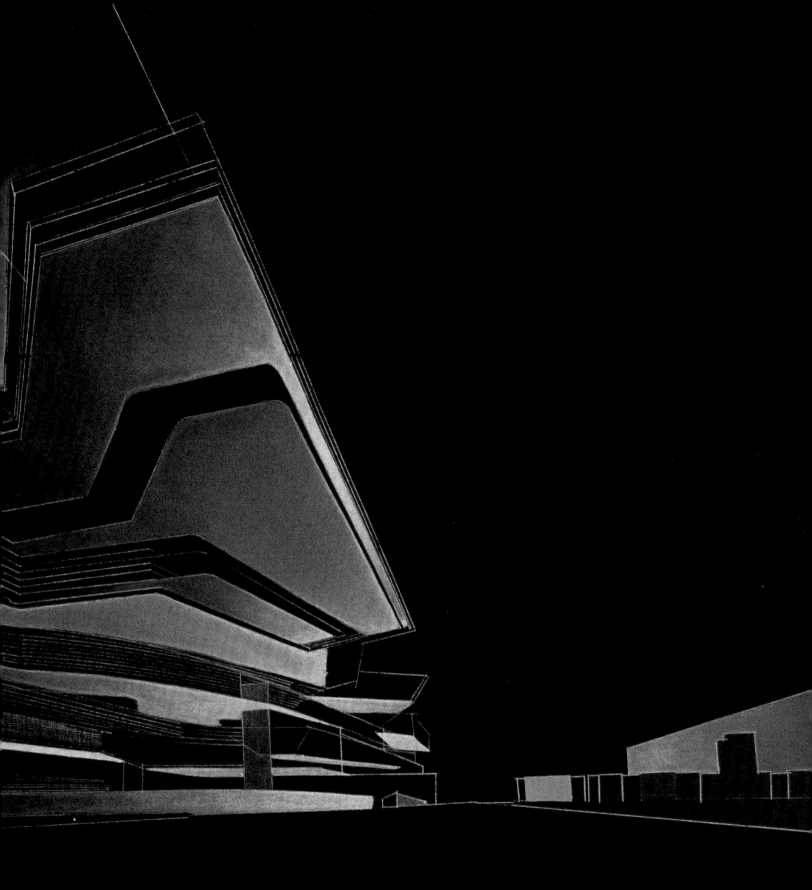

NATIONAL LIBRARY
OF QUEBEC

Montreal, Canada. 2001

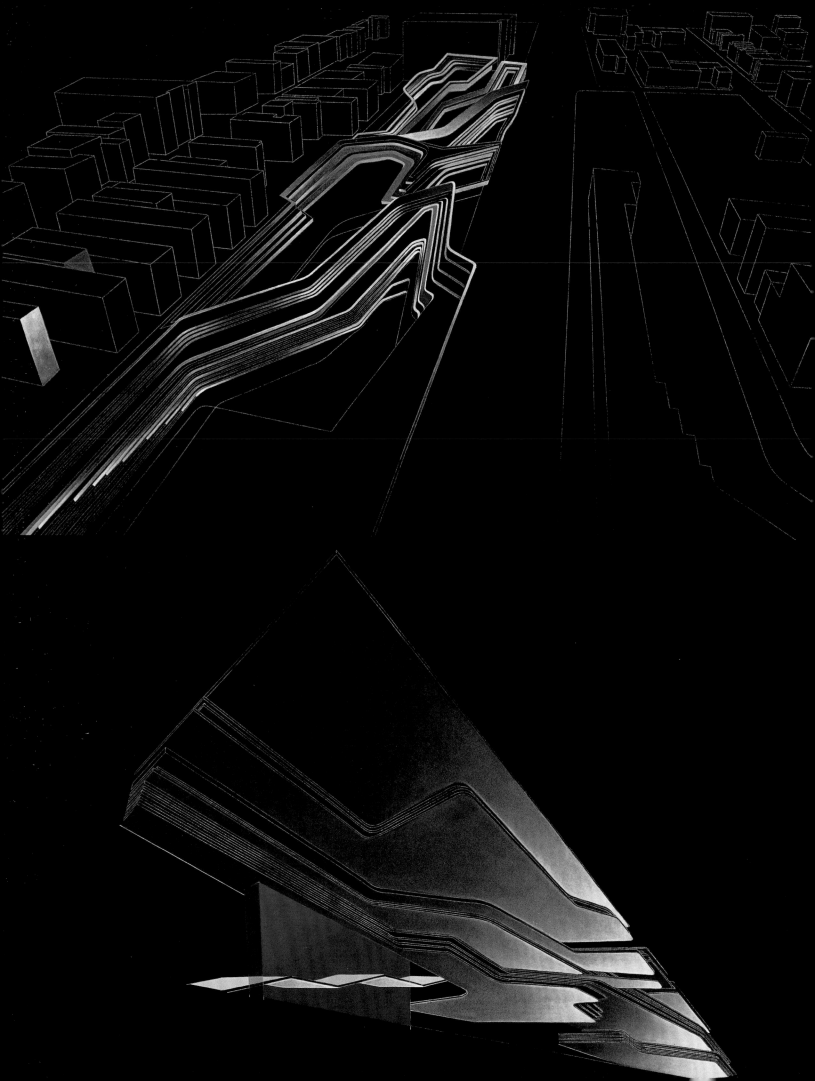

Project
NATIONAL LIBRARY OF QUEBEC

Location
MONTREAL, CANADA

Clinent
LA GRANDE BIBLIOTHEQUE DU QUEBEC

Area/Size
35 000 m²

Pages 104–105:
EXTERIOR PERSPECTIVE
Acrylic on black cartridge, 84.1 x 59.4 cm
2000

Page 106 top:
EARLY STUDIES – AERIAL VIEW
Acrylic on black cartridge, 84.1 x 59.4 cm
2000

Page 106 bottom:
EARLY STUDIES – FISH EYE VIEW
Acrylic on black cartridge, 84.1 x 59.4 cm
2000

The ramifications of Hadid's "tree of knowledge" are visible both in the general images to the left and in the sketches below. The complexity of the system is justified by the different functions of the library and the categories of knowledge.

Die Verästelungen von Hadids „Wissensbaum" sind sowohl in den allgemeinen Ansichten als auch in den Zeichnungen unten zu erkennen. Die Komplexität des Systems ist angesichts der verschiedenen Funktionen der Bibliothek und ihrer unterschiedlichen Fachgebiete durchaus gerechtfertigt.

Les ramifications de « l'arbre de la connaissance » proposé par Hadid apparaissent dans les images d'ensemble à gauche et les croquis ci-dessous. La complexité de ce système se justifie par les différentes fonctions de la bibliothèque et des catégories de la connaissance.

In January 2000, the government of the province of Quebec launched its first international architecture competition for the Grande Bibliothèque du Québec. Jury members included Phyllis Lambert, the founder of the Canadian Center for Architecture, and Bernard Tschumi. The competition was won by Patkau Architects (Vancouver), Croft-Pelletier (Quebec), and Gilles Guité from Montreal. Zaha Hadid, associated with Boutin Ramoisy Tremblay (Quebec), was one of the five finalists. The project posed the difficulty of having a variety of different services, including a 24-hour access area. Hadid approached this aspect of the program requirements by creating "localities," or self-contained environments related to the rest of the building by context. Basing her design on the idea of a "tree of knowledge" with "veins eroding the solid mass of the building" and serving as circulation, internal organization leads visitors along readily identifiable paths leading from general knowledge to more and more particular or specialized content. Humanities and the arts form one element of the design/content while history and the sciences constitute another of the "two intertwining trees" in the design. This concept allows for connections to be made between the two larger disciplines, for example, where economics are concerned. A "main public void" forms the front of the building revealing its different levels and functions. Zaha Hadid explains that here the "mass is undercut like an overhanging cliff." The book collections are set in "terraced valleys," and reading rooms "conceived in analogy with the canopy level of trees" are located at the top of the building with filtered natural light. Attention is paid in the design to creating zones of silence for these reading rooms.

Im Januar 2000 schrieb die Regierung der Provinz Québec ihren ersten internationalen Wettbewerb für die Grande Bibliothèque du Québec aus. Zu den Mitgliedern der Jury zählten u. a. Phyllis Lambert, Gründerin des Canadian Center for Architecture, und Bernard Tschumi. Der erste Preis ging an Patkau Architects (Vancouver), Croft-Pelletier (Québec) und Gilles Guité aus Montreal. Zaha Hadid, in Zusammenarbeit mit Boutin Ramoisy Tremblay (Québec), zählte zu den fünf Finalisten. Das Projekt sah sich vor die Schwierigkeit gestellt, die verschiedensten Nutzungen zu ermöglichen, darunter auch einen rund um die Uhr zugänglichen Bereich. Hadid stellte sich diesem Aspekt des Programms, indem sie verschiedene „Lokalitäten" schuf, separate Bereiche, die durch den Gesamtkontext an die übrigen Gebäudebereiche angebunden waren. Ihr Entwurf basierte auf dem Motiv eines „Wissensbaums", dessen „Adern die Masse des Baus von innen durchziehen" und zugleich als Verkehrsfläche dienen. Die interne Organisation des Gebäudes führt die Besucher dank eines leicht lesbaren Leitsystems von allgemeineren Wissensgebieten zu immer fachspezifischeren Beständen. Ein Element des Entwurfs (und der Bestände) sind Geisteswissenschaften und Kunst, während Geschichte und Naturwissenschaften den zweiten der „beiden ineinander verzweigten Bäume" darstellen. Das Konzept ermöglicht Querverbindungen zwischen den beiden großen Disziplinen, etwa im Bereich Wirtschaft. Ein „öffentlich zugänglicher, zentraler Leerraum" bildet die Front des Gebäudes und bietet Einblick in die verschiedenen Ebenen und Funktionen des Baus. Zaha Hadid zufolge wird „die Masse [hier] wie eine überhängende Klippe untergraben". Die Buchbestände sind in „terrassenförmig angelegten Tälern" untergebracht, während die Lesesäle „wie die Laubkrone von Bäumen" in der oberen Ebene des Gebäudes liegen und mit gefiltertem, natürlichem Licht versorgt werden. Besondere Aufmerksamkeit kam der Schaffung von Ruhezonen für die Lesesäle zu.

En 2000, le gouvernement de la province du Québec lança un concours international d'architecture pour la Grande bibliothèque du Québec. Le jury comprenait notamment Phyllis Lambert, fondatrice du Centre canadien d'architecture, et Bernard Tschumi. La compétition fut remportée par Patkau Architects (Vancouver), Croft-Pelletier (Québec) et Gille Guité de Montréal. Zaha Hadid, associée à Boutin Ramoisy Tremblay (Québec), fut parmi les cinq finalistes. La difficulté du projet tenait à la variété des services qu'il devait proposer, dont un accès 24 h/24. Hadid traita cet aspect par la création de « points stratégiques » ou environnements autonomes liés au reste du bâtiment par leur contexte, basant son projet sur l'idée d'un « arbre de la connaissance » aux « veines [servant de circulations] venant éroder la masse pleine du bâtiment ». L'organisation interne conduit les visiteurs le long de cheminements identifiables, des connaissances générales vers des contenus de plus en plus spécialisés. Les humanités et les arts forment l'un des éléments de « contenu/plan », tandis que l'histoire et les sciences constituent l'un des « deux arbres entrelacés » du projet. Ce concept laisse la place à des connexions entre deux grandes branches, l'économie. Un « vide principal public » forme la façade avant du bâtiment, révélant ses différents niveaux et fonctions. Zaha Hadid explique que « la masse est découpée par le dessous comme une colline suspendue ». Les collections de livres sont disposées dans des « vallées terrassées », et les salles de lecture, « conçues par analogie avec le niveau de la canopée des arbres », se trouvent partie supérieure du bâtiment et bénéficient d'un éclairage naturel filtré. Le projet s'est attaché à créer des zones de silence.

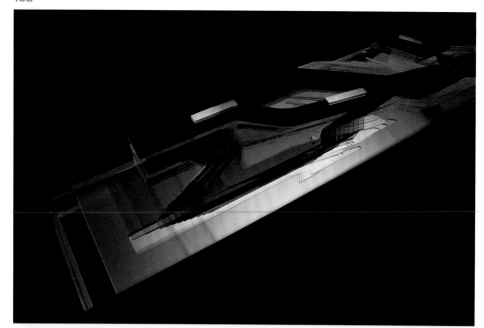

Overlapping layers and intertwined elements again recall natural systems without falling into the trap of attempting too literal an interpretation.

Einander überlagernde Schichten erinnern an natürliche Systeme, ohne den Fehler zu begehen, eine allzu wörtliche Interpretation zu versuchen.

Les strates superposées et les éléments imbriqués rappellent des systèmes naturels sans tomber dans le piège de tendre vers une interprétation trop littérale.

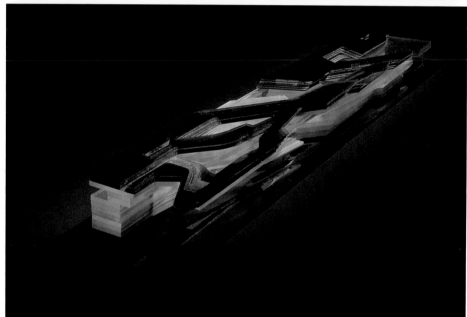

Model images and other visualizations of the project do render explicit the idea of the "tree of knowledge," albeit without touching on what might be considered purely "organic" architecture.

Modellansichten und weitere Visualisierungen des Projekts illustrieren das Konzept des „Wissensbaums", ohne dabei als rein „organische" Architektur daherzukommen.

Des maquettes et autres visualisations du projet explicitent l'idée de « l'arbre de la connaissance » sans pour autant se rapprocher de ce que l'on pourrait voir comme une architecture purement « organique ».

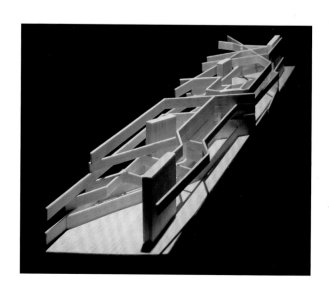

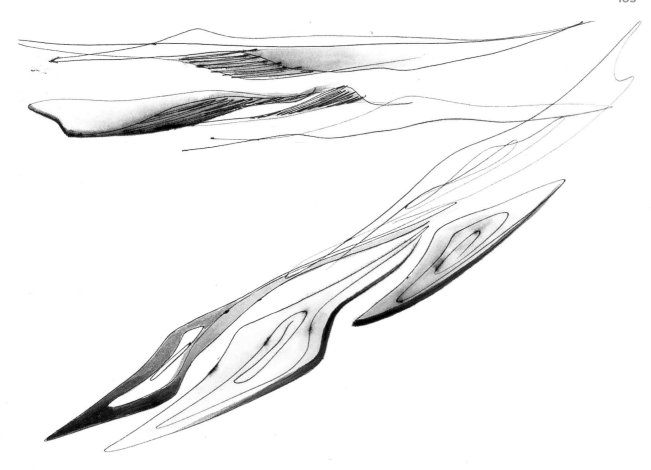

BUILT WORK

MOONSOON RESTAURANT

Sapporo, Japan. 1989–90

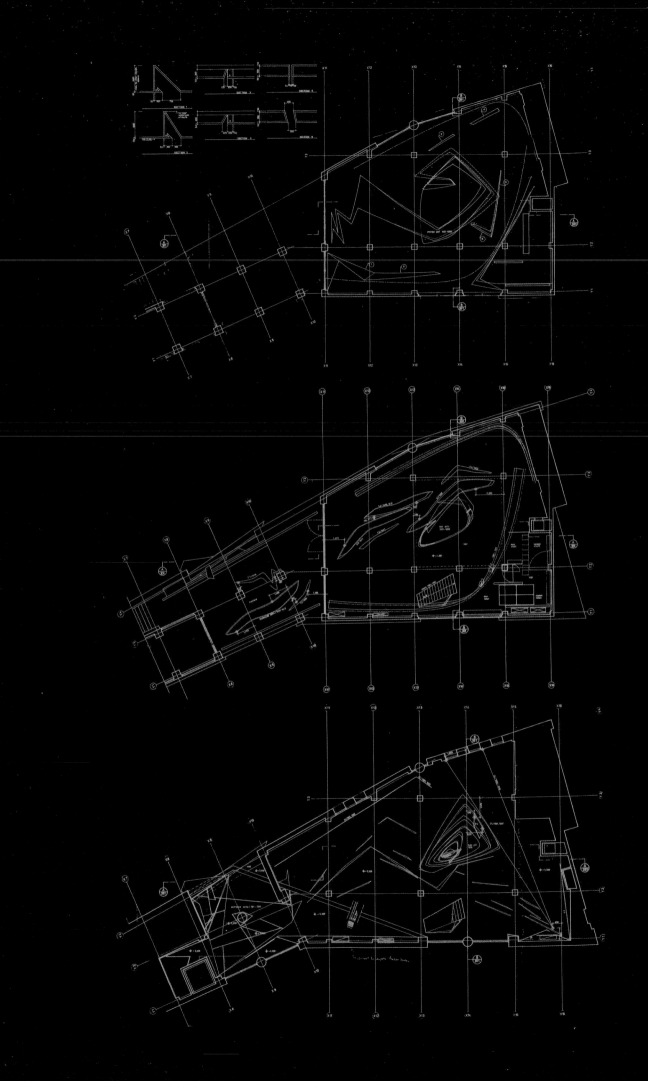

Project
MOONSOON RESTAURANT

Location
SAPPORO, JAPAN

Client
JASMAC CORPORATION, JAPAN

Area/Size
435 m² (2 FLOORS)

Although perhaps more emphatic than later work, Moonsoon shows the consistent and early use of the idea of an overall design that takes in not only furniture, but the architecture itself, to create a coherent whole.

Obwohl das Moonsoon dramatischer anmutet als spätere Projekte, zeigt es die frühe und konsequente Umsetzung eines Gesamtkonzepts, das nicht nur das Mobiliar, sondern auch die Architektur selbst mit einbezieht, um ein schlüssiges Gesamtbild zu erzielen.

Peut-être plus emphatique que ses réalisations à venir, le restaurant Moonsoon montre la pratique, précoce chez Hadid, d'une conception d'ensemble qui prend en charge non seulement l'architecture elle-même mais aussi le mobilier afin de créer un tout cohérent.

Zaha Hadid created this restaurant in northern Japan after the 1988 MoMA exhibition *Deconstructivist Architecture* in which her Hong Kong Peak project was featured. Her client, Michihiro Kuzawa, also commissioned Aldo Rossi's iconic Palace Hotel in Hakata, southern Japan. Laid out on two floors of a nightclub—one for formal dining and the other for a "relaxed lounge"—the design features contrasting environments that the architect compares to fire and ice. The ground floor (ice) is conceived in tones of gray, using glass and metal. As the architect stated: "Tables are sharp fragments of ice: a raised floor level drifts like an iceberg across the space." Hadid refers to the celebrated local tradition of ice sculptures in winter in Sapporo as being a source of inspiration for this space. The upper floor, connected to the ground, via a fiberglass spiral above the bar, was done in yellow, orange, and red. The spiraling connection bears early proof of Hadid's desire to create coherent environments, even when she indulges in specific, and rather exuberant, contrasts, as is the case in the Moonsoon Restaurant. Biomorphic sofas that can be configured in numerous ways are featured for the seating. Warmer and softer than the ground-floor design, the upper level contrasts not only in materials and colors but also in overall mood.

Zaha Hadid realisierte dieses Restaurant in Nordjapan im Anschluss an die MoMA-Ausstellung *Deconstructivist Architecture* (1988), bei der ihr Hong-Kong-Peak-Projekt präsentiert worden war. Ihr Klient, Michihiro Kuzawa, hatte bereits das von Aldo Rossi entworfene Palace Hotel im südjapanischen Hakata in Auftrag gegeben. Der Entwurf umfasst zwei Ebenen eines Nachtklubs – ein förmliches Restaurant und eine zwanglose Lounge – und definiert dabei zwei höchst unterschiedliche Designkontexte, die die Architektin mit Feuer und Eis vergleicht. Das Erdgeschoss (Eis) wurde in Grautönen gehalten, wobei Glas und Metall zum Einsatz kamen. Die Architektin erklärt: „Die Tische sind scharfkantige Fragmente aus Eis: ein Bodenpodest schiebt sich wie ein Eisberg durch den Raum." Hadid nimmt hierbei auf die berühmte regionale Tradition der Eisskulpturen in Sapporo Bezug, von denen sie sich für diesen Raum inspirieren ließ. Das obere Geschoss, das durch eine Spirale aus Glasfaser über der Bar mit der unteren Ebene verbunden ist, wurde in Gelb-, Orange- und Rottönen gehalten. Die spiralförmige Verbindung ist ein früher Beleg für Hadids Bestreben, räumliche Umfelder als Kontinuum zu gestalten, selbst wenn sie dabei – wie hier beim Moonsoon Restaurant – in höchst eigenwilligen, geradezu überbordenden Kontrasten schwelgt. Die biomorphen Sofas lassen sich unterschiedlich gestalten und bieten Sitzgelegenheiten. Das obere Geschoss, wärmer und weicher gehalten als das untere, hebt sich nicht nur in Materialien und Farben, sondern in der gesamten Stimmung vom Erdgeschoss ab.

Zaha Hadid a conçu ce restaurant de Sapporo (nord du Japon), après l'exposition de 1988 au MoMA « Deconstructivist Architecture » où avait été présenté son projet du Hong Kong Peak. Son client, Michihiro Kuzawa, était le commanditaire du fameux Palace Hotel d'Aldo Rossi à Hakata, dans le sud du Japon. Aménagé sur les deux niveaux d'un night club – le premier pour les dîners for-

mels, le second réservé à un « lounge décontracté » – le concept met en scène des environnements contrastés comparés par l'architecte au feu et à la glace. Le rez-de-chaussée (la glace) fait appel à diverses tonalités de gris, au verre et au métal. « Les tables sont des fragments de glace aux arêtes vives : un sol surélevé flotte comme un iceberg dans l'espace », commente Hadid. Son inspiration se réfère ici à une célèbre tradition locale de sculpture de la glace en hiver. L'étage, relié au rez-de-chaussée par une spirale en fibre de verre qui passe au-dessus du bar, est traité dans les tons de jaune, orange et rouge. Cette connexion dynamique est une des premières illustrations du désir d'Hadid de créer des environnements cohérents même lorsqu'elle cultive à plaisir, comme ici, des contrastes assez exubérants. Des canapés biomorphiques configurables de multiples façons accueillent les clients. Plus chaleureux et moins agressif que le rez-de-chaussée, l'étage contraste avec lui non seulement par ses matériaux et ses couleurs mais aussi par son atmosphère.

VITRA FIRE STATION

Weil am Rhein, Germany. 1991–93

Project
VITRA
FIRE STATION

Location
WEIL AM RHEIN, GERMANY

Client
VITRA INTERNATIONAL AG

Area/Size
852 m²

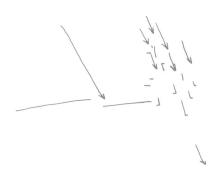

BIRD'S EYE VIEW
Acrylic on black cartridge, 127.5 x 96 cm
1999

A painterly style is affirmed in the presentation seen on the left page and in the sketches above, rendering the final form of the building somewhat difficult to understand.

Sowohl die Präsentation links als auch die Skizzen oben zeugen von einem ausgesprochen malerischen Stil, der es nicht ganz leicht macht, sich die endgültige Form des Baus zu erschließen.

Le style pictural affirmé de la représentation du projet page de gauche et des croquis ci-dessus, ne facilite pas la compréhension de la forme finale de la construction.

Part of the campus of buildings by exceptional architects brought together by Vitra chief Rolf Fehlbaum, the Fire Station is one of Zaha Hadid's first efforts to translate her spectacular drawings into built form. Here, despite the surprisingly angular design, interior space is well managed to create an architecturally spectacular facility. Perhaps even more important, the architect has taken into account the large neighboring factory buildings and used the Fire Station to structure the street that it is set on. The building was "envisaged as a linear landscaped zone, almost as if it were the artificial extension of the linear patterns of the adjacent agricultural fields and vineyards," which also makes it an interesting predecessor to the nearby LF One project (see page 130). Hadid meant the linear stretch of her building also to shield the Vitra complex from neighboring structures. According to the office description of the structure: "The space-defining and screening functions of the building were the point of departure for the development of the architectural concept: a linear, layered series of walls. The program of the Fire Station inhabits the spaces between these walls, which puncture, tilt, and break according to the functional requirements. The building is hermetic from a frontal reading, revealing the interiors only from a perpendicular viewpoint." It may be a moot point in this context that the structure was never really used as a fire station; rather it became the most visible and successful symbol of the architectural experimentation that Rolf Fehlbaum was willing to envisage, and the confirmation that Zaha Hadid's buildings would be as interesting as her drawings.

Die Feuerwache ist Teil eines größeren Campus, für den bedeutende Architekten auf Einladung des Vitra-Direktors Rolf Fehlbaum verschiedene Bauten gestaltet haben. Sie ist einer der ersten Versuche Hadids, ihre spektakulären Zeichnungen in reale Bauten umzusetzen. Trotz des überraschend kantigen Entwurfs wurde der Innenraum gelungen aufgeteilt, sodass ein architektonisch spektakulärer Bau entstand. Entscheidender ist jedoch womöglich die Tatsache, dass die Architektin die umliegenden Fabrikgebäude berücksichtigte und die Feuerwache nutzte, um die Straße, an der sie liegt, zu strukturieren. Der Bau war „als linear gestaltete Landschaft konzipiert, geradezu wie eine künstliche Weiterführung der Geradlinigkeit der angrenzenden Felder und Weinberge". Dieser Aspekt macht das Projekt darüber hinaus zu einem interessanten Vorläufer des nahe gelegenen LF One (Seite 130). Hadid hatte ihr Gebäude u. a. deshalb so gestreckt, um das Vitra-Gelände von der benachbarten Bebauung abzuschirmen. Das Büro

beschreibt den Bau wie folgt: „Die raumbildenden und abschirmenden Funktionen des Gebäudes waren Ausgangspunkt des architektonischen Konzepts: einer linearen, schichtartigen Staffelung von Wänden. Das Programm der Feuerwache ist zwischen diesen Wänden untergebracht, die je nach funktionellen Erfordernissen durchbohrt, geneigt oder durchbrochen sind. Von vorn gibt sich der Bau hermetisch verschlossen, nur wenn man direkt davor steht, ist ein Blick ins Innere möglich." Es dürfte kaum relevant sein, dass der Bau nie wirklich als Feuerwache genutzt wurde. Stattdessen ist er eines der sichtbarsten und gelungensten Symbole für Rolf Fehlbaums Offenheit für architektonische Experimente und zugleich die Bestätigung, dass Zaha Hadids Bauten tatsächlich ebenso aufregend sind wie ihre Zeichnungen.

Ce poste d'incendie, qui est l'un des composants du campus industriel réalisé par quelques brillants architectes réunis à l'initiative du président de Vitra, Rolf Fehlbaum, est l'une des premières tentatives de Zaha Hadid de traduire ses spectaculaires dessins et plans sous forme bâtie. En dépit d'un aspect étonnament anguleux, l'espace interne est parfaitement géré tout en atteignant un niveau de qualité architecturale spectaculaire. Encore plus important peut-être, l'architecte a pris en compte les vastes bâtiments industriels voisins et mis à profit son projet pour structurer la rue qui le dessert. Le bâtiment a été « envisagé comme une zone paysagère linéaire, comme s'il formait une extension artificielle du mode linéaire des champs et vignobles des environs immédiats », ce qui en fait également un précurseur intéressant du tout proche LF One (voir page 130). Hadid voulait également que l'étirement linéaire du poste protège aussi le complexe Vitra de diverses constructions voisines. Selon le descriptif de l'agence : « Les fonctions de définitions de l'espace et d'écran protecteur du bâtiment ont été le point de départ du développement du concept architectural : une séquence linéaire de strates de murs. Les fonctions programmatiques de ce poste d'incendie occupent les espaces entre les murs qui sont percés, s'inclinent et se rompent selon les impératifs fonctionnels. Le bâtiment est hermétique en lecture frontale, ne révélant son intérieur que d'un point de vue perpendiculaire. » On pourrait discuter du fait que cette construction n'ait jamais été vraiment utilisée comme poste d'incendie, mais est devenue en fait le symbole le plus connu des expérimentations architecturales envisagées par Rolf Fehlbaum, et la confirmation que les constructions de Zaha Hadid pouvaient se montrer aussi intéressantes que ses dessins.

AERIAL SITE PLAN
Acrylic on black cartridge, 263 x 113 cm
1991

Lines of force that tie the building together, but also relate it to its site, and a fragmented imagery push the visualization of the project to its utmost refinement and dynamic expression.

Durch Feldlinien, die den Bau zusammenhalten, ihn aber auch in Bezug zu seinem Standort setzen, und die fragmentarische Formensprache gewinnt die Visualisierung des Projekts höchste Raffinesse und dynamischen Ausdruck.

Les lignes de force qui sous-tendent le projet mais aussi le rattachent à son site et l'imagerie fragmentée entraînent cette visualisation vers une expression dynamique et un raffinement suprême.

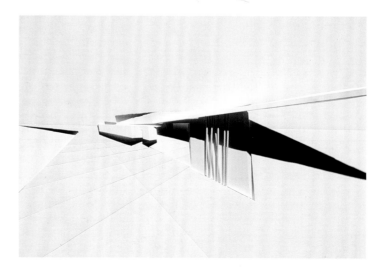

Page 121:
SILVER PAINTING
Acrylic on black cartridge
1992

With its sharply defined walls and skewed
surfaces, the building looks completely different
depending on what angle it is viewed from. Project
sketches on this page remain almost abstract.

Wegen der scharf konturierten Wände und schief-
winkligen Flächen ist die Wirkung des Baus gänzlich
vom Blickwinkel abhängig. Die Projektskizzen auf
dieser Seite bleiben fast vollkommen abstrakt.

Par ces murs se coupant à angle aigu et ses
plans inclinés, la petite construction prend des
apparences totalement différentes selon l'angle
de vision du spectateur. Les croquis ci-dessus
semblent presque abstraits.

Concrete surfaces alternate with unexpected openings, and the net result is that the precise function of the building is not immediately obvious.

Betonflächen und überraschende Öffnungen wechseln einander ab. In der Gesamtwirkung ist die Funktion des Baus nicht unmittelbar erkennbar.

Les plans en béton alternent avec des ouvertures surprenantes : la fonction précise du bâtiment n'est absolument pas évidente.

Skewed and grouped metal columns emphasize the dynamic impression generated by the more weighty concrete volumes. Below, fire trucks make their appearance.

Schief stehende, zu Gruppen gebündelte Stützen unterstreichen den dynamischen Eindruck der massiveren Betonvolumina. Unten der Auftritt der Feuerwehrwagen.

Des colonnes métalliques regroupées et inclinées mettent en valeur l'impression de dynamique générée par des volumes de béton nettement plus pesants. Ci-dessous, les camions de pompiers font leur apparition.

In a sense, the architecture is very close to the original drawings and images in that it is refined and nearly abstract in its disposition of volumes, surfaces, and lighting.

In gewisser Weise bleibt die Architektur sehr nah an den ursprünglichen Entwurfszeichnungen, ist anspruchsvoll und geradezu abstrakt in der Anordnung der Volumina, der Oberflächen und der Lichtführung.

En un sens, cette architecture est très proche des dessins et images d'origine dans sa disposition raffinée et presque abstraite des volumes, des surfaces et des éclairages.

LANDSCAPE FORMATION ONE (LF ONE)

Weil am Rhein, Germany. 1996–99

Project
LANDSCAPE FORMATION ONE (LF ONE)

Location
WEIL AM RHEIN, GERMANY

Client
CITY OF WEIL AM RHEIN

Area/Size
845 m²

An early example of the intertwining of volumes, here related to the very forms of the land, as the title of the project suggests. The imagery here is sculptural, and suggests movement more than it does precise aspects of the functions of the building.

Ein frühes Beispiel für ineinander greifende Baukörper, die hier auf die Landschaftsformation selbst Bezug nehmen, wie schon der Projekttitel nahelegt. Die Formensprache ist skulptural und vermittelt eher Dynamik, als spezifische Funktionsaspekte des Baus offenzulegen.

Cet exemple précoce de l'imbrication de volumes – ici liée à la forme même du sol – comme le nom du projet le suggère d'ailleurs. L'image est sculpturale et suggère davantage le mouvement qu'elle ne précise les aspects fonctionnels du bâtiment.

Built for the 1999 Landesgartenschau garden show hosted by Weil am Rhein, this structure was conceived as a series of paths that in some respects integrate themselves directly into the surrounding gardens. Located close to the Vitra factories, where such architects as Frank Gehry, Tadao Ando, Álvaro Siza, and Zaha Hadid herself have built, this 750-square-meter building includes a restaurant, offices, and an exhibition space. Made of three distinct concrete strands, the concrete structure is inserted into its environment so as to maximize its temperature stability both in winter and in summer. With its terraces and walkways, the building seems not to be an alien presence as its complex design might suggest, and as Zaha Hadid's reputation might have led some to expect. Rather, it blends gently into the landscape and fulfills its assigned role admirably well. The fact that this design has its source of inspiration in the natural environment is clearly confirmed by Hadid, who says: "This exhibition hall for an international gardening show is part of a sequence of projects that try to elicit new fluid spatialities from the study of natural landscape formations such as river deltas, mountain ranges, forests, deserts, canyons, ice flows, and oceans. The most important general characteristics of landscape spaces, as distinct from traditional urban and architectural spaces, are the multitude of subtle territorial definitions as well as the smoothness of transitions [...] This means that we abandon architecture and surrender to nature; rather, the point here is to seek out potentially productive analogies to inspire the invention of new artificial landforms, pertinent to our contemporary complex and multiple life-processes."

Dieser Bau wurde für die Landesgartenschau 1999 in Weil am Rhein entworfen und als eine Reihe von Wegen konzipiert, die das Projekt in gewisser Weise unmittelbar in die umliegenden Gartenanlagen integrieren. Das 750 m² große Gebäude umfasst ein Restaurant, Büro- und Ausstellungsräume und liegt unweit des Vitra-Werksgeländes, für das Architekten wie Frank Gehry, Tadao Ando, Álvaro Siza und Zaha Hadid selbst Bauten realisieren konnten. Der Betonbau setzt sich aus drei separaten Strängen zusammen und wurde in das Terrain hineingebaut, um winters wie sommers maximale Temperaturstabilität zu gewährleisten. Mit seinen Terrassen und Wegen wirkt der Bau weit weniger fremdartig, als der komplexe Entwurf hätte vermuten lassen und als es so manche von Zaha Hadid erwartet hatten. Vielmehr fügt er sich sanft in die Landschaft ein und wird seiner Aufgabe bewundernswert gerecht. Dass der Entwurf von der Natur inspiriert wurde, wird von Hadid bestätigt: „Diese Ausstellungshalle für eine internationale Gartenschau gehört zu einer Reihe von Bauten, die neue, fließende Raumqualitäten aus natürlichen Landschaftsformationen wie Flussmündungen, Gebirgszügen, Wäldern, Wüsten, Schluchten, wandernden Gletschern und Meeren abzuleiten versuchen. Das entscheidendste Merkmal von Landschaftsräumen, anders als bei traditionellen urbanen und architektonischen Räumen, ist die Vielzahl subtiler Terraingestaltungen und sanfter Übergänge [...] Das heißt nicht

etwa, dass wir uns von der Architektur lösen und der Natur anheimgeben. Der Punkt ist vielmehr, dass wir nach potenziell produktiven Analogien suchen, um

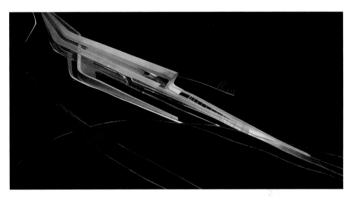

neuartige künstliche Landschaftsformationen zu entwerfen, die unseren heutigen komplexen und vielschichtigen Lebensprozessen gerecht werden."

Réalisé pour le Landesgartenschau 1999 (exposition de jardins) de Weil am Rhein, cette structure a été conçue autour d'une série de cheminements qui s'intégraient directement aux jardins environnants. Proche de l'usine Vitra, où avaient construit des architectes comme Frank Gehry, Tadao Ando, Álvaro Siza et Zaha Hadid elle-même, cette réalisation de 750 m² comprend un restaurant, des bureaux et un espace d'expositions. Composée de trois éléments longilignes distincts, cette structure en béton s'insère dans son environnement pour optimiser sa stabilité thermique aussi bien en été qu'en hiver. Avec ses terrasses et ses passages, le bâtiment ne donne pas l'effet d'une présence extraterrestre comme on aurait pu le penser ou comme la réputation de Zaha Hadid aurait pu le faire croire. Il se fond au contraire délicatement dans le paysage et remplit admirablement le rôle qui lui a été assigné. Hadid confirme que l'inspiration de ce projet vient de son environnement naturel : « Ce hall pour une exposition internationale sur le jardin fait partie d'une séquence de projets qui essaient d'éliciter de nouvelles spatialités à partir de l'étude de formations naturelles paysagères comme les rivières, les deltas, les chaînes de montagne, les forêts, les déserts, les canyons, les glaciers et les océans. Les caractéristiques générales les plus importantes des espaces paysagers, à distinguer des espaces urbains et architecturaux traditionnels, tiennent à une multitude de définitions subtiles des territoires et à la subtilité de leurs transitions [...] Ceci signifie que nous abandonnons l'architecture pour nous rendre à la nature ; mais l'enjeu ici est plutôt de rechercher des analogies potentiellement productives pour inspirer l'invention de nouveaux modelés artificiels, pertinents dans le cadre de nos modes de vie contemporains, complexes et multiples. »

ELEVATIONS
White cardboard and foamcore, 181 x 96 cm
1996

Hadid's images of the project sometimes approach apparent abstraction (bottom of left page), but ultimately all of the forms she depicts are imagined as coherent parts of an architectural whole.

Hadids Visualisierungen des Projekts sind mitunter geradezu abstrakt (linke Seite, unten). Letztendlich sind jedoch alle dargestellten Formen als schlüssige Bestandteile eines architektonischen Gesamtbilds konzipiert.

Les images du projet frôlent parfois l'abstraction (page de gauche en bas) mais finalement toutes les formes représentées doivent être vues comme les parties d'un tout architectural cohérent.

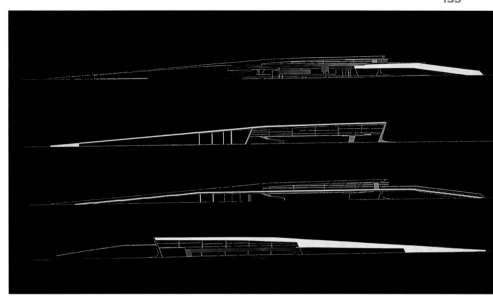

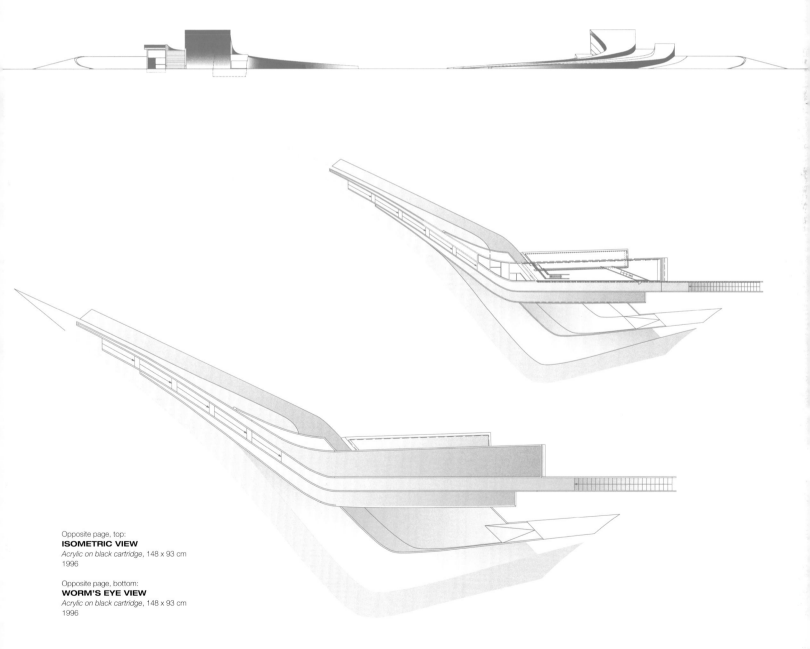

Opposite page, top:
ISOMETRIC VIEW
Acrylic on black cartridge, 148 x 93 cm
1996

Opposite page, bottom:
WORM'S EYE VIEW
Acrylic on black cartridge, 148 x 93 cm
1996

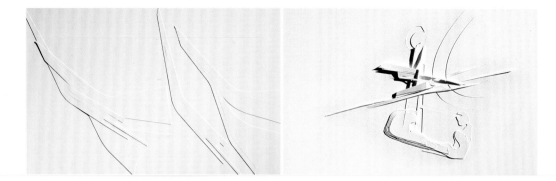

The lines of force that Zaha Hadid extracts from the site are more symbiotic with the earth than they are intended to appear to be in true continuity with the landscape. They emerge from the earth and become something else.

Die Feldlinien, die Zaha Hadid aus dem Terrain herausarbeitet, bleiben eher symbiotisch mit der Erde verbunden, als das landschaftliche Kontinuum fortzusetzen. Sie tauchen aus dem Boden auf und werden zu etwas anderem.

Les lignes de forces que Zaha Hadid extrait du site viennent davantage en symbiose avec les profondeurs de la terre elle-même que d'une simple continuité du paysage. Elles émergent du sol pour se transformer en quelque chose d'autre.

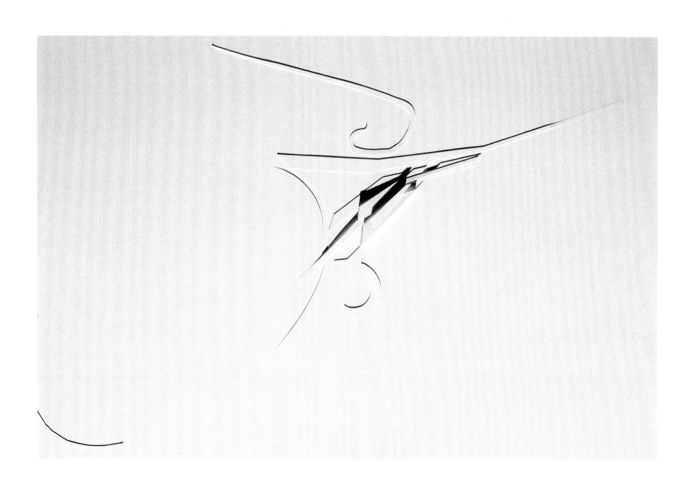

With its ramp rising up from ground level and leading up toward the main body of the building, the structure challenges traditional ideas of levels in architecture.

Mit seiner Rampe, die sich von Bodenhöhe zum Hauptvolumen des Gebäudes hin aufschwingt, hinterfragt der Bau traditionelle Vorstellungen von Geschossebenen in der Architektur.

Par cette rampe qui s'élève du sol et mène au corps principal du bâtiment, le projet remet en question les conceptions traditionnelles des niveaux en architecture.

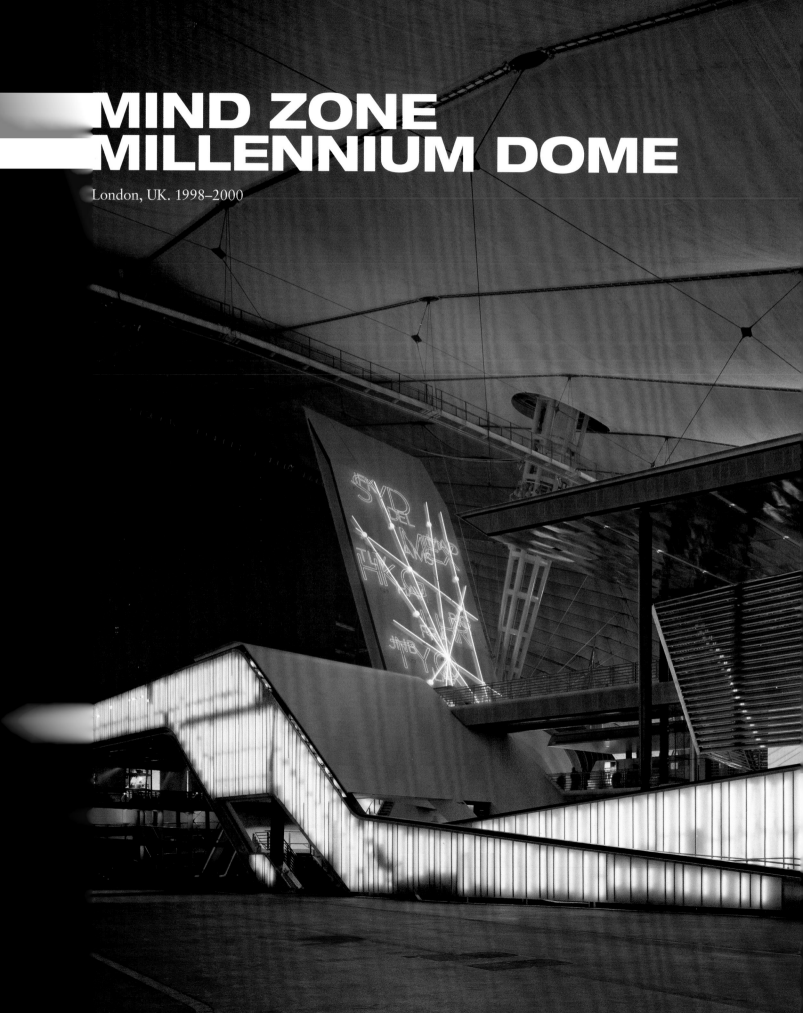

MIND ZONE
MILLENNIUM DOME

London, UK. 1998–2000

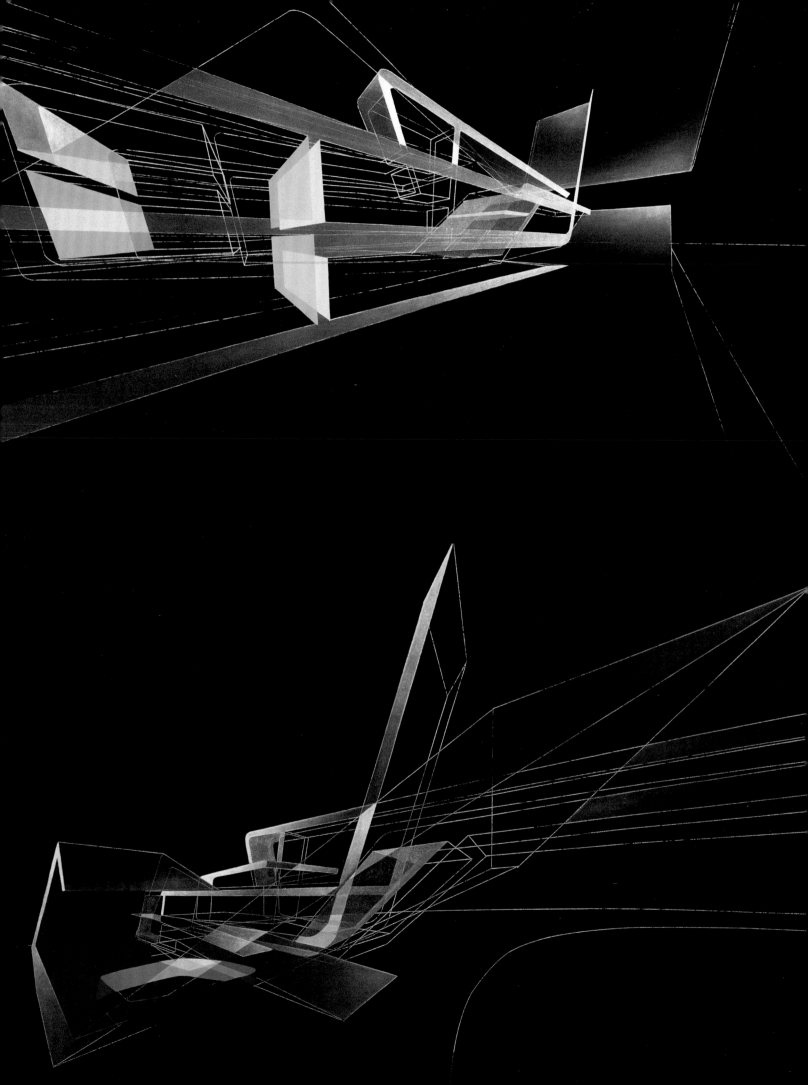

Project
MIND ZONE MILLENNIUM DOME

Location
LONDON, UK

Client
THE NEW MILLENNIUM EXPERIENCE CO. LTD.

Area/Size
2500 m²

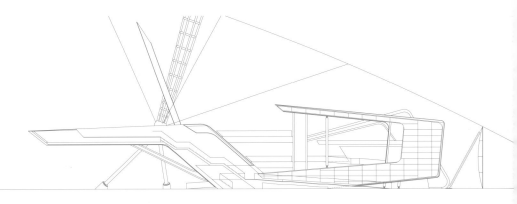

INTERIOR PERSPECTIVE
Acrylic on black cartridge, 84.1 x 59.4 cm
1998

INTERIOR PERSPECTIVE
Acrylic on black cartridge, 84.1 x 59.4 cm
1998

Set beneath London's Millennium Dome, the Mind Zone could dispense with any particular relation to the site, aside from the material constraints of the allotted space. Here, Hadid's images seem to suggest the Dome only for purposes of placement and height.

Wegen ihrer Lage unter dem Dach des Millennium Dome kam die Mind Zone ohne engeren Bezug zur Umgebung aus, abgesehen von den materiellen Beschränkungen des zugewiesenen Standorts. Hadids Bilder scheinen den Kuppelbau hier nur zu Zwecken der Platzierung und Höhe anzudeuten.

Installée sous le Millennium Dome à Londres, la Mind Zone pouvait se libérer de toute relation précise au terrain, en dehors des contraintes matérielles de l'espace alloué. Ici, les images de Hadid ne semblent suggérer le Dôme que pour indiquer les contraintes de placement et de hauteur qu'il imposait.

Situated beneath the Millennium Dome, Zaha Hadid's Mind Zone stood out with its spectacular cantilevered steel structure. As the designer says: "Our minds are amazingly complex machines and our aim is to unravel some of their mysteries in a truly memorable fashion." Working with a number of talented artists, such as Ron Mueck, Gavin Turk, Langlands & Bell, Helen Chadwick, and Richard Deacon, Hadid succeeded in creating spaces that appear to defy gravity and to prepare the visitor for the technologically oriented exhibits within the pavilion. Clearly, there was some danger for Hadid in participating in this circus-like assembly of pavilions, but she showed by the force of her design that good architecture can impose itself even in difficult conditions. One of 14 individual exhibition spaces within the Millennium Dome, the Mind Zone was controlled by Hadid both from architectural and a curatorial point of view, with the assistance for the artist liaison of Doris Lockhart-Saatchi. Here, as in many of her works, she formed a continuous surface "that allows for a fluid journey through the space," encompassing floors, walls, and ceilings. According to the architect's description of the project: "As a narrative strategy, the three elements complement the primary mental functions—'input,' 'process,' and 'output'—represented variously through perspective and visual distortion, explanatory exhibits, sculpture, computers, audiovisual installations, and interactive elements. The design strategy avoids being overtly pedagogical and is interactive and thought provoking." Essentially made of synthetic materials such as lightweight transparent panels with glass-fiber skins and an aluminum honeycomb structure, the pavilion, destined to last one year, sought to "create an ephemeral temporal quality."

Unter dem Dach des Millennium Dome fiel Zaha Hadids Mind Zone als spektakulär auskragende Stahlkonstruktion auf. Die Architektin merkt an: „Unser Verstand ist eine überwältigend komplexe Maschine, und unser Ziel ist es, einige seiner Geheimnisse auf wirklich eindrucksvolle Weise zu lüften." In Zusammenarbeit mit einer ganzen Reihe begabter Künstler wie Ron Mueck, Gavin Turk, Langlands & Bell, Helen Chadwick und Richard Deacon gelang es Hadid, Räume zu schaffen, die der Schwerkraft zu trotzen schienen und den Besucher auf die technologisch orientierten Exponate im Pavillon einstimmten. Ganz offensichtlich war es für Hadid riskant, sich an einer solch zirkushaften Ansammlung von Pavillons zu beteiligen, doch die Ausdruckskraft ihres Entwurfs zeigte, dass gute Architektur sich selbst unter schwierigen Bedingungen behaupten kann. Die Mind Zone war einer von insgesamt 14 unabhängigen Ausstellungsbereichen innerhalb des Millennium Dome und wurde von Zaha Hadid sowohl architektonisch als auch kuratorisch betreut. Unterstützt wurde sie bei der Kooperation mit den Künstlern von Doris Lockhart-Saatchi. Hier, wie auch bei anderen Arbeiten, schuf Hadid eine durchgehende Oberfläche für Böden, Wände und Decken, „was eine fließende Reise durch den Raum erlaubt". Die Architektin beschreibt das Projekt wie folgt: „Unsere narrative Strategie war es, eine Beziehung zwischen den drei Elementen [des Pavillons] und den primären mentalen Funktionen – Eingabe, Verarbeitung, Ausgabe – herzustellen. Diese werden durch perspektivische und optische Verzerrungen, erläuternde Exponate, Skulpturen, Computer, audiovisuelle Installationen und interaktive Elemente anschaulich. Das Design vermeidet es, allzu pädagogisch zu wirken, ist interaktiv und regt zum Nachdenken an." Der Pavillon, überwiegend aus synthetischen Materialien gefertigt, etwa aus transparenten Leichtbauelementen mit Glasfaserhaut und einer honigwabenähnlichen Aluminiumstruktur, war für die Dauer eines Jahres konzipiert und darauf angelegt, eine „flüchtige, temporäre Qualität" zu vermitteln.

L'un des quatorze espaces d'expositions aménagés sous le Millennium Dome, cette Mind Zone (zone de l'esprit) était l'œuvre de Zaha Hadid, aussi bien pour son architecture que pour son contenu, établi avec l'assistance pour les relations avec les artistes de Doris Lockhart-Saatchi. « Notre esprit est une machine étonnamment complexe et notre but est de révéler certains de ses mystères de manière mémorable », a déclaré l'architecte. Travaillant avec des artistes de talent comme Ron Mueck, Gavin Turk, Langlands & Bell, Helen Chadwick et Richard Deacon, Hadid a réussi à créer des espaces qui semblent défier la gravité et préparer le visiteur à la découverte des pièces exposées de nature technologique. Participer à cet assemblage disparate de pavillons n'était pas sans danger, mais elle a montré par la force de son projet qu'une bonne architecture pouvait s'imposer, même dans les conditions difficiles. Implantée au cœur du dispositif du dôme à l'atmosphère d'exposition universelle, la Mind Zone se singularisait par une structure d'acier en porte-à-faux spectaculaire. Comme dans beaucoup de ses réalisations, Hadid avait créé un plan continu « qui permet un itinéraire fluide à travers l'espace », comprenant les sols, les murs et les plafonds. Selon le descriptif du projet : « Dans le cadre d'une stratégie narrative, les trois éléments viennent en illustration des trois grandes fonctions mentales – réception, traitement, émission – représentées de façons variées par des perspectives et des distorsions visuelles, des éléments explicatifs, des sculptures, des ordinateurs, des installations audiovisuelles et des éléments interactifs. La stratégie du projet évite la stricte pédagogie ; elle est interactive et provoque la réflexion. » Essentiellement réalisé en matériaux synthétiques, dont des panneaux transparents légers à peau en fibre de verre et une structure en nid d'abeille en aluminium, le pavillon, conçu pour durer une année, cherchait à « créer une qualité temporelle éphémère ».

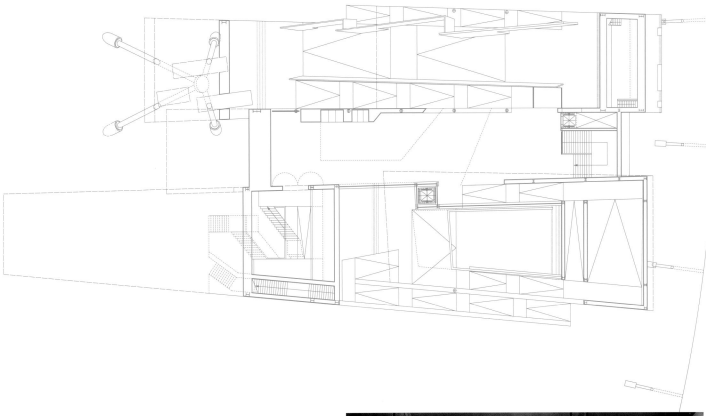

The actual structure was inserted into what might be called a miniature version of a universal exposition—with various pavilions and themes, hence the scintillating light scheme seen in these images. Tilted planes and volumes make it difficult to distinguish the structure's interior from its outside appearance.

Der Bau war gewissermaßen in eine Weltausstellung en miniature integriert – mit verschiedenen Pavillons und Themen –, daher auch die funkelnden Lichteffekte auf den Abbildungen. Schiefe Ebenen und Volumina erschweren es, vom Außenbau auf den Innenraum der Konstruktion zu schließen.

La structure s'insérait dans une autre plus vaste, version miniature d'une exposition universelle développée à travers de multiples pavillons et thématiques que montrent les plans lumineux présents sur ces photographies. Les plans et les volumes inclinés ne facilitent pas la compréhension extérieure de l'intérieur de la structure.

HOENHEIM-NORD
TERMINUS

Strasbourg, France. 1998–2001

Project
HOENHEIM-NORD TERMINUS

Location
STRASBOURG, FRANCE

Client
COMMUNAUTE URBAINE DE STRASBOURG, COMPAGNIE DES TRANSPORTS STRASBOURGEOIS

Area/Size
3000 m² STATION
25 000 m² PARKING/VRD

Below, right:
AERIAL VIEW
Acrylic on black cartridge, 84.1 x 59.4 cm
1998

Skewed columns emphasize what is already inherent in the project—its movement and integration into the tramway system of Strasbourg.

Geneigte Stützen betonen, was ohnehin integraler Bestandteil des Projekts ist – seine Dynamik und Einbindung in das Straßburger Straßenbahnsystem.

Des colonnes inclinées mettent en valeur ce qui est inhérent au projet : sa dynamique de mouvement et l'intégration au système des tramways de Strasbourg.

As part of a tramway system installed by the French eastern city of Strasbourg, one of the two homes of the European Parliament, Zaha Hadid created a station and car park for 700 vehicles at the northern end of Line B (Hoenheim Gare to Lingolsheim, a distance of 14.7 kilometers). It may be interesting to note that the city had invited such reputed artists as Mario Merz and Barbara Kruger to participate in the first phase of the tramway operation, and that Hadid's interventions, in many images, almost appear to be more of a work of art on a large scale than a piece of architecture. As the former mayor of Strasbourg and former French Minister of Culture Catherine Trautmann put it: "Public transport is an especially effective means of increasing people's awareness of the art of their time and an outlet for contemporary art distinct from traditional venues." Hadid imagined the design as a set of overlapping fields or directional lines that are formed by the movement of cars, trams, bicycles, or people on foot. Made up of a waiting space, bicycle storage area, toilets, and a shop, the station is animated by lines that continue in the overall pattern of the plan, appearing inside sometimes as narrow openings in the concrete ceilings or walls. The parking spots, each marked by thin vertical lamps, are initially organized along a north-south axis, but then curve gently in a rhythm suggested by the boundaries of the site. Like the LF One (see page 130) or Vitra (see page 116) projects, the Strasbourg project experiments with the idea of "artificial nature [...] one that blurs the boundaries between natural and artificial environments" with the goal of "improving civic life for Strasbourg," according to the architect.

Für das Straßenbahnnetz von Straßburg, einem der beiden Sitze des Europäischen Parlaments, realisierte Zaha Hadid eine Haltestelle und einen Parkplatz mit 700 Stellplätzen an der nördlichen Endstation der Linie B (Bahnhof Hoenheim bis Lingolsheim, eine Strecke von 14,7 km). Interessant ist sicherlich, dass die Stadt so renommierte Künstler wie Mario Merz und Barbara Kruger eingeladen hatte, um sich an der ersten Erschließungsphase des Straßenbahnnetzes zu beteiligen, und dass Hadids Straßburger Interventionen auf vielen Bildern fast eher wie ein großes Kunstprojekt als wie Architektur wirken. Catherine Trautmann, frühere Bürgermeisterin von Straßburg und ehemalige französische Kultusministerin, formulierte einmal: „Der öffentliche Nahverkehr ist eines der effektivsten Mittel, um das Bewusstsein der Menschen für die Kunst ihrer Zeit zu schärfen, und zugleich eine Arena für zeitgenössische Kunst jenseits der traditionellen Institutionen." Hadid entwickelte den Entwurf als einander überlagernde Felder oder Spurmarkierungen, die sich aus den Bewegungsmustern der Autos, Straßenbahnen, Fahrräder und Fußgänger ergeben. Die Haltestelle mit Wartebereich, Fahrradstellplatz, Toiletten und Ladengeschäft wird von den Linienmarkierungen belebt, die sich durch den gesamten Grundriss ziehen und im Innern der Haltestelle z. T. als schmale Öffnungen in den Betondecken und -wänden in Erscheinung treten. Die Parkplätze, markiert von schlanken vertikalen Laternen, orientieren sich zunächst entlang einer Nord-Süd-Achse, folgen dann aber in sanftem Schwung einem von

der Grundstücksgrenze angedeuteten Rhythmus. Wie das Projekt LF One (siehe Seite 130) oder die Feuerwache für Vitra (siehe Seite 116), so experimentiert auch das Straßburger Projekt mit der Idee einer „künstlichen Natur [...], einer, in der die Grenzen zwischen natürlicher und künstlicher Umwelt verschwimmen", um der Architektin zufolge „das öffentliche Leben in Straßburg zu verbessern".

C'est dans le cadre du nouveau réseau de transport par tramway, créé par Strasbourg – l'un des deux sièges du Parlement européen – que Zaha Hadid a conçu cette gare complétée par un parking de 700 places à l'extrémité nord de la Ligne B (Hoenheim Gare–Lingolsheim, 14,7 km). On peut noter que la ville avait invité des artistes aussi réputés que Mario Merz et Barbara Kruger à participer à la première phase de la création du tramway et que les interventions de Zaha Hadid, dans de nombreuses images, font davantage penser à des œuvres d'art de grandes dimensions qu'à une réalisation architecturale. Comme l'ancienne maire de Strasbourg et ancienne ministre de la Culture, Catherine Trautmann, l'a déclaré : « Le transport public est un moyen particulièrement efficace d'accroître la prise de conscience de l'art de son temps par le public, et un lieu d'expositions qui se différencie des points d'accueil traditionnels. » Hadid a imaginé son projet comme un ensemble de plans ou de d'axes superposés, générés par le mouvement des trams, des voitures, des vélos ou des piétons. Comprenant une salle d'attente, des garages à vélos, des toilettes et une boutique, la gare est animée par des axes visuels qui se poursuivent sur l'ensemble du plan, apparaissant parfois sous la forme d'étroites ouvertures pratiquées dans les murs ou les plafonds en béton. Les emplacements de parking, chacun signalé par une mince lampe verticale, s'organisent d'abord sur un axe nord-sud, puis s'incurvent doucement en suivant les limites du terrain. Comme pour LF One (voir page 130) ou Vitra (voir page 116), le projet strasbourgeois joue de l'idée de « nature artificielle... qui bouscule les frontières entre environnements naturels et artificiels », dans le but « d'améliorer la vie citoyenne à Strasbourg », précise l'architecte.

The irregular leaning columns support an apparently massive, cantilevered roof. Left, the irregular parking lots of the station, also seen in the drawing and image on the upper right page.

Die unregelmäßig angeordneten, schiefen Stützen tragen ein monumentales, auskragendes Dach. Links, die asymmetrisch angelegten Parkplätze der Station, auch in der Zeichnung und Aufnahme rechts oben zu sehen.

Les colonnes inclinées irrégulièrement disposées soutiennent une toiture en porte-à-faux d'apparence massive. À gauche, les emplacements de parking positionnés en biais, que l'on voit également dans le dessin et la photographie en haut de la page de gauche.

Below, an aerial view of the station shows the slightly curving pattern of the parking lots, also to the right. The treatment of the parking area surface also appears from abore to be a continuation of the volume of the building itself.

Eine Luftaufnahme der Endstation, unten, zeigt die geschwungene Anordnung der Parkplätze, auch rechts im Bild. Von oben gesehen wird deutlich, dass die Gestaltung der Parkflächen und der eigentliche Baukörper ein Gesamtbild ergeben.

Ci-dessous, une vue aérienne de la gare montrant la disposition légèrement incurvée des emplacements de parking à droite. Le traitement de ces parkings de surface est ainsi en continuité avec le mouvement du bâtiment lui-même.

Night lighting of the main canopy and the parking area emphasizes the unexpected nature of the architecture and the landscape treatment around it.

Die nächtliche Beleuchtung des Hauptdachs und des Parkplatzes unterstreicht die überraschenden Aspekte der Architektur und der Landschaftsgestaltung.

L'éclairage nocturne de l'auvent principal et de la zone des parkings souligne la nature surprenante de l'architecture et du traitement du paysage environnant.

Rectangular lights also mark the ceiling of the canopy, whose columns and cantilevered design suggest a continuity of movement with the tramway itself.

Rechteckige Leuchten durchziehen auch die Dachkonstruktion, die mit ihren Stützen und der auskragenden Form die Bewegung der Straßenbahnen aufzugreifen scheint.

Des luminaires rectangulaires ponctuent la sousface de l'auvent dont les colonnes et le porte-àfaux suggèrent une continuité de mouvement avec le tramway.

BERGISEL SKI JUMP

Innsbruck, Austria. 1999–2002

Project
BERGISEL SKI JUMP
Location
INNSBRUCK, AUSTRIA
Client
AUSTRIAN SKI FEDERATION
Area/Size
91 m (HEIGHT 49 m)

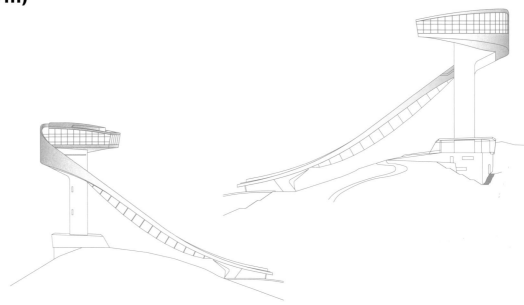

The wrapping form of the Bergisel Ski Jump suggests its function, of course, but also defines a relationship to the mountain landscape, as though the ramp emerged from the slope or vice versa.

Die in sich geschwungene Form der Bergisel-Skischanze ist zunächst ein Verweis auf ihre Funktion, definiert jedoch auch ihr Verhältnis zur Berglandschaft – als sei die Schanze aus dem Hang herausgewachsen.

La forme enveloppante du tremplin de saut à ski de Bergisel évoque bien entendu sa fonction, mais définit également une relation avec le paysage de montagne, comme si la rampe émergeait de la pente ou celle-ci se fondait avec elle.

Created in 1926, the Bergisel Ski Jump has been well known almost since its construction, and was the site of the 1964 and 1976 Winter Olympic competitions. The schedule of international ski jumping events is such that local authorities could allow only one year from demolition to opening the new facility. Cleverly, the Ski Jump includes a steel-plate-clad café situated 10 meters above the jumping ramp, and it is apparent in the design that the Austrian Ski Federation wanted to create a monument as much as they sought a high-quality sports facility. Seating 150 people, the café boasts a 360° view of the city and mountain scenery. In spite of local resistance to contemporary architecture of notable quality, both Hadid and Dominique Perrault (Innsbruck Town Hall) have succeeded in breaking into this Tyrolean stronghold of traditionalism. Forty-eight meters tall and seven by seven meters on the ground, the concrete structure has already permitted long flights, such as the 134.5-meter jump achieved here by Sven Hannawald in January 2002. Hadid has described the structure as an "organic hybrid"—a sort of mixture of a tower and a bridge—but it succeeds in abstracting the speed of motion and flight that characterizes the most spectacular of winter sports events.

Die Bergisel-Skischanze von 1926 war seit ihrer Eröffnung berühmt und Schauplatz der Olympischen Winterspiele 1964 und 1976. Aufgrund festliegender Termine für die internationalen Skisprungwettbewerbe hatte die örtliche Gemeinde nur ein Jahr Zeit vom Abriss der alten bis zur Eröffnung der neuen Schanze. Ein geschickter Zug war die Realisierung eines mit Stahl verblendeten Cafés 10 m oberhalb der Absprungrampe – eine Entscheidung, die deutlich macht, dass sich der Österreichische Skiverband ebenso sehr ein Monument, wie eine hochkarätige Sporteinrichtung wünschte. Das Café bietet Raum für 150 Gäste und

einen Rundblick über Stadt und Berglandschaft. Trotz regionaler Proteste gegen solch anspruchsvolle zeitgenössische Architektur gelang es Hadid – ebenso wie Dominique Perrault (Rathaus Innsbruck) –, diese Tiroler Hochburg des Traditionalismus zu erobern. Die 48 m hohe Betonkonstruktion der Schanze mit einer Grundfläche von 7 x 7 m hat weite Sprünge möglich gemacht, darunter Sven Hannawalds 134,5 m weiten Sprung im Januar 2002. Hadid beschrieb den Bau als „organische Hybride" – eine Art Kreuzung von Turm und Brücke. Gelungen abstrahiert die Schanze die Geschwindigkeit von Abfahrt und Skiflug, die eines der spektakulärsten Wintersportereignisse auszeichnet.

Créé en 1926, le tremplin de saut à ski de Bergisel, amplement publié dès son chantier, a été le site de compétitions olympiques d'hiver en 1964 et 1976. Le programme des rencontres internationales de ce sport est tel que les autorités ne pouvaient se permettre qu'un délai d'une seule année entre la démolition et l'inauguration du nouvel équipement. Il intègre de façon intelligente un café plaqué d'acier situé 10 m au-dessus de la piste de saut. Le projet montre que la Fédération autrichienne de ski souhaitait autant créer un monument qu'une installation sportive de haute qualité. Le café de 150 places offre une vue à 360° sur la ville et les montagnes. Malgré les résistances locales à l'architecture contemporaine de qualité, Zaha Hadid et Dominique Perrault (pour l'hôtel de ville d'Innsbruck) ont réussi à lui faire une place dans ce fief traditionnaliste. Haute de 48 m et de 7 x 7 m de section à la base, la structure en béton a déjà permis des records comme le saut de 134,5 m accompli par Sven Hannawald en janvier 2002. Hadid a décrit ce projet comme un « hybride organique » – sorte de croisement de tour et de pont – qui réussi à donner une image abstraite de la vitesse, du mouvement et de l'envol qui caractérisent l'un des sports d'hiver les plus spectaculaires.

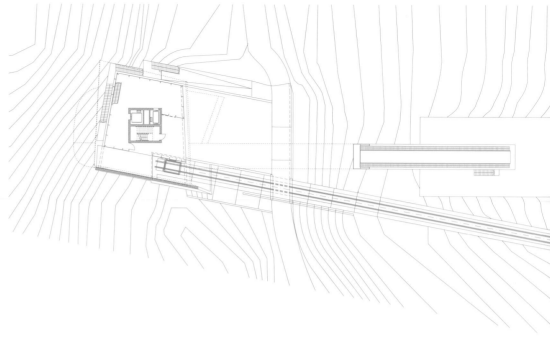

The daring forms of the Ski Jump relate to the vertiginous mountains nearby, but also to the soaring activity for which it was built.

Die gewagte Formgebung der Skischanze nimmt Bezug auf die atemberaubenden Gipfel der Umgebung, ebenso wie auf den hochfliegenden Sport, dem sie dient.

Les formes audacieuses de ce tremplin sont en relation avec les montagnes vertigineuses qui l'entourent, mais aussi à l'activité sportive à laquelle il est dédié.

As the section drawing below makes evident, there is something of an anthropomorphic suggestion in the "head" and "body" of the Ski Jump, but, as always, Zaha Hadid avoids becoming too literal. As is often the case in her work, night lighting is important.

Wie die Schnittzeichnung unten deutlich macht, klingt in „Kopf" und „Torso" der Skischanze etwas Anthropomorphes mit, doch wie immer vermeidet Zaha Hadid eine zu offensichtliche Allegorie. Wie oft in ihrem Werk, ist auch hier die nächtliche Beleuchtung wichtig.

Comme le montre avec clarté le dessin de coupe ci-dessous, on peut noter une sorte d'allusion anthropomorphique (avec une « tête » et un « corps ») dans ce tremplin, mais comme toujours, Zaha Hadid évite toute littéralité trop marquée. Comme souvent chez elle, l'éclairage est important.

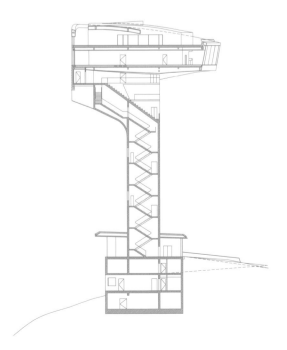

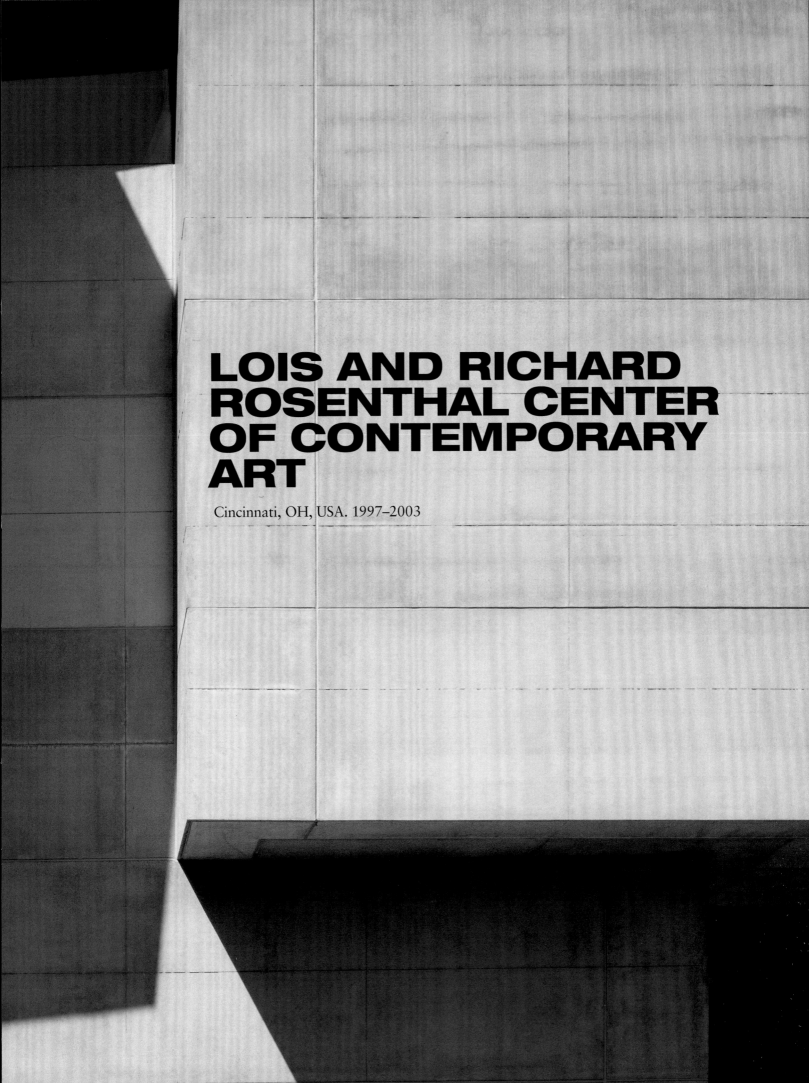

LOIS AND RICHARD ROSENTHAL CENTER OF CONTEMPORARY ART

Cincinnati, OH, USA. 1997–2003

Project
LOIS AND RICHARD ROSENTHAL CENTER OF CONTEMPORARY ART

Location
CINCINNATI, OH, USA

Client
THE CONTEMPORARY ARTS CENTER

Area/Size
8500 m²

The complex composition, this time in an essentially rectilinear format, contains numerous surprises, such as the thin columns and full-height glazing at the entrance level, giving the impression that the weighty part of the building is at the top rather than the bottom.

Die komplexe Komposition, diesmal überwiegend geradlinig, birgt zahlreiche Überraschungen, etwa die schlanken Stützen und eine geschosshohe Verglasung der Eingangsebene. So entsteht der Eindruck, der schwerere Teil des Baus befinde sich im oberen statt im unteren Bereich.

La composition complexe, cette fois dans un format essentiellement orthogonal, réserve néanmoins de multiples surprises, comme les colonnes fines et la paroi vitrée toute en hauteur du niveau de l'entrée qui donne l'impression que la partie lourde du bâtiment se trouve à son sommet plutôt qu'à sa base.

With the opening of the Rosenthal Center, Zaha Hadid became, surprisingly enough, the first woman to design an American art museum. Even more surprising for the usually angular and complicated Hadid, her new museum fits nicely into a city street of mixed architectural merit. Indeed, the only thing that signals the presence of an architectural "star" in this unlikely location is the closed succession of cantilevered boxes that looks onto 6th Street. True, Marcel Breuer's Whitney Museum on Madison Avenue presents similarly blind volumes of stone to the street. Then, too, this is the very institution that dared to defy the strictures of Puritan America by exhibiting the controversial photographs of Robert Mapplethorpe, becoming embroiled in a famous obscenity trial. Measuring about 8500 square meters, this is not a very large building, but it does signal the arrival of Hadid as a serious builder as opposed to a largely theoretical designer. Poured-in-place concrete floors seem to curve effortlessly into walls near the entrance, and visitors see heavy painted black, steel, ramp-stairs that rise almost 30 meters up to skylights. Each flight of stairs weighs 15 tons, as much as the construction cranes could carry. This staircase is the central mediating feature of the Center, leading to the exhibition space and providing a continuous focal point for the movement of visitors. Hadid's architecture relies on the art it will exhibit to bring its exhibition spaces to life, even if some artists may find her spaces challenging or difficult. This is less an act of artistic freedom than Gehry's Guggenheim Bilbao, but it remains a significant step forward for quality architecture in the context of America's often barren provincial cities.

Mit der Eröffnung des Rosenthal Centers wurde Zaha Hadid überraschenderweise zur ersten Frau, die je ein amerikanisches Kunstmuseum entworfen hatte. Noch überraschender für Hadid, deren Bauten sonst eher spitzwinklig und kompliziert wirken, war die Tatsache, dass sich das neue Museum geradezu nahtlos in den Straßenzug einfügt, dessen Bebauung von höchst unterschiedlicher architektonischer Qualität ist. Tatsächlich ist der einzige Hinweis darauf, dass hier eine Stararchitektin am Werk war, die enge Folge auskragender Boxen zur 6. Straße hin. Zwar präsentiert sich auch das Whitney Museum auf der New Yorker Madison Avenue, ein Bau von Marcel Breuer, mit ähnlich geschlossenen Volumina aus Stein zur Straßenfront hin. Doch immerhin war das Whitney jene Institution, die es gewagt hatte, sich den engstirnigen Moralvorstellungen der puritanischen amerikanischen Gesellschaft zu verweigern, als sie die kontroversen Fotografien Robert Mapplethorpes ausstellte und sich schließlich bekanntermaßen wegen „Obszönität" vor Gericht verantworten musste. Mit 8500 m² ist der Bau in Cincinnati nicht sonderlich groß, signalisiert jedoch, dass Hadid nun als ernstzunehmende, tatsächlich bauende Architektin auftritt, statt überwiegend theoretisch zu entwerfen. Die Böden aus Ortbeton scheinen im Eingangsbereich nahtlos in die Wände überzugehen. Besucher sehen sich schweren, rampenähnlichen Treppen aus schwarz gestrichenem Stahl gegenüber, die fast 30 m hoch bis zu den Oberlichtern hin aufsteigen. Jeder einzelne Treppenabschnitt wiegt 15 t, die Maximallast, die mit den Baukränen zu bewegen war. Das Treppenhaus ist die zentrale Drehscheibe des Centers, es erschließt die Ausstellungsräume und wird zugleich zum ständigen Brennpunkt der sich bewegenden Besucherströme. Hadids Architektur ist auf die hier präsentierte Kunst angewiesen, damit sich die Ausstellungsräume mit Leben füllen, wenngleich manche Künstler ihre Räume schwer zu bespielen finden. Auch wenn dieser Bau wohl nicht so ein architektonischer Befreiungsschlag ist wie Gehrys Guggenheim-Museum in Bilbao, so ist er doch ein entscheidender Schritt hin zu mehr qualitätvoller Architektur in Amerikas oft vernachlässigten Provinzstädten.

Avec l'ouverture du Centre Rosenthal, Zaha Hadid est devenue la première femme architecte à avoir conçu un musée d'art aux État-Unis. Plus surprenant encore pour les projets habituellement complexes de Zaha Hadid, celui-ci s'intégrait plaisamment dans une rue d'intérêt architectural discutable. En fait, la seule chose qui signale la présence d'une « star » architecturale à cette adresse improbable est l'empilement de boîtes en porte-à-faux qui donne sur 6th Street. Le Whitney Museum de Marcel Breuer sur Madison Avenue (New York) présente lui aussi des volumes clos similaires donnant sur la rue. C'est aussi cette même institution qui avait osé défier les codes de l'Amérique puritaine en exposant les photographies si controversées de Robert Mapplethorpe, déclenchant un célèbre procès pour obscénité. Le bâtiment n'est pas vraiment très vaste – 8500 m² – mais a signalé l'arrivée de Hadid comme architecte de terrain dans le cercle des grands constructeurs, contrastant avec sa carrière antérieure essentiellement consacrée à la théorie. Les sols en béton coulés en place semblent se recourber sans effort vers l'entrée pour se transformer en murs. Les visiteurs sont happés par de lourdes rampes escaliers d'acier laqué noir qui s'élèvent à près de 30 m jusqu'aux verrières. Chaque volée de marches pèse 15 tonnes, le maximum de ce que les grues pouvaient accepter. Cet escalier, élément central de circulation du musée, conduit aux salles d'expositions et constitue un point d'attraction. L'architecture de Zaha Hadid laisse aux expositions à venir le soin d'animer les espaces, même si certains artistes les trouvent difficiles ou problématiques. Le Centre Rosenthal est moins un acte de liberté esthétique que le Guggenheim de Gehry à Bilbao, mais il marque néanmoins une avancée significative dans le domaine de la qualité architecturale des villes américaines de province.

Drawings and images of the building show its sculptural exterior composition, corresponding naturally to required programmatic elements within.

Zeichnungen und Ansichten des Gebäudes veranschaulichen die Komposition des Außenbaus, die zugleich natürliches Pendant zu den erforderlichen programmatischen Elementen des Innenbaus sind.

Les dessins et les photographies montrent le caractère sculptural de la composition des façades, qui correspond bien sûr à la programmation interne.

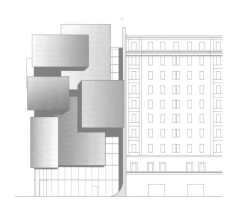

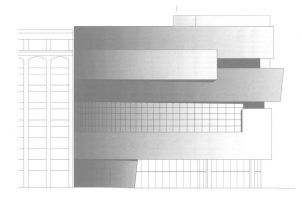

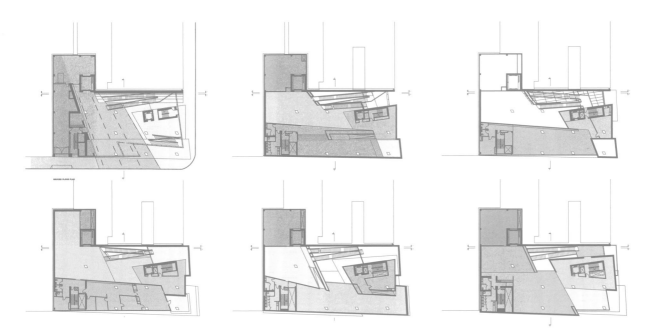

SECOND FLOOR PLAN

To the left is *Cloud Prototype No. 1*, 2003 (fiberglass and titanium alloy foil, 3.35 x 4.47 x 2.44 meters) by Iñigo Manglano-Ovalle, in the stairway in
Cincinnati. Floor plans (above) seem to correspond
in their spirit to the interior view seen on the right.

Links im Bild *Cloud Prototype No. 1*, 2003 (Glasfaser und Folie aus Titanlegierung, 3,35 x 4,47 x 2,44
Meter) von Iñigo Manglano-Ovalle im Treppenhaus
des Museums in Cincinnati. Die Etagengrundrisse
(oben) zeugen von demselben Geist wie die Innenansicht rechts.

À gauche, *Cloud Prototype No. 1*, 2003 (fibre
de verre et tôle d'alliage de titane, 3,35 x 4,47 x
2,44 m) d'Inigo Manglano-Ovalle, dans la cage
d'escalier du musée. Les niveaux (ci-dessus)
semblent correspondre dans leur esprit à la vue de
l'intérieur (à droite).

COMPOSITION
Acrylic on black cartridge, 125 x 90 cm
1997

A complexity that might appear Piranesian in inspiration can be seen in these images of the stairway of the building. Light, floating forms alternate with stable, massive blocks.

Die Ansichten des Treppenhauses verraten eine Komplexität, die durchaus von Piranesi inspiriert sein könnte. Leichte, schwebende Formen und statische, massive Blöcke wechseln einander ab.

Une complexité qui pourrait sembler d'inspiration piranésienne se perçoit dans ces images de la cage d'escalier. Des formes légères en suspension alternent avec des blocs massifs et stables.

ORDRUPGAARD
MUSEUM EXTENSION

Copenhagen, Denmark. 2001–05

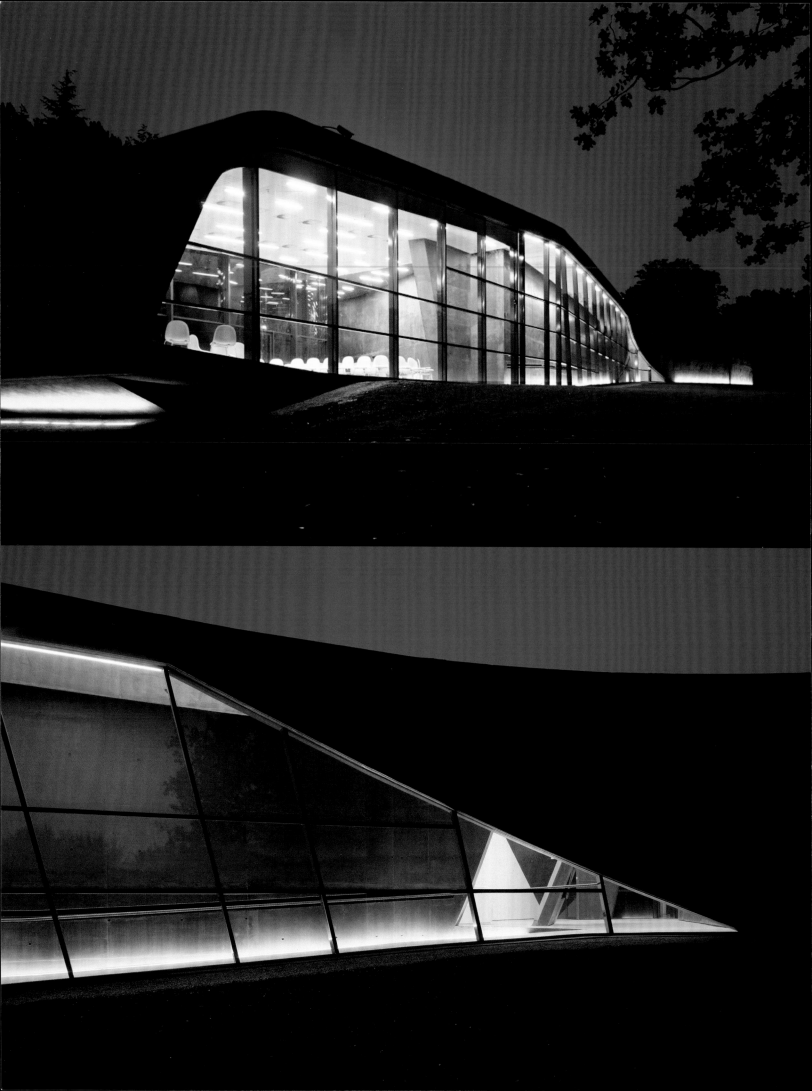

Project
ORDRUPGAARD MUSEUM EXTENSION

Location
COPENHAGEN, DENMARK

Client
DANISH MINISTRY OF CULTURE, ORDRUPGAARD MUSEUM

Area/Size
1150 m²

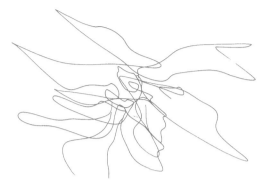

The dramatic lines of the building, where horizontals and verticals are inevitably skewed or curved, are rendered in these evening views where transparency and opacity stand in stark contrast.

Die dramatischen Linien des Baus, dessen Horizontalen und Vertikalen durchweg schief oder geschwungen sind, werden an diesen Nachtansichten deutlich, auf denen Transparenz und Opazität in scharfem Kontrast zueinander stehen.

Ces vues prises en fin de journée mettent en valeur les lignes spectaculaires du bâtiment dans lequel les horizontales et les verticales partent inévitablement en biais. Le dialogue de la transparence et de l'opacité créent de puissants contrastes.

For this extension of the existing Ordrupgaard Museum, a Danish state museum for 19th-century French and Danish art lodged in the former mansion of the collector Wilhelm Hansen, Zaha Hadid again called on the idea of a distinct relationship between the landscape setting and the new building: "The new extension seeks to establish a new landscape within the territory of its architecture, at the same time allowing new relations with the existing conditions. The logic of the existing landscape is abstracted in the geometry; new contours extend into the collection developing an alternate ground where occupancy and use are extended." Built by the Danish Ministry of Culture, Fonden Realdania, and Augustin Fonden, the new structure is 87 meters long and 20 meters wide, plus a five meter passage to the old structure. Made of cast black lava concrete, the structure's complex curving geometry suggested an on-site molding process with the self-consolidating concrete pressed into forms from below or pumped into an outer shell through holes. With walls curving into ceilings or floors, the Extension experiments successfully with continuous space, where the straight lines that characterize the original museum are the exception rather than the rule. Indeed, the architect insists on fluidity even in the transition from inside to outside and from one building to the other. "The critique of the edge is thus replaced by a notion of fluid interaction between the garden and the interior program," she says, "and it acts as a constant instrument of gradation that allows for different conditions to appear without necessarily breaking the volume up." Glazing shows the relationship of the building to its topography, while openings in the continuous shell provide ample opportunities for movement from one area to another.

Der Erweiterungsbau ergänzt das Ordrupgaard Museum, eine staatliche Sammlung dänischer und französischer Kunst des 19. Jahrhunderts im ehemaligen Anwesen des Sammlers Wilhelm Hansen. Auch hier entschied sich Zaha Hadid wieder für die Schaffung einer sehr eigenen Wechselbeziehung von Standort und Neubau: „Der neue Erweiterungsbau will mit seiner Architektur eine neue Landschaft schaffen und zugleich neue Beziehungen zur bestehenden Topografie knüpfen. Die Logik der bestehenden Landschaft wird geometrisch abstrahiert; neue Konturen greifen in die Sammlungsräume ein und definieren ein alternatives Terrain, das gängige Nutzungsbegriffe sprengt." Der 87 m lange und 20 m breite Neubau ist durch einen 5 m langen Gang mit dem Altbau verbunden; die Baukosten teilten sich das dänische Kultusministerium, die Fonden Realdania sowie die Augustin Fonden. Der Bau aus schwarzem Lava-Ortbeton erforderte aufgrund seiner komplexen geschwungenen Form einen Fertigungsprozess vor Ort, bei dem selbstverdichtender Beton von unten in die Schalung gepresst oder von außen durch Öffnungen in eine Außenschalung gepumpt wurde. Mit seinen geschwungenen Wänden, die in Böden und Decken übergehen, ist der Erweiterungsbau ein gelungenes Experiment, dessen Resultat ein Raumkontinuum ist, in dem die rechten Winkel, die das Haupthaus prägen, eher die Ausnahme als die Regel sind. Tatsächlich beharrt die Architektin selbst beim Übergang vom Innen- zum Außenraum oder von einem Gebäude zum anderen auf dieser fließenden Ästhetik. „So wird die Kritik des rechten Winkels von einem Konzept fließender Interaktion zwischen Garten und Innenraumprogramm abgelöst", sagt Hadid. „Diese dient der kontinuierlichen Abstufung, durch die sich verschiedene Bereiche definieren lassen, ohne im Raumkörper notwendigerweise Zäsuren zu schaffen." Die Verglasung lässt die Beziehung zwischen Gebäude und Topografie deutlich werden. Dank verschiedener Durchgänge in der kontinuierlichen Raumschale entstehen zahlreiche Übergangsmöglichkeiten zwischen den verschiedenen Bereichen.

Pour cette extension du Musée d'Ordrupgaard, consacré à l'art danois et français du XIXᵉ siècle situé dans l'ancienne résidence du collectionneur Wilhelm Hanse, Zaha Hadid a refris l'idée d'une relation distincte entre le cadre paysager et le nouveau bâtiment : « La nouvelle extension cherche à établir un nouveau paysage à l'intérieur du territoire de son architecture, tout en permettant de nouvelles relations avec l'environnement existant. La logique du paysage existant est tirée de la géométrie ; de nouvelles formes de contours se développent à travers la collection et créent un sol alternatif dont l'occupation et l'utilisation s'emparent. » Construit par le ministère danois de la Culture, la Fonden Realdania et Augustin Fonden, le nouveau bâtiment mesure 87 m de long et 20 de large, sans compter un passage de 5 m de large vers l'ancienne structure. Réalisées en béton de lave noire, les formes incurvées et complexes sont le résultat d'un processus de moulage *in situ* au cours duquel le béton était pressé dans les formes par le dessous, ou pompé vers une coque extérieure par des ouvertures. Les murs blancs évoluent en plafonds ou murs pour donner un espace continu dans lequel les lignes orthogonales de l'ancien musée sont l'exception plutôt que la règle. L'architecte insiste d'ailleurs sur la fluidité, y compris dans la transition entre l'intérieur et l'extérieur ou d'un bâtiment à l'autre. « Le point critique de la limite est ainsi remplacé par une notion d'interaction fluide entre le jardin et le programme interne, dit-elle, et agit comme une instrument permanent de progression, qui révèle les différents états, sans nécessairement rompre le volume vers le haut. » Des vitrages font comprendre la relation entre le bâtiment et la topographie, tandis que les ouvertures dans la coque offrent de multiples opportunités de mouvement d'une partie du musée à l'autre.

A plan (below) shows how the new extension with its curves and irregular forms relates to the original, orthogonal building. The natural setting is reflected in glazed surfaces seen to the left.

Ein Grundriss (unten) macht das Verhältnis des neuen Erweiterungsbaus mit seinen geschwungenen Linien und unregelmäßigen Formen zum orthogonal geprägten Altbau deutlich. Die Umgebung spiegelt sich in den verglasten Flächen, wie links zu sehen.

Le plan (ci-dessous) montre comment la nouvelle extension de formes et courbes irrégulières entre en relation avec le bâtiment d'origine qui est orthogonal. Sur les images de gauche, le cadre naturel se reflète dans les surfaces vitrées.

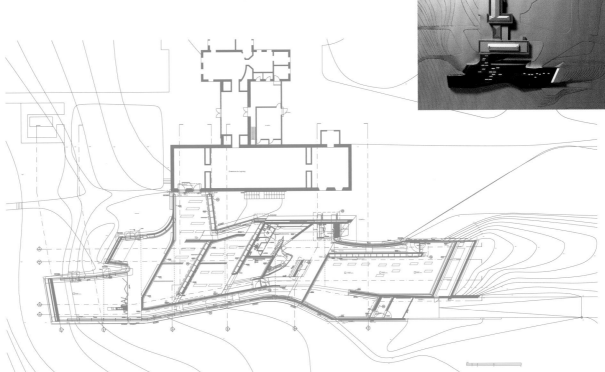

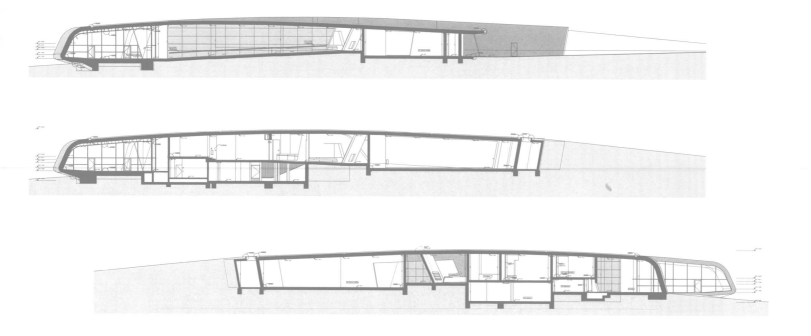

Sections of the building and the image below shows its generous openings, relationship to the natural setting and to the existing, much more traditionally designed structure.

Schnitte des Gebäudes und die Aufnahmen unten zeigen die großzügigen Öffnungen sowie das Verhältnis des Baus zur Landschaft und dem weitaus traditionelleren Altbau.

Les coupes et les images ci-dessous montrent les généreuses ouvertures et la relation avec le cadre naturel et le bâtiment existant beaucoup plus traditionnel.

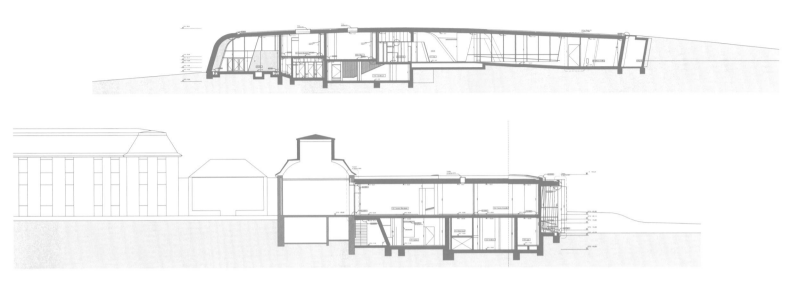

Through glazing and reflections, as well as in openings to the sky (right), the structure demonstrates a willful interpenetration with nature, while defining its own environment, which appears to spring from the site.

Mit seiner Verglasung und den Spiegeleffekten, ebenso wie den Öffnungen im Dach (rechts), lässt sich der Bau bewusst von der Natur durchdringen und definiert zugleich sein eigenes Umfeld, das vom Grundstück inspiriert scheint.

Par le biais des reflets, des transparences et des ouvertures vers le ciel (à droite), le bâtiment témoigne d'une interpénétration volontaire avec la nature, tout en définissant son propre environnement qui semble jaillir du sol.

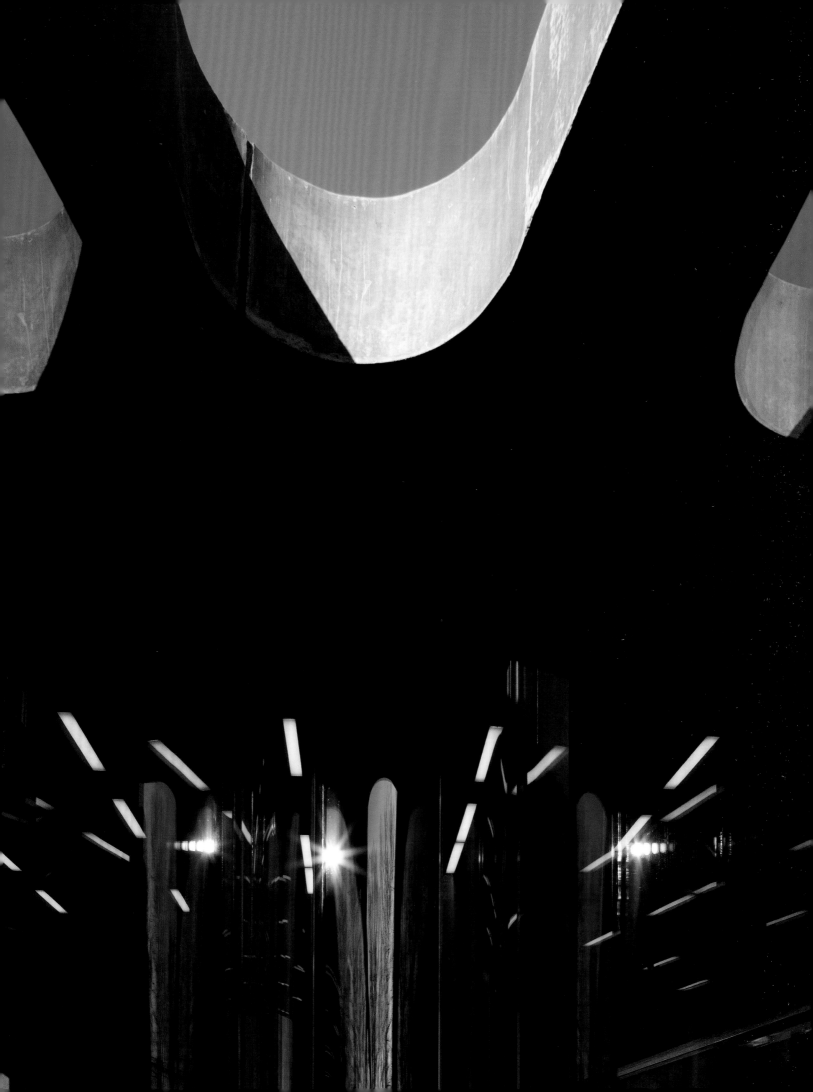

PHAENO
SCIENCE CENTER

Wolfsburg, Germany. 2000–05

Project
PHAENO SCIENCE CENTER

Location
WOLFSBURG, GERMANY

Client
NEULAND WOHNBAUGESELLSCHAFT MBH

Area/Size
12 000 m² SCIENCE CENTER
15 000 m² UNDERGROUND CAR PARK

On a larger scale than Hadid's earlier built work, the Phaeno Science Center appears to rear up from its setting, its irregular window pattern and fairly austere façade defining a new presence in contemporary architecture.

In größerem Maßstab als Hadids früher realisierte Bauten scheint das Phaeno-Wissenschaftszentrum aus seinem Umfeld aufzusteigen. Mit seinen unregelmäßig angeordneten Fensteröffnungen und der eher strengen Fassade definiert es eine neue Art von Präsenz in der zeitgenössischen Architektur.

De plus grande échelle que les premières réalisations de Zaha Hadid, le Centre des sciences Phaeno semble se dresser par rapport à son cadre. Le rythme irrégulier de ses ouvertures et sa façade assez austère définissent une forme de présence qui est nouvelle en architecture contemporaine.

The client for this building was the City of Wolfsburg and the user, the Phaeno Foundation. The construction cost was 79 million euros. Winner of an international competition in January 2000, Zaha Hadid imagined a structure that contains no less than 27 000 cubic meters of concrete, and yet is suspended, in good part, some seven meters above the ground. Explaining the unusual public space created beneath the Science Center, Hadid states: "The free ground is a modernist idea, but it was never an animated space. That's what I try to create." Located near the town's central train station and across the tracks from the VW manufacturing plant, the new building rests on ten asymmetrical cones, some of which contain a shop, a bar, and a bistro, as well as the museum entrance. The same cones penetrate the building and hold up the roof. The structure is nothing if not complex. Hadid states: "Phaeno is the most ambitious and complete statement of our quest for complex, dynamic, and fluid spaces. The visitor is faced with a degree of complexity and strangeness, ruled by a very specific system based on an unusual volumetric structural logic." As it is described by the users: "Phaeno provides hands-on, entertaining access to the phenomena of natural science and the principles of technology. Around 180 000 visitors are expected to play and experiment each year with its over 300 exhibits in the visitor labs, in the Ideas Forum, and in the Science Theater." Total visitor space is 9000 square meters with 5900 square meters devoted to the "exhibition landscape"; 54 square meters and 10 workplaces for the biology and chemistry lab; 118 square meters and 16 workplaces for the physics and technology lab; a 560-square-meter, 250-seat Science Theater; and the 370-square-meter Ideas Forum. Obviously sensitive to questions raised about the complexity of the building, Hadid declares: "Nobody thinks that landscape is strange because God made it, but if I make it, people think it's strange."

Auftraggeber für den Bau waren die Stadt Wolfsburg und der Gebäudenutzer, die Phaeno-Stiftung. Die Baukosten beliefen sich auf 79 Millionen Euro. Der Entwurf, der sich im Januar 2000 in einem Wettbewerb durchsetzen konnte, war von Zaha Hadid als Struktur aus nicht weniger als 27 000 m³ Beton konzipiert worden. Dennoch schwebt der Bau zu weiten Teilen etwa 7 m über dem Boden. In einer Stellungnahme zu dem so geschaffenen öffentlichen Raum unterhalb des Wissenschaftszentrums macht Zaha Hadid deutlich: „Der freie Baugrund ist eine Idee der Moderne, jedoch war er nie ein belebter Raum. Genau diesen versuche ich zu schaffen." Unweit des Bahnhofs und gegenüber der VW-Autostadt gelegen, erhebt sich der Bau auf zehn asymmetrischen kegelförmigen Stützen, in denen u. a. ein Geschäft, eine Bar, ein Bistro sowie der Museumseingang untergebracht sind. Die Stützen durchbohren die gesamte Konstruktion und tragen auch das Dach. Das Gebäude ist überaus komplex. Hadid erklärt: „Das Phaeno ist die bisher ehrgeizigste, umfassendste Manifestation unserer Suche nach komplexen, dynamischen und fließenden Räumen. Der Besucher sieht sich einer Komplexität

und Fremdheit gegenüber, die von einem sehr speziellen System gesteuert wird, das auf einer außergewöhnlichen volumetrischen strukturellen Logik gründet." Die Stiftung beschreibt den Komplex wie folgt: „Das Phaeno macht naturwissenschaftliche Phänomene und technische Vorgänge zugänglich – unterhaltsam und zum Anfassen. Pro Jahr werden etwa 180 000 Besucher erwartet, um mit den über 300 Exponaten in den Besucherlaboren, dem Ideenforum und dem Wissenschaftstheater zu spielen und zu experimentieren." Die Besucherfläche beträgt insgesamt 9000 m², davon entfallen 5900 m² auf die „Ausstellungslandschaft", 54 m² auf die zehn Arbeitsplätze im Biologie- und Chemielabor, 118 m² auf die 16 Arbeitsplätze im Physik- und Techniklabor, 560 m² auf ein Wissenschaftstheater mit 250 Plätzen und 370 m² auf das Ideenforum. Offenbar sensibel für die Fragen, die bezüglich der Komplexität des Gebäudes laut geworden sind, erklärt Hadid: „Niemand findet Landschaften seltsam, schließlich hat Gott sie geschaffen; wenn ich sie schaffe, findet man sie merkwürdig."

Le commanditaire de ce bâtiment de était la ville elle-même, et l'utilisateur final, la Fondation Phaeno. Pour un budget de 79 millions d'euros. Pour ce projet, dont elle a remporté le concours international en janvier 2000, Zaha Hadid a conçu une structure qui a demandé pas moins de 27 000 m³ de béton tout en étant pour une bonne partie suspendue, parfois à quelque 7 m au-dessus du sol. Pour expliquer la création de l'espace public inhabituel sous le Centre des Sciences, Zaha Hadid précise : « Le sol libre est une idée moderniste, mais ce ne fut jamais un espace animé. C'est ce que j'ai essayé de faire. » Situé près de la gare principale, de l'autre côté des voies de desserte de l'usine Volkswagen, le bâtiment repose sur dix cônes asymétriques, dont certains contiennent une boutique, un café, un bistro ou l'entrée du musée. Les mêmes cônes pénètrent le bâtiment et soutiennent la couverture. La structure est d'une très grande complexité. Selon Zaha Hadid : « Phaeno est matérialisation la plus ambitieuse et la plus complète de nos recherches sur les espaces complexes dynamiques et fluides. Le visiteur est confronté à un degré élevé de complexité et d'étrangeté, régi par un système très spécifique reposant sur une logique structurelle volumétrique inhabituelle. » Selon la description donnée, « Phaeno offre un accès libre, pratique et engageant aux phénomènes des sciences naturelles et aux principes de la technologie. Environ 180 000 visiteurs sont attendus chaque année pour découvrir et expérimenter les trois cent pièces exposées dans les laboratoires, le Forum des idées et le Théâtre de la Science. » Neuf mille mètres carrés sont consacrés à la visite, dont 5900 m² destinés au « paysage d'expositions » ; 54 m² et 10 postes de travail au laboratoire de biologie et de chimie ; 118 m² et 16 postes à celui de physique et de technologie ; 560 m² et 250 places au Théâtre de la Science ; et 370 m² au Forum des Idées. Sensible aux questions soulevées par la complexité du bâtiment, Zaha Hadid a déclaré : « Personne ne pense qu'un paysage est étrange, parce que Dieu l'a créé, mais si c'est moi qui le conçoit, les gens pensent qu'il est bizarre. »

The strong cantilever visible in images here and in the elevations bottom right are surely characteristic of Zaha Hadid's designs, but here, as always, the actual form of the building is a surprise, and needs to be viewed from every angle to be fully understood.

Die in den Aufnahmen hier und den Aufrissen unten rechts deutlich sichtbare Auskragung ist ohne Frage typisch für Hadids Entwürfe. Dennoch ist die tatsächliche Form des Gebäudes hier, wie auch sonst, eine Überraschung und muss aus jedem Blickwinkel betrachtet werden, um wirklich verstanden zu werden.

Le puissant porte-à-faux, visible sur ces images et dans l'élévation ci-dessous à droite, est certainement caractéristique du style de Zaha Hadid mais, comme toujours, la forme réelle du bâtiment reste une surprise et doit être observée sous tous ses angles pour être pleinement appréhendée.

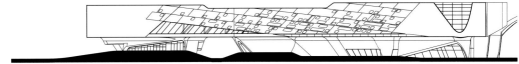

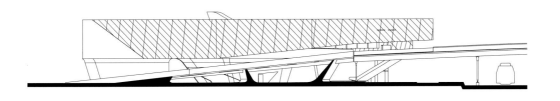

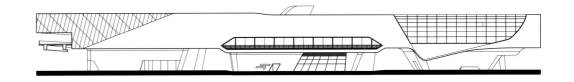

With its deliberate irregularity and forward-leaning design, the building almost appears to be in motion despite its consequential mass. A large inverted bell-shaped window further adds to the structure's sculptural presence.

Dank seiner bewussten Unregelmäßigkeit und der Neigung nach vorn wirkt der Bau geradezu wie in Bewegung – trotz seiner nicht unerheblichen Masse. Das große Fenster in Form einer auf dem Kopf stehenden Gauß-Kurve steigert die skulpturale Präsenz des Baus zusätzlich.

Par le biais de ses ouvertures volontairement irrégulières et de son inclinaison vers l'avant, le bâtiment semble pratiquement en mouvement malgré sa masse conséquente. Une importante baie en forme de cloche inversée renforce la présence sculpturale du musée.

Here, we see the dark interior with its irregular glazing admitting some natural light, together with some views to the exterior.

Diese Ansicht zeigt die dunkle Atmosphäre im Innern des Baus, in den die unregelmäßigen Fenster natürliches Licht einfallen lassen und vereinzelt Durchblicke nach draußen erlauben.

Image de l'atmosphère intérieure sombre et des ouvertures à implantation irrégulière qui laissent passer un peu de lumière naturelle et offrent quelques perspectives sur l'extérieur.

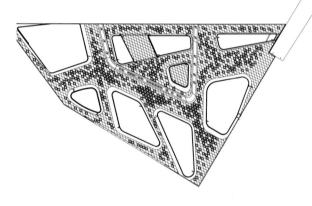

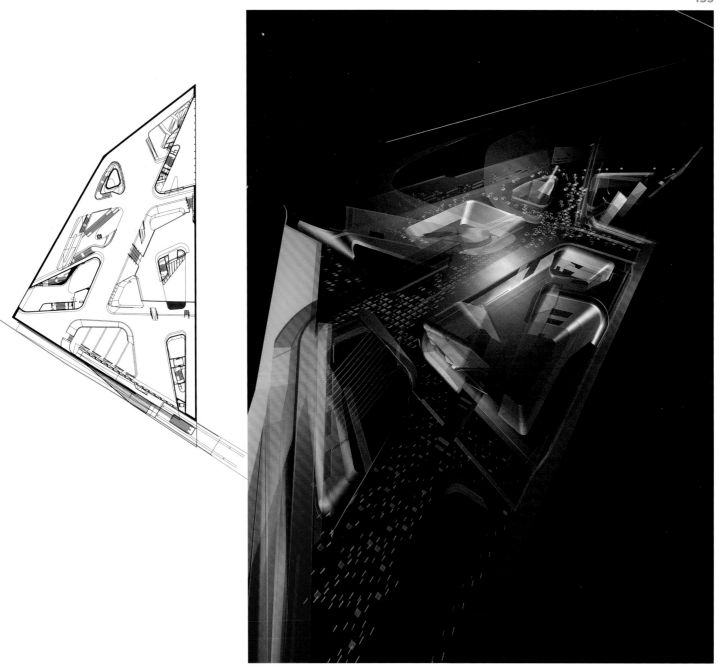

Hadid's forms seem to have something of the apparent irregularity of nature. Ideally, her architecture is not organic per se, but it is composed by means of a layered process and a continual superposing of elements, resulting in a logic that is fundamentally natural.

Hadids Formen haben etwas von der deutlichen Unregelmäßigkeit der Natur. Im Idealfall ist ihre Architektur jedoch nicht organisch, sondern entsteht im Zuge eines Schichtprozesses und einer kontinuierlichen Übereinanderlagerung von Elementen, woraus eine im Kern natürliche Logik erwächst.

Les formes de Hadid possèdent quelque chose de l'irrégularité apparente de la nature. Son architecture n'est pas organique en soi, mais se compose dans un processus de strates et de superpositions continues des éléments pour exprimer une logique fondamentalement naturelle.

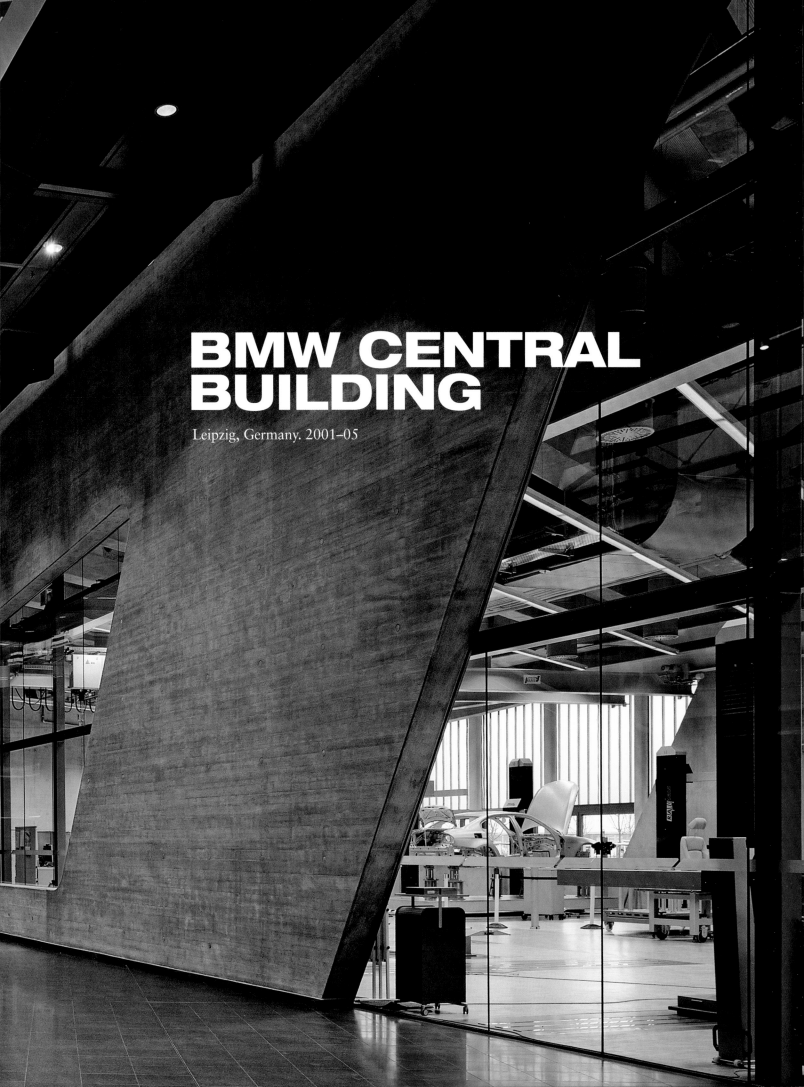

BMW CENTRAL BUILDING

Leipzig, Germany. 2001–05

Project
BMW CENTRAL BUILDING

Location
LEIPZIG, GERMANY

Client
BMW AG

Area/Size
25 000 m²

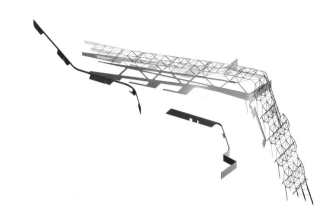

Zaha Hadid speaks of the transition between manufacturing and public space in terms of "mediation" and her very interesting ambition here is to reconcile the movement of car assembly with that of office and individual traffic.

Zaha Hadid beschreibt den Übergang zwischen industrieller Fertigung und öffentlichem Raum als „Mediation". Ihr zweifellos interessantes Anliegen ist hier, die Dynamik der Fließbänder in der Autofertigung und die Dynamik der Büros und der individuellen Fortbewegung miteinander zu verbinden.

Zaha Hadid parle de la transition entre les espaces réservés à la construction des voitures et ceux ouverts au public en termes de « médiation ». Son ambition est ici de réconcilier le mouvement de l'assemblage des voitures avec les déplacements des individus, visiteurs ou employés.

Simply put, in the words of the architect: "It was the client's objective to translate industrial architecture into an aesthetic concept that complies equally with representational and functional requirements. In the transition zones between manufacturing halls and public space the Central Building acts as a 'mediator,' impressing a positive permanent impact upon the eye of the beholder in a restrained semiotic way." Zaha Hadid was asked to design this building, described as the "nerve center of the whole factory complex," subsequent to an April 2002 competition she won, when the layout of adjacent manufacturing buildings had already been decided. Suppliers chosen for the rest of the factory provided many prefabricated elements, in harmony with the "industrial approach to office spaces" decided by BMW. Used as the entrance to the entire plant, the Central Building connects the three main manufacturing departments. The nerve-center concept is rendered all the more clear in that "the central area as a 'market place' is intended to enhance communication by providing staff with an area in which to avail themselves of personal and administrative services." A system of cascading floors allows views of different parts of the manufacturing process, ranging from assembly to the auditing area, described as "a central focus of everybody's attention." The building itself is made with "self-compacting concrete and a roof structure assembled with a series of H-steel beams." The architect intends to use the architecture to create an "overall transparency of the internal organization," but also to mix functions "to avoid the traditional segregation of status groups." Particular attention was also paid to the inevitable parking area in front of the building by "turning it into a dynamic spectacle in its own right."

Die Architektin fasst in einfachen Worten zusammen: „Die Absicht des Auftraggebers war es, Industriearchitektur in ein ästhetisches Konzept zu übersetzen, das repräsentativen und funktionalen Anforderungen gleichermaßen gerecht wird. In den Übergangszonen zwischen den Werkshallen und den öffentlichen Bereichen wird das Zentralgebäude zum ‚Vermittler' und hinterlässt beim Betrachter auf verhalten semiotische Weise bleibenden Eindruck." Zaha Hadid erhielt den Auftrag für dieses Gebäude, das als „Nervenzentrum der gesamten Fabrikanlage" dienen soll, nachdem sie im April 2002 den entsprechenden Wettbewerb gewonnen hatte. Die Lage der benachbarten Werksbauten stand zu diesem Zeitpunkt bereits fest. Zulieferer für die übrigen Gebäude lieferten vorgefertigte Bauelemente, die der von BMW gewünschten „industriellen Anmutung des Bürogebäudes" entsprachen. Das Zentralgebäude, zugleich Zugang zum gesamten Werksgelände, verbindet drei Hauptfertigungsbereiche. Besonders deutlich

wird die konzeptuelle Vorstellung von einem „Nervenzentrum" daran, dass „der Kernbereich als ‚Marktplatz' dazu dienen soll, Kommunikation zu fördern, indem er der Belegschaft einen Raum bietet, in dem sie Service- und Verwaltungsleistungen nutzen kann". Ein stufenartiges Etagensystem erlaubt Einblicke in verschiedene Fertigungsprozesse, von der Montage bis zur Revision – ein „zentraler Blickpunkt für alle". Der Bau selbst wurde aus „selbstverdichtendem Beton und einer Dachkonstruktion aus Breitflanschträgern" realisiert. Absicht der Architektin ist es, „die interne Organisationsstruktur insgesamt transparent" werden zu lassen, und „die traditionelle Trennung der verschiedenen Berufsgruppen zu vermeiden". Besondere Aufmerksamkeit wurde auch dem unvermeidlichen Parkplatz vor dem Gebäude gewidmet, der als „dynamisches Schauspiel" interpretiert wurde.

L'architecte explique avec simplicité son projet : « L'objectif du client était de traduire une architecture industrielle dans un concept esthétique qui corresponde autant à ses attentes en matière de fonctions que de représentation. Dans les zones de transition entre les halls de fabrication et l'espace public, ce Bâtiment central joue un rôle de "médiateur" qui s'impose en permanence positivement au regard du spectateur d'une manière sémiotique subtile. » C'est en 2002 que Zaha Hadid remporté le concours pour ce « centre nerveux du complexe industriel BMW », alors que les plans des bâtiments de fabrication adjacents avaient déjà été décidés. Les sous-traitants choisis pour le reste de l'usine ont fourni de nombreux éléments préfabriqués correspondant à « l'approche industrielle des espaces de bureaux » décidée par BMW. Servant d'entrée au complexe, le bâtiment connecte les trois principaux départements de fabrication. Le concept de centre nerveux est d'autant plus clair dans ce traitement que « la zone centrale est considérée comme une "place de marché" qui facilite la communication, en permettant au personnel de bénéficier d'un espace où il peut profiter de multiples services administratifs et individuels. » Un système de plateaux en cascade ouvre des perspectives sur différentes phases du processus de fabrication, de l'assemblage au contrôle, décrit comme « le focus de l'attention de chacun ». Le bâtiment lui-même est en « béton autocompactant. La structure de couverture est en poutres d'acier à profil en H. » L'architecte voulait mettre à profit l'architecture pour créer « une transparence globale de l'organisation interne », mais également pour mélanger les fonctions « afin d'éviter la ségrégation traditionnelle des statuts des groupes ». Une attention particulière a également été portée à l'inévitable parking devant le bâtiment, en « le transformant en un spectacle dynamique en soi ».

As the examples on these two pages demonstrate, the reality of Zaha Hadid Architects' built work corresponds quite closely to the surprise engendered by and the dynamism of the drawings.

Wie die Beispiele auf diesen beiden Seiten unter Beweis stellen, entspricht die Realität der gebauten Projekte recht genau der Atmosphäre, die die Zeichnungen Hadids vermitteln, so überraschend und dynamisch sie auch sein mögen.

Comme le montrent les exemples donnés par ces deux pages, aussi surprenants et dynamiques puissent être les plans et dessins de Zaha Hadid Architects, la réalité du bâti correspond d'assez près à l'impression qu'ils donnent.

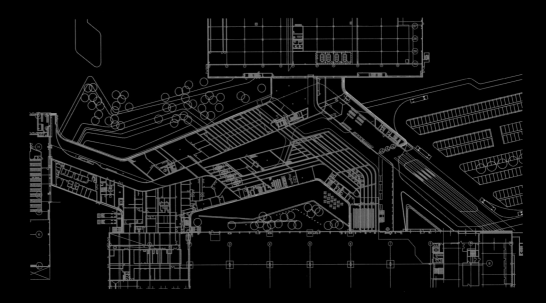

Despite the rather unexpected appearance of the perspective drawings from Zaha Hadid Architects, the photos to the left give a very similar impression. And plans like the one above reveal a high degree of organization that is far from the purely "aesthetic" impression that some people have of the architect's work.

Trotz der recht ungewöhnlichen Optik der Perspektivzeichnungen Hadids, vermitteln die Aufnahmen auf der linken Seite einen ähnlichen Eindruck. Grundrisse wie der hier gezeigte (oben) zeugen von einem hohen Grad an Organisation, die alles andere als rein „ästhetisch" ist, obwohl manche das Werk der Architektin dafür halten.

Malgré l'aspect assez surprenant de ces perspectives dessinées, les photos de gauche donnent une impression très similaire. Les plans, comme celui ci-dessus, révèlent un degré élevé d'organisation, loin de l'impression purement « esthétique » que certains ont de l'œuvre de l'architecte.

Although elements such as the beams give an industrial feel to the space, there is an openness and clarity that emerge from the continuous volumes, created almost less by the architect than by the needs of the building itself.

Obwohl der Raum durch Elemente wie die Stützen einen industriellen Charakter erhält, ist er auch von einer Offenheit und Klarheit, die aus der Kontinuität der Volumina entsteht, die wiederum weniger von der Architektin geschaffen, als vielmehr aus den Anforderungen des Gebäudes zu erwachsen scheinen.

Même si des éléments comme les poutres c une impression d'installation industrielle, on o une ouverture et une clarté dans ces volume continus qui semblent moins créés par l'arc que par les besoins du bâtiment.

Sweeping bands and broad curves that seem to complement the straight lines here create an impression of unbroken movement. Though there is certainly complexity in the plan, the spaces seem to be completely clear and open.

Dynamisch ausgreifende Bänder und weite Schwünge scheinen alle geraden Linien zu ergänzen und schaffen den Eindruck ungebrochener Bewegung. Obwohl der Grundriss durchaus komplex ist, wirken die Räume absolut klar und offen.

Des bandeaux enveloppants et des courbes généreuses semblent venir en complément des axes rectilignes pour donner une impression de mouvement sans rupture. Bien que le plan soit certainement complexe, les espaces restent entièrement lisibles et ouverts.

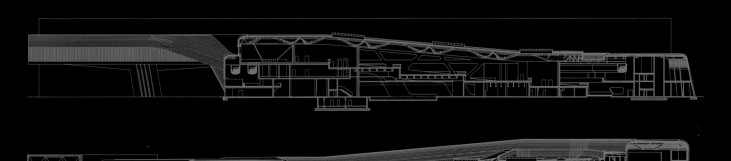

HOTEL
PUERTA AMÉRICA

Madrid, Spain. 2003–05

Project

HOTEL
PUERTA AMÉRICA

Location
MADRID, SPAIN

Client
HOTELES SILKEN, GRUPO URVASCO

Area/Size
1200 m²

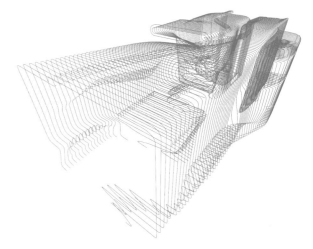

With its 12 floors and 342 rooms, the Puerta América is relatively large on the scale of the fashionable "designer" hotels that have sprung up all over the world in the past 15 years. Run by the Silken Group, the Puerta América does pose some questions about the nature of the collaboration of no less than 19 internationally recognized architects and designers. As the promotional material for the hotel declares: "At the Hotel Puerta América, the guest discovers the finest cutting-edge design and architecture almost without even realizing it." This may or may not be flattering for the talents involved. Jean Nouvel designed the façade and the 12th floor of this very unusual collaborative project with a location not far from the airport, but less central than might have been hoped. The first floor, "characterized by the fluidity of the spaces based on new developments in digital design," is the work of Zaha Hadid. Other figures involved include David Chipperfield, Marc Newson, Arata Isozaki, and John Pawson. Zaha Hadid explains that the client gave her full leeway to design the floor, including 30 rooms and the common areas. She sought clearly to create "a fluid space and a seamless experience." As she stated: "We took the opportunity to create a new domestic language of architecture, driven by new developments in digital design and enhanced manufacturing capabilities. This new dialogue emphasizes the complex and continuous nature of the design and the merging of disparate forms and texture." From the elevator area to the rooms, all the surfaces are continuous flowing spaces. Within the rooms, colored in black or white and sometimes orange, all surfaces are continuous—desk, bed, and bathroom are all seamlessly united, as are floors and ceilings to the walls. The architect used digital designs "directly transferred from our computer generated files to CNC milling machines which are used to create wooden (MDF) molds for the thermoforming process of the white LG HI-MACS surface." It is this process and the thermoformable material that allowed the architects to obtain a truly seamless surface throughout.

Mit zwölf Stockwerken und 342 Zimmern ist das Puerta América ein vergleichsweise großes „Designerhotel", wie sie in den letzten 15 Jahren in Mode gekommen und weltweit aus dem Boden geschossen sind. Betrieben wird das Puerta América von der Silken-Gruppe. Ein Hotel wie dieses wirft die Frage auf, wie eine Kooperation von nicht weniger als 19 international renommierten Architekten und Designern wohl aussehen mag. Im Werbematerial des Hotels heißt es: „Im Hotel Puerta América entdeckt der Gast anspruchsvollstes, hochmodernes Design und Architektur fast nebenbei." Ob dies nun als Kompliment für die Beteiligten zu verstehen ist, sei dahingestellt. Jean Nouvel gestaltete die Fassade und die zwölfte Etage dieses ungewöhnlichen Gemeinschaftsprojekts, das nicht weit vom Flughafen, jedoch nicht ganz so zentral liegt, wie man sich hätte wünschen können. Zaha Hadids Werk ist die erste Etage, „charakterisiert durch fließende Räume, deren Realisierung dank neuartiger digitaler Entwurfswerkzeuge möglich war". Beteiligt waren außerdem David Chipperfield, Marc Newson, Arata Isozaki und John Pawson. Zaha Hadid berichtet, der Auftraggeber habe ihr freie Hand bei der Gestaltung der gesamten Etage einschließlich der 30 Zimmer und der Gemeinschaftsflächen gelassen. Es ging ihr ganz offensichtlich darum, „fließende Räume und ein Raumerlebnis ohne Kanten" zu gestalten. Sie führt aus: „Wir nutzten die

Gelegenheit, eine neuartige Form von Wohnarchitektur zu prägen, getragen von neuen Entwicklungen in der digitalen Gestaltung und neuen Fertigungsmöglichkeiten. Dieser neue Dialog unterstreicht die Komplexität und Kontinuität des Entwurfs und das Verschmelzen unterschiedlichster Formen und Texturen." Von den Aufzügen bis hin zu den Zimmern sind sämtliche Oberflächen nahtlos fließend gestaltet. Auch in den Zimmern selbst, die in Schwarz oder Weiß oder vereinzelt in Orange gehalten sind, sind alle Oberflächen als Kontinuum definiert – Schreibtisch, Bett und Badezimmer gehen fugenlos ineinander über, ebenso wie Böden und Decken nahtlos in Wände übergehen. Die Architektin arbeitete mit digitalen Entwürfen, die „mithilfe unserer Computerdateien direkt in die CNC-Fertigungsmaschinen eingespeist wurden, mit denen Gussformen aus MDF erstellt wurden, die für den Wärmeformungsprozess der weißen LG-HI-MACS-Oberflächen erforderlich waren". Dieser Prozess und das thermoformbare Material erlaubten der Architektin, überall tatsächlich nahtlose Oberflächen zu realisieren.

Comptant 12 niveaux et 342 chambres, le Puerta América est un « designer hôtel » relativement vaste pour cette catégorie, qui a essaimé dans le monde entier depuis une quinzaine d'années. Géré par le Silken Group, le Puerta América soulève certainement des questions sur la problématique que peut poser un appel à collaborations multiples, lancé à pas moins de dix-neuf architectes et designers de réputation internationale. Comme l'hôtel l'annonce dans ses documents promotionnels : « À l'hôtel Puerta América, l'hôte découvre l'avant-garde la plus raffinée du design et de l'architecture, presque sans le réaliser … » – une remarque qui peut être diversement appréciée par les talents choisis pour y œuvrer. Jean Nouvel a conçu la façade et le 12e niveau de ce projet très original situé à proximité de l'aéroport de Barrajas, donc moins central qu'on aurait pu le souhaiter. Le rez-de-chaussée, « caractérisé par la fluidité des espaces obtenue grâce à de nouveaux développements de la conception assistée par ordinateur », est l'œuvre de Zaha Hadid. Parmi les autres intervenants figurent David Chipperfield, Marc Newson, Arata Isozaki et John Pawson. Zaha Hadid a expliqué que son client lui avait laissé toute liberté pour sa partie du projet qui couvrait 30 chambres et les parties communes. Elle a cherché à créer « un espace fluide dans une expérience continue, sans rupture … Nous avons ainsi eu l'opportunité de créer un nouveau langage domestique de l'architecture, grâce à de récents développements en CAO associés à de nouvelles possibilités de fabrication. Ce dialogue met en exergue la nature complexe et continue du projet et la fusion de formes et de textures disparates. » De la zone des ascenseurs jusqu'aux chambres, toutes les surfaces sont traitées en espaces fluides continus. À l'intérieur des chambres, colorées en noir ou blanc ou parfois en orange, toutes les surfaces sont dans la continuité : lit, bureau, salle de bains sont pris dans une sorte flux, de même que les sols, les plafonds et les murs. L'architecte a utilisé des techniques numériques « à transfert direct entre nos ordinateurs et les machines de fabrication également pilotées par informatique, qui servent à créer des moules en bois (MDF) pour le thermoformage des plans en LG HI-MACS blanc ». C'est ce processus et le matériau thermoformable utilisé qui ont permis d'obtenir des plans sans la moindre rupture.

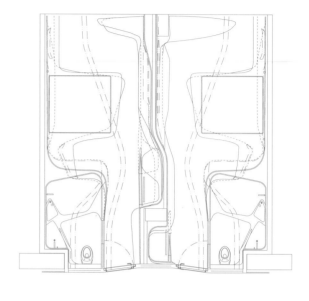

Whether in black or white, the principle of the Zaha Hadid rooms at the Hotel Puerta América is the same—an astonishing continuity between walls, ceilings, and floors, as well as the furniture, which seems to emerge fully formed from the very substance of the space.

Ob nun in Schwarz oder Weiß, das Prinzip der von Zaha Hadid gestalteten Zimmer im Hotel Puerta América bleibt dasselbe – eine überraschende Kontinuität von Wänden, Decken und Böden, bis hin zum gesamten Mobiliar der Zimmer, das formvollendet aus dem Raum herauszuwachsen scheint.

Que ces chambres de l'Hôtel Puerta América soient traitées en blanc ou noir, leur principe d'aménagement reste le même : une étonnante continuité entre les murs, les plafonds, les sols et le mobilier intégré qui semble émerger sous sa forme définitive de la substance même de l'espace.

A drawing (below) shows how the continuity of the space is imagined, while images taken in a white room show how colored lighting can change the ambiance.

Eine Zeichnung (unten) veranschaulicht, wie das räumliche Kontinuum entwickelt wurde. Die in einem weißen Zimmer entstandenen Aufnahmen zeigen, wie farbige Beleuchtung die Stimmung verändern kann.

Le dessin ci-dessous montre l'approche de continuité de l'espace. Les images prises dans une des chambres blanches illustrent les changements d'ambiance apportés par l'éclairage.

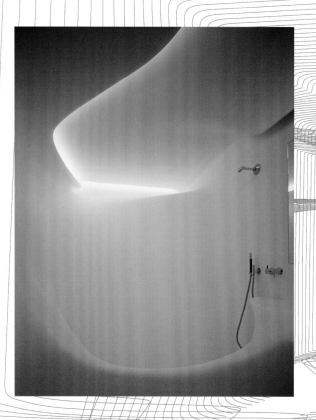

MAGGIE'S CANCER CARE CENTRE FIFE

Kirkcaldy, Fife, Scotland, UK. 2001–06

Project
MAGGIE'S CANCER CARE CENTRE FIFE

Location
KIRKCALDY, FIFE, SCOTLAND, UK

Client
MAGGIE'S CANCER CARING CENTRES

Area/Size
250 m²

A dramatic wedge-like form seen from below in the image on the left page, and in elevations above on this page, the Centre is cantilevered in part over a natural slope.

Das Centre ist ein dramatisches, keilförmiges Volumen, das links in der Untersicht und oben auf Aufrissen zu sehen ist und teilweise über einen natürlichen Abhang auskragt.

Avec sa forme de cale spectaculaire (vue en contrebas page de gauche et dans les élévations de cette page), le Centre est en partie en porte-à-faux au-dessus d'une pente naturelle.

Maggie's Centres are a network of daycare facilities in the United Kingdom founded by and named after Maggie Keswick Jencks, the late wife of the architecture critic Charles Jencks. An emphasis on architectural quality has been placed on recent designs, including Frank O. Gehry's first building in the United Kingdom, the Maggie's Centre in Dundee, and the new building in London, at Charing Cross Hospital, by Richard Rogers. Maggie's Centre Fife was the first building by Zaha Hadid to be built in the United Kingdom. Located at Victoria Hospital in Kirkcaldy, the brief required a "relaxed atmosphere where people can access additional support outside of the more clinical hospital environment." Hadid knew Maggie Keswick Jencks and says: "She had a unique ability to make everyone feel special by giving them the time and space to express and be themselves. As a friend of mine, it was important that this unique quality was in some way translated into my design for Maggie's Fife. I hope that the look and feel of the Centre in some way enhances a visitor's experience and provides a warm and welcoming place for them to relax and access the support they need." Located at the edge of a hollow area, the building is envisaged as a transitional space between the natural environment and the neighboring hospital. Hadid used a folding surface to link the two different environments, and shimmering black ceiling and walls, coated with black liquid polyurethane with silicon carbide grit combined with translucent and clear glass elevations. Sharply angled overhangs and a concrete plinth that extends into the site emphasize the feeling of continuity created by the architect.

Die Maggie's Centres in Großbritannien sind Tageskliniken, die von Maggie Keswick Jencks, der verstorbenen Frau des Architekturkritikers Charles Jencks, gegründet und nach ihr benannt wurden. Bei neueren Bauten für die Organisation wurde besonderer Wert auf architektonische Qualität gelegt, etwa bei Frank O. Gehrys erstem Bau in Großbritannien, dem Maggie's Centre in Dundee, oder einem von Richard Rogers realisierten Neubau am Londoner Charing Cross Hospital. Maggie's Centre Fife war Hadids erstes realisiertes Bauvorhaben in Großbritannien. Der an das Victoria Hospital in Kirkcaldy angeschlossene Bau sollte laut Vorgaben eine „entspannte Atmosphäre schaffen, in der Patienten außerhalb des eher klinischen Krankenhausumfelds Hilfe in Anspruch nehmen können". Hadid kannte Maggie Keswick Jencks persönlich und sagt über sie: „Sie hatte die einzigartige Fähigkeit, jedem das Gefühl zu geben, etwas Besonderes zu sein, indem sie einem Zeit und Raum gab, sich auszudrücken und man selbst zu sein. Weil sie eine Freundin war, ist es mir wichtig, diese Einzigartigkeit in

meinem Entwurf für Maggie's Fife umzusetzen. Ich hoffe, das Zentrum kann die Erfahrungen der Patienten durch sein Erscheinungsbild und seine Atmosphäre in irgendeiner Weise leichter machen und ihnen ein warmer Ort sein, an dem sie sich willkommen fühlen, entspannen können und die Hilfe bekommen, die sie brauchen." An der Kante einer Bodensenke gelegen, fungiert der Bau als Übergang zwischen Landschaft und dem benachbarten Krankenhaus. Um zwischen den beiden Umfeldern zu vermitteln, arbeitete Hadid mit einer gefalteten Außenhaut, schimmernden schwarzen Decken und Wänden, die mit flüssigem schwarzem Polyurethan und Siliziumkarbidsand versiegelt wurden, sowie mit Milch- und Klarverglasung. Scharfkantige Überstände und ein in das Grundstück ausgreifender Betonsockel verstärken den Eindruck eines von der Architektin definierten Raumkontinuums.

Les Centres Maggie sont un réseau de dispensaires britannique qui a pris le nom de sa fondatrice Maggie Keswick Jencks, épouse disparue du critique d'architecture Charles Jencks. La Fondation, qui s'intéresse à la qualité architecturale, a récemment fait travailler Frank Gehry, qui a ainsi réalisé son premier projet au Royaume-Uni, à Dundee, et Richard Rogers pour un nouveau bâtiment à l'hôpital de Charing Cross à Londres. Le Maggie's Centre Fife est la première réalisation de Zaha Hadid en Grande-Bretagne. Situé dans l'hôpital Victoria à Kirkcaldy, il répond parfaitement à son programme : « Créer une atmosphère détendue où les gens peuvent recevoir un soutien supplémentaire en dehors d'un environnement plus clinique. » Hadid qui connaissait Maggie Keswick Jencks a déclaré : « Elle avait cette capacité unique à faire que chacun se sente quelqu'un de spécial en lui offrant le temps et l'espace pour s'exprimer. Elle était l'une de mes amies et j'ai pensé qu'il était important que cette qualité humaine exceptionnelle se traduise d'une certaine façon dans mon projet. J'espère que le style et le ressenti du Centre rendent plus agréable le passage de chaque patient, en lui proposant un lieu chaleureux et accueillant où il peut se détendre et avoir accès aux soutiens dont il a besoin. » Situé en bordure d'une zone en creux, le bâtiment est conçu comme un espace de transition entre l'environnement naturel et l'hôpital voisin. Hadid a utilisé un principe de plan replié pour relier ces deux environnements. Les murs et les plafonds enduits d'un polyuréthane noir liquide à trame de silicone de carbone sont de couleur noire luisante, et interrompus par des élévations de verre translucide ou transparent. Des porte-à-faux fortement inclinés et une plinthe en béton qui se prolonge sur le terrain mettent en valeur le sentiment de continuité recherché par l'architecte.

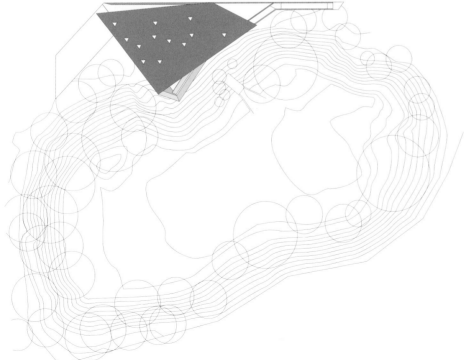

A night view (above) shows the Centre with the Victoria Hospital behind it. To the left, a site plan showing the building as a dark quadrilateral at the top of the drawing.

Eine nächtliche Ansicht (oben) zeigt das Centre mit dem Victoria Hospital im Hintergrund. Links ein Lageplan, der den Bau als dunkles Tetragon im oberen Bereich der Zeichnung zeigt.

Une vue de nuit (ci-dessus) montre le Centre devant le Victoria Hospital. À gauche, le plan au sol montre en partie haute le nouveau bâtiment sous la forme d'un quadrilatère noir.

The Centre faces greenery on one side and the Hospital on the other, rising up from its site with this situation as part of the natural solution devised by Zaha Hadid in this instance. Its dark volume contrasts with the surroundings, but glazing provides ample connection to the environment.

Das Centre grenzt auf einer Seite an Grünflächen, auf der anderen an das Krankenhaus und erhebt sich auf seinem Grundstück in einem Kontext, den Hadid hier als natürliche Lösung entwickelt hat. Sein dunkler Baukörper kontrastiert mit dem Umfeld, doch die großzügige Verglasung sorgt für eine klare Einbindung in die Umgebung.

Le Centre donne sur des espaces verts d'un côté et sur l'hôpital de l'autre. Sa surélévation par rapport au sol fait partie de la solution d'intégration à la nature recherchée par Zaha Hadid. Les volumes sombres contrastent avec leur environnement, mais les baies vitrées procurent un lien généreux avec la nature.

Triangular windows and openings dot an interior space. Models show the folded form with its and sharp angles. Right page, interior views emphasizing the frequent exterior views afforded by full-height glazing.

Dreiecksfenster und Wandöffnungen durchziehen einen der Innenräume. Modelle zeigen die gefaltete Bauform mit ihren Oberlichtern und scharfen Kanten. Innenansichten (rechts) unterstreichen die vielfältigen Ausblicke durch die deckenhohe Verglasung.

L'espace intérieur se caractérise par des fenêtres et des ouvertures triangulaires. Les maquettes montrent la forme pliée, les verrières et les angles vifs. À droite, vues illustrant les nombreuses perspectives des ouvertures en hauteur.

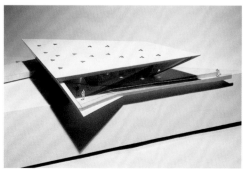
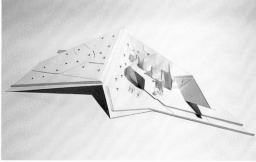

NORDPARK
RAILWAY STATIONS

Innsbruck, Austria. 2004–07

Project
NORDPARK RAILWAY STATIONS

Location
INNSBRUCK, AUSTRIA

Client
INNSBRUCKER NORDKETTENBAHNEN GMBH, PUBLIC PRIVATE PARTNERSHIP

Area/Size
2500 m²

The spectacular arched opening seen in the image to the left emphasizes the possible similarity of this project to the ice formations seen in the region. Below, forms of the stations on the line.

Die spektakuläre geschwungene Öffnung links im Bild unterstreicht die Ähnlichkeit des Projekts mit Eisformationen in der Gegend. Unten die formale Gestaltung der einzelnen Stationen der Bergbahn.

La spectaculaire ouverture en arc (à gauche) renforce l'impression de similarité avec les formations glaciaires de la région. Ci-dessous, les différentes gares construites le long de la ligne.

Inaugurated on December 1, 2007, the Nordpark Cable Railway consists of four new stations and a cable-stayed suspension bridge over the River Inn. The roof surface of the four stations built for the INKB (Innsbrucker Nordkettenbahnen GmbH) Public Private Partnership is a total of 2500 square meters. The railway runs from the Congress Station in the center of the city, up the Nordkette Mountain to the Hungerburg Station, 288 meters above Innsbruck. Hadid had previously completed the Bergisel Ski Jump in the Austrian city (1999–2002; see page 156). The architect won a 2005 competition for the Nordpark project together with the contractor Strabag. Adapting her designs to the specific locations of each station, Zaha Hadid employed "an overall language of fluidity." According to the architect: "We studied natural phenomena, such as glacial moraines and ice movements, as we wanted each station to use the fluid language of natural ice formations, like a frozen stream on the mountainside." Double-curvature glass on top of concrete plinths forms an "artificial landscape." Recently available fabrication methods, such as CNC milling and glass thermoforming, allowed the use of computer design and production with some techniques borrowed from the automotive industry.

Der am 1. Dezember 2007 eingeweihte Abschnitt der Nordkettenbahn besteht aus vier neuen Stationen und einer Schrägseilbrücke über den Inn. Die Dachfläche der vier Stationen, die für die INKB (Innsbrucker Nordkettenbahnen GmbH) gebaut werden, beläuft sich auf insgesamt 2500 m². Die Bahnstrecke führt von der Haltestelle Congress (im Zentrum der Stadt) über die Nordkette bis hinauf zur Station Hungerburg, 288 m oberhalb von Innsbruck gelegen. Zuvor hatte Hadid bereits die Bergisel-Skischanze in der österreichischen Stadt realisiert (1999–2002; Seite 156). 2005 gewann die Architektin gemeinsam mit dem Bauunternehmen Strabag den Wettbewerb für die Nordkettenbahn. Hadid entschied sich für „eine insgesamt fließende Formensprache" und passte ihren Entwurf an die jeweiligen örtlichen Gegebenheiten der Stationen an. Die Architektin führt aus: „Wir setzten uns mit natürlichen Phänomenen wie Gletschermoränen und Eisbewegungen auseinander, weil wir wollten, dass jede Station die fließende Formensprache natürlicher Eisformationen aufgreift wie z. B. einen gefrorenen Gebirgsfluss." Die doppelt geschwungenen Glaselemente ruhen auf Betonsockeln und bilden eine „künstliche Landschaft". Erst seit Kurzem verfügbare Fertigungsmethoden, wie CNC-Fräsen oder das Thermoformen von Glas, machten es möglich, computergestützte Entwürfe und Fertigungstechniken einzusetzen, wobei einige Techniken der Autoindustrie entlehnt sind.

Mis en service le 1er décembre 2007, le funiculaire du Nordpark comprend quatre gares nouvelles et un pont à haubans sur l'Inn. La surface totale de ces quatre gares construites pour l'INKB (Innsbrucker Nordkettenbahnen GmbH) s'élève à 2500 m². Le funiculaire part de la gare Congress au centre de la ville pour rejoindre celle d'Hungenburg dans la chaîne montagneuse de la Nordkette, à 288 m au-dessus d'Innsbruck. Hadid avait précédemment réalisé le tremplin de saut à ski de Bergisel pour cette même ville autrichienne (1999–2002, voir page 156). Associée au constructeur Strabag, elle a remporté le concours pour ce projet en 2005. Adaptant ses plans aux conditions spécifiques de chaque gare, Zaha Hadid a utilisé un « langage global de fluidité ». « Nous avons étudié certains phénomènes naturels explique-t-elle, comme les moraines glaciaires et les mouvements de la glace, car nous voulions que chaque gare reprenne le langage tout de fluidité des formations glaciaires naturelles, dont par exemple un torrent gelé au flanc de la montagne. » Des couvertures en verre à double courbure forment un « paysage artificiel ». Des méthodes d'usinage à commande numérique et de thermoformage récemment développées et empruntées à l'industrie automobile ont permis d'utiliser directement les plans établis par ordinateur.

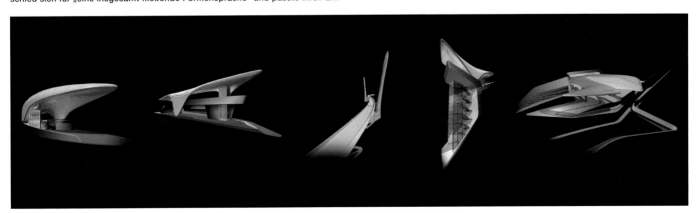

Interior and exterior views, as well as a section, drawing, and plan of the railway line, give an impression of the scale and nature of the project. The section below shows that the strongly cantilevered canopy hovers over a more purely functional station zone. Below, a full site map of the railway line.

Innen- und Außenansichten, Schnitt, Zeichnung und Kartenansicht der Bergbahn vermitteln einen Eindruck von Größenordnung und Art des Projekts. Der Schnitt unten zeigt, wie das stark auskragende Dach über der funktional konzipierten Station schwebt. Unten eine Überblickskarte vom Gelände der Bergbahn.

Les vues internes et externes ainsi qu'une coupe, un dessin et un plan de la ligne permettent de mieux saisir l'échelle et la nature du projet. La coupe ci-dessous montre que le puissant porte-à-faux de l'auvent abrite une section purement fonctionnelle de la station. Ci-dessous, la carte du parcours du funiculaire.

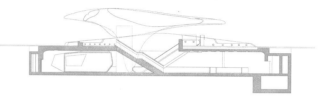

The arching canopy above the station appears to float in space, revealing a panorama of the Alps in the background. As always, night lighting was carefully studied.

Das geschwungene Dach über der Station scheint zu schweben; hinter ihm zeichnet sich das Alpen-panorama ab. Die nächtliche Beleuchtung ist wie immer sorgfältig ausgearbeitet.

L'immense auvent semble flotter dans l'espace audessus de la station, sur fond de chaîne de montagnes. Comme toujours chez Zaha Hadid, l'éclairage nocturne est soigneusement étudié.

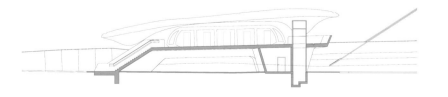

The canopies, station platforms, and other elements of the design are carefully considered to be fully functional at the same time as they are evocative and surprising. Most of all, the main architectural elements have a strong relationship to their site, without being "figurative" in any sense.

Dächer, Bahnsteige und andere Elemente des Entwurfs sind sorgfältig durchdacht, uneingeschränkt funktional und zugleich suggestiv und überraschend. In erster Linie jedoch nehmen die wichtigsten architektonischen Elemente starken Bezug auf ihre Umgebung, ohne diese allzu „wörtlich" zu interpretieren.

Les auvents, les quais des stations et les autres composants ont été étudiés pour être à la fois pleinement fonctionnels et en même temps surprenants et évocateurs. Mais surtout, les principaux éléments architecturaux entretiennent une forte relation avec le site sans être en quoi que ce soit « figuratifs ».

Below, a night view emphasizes the organic curves of the architecture against the straighter lines of the stairway. Although individual cladding panels are all but unique, they give the impression of participating in a deformed grid.

Eine Nachtansicht (unten), lässt die organischen Schwünge der Architektur im Kontrast zur geradlinigeren Treppe besonders deutlich werden. Obwohl die einzelnen Segmente der Verkleidung Unikate sind, wirken sie wie Bestandteile eines verzerrten Rasters.

Ci-dessous, une vue de nuit qui souligne les courbes organiques de l'architecture par contraste avec les lignes rigides de l'escalier. Chaque panneau d'habillage est de forme unique et donne l'impression de faire partie d'une trame déformée.

The sweeping lines of the architecture, especially seen against their natural backdrop, suggest the movement of the mountain itself, or its slowly eroding sheets of ice.

Die dramatische Linienführung der Architektur, besonders vor dem landschaftlichen Hintergrund, spiegelt die Bewegung des Berges selbst bzw. seiner nach und nach erodierenden Eisfelder.

Les lignes enveloppantes de l'architecture, en particulier si on la considère dans son cadre naturel, suggèrent presque le mouvement des montagnes ou des glaces soumises à une lente érosion.

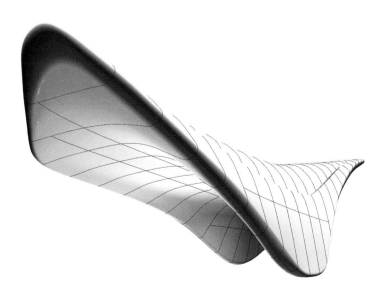

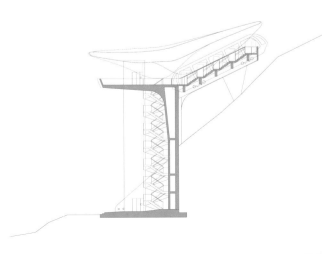

Like gently eroded ice caves, the station canopies seen here are the product of a grid deformed using computer-assisted design, and yet it is their "natural" appearance in this location that strikes the viewer before any reference to technology.

Die hier abgebildeten Stationsdächer wirken wie durch sanfte Erosion glatt geschliffene Eishöhlen. Sie sind das Resultat einer rechnergestützten Rasterverzerrung, doch dem Betrachter fällt vor allem auf, wie „natürlich" sie an diesem Ort wirken, noch bevor sich technische Bezüge aufdrängen.

Comme des grottes de glace délicatement érodées, les auvents des différentes stations sont issus de la déformation d'une trame créée par ordinateur même si c'est leur aspect « naturel » qui frappe le spectateur avant toute référence technologique.

Where tramway stations might tend to allow views of their setting only as an incidental, accessory aspect of their design, Zaha Hadid clearly takes the alpine setting into account and thus gives the structures a real connection to the mountains.

Während Straßenbahnstationen den Blick in ihr Umfeld zumeist eher beiläufig freigeben und die Umgebung ein nebensächlicher Aspekt ihres Designs sein mag, nimmt Zaha Hadid hier ganz offensichtlich Bezug auf die Berge und bindet die Bauten greifbar in die Alpenlandschaft ein.

Alors que les stations de tramway ne se préoccupent que rarement de leur cadre, Zaha Hadid a clairement pris en compte l'environnement alpin pour créer un lien réel entre ses constructions et les montagnes.

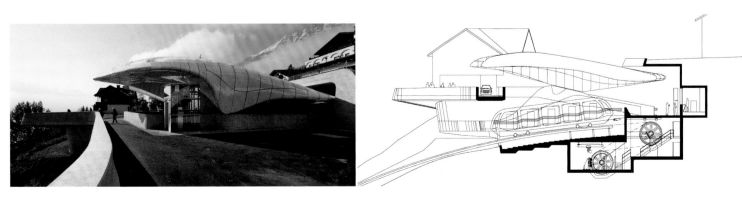

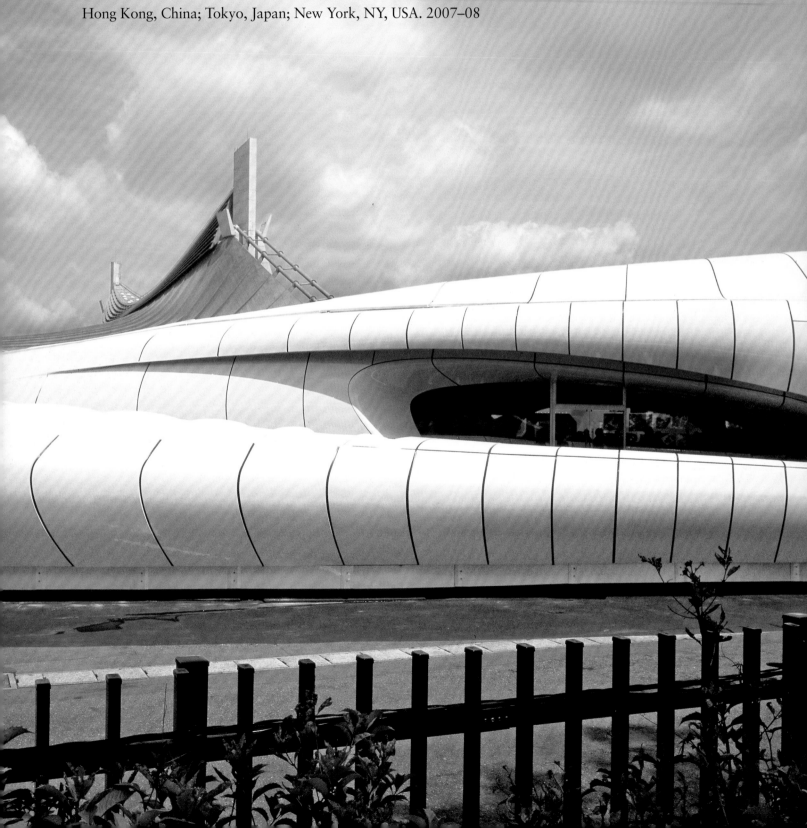

MOBILE ART,
CHANEL CONTEMPORARY
ART CONTAINER

Hong Kong, China; Tokyo, Japan; New York, NY, USA. 2007–08

Project

MOBILE ART, CHANEL CONTEMPORARY ART CONTAINER

Location
HONG KONG, CHINA; TOKYO, JAPAN; NEW YORK, NY, USA

Client
CHANEL

Area/Size
29 x 45 m, TOTAL 700 m²

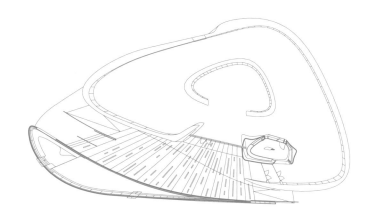

Seen in its Central Park (New York) location, the Container might well bring to mind an alien craft that has just landed. Lighting extends this effect into the immediate environment.

Der Container, hier im New Yorker Central Park, wirkt wie ein soeben gelandetes Raumschiff. Durch die Beleuchtung überträgt sich dieser Eindruck auch auf die unmittelbare Umgebung.

Photographié à Central Park à New York, le Container pourrait faire penser à un vaisseau extraterrestre échoué là par hasard. L'éclairage étend cet effet à son environnement immédiat.

Commissioned by Chanel designer Karl Lagerfeld, this traveling exhibition pavilion "is a celebration of the iconic work of Chanel, unmistakable for its smooth layering of exquisite details that together create an elegant, cohesive whole." Made of a series of continuous arch-shaped elements with a 65-square-meter central courtyard and a partially glazed adjustable ceiling, the pavilion is described as a "new artificial landscape for art installations." Twenty-nine meters long with a usable floor area of 700 square meters, the structure is six meters high, with a floor raised one meter above ground level. Conceived for easy dismounting and shipment, the Chanel pavilion has structural segments with a maximum width of 2.25 meters. Inspired to some extent by Chanel's famous quilted 2.55 handbag, the pavilion was erected in Hong Kong in March 2008, when Hadid commented: "The complexity and technological advances in digital imaging software and construction techniques have made the architecture of the Mobile Art pavilion possible. It is an architectural language of fluidity and nature, driven by new digital design, and manufacturing processes have enabled us to create the pavilion's totally organic forms—instead of the serial order of repetition that marks the architecture of the industrial 20th century." When the project was first shown at the 2007 Venice art Biennale, Karl Lagerfeld said of Hadid: "She is the first architect to find a way to part with the all-dominating post-Bauhaus aesthetic. The value of her designs is similar to that of great poetry. The potential of her imagination is enormous." The pavilion has been seen in Tokyo and in Central Park (New York, 2008).

Der von Chanel-Chefcouturier Karl Lagerfeld in Auftrag gegebene, mobile Ausstellungspavillon „ist eine Hommage an die stilbildenden Entwürfe Chanels, die dank ihrer exquisit aufeinander abgestimmten Details elegante, stimmige Gesamtkunstwerke sind". Der aus geschwungenen Teilsegmenten gefertigte Pavillon mit einem 65 m² großen Innenhof und einem teilverglasten, regulierbaren Dach gilt als „neuartige, künstliche Landschaft für Kunstausstellungen". Die Konstruktion ist 29 m lang, hat eine Nutzfläche von 700 m², ist 6 m hoch und 1 m über dem Boden aufgeständert. Der Chanel-Pavillon besteht aus Konstruktionselementen, die maximal 2,25 m breit sind, um Demontage und Transport zu erleichtern. Inspiriert wurde der Pavillon auch von Chanels berühmter gesteppter Handtasche „2.55"; installiert wurde er erstmals im März 2008 in Hongkong. Hadid merkt an: „Die Komplexität und technologische Weiterentwicklung digitaler

Konstruktionssoftware und -techniken haben die Architektur des mobilen Kunstpavillons erst möglich gemacht. Die fließende und natürliche Architektursprache ist getragen von neuen digitalen Entwurfstechniken und Fertigungsprozessen, mit deren Hilfe sich die organische Formensprache des Pavillons realisieren ließ, statt zwingend einem seriellen Wiederholungsmuster zu folgen, das die Architektur des technischen 20. Jahrhunderts geprägt hat." Als das Projekt auf der Biennale in Venedig 2007 erstmals vorgestellt wurde, sagte Lagerfeld über Hadid: „Sie ist die erste Architektin, die einen Weg gefunden hat, sich von der alles beherrschenden Post-Bauhaus-Ästhetik zu lösen. Ihre Entwürfe sind vergleichbar mit großer Dichtung. Ihre Vorstellungskraft hat ein enormes Potenzial." Der Pavillon ist inzwischen auch in Tokio und im Central Park (New York, 2008) zu sehen gewesen.

Commandé par le styliste de Chanel, Karl Lagerfeld, ce pavillon d'expositions itinérant « est une célébration de l'œuvre iconique de Chanel, unique par sa réunion délicate de détails exquis qui, assemblés, créent un ensemble élégant et cohérent ». Composé d'une succession d'éléments en arcs regroupés autour d'une cour centrale de 65 m² et d'un plafond transformable partiellement vitré, le pavillon est présenté comme « un nouveau paysage artificiel pour installations artistiques ». De 45 m de long et 29 m de large pour une surface utile de 700 m², il mesure 6 m de haut. Son plancher est surélevé d'un mètre par rapport au sol. Prévu pour être aisément démonté et transporté, il se compose d'éléments structurels d'une largeur maximum de 2,25 m. Inspiré dans un certaine mesure du célèbre sac matelassé 2.55 de Chanel, il a été monté à Hongkong en mars 2008. À cette occasion, Hadid a déclaré : « La complexité et les progrès technologiques intervenus dans les logiciels d'imagerie numérique et les techniques de construction ont rendu possible l'architecture de ce Mobile Art Pavillon. C'est un langage architectural de fluidité et de naturel, piloté par de nouvelles techniques de conception et processus de fabrication numériques qui nous ont permis de créer des formes totalement organiques, à la place de l'ordre répétitif sériel qui caractérise l'architecture du XXe siècle industriel. » Lorsque le projet a été présenté pour la première fois à la Biennale artistique de Venise en 2007, Karl Lagerfeld a dit de Hadid : « Elle est le premier architecte à trouver une voie qui s'écarte de l'esthétique dominatrice du Bauhaus. La valeur de sa création est similaire à celle de la forme poétique la plus élevée. Son potentiel d'imagination est énorme. » Le pavillon a été monté à Tokyo et à Central Park (New York, automne 2008).

Seen in its Tokyo setting (above), at night, the Art Container appears to radiate out into the space that it occupies, inviting visitors to enter. To the left, another picture of it in its New York venue (Central Park).

Der hier in einer nächtlichen Ansicht an seinem Standort in Tokio gezeigte Art Container (oben) scheint in sein Umfeld auszustrahlen und lädt Gäste zu einem Besuch ein. Links eine weitere Ansicht am New Yorker Standort (Central Park).

Installé à Tokyo (ci-dessus), l'Art Container semble irradier dans l'espace qui l'entoure, et invite ainsi les visiteurs à entrer. À gauche, une autre image de son installation dans Central Park à New York.

In the three images on this page, the Chanel Art Container is seen in Hong Kong, a more densely urban setting than the Central Park location for example, and yet the structure appears very much at ease, flowing into its site and suggesting clearly that the rigidity of surrounding towers is not the only way forward for contemporary architecture and design.

Die drei Aufnahmen auf dieser Seite zeigen den Chanel Art Container in Hongkong, einem urbanen Umfeld mit dichterer Bebauung als etwa der Central Park. Dennoch scheint sich der Bau wie selbstverständlich einzufügen, verschmilzt mit seinem Standort und macht deutlich, dass die formale Strenge der ihn umgebenden Hochhausbauten zukünftig keineswegs die einzige Option für zeitgenössische Architektur und Design ist.

Dans ces trois représentations, le Chanel Art Container est photographié à Hongkong dans un contexte beaucoup plus construit qu'à Central Park. Il y semble néanmoins très à l'aise. Se glissant dans son site, il suggère que la rigidité géométrique des tours environnantes n'est pas la seule voie de l'architecture et du design contemporains.

The interiors of the Container continue the curvi-linear, enveloping design that is visible from the outside.

In den Innenräumen des Containers setzt sich das geschwungene, kapselartige Design fort, das schon außen sichtbar ist.

L'intérieur du Container reprend le plan curviligne enveloppant de l'extérieur.

Although the point is to present the products of Chanel, in full agreement with Chanel designer Karl Lagerfeld, Zaha Hadid has also created a work that indirectly suggests that the products concerned are at the cutting edge of design.

Obwohl es hier, nach enger Absprache mit Chanel-Designer Karl Lagerfeld, in erster Linie darum geht, Produkte von Chanel zu präsentieren, gelang es Zaha Hadid zudem, ein Werk zu schaffen, das implizit andeutet, wie innovativ das Design dieser Produkte ist.

Bien que l'objectif soit de présenter les produits Chanel, en accord avec le styliste de la marque, Karl Lagerfeld, Zaha Hadid a également créé une œuvre qui suggère indirectement la modernité de pointe de ces produits.

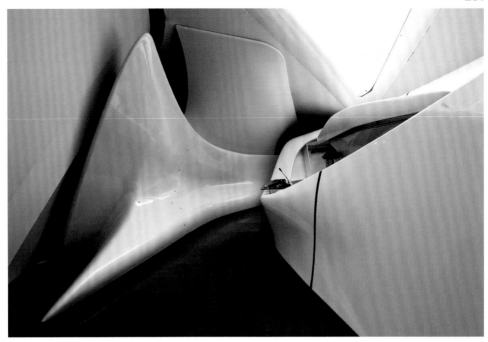

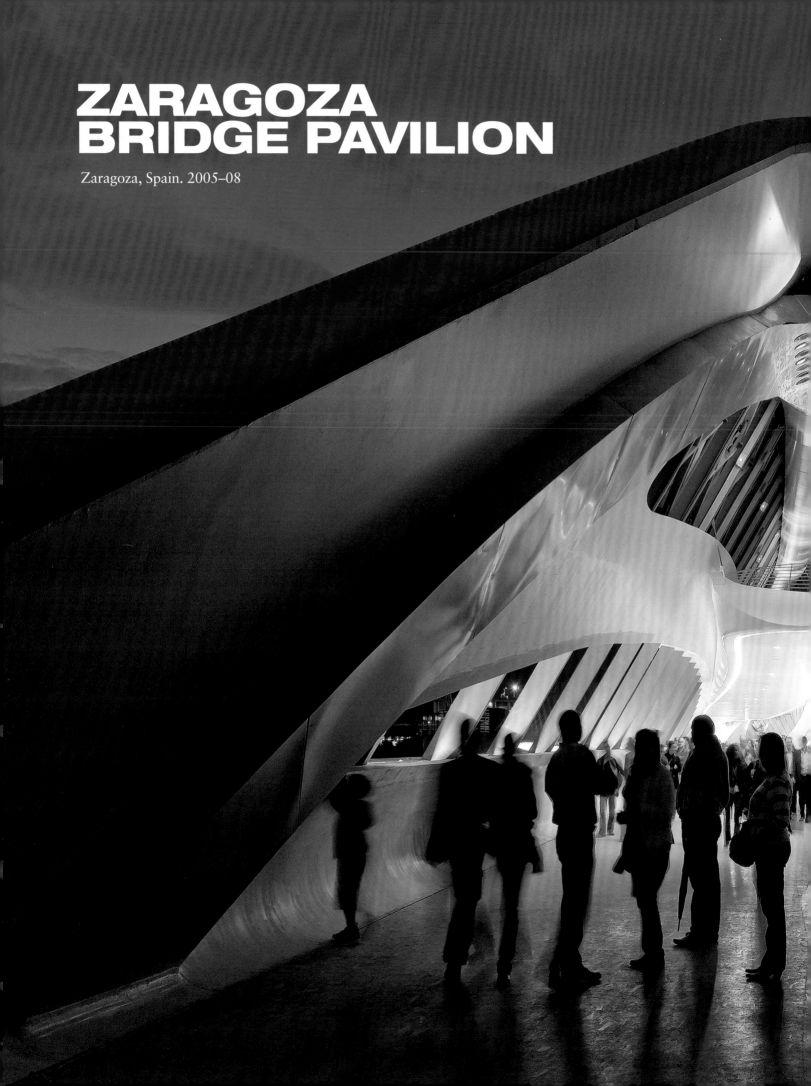

ZARAGOZA
BRIDGE PAVILION

Zaragoza, Spain. 2005–08

Project
ZARAGOZA BRIDGE PAVILION

Location
ZARAGOZA, SPAIN

Client
EXPOAGUA ZARAGOZA 2008

Area/Size
TOTAL FLOOR AREA: 6415 m²
(LENGTH 270 m, HEIGHT 30 m)

The expressive continuity and mixture of forms and materials seen here are nothing short of remarkable. There is a real sense that this is a new type of architecture, which nonetheless has an innate legitimacy.

Die hier deutlich sichtbare expressive Kontinuität sowie die Kombination von Formen und Materialien sind ohne Frage höchst beeindruckend. Hier spürt man, dass dies eine vollkommen neue Form von Architektur ist, die eine ganz eigene Legitimität besitzt.

La continuité expressive et le mélange de formes et de matériaux sont en tous points remarquables. On a le sentiment très fort de se trouver devant un nouveau type d'architecture qui n'en possède pas moins une légitimité innée.

This interactive exhibition structure with a focus on water and sustainability, themes of Expo 2008 in Zaragoza, has a total floor area of 6415 square meters, and an exhibition area of 3915 square meters. The pedestrian bridge that is part of the scheme occupies a further 2500 square meters. The Pavilion is "organized around four main objects or pods that perform both as structural elements and as spatial enclosures." Each diamond-shaped pod corresponds to a specific exhibition area. Because loads are distributed between the pods rather than being borne by a central element, the resulting load-bearing members can be smaller. The bridge section of the pavilion spans 85 meters, from an Ebro River island to the Expo site. The architect explains: "the long pod that houses the pedestrian bridge spans 185 meters from the right riverbank to the bridge's middle support on an island, where the three exhibition pods are grafted on, spanning from the island to the left bank." Interiors vary from softly lit, air-conditioned enclosures focused on the works exhibited, to open, naturally ventilated areas with views of the river and the exhibition grounds. Twenty-six thousand flat panels organized in 300 different color combinations cover the upper part of the bridge, forming an array of optical patterns reminiscent of the skin of a shark. The lower part of the structure is constituted by a 275-meter long double-curved structural monocoque steel deck. While a number of Hadid's buildings have had a deep relation to the land, this form appears to move across the river in an almost organic flow, taking in the air and water that surrounds it.

Der interaktive Ausstellungsbau befasst sich primär mit zwei Themen der Expo 2008 im spanischen Saragossa: mit Wasser und Nachhaltigkeit. Seine gesamte Geschossfläche beträgt 6415 m², die Ausstellungsfläche als solche 3915 m². Der Fußgängerüberweg, Teil des Entwurfs, nimmt weitere 2500 m² in Anspruch. Der Pavillon ist „um vier zentrale Objekte oder Kapseln organisiert, die sowohl als konstruktive Elemente dienen als auch als umbaute räumliche Einheiten". Jede der rautenförmigen Kapseln bietet eine eigenständige Ausstellungsfläche. Weil sich die Lasten auf die verschiedenen Kapseln verteilen, statt auf einem zentralen Konstruktionselement zu ruhen, können die tragenden Elemente kleiner ausfallen. Der Brückenabschnitt erstreckt sich 85 m weit von einer Insel im Ebro hinüber zum Expogelände. Die Architektin führt aus: „Eine lange Kapsel erstreckt sich vom rechten Ufer bis hinüber zur Insel, wo die übrigen drei Kapseln, die von der Insel zum linken Ufer verlaufen, ‚eingepfropft' sind." Das Spektrum des Inneren reicht von schlichten Räumen, deren Fokus auf den Exponaten liegt, bis hin zu offenen Bereichen mit Aussicht auf den Fluss und das Ausstellungsgelände. Der Bau ist mit 29 000 dreieckigen „Schuppen" überzogen, die an eine Haifischhaut denken lassen und aus nachhaltigen Materialien gefertigt sind. Viele von ihnen lassen sich öffnen; sie bilden die Außenhaut des insgesamt 275 m langen Baus. Während zahlreiche Gebäude Hadids eng mit der Erde verbunden sind, scheint sich dieses Bauwerk geradezu organisch über den Fluss zu schwingen und dabei Luft und Wasser der Umgebung in sich aufzunehmen.

Cette structure pour expositions interactives sur les thèmes de l'eau et du développement durable (ceux de l'Expo 2008 organisée à Saragosse), représente une surface totale de 6415 m² pour un espace d'expositions de 3915 m² et un pont piétonnier de 2500 m². Le pavillon « s'organise autour de quatre objets principaux ou *pods* qui sont à la fois des éléments structurels et des espaces enclos ». Chaque *pod* en forme de diamant correspond à une zone d'exposition spécifique. Comme les charges sont distribuées entre ces éléments au lieu d'être soutenues par un élément central, les fermes porteuses peuvent être de dimensions réduites. La partie franchissement, entre une île sur l'Èbre et l'entrée du site de l'Expo, est d'une portée de 85 m. « Un *pod* allongé se projette de la rive du fleuve vers l'île, tandis que les trois autres se greffent sur lui, en passant de l'île vers l'autre rive. » Les espaces intérieurs vont de simples volumes consacrés aux expositions à des zones ouvertes offrant des vues sur le fleuve et les autres pavillons de l'Expo. Vingt-neuf mille *shingles* triangulaires faits de matériaux écologiques, que l'on a pu comparer à une peau de requin, recouvrent la construction. Un bon nombre d'entre eux sont mobiles pour ménager des ouvertures dans la peau de cette structure de 275 m de long. Si de nombreuses réalisations de Hadid expriment une forte relation avec le sol, cette forme originale semble se projeter au-dessus du fleuve dans un mouvement de flux quasi organique qui aspire l'air et l'eau environnants.

The concept of the inhabited bridge, of course, goes back to medieval times if not before, but Zaha Hadid here gives the genre a totally new incarnation, with its quasi-organic forms flowing across the river while achieving the other programmatic goals.

Das Konzept der bewohnten Brücke reicht bis ins Mittelalter, wenn nicht gar weiter zurück. Dennoch verhilft Zaha Hadid diesem Bautyp zu einer gänzlich neuartigen Verkörperung. Mit ihren quasi organischen Formen scheint die Brücke über den Fluss zu fließen und wird den vielen programmatischen Anforderungen gerecht.

Le concept de pont habité remonte au moins à l'époque médiévale, mais Zaha Hadid en offre ici une incarnation entièrement nouvelle à travers des formes quasi organiques qui semblent glisser au-dessus du fleuve tout en remplissant de multiples objectifs programmatiques.

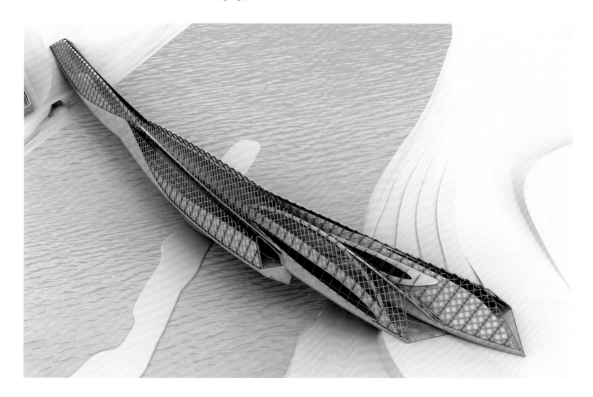

Where regularity has been banished, each element of the interior offers surprises to visitors, and indeed appearances change according to the angle of view or the direction of movement. This runs quite contrary to modernist regularity.

Wo jegliche Regelmäßigkeit verbannt wurde, verstehen sämtliche Elemente des Innenraums, die Besucher zu überraschen. Im Grunde wandeln sich die Ansichten je nach Blickwinkel oder Bewegungsrichtung – ein starker Kontrast zu modernistischer Regelmäßigkeit.

La régularité a été bannie et chaque élément de l'intérieur offre de nouvelles surprises aux visiteurs. Des changements d'apparence se manifestent selon l'angle de vue et le déplacement de chacun. On est ici à l'opposé de la régularité formelle moderniste.

Though organic or skeletal forms do not appear to be too distant from these views, Zaha Hadid has always steered clear of any literal interpretation of living creatures. She does relate more specifically to landscape, of course; in this instance, the crossing of a river.

Obwohl organische oder skelettartige Formen nicht allzu weit von diesen Ansichten entfernt sind, hat Zaha Hadid es stets vermieden, lebende Wesen allzu wörtlich zu interpretieren. Tatsächlich orientiert sie sich eher an landschaftlichen Situationen; in diesem Fall an der Überquerung eines Flusses.

Si ces vues peuvent faire penser à des formes organiques ou squelettiques, Zaha Hadid reste toujours nettement à l'écart de l'interprétation littérale de créatures vivantes. Elle s'intéresse plus spécifiquement au paysage et, ici, au franchissement d'un fleuve.

MAXXI: NATIONAL MUSEUM OF XXI CENTURY ARTS

Rome, Italy. 1998–2009

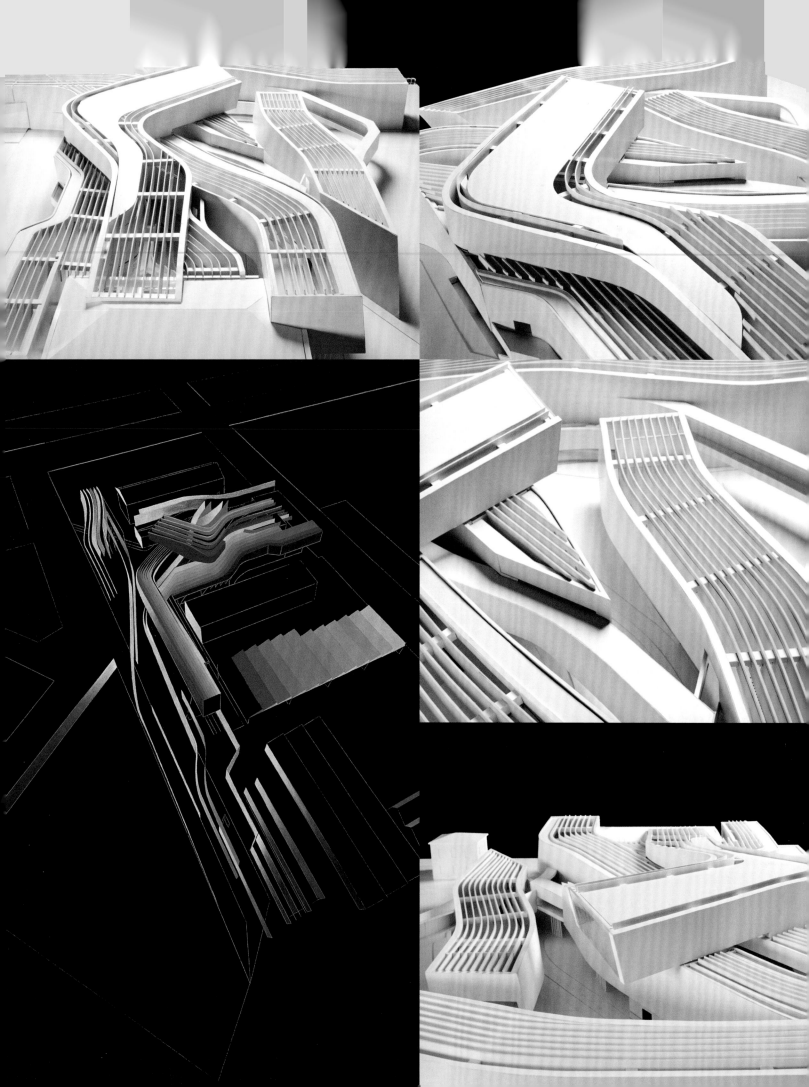

MAXXI: NATIONAL MUSEUM OF XXI CENTURY ARTS

Location
ROME, ITALY

Client
ITALIAN MINISTRY OF CULTURE

Area/Size
30 000 m²

Opposite page, bottom left:
PART OF A SERIES OF 5 COMPETITION PAINTINGS
Acrylic on black cartridge, 172.5 x 93 cm
1998

The process of weaving and intertwining forms, seen on a much smaller scale in earlier works of Zaha Hadid, here reaches a kind of apotheosis, interconnecting and relating every volume.

Das Verflechten und Ineinandergreifen von Formen, in viel kleinerem Maßstab schon bei früheren Projekten Hadids zu sehen, erreicht hier eine Art Apotheose, durchdringt und verbindet sämtliche Baukörper.

Le processus de formes entrelacées, vu à plus petite échelle dans certaines œuvres antérieures de Zaha Hadid, atteint ici à une sorte d'apothéose dans l'interconnexion de tous les volumes.

The client for this project was the Italian Ministry of Culture. Given the date of its conception, its forms may be more related to earlier work of Zaha Hadid, such as her Landscape Formation One (LF One, 1996–99; see page 130), than to her most recent designs. The difference here is, of course, the location is no longer related to a natural setting, but rather to the city. Hadid's description of the project explains: "By intertwining the circulation with the urban context, the building shares a public dimension with the city, overlapping tendril-like paths and open space. In addition to the circulatory relationship, the architectural elements are also geometrically aligned with the urban grids that join at the site." Allowing both visitors and curators a good deal of freedom for their movement through the space, or interpretation of its potential, Hadid further explains: "The drift through the Center is a trajectory through varied ambiences, filtered spectacles, and differentiated luminosity. Whilst offering a new freedom in the curators' palette, this in turn digests and recomposes the experience of art spectatorship as liberated dialogue with artifact and environment." The idea of drifting through the space is essential to the concept of the building, as opposed to a predetermined set of "key points." Nor is this interpretation related only to the question of architecture. "We take this opportunity, in the adventure of designing such a forward-looking institution, to confront the material and conceptual dissonance evoked by art practice since the late 1960s. The paths lead away from the 'object' and its correlative sanctifying, toward fields of multiple associations that are anticipative of the necessity to change," again according to the architect. The dissolution of such typical museum elements as the vertical wall intended to hang paintings here allows for walls that turn into ceilings or are transformed into windows. Surely related to the later work that provides for flowing spatial continuity, the MAXXI might be considered a transition toward that increasingly marked theme in Zaha Hadid's work.

Bauherr dieses Projekts war das italienische Kultusministerium. Angesichts des Entwurfsdatums ist die Formensprache des Baus wohl eher dem Frühwerk Zaha Hadids zuzuordnen, etwa der Landscape Formation One (LF One, 1996–99; siehe Seite 130), als der Mehrzahl neuerer Entwürfe. Allerdings sucht das Projekt in Rom weniger einen Bezug zur Natur als vielmehr zur Stadt. Hadids Beschreibung erläutert: „Bau und Stadt haben eine gemeinsame öffentliche Dimension: die Verkehrsflächen sind in den urbanen Kontext eingewoben, die sich rankenden Pfade und offenen Plätze überschneiden einander. Abgesehen von Ähnlichkeiten in der Verkehrsführung wurden die architektonischen Elemente außerdem geometrisch nach dem urbanen Raster ausgerichtet, das an das Grundstück anschließt." Besuchern und Kuratoren wird erhebliche Freiheit gelassen, sich im Raum zu bewegen und sein Potenzial zu interpretieren, wie Hadid weiter ausführt: „Sich durch den Bau treiben zu lassen, ist wie eine Reise durch verschiedene Atmosphären, modulierte Ereignisfelder und differenzierte Lichtverhältnisse. Hierdurch entsteht zum einen neuer kuratorischer Spielraum, zum anderen wird die Kunsterfahrung als befreiter Dialog mit dem Kunstwerk und seinem Umfeld neu gedacht." Die Idee, sich durch den Raum treiben zu lassen, spielt hier eine zentrale Rolle, im Gegensatz zu Konzepten, die sich an klar definierten „Schlüsselpunkten" orientieren. Dieser Ansatz beschränkt sich jedoch nicht auf die Architektur. „Es war ein Abenteuer, eine so zukunftsweisende Institution gestalten zu können, und so nutzten wir die Gelegenheit, der Dissonanz zwischen Materialität und Konzept, die die Kunstpraxis seit den 1960er-Jahren prägt, die Stirn zu bieten. Unser Ansatz verabschiedet sich vom ‚Objekt' und der daraus resultierenden Überhöhung des Kontexts und setzt stattdessen auf assoziativ vielschichtige Felder als Signal für einen dringend notwendigen Wandel", so die Architektin. Die Loslösung von typischen Museumselementen, wie vertikalen Wandflächen zur Hängung von Gemälden, ermöglichte die Gestaltung von Wänden, die fließend in Decken oder Fensteröffnungen übergehen. Das MAXXI, das mit späteren Projekten verwandt ist, die sich durch ein fließendes Raumkontinuum auszeichnen, lässt sich als Bindeglied zu einem Thema im Werk Hadids verstehen, das sich immer deutlicher abzuzeichnen beginnt.

Le client de ce projet était le ministère de la Culture italien. Étant donné sa date de conception, ses formes peuvent paraître davantage liées à l'œuvre antérieure de Zaha Hadid, comme sa Landscape Formation One (LF One, 1996–99, voir page 130), qu'à ses projets les plus récents. La différence tient ici, bien sûr, au site qui ne s'apparente pas à un cadre naturel, mais plutôt à celui d'une ville. La description du projet par l'architecte est éclairante : « En entrelaçant sa circulation au contexte urbain, le bâtiment partage sa dimension publique avec la ville, superposant les cheminements qui évoquent des tiges végétales à l'espace ouvert. En dehors de cette relation circulatoire, les éléments architecturaux s'alignent géométriquement avec les trames urbaines qui se rejoignent sur le site. » En offrant aux visiteurs comme aux conservateurs une grande liberté de déplacement dans le volume, ou dans l'interprétation de son potentiel, « le mouvement à travers le musée est une trajectoire à travers des ambiances diversifiées, des vues filtrées et des atmosphères lumineuses différenciées. Tout en offrant une liberté nouvelle à la palette du conservateur, ce phénomène digère et recompose successivement l'expérience du spectateur de l'art, en l'invitant à un dialogue libéré avec les artéfacts et l'environnement. » L'idée de mouvement à travers l'espace est essentielle au concept de cette réalisation, par opposition à un ensemble prédéterminé de « points clés ». L'interprétation n'est pas reliée à la seule question de l'architecture. « Nous saisissons l'opportunité, dans cette aventure que représente la conception d'une institution aussi avancée, de confronter la dissonance matérielle et conceptuelle que connaît la pratique artistique depuis la fin des années 1960. Les cheminements éloignent de "l'objet" et de sa sanctification corrélative, pour aller vers des domaines d'associations multiples qui anticipent la nécessité du changement. » La dissolution des éléments typiques d'un musée comme le mur vertical destiné à suspendre des tableaux permet aux murs de se transformer en plafonds ou en fenêtres. En lien avec son travail ultérieur axé sur la continuité spatiale fluide, le MAXXI peut être considéré comme une transition vers ce thème de plus en plus marqué dans l'œuvre de Zaha Hadid.

An aerial view and the image of the space below the building show how it is firmly connected to its site, allowing pedestrians to approach without necessarily entering.

Eine Luftaufnahme und eine Ansicht des Bereichs unterhalb des Gebäudes zeigen, wie präzise der Komplex in sein Umfeld eingebettet wurde. Fußgänger haben Zugang, auch ohne den Bau betreten zu müssen.

Une vue aérienne et une image de l'entrée du musée montrent sa relation particulière au site, qui permet aux piétons de s'en approcher sans nécessairement y entrer.

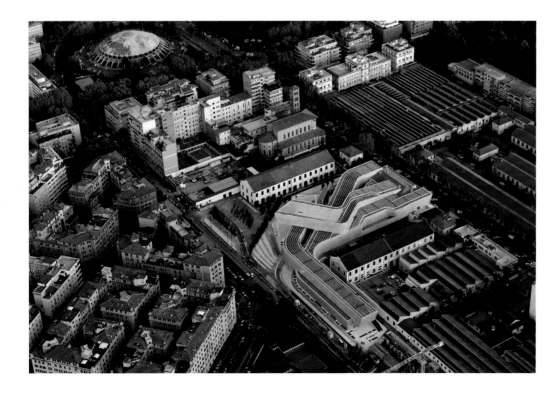

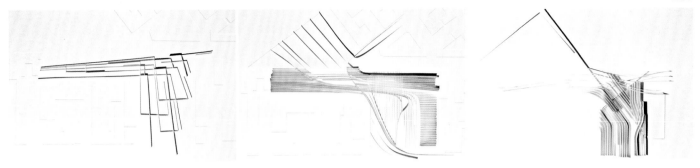

The complex sense of movement seen in these images might almost bring to mind the forms generated by the requirements of a railway yard, for example. Though apparently a tangle of shapes, each curve corresponds to a carefully considered need.

Der komplexe Eindruck von Bewegung, den diese Abbildungen vermitteln, erinnert fast an die formale Gestaltung eines Rangierbahnhofs. Was wie ein Gewirr geschwungener Stränge wirkt, ist aber auf sorgsam ermittelte Erfordernisse zugeschnitten.

Le sentiment complexe de mouvement que l'on perçoit dans ces images pourrait presque évoquer les formes d'une gare de triage. Cet écheveau de formes correspond en fait à des besoins attentivement pris en compte.

Again here, the light openings of the building serve as an invitation to visit, or to explore the space in a free, unfettered way.

Auch hier laden erleuchtete Fassadenöffnungen zum Besuch ein – oder dazu, das Areal ungezwungen zu erkunden.

Les ouvertures du bâtiment sur l'extérieur sont une invitation à le visiter ou à explorer son volume de la manière la plus libre qui soit.

With its emphasis on horizontal lines and cantilevered volumes, the architecture is marked by a willful contrast between opaque surfaces and glazed or open sections.

Der Baukörper mit seiner auffälligen Horizontalität und den Auskragungen zeichnet sich durch einen gezielten Kontrast zwischen geschlossenen Flächen und verglasten oder offenen Zonen aus.

Tout en mettant l'accent sur l'horizontalité et les volumes en porte-à-faux, l'architecture est marquée par un contraste recherché entre les plans aveugles et les parties vitrées.

Rather than the rectilinear order that is more familiar in modern architecture, Hadid employs a flowing scheme to interiors as well as the exterior—each level curves or slices into the next.

Statt eines in der Moderne üblicheren, rechtwinkligen Ordnungsprinzips setzt Hadid bei Innen- wie Außenbau auf fließende Formen – jede Ebene fügt sich fließend in die jeweils nächste ein oder überschneidet sie.

Au lieu de se conformer à l'ordre rectiligne et familier de l'architecture moderne, Hadid recourt à un vocabulaire tout de fluidité, aussi bien à l'extérieur qu'à l'intérieur. Chaque niveau s'imbrique avec fluidité ou se croise avec un autre.

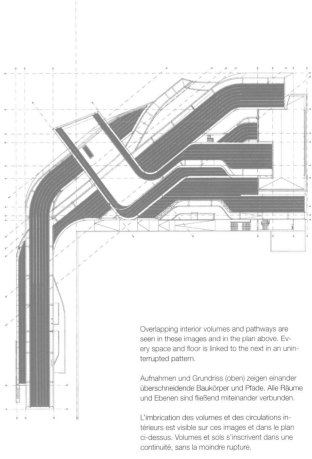

Overlapping interior volumes and pathways are seen in these images and in the plan above. Every space and floor is linked to the next in an uninterrupted pattern.

Aufnahmen und Grundriss (oben) zeigen einander überschneidende Baukörper und Pfade. Alle Räume und Ebenen sind fließend miteinander verbunden.

L'imbrication des volumes et des circulations intérieurs est visible sur ces images et dans le plan ci-dessus. Volumes et sols s'inscrivent dans une continuité, sans la moindre rupture.

SHEIKH ZAYED BRIDGE

Abu Dhabi, UAE. 1997–2010

Project
SHEIKH ZAYED BRIDGE

Location
ABU DHABI, UAE

Client
ABU DHABI MUNICIPALITY

Length
842 m

Although it was a long time in preparation, the bridge offers an evident and iconic entrance pathway to the city of Abu Dhabi.

Ungeachtet ihrer langen Planungsphase ist die Brücke längst zum unübersehbaren Eingang und Wahrzeichen für Abu Dhabi geworden.

Projet et chantier de longue haleine, le pont constitue aujourd'hui une porte d'entrée iconique de la ville d'Abu Dhabi.

This bridge, which links Abu Dhabi Island with the mainland, including Dubai and the international airport, presented an engineering challenge with its sculptural forms, the complex geometry of its steel arches, and solid concrete piers. As Hadid's office description has it: "A collection, or strands of structures, gathered on one shore, are lifted and 'propelled' over the length of the channel. A sinusoidal waveform provides the structural silhouette shape across the channel." The main 234-meter-long arch of the bridge rises to a height of 60 meters above the water with the road some 40 meters below that. The four-lane structure with pedestrian walkways in each direction is the third bridge to link Abu Dhabi Island to the mainland, and is 68 meters in width, and a total of 842 meters long. Although other architects like Ben van Berkel have designed major bridges (UNStudio, Erasmus Bridge, Rotterdam, The Netherlands, 1996), Hadid's foray into this area, often reserved for engineers, is a confirmation of the range of her interests and ability to renew particularly codified structural forms. Where bridges often have static, symmetrical forms for reasons of stability, Hadid dares here to introduce complex notions of movement into the design. The project description makes this dynamic element apparent: "The mainland is the launch pad for the bridge structure emerging from the ground and approach road. The road decks are cantilevered on each side of the spine structure. Steel arches rise and spring from mass concrete piers asymmetrically, in length, between the road decks to mark the mainland and the navigation channels. The spine splits and splays from one shore along the central void position, diverging under the road decks to the outside of the roadways at the other end of the bridge."

Die Brücke, die Abu-Dhabi-Insel mit dem Festland verbindet, auf dem auch Dubai und der internationale Flughafen liegen, war schon aufgrund ihrer skulpturalen Form, der komplexen Geometrie ihrer Stahlbögen und ihrer massiven Betonstützpfeiler eine ingenieurtechnische Herausforderung. Hadids Büro schreibt: „Ein Strang konstruktiver Elemente wird an einem der Ufer gebündelt und über die gesamte Breite des Kanals ‚geschleudert'. Eine sinusförmige Welle prägt die Silhouette der Konstruktion über dem Kanal." Der 234 m lange Hauptbogen der Brücke erhebt sich bis zu 60 m über den Wasserspiegel, die Straße verläuft gut 40 m tiefer. Das doppelt vierspurige Bauwerk mit Fußgängerpassage in beiden Richtungen, 68 m breit und insgesamt 842 m lang, ist die dritte Brücke zwischen Abu-Dhabi-Insel und dem Festland. Obwohl auch andere Architekten wie Ben van Berkel große Brücken geplant haben (UNStudio, Erasmusbrücke, Rotterdam, Niederlande, 1996), belegt Hadids Vorstoß auf diesem Gebiet – das

oft als Domäne von Ingenieuren gilt – die Bandbreite ihres Interesses und ihre Fähigkeit, besonders kodifizierte Bauformen grundlegend zu erneuern. Während Brücken aus Gründen der Stabilität oft statisch oder symmetrisch gestaltet werden, wagt es Hadid hier, komplexe Bilder von Bewegung in den Entwurf einfließen zu lassen. Die Projektbeschreibung lässt dieses dynamische Element deutlich werden: „Das Festland dient als Abschussrampe für eine Brückenkonstruktion, die aus dem Boden wächst und sich der Straße nähert. Die Straßendecks kragen beidseitig über die Mittelträgerkonstruktion aus. Stahlbögen steigen auf, entspringen in Längsrichtung zwischen den Straßendecks asymmetrisch aus den massiven Betonstützpfeilern und markieren das Festland und die Schifffahrtsrinnen. Der Mittelträger spaltet sich, spreizt sich vom Ufer aus beiderseits eines zentralen Leerraums auf und wölbt sich unterhalb der Straßendecks nach außen, hinüber zum anderen Ende der Brücke."

Ce pont, qui relie l'île d'Abu Dhabi au continent, Dubaï et l'aéroport international, a représenté un défi par ses formes sculpturales, la géométrie complexe de ses arches d'acier et de ses piles massives de béton. Selon le descriptif de l'agence : « Une collection, ou éléments de structures, réunie sur une rive est soulevée et "propulsée" sur toute la largeur du chenal. Une forme en vague sinusoïdale constitue la silhouette structurelle de ce franchissement. » L'arc principal de 234 m de long s'élève à 60 m au-dessus des eaux pour 40 m du tablier à quatre voies. Celui-ci, qui mesure 68 m de large et 842 m de long, comprend également une voie piétonnière dans chaque sens. Ce point est le troisième à relier Abu Dhabi au continent. Si d'autres architectes, comme Ben van Berkel, ont eux aussi conçu des ponts de grande taille (UN-Studio, pont Érasme, Rotterdam, Pay-Bas, 1996), ce nouvel ouvrage est une confirmation de la variété des intérêts de Hadid et de sa capacité à renouveler des formes structurelles particulièrement codifiées, et ce dans un secteur qui est souvent la chasse gardée des ingénieurs. Alors que les ponts présentent souvent des formes statiques et symétriques pour des raisons de stabilité, Hadid a osé introduire des notions complexes de mouvement. Sa description met l'accent sur ce dynamisme : « La rive du continent est la base de lancement de la structure du pont qui jaillit du sol et de la voie d'approche. Les tabliers sont en porte-à-faux au-dessus de la structure. Les arcs d'acier s'élèvent et jaillissent asymétriquement de la masse des piles de béton, dans l'axe longitudinal, entre les tabliers, le continent et les canaux de navigation. Partie de la rive, la colonne vertébrale se sépare et s'évase le long du vide central, divergeant sous les tabliers et s'écartant à l'extérieur des voies, à l'autre extrémité du pont. »

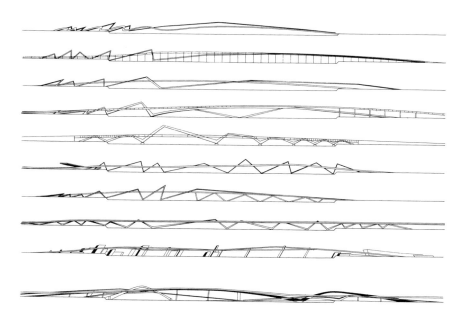

Night lighting, which changes in subtle, non-repetitive ways, is an integral part of the scheme, making the bridge stand out in the dark. Left, sketches for the bridge design.

Die nächtliche Beleuchtung, die als Zufallssequenz subtil in ihrer Farbigkeit wechselt, ist integraler Bestandteil des Entwurfs und hebt die Brücke im Dunkeln hervor. Links Skizzen des Entwurfs.

L'éclairage nocturne qui se modifie en permanence selon un rythme non répétitif fait partie intégrante du projet. Le pont se détache sur le fond du ciel nocturne. À gauche, croquis de conception.

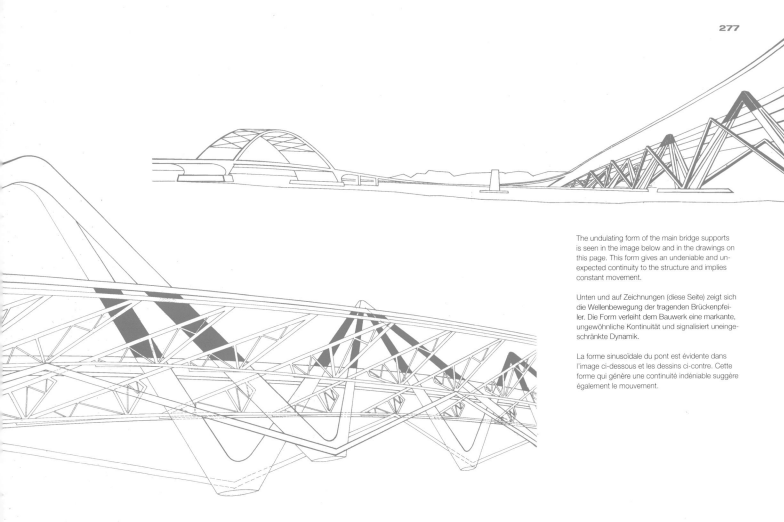

The undulating form of the main bridge supports is seen in the image below and in the drawings on this page. This form gives an undeniable and unexpected continuity to the structure and implies constant movement.

Unten und auf Zeichnungen (diese Seite) zeigt sich die Wellenbewegung der tragenden Brückenpfeiler. Die Form verleiht dem Bauwerk eine markante, ungewöhnliche Kontinuität und signalisiert uneingeschränkte Dynamik.

La forme sinusoïdale du pont est évidente dans l'image ci-dessous et les dessins ci-contre. Cette forme qui génère une continuité indéniable suggère également le mouvement.

GUANGZHOU
OPERA HOUSE

Guangzhou, China. 2003–10

Project
GUANGZHOU OPERA HOUSE

Location
GUANGZHOU, CHINA

Cliente
GUANGZHOU MUNICIPAL GOVERNMENT

Area/Size
70 000 m²

Lying low on the water against a backdrop of towers, the opera house has something of the iconic drama of the Sydney Opera House without adopting any such literal device as the "shell" forms of Utzon.

Der niedrige Bau am Wasser liegt vor einer Hochhauskulisse. Das Opernhaus ist ähnlich dramatisch wie die Oper in Sydney, ohne jedoch auf so allegorische Stilmittel wie die „Muschelformen" Utzons zurückzugreifen.

Tapis en bordure du fleuve devant un panorama de tours, l'opéra possède en partie la qualité iconique de celui de Sydney, sans se référer à des formes aussi littérales que les « coquilles » d'Utzon.

Built for the Guangzhou Municipal Government, this 70 000-square-meter structure overlooks the Pearl River in the Guangzhou cultural development area. Guangzhou (known earlier as Canton), a city of nearly 10 million people and a river port, is located 120 kilometers northwest of Hong Kong. The site of the opera house, adjacent to a proposed municipal museum and a "metropolitan activities zone," is set against the background of the tall buildings of Zhujiang New Town, a particularly spectacular location leading to the Haixinsha Tourist Park Island. The architect speaks of a "twin boulder design" and of landforms to describe the facility that includes a 1800-seat grand theater, entrance lobby, lounge, multifunction hall, and support facilities. An internal street leading on one side to the planned museum site has a café, bar, restaurant, and retail areas on one side, dividing the two main volumes. Inscribed in the urban context of the changing city in a strategic location at the foot of Zhujiang Boulevard, a central avenue of the city, the architectural design also adapts a variation on Hadid's theme of forms inspired by the land. One of the largest performing arts centers in South China and one of the three biggest theaters in the country, the Guangzhou Opera House is Zaha Hadid's first completed work in China.

Der für die Stadt Guangzhou errichtete 70 000 m² große Komplex liegt in einem neuen Kulturviertel mit Blick auf den Perlfluss. Guangzhou (früher Kanton), eine Hafenstadt mit fast 10 Millionen Einwohnern, liegt 120 km nordwestlich von Hongkong. Das Grundstück des Opernhauses grenzt an ein geplantes Stadtmuseum und eine „urbane Zone". Die Hochhäuser des neuen Stadtviertels Zhujiang bilden seine Kulisse – ein spektakulärer Ort auf dem Weg zur Insel Haixinsha. Die Architektin spricht vom Motiv eines „Zwillingsfelsens" und von geologischen Formationen, wenn sie den Bau beschreibt, der einen großen Theatersaal mit 1800 Plätzen, Lobby, Halle, Multifunktionssaal und Versorgungseinrichtungen umfasst. Eine durch das Grundstück verlaufende Promenade, die beide Baukörper trennt und zum geplanten Museum führt, wird an der einen Seite von einem Café, einer Bar, einem Restaurant und Ladenflächen gesäumt. Der Entwurf, eingeschrieben in den urbanen Kontext der sich wandelnden Stadt und strategisch unterhalb des zentralen Zhujiang Boulevard gelegen, ist zudem eine Variation des Motivs landschaftlich inspirierter Formen, ein ständiges Thema bei Hadid. Das Opernhaus in Guangzhou, eines der größten Zentren für darstellende Künste in Südchina und zugleich eines der drei größten Theater des Landes, ist Hadids erster realisierter Bau in China.

Guangzhou (Canton) est une ville de près de 10 millions d'habitants et un grand port fluvial à 120 km au nord-ouest de Hongkong. Édifiée pour la municipalité, cette construction de 70 000 m² domine la rivière des Perles, située en pleine zone de développement à vocation culturelle. Ce site, adjacent à un musée municipal qui devrait être construit et à une « zone d'activités métropolitaines », se présente sur le fond des immeubles de grande hauteur de la ville nouvelle de Zhujiang. Il occupe donc un emplacement particulièrement spectaculaire, qui est également la porte d'accès au parc touristique de l'île d'Haixinsha. L'architecte parle « d'un design de double rocher » et de modelé naturel pour décrire cette réalisation qui comprend un théâtre de 1800 places, un hall d'entrée, un salon, un hall polyvalent et des installations techniques. La rue intérieure, qui conduit vers le site du futur musée, est dotée d'un café, d'un bar, d'un restaurant et de commerces divisant les deux volumes principaux. Inscrit dans le contexte urbain d'une ville en plein changement, situé sur un site stratégique au départ du boulevard Zhujiang, l'avenue centrale de la ville nouvelle, ce projet architectural est encore une fois une variation du thème « hadidien » des formes inspirées par la terre. Faisant partie des plus grands centres des arts du spectacle de la Chine du Sud et des trois plus grands théâtres du pays, cet opéra est la première œuvre achevée par Zaha Hadid en Chine.

An overall view of the main concert hall (above) and a section drawing below demonstrate how the architects impose their own style on spaces that are also in good part determined by seating and acoustics.

Ein Blick in den großen Konzertsaal (oben) und ein Querschnitt unten belegen, wie die Architekten es verstehen, auch solchen Räumen ihre Handschrift zu verleihen, die vor allem von Kriterien wie Kapazität und Akustik definiert werden.

Cette vue générale de la salle de concerts principale (ci-dessus) et la coupe ci-dessous montrent comment les architectes ont imposé leur style à des volumes déterminés en grande partie par le nombre de sièges et l'acoustique.

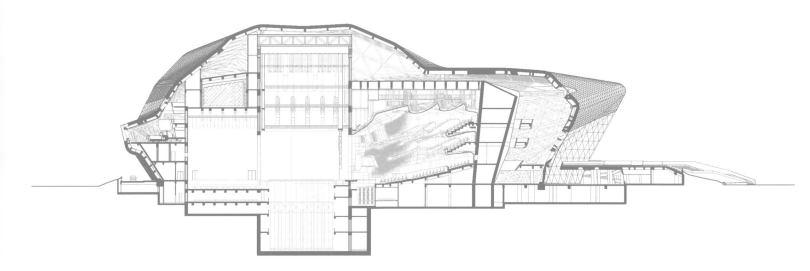

A ballet rehearsal area has the same kind of flowing, light-filled atmosphere as much of the rest of the building, whereas often such spaces are treated by architects as an afterthought.

Ein Probenraum für das Ballett hat dieselbe fließende, lichtdurchflutete Atmosphäre wie weite Bereiche des Komplexes, obwohl Architekten solche Räumlichkeiten häufig nachrangig behandeln.

Répétition d'un ballet dans une salle qui bénéficie de la même atmosphère fluide et lumineuse que le reste du bâtiment, alors que ce type d'espace est souvent négligé par les architectes.

Foyer space with a triangulated frame that defines seemingly uninterrupted and continuous volumes. The synthesis of exterior and interior design is evident here.

Ein Bereich des Foyers mit einem Rastermotiv in Dreiecksform. Auch hier gehen die Räume ununterbrochen und fließend ineinander über. Deutlich erkennbar ist die Synthese von Außen- und Innenbau.

La structure triangulée du foyer dessine des volumes apparemment continus sans interruption. La synthèse de la conception de l'intérieur et de l'extérieur est particulièrement évidente ici.

GLASGOW RIVERSIDE MUSEUM

Glasgow, Scotland, UK. 2004–11

Project
GLASGOW RIVERSIDE MUSEUM

Location
GLASGOW, SCOTLAND, UK

Client
GLASGOW CITY COUNCIL

Exhibition Area
6000 m²

Total Area
11 000 m²

Flowing and curvilinear in plan, as seen in the aerial view to the left, the building appears to be more angular and rectilinear when seen from ground level.

Während der Bau im Luftbild links fließend und geschwungen wirkt, gibt er sich zu ebener Erde deutlich geradliniger und eckiger.

De plan fluide et tout en courbe quand on le voit du ciel, le bâtiment semble plus anguleux et rectiligne vu au niveau du sol.

Built for the Glasgow City Council at 22 Trongate in Glasgow, this 11 000-square-meter museum has 6000 square meters of exhibition space. The architect speaks of a "wave" or a "pleated movement" in describing the building that has a café and corporate entertainment space at one end with a view of the Clyde River. As it is described: "The building, open at opposite ends, positions itself in a tunnel-like configuration between the city and the Clyde. In doing so it becomes porous to its context. However, the connection from one to the other is where the building diverts to create a journey away from the external context into the world of the exhibits. Here the interior path becomes a mediator between the city and the river that can either be hermetic or porous depending on the exhibition layout. Thus the museum positions itself symbolically and functionally as open and fluid with its engagement of context and content." The office has also developed the landscape scheme for the area around the building with the idea of a single surface laid across the site, with fluid changes in levels and blurred boundaries between hard and soft landscape. A shallow pond to the west side for occasional use by boat enthusiasts further links the building with the Clyde and the museum's visitors. One of a number of projects by recognized architects in Glasgow, the Riverside Museum of Transport underlines the desire of the city to confirm and develop its position as the cultural capital of Scotland.

Das 11 000 m² große, von der Stadt Glasgow in Auftrag gegebene Museum liegt an der Trongate 22 in Glasgow und umfasst über 6000 m² Ausstellungsfläche. Die Architektin bezeichnet den Bau, der an seiner Stirnseite neben einem Café auch einen Veranstaltungsraum mit Blick auf den Clyde bietet, als „Welle" oder „gestauchte Bewegung". Laut Projektbeschreibung ist „der Bau eine tunnelartige Halle, die sich an den Schmalseiten zur Stadt bzw. zum Fluss hin öffnet. So wird er an beiden Seiten durchlässig für sein Umfeld. Exakt an dieser Schnittstelle faltet sich der Bau nach innen und lädt ein zu einer Reise in die Welt der Ausstellung. Der Pfad im Innern des Museums wird zum Vermittler zwischen Stadt und Fluss und lässt sich je nach Ausstellungskonzept geschlossen oder offen konfigurieren. Auf diese Weise positioniert sich das Museum symbolisch wie funktional als offen und fließend im Umgang mit kontextuellen und inhaltlichen Fragen." Hadids Büro entwickelte auch die Grünflächenplanung als durchgängige Geländeoberfläche mit fließenden Übergängen zwischen unterschiedlichen Ebenen sowie „harter" und „weicher" Landschaft. Nach Westen signalisiert ein flacher Teich, auch für Bootsliebhaber nutzbar, die Anbindung des Baus an den Clyde. Das Museum of Transport ist eines von mehreren Projekten in Glasgow, die von bekannten Architekten gestaltet werden, ein Zeichen für das Engagement der Stadt, sich zunehmend als kulturelles Zentrum Schottlands zu profilieren.

Construit pour la ville de Glasgow, au 22 Trongate Street, ce musée de 11 000 m² dispose de 6000 m² de salles d'expositions. L'architecte parle d'une « vague » ou d'un « mouvement plissé » pour décrire ce bâtiment qui possède également un espace pour réceptions et un café donnant sur la Clyde. « Le bâtiment est comme un hangar en forme de tunnel, ouvert à ses deux extrémités opposées sur la ville et sur la Clyde. Il devient ainsi poreux des deux côtés par rapport à son contexte. Cependant, la connexion de l'un à l'autre s'effectue selon un parcours divergeant qui mène du monde extérieur à l'univers des pièces exposées. Médiateur entre la ville et le fleuve, le cheminement peut donc être hermétique ou poreux en fonction du plan de l'exposition. Ainsi le musée se positionne symboliquement et fonctionnellement comme ouvert et fluide dans son rapport avec son contexte et son contenu. » L'agence a également réalisé l'aménagement paysager pour l'environnement du musée qui se présente comme une surface d'un seul tenant avec des changements de niveaux tout en douceur et des transitions fluides entres les paysages « durs » et « mous ». À l'ouest, un étang peu profond, que peuvent utiliser les amateurs de la barque, met en valeur la continuité du bâtiment avec la Clyde. Faisant partie de divers projets signés par des architectes de renom à Glasgow, le musée des Transports incarne le désir de la ville de confirmer et de développer son rôle de capitale culturelle de l'Écosse.

Seen from the exterior, the spectacular glazed façade seems to reveal a great assortment of vehicles as though they might be speeding toward the visitor.

Von außen ist durch die spektakuläre Glasfassade eine Vielzahl von Fahrzeugen zu sehen, die auf den Betrachter zuzurasen scheinen.

Vue de l'extérieur, la spectaculaire façade vitrée révèle toute une gamme de véhicules qui semblent se précipiter à la rencontre du visiteur.

Some displays set vehicles apart from the architectural volumes by means of contrast (right), while bicycles seem to fly around the space in a great circle.

In einigen Fällen wurde die Präsentation der Exponate als Kontrast zur Architektur konzipiert (rechts), während Fahrräder in ausholendem Schwung durch den Raum zu fliegen scheinen.

Certaines présentations se détachent de l'architecture (à droite) tandis que des vélos semblent parcourir l'espace dans un immense cercle.

LONDON
AQUATICS CENTRE
London, UK. 2005–11

Project
LONDON AQUATICS CENTRE

Location
LONDON, UK

Client
OLYMPIC DELIVERY AUTHORITY

Area/Size
20 000 m²

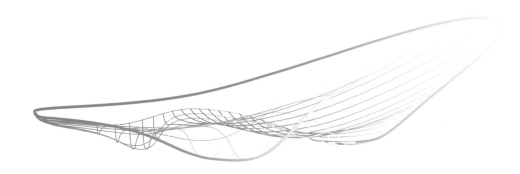

The light, curving roof of the complex is one of its main architectural features—seen here from the interior and in a drawing.

Das leicht geschwungene Dach ist eines der markantesten baulichen Merkmale des Komplexes – hier eine Innenansicht und eine Zeichnung.

Légère et incurvée, l'immense toiture est une des caractéristiques principales de l'architecture de ce Centre. Elle est vue ici de l'intérieur et sur un dessin.

The Aquatics Centre, a sports facility for the 2012 Summer Olympics and future "legacy" use, has an area of 20 000 square meters. Zaha Hadid makes it clear that the architecture is "inspired by the fluid geometry of water in motion." An undulating roof rises from the ground and encloses the swimming pools in a "unifying gesture of fluidity." Part of the Olympic Park Master Plan, the facility is located on its southeastern corner. A new pedestrian access to the Olympic Park via the east–west bridge (called the Stratford City Bridge) passes directly over the Centre, serving as a primary gateway to the Park. The structure is laid out perpendicularly to the bridge and contains three pools, one for training, one for the swimming events, and the other for diving—with seating for 17 500 people for the main competition pool and diving, and 5000 seats for water polo. The architects explain: "The overall strategy is to frame the base of the pool hall as a podium connected to the Stratford City Bridge." The steel and aluminum roof with double-curvature parabolic arches is most probably the "signature" element of the complex, filled with glazing where it rises above the podium. The London Aquatics Centre was completed on budget and on schedule, on July 21, 2011.

Das Aquatics Centre, eine Sporteinrichtung für die Olympischen Sommerspiele 2012 und darüber hinaus, hat eine Nutzfläche von 20 000 m². Zaha Hadid betont, die Architektur sei „inspiriert von der fließenden Geometrie bewegten Wassers". Ein geschwungenes Dach steigt vom Boden auf und überfängt die Schwimmbecken in einer „einenden, fließenden Geste". Der Bau ist Teil des Masterplans für den olympischen Park und liegt an dessen südöstlicher Ecke. Eine neue Fußgängerbrücke, die Stratford City Bridge, verläuft in Ost-West-Richtung teilweise über den Komplex hinweg und ist zugleich eine der Hauptadern im Fußgängerschließungskonzept des Parks. Der Komplex verläuft im rechten Winkel zur Stratford City Bridge und umfasst drei Schwimmbecken, ein Trainingsbecken, ein Wettkampfbecken sowie ein Sprungbecken – wobei das zentrale Wettkampfbecken und das Sprungbecken Platz für 17 500 Zuschauer bieten, 5000 Plätze bei Wasserpolospielen. Die Architekten erklären: „Zentrale Strategie war es, die Grundebene der Schwimmhalle als Sockel an die Stratford City Bridge anzubinden." Das parabolisch zweifach geschwungene Dach aus Stahl und Aluminium, das über der Tribüne verglast ist, ist fraglos das eigentliche Wahrzeichen des Gebäudes. Das London Aquatics Centre konnte im Rahmen des gesetzten Budgets gebaut und pünktlich am 21. Juli 2011 in Betrieb genommen werden.

Pour Zaha Hadid, ces installations nautiques de 20 000 m² réalisées pour les Jeux olympiques de Londres en 2012 mais qui seront utilisées longtemps après « s'inspirent de la géométrie fluide de l'eau en mouvement ». Une immense toiture ondulée qui part du sol recouvre les bassins de natation dans un « geste de fluidité unificatrice ». Ce stade est situé à l'angle sud-est du plan directeur du Parc olympique. L'accès principal au Parc se fait par un nouveau pont piétonnier (Stratford City Bridge) passant directement au-dessus des voies de chemin de fer. Le bâtiment implanté perpendiculairement au pont contient trois bassins : un pour l'entraînement, un pour les compétitions et le troisième pour le plongeon. 17 500 sièges étaient prévus pour les grandes compétitions de natation et de plongeon, 5000 pour les matches de water polo. Comme l'expliquent les architectes : « La stratégie d'ensemble est de faire de la base du bâtiment des bassins un podium connecté au pont de Stratford. » La toiture en acier et aluminium à arcs paraboliques à double courbure est la « signature » visible de cette architecture amplement vitrée à partir du podium. Ces installations sportives ont été achevées le 21 juillet 2011 dans les délais et selon le budget alloué.

Above, a computer-generated image shows the roof of the complex as well as the landscaping of the site. Left, two pictures taken in 2013 during the transformation of the Centre to its final form after the 2012 Olympics. The curvature of the roof is clearly visible.

Eine Simulation (oben) zeigt das Dach des Komplexes und die Landschaftsplanung des Geländes. Links zwei Aufnahmen von 2013 beim Umbau des Centres in seine endgültige nacholympische Form. Der Schwung des Dachs ist deutlich zu erkennen.

Ci-dessus, rendu par ordinateur du complexe, de sa toiture et de l'aménagement paysager du site. À gauche, deux images prises en 2013 pendant la transformation du Centre après les Jeux olympiques 2012. La courbe du toit s'impose dans le paysage.

Drawings show the elegant supporting structure of the roof. Below, a computer-generated image with the overhanging roof and broadly glazed façade.

Zeichnungen veranschaulichen die Eleganz des Dachtragwerks. Die Simulation unten zeigt den Dachüberstand und die großzügig verglaste Fassade

Deux dessins montrant l'élégante structure de la toiture. Ci-dessous, image de synthèse du surplomb du toit et de la vaste façade vitrée.

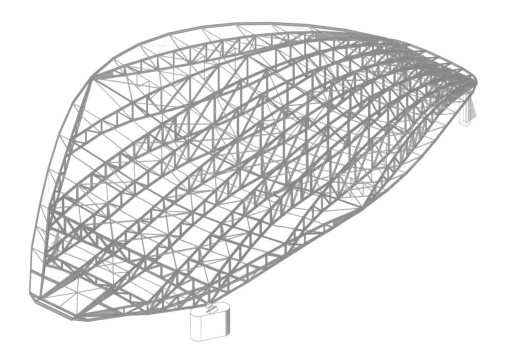

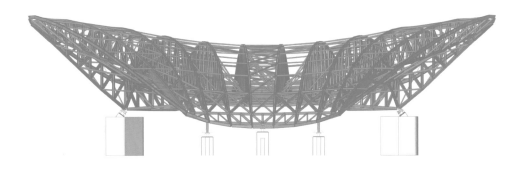

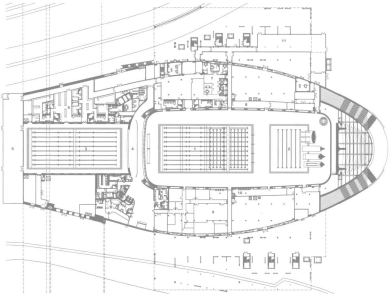

The curving ceiling and the broad continuity of the swimming pool and grandstands create a coherent sporting environment—something that is rarer than it might seem. Left, a plan of the area.

Durch die geschwungene Decke und die kontinuierliche Linienführung von Becken und Tribünen entsteht ein überzeugendes Umfeld für sportliche Wettkämpfe – was seltener ist als man erwarten könnte. Links ein Grundriss des Bereichs.

Le plafond incurvé et la continuité entre les bassins et les gradins créent un environnement sportif cohérent, un fait plus rare qu'on ne le pense. A gauche, plan de la même partie du Centre.

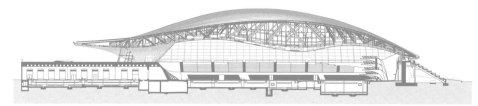

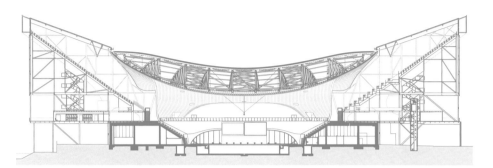

Section drawings make apparent the dynamic impact of the broadly curving roof. Although Hadid is not given to specific references to the animal world, the image of a ray does come to mind.

Querschnitte veranschaulichen die dynamische Wirkung des ausgreifend geschwungenen Dachs. Auch wenn Hadid kaum Bezüge zur Tierwelt herstellt, lässt sich hier das Bild eines Rochens ahnen.

Ces coupes montrent l'impact dynamique de la courbure du toit. Bien qu'Hadid n'ait pas fait de références spécifiques au monde aquatique, l'image d'une raie géante vient à l'esprit.

The curvature of the diving platforms also brings an added architectural element to the swimming complex, again linking specifically to Hadid's aesthetic sense of continuity and movement.

Die geschwungene Form der Sprungtürme in der Schwimmhalle ist eine weitere architektonische Geste und fügt sich schlüssig in Hadids Ästhetik, die von fließenden, dynamischen Räumen geprägt ist.

La courbe du plongeoir est en soi un élément architectural, là encore caractéristique du sens esthétique de la continuité et du mouvement chez Hadid.

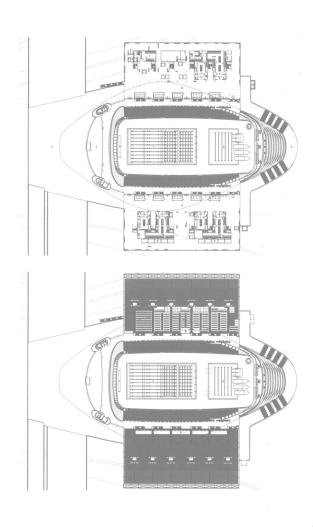

Above, a training pool is rendered attractive by the overhead lighting system, arrayed in continuous rows like the swimming lanes themselves.

Das Trainingsbecken oben gewinnt besonders durch seine Lichtdecke, gestaltet als Reihensystem in Anlehnung an die Schwimmbahnen.

Ci-dessus, un bassin d'entraînement est rendu plus spectaculaire encore par le système d'éclairage zénithal, disposé en lignes suivant celles des bassins.

Left, the same training pool and, above left, the powerful curvature of a concrete stairway near the swimming pools.

Links dasselbe Trainingsbecken; oben links der beeindruckende Schwung einer Betontreppe neben den Schwimmbecken.

À gauche, le même bassin d'entraînement et, ci-dessus à gauche, la puissante courbe d'un escalier de béton situé près des bassins.

CMA CGM TOWER

Marseille, France. 2006–11

Project
CMA CGM TOWER
Location
MARSEILLE, FRANCE
Client
CMA CGM
Area/Size
93 200 m²
HEIGHT 33 FLOORS/147 m

Left, a view of the tower gives the impression that it is actually set on the elevated motorway that passes near its base. This page, drawings emphasize the leaning, flowing movement of the structure.

Auf der Aufnahme links erscheint es so, als stünde der Turm direkt auf der Stadtautobahn nahe des Sockels. Die Zeichnungen auf dieser Seite betonen die schiefwinklig fließende Dynamik des Baus.

À gauche, vue de la tour donnant l'impression qu'elle prend appui sur l'autoroute passant à son pied. Ci-dessus, dessins mettant en évidence le caractère fluide du projet.

This 93 200-square-meter tower is located approximately one kilometer north of the historic center of Marseille in the Euroméditerranée development zone near the city's commercial port. It is located 100 meters from the edge of the water near an elevated motorway. The project is divided into two parts, with the tower itself offering 56 600 square meters of space, and an annex that measures 36 600 square meters. Designed for 2700 employees, with parking for 700 cars and 200 motorcycles, the complex includes a corporate restaurant that seats 800 people. A gym and auditorium are also part of the facility. The architects explain: "The design strategy to deal with an awkward, elongated site was to break down the volume of the façade into vertical segments and differentiate them using light and dark glazing. These are then offset to one another with the clear glazing set forward as a separate skin which is articulated architecturally by incorporating the peripheral structural columns." The apparently diverging elements of the tower echo the split in the motorway that runs on either side of the site. In a city with few tall buildings, the CMA CGM Tower offers hope of regeneration that goes beyond the immediate district.

Das Hochhaus mit einer Fläche von 93 200 m² liegt rund einen Kilometer nördlich der historischen Altstadt von Marseille im Bauerschließungsgebiet Euroméditerranée, nicht weit vom Frachthafen der Stadt. Der Bau befindet sich 100 m vom Wasser entfernt an einer Hochstraße. Die Anlage gliedert sich in zwei Teile: dem Turm mit 56 600 m² Nutzfläche und einem Nebengebäude mit 36 000 m² Fläche. Der für 2700 Mitarbeiter geplante Komplex umfasst Stellplätze für 700 Pkw und 200 Motorräder sowie ein Firmenrestaurant mit 800 Plätzen. Hinzu kommen ein Fitnessbereich und ein Auditorium. Die Architekten erklären: „Als Planungsstrategie für das problematische, gestreckte Baugrundstück entschie-

den wir uns, die Fassade in vertikale Segmente aufzulösen und durch dunkle und hellere Verglasung zu differenzieren. Diese sind voneinander abgesetzt durch das Vorhängen der Klarverglasung als separate Gebäudehaut, die architektonisch durch Einbindung tragender Stützen artikuliert wird." Die deutlich divergierenden Elemente des Turms spiegeln motivisch die Schnellstraße, die das Grundstück beidseitig einfasst. In einer Stadt mit nur wenigen Hochhausbauten ist der CMA CGM Tower ein Hoffnungsschimmer, dass die Stadterneuerungsbemühungen über den unmittelbaren Stadtkern hinausgehen.

Cette tour de 93 200 m² s'élève à un kilomètre environ au nord du centre historique de Marseille dans la zone de rénovation urbaine appelée Euroméditerranée à proximité du port commercial et à 100 mètres seulement du rivage, derrière une autoroute suspendue. Le projet se divise en deux parties : la tour elle-même, de 56 600 m², et une annexe de 36 600 m². Conçu pour 2700 employés, l'ensemble comprend également un parking pour 700 voitures et 200 motos, un restaurant de 800 couverts, un gymnase et un auditorium. Pour Zaha Hadid : « La stratégie de conception de ce projet a dû prendre en compte le caractère difficile d'un terrain tout en longueur, et pour ce faire rompre le volume de la façade en segments verticaux, différenciés par un vitrage clair ou sombre, devant lesquels a été tendue une peau indépendante en verre clair, architecturalement articulée par l'intégration des colonnes structurelles périphériques. » Les éléments en divergence apparente font écho à l'embranchement de l'autoroute qui encadre le site. Dans une ville qui ne compte pas beaucoup de tours, celle de la CMA CGM est un appel à une renaissance urbaine qui se fait entendre au-delà de son quartier.

The commercial port district where the tower is located is by no means central, but the upward sweep of the structure gives a decidedly dynamic aspect to the image. Below, elevation drawings.

Das Industriehafenviertel, in dem der Turm steht, ist alles andere als zentral, der aufwärtsstrebende Schwung verleiht dem Bau eine besondere Dynamik. Unten Aufrisse.

Située dans le contexte du port commercial de Marseille, la structure semble surgir du sol dans un geste dynamique. Ci-dessous, dessins d'élévations.

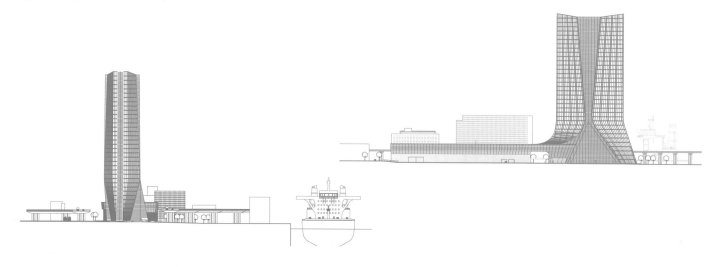

As it happens, the white curves of the bathroom fixtures displayed by the client fit into the overall design in a coherent way, creating neither contradiction nor contrast.

Die Formgebung der weißen Sanitäreinbauten im Ausstellungsraum fügt sich schlüssig in den Gesamtentwurf, ohne Widerspruch oder Kontrast.

Le design des éléments de salles de bains présentés par le client se fondent de manière cohérente dans le projet, sans contradiction ni contraste.

The space surely has a very contemporary feeling and yet it also evokes natural forms, perhaps caves in the case of the images seen here.

Obwohl die Räume dezidiert zeitgenössisch sind, ist die Nähe zu natürlichen Formen spürbar – die Aufnahmen wecken Assoziationen an Höhlen.

L'espace est évidemment d'esprit très contemporain et évoque cependant des formes naturelles. On pourrait même penser, comme ici, à des cavernes.

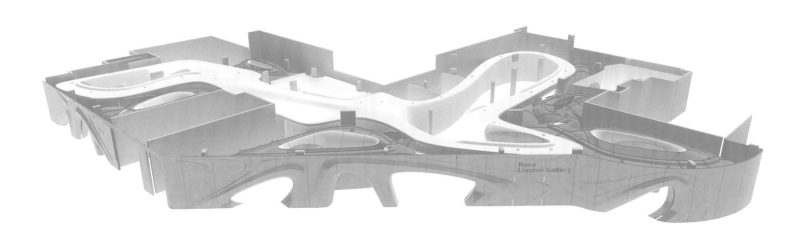

The client makes bathroom fixtures, including toilets, which here find an elegance in their architectural setting that is not contradictory with their forms, but rather complements their own curves.

Der Auftraggeber ist Hersteller von Sanitäreinbauten. Selbst Toiletten fügen sich hier elegant in ein bauliches Umfeld, das keine Kontraste, sondern ein formales Pendant bildet.

Le client est un fabricant d'appareils sanitaires, et même ses cuvettes de toilette expriment dans ce cadre architectural une élégance de courbes en accord avec leur cadre.

PIERRESVIVES

Montpellier, France. 2002–12

Project
PIERRESVIVES

Location
MONTPELLIER, FRANCE

Client
DEPARTEMENT DE L'HERAULT

Area/Size
BUILDING 28 500 m²
SITE 35 000 m²

The exterior forms of the building, together with the drawing above, give a very decided impression of forward movement but also of architectural continuity, as opposed to the stability that was so sought after in the past.

Die Formgebung des Außenbaus und die Zeichnung (oben) zeugen deutlich von vorwärtsstrebender Dynamik und fließender Kontinuität – im Gegensatz zu einer in der Vergangenheit oft angestrebten statischen Stabilität.

Les formes extérieures du bâtiment et le dessin ci-dessus donnent une impression très forte de forme en mouvement, mais aussi de continuité architecturale, contrairement au sentiment de stabilité si recherché dans l'architecture du passé.

The program for this 28 500-square-meter complex includes archives, a library, and offices for the sports department of the Hérault region of France, in the city of Montpellier. The site measures 35 000 square meters. The three elements of the project are melded together in a form likened to a "horizontal tree trunk," with the archives in the base, the library above, and the sports department offices on top. Each level is progressively more porous or open. Branches come out of this trunk providing access to the different areas of the building. Public entrances are on the west and service entrances on the opposite side. A road provides access to both sides of the structure. A very large cantilevered canopy marks the main doors. A central "linear lobby" links the different parts of the complex, but functions are kept clearly delineated, especially above ground level. Different layouts are provided according to the required functions. Auditoriums and meeting rooms shared by the institutions are located near the central part of the main public artery of the building. Zaha Hadid states: "Its conception is one of the most ambitious and comprehensive assertions of our will to create dynamic and fluid spaces. It blends formal geometric complexity with bold structures and an innovative use of materials. Architectural creation involves pushing the boundaries—and I believe that Pierresvives is an excellent demonstration of that." The building was inaugurated on September 13, 2012.

Das Programm des 28 500 m² großen Komplexes umfasst ein Archiv, eine Bibliothek und Büros für die Sportverwaltung des südfranzösischen Departements Hérault und liegt auf einem 35 000 m² großen Grundstück in Montpellier. Die drei funktionalen Elemente verschmelzen zu einem „horizontalen Baumstamm": das Archiv zuunterst, die Bibliothek darüber, die Büros der Sportverwaltung ganz oben. Die einzelnen Ebenen sind mit zunehmender Höhe durchlässiger und offener gehalten. Erschlossen werden die verschiedenen Zonen über „Verzweigungen" im „Stamm". Besuchereingänge sind nach Westen, die Personaleingänge zur gegenüberliegenden Seite orientiert. Eine Straße erschließt den Komplex von beiden Seiten. Über dem Haupteingang schiebt sich der Bau als mächtiger Ausleger heraus. Ein geradliniges Hauptfoyer verbindet die verschiedenen Bereiche, den-noch sind die Funktionen klar differenziert, gerade in den Obergeschossen. Zudem sind den Funktionen individuelle Grundrisse zugewiesen. Gemeinsam genutzte Auditorien und Konferenzräume liegen in einer zentralen Zone, der Hauptschlagader des Baus. Zaha Hadid erklärt: „Der Entwurf ist eine der bisher ambitioniertesten und konsequentesten Umsetzungen unserer Vision von dynamischen, fließenden Räumen. Hier verschmelzen formal-geometrische Komplexität und gewagte Formen mit einer innovativen Nutzung baulicher Materialien. Kreative Architektur geht immer über Grenzen – ich bin überzeugt, dass Pierresvives der beste Beweis hierfür ist." Der Bau wurde am 13. September 2012 eingeweiht.

Le programme de ce complexe de 28 500 m² édifié sur un terrain de 35 000 m², conçu pour la direction des sports du département de l'Hérault à Montpellier, comprend des bureaux, une bibliothèque et des archives. Les trois composantes du projet sont fondues dans une forme comparable à un « tronc d'arbre horizontal ». Les archives occupent la base, la bibliothèque est implantée au-dessus et les bureaux au dernier niveau. Progressivement, les niveaux sont de plus en plus ouverts et poreux. Des « branches » poussent de ce tronc pour permettre l'accès aux différentes parties de l'immeuble. Les entrées pour le public sont situées sur la façade ouest et celles de service à l'est. Une route dessert les deux côtés du bâtiment. Un grand auvent en porte-à-faux signale l'entrée principale. Un « hall linéaire » central relie les différentes parties de l'ensemble, mais les fonctions restent clairement délimitées et caractérisées par leur plan, en particulier au-dessus du rez-de-chaussée. Les auditoriums et salles de réunion partagées par les différents départements sont implantés à proximité de la section centrale de l'axe de circulation principal. Pour Zaha Hadid, « ce projet est l'une des affirmations les plus ambitieuses et les plus complètes de notre volonté de créer des espaces fluides et dynamiques. Il associe une complexité géométrique formelle à des structures audacieuses et une utilisation novatrice des matériaux. La création architecturale signifie aussi savoir repousser les frontières, et je crois que les Pierresvives en sont une excellente démonstration. » Le bâtiment a été inauguré le 12 septembre 2012.

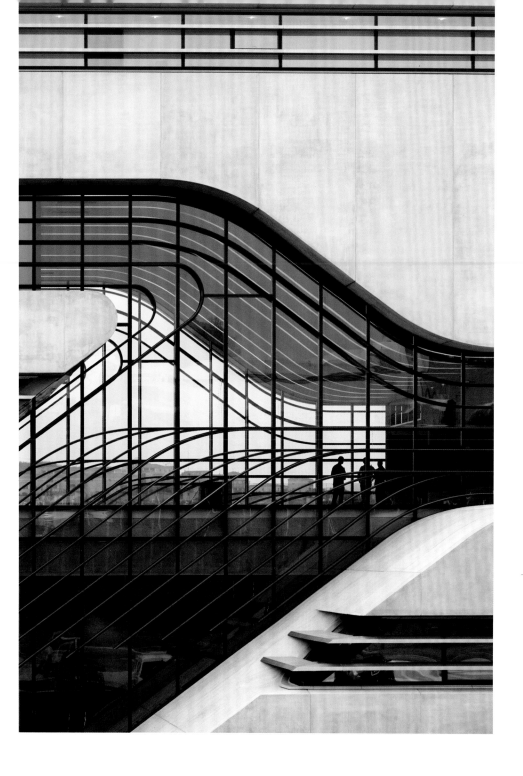

Although Hadid does not seek references to specific existing systems aside from geology, here the viewer is tempted to make a relation to aerodynamics, or aircraft forms.

Auch wenn Hadid – abgesehen von der Geologie – selten auf spezifische Systeme Bezug nimmt, legen diese Ansichten Referenzen an Aerodynamik oder den Flugzeugbau nahe.

Même si Hadid ne recherche pas ses références dans des systèmes spécifiques existants, en dehors de la géologie, le visiteur ne peut s'empêcher de penser à l'aérodynamique ou à des formes d'avion.

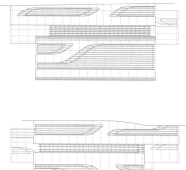

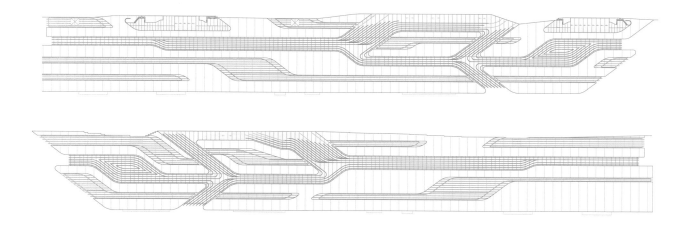

The undeniable elegance of these images may also bring to mind electronic circuitry or even wave forms. In any case, opacity and transparency are opposed and played upon.

Die auffällige Eleganz dieser Ansichten lässt auch an elektronische Schaltbilder oder Wellen denken. Jedenfalls wird motivisch mit Transparenz und Geschlossenheit gespielt und kontrastiert.

L'élégance indéniable de ces images peut aussi rappeler des circuits électroniques ou même des formes de vagues. Le jeu entre l'opacité et la transparence est permanent.

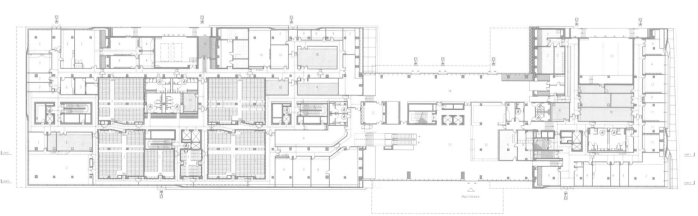

Main Entrance

Left, a floor plan shows rational space division, perhaps to an even higher degree than might be assumed from the exterior appearance of the building. Left, and above, reflections on the floor appear to multiply the sense of space inside the building.

Ein Grundriss (links) zeugt von rationaler Raumaufteilung, stärker noch, als es der Außenbau vermuten ließe. Links und oben: Spiegelungen im Boden verstärken die Raumtiefe.

À gauche, plan au sol montrant la division rationnelle de l'espace, plus précise que ce que l'on pourrait imaginer à partir de l'aspect extérieur du bâtiment. À gauche et en haut, les reflets au sol accentuent la profondeur de l'espace.

Sweeping floors and stairs are lit with a carefully designed system that is also integrated into the overall architectural concept.

Geschwungene Decken und Treppenanlagen sind mit einem speziell geplanten Lichtsystem ausgestattet, das sich in den Gesamtentwurf fügt.

Les sols et les escaliers sont éclairés par des systèmes d'éclairage soigneusement conçus, intégrés dans le concept global de l'architecture.

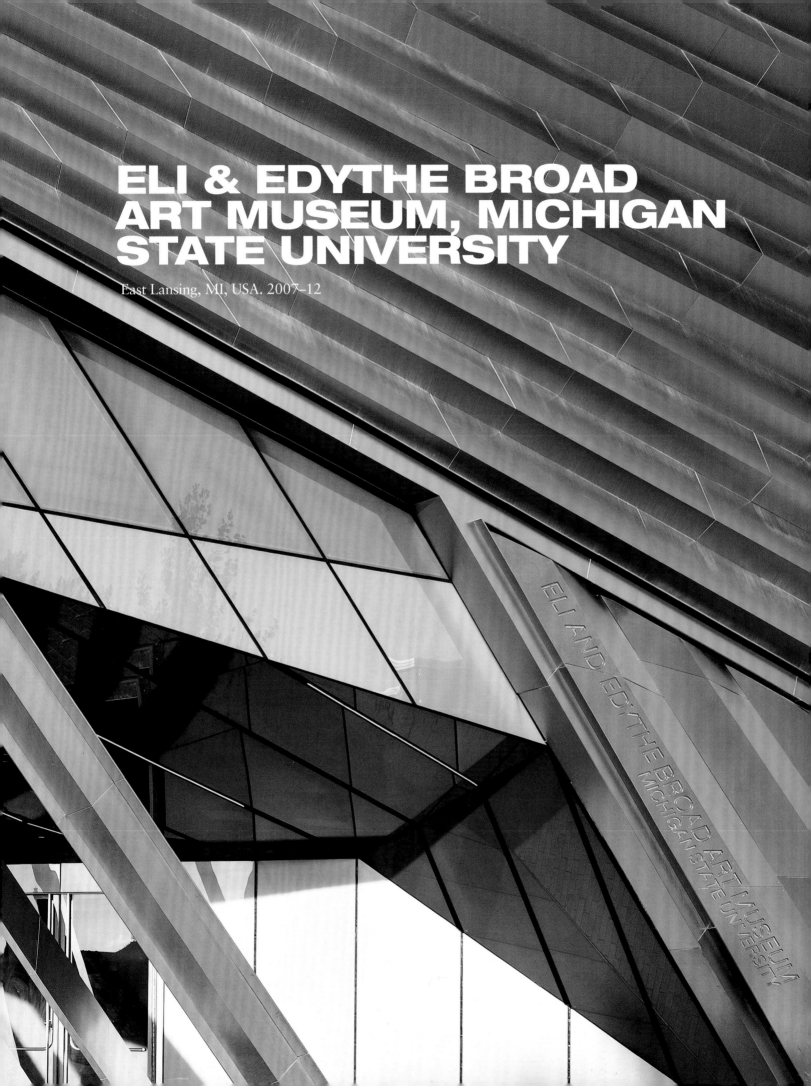

ELI & EDYTHE BROAD ART MUSEUM, MICHIGAN STATE UNIVERSITY

East Lansing, MI, USA. 2007–12

Project

ELI & EDYTHE BROAD ART MUSEUM, MICHIGAN STATE UNIVERSITY

Location
EAST LANSING, MI, USA

Client
MICHIGAN STATE UNIVERSITY

Area/Size
4274 m²

The folded shape of the building emerges from the earth like a natural rock outcropping might. Although straight lines dominate, there is an accordion-like effect that renders the structure even more unexpected than it would be with more regular lines.

Der gefaltete Korpus des Gebäudes ragt aus dem Boden auf wie ein Felsen. Obwohl hier gerade Linien dominieren, wirkt der Bau durch seinen Ziehharmonikaeffekt ungewöhnlicher, als es bei regelmäßiger Linienführung der Fall gewesen wäre.

La forme très particulière, comme « pliée », du musée semble jaillir du sol à la manière d'un rocher. Si les lignes droites dominent, l'effet d'accordéon surprend néanmoins.

The Broad Art Museum is intended essentially for contemporary art, but it also has a study collection with pieces ranging back to Greek and Roman art. It opened on November 10, 2012, and has an area of 4274 square meters. The building includes gallery space for special exhibitions, modern and contemporary art, new media, photography, and works on paper. The three-level museum (lower level, ground floor, and second floor) includes two-level spaces that provide space for large-scale installations. Other features include an education area, a café, shop, and outdoor sculpture park and pedestrian plaza. Zaha Hadid emphasizes the importance of the connecting paths and nearby Grand River Avenue in the design concept. The architects state: "Generating two dimensional planes from these lines of circulation and visual connections, the formal composition of the museum is achieved by folding these planes in three-dimensional space to define an interior landscape which brings together and negotiates the different pathways on which people move through and around the site." This structure has an exterior rainscreen system of steel framing clad with stainless-steel pleated panels. The architect's statement concludes: "The Broad Art Museum presents as a sharp, directed body, comprising directional pleats that reflect the topographic and circulatory characteristics of its surrounding landscape. Its outer skin echoes these different directions and orientations, giving the building an ever-changing appearance that arouses curiosity yet never quite reveals its content. This open character underlines the museum's function as a cultural hub for the community."

Das Broad Art Museum wurde primär für zeitgenössische Kunst geplant, umfasst jedoch auch eine Studiensammlung mit Werken der griechischen und römischen Antike. Der 4274 m² große Bau wurde am 10. November 2012 eröffnet und bietet Platz für Sonderausstellungen, für moderne und zeitgenössische Kunst, neue Medien, Fotografie und Grafik. Auf den drei Ebenen des Museums (Unter- und Erdgeschoss sowie erstes Stockwerk) wurden auch doppelgeschossige Zonen für raumgreifende Installationen geschaffen. Außerdem gehören ein Bereich für Museumspädagogik, ein Café, ein Museumsshop, ein Skulpturengarten und ein Vorplatz zu dem Museum. Hadid betont die Bedeutung der Verbindungswege und der Nähe zur Grand River Avenue für den Entwurf. Die Architekten erklären: „Aus den Linien der Verkehrsflüsse und Sichtachsen entstanden zunächst zweidimensionale Ebenen. Die formale Komposition ergab sich aus der Faltung dieser Ebenen zu einem dreidimensionalen Raum, einer Raumlandschaft, in der die Pfade durch und um das Gelände herum verbunden werden." Ummantelt ist der Bau mit einer Fassade aus gefalteten Edelstahlpaneelen über einer Stahlrahmenkonstruktion. Die Architekten fassen zusammen: „Das Broad Art Museum ist ein scharfer, gerichteter Korpus, eine Komposition aus Einzelsegmenten mit gerichteten Faltungen, die die Topografie und die Verkehrswege der umgebenden Landschaft reflektieren. Die Außenhaut spiegelt diese verschiedenen Richtungen und verleiht dem Bau eine changierende Erscheinung, die Neugier

weckt, ohne das Innere völlig zu enthüllen. Dieser offene Charakter unterstreicht die Bedeutung des Museums als kultureller Brennpunkt der Gemeinde."

Le Broad Art Museum, essentiellement consacré à l'art contemporain, possède également une collection historique dont les œuvres remontent à Rome et à la Grèce. De 4274 m² de surface, le bâtiment a ouvert ses portes le 10 novembre 2012. Il comprend des galeries pour l'art contemporain et moderne, pour les expositions temporaires, les nouveaux médias, la photographie et les travaux sur papier, réparties sur trois niveaux (sous-sol, rez-de-chaussée et étage). Certaines salles s'élèvent sur deux niveaux ce qui permet d'accueillir des installations et des œuvres de grandes dimensions. Il possède également des équipements éducatifs, un café, une boutique, un parc de sculptures et une plazza. Zaha Hadid a insisté dans sa conception sur les liens avec le quartier et la Grand River Avenue. « À partir des plans bidimensionnels créés par ces axes de circulation et ces connexions visuelles, la composition formelle du musée replie ces plans en espaces tridimensionnels pour définir un paysage intérieur réunissant et négociant les différents passages et parcours empruntées par les visiteurs dans le site et tout autour. » Le bâtiment est enveloppé d'un système de façade ventilée en panneaux plaqués d'acier inoxydable. « Le Broad Art Museum présente des masses à angles vifs, en basculement, dont les plis directionnels reflètent les caractéristiques topographiques et de circulation du paysage environnant. Sa peau externe fait écho aux différentes directions et orientations, donnant au bâtiment un aspect continuellement changeant qui éveille la curiosité sans jamais vraiment révéler son contenu. Ce caractère ouvert met en valeur la fonction du musée, plate-forme d'échanges culturels de la communauté à laquelle il appartient. »

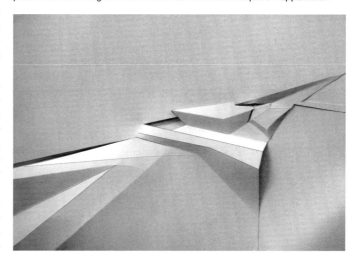

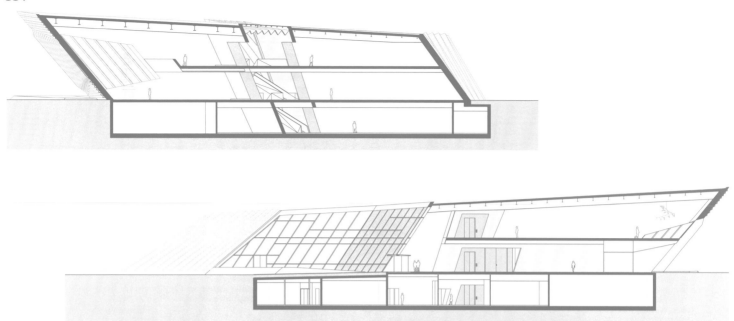

Shifted and cantilevered forms are revealed in images, but also, even more clearly, in the section drawings seen here.

Die Ansichten zeigen deutlich die Verschiebungen und Auskragungen des Baukörpers. Noch deutlicher wird dies in den Querschnitten.

Les formes inclinées ou en porte-à-faux sont prépondérantes comme le montrent ces images et, encore plus clairement, les coupes ci-contre.

Night lighting emphasizes the unusual forms of the structure, where angles and straight lines dominate, as opposed to the flowing curves often most evident in Hadid's buildings.

Die abendliche Beleuchtung unterstreicht die ungewöhnlichen Formen des Baus. Hier dominieren Winkel und gerade Linien, anders als die sanften Schwünge, die Hadids Entwürfe zumeist auszeichnen.

L'éclairage nocturne met en valeur les formes inhabituelles de ce projet dans lequel les lignes droites et les plans inclinés dominent, à l'opposé des formes en courbes et flux généralement très présentes chez Hadid.

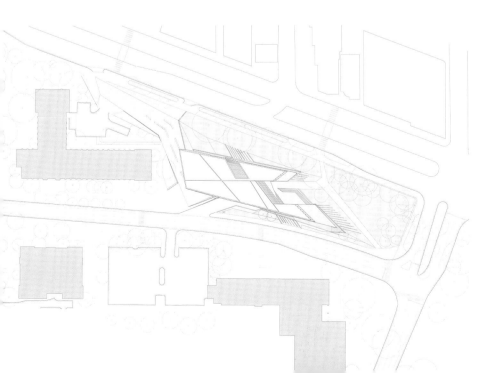

The image above shows how natural light is
brought into the building, while the site plan demonstrates the relation of the structure's fractured forms
with its surroundings.

Die Aufnahme oben zeigt, wie natürliches Licht in
den Bau gelangt. Der Lageplan unten illustriert das
Zusammenspiel der zersplitterten Formen des Baus
mit dem Umfeld.

L'image ci-dessus montre la manière dont l'éclairage naturel pénètre dans le bâtiment. Le plan ci-
contre illustre la relation entre les formes fracturées
du musée et son environnement.

Generous interior volumes feature a great deal of natural light. Strong angular forms carry the exterior design inside the building.

In die großzügigen Innenräume fällt reichlich Tageslicht ein. Markante Winkel übertragen die Ästhetik des Außenbaus ins Innere des Gebäudes.

Les généreux volumes intérieurs laissent pénétrer une énorme quantité de lumière naturelle. Les formes puissantes et anguleuses reprennent à l'intérieur le style de l'extérieur.

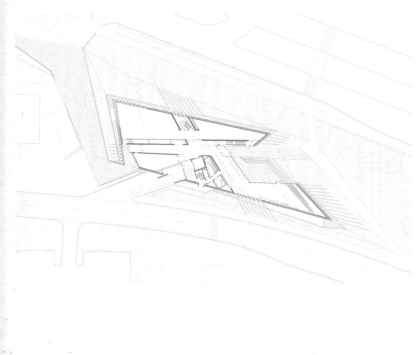

Even stairways are designed with the overall concept in mind, all very much in the style that Hadid has mastered—here in an increasingly mature and complete way.

Auch Treppenhäuser wurden im Sinne des Gesamtentwurfs gestaltet, in dem Stil, den Hadid meisterlich beherrscht – hier mit zunehmender Reife und Konsequenz.

Les escaliers font également partie du concept formel global, dans un style maîtrisé par Hadid de façon de plus en plus mature et achevée.

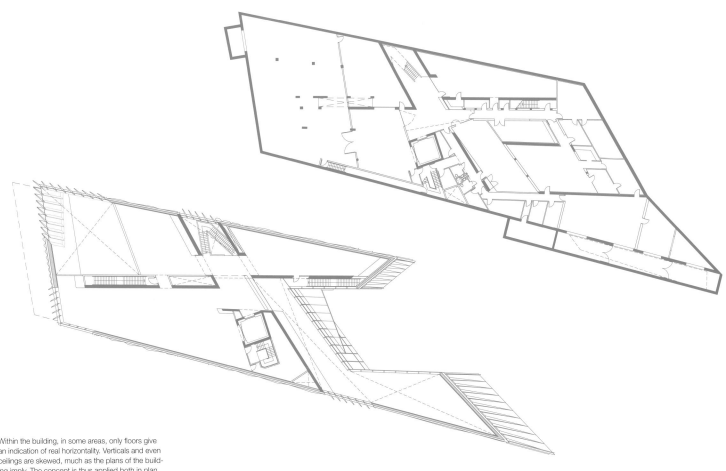

Within the building, in some areas, only floors give an indication of real horizontality. Verticals and even ceilings are skewed, much as the plans of the building imply. The concept is thus applied both in plan and in section.

In manchen Bereichen des Baus sind ausschließlich die Böden ein klarer Indikator für Horizontalität. Wände und selbst Decken sind geneigt, eine Schiefwinkligkeit, die auch der Grundriss reflektiert. Das Konzept wird schlüssig in Grund- und Aufriss umgesetzt.

Dans certaines zones du bâtiment, seuls les sols offrent un repère horizontal. Les murs et même les plafonds sont inclinés, suivant le plan du projet. Le concept est aussi bien appliqué en plan qu'en section.

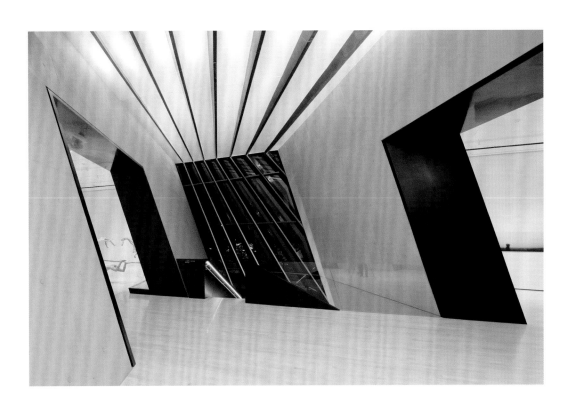

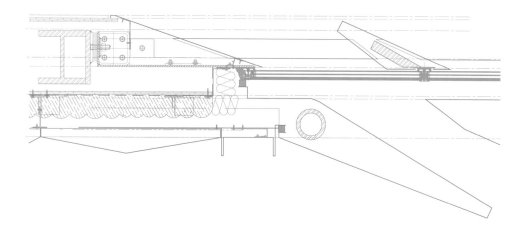

Although actual decorative elements are rare, the design is clearly thought out down to the smallest detail.

Auch wenn hier kaum dekorative Elemente zu finden sind, ist der Entwurf offensichtlich bis ins letzte Detail durchgeplant.

Bien que les éléments décoratifs soient rares, le projet est pensé jusque dans ses moindres détails.

The architectural design actually seeks to redefine built space, an ambitious goal that is at the heart of Zaha Hadid's approach—to reform space.

Der architektonische Entwurf will nicht weniger, als gebauten Raum neu definieren – ein ehrgeiziges Ziel, das ein zentrales Anliegen Hadids ist: die grundlegende Raumerneuerung.

La conception architecturale a cherché à redéfinir l'espace construit, objectif ambitieux au cœur de l'approche d'Hadid : re-former l'espace.

GALAXY SOHO

Beijing, China. 2008–12

Project
GALAXY SOHO

Location
BEIJING, CHINA

Client
SOHO CHINA

Area/Size
332 857 m²

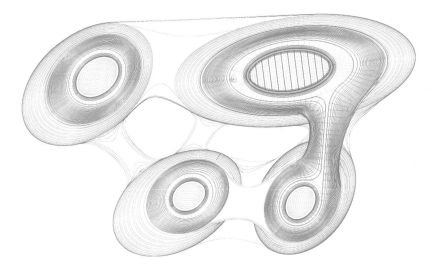

The amoeboid forms of the plan, actually made up of a series of interconnected ovals, are translated into the architectural volumes seen on the left page.

Die Amöbenform des Grundrisses basiert auf einer Reihe verbundener Ovale. Links im Bild die Umsetzung der Form in reale Baukörper.

Les formes amibiennes du plan, composé de quatre ovales reliés, se retrouvent dans les volumes architecturaux intérieurs (page de gauche).

This mixed-use (office and retail) building located in central Beijing, was built in just 30 months, which, considering its area of 332 857 square meters, is no small accomplishment. The architect explains: "Its architecture is a composition of four continuous, flowing volumes that are set apart, fused or linked by stretched bridges. These volumes adapt to each other in all directions, generating a panoramic architecture without corners or abrupt transitions that break the fluidity of its formal composition." Zaha Hadid compares the interior courts of the complex to traditional Chinese architecture, though she has eschewed from taking the rectilinear approach seen in such Chinese monuments as the Forbidden City. Rather, ovoid shapes of different dimensions coalesce into a convincing whole, where visitors experience shifts of scale inside the complex that have a fundamental relation to the overall plan. As the architect puts it, they find "intimate spaces that follow the same coherent formal logic of continuous curvilinearity." Curves are present not only in plan, but also in section, giving a flowing appearance that can readily be identified as a design by Zaha Hadid.

Der Büro- und Gewerbekomplex im Stadtzentrum von Peking wurde in nur 30 Monaten gebaut – angesichts einer Nutzfläche von 332 857 m² keine geringe Leistung. Die Architektin erklärt: „Die architektonische Komposition besteht aus vier fließenden Baukörpern, die durch Stege separiert, miteinander verschmolzen oder verbunden werden. Die Baukörper sind allseitig aufeinander abgestimmt, schaffen eine ‚Panorama-Architektur' ohne Ecken oder Kanten, die den Fluss der Komposition unterbrechen würden." Zaha Hadid vergleicht die Innenhöfe des Komplexes mit dem traditionellen chinesischen Hofhaus, wenngleich sie auf rechte Winkel verzichtet, wie man sie von chinesischen Monumenten wie der Verbotenen Stadt kennt. Vielmehr verschmelzen hier ovale Formen unterschied-

licher Größenordnung zu einem schlüssigen Ganzen. Im Inneren des Baus wird dieser Maßstabswechsel, stets überzeugend aus dem Gesamtentwurf abgeleitet, für Besucher nachvollziehbar. Der Architektin zufolge erleben die Besucher „einladende Räume", die „konsequent eine fließende Formensprache sprechen". Die geschwungene Linienführung zeigt sich nicht nur im Grundriss, sondern auch im Querschnitt: So entsteht ein Gesamtbild fließender Formen, das sich unmittelbar als Entwurf Zaha Hadids zu erkennen gibt.

Cet immeuble mixte (bureaux et commerces) du centre de Pékin a été construit en 30 mois ce qui, considérant sa surface de 332 857 m², n'est pas un mince exploit. Comme l'explique Zaha Hadid : « Son architecture est une composition de quatre volumes en flux continu qui sont séparés, fusionnés ou reliés par des passerelles étirées. Chaque volume s'adapte aux autres dans toutes les directions pour donner naissance à une architecture panoramique sans angles ni transitions abruptes qui puisse rompre la fluidité de sa composition formelle. » L'architecte compare les cours intérieures du complexe à l'architecture traditionnelle chinoise, bien qu'elle se soit tenue à l'écart de la rectilinéarité typique de monuments chinois comme la Cité interdite, par exemple. Elle a dessiné au contraire des formes ovoïdes de différentes dimensions qui se fondent en un ensemble convaincant, dans lequel le visiteur découvre des changements d'échelle mais toujours dans une relation fondamentale avec le plan d'ensemble. Comme Zaha Hadid l'exprime : « Les espaces intimes suivent la même logique formelle cohérente de curvilinéarité continue. » Les courbes se retrouvent non seulement en plan mais aussi en coupe, dans une fluidité apparente, indéniablement caractéristique du style de Zaha Hadid.

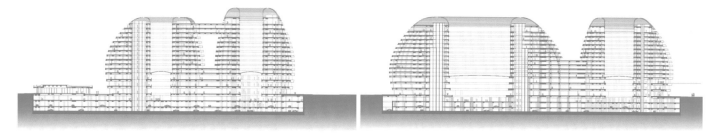

The layered curvature of the structure might bring to mind certain natural phenomena, such as erosion, but the effect of the building is a convivial and efficient one.

Die Schichtung des geschwungenen Baus lässt an geologische Phänomene wie Erosion denken. Dabei wirkt der Komplex einladend und räumlich effizient.

Les courbes stratifiées du complexe pourraient rappeler certains phénomènes naturels comme l'érosion, mais le résultat reste convivial et efficace.

Images emphasize the unusual mixture of natural and artificial forms that have been found in this instance—mountains, rivers, and contemporary architecture meet here.

Die Ansichten unterstreichen die ungewöhnliche Kombination natürlicher und künstlicher Formen, die hier zu erkennen sind – ein Zusammentreffen von Bergen, Flüssen und zeitgenössischer Architektur.

Les images mettent en valeur un mélange curieux de formes naturelles et artificielles, comme celle de montagnes, de rivières et d'éléments de l'architecture contemporaine.

The white curves of the interior have a decidedly contemporary appearance, with ample public space and a generous skylight.

Der Innenbau ist mit seinen geschwungenen weißen Linien eindeutig zeitgenössisch und bietet weitläufige öffentliche Verkehrsflächen und ein großzügiges Oberlicht.

Les courbes blanches que l'on retrouve à l'intérieur ont un aspect résolument contemporain. Elles déterminent de vastes espaces publics et bénéficient d'un généreux éclairage zénithal.

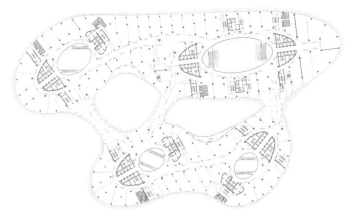

A plan and images of the exterior of the building show the high degree of relation between inside and outside.

Grundriss und Ansichten des Außenbaus veranschaulichen die klaren Bezüge zwischen innen und außen.

Un plan et une image de l'extérieur montrent la relation extrêmement étroite qu'entretiennent l'intérieur et l'extérieur.

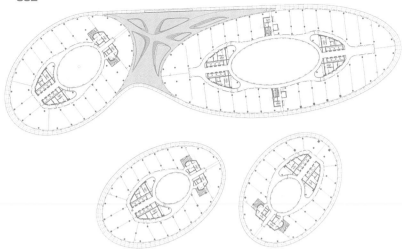

A plan showing the large connected oval shapes reveals the exterior courtyard spaces that can be seen under various angles in these images.

Ein Grundriss zeigt die großflächigen verbundenen ovalen Zonen und zugleich die Innenhofbereiche, die auf diesen Ansichten aus verschiedenen Blickwinkeln zu sehen sind.

Plan montrant les quatre composants ovales du complexe et les cours qui les connectent, aperçues sur ces images.

HEYDAR ALIYEV
CULTURAL CENTER

Baku, Azerbaijan. 2007–13

Project
HEYDAR ALIYEV CULTURAL CENTER

Location
BAKU, AZERBAIJAN

Client
THE REPUBLIC OF AZERBAIJAN

Floor area
52 417 m²

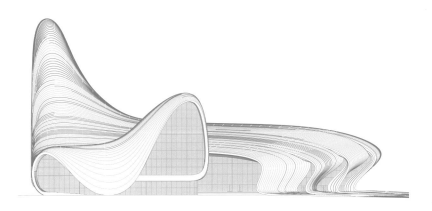

The real strength of Hadid's approach becomes apparent in these interior views where natural light and broad, flowing curves make for convivial spaces that are intimately linked to the exterior forms seen in the drawing on this page.

Die besondere Stärke von Hadids Ansatz wird auf diesen Innenansichten deutlich: Tageslicht und ausgreifende, fließende Formen schaffen einladende Räumlichkeiten, die eng mit dem Außenbau verknüpft sind, wie die Zeichnung oben belegt.

La force de l'approche d'Hadid s'impose d'elle-même dans ces vues intérieures. L'éclairage naturel et la fluidité des courbes créent des espaces conviviaux intimement liés aux formes extérieures (dessin ci-dessus).

This mixed-use cultural center has a total floor area of 101 801 square meters and a 15 514-square-meter footprint. The structure houses a conference hall with three auditoriums, a library, and a museum. It is named after a former president of Azerbaijan. The architect describes the design as a "fluid form which emerges by the folding of the landscape's natural topography and by the wrapping of individual functions of the Center." The functions and the entrances are represented by folds in a continuous surface. The museum faces a landscaped area and has a glass façade that emphasizes the permeability of the architecture, where the "interior is an extension of the natural topography." The library faces north, controlling natural light. Ramps and bridges connect the library with the other elements of the overall program. The conference hall is imagined as one large area that can be subdivided into three smaller spaces. The Center was inaugurated on March 11, 2012, by the current president of Azerbaijan, Ilham Aliyev, who happens to be a son of Heydar Aliyev, but this was considered a "soft" opening. The actual opening of the building, delayed by a fire in late 2012, occurred in 2013.

Das Kulturzentrum mit gemischter Nutzung hat eine Gesamtnutzfläche von 101 801 m² auf einer Grundfläche von 15 514 m². Untergebracht sind hier eine Kongresshalle mit drei Auditorien, eine Bibliothek und ein Museum. Benannt ist der Bau nach einem ehemaligen Präsidenten Aserbaidschans. Die Architektin beschreibt den Entwurf als „fließende Form, die sich aus den Faltungen der natürlichen Topografie der Landschaft entwickelt und die verschiedenen Funktionen des Zentrums umschließt". Funktionen und Eingänge werden durch Faltungen in der fließenden Gebäudehaut markiert. Das Museum orientiert sich zu Grünflächen und hat eine Glasfassade, die zugleich Durchlässigkeit signalisiert und den „Innenraum als Erweiterung der Topografie" präsentiert. Um den Lichteinfall zu regulieren, wurde die Bibliothek nach Norden ausgerichtet; Rampen und Brücken verbinden sie mit den übrigen Bereichen des Gesamtprogramms. Die Kongresshalle wurde als großer Saal geplant, der sich in drei kleinere Räume unterteilen lässt. Am 11. März 2012 wurde das Zentrum vom aserbaidschanischen Präsidenten Ilham Aliyev (dem Sohn Heydar Aliyevs) vorab eingeweiht. Die offizielle Eröffnung verzögerte sich 2012 durch einen Brand und erfolgte 2013.

Dédié au précédent président de l'Azerbaïdjan, ce centre culturel représente une surface totale de 101 801 m² pour une emprise au sol de 15 514 m². Il abrite un centre de conférences comptant trois auditoriums, une bibliothèque et un musée. Zaha Hadid présente ce projet comme « une forme fluide qui émerge des plis de la topographie naturelle du paysage et enveloppe les différentes fonctions du Centre ». Ces fonctions et les différentes entrées sont matérialisées par des plis mis en forme dans une surface continue. La façade du musée qui donne sur une aire paysagée met en évidence la perméabilité de cette architecture dans laquelle « l'intérieur est une extension de la topographie naturelle ». La bibliothèque est orientée au nord pour mieux contrôler l'éclairage naturel. Des rampes et des passerelles la relient à d'autres éléments du programme. La salle de conférence est un vaste volume qui peut se subdiviser en trois espaces. Le Centre a été l'objet d'une pré-inauguraiton le 11 mars 2012 par le président actuel du pays, Ilham Aliyev, fils de Heydar Aliyev, mais son ouverture définitive, retardée par un incendie fin 2012, n'a eu lieu qu'en 2013.

Inside, an emphasis on white or light colors makes the contours of the volumes difficult to discern in a precise way—it is rather an impression of light and space that is present for visitors. The concert hall also partakes of this architectural continuity.

Überwiegend weiße und helle Farbtöne im Innern des Gebäudes sorgen dafür, dass die Konturen der Volumina verschwimmen – für die Besucher ist eher der Eindruck von Licht und Raumtiefe prägend. Auch der Konzertsaal fügt sich in das fließende Gesamtbild.

À l'intérieur, l'accent mis sur le blanc ou les couleurs légères perturbent la perception précise des volumes. Une impression de lumière et d'espace se crée. La salle de concert est traitée dans la continuité architecturale de l'œuvre.

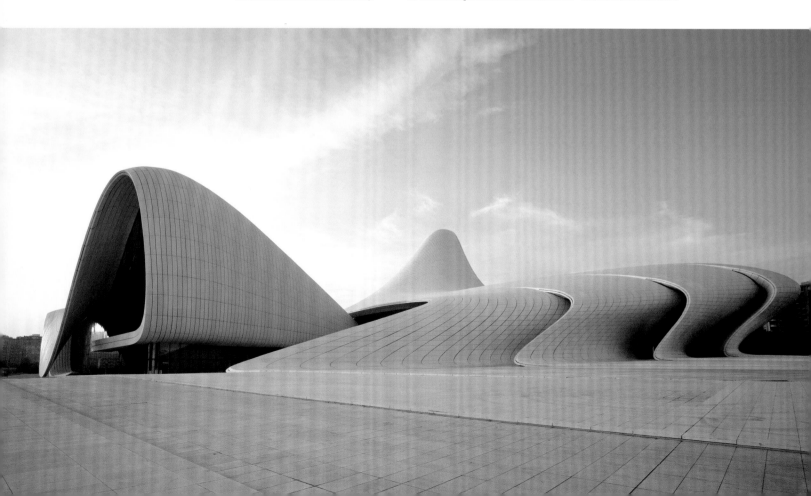

The geological inspiration of the architect can be seen both in the drawing to the right and in the image on the opposite page. Overlapping layers, like a folded landscape, give birth to the building's essential forms.

Zeichnung (rechts) und Ansicht (gegenüber) verraten, dass der Entwurf von geologischen Formen inspiriert ist. Aus einander überlagernden Schichten, wie die Faltungen einer Landschaft, entwickeln sich die formalen Kernelemente des Baus.

L'inspiration géologique de l'architecte est visible dans le dessin à droite et l'image ci-contre. Les strates superposées, comme une sorte de paysage de plis, donnent naissance aux formes essentielles du bâtiment.

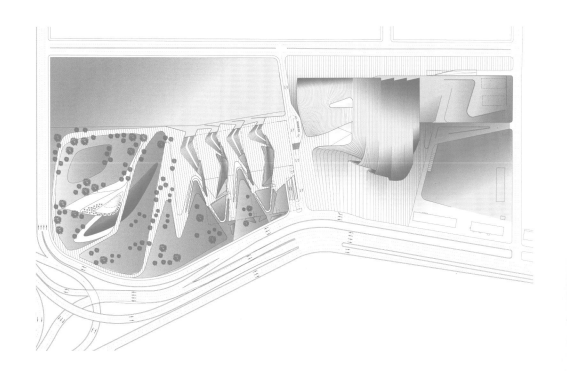

On occasion, the bright, white curves of the design turn into forms that appear to be essentially sculptural in their inspiration. Rather than only following function, form takes on a life of its own.

Hier und da wirken die weißen Schwünge des Entwurfs geradezu skulptural. Statt nur der Funktion zu folgen, gewinnt die Form hier deutlich an Eigendynamik.

Parfois, les courbes puissantes, traitées en blanc, se font sculpture. Plutôt que de se contenter de suivre la fonction, la forme mène sa vie en toute indépendance.

Even a glazed passage and a stairwell seem to grow in a natural way out of the walls, floors, and ceilings. Drawings reveal the overall continuity and forms of the structure.

Auch der verglaste Treppenaufgang scheint organisch aus Wänden, Böden und Decken hervor-zuwachsen. Die Zeichnung veranschaulicht die Kontinuität und Formensprache der Gesamtanlage.

Même un passage vitré et cet escalier semblent être issus des murs, des sols et des plafonds. Les dessins montrent la continuité d'ensemble des formes.

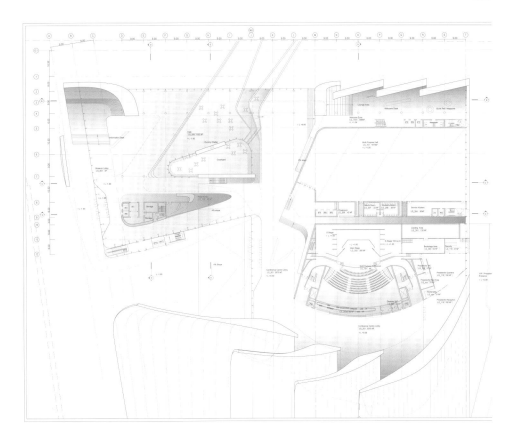

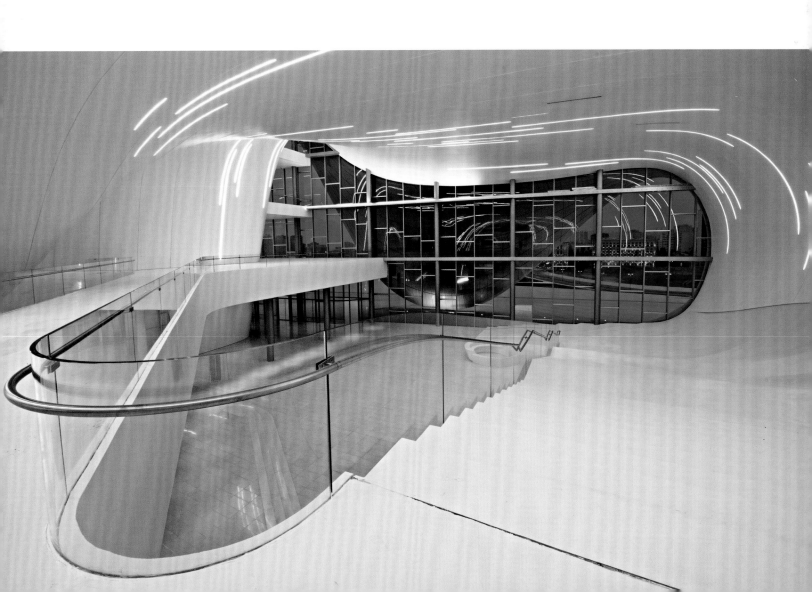

ON SITE

SALERNO MARITIME TERMINAL

Salerno, Italy. 2000–13

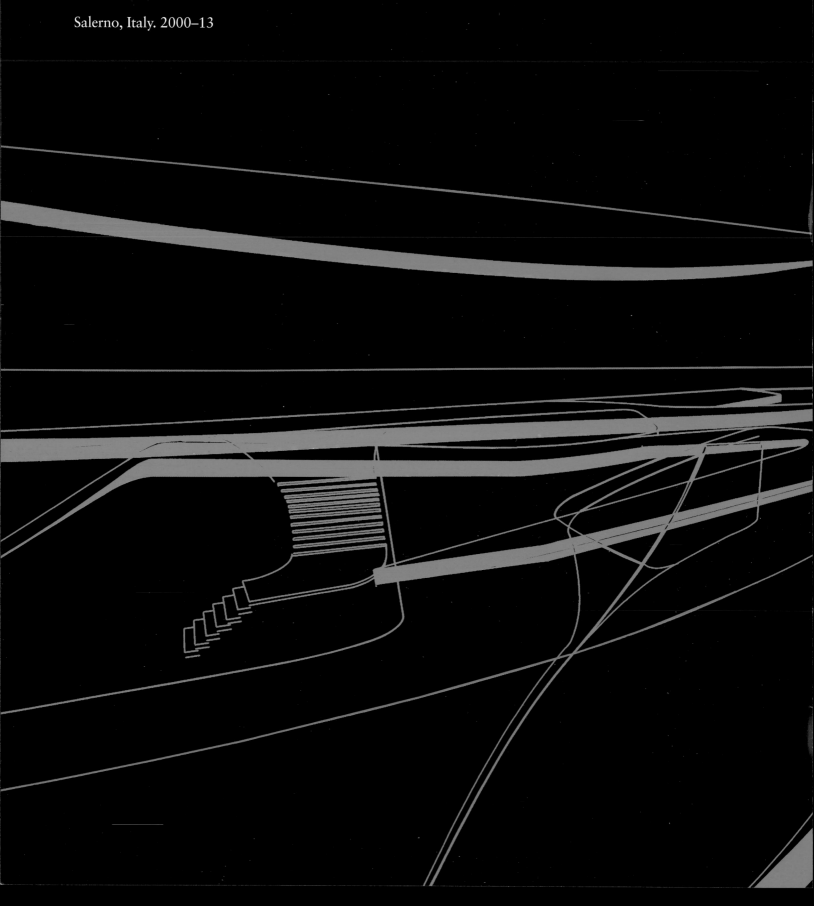

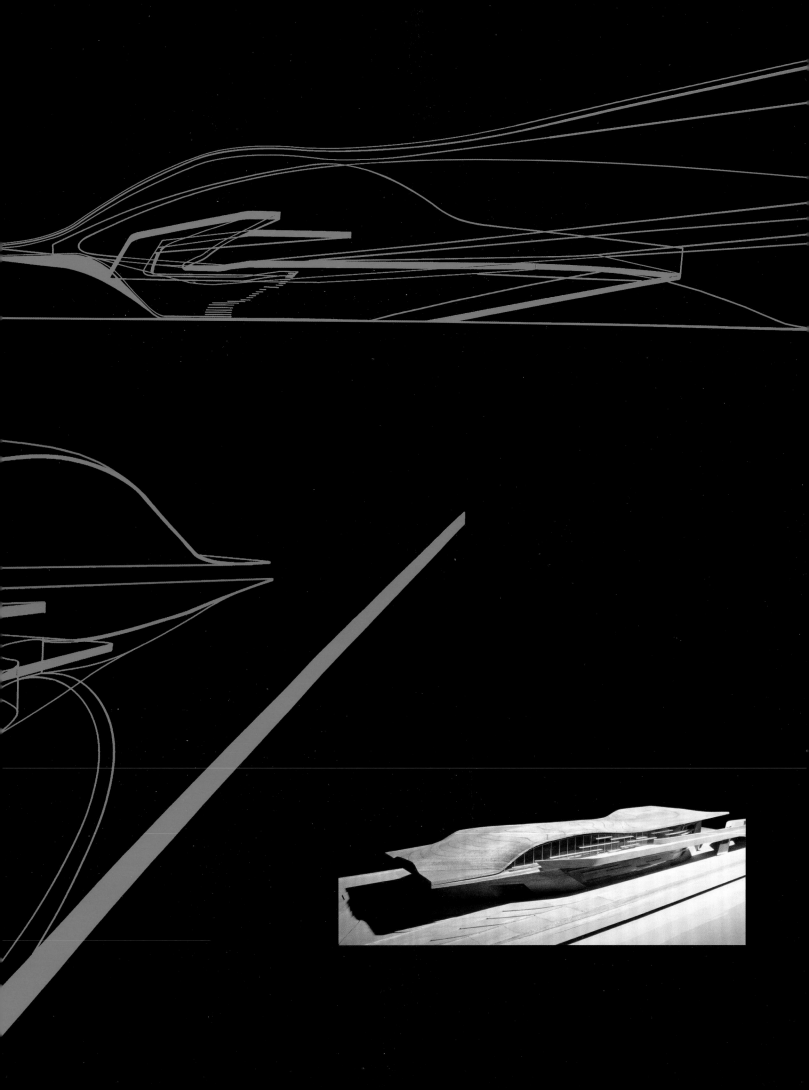

Project
SALERNO MARITIME TERMINAL

Location
SALERNO, ITALY

Client
COMUNE DI SALERNO

Area/Size
4500 m²

Raising the structure up above its platform and cantilevering it forward gives the Terminal a very definite sense of movement. Though few ships have such a dynamic, futuristic profile, the familiar image of a seagoing vessel is nonetheless evoked.

Durch das Aufständern des Baus auf eine Plattform und die Auskragung nach vorn wirkt das Terminal, als sei es in Bewegung. Obwohl nur wenige Schiffe ein solch dynamisches, futuristisches Profil haben, lässt sich hierin dennoch ein Anspielung auf in See stechende Schiffe sehen.

Le soulèvement de la structure largement au-dessus du tablier et son porte-à-faux vers l'avant créent un sentiment très précis de mouvement. Même si peu de bateaux présentent un profil dynamique aussi futuriste, l'image d'un vaisseau prenant la mer vient néanmoins à l'esprit.

Salerno is a city of about 140 000 people on the Gulf of Salerno in southwestern Italy. Zaha Hadid compares the new Ferry Terminal to an oyster because "the building has a hard shell that encloses soft, fluid elements within." The architect emphasizes on the "insistently differentiated spaces" and the dynamic nature of the design—where passengers "drift" rather than being given a clear orientation. Instead, lighting guides visitors through the building and serves to make the structure stand out in the port at night. The facility includes administrative offices and terminals for ferries and cruise ships. A distinction is made between the "fast and intense" movement of daily ferry passengers, who buy tickets and go up ramps to the ferry, and cruise passengers. In an interesting variation on her interest in landforms, Zaha Hadid explains that this Maritime Terminal is intended to offer a "smooth transition between the land and the sea, an artificial landform that is constantly mediating, as if melting, from the solid into the liquid." It might be noted in passing that the dissolution of architectural forms, traditionally rectilinear, into a fluid continuity is a constant theme of Zaha Hadid, expressed here in terms of the specific site and function of the Terminal.

Salerno hat 140 000 Einwohner und liegt im Südwesten Italiens, am Golf von Salerno. Zaha Hadid vergleicht das neue Fährterminal mit einer Auster: „Der Bau hat eine harte Schale, die weiche, fließende Elemente umschließt." Die Architektin legt besonderen Wert auf die „überaus differenziert ausgearbeiteten Räume" und die Dynamik des Entwurfs – ein Bau, in dem sich die Passagiere „treiben" lassen können, statt klare Richtungsvorgaben zu bekommen. Vielmehr werden die Besucher durch das Gebäude mithilfe von Licht geleitet, das den Bau bei Nacht im Hafen erstrahlen lässt. In der Einrichtung befinden sich Verwaltungsbüros und Terminals für Fähren und Kreuzfahrtschiffe. Unterschieden wird einerseits zwischen den „schnellen, intensiven" Strömen der täglichen Fährpassagiere, die ihre Fahrkarten kaufen und die Rampen zu den Fährschiffen hinauflaufen, sowie andererseits den Kreuzfahrtgästen. Es ist eine interessante Variante von Hadids Interesse an geologischen Formationen, dass die Architektin das Hafenterminal als „sanften Übergang zwischen Land und See" versteht, als „künstliche geologische Formation, die unablässig zwischen festen und flüssigen Aggregatzuständen vermittelt, sie womöglich sogar schmelzend ineinander übergehen lässt". Man könnte nebenbei darauf hinweisen, dass die Auflösung architektonischer, traditionell rechtwinkliger Formen zu einem fließenden räumlichen Kontinuum ein ständiges Thema bei Hadid ist, wie hier an der spezifischen Lage und Funktion des Terminals zu sehen ist.

Salerne est une ville d'environ 140 000 habitants située au bord du golfe du même nom en Italie du Sud. Zaha Hadid compare ce nouveau terminal de ferry à une huître car « le bâtiment se présente sous forme d'une coquille rigide qui enferme des éléments mous et fluides ». L'architecte met l'accent sur « les espaces différenciés avec insistance » et la nature dynamique du projet dans lequel les voyageurs se propulsent plutôt que de suivre une orientation précise reçue. L'éclairage les guide à travers les installations et distingue le bâtiment la nuit. Il comprend des bureaux administratifs et des installations portuaires pour ferries et bateaux de croisière. Une distinction est faite entre le mouvement « rapide et intense » des passagers des ferries quotidiens, qui prennent leur billet et empruntent des rampes vers leur bateau, et les voyageurs de croisière. Dans une variante intéressante de son intérêt pour les modelés naturels, Zaha Hadid explique que ce terminal veut offrir « une transition douce entre la terre et la mer, un modelé artificiel constamment mis en médiation, comme en fusion, du solide au liquide ». On peut noter au passage que la dissolution des formes architecturales traditionnellement rectilignes, en continuité fluide, est un thème constant chez Zaha Hadid, qui s'exprime ici en termes de spécificité par rapport au site et à la fonction de ce Terminal.

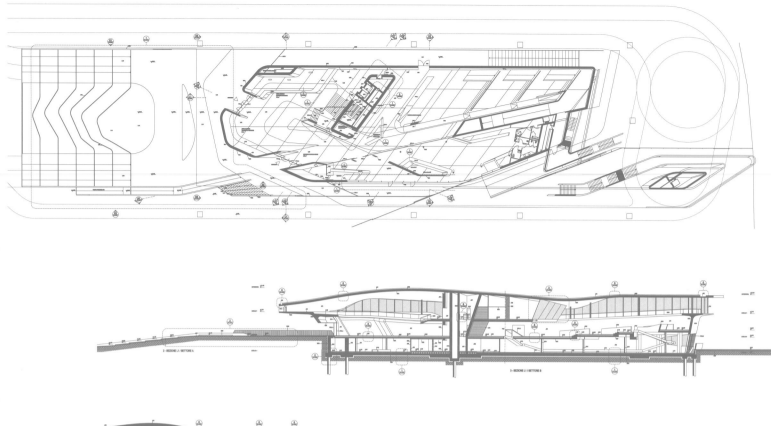

The layered, intertwined approach of the architects is particularly well suited to a terminal destined to handle a continuous flow of travelers. As always, the interior and exterior of the building are designed in complete harmony.

Der schichtartige, ineinander greifende Stil der Architektin passt besonders gut zu einem Terminal, das in Zukunft einem unablässigen Passagierstrom gerecht werden muss. Wie immer wurden Innen- und Außenbau absolut harmonisch gestaltet.

Cette approche de stratifications et d'entrelacements est particulièrement bien adaptée à un terminal destiné à gérer un flux continu de voyageurs. Comme toujours, l'intérieur et l'extérieur du bâtiment sont en complète harmonie.

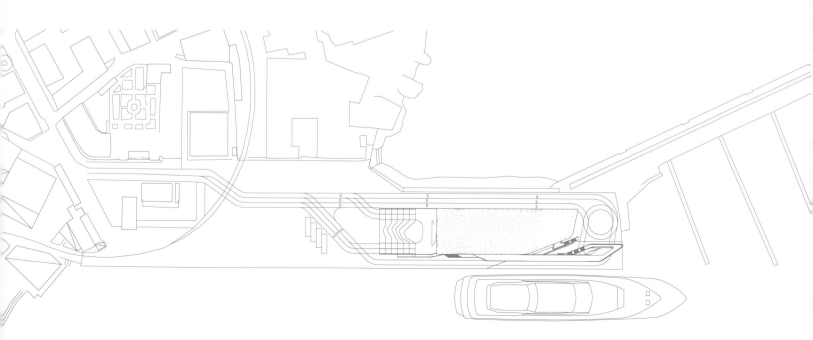

INNOVATION TOWER

Hong Kong, China. 2007–13

Project
INNOVATION TOWER
Location
HONG KONG, CHINA
Client
HONG KONG POLYTECHNIC UNIVERSITY

Three renderings (left) show the stacked and for-ward-leaning nature of the design, while a site plan (below) shows that even if the building itself may appear unusual, it is designed to become an integral part of its urban environment.

Drei Darstellungen (links) illustrieren die Schichtung und die nach vorn geneigte Form des Entwurfs. Ein Lageplan (unten) belegt, dass das Bauwerk trotz seiner ungewöhnlichen Optik so angelegt wurde, dass es sich nahtlos in sein urbanes Umfeld fügt.

Trois rendus (à gauche) illustrent le concept d'empilement et d'inclinaison vers l'avant du projet. Le plan du terrain (ci-dessous) montre que même si la masse du bâtiment peut surprendre, elle est conçue pour faire partie intégrante de son environnement urbain.

Intended for the School of Design Development of the Hong Kong Polytechnic University, this 15 000-square-meter, 76-meter-high building will serve 1450 people. The idea of the tower is the "dissolution of the classic typology" in favor of fluid forms, such as internal and external courtyards. Aiming to take advantage of a "void" on the north side of its campus, the structure clearly seeks to draw in users through the podium entrance and "organization" sequence. Careful attention is paid to circulation patterns. The architect states: "The long integrated path from Suen Chi Sun Memorial Square guides the visitor to the main entrance, and from here a generous and welcoming space invitingly leads visitors to supporting public facilities (shop, cafeteria, museum) through a generous open exhibition 'showcase' spanning over two levels between podium and ground level." Within, glazed work areas line a four-story escalator that leads upward, encouraging visitors and users to view and perhaps further explore the activities within. Divided into "learning clusters" and central facilities, the tower provides the space necessary for each activity, but also encourages "dialogue between respective volumes," an idea that applies to the architecture as well as to the use of the building. The layered, articulated form of the building might bring to mind some natural rock formations.

In dem 15 000 m² großen und 76 m hohen Gebäude für das Institut für Designentwicklung der Polytechnischen Universität Hongkong sollen 1450 Nutzer untergebracht werden. Das Hochhaus fußt auf der Idee, die „klassische Typologie aufzuheben" und stattdessen mit fließenden Formen zu arbeiten, etwa mit Innenhöfen und Terrassen. Der Bau wurde so konzipiert, dass ein „Vakuum" auf der nördlichen Seite des Campusgeländes genutzt wird; hierbei geht es ganz offensichtlich darum, die Nutzer durch den auf einem Podium liegenden Eingangsbereich sowie eine „Organisationssequenz" in den Bau hineinzuziehen. Die Verkehrsabläufe wurden in ihrer Struktur höchst sorgsam geplant. Die Architektin erklärt: „Ein lang gestreckter, in das Gelände eingebundener Zugangsweg vom Suen Chi Sun Memorial Square führt die Besucher zum Haupteingang. Hier heißt ein großzügiger und einladender Bereich die Besucher willkommen und führt sie durch eine großzügige Ausstellungszone, die sich zwischen Podium und Erdgeschoss über zwei Ebenen erstreckt, zu den sekundären Gemeinschaftseinrichtungen (Shop, Caféteria, Museum)." Im Innern des Baus flankieren verglaste Arbeitsbereiche eine vier Stockwerke erschließende Rolltreppe, die nach oben führt und Besucher und Nutzer einlädt, die hier stattfindenden Aktivitäten zu beobachten und vielleicht näher zu erkunden. Der Turm selbst ist in „Lern-Cluster" und Zentraleinrichtungen untergliedert und bietet ausreichend Raum für alle Bereiche, regt jedoch auch den „Dialog zwischen den jeweiligen Volumina" an, ein Motto, das für die Architektur als solche ebenso wie für die Gebäudenutzung gilt. Die schichtartig aufgebaute, klar gegliederte Form des Baus könnte an natürliche Gesteinsformationen erinnern.

Conçu pour l'École de design de l'Université polytechnique de Hong-kong, ce bâtiment de 15 000 m² et 76 mètres de haut accueillera 1450 personnes. Le concept retenu est celui d'une « dissolution de la typologie classique » dans des formes fluides, illustrées par des cours intérieures et extérieures. Pour profiter d'un « vide » sur la façade nord du campus, le bâtiment cherche visiblement à attirer à lui les visiteurs par son podium de l'entrée et la séquence de son « organisation ». Un souci attentif est porté aux circulations. « Le long cheminement intégré qui part de la place du Mémorial de Suen Chi Sun guide le visiteur vers l'entrée principale, où un espace généreux et accueillant l'introduit à divers services – boutique, cafeteria, musée – à travers une "vitrine" d'exposition amplement ouverte s'étendant sur deux niveaux entre le podium et le rez-de-chaussée », explique l'architecte. À l'intérieur, les zones de travail vitrées sont bordées d'un escalier mécanique desservant quatre niveaux, qui encourage les visiteurs et les utilisateurs à voir et peut-être explorer davantage les activités qui s'y déroulent. Divisé en « îlots d'apprentissage » et équipements centraux, la tour offre à chaque activité l'espace dont elle a besoin, tout en « encourageant le dialogue entre les volumes respectifs », idée qui s'applique aussi bien à l'architecture qu'à l'utilisation de l'immeuble. La forme stratifiée et articulée peut faire penser à certaines formations rocheuses naturelles.

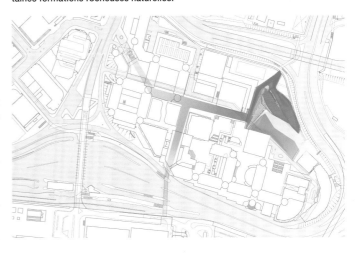

SERPENTINE SACKLER GALLERY

London, UK. 2010–13

Project
SERPENTINE SACKLER GALLERY

Location
LONDON, UK

Client
SERPENTINE GALLERY

Area/Size
900 m²

The Magazine was designed like a Palladian villa. Below, the restored 1805 structure is seen with the Hadid extension on the left. Left page, the forms of Zaha Hadid's addition.

Das historische Depot wurde als Palladianische Villa gestaltet. Unten der 1805 modifizierte Bau mit Hadids Erweiterung (links). Linke Seite: Die Formensprache des Hadid-Anbaus.

L'ancien entrepôt de poudre a pris au XIXᵉ siècle l'aspect d'une villa palladienne. Ci-dessous le bâtiment de 1805 restauré et, à gauche, l'extension de Zaha Hadid. Page de gauche, vue partielle de l'extension traitée dans le style caractéristique de l'architecte.

The Serpentine Sackler Gallery is located on the north side of the Serpentine Bridge in Kensington Gardens, not far from the original Gallery building. In 2010 the Serpentine Gallery won a tender from the Royal Parks over Damien Hirst, who wanted to show his collection there, to lease the building for 25 years. The 900-square-meter facility includes a new gallery, restaurant, and social space. The project occupies the Magazine, a former gunpowder store that is a Grade II listed Neoclassical building that had never previously been open to the public. In 1805, the Magazine was enlarged in the form of a Palladian villa, though its core dates from 1765. Zaha Hadid created a very contemporary extension to the building, her first permanent structure in central London. She of course designed the London Aquatics Centre for the 2012 Summer Olympic Games located in the east of London, as well as the first in the series of temporary Serpentine Gallery Pavilions in 2000. The curved white roof of the extension swoops down as far as the ground, giving it a tentlike appearance, and recalling to some extent the surfaces of her Mobile Art Pavilion, created for Chanel and now permanently located at the Institut du Monde Arabe in Paris. The sides of the extension are fully glazed. Arabella Lennox-Boyd designed the landscaping around the facility.

Die Serpentine Sackler Gallery liegt nördlich der Serpentine Bridge in Kensington Gardens, nicht weit vom Stammhaus der Galerie. 2010 hatte sich die Galerie in einer Ausschreibung der Royal Parks gegen Damien Hirst durchsetzen können, der in den Räumen seine Sammlung zeigen wollte. Der Pachtvertrag hat eine Laufzeit von 25 Jahren. Auf 900 m² werden eine neue Galerie, ein Restaurant sowie öffentliche Bereiche untergebracht. Genutzt wird hierfür ein historisches Depot für Schießpulver, ein denkmalgeschütztes neoklassizistisches Gebäude, das bisher nicht öffentlich zugänglich war. 1805 wurde das Depot, ursprünglich 1765 erbaut, in Form einer Palladianischen Villa erweitert. Zaha Hadid entwarf einen deutlich zeitgenössischen Anbau, ihr erstes bleibendes Projekt in der Londoner Innenstadt. Zuvor hatte sie bereits das London Aquatics Centre für die Olympischen Sommerspiele 2012 im Osten der Stadt sowie 2000 den ersten temporären Sommerpavillon der Serpentine Gallery realisiert. Das geschwungene weiße Dach des Anbaus reicht bis auf den Boden hinab, erinnert an ein Zelt und in Teilen an die Oberflächengestaltung von Hadids Mobile Art Pavilion für Chanel, der inzwischen dauerhaft am Institut du monde arabe in Paris installiert ist. Die Seitenwände der Serpentine-Erweiterung sind vollständig verglast; die Landschaftsgestaltung lag in den Händen von Arabella Lennox-Boyd.

La Serpentine Sackler Gallery s'élève dans les jardins de Kensington au nord du pont sur la Serpentine et non loin de la Serpentine Gallery. En 2010, celle-ci s'est vue attribuer les lieux pour 25 ans par l'administration des Parcs royaux, face à Damien Hirst qui souhaitait y présenter sa collection. Le bâtiment de 900 m² comprend une galerie d'exposition, un restaurant et des espaces de réception. Jadis appelé le « Magazine », il s'agissait d'un ancien entrepôt militaire de poudre classé monument historique qui n'avait jamais été ouvert au public. Datant de 1765, l'entrepôt avait été transformé en 1805 en une villa de style palladien. Zaha Hadid a créé là une extension d'esprit très contemporain qui constitue sa première réalisation permanente au centre de Londres. Elle avait auparavant conçu le premier de la série de pavillons d'été temporaires de la Serpentine Gallery en 2000 et le London Aquatics Centre pour les Jeux olympiques de 2012 à l'est de la capitale. La toiture incurvée blanche de l'extension descend jusqu'au sol, donnant à l'ensemble un aspect de tente, rappelant un peu le pavillon Mobile Art créé pour Chanel aujourd'hui installé au pied de l'Institut du monde arabe à Paris. Les façades sont entièrement vitrées. Arabella Lennox-Boyd a conçu les aménagements paysagers autour de la galerie.

CAPITAL HILL
RESIDENCE

Moscow, Russia. 2006–14

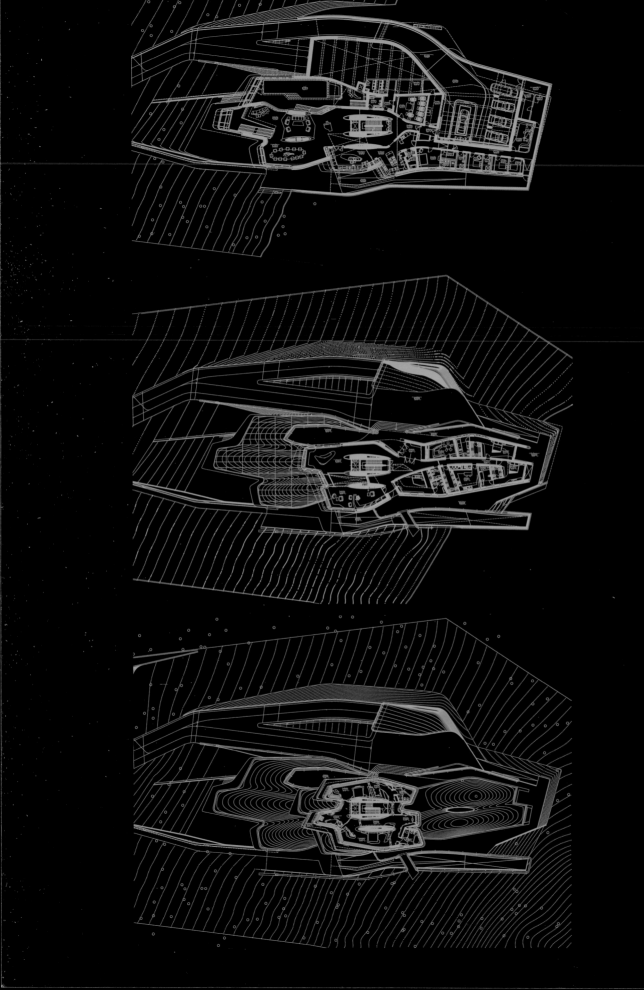

Project
CAPITAL HILL RESIDENCE
Location
MOSCOW, RUSSIA
Client
PRIVATE CLIENT
Area/Size
2650 m²

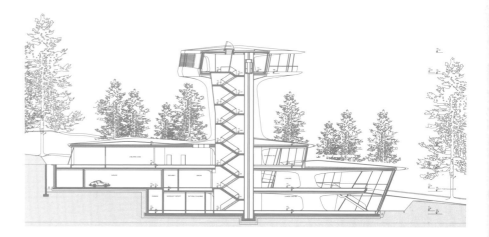

Drawings to the left and a section above certainly do not bring to mind a traditional residence in any sense. The tower looks over the trees, and sits on a base whose flowing organizational scheme appears to be closely related to landscape lines of force.

Die Zeichnungen links und der Schnitt oben lassen sicherlich nicht an einen Wohnsitz im traditionellen Sinne denken. Der Turm überragt die Bäume und ruht auf einem Sockel, dessen fließende räumliche Organisation eng an die Feldlinien der Landschaft anzuknüpfen scheint.

Les dessins de gauche et la coupe ci-dessus n'évoquent en rien une résidence privée classique. La tour dépasse la cime des arbres et repose sur une base dont la structure semble étroitement liée aux lignes de force du paysage.

This is a rare example of a private villa designed by Zaha Hadid. Essentially inscribed in the forest topography, the house, set on a north-facing hillside with pine and birch trees up to 20 meters high, has a 22-meter-high volume intended to allow the owners panoramic views. Its main materials both inside and out are precast and cast-in-place concrete, steel, and glass. Hadid describes the concept as "organic inter-articulation" that allows for "intricately layered spatial formation that presents itself as a unified whole with each component referring to its local topography." The lower part of the house appears to emerge from the existing landscape or rather to create its own artificial landscape in harmony with the site, and, indeed, it is partly embedded in the hillside. A first level, below grade, contains leisure space, including a living room, massage and fitness spaces, and a sauna and hamam. The living room and dining areas, kitchen, indoor swimming pool, and parking are located at ground level. The double-height entrance, study, guest room, and a child's room are on the first floor with the master bedroom and a lounge with an exterior terrace on the top level. Three concrete columns or "legs" form the structure, with technical elements inside them. A transparent glass elevator and a staircase are set between these legs. The architect explains: "The general concept for the design of the villa responds to a strategy that extends the exterior topography to the interior of the building, while its geometrical definition is derived from the surrounding environment of flowing terrain levels that are stretched to generate the new landscape, proposing a continuous integration between interior and exterior spaces."

Dies ist ein seltenes Beispiel für einen privaten Wohnbau nach Entwürfen Zaha Hadids. Das Haus, eingeschrieben in die bewaldete Topografie, liegt an der Nordseite eines mit Kiefern und Birken bestandenen Hügels, dessen Baumbestand bis zu 20 m hoch ist. Ein 22 m hoher Baukörper soll den Besitzern Panoramablicke bieten. Innen- und Außenbau bestehen aus Betonformteilen sowie Ortbeton, Stahl und Glas. Hadid beschreibt das Konzept als „organische Interartikulation", die erlaubt, eine „feinst abgestimmte, geschichtete Raumformation [zu schaffen], die sich als harmonische Gesamteinheit präsentiert und mit jeder Komponente Bezug auf die örtliche Topografie nimmt". Der untere Bereich des Hauses scheint aus dem landschaftlichen Umfeld zu erwachsen oder vielmehr eine neue künstliche Landschaft zu definieren, die sich harmonisch in das Terrain fügt und tatsächlich teilweise in den Hügel versenkt ist. In der ersten Ebene, unter Bodenniveau, befinden sich Freizeiträume, etwa ein Wohnzimmer, Massage- und Fitnessräume, eine Sauna und ein Hamam. Im Erdgeschoss liegen ein

weiteres Wohnzimmer, Essbereiche, eine Küche, ein Schwimmbad und Garagen. Der Eingangsbereich mit doppelter Geschosshöhe, das Arbeitszimmer, Gästezimmer und Kinderzimmer liegen im ersten Stock. Das Hauptschlafzimmer und eine Lounge mit Außenterrasse befinden sich in der obersten Etage. Drei Betonpfeiler oder „Beine", in denen die Haustechnik untergebracht ist, bilden die Struktur des Baus. Zwischen diesen „Beinen" sind ein gläserner Aufzug und das Treppenhaus eingespannt. Die Architektin erklärt: „Das Grundkonzept für den Entwurf der Villa erwächst aus einer Strategie, die die Topografie des Außenraums in das Innere des Baus ausdehnt. Die geometrische Form leitet sich aus der landschaftlichen Umgebung ab, deren fließende Geländeebenen erweitert werden, um so eine neue Landschaft zu erzeugen und ein integratives Kontinuum zwischen Innen- und Außenräumen zu schaffen."

Capital Hill est un des rares exemples de résidence privée conçue par Zaha Hadid. S'inscrivant pour l'essentiel dans un cadre forestier de pins et de bouleaux mesurant jusqu'à 20 m de haut, elle est implantée au flanc d'une colline orientée au nord. Le volume vertical de 22 m de haut offre aux propriétaires une vue panoramique. L'ensemble est réalisé en grande partie en béton préfabriqué ou coulé sur place, en verre et en acier, aussi bien pour l'extérieur que pour l'intérieur. Hadid présente son concept comme une « interarticulation organique » qui se prête à « une formation spatiale aux strates imbriquées, se présentant comme un tout unifié dont chaque composant se réfère à la topographie du lieu ». L'espace inférieur de la maison, en partie pris dans le flanc de la colline, semble émerger du paysage, voire même créer son propre paysage en harmonie avec le site. Le premier niveau, en sous-sol, contient des pièces réservées aux loisirs, un séjour, une salle de massages et de sport, un sauna et un hammam. Au-rez-de-chaussée, se trouvent le séjour principal, la zone des repas, la cuisine, une piscine intérieure et un garage. L'entrée double hauteur, le bureau, la chambre d'amis et une chambre d'enfant occupent l'étage, tandis que la chambre principale et un salon avec terrasse se réservent le dernier niveau. Trois colonnes de béton ou « jambes » qui constituent la structure contiennent divers éléments techniques. Un ascenseur en verre transparent et un escalier se glisse entre elles. Pour l'architecte : « Le concept global de cette villa répond à une stratégie qui étend la topographie de l'extérieur vers l'intérieur, par le biais d'une définition géométrique issue de l'environnement créé par les niveaux du terrain qui s'étirent pour dessiner un nouveau paysage et initier une intégration continue entre espaces externes et internes. »

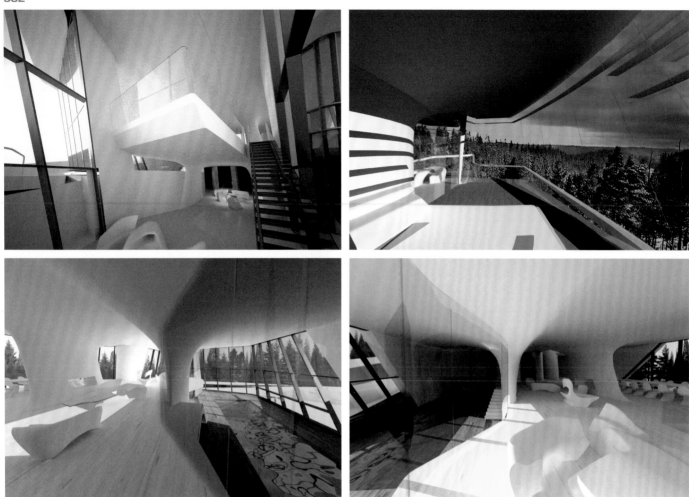

Zaha Hadid Architects' use of continuous space with integrated furniture elements is closely related to the dynamic exterior appearance of the residence, part science fiction and part organic flow.

Die wie aus einem Guss gestalteten Räume mit eingebauten Möbelelementen, so typisch für das Büro Hadids, knüpfen stilistisch eng an den dynamischen Außenbau der Villa an – teils Science-Fiction, teils organisches Fließen.

Entre science-fiction et flux organique, le principe d'espace continu et d'éléments de mobilier intégrés est étroitement lié à l'aspect extérieur dynamique de cette résidence.

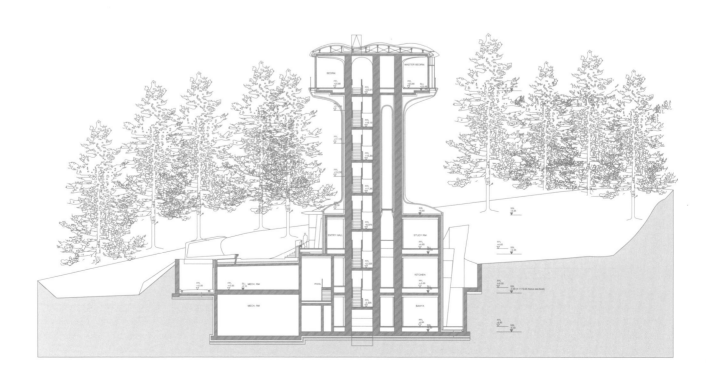

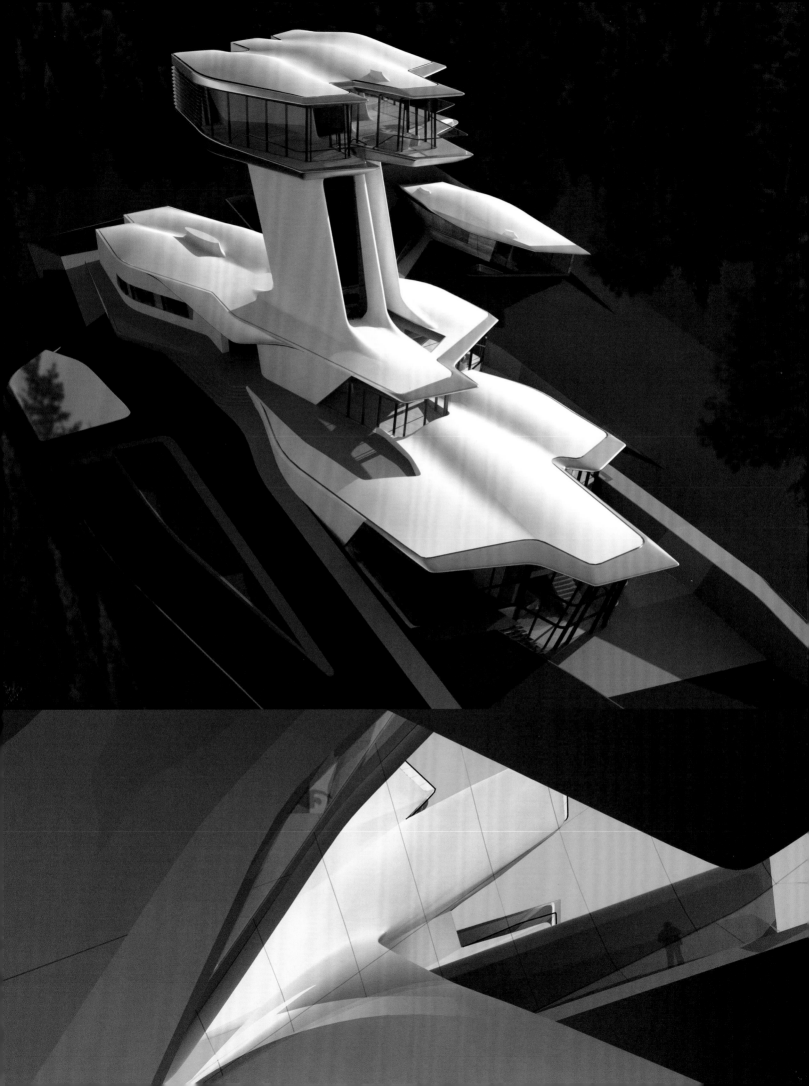

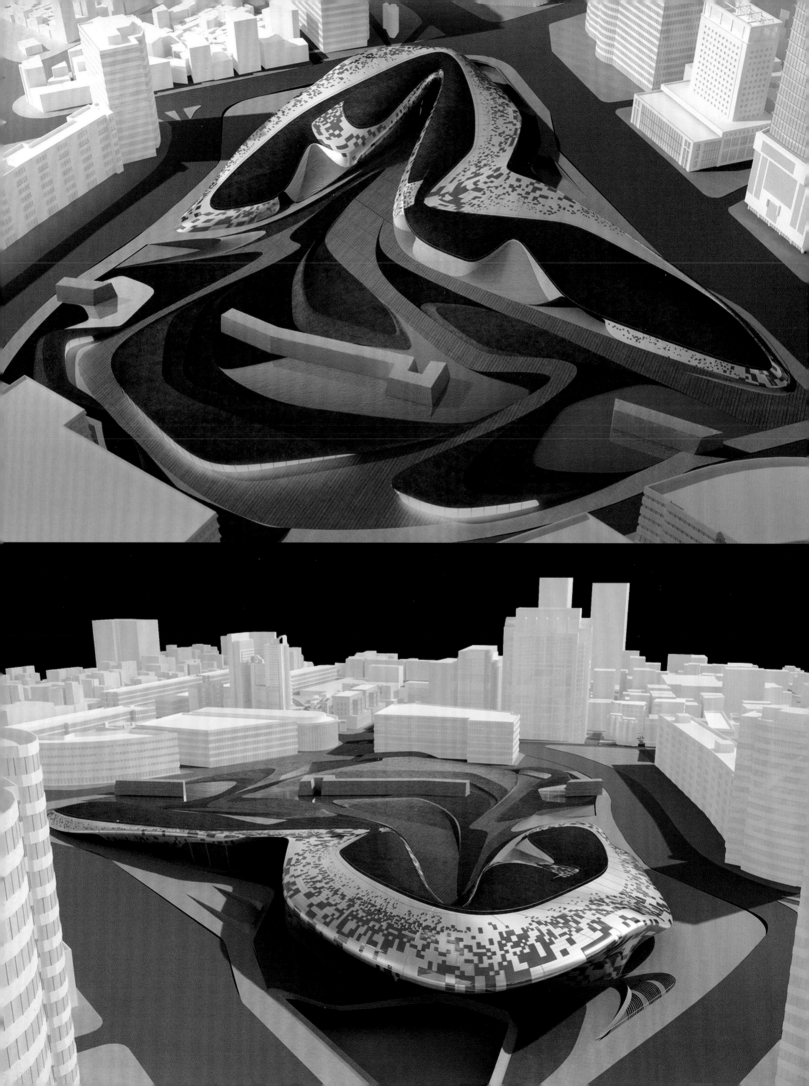

DONGDAEMUN WORLD DESIGN PARK AND PLAZA

Seoul, South Korea. 2007–14

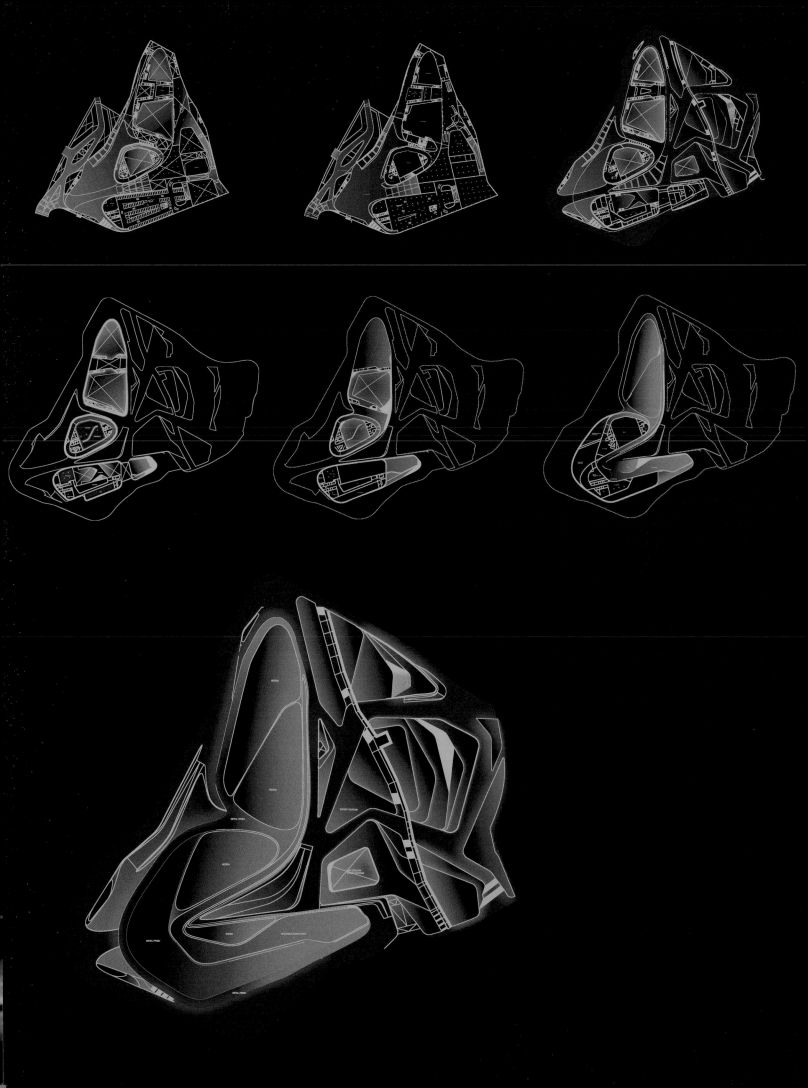

Project
DONGDAEMUN WORLD DESIGN PARK AND PLAZA

Location
SEOUL, SOUTH KOREA

Client
SEOUL METROPOLITAN GOVERNMENT

Area/Size
83 000 m² + PARK 30 000 m²

This Park and design complex takes Hadid's ideas about the integration of architecture and landscape to new heights and is located in central Seoul. With the firm intention to renew learning about design, the architect has sought to create a type of "anticipatory architecture" that is able to change with its circumstances and use. She says further that "this project is governed by the belief that architecture must 'enable people to think the unthinkable.'" Interior and exterior surfaces are continuous, encouraging the idea of a flowing, "seamless" connection between the park and contemporary design activities. Architecture and landscape are clearly part of the same complex, and are marked by the same creativity in the World Design Park. The name Dongdaemun means "Great East Gate," in reference to the wall that formerly surrounded Seoul. Hadid's site makes use of remnants of that wall to create continuity that is not only physical—in the sense of the landscape that emerges from the ground—but also historical due to the presence of the wall. Hadid refers to bringing the residents of Seoul or the visitors to the Park and Center "back to nature." She states: "Our language of building and engineering is organic insofar as each program is physically connected by some form of building tissue such as bridge, path, outdoor plaza or performance area, enclosure, and canopy." An underground shopping and dining area, meant as a continuation of the design-oriented environment above, is also "folded into" the ground-level landscape. Voids and undulations in the park surface allow the everyday public to see the spaces below grade and thus, perhaps, to become interested in design. The central concepts of the project according to the architect are "transparency, porosity, and sustainability," with solar panels, double-skin façades, rainwater recycling, and passive energy systems integrated into the design. Wetland areas in the park highlight the existence of biodiversity in the heart of one of the world's largest cities.

Dieser Park und der Designkomplex mitten in Seoul zeigen, dass Hadids Überlegungen zur Integration von Architektur und Landschaft neue Gipfel erreicht haben. Mit dem klaren Anliegen, innovative Formen für die Vermittlung von Design zu finden, bemühte sich die Architektin, eine Art „antizipatorischer Architektur" zu schaffen, die in der Lage ist, sich Bedingungen und Nutzungen anzupassen. Darüber hinaus verkörpert das Projekt in ihren Augen „die Überzeugung, dass Architektur ‚Menschen befähigen sollte, das Undenkbare zu denken'". Die Oberflächen innen und außen sind als Kontinuum gestaltet und unterstreichen die Idee einer fließenden, „nahtlosen" Verbindung zwischen Park und zeitgenössischer Designpraxis. Architektur und Landschaft sind eindeutig Teil desselben Komplexes und zeichnen sich durch dieselbe Kreativität aus wie der World Design Park. Der Name Dongdaemun bedeutet „Großes Osttor" und bezieht sich auf Seouls frühere Stadtmauer. Hadids Anlage bindet erhaltene Fragmente der Mauer mit ein und erzeugt so ein Kontinuum, das nicht nur physisch ist – etwa in Form der Landschaft, die aus dem Boden aufzusteigen scheint –, sondern dank der Präsenz der Mauer auch eine historische Qualität besitzt. Hadid geht es darum, die Bürger von Seoul und die Besucher des Parks und des Centers wieder „zurück zur Natur" zu bringen. Sie meint: „Die Sprache unseres Bauens und unserer Ingenieurkunst ist insofern organisch, als dass jeder Aspekt des Programms mit einem Teil des Gebäudegeflechts physisch verbunden ist, etwa durch eine Brücke, einen Weg, einen Platz oder eine Bühne, eine Umbauung, ein Dach." Eine unterirdische Einkaufs- und Gastronomiezone, konzipiert als Fortsetzung des darüberliegenden, designorientierten Umfelds, ist ebenfalls in die ebenerdige Landschaft „eingelassen". Einschnitte und Wellen in den Bodenflächen des Parks geben den Passanten Einblicke in die Räume unter der Erde und wecken so womöglich deren Interesse für Design. Der Architektin zufolge sind die Schlüsselideen des Projekts „Transparenz, Durchlässigkeit und Nachhaltigkeit", die unter anderem durch Solarmodule, Doppelfassaden, Regenwasseraufbereitung und Passivenergiesysteme erzielt werden, die in den Entwurf eingearbeitet wurden. Feuchtgebiete im Park unterstreichen die biologische Vielfalt in einer der größten Städte der Welt.

Ce projet, destiné au centre de Séoul, porte à de nouveaux sommets l'intégration de l'architecture et du paysage chez Zaha Hadid. Dans l'intention revendiquée de renouveler l'apprentissage du design, l'architecte a cherché à créer un type « d'architecture anticipatrice », en mesure d'évoluer avec les circonstances et les utilisations. Elle ajoute que « ce projet est régi par la conviction que l'on doit pouvoir "permettre aux gens de penser l'impensable" ». Les plans intérieurs et extérieurs continus favorisent la connexion fluide, « sans rupture », entre le parc et les activités de design. L'architecture et le paysage font ici clairement partie d'un même ensemble, relèvent de la même créativité. Le terme de Dongdaemun signifie « Grande porte de l'Ouest », en référence aux remparts qui entouraient jadis la capitale coréenne. L'aménagement du terrain met à profit des vestiges de cette muraille pour créer une continuité qui n'est donc pas seulement physique, mais aussi historique. Hadid parle de « ramener vers la nature » les visiteurs du Parc et du Centre : « Notre langage constructif et d'ingénierie est organique dans la mesure où chaque programme est physiquement connecté par une forme ou une autre de tissu bâti, tel un pont, un cheminement, une place, un lieu pour spectacles, un espace clos, un auvent. » Un petit complexe de boutiques et de restaurants en sous-sol, qui se veut dans la continuité de l'environnement consacré au design à l'air libre, permet à chacun de visiter ces espaces souterrains, et peut-être de s'intéresser au design. Les concepts centraux du projet sont « la transparence, la porosité et le développement durable », illustrés par des panneaux solaires, des façades à double-peau, le recyclage de l'eau de pluie et des systèmes d'énergie passive intégrés dès la conception. Quelques zones humides dans le parc soulignent la présence d'une certaine biodiversité au cœur même de l'une des plus grandes villes du monde.

SOHO PEAKS

Beijing, China. 2009–14

Project
SOHO PEAKS

Location
BEIJING, CHINA

Client
SOHO CHINA LTD.

Floor area
GROSS FLOOR AREA 521 265 m²

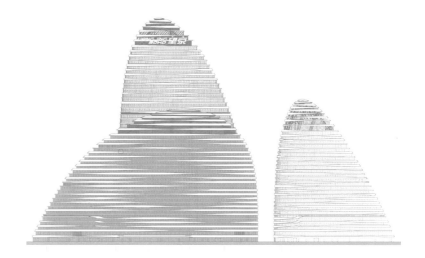

Further exploring her interest in forms that appear to have a relation to nature, Zaha Hadid articulates the volumes of the complex like a group of curved hills, while inserting them into the somewhat irregular site.

Zaha Hadid vertieft ihr Interesse an Formen, die von der Natur inspiriert scheinen, und gestaltet die Baukörper des Komplexes wie eine Hügellandschaft. Zugleich integriert sie sie in das eher unregelmäßige Grundstück.

Approfondissant son exploration de formes inspirées de la nature, Zaha Hadid a articulé ses trois volumes comme un groupe de collines inséré dans un terrain de forme assez irrégulière.

This is a second Beijing project developed by Zaha Hadid for SOHO China, the largest prime office real-estate developer in China. Formerly called Wangjing SOHO, it is located about halfway between the new Capital Airport and the city center in the Wangjing district. As the architects describe this very large project (521 265 square meters of gross floor area): "Like Chinese fans, the volumes appear to move around each other in an intricate dance, each embracing the other from a continuously changing angle. This interplay creates a vibrant architectural complex that is enhanced by an equally dynamic external skin, which continuously varies in density creating a shimmering, exciting presence." Reaching a maximum height of 200 meters, with two retail and 37 office floors above grade, the complex has curved volumes that wrap around each other and are united by a retail podium with a three-story "connective atrium." The differentiation of the volumes allows for a variety of views of the city and also implies that visitors coming into Beijing, or leaving, will perceive SOHO Peaks in different ways. Despite the originality of the forms of the architecture, a standard 8.4-meter office grid is used, and vertical transportation and services are designed with careful attention to practical aspects that allow for flexible use of the buildings. Parking is provided on three basement levels.

Das Projekt ist ein zweiter Entwurf Zaha Hadids für SOHO China, den größten Bauentwickler Chinas für gehobene Büroflächen. Der Komplex, vormals Wangjing SOHO, liegt auf etwa halbem Weg zwischen dem neuen Hauptstadtflughafen und dem Zentrum des Stadtteils Wangjing. Die Architekten beschreiben ihr Großprojekt (Bruttogeschossfläche 521 265 m²): „Die Baukörper scheinen sich, wie chinesische Fächer, in immer neuen Winkeln im Tanz umeinander zu bewegen. Durch dieses Zusammenspiel entsteht ein pulsierender Baukomplex mit einer ebenso dynamischen Gebäudehaut, die sich in ständig wandelnder, schimmernder Intensität präsentiert." Der Komplex erreicht eine Höhe von bis zu 200 m und umfasst zwei Obergeschosse mit Gewerbe- und weitere 37 Etagen mit Büroflächen. Die gewölbten Baukörper greifen ineinander und teilen sich

ein gemeinsames Sockelgeschoss und ein dreistöckiges „Verbindungs-Atrium". Dank der unterschiedlich differenzierten Baukörper ergeben sich abwechslungsreiche Ausblicke auf die Stadt, zugleich bieten sich Peking-Besuchern auf der An- oder Abreise immer wieder verschiedene Blickwinkel auf SOHO Peaks. Trotz der ungewöhnlichen Bauform wurden die Büroetagen mit einem Raster von 8,4 m geplant. Vertikale Verkehrs- und Versorgungsstränge wurden konsequent nach praktischen Gesichtspunkten konzipiert, um die flexible Nutzung der Gebäude zu ermöglichen. Parkflächen stehen auf drei Untergeschossen zur Verfügung.

Ce projet pékinois est le second réalisé par Zaha Hadid pour SOHO China, le plus important promoteur d'immeubles de bureaux haut de gamme en Chine. Anciennement appelé Wangjing SOHO, ce complexe est situé dans le district de Wangjing à mi-distance entre le nouvel aéroport international et le centre de la capitale. Les architectes décrivent ainsi ce très important projet de 521 265 m² de surface brute : « Un peu comme un jeu d'éventails chinois, les volumes semblent tourner les uns autour des autres dans un ballet complexe, chacun semblant donner à l'autre une accolade sous des angles qui se modifient en permanence. Ce jeu savant explique l'aspect dynamique de ce complexe architectural. Son impact visuel est renforcé par une peau dont la densité, qui varie continuellement, participe à la présence miroitante et attirante de l'ensemble. » D'une hauteur maximum de 200 m, comptant deux niveaux de magasins et 37 de bureaux, ce complexe développe ses volumes incurvés à partir d'une base consacrée aux commerces et à un « atrium de connexion » de trois étages de haut. La variété des volumes a permis de multiplier les vues sur la ville et fait que les automobilistes arrivant dans Pékin ou en en revenant perçoivent les bâtiments de façon différente. Derrière ces formes architecturales originales, l'organisation des espaces ne s'appuie pas moins sur une trame rigoureuse de 8,4 m de côté tandis que les circulations verticales et les équipements techniques sont conçus avec un soin particulier pour permettre une grande souplesse d'utilisation. Les parkings occupent trois niveaux en sous-sol.

A rendering of an interior space carries the former name of the complex, Wangjing SOHO, but, as always, underlines the willful continuity established by the architect between interior and exterior forms.

Diese Darstellung eines Innenbereichs zeigt noch den alten Namen des Komplexes, Wangjing SOHO, betont aber auch die von der Architektin – innen wie außen – konsequent umgesetzte Kontinuität der Formensprache.

Image de synthèse du hall d'accueil portant encore l'ancien nom du projet, Wangjing SOHO. Elle exprime clairement la continuité voulue entre les formes externes et internes.

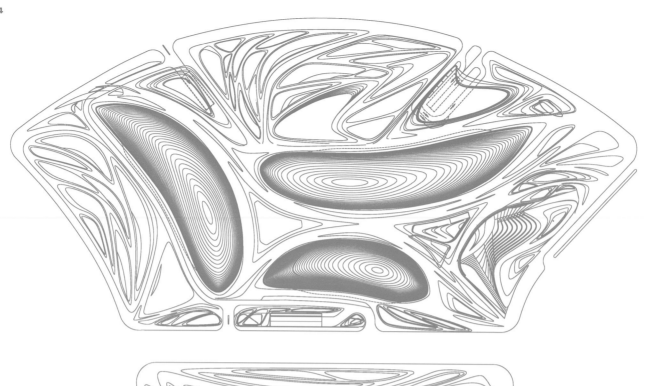

Left page, a site plan with the curvilinear footprint of the complex, and an interior rendering. On this page, renderings highlight the curvature of the volumes and the flowing space imagined by Zaha Hadid. Left, a section drawing showing the relative building heights.

Auf der linken Seite ein Lageplan mit den geschwungenen Konturen des Komplexes sowie das Bild eines Innenbereichs. Die Darstellungen auf dieser Seite unterstreichen die Wölbung der Baukörper und Hadids fließende Räume. Ein Querschnitt links illustriert die Größenverhältnisse der Bauten.

Page de gauche, plan du terrain montrant l'empreinte au sol du complexe et vue de l'intérieur. Sur cette page, images de synthèse illustrant la fluidité de l'espace imaginé par Zaha Hadid. À gauche, coupe illustrant les différentes hauteurs des tours.

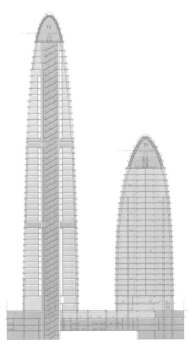

CITYLIFE

Milan, Italy. 2004–16

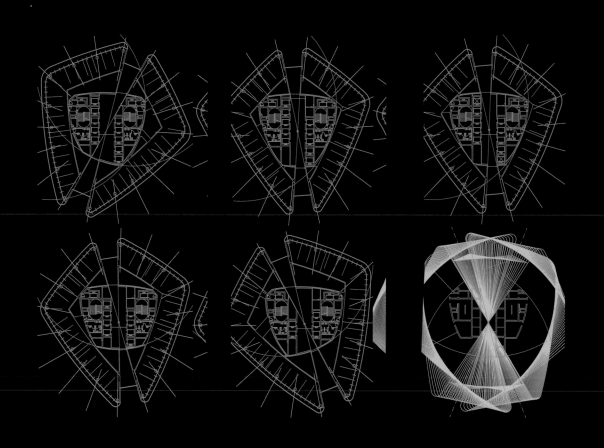
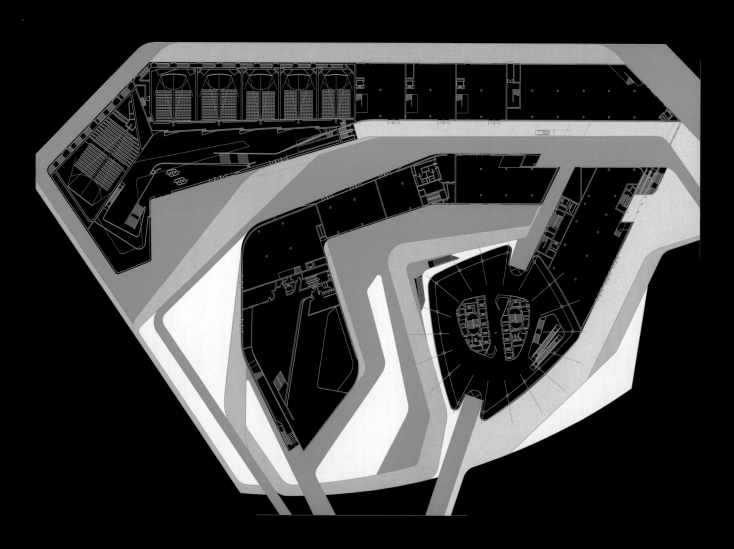

Project
CITYLIFE

Location
MILAN, ITALY

Client
CITYLIFE CONSORTIUM - MILAN

Floor area
TOTAL 160 700 m²

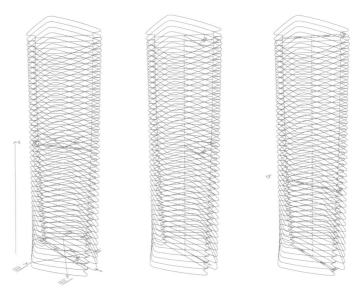

As usual, the plans and drawings of this tower show a great deal of innovation and variety, ensuring that the building will look different from every angle and assume something of the dynamics imparted to lower buildings by Hadid with layering and intertwining.

Wie sonst auch, zeugen die Grundrisse und Zeichnungen des Turms von außergewöhnlicher Innovation und Variation, weshalb der Bau aus jeder Perspektive anders wirkt und etwas von jener Dynamik gewinnt, die Hadid bei ihren niedrigeren Bauten durch Schichtungen und das Ineinandergreifen von Formen erzielt.

Comme d'habitude, les plans et croquis de cette tour témoignent d'un niveau élevé d'innovation et de variété. L'immeuble présentera des profils différents selon les angles de vue. Il déclinera ainsi en partie, par des stratifications et des entrelacements formels, la dynamique des immeubles bas signés Zaha Hadid.

Located on the site of the former Milan fairgrounds, this project includes a park, three office towers, retail buildings, residential structures, education and social facilities, and a museum. Four architects are involved—Zaha Hadid, Arata Isozaki, Daniel Libeskind, and Pier Paolo Maggiora. Hadid's part of the complex is a 43-story, 190-meter-high, 67 000-square-meter office tower, a connected three-level retail mall (15 000 square meters), and a 300-unit housing complex, including 6 buildings ranging in height from 3 to 14 stories. The tower has an upward spiral form, "a strong optimistic icon, contributing to the new skyline of Milan." In contrast with this vertical element, the residential part of the project has been designed in a horizontal mode, made of "meandering lines" that create a series of semi-public gardens for inhabitants. The architect creates a "seamless" transition between the two entities. A continuous line in the ground rises up through the glazed split in the tower. Zaha Hadid states, with reference to the projects of the other architects as well as her own design: "We had from the very beginning a very clear way to read the project. I think that the dynamic of this goes between the three towers with their different heights and the whole central area. It is very exciting and offers an interesting discourse between the tall buildings and the entire skyline."

Das Projekt auf dem ehemaligen Mailänder Messegelände umfasst einen Park, drei Bürohochhäuser, Einkaufszentren, Wohnbauten, Bildungs- und Sozialeinrichtungen sowie ein Museum. Beteiligt sind vier Architekten – Zaha Hadid, Arata Isozaki, Daniel Libeskind und Pier Paolo Maggiora. Hadids Beitrag ist ein 43-stöckiger, 190 m hoher, 67 000 m² großer Büroturm, ein damit verbundenes dreigeschossiges Einkaufszentrum (15 000 m²) sowie ein Wohnkomplex mit 300 Wohnungen, verteilt über sechs Bauten mit je 3 bis 14 Stockwerken. Der Turm wirkt wie eine sich nach oben schraubende Spirale, „ein ausdrucksstarkes, optimistisches Wahrzeichen, das das neue Stadtpanorama von Mailand bereichert". Anders als dieses vertikale Element wurden die Wohnbauten des Projekts horizontal gestaltet und präsentieren sich als „„mäandernde Linien", zwischen denen mehrere halböffentliche Gartenanlagen für die Bewohner entstehen. Der Architektin gelingt eine „nahtlose" Verknüpfung der beiden Einheiten. Eine durchgehende Linie zieht sich von unten als verglaste Spalte bis an die Spitze des Turms. Zaha Hadid betont im Hinblick auf die Bauten der Kollegen ebenso wie ihre eigenen: „Von Anfang an hatten wir eine sehr klar Vorstellung davon, wie wir das Projekt interpretieren wollten. Diese Dynamik zieht sich meiner Ansicht nach trotz der unterschiedlichen Höhe durch alle drei Türme und den gesamten zentralen Bereich. Das ist sehr aufregend und stößt einen interessanten Diskurs zwischen den hohen Bauten und der gesamten Skyline [der Stadt] an."

Prévu sur les anciens terrains de la Foire de Milan, ce projet comprend 3 tours de bureaux, des immeubles commerciaux, des constructions résidentielles, des équipements éducatifs et sociaux, un musée et un parc. Quatre architectes ont été appelés à y participer : Zaha Hadid, Arata Isozaki, Daniel Libeskind et Pier Paolo Maggiora. Le projet pris en charge par Hadid est une tour de bureaux de 43 niveaux, 190 m de haut et 67 000 m² de surface, un centre commercial sur 3 niveaux de 15 000 m² et un ensemble de 300 appartements en 6 immeubles de 3 à 14 niveaux. La tour présente une forme spiralée, « icône puissante et optimiste qui apporte sa contribution au nouveau panorama urbain milanais ». Par contraste avec cet élément vertical, la partie résidentielle conçue sur un plan horizontal se compose de « méandres » qui délimitent une succession de jardins semi-publics. L'architecte a créé une transition « sans rupture » entre les deux entités. Une ligne continue tracée dans le sol s'élève le long du flanc vitré de la tour. Zaha Hadid a déclaré en se référant aux projets des autres architectes et au sien : « Dès le départ, nous avions une vision claire de la manière de rendre ce projet lisible. Je crois qu'une dynamique se dégage entre les trois tours, leurs différentes hauteurs, et la zone centrale. C'est très stimulant et cela provoque des échanges intéressants entre ces immeubles élevés et le panorama urbain. »

Zaha Hadid's tower (left, above) is complemented by a series of lower buildings devoted to retail and housing, on this former site of the Fiera Milano.

Zaha Hadids Turm (oben links) auf dem ehemaligen Mailänder Messegelände wird von einer Reihe niedriger Bauten begleitet, in denen Geschäfte und Wohnungen untergebracht werden sollen.

La tour de Zaha Hadid (ci-dessus, à gauche) sur l'ancien site de la Foire de Milan, s'accompagne d'une série de bâtiments de faible hauteur dédiés à des commerces et des logements.

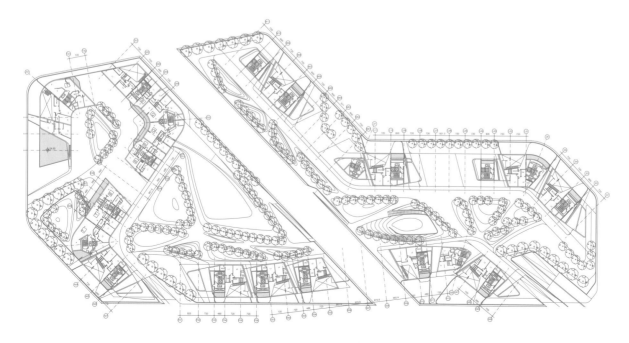

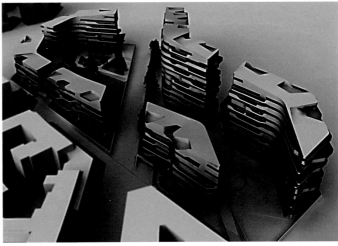

In the layered design of the housing structure, Zaha Hadid introduces a fairly high volume of vegetation to echo the surrounding park space, as can be seen in the perspective view below. Her series of lower buildings form a complex unity that is visible in model views or site plans (left page, bottom).

In den schichtartigen Entwurf der Wohnbauten integriert Hadid ein vergleichsweise hohes Maß an Vegetation und knüpft damit an die umliegenden Parkanlagen an, wie unten zu sehen. Die niedrigen Bauten bilden eine komplexe Einheit, was an den Modellansichten und Grundstücksplänen (linke Seite, unten) deutlich wird.

Dans le plan en strates de l'immeuble de logements, Zaha Hadid a introduit un volume de végétation assez élevé en rappel du parc environnant, comme le montre la vue en perspective ci-dessous. Ses immeubles bas participent à une unité complexe qui est visible dans les maquettes et les plans au sol (page de gauche, en bas).

NEW NATIONAL
STADIUM OF JAPAN

Tokyo, Japan. 2012–19

Project
NEW NATIONAL STADIUM OF JAPAN

Location
TOKYO, JAPAN

Client
JAPAN SPORTS COUNCIL

Area/Size
290 000 m²

The architects emphasize the "iconic" nature of the stadium roof, and also its connections to the city. It is located near the Gaienmae Station on the Ginza Line of the Tokyo subway in the heart of the Japanese capital.

Die Architekten betonen den unverwechselbaren Charakter des Stadiondachs sowie seine Anbindung an die Stadt. Das Stadion liegt in der Nähe des Bahnhofs Gaienmae an der U-Bahn-Linie Ginza im Herzen der japanischen Hauptstadt.

L'architecte s'est attachée à la nature « iconique » de la toiture du stade et au système de connexions avec la ville. Le stade est situé près de la gare de Gaienmae, sur la ligne Ginza du métro de Tokyo, au cœur de la capitale japonaise.

On November 15, 2012, Zaha Hadid was declared the winner of the competition for the new Tokyo National Stadium. The competition was launched in the prospect of the 2020 Summer Olympic Games. With an area of 290 000 square meters, the stadium is designed for a capacity of 80 000 people. With an "iconic silhouette" defined by its roof design, the structure will have retractable, lightweight, translucent membranes arrayed on long-spanning structural ribs to protect the public and playing field from the weather. The architects explain: "It is a piece of the city's fabric, an urban connector that enhances and modulates people moving through the site from different directions and points of access. The elevated ground connections govern the flow of people through the site, effectively carving the geometric forms of the building." The project is based on the refurbishment of the older Kasumigaoka National Stadium (1958), which served as the main venue for the 1964 Tokyo Olympic Games. Competition entries from Alastair Ray Richardson (Cox Architecture) and Kazuyo Sejima (SANAA) ranked respectively second and third.

Am 15. November 2012 ging Zaha Hadid als Siegerin aus dem Wettbewerb für das neue Nationalstadion in Tokio hervor. Die Ausschreibung stand im Zusammenhang mit der Olympiabewerbung Tokios für die Sommerspiele 2020. Mit einer Fläche von 290 000 m² soll das Stadium Platz für 80 000 Zuschauer bieten. Seine unverwechselbare Silhouette verdankt der Bau vor allem seinem Dach – einer ein- und ausfahrbaren Leichtbaukonstruktion mit weitspannendem Rippentragwerk und lichtdurchlässigen Membranen, die Zuschauern und Spielfeld Wetterschutz bieten. Die Architekten erklären: Der Entwurf „fügt sich in die Textur der Stadt, ist ein urbanes Bindeglied, das den Verkehrsfluss über das Stadiongelände hinweg aus verschiedenen Richtungen und Zugangspunkten verbessert und moduliert. Fußgänger werden über eine erhöhtes Wegesystem durch das Gelände geleitet, das zugleich die Geometrie des Baus definiert." Ausgangspunkt des Projekts ist der Umbau des alten Kasumigaoka-Nationalstadions (1958), das 1964 zentraler Austragungsort der Olympischen Spiele in Tokio war. Die Wettbewerbsbeiträge von Alastair Ray Richardson (Cox Architecture) und Kazuyo Sejima (SANAA) erreichten den zweiten und dritten Platz.

C'est le 15 novembre 2012 que Zaha Hadid a remporté le concours pour le nouveau stade national de Tokyo, projet lancé dans la perspective de la tenue des Jeux olympique d'été de 2020 au Japon. D'une surface utile de 290 000 m², le stade offrira une capacité de 80 000 places. Sa silhouette « iconique » est définie par la structure de sa couverture qui fait appel à de légères membranes translucides rétractables tendues sur des nervures structurelles de longue portée qui protégeront le public et les joueurs des intempéries ou du soleil. « C'est un élément du tissu urbain, expliquent les architectes, une connexion urbaine facilitant les mouvements des foules qui se déplaceront sur le site dans différentes directions et à partir de divers points d'accès. Des liaisons surélevées orientent les flux de spectateurs à travers le stade en sculptant une forme géométrique. » Le projet part de la modernisation de l'ancien stade national de Kasumigaoka (1958) qui avait été le centre des Jeux olympiques de 1964. Lors du concours, Alastair Ray Richardson (Cox Architecture) et Kazuyo Sejima (SANAA) sont arrivés respectivement second et troisième derrière Zaha Hadid.

ONE-NORTH
MASTER PLAN

Singapore, Singapore. 2001–21

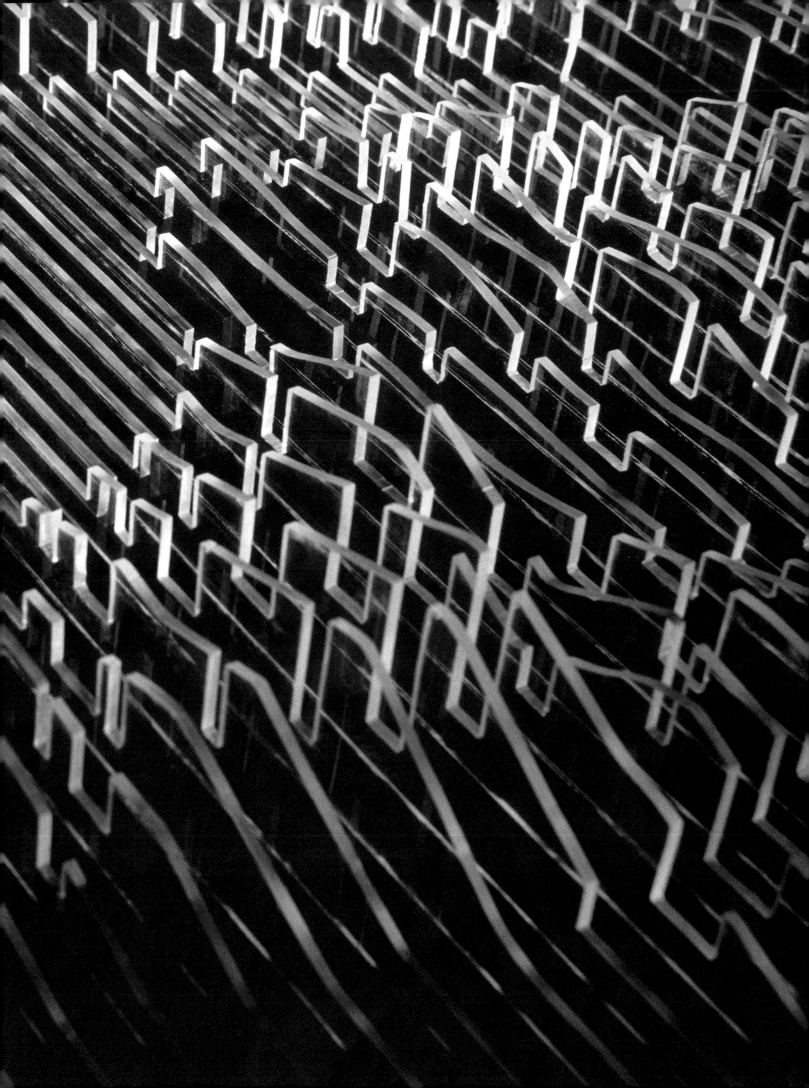

Project
ONE-NORTH MASTER PLAN

Location
SINGAPORE, SINGAPORE

Client
SCIENCE HUB DEVELOPMENT GROUP (SHDG)
JURONG TOWN CORPORATION (JTC)

Area/Size
BUILDING 5 000 000 m²

Intended for an area of 200 hectares with five million square meters of floor area and a projected population of 138 000 people, the one-north master plan responds to and regenerates the urban pattern, bringing an organic scheme into direct contact with the more traditional lines of the city.

Der Masterplan, konzipiert für ein 200 ha großes Gebiet mit 5 Millionen m² Geschossfläche und eine Bevölkerung von voraussichtlich 138 000 Bewohnern, fügt sich in die urbane Struktur und erneuert sie zugleich. Mit seinem organischen Konzept knüpft er an die eher traditionellen Achsen der Stadt an.

Conçu pour une zone de 200 hectares et prévoyant 5 millions de m² de surface bâtie pour une population de 138 000 habitants, le Plan directeur one-north répond au besoin de rénovation du tissu urbain et introduit un schéma organique en contact direct avec les profils plus traditionnels de la ville.

This is an urban master plan developed for the Science Hub Development Group (SHDG). The architect relates this "possibility of an urban architecture that exploits the spatial repertoire and morphology of natural landscape formations" to her earliest work and in particular to the Hong Kong Peak (1982–83), but here applies her ideas to a whole neighborhood. The forms of the plan bring to mind a series of dunes, imagery present in other aspects of Hadid's work, emphasized by the undulating roofs of the area that often join together. Though the plan calls for a number of "microenvironments" within the overall urban scheme, it is clear that the goal is to engender a sense of continuity within a sufficient matrix of different solutions, including varying heights and building sizes. A curving or "softly swaying" pattern of streets allows the master plan to integrate itself into the varying street alignments that surround the zone concerned. The architect describes the scheme as embodying "flexibility without chaos.... The proposed morphological system allows for infinite variation within the bounds of a strong formal coherence and lawfulness. This," she says, "is a great advantage of working with a 'natural' geometry rather than with a strict Platonic geometry." Pedestrian and public transport on a level five meters above ground is envisaged on raised plazas connected to the street level by ramps or broad staircases. This is certainly an effort to develop an artificial landscape that in many ways takes its cues from nature.

Entwickelt wurde dieser urbane Masterplan für die Science Hub Development Group (SHDG). Der Architektin zufolge ist diese „Gelegenheit, eine urbane Architektur zu gestalten, die das räumliche Repertoire und die Morphologie natürlicher Landschaftsformationen auslotet", im Zusammenhang mit ihren frühesten Projekten zu sehen, insbesondere dem Peak in Hongkong (1982–83); allerdings wendet sie ihre Ideen hier auf ein ganzes Stadtviertel an. Von seiner Formgebung her erinnert der Plan an Dünengruppen, ein Motiv, das auch in anderen Bereichen von Hadids Werk anzutreffen ist. Unterstrichen wird dieser Eindruck von den sich wellenförmig abzeichnenden Dächern des Viertels, die häufig miteinander verbunden sind. Obwohl der städtebauliche Gesamtentwurf (den planerischen Vorgaben entsprechend) verschiedene „Mikro-Umfelder" vorsieht, ist klar, dass hier der Eindruck von Geschlossenheit entstehen soll – und dies im Rahmen einer ausreichend breit gefächerten Matrix unterschiedlicher Einzellösungen, wie etwa variierenden Bauhöhen und Gebäudegrößen. Dank eines

geschwungenen, sich „sanft wiegenden" Straßenrasters fügt sich der Masterplan in die unterschiedlichen Straßenverläufe des umliegenden Gebiets ein. Die Architektin beschreibt das Konzept als Inbegriff von „Flexibilität ohne Chaos ... Das vorgeschlagene morphologische System erschließt unendlich viele Variationsmöglichkeiten, ist aber dennoch von formaler Kohärenz und Gesetzmäßigkeit. Dies ist der große Vorteil", betont sie, „wenn man mit einer ‚natürlichen', statt einer streng platonischen Geometrie arbeitet." Fußgänger- und öffentlicher Nahverkehr sollen auf ein erhöhtes Niveau 5 m über dem Boden verlegt werden, das über Rampen oder breite Treppen an die Straßenebene angeschlossen wird. Dies ist fraglos der Versuch, eine künstliche Landschaft zu entwickeln, die in vielerlei Hinsicht von der Natur inspiriert ist.

Ce plan directeur d'urbanisme a été mis au point pour le Science Hub Development Group (SHDG). L'architecte relie cette « possibilité d'une architecture urbaine qui exploite le répertoire spatial et la morphologie des formations naturelles du paysage » à ses premiers travaux et en particulier au projet du Hong Kong Peak (1982-83), mais applique ici ses idées à tout un quartier. Les formes du plan rappellent une succession de dunes, à travers une imagerie que l'on retrouve dans plusieurs projets d'Hadid, impression renforcée par l'ondulation des toitures qui se rejoignent souvent. Si le projet génère un certain nombre de « micro-environnements » dans le cadre du schéma urbain d'ensemble, il est clair que l'objectif est de créer un sentiment de continuité à l'intérieur d'une matrice de solutions différentes, dont les variables comprennent les hauteurs et les autres dimensions des constructions. Le dessin des rues incurvées ou « légèrement déportées » permet à ce schéma directeur de s'intégrer dans les divers alignements des axes existants autour de la zone concernée. L'architecte voit dans son projet une incarnation « de flexibilité sans chaos ... le système morphologique proposé autorise une infinité de variations dans les limites d'une forte cohérence et d'une légitimité formelles. C'est le grand avantage de travailler à partir d'une géométrie "naturelle" plutôt qu'une stricte approche platonicienne. » La présence des piétons et des transports publics est envisagée à cinq mètres au-dessus du sol sur des plazzas surélevées connectées au niveau de la rue par des rampes ou de larges escaliers. Ce projet illustre une tentative de développer un paysage artificiel qui, à de nombreux égards, trouve ses raisons dans la nature même.

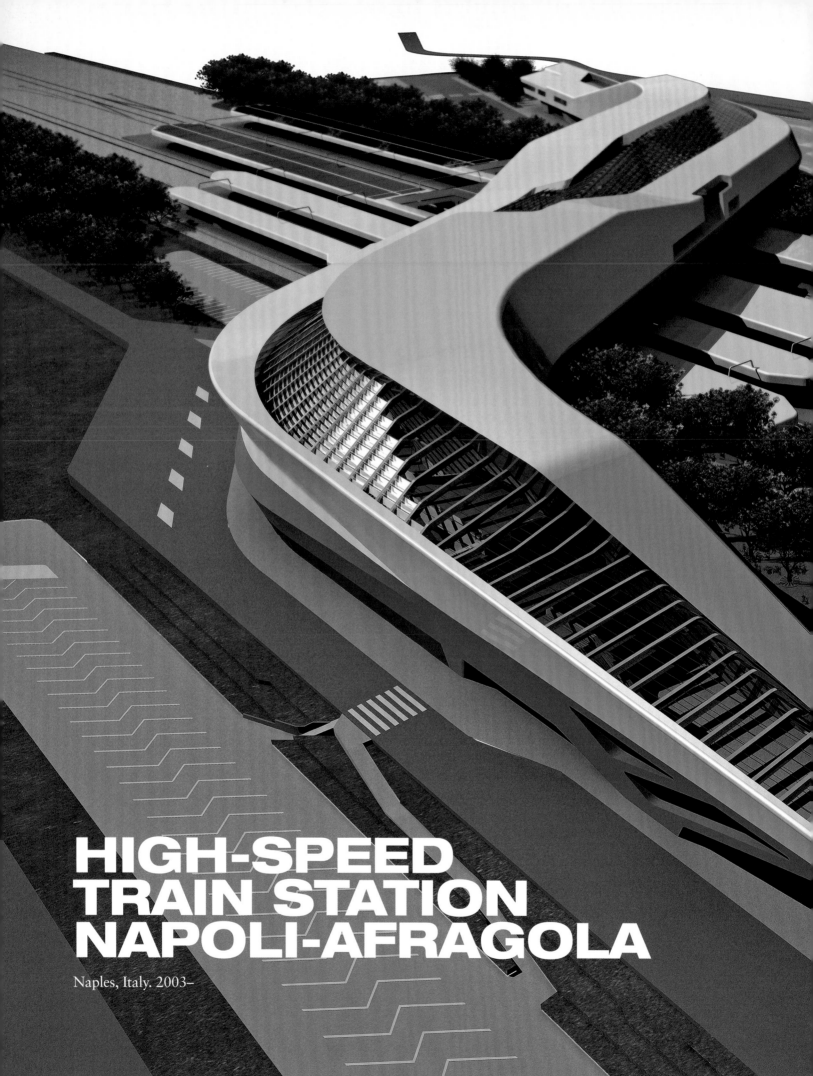

HIGH-SPEED
TRAIN STATION
NAPOLI-AFRAGOLA

Naples, Italy. 2003–

Project
HIGH-SPEED TRAIN STATION NAPOLI-AFRAGOLA

Location
NAPLES, ITALY

Client
RFI S. P. A.

Area/Size
30 000 m²

The low-lying form of the Station undeniably carries an evocation of the high-speed trains it is meant to serve, though this form is more complex than any train. To the left, a dramatic atrium space that seems to be carved out of a preexisting mass.

Die geduckte Form des Bahnhofs spielt zweifellos auf die Hochgeschwindigkeitszüge an, für die er vorgesehen ist, auch wenn seine formale Gestaltung wesentlich komplexer ist als jeder Zug. Links ein dramatisches Atrium, das wie aus einem Monolith herausgeschnitten wirkt.

Les formes surbaissées de la gare évoquent indéniablement les trains à grande vitesse qu'elle accueillera, même si sa forme est beaucoup plus complexe que ceux-ci. À gauche, le volume spectaculaire de l'atrium qui semble sculpté dans un bloc préexistant.

Zaha Hadid's project for the new high-speed train station of Naples was selected in November 2003 from a shortlist of 10 firms. Hadid described the fluid design as a "bridge above the tracks announcing the approach to the city." By elevating the structure in the landscape, its function as a gateway to Naples is defined. Making it into a bridge over the tracks permits the station to function more as a link to the developing business area of the site than as a barrier to the movement of pedestrians. Nor does the bridge have a main entrance and a rear façade as most similar structures do; the architect decided clearly to give equal weight to the two entrances, with the "central functions" of the station ideally placed at the center of the bridge, confirming the desired equilibrium. With its diagonal setting vis-à-vis the tracks and proposed linear parks on either side, the station immediately assumes an unusual appearance that is nonetheless integrated into the site, or the "surrounding man-made landscape." As is implied by its fluid design, the station is all about movement and the connection of various forms of transport. The impression of fluidity and movement is accentuated through the design of the interior "like a river that has carved a riverbed or canyon through solid rock." Likewise, Hadid's design seeks to generate lines of movement of people that flow through the space and define it. A shopping concourse is located above the ticketing and access level, with a main opening that allows light from above to reach the lower floors, forming a central space that is intended to mark the interior architecture.

Zaha Hadids Projekt für einen neuen Bahnhof für Hochgeschwindigkeitszüge in Neapel wurde 2003 aus einer engeren Wahl von zehn Bewerbern ausgewählt. Hadid beschreibt das fließende Design als „Brücke über den Gleisen, die die Ankunft in der Stadt signalisiert". Durch die erhöhte Positionierung des Baus in der Landschaft wird seine Funktion als Tor nach Neapel deutlich. Die Gestaltung als Brücke über den Gleisen lässt den Bahnhof als Bindeglied zum neu entstehenden Geschäftsviertel auf dem Gelände erscheinen, statt als Barriere für den Fußgängerverkehr. Darüber hinaus hat die Brücke keinen Haupteingang und keine Rückseite, wie die meisten vergleichbaren Bauten; die Architektin entschied sich ganz bewusst dafür, beiden Eingängen gleich viel Gewicht beizumessen. Die „zentralen Funktionen" des Bahnhofs liegen ideal positioniert in der Mitte der Brücke, was die gewünschte Ausgewogenheit unterstreicht. Durch seinen diagonalen Verlauf über den Gleisen und die geplanten geradlinigen Park-

anlagen zu beiden Seiten ist der Bahnhof eine ungewöhnliche Erscheinung, die dennoch in das Gelände bzw. das „künstliche landschaftliche Umfeld" integriert scheint. Wie das fließende Design ahnen lässt, symbolisiert der Bahnhof in erster Linie dynamische Bewegung und eine Schnittstelle verschiedener Verkehrsmittel. Betont wird der fließende, dynamische Eindruck auch durch die Gestaltung der Innenräume, die „wie ein Fluss wirken, der sich ein Bett oder gar eine Schlucht durch den Felsen gegraben hat". Zugleich will Hadids Entwurf dynamische Wegesysteme für die Menschen schaffen, die durch den Raum strömen und ihn prägen. Über der Fahrkarten- und Eingangsebene liegt eine Einkaufspassage. Ein zentrales Oberlicht lässt Helligkeit in die unteren Ebenen fallen und definiert einen Hauptraum, der die Architektur im Innern des Baus prägt.

Le projet de Zaha Hadid pour la nouvelle gare de Naples destinée aux trains à grande vitesse a été choisi en novembre 2003 parmi dix autres propositions. Hadid décrit cette réalisation marquée par la fluidité comme « un pont au-dessus des voies qui annonce l'approche de la ville ». Le fait de surélever le bâtiment dans le paysage définit ainsi mieux sa fonction de porte de la cité. Le concept de franchissement permet à la gare de se présenter davantage comme un lien avec le quartier de bureaux du site, et non comme une barrière. Ce bâtiment-pont ne possède ni entrée principale ni façade arrière comme beaucoup de constructions similaires. L'architecte a décidé d'accorder la même importance aux deux entrées, les « fonctions centrales » de la gare étant idéalement implantées au centre, confirmant ainsi l'équilibre recherché. Par son orientation en diagonale par rapport aux voies et grâce aux deux parcs de forme allongée prévus sur chacun de ses côtés, la gare prend un aspect original qui ne s'intègre pas moins dans le site ou « le paysage artificiel environnant ». Comme l'implique la fluidité de ses plans, elle s'organise autour de principes de mouvements et de connexions entre les divers modes de transport. L'impression de fluidité et de dynamique est accentuée par le dessin des volumes intérieurs, « comme une rivière qui aurait creusé son lit ou un canyon dans la roche ». De même, le projet cherche à matérialiser les axes de déplacement des usagers qui sillonnent l'espace tout en le définissant. Un centre commercial est aménagé au-dessus du niveau d'arrivée et de la billetterie, tandis qu'une longue ouverture en toiture permet à la lumière naturelle d'atteindre les niveaux inférieurs tout en délimitant l'espace central autour duquel s'organise l'architecture intérieure.

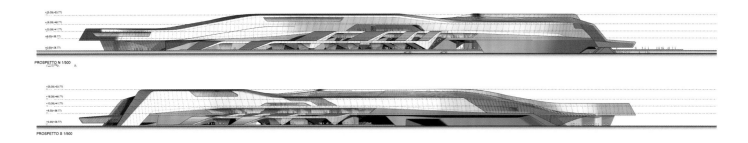

PROSPETTO N 1/500

PROSPETTO S 1/500

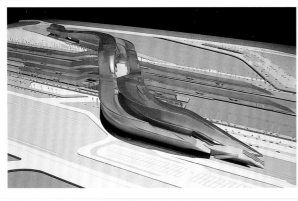
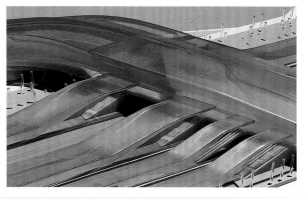

Layered forms and in particular a snaking volume that runs over the tracks allowing passengers to reach their trains create as dynamic a form in plan as in elevation.

Übereinander geschichtete Formen und vor allem der geschwungene Baukörper, der die Gleise überspannt und den Reisenden Zugang zu den Zügen bietet, bilden ein dynamisches Ganzes in Grund- und Aufriss.

Les formes stratifiées, et en particulier le volume qui serpente au-dessus des voies et permet aux passagers d'accéder aux trains, créent une forme aussi dynamique en plan qu'en élévation.

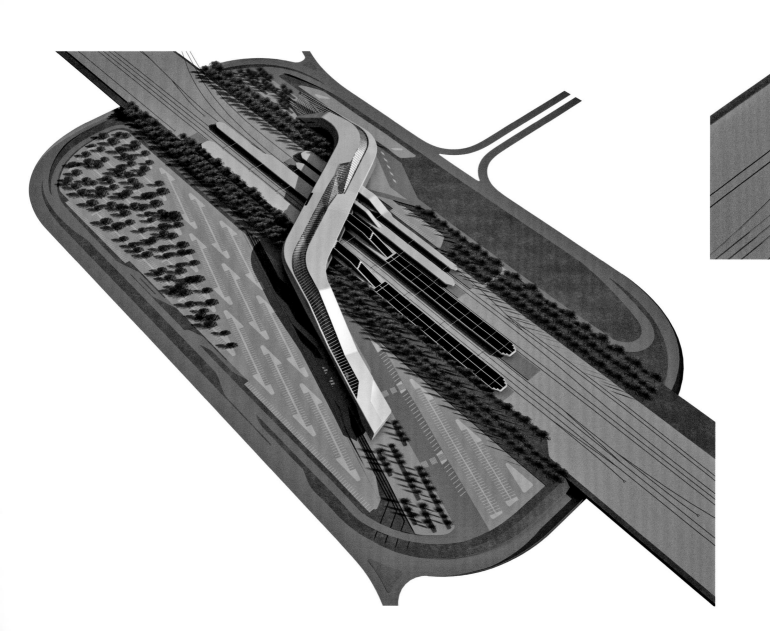

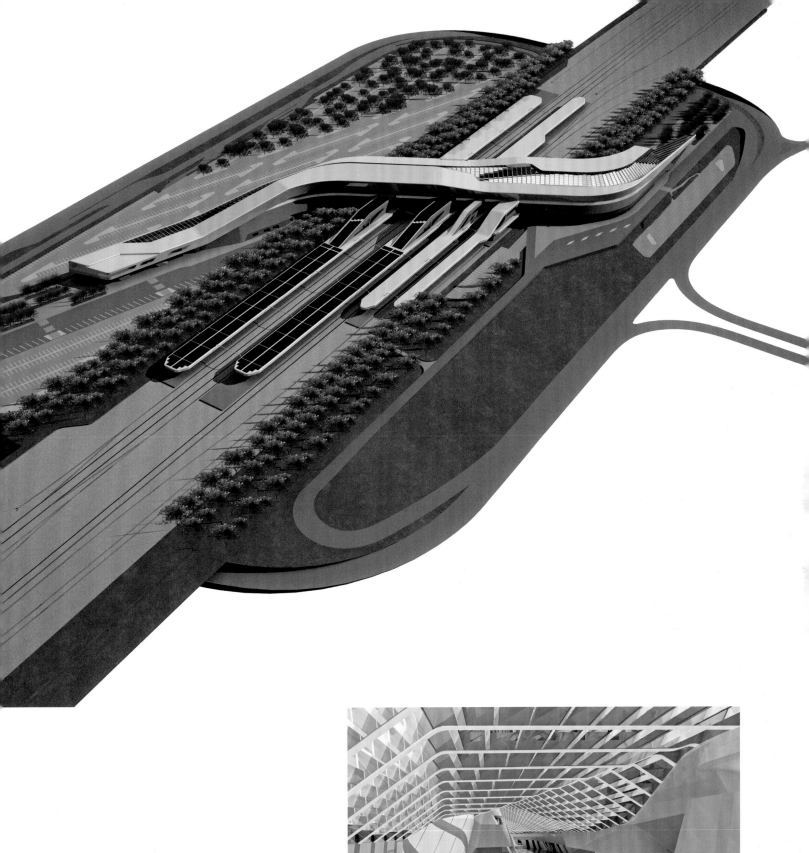

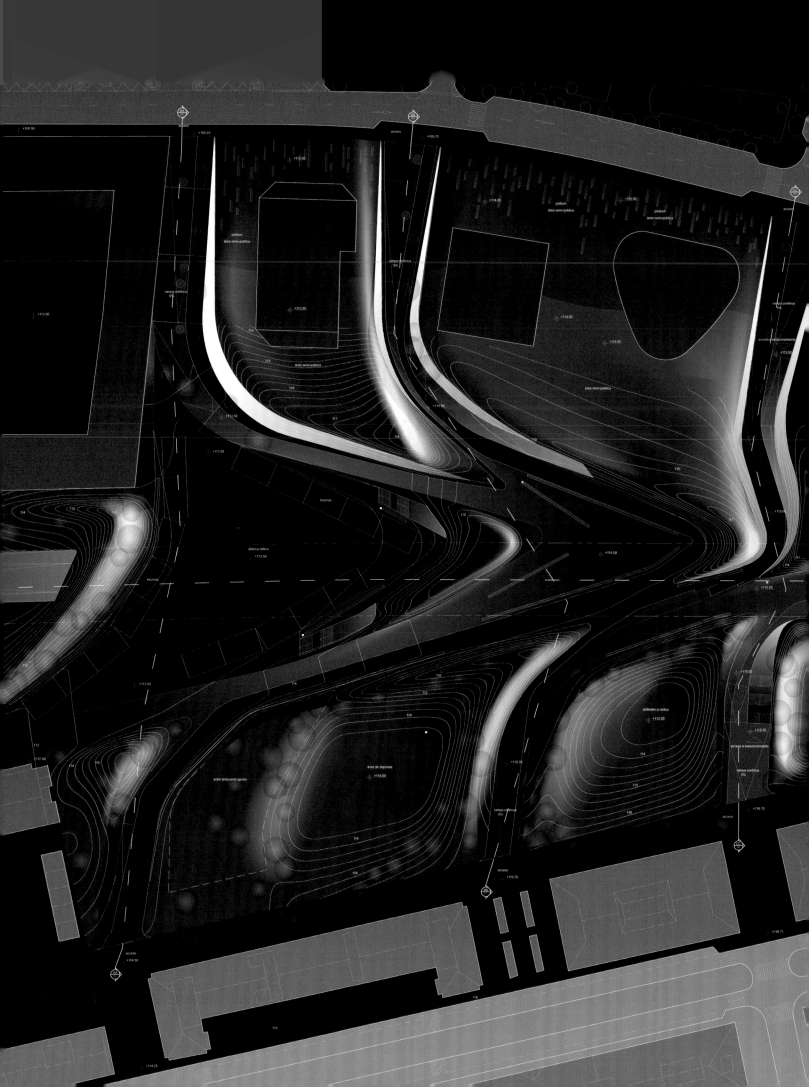

EUSKOTREN
HEADQUARTERS AND
URBAN PLANNING

Durango, Spain. First phase: 2004–

Project
EUSKOTREN HEADQUARTERS AND URBAN PLANNING

Location
DURANGO, SPAIN

Client
EUSKOTREN/ETS RED FERROVIARIA VASCA

Area/Size
HEADQUARTERS 7291 m²
COMMERCIAL AND LEISURE CENTER 9576 m²

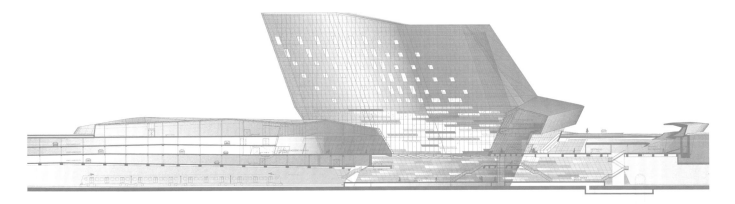

Here again, the layering, interpenetrating style of Zaha Hadid Architects is well suited to the mixed-use complexity of the scheme, incorporating offices, residential space, and a train station.

Auch hier wird der schichtartige, ineinander greifende Stil von Zaha Hadid der Komplexität einer gemischt genutzten Anlage, zu der Büros, Wohnflächen und ein Bahnhof gehören, optimal gerecht.

L'approche de stratification et d'interpénétration de Zaha Hadid Architects s'adapte bien à la complexité de ce projet mixte, incluant des bureaux, des logements et une gare de chemin de fer.

Zaha Hadid's design was selected from a shortlist of five international firms by a jury that commented: "Hadid's design combines the functional necessities of Euskotren with a new vision for the future." Durango is located approximately 25 kilometers from the city of Bilbao, and Euskotren is the Basque railway company. The program here calls for the corporate headquarters, but also a train station, five residential buildings, and a park. Part of the task of the architect in this instance was to contribute to the urban regeneration of Durango. A commercial and leisure center is located below grade with parking areas in this seven-story, 7291-square-meter proposal. The Durango Station is set underground and has an independent ground-level entrance. Hadid studied pedestrian circulation in particular, proposing a reorganization using flow diagrams. Burying a certain number of train lines in the area makes way for new park spaces at ground level, emphasizing the regeneration of the area. The architect writes: "Topographic differentiations and ground-level changes are employed to create self-separation and allow programmatic connections across the site to the car park, buildings, and adjacent streets." The separation referred to is that of the public and private areas, including residential space.

Zaha Hadids Entwurf wurde aus einer engeren Wahl von fünf internationalen Büros ausgesucht. Die Jury begründete das so: „Zaha Hadids Entwurf verbindet die funktionalen Anforderungen von Euskotren mit einer neuen Vision für die Zukunft." Durango liegt etwa 25 km von Bilbao entfernt, Euskotren ist die baskische Eisenbahngesellschaft. Das Programm erforderte eine Firmenzentrale sowie einen Bahnhof, fünf Wohnbauten und einen Park. Teil der Aufgabe der Architektin war es, zur Stadterneuerung von Durango beizutragen. Der siebenstöckige Entwurf mit 7291 m² schließt ein Einkaufs- und Freizeitzentrum mit Parkplätzen im Untergeschoss ein. Auch der Bahnhof liegt unterirdisch und hat einen separaten Eingang auf Straßenebene. Hadid setzte sich besonders mit den

Fußgängerströmen auseinander und plädierte für eine Neuorganisation ausgehend von Flussdiagrammen. Die Verlegung verschiedener Zuglinien unter die Erde schafft Raum für neue Parkplätze auf Straßenebene und unterstützt die Stadterneuerungsbemühungen im Viertel. Die Architektin schreibt: „Topografische Differenzierungen und Veränderungen zu ebener Erde dienen der Abgrenzung und ermöglichen programmatische Verknüpfungen über das gesamte Gelände hinweg, bis hin zum Parkplatz, den Gebäuden und den angrenzenden Straßen." Die hier erwähnte Abgrenzung bezieht sich auf die Differenzierung öffentlicher und privater Bereiche, etwa bei den Wohnbauten.

Ce projet de Zaha Hadid a été sélectionné parmi ceux de cinq agences internationales par un jury qui a ainsi justifié son choix : « Le projet Hadid associe les nécessités fonctionnelles d'Euskotren et une nouvelle vision du futur. » Euskotren est la compagnie des chemins de fer basque. Le programme comprend le siège de l'entreprise, une gare, cinq immeubles résidentiels et un parc. Une partie de la tâche de l'architecte a été de s'intégrer dans les plans de rénovation urbaine de Durango, ville située à 25 km environ de Bilbao. Ce projet de 7291 m² sur sept niveaux comprend également un centre commercial et de loisirs en sous-sol accompagné de parkings. La gare souterraine possède une entrée indépendante à l'air libre. Hadid a particulièrement étudié la circulation piétonnière et proposé de l'organiser en fonction de diagrammes de flux. L'enfouissement d'un certain nombre de voies a permis de dégager de la place pour créer un parc en surface et mieux s'intégrer à la rénovation de cette zone. Selon Zaha Hadid : « Les différenciations topographiques et les modifications du niveau du sol permettent de créer une autoséparation et de faciliter les connexions programmatiques sur l'ensemble du site, entre parkings, immeubles et rues adjacentes. » La séparation qu'elle mentionne est celle qui figure entre domaines public et privé, ce dernier comprenant les immeubles d'appartements.

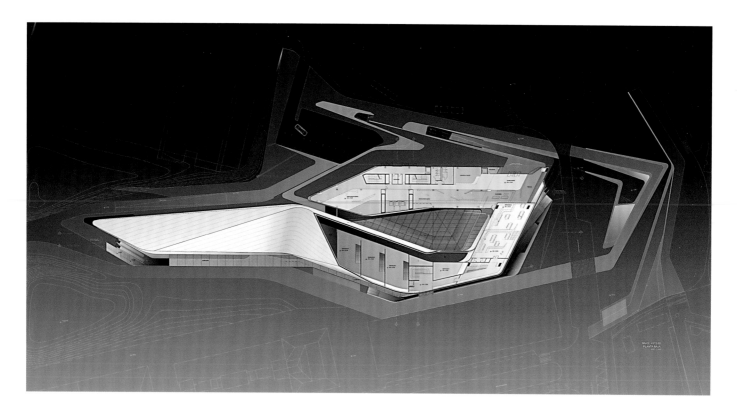

Despite its willfully innovative aesthetics, it is clear from the site drawing below that the architect has carefully considered the urban situation of the complex, making its own lines flow into and around those of the environment.

Wie die Zeichnung unten zeigt, hat die Architektin die urbane Lage des Komplexes ungeachtet der eigenwillig innovativen Ästhetik umfassend berücksichtigt. Die Linienführung fügt sich fließend in die Linien der Umgebung ein.

Malgré son esthétique innovante, il est évident d'après les plans ci-dessous que l'architecte a étudié avec soin l'intégration urbaine du complexe dont les axes s'intègrent à ceux de son environnement.

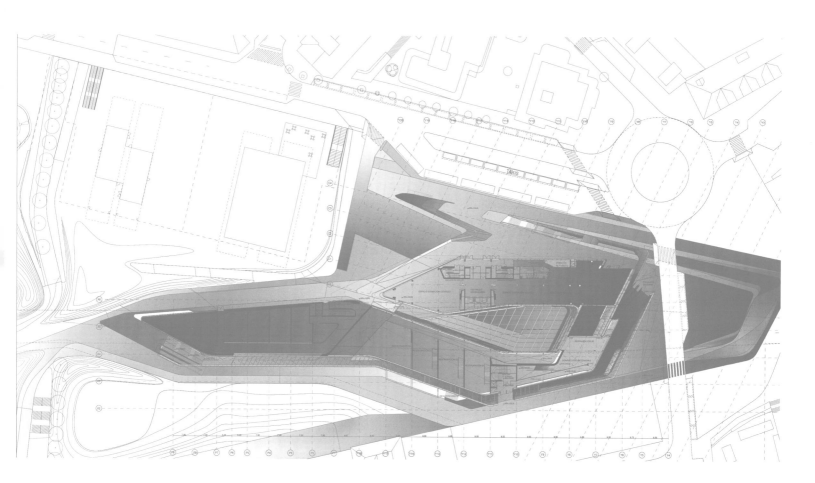

Showing the profile of the building against the neighboring structures and its situation within the city, the drawings above show that exhaustive research has gone into the project not only with respect to the program but also to its urban presence.

Die Zeichnungen oben zeigen die Konturen des Gebäudes vor dem Hintergrund der Nachbarbauten sowie seine Lage in der Stadt und belegen, welch umfassende Recherchen in das Projekt eingeflossen sind – nicht nur im Hinblick auf das Programm, sondern auch auf seine urbane Präsenz.

Le dessin ci-dessus, qui représente le profil du bâtiment, sa situation dans la ville et les constructions avoisinantes, montre qu'une recherche poussée a été menée non seulement sur le programme mais aussi sur la présence urbaine de ce projet.

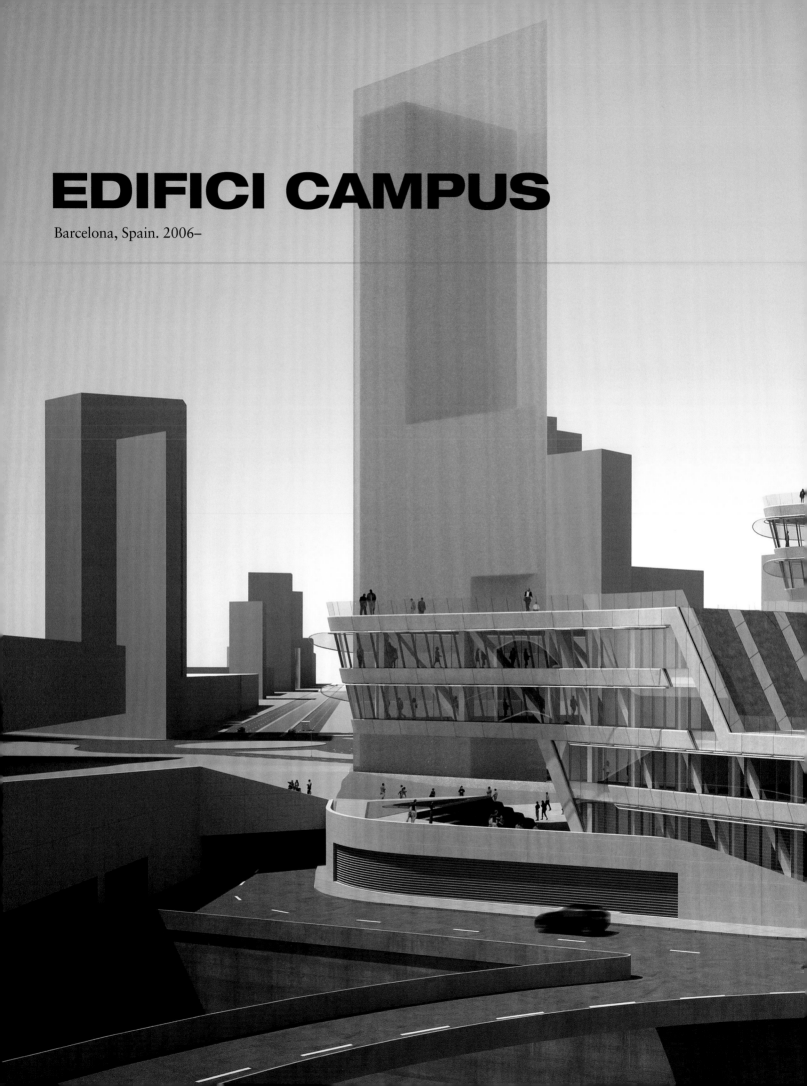

EDIFICI CAMPUS

Barcelona, Spain. 2006–

Project
EDIFICI CAMPUS

Location
BARCELONA, SPAIN

Client
EL CONSORCI – ZONA FRANCA DE BARCELONA, CONSORCI DEL CAMPUS INTERUNIVERSITARI DEL BESÒS

Area/Size
27 650 m²

The sweeping lines of light and ramps or stairways that run through the spaces seen in the perspectives to the left echo the spiraling nature of the complex. A sketch, above, makes sense only if the actual design of the building is grasped (see next double page).

Die dramatischen Lichtbänder, Rampen und Treppen, die die Räume durchziehen und in den Ansichten links zu sehen sind, spiegeln die spiralförmige Anlage des Komplexes. Die Skizze oben erschließt sich nur, wenn man das tatsächliche Design des Gebäudes kennt (folgende Doppelseite).

Les lignes enveloppantes des axes d'éclairages et des rampes ou escaliers qui courent à travers l'espace observables dans les perspectives à gauche illustrent la conception en spirale de ce complexe. Le croquis, ci-dessus, ne se comprend que par rapport à une illustration du projet réalisé (voir double-page suivante).

This complex combines 12 150 square meters of office space and retail, with 8500 square meters of university facilities, including an exhibition area and auditorium. A further 7000 square meters are dedicated to parking areas. This somewhat unusual mixture of activities is intended to facilitate bridge building between the worlds of education, research, and business. Indeed, Hadid's plan willfully mixes activities where others might have sought a more complete division of the client spaces. Located at the water's edge, the main structure is a spiraling tower set at the dividing point of Barcelona and the neighboring town of Besòs, near the Edifici Forum built by Herzog & de Meuron (2000–04). Hadid says that the spiral design will stimulate "the seamless integration of the city fabric, connecting in a dynamic way the different surrounding areas." Hadid's description of the building, with its curved, shifting floor plates, is indicative of the overall ambition of the project: "The fluid character of the tower is generated through an intrinsically dynamic composition of volumes that dissolves the classic typology of the tower and the podium into a seamless piece. The building uses the site's inclined topography to redesign the landscape in order to create seamless accessibility between the new campus and the forum. Through the use of cantilevers, the building lifts from the street level, releasing the ground to be occupied by civic/public uses. The continuous, 'choreographed,' spiral movement 'weaves' a series of public spaces, connecting the campus, through the courtyards and under the cantilevers, to the Forum beyond."

Dieser Komplex umfasst 12 150 m² Büro- und Gewerbeflächen sowie 8500 m² für Universitätseinrichtungen, darunter auch eine Ausstellungsfläche und ein Auditorium. Weitere 7000 m² entfallen auf Parkplätze. Diese eher ungewöhnliche Kombination soll den Brückenschlag zwischen Bildung, Forschung und Wirtschaft fördern. Tatsächlich mischt Hadids Grundriss ganz bewusst verschiedene Nutzungen, wo andere vielleicht eine vollständige Trennung der Räumlichkeiten nach Nutzern angestrebt hätten. Der zentrale, direkt am Ufer gelegene Baukörper ist ein spiralförmig gedrehter Turm und liegt an der Stadtgrenze von Barcelona und Besòs, unweit des Edifici Forum von Herzog & de Meuron (2000–04). Hadid geht davon aus, dass der spiralförmige Entwurf „eine nahtlose Integration in das Geflecht der Stadt" anregen und den Komplex „auf dynamische Weise mit den verschiedenen angrenzenden Stadtvierteln verbinden wird". Hadids Beschreibung des Gebäudes mit seinen geschwungenen, gegeneinander verschobenen Geschossen zeugt vom Ehrgeiz des gesamten Projekts: „Der fließende Charakter des Turms entsteht durch eine dynamische Komposition der Baukörper, die die klassischen Typologien von Turm und Sockelbau zu einem nahtlosen Ganzen verschmilzt. Der Bau macht sich die leichte Neigung des Geländes zunutze, um den landschaftlichen Kontext neu zu definieren und neue nahtlose Verkehrswege zwischen dem neuen Campus und dem Forum zu schaffen. Mithilfe von Auslegern wird der Bau über die Straße angehoben, der Boden wird frei für öffentliche Nutzung. Die kontinuierliche, ‚choreografierte' Spiralbewegung ‚verwebt' unterschiedliche öffentliche Räume miteinander und bindet den Campus durch seine Innenhöfe und die Verkehrszonen unterhalb der Auskragungen an das Forum an."

Ce complexe regroupe 12 150 m² de bureaux et de commerces, 8500 m² d'installations universitaires, dont un lieu d'expositions et un auditorium, et 7000 m² de parkings. Ce mélange assez peu courant d'activités a pour ambition de faciliter les liens entre les univers de l'éducation, de la recherche et des affaires. Le plan de Zaha Hadid mixe ainsi volontairement des activités que d'autres auraient pu vouloir séparer. Érigée en bordure de la mer, la construction principale est une tour en spirale dressée à la limite des communes de Barcelone et de Besòs, à proximité du Forum construit par Herzog & de Meuron (2000–04). Pour Hadid, cette spirale devrait stimuler « l'intégration sans rupture du tissu urbain, et connecter de manière dynamique les différentes zones environnantes ». Sa description du bâtiment à plateaux aux contours incurvés coulissant les uns sur les autres exprime les objectifs du projet : « Le caractère fluide de la tour naît d'une composition intrinsèquement dynamique de volumes qui dissolvent la typologie classique de la tour et du podium dans un ensemble continu, sans rupture. Le bâtiment utilise la pente du terrain pour redessiner le paysage et permettre une accessibilité sans césure entre le nouveau campus et le Forum. Ses porte-à-faux, qui semblent le soulever par rapport à la rue, libèrent le sol pour des activités civiques et/ou publiques. Le mouvement, continu en spirale "chorégraphié", "tisse" une série d'espaces publics, connectant le campus, par des cours et des espaces sous les porte-à-faux, au Forum situé plus bas. »

Though cantilevered forms are frequent in the architecture of Zaha Hadid, here they appear to define the building as it rises, allowing for generous terraces at several points. Section drawings below show that the usable floor area is certainly not diminished for the purposes of the architectural effect.

Obwohl auskragende Formen in der Architektur Zaha Hadids keine Seltenheit sind, scheinen sie hier den Bau mit zunehmender Höhe zu definieren und schaffen an mehreren Stellen großzügige Terrassen. Die Schnittzeichnungen unten belegen, dass die Nutzfläche pro Geschoss keineswegs dem architektonischen Effekt geopfert wird.

Les formes en porte-à-faux sont fréquentes dans l'architecture de Zaha Hadid. Ici, elles semblent définir le bâtiment et permettent la projection de généreuses terrasses à plusieurs endroits. Les coupes ci-dessous montrent que les surfaces de sol utiles ne sont en rien diminuées par ces effets architecturaux.

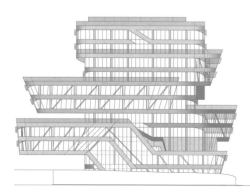
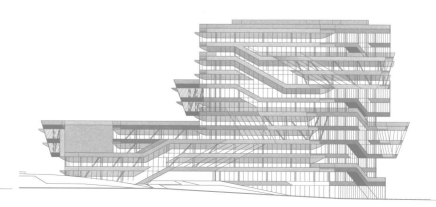

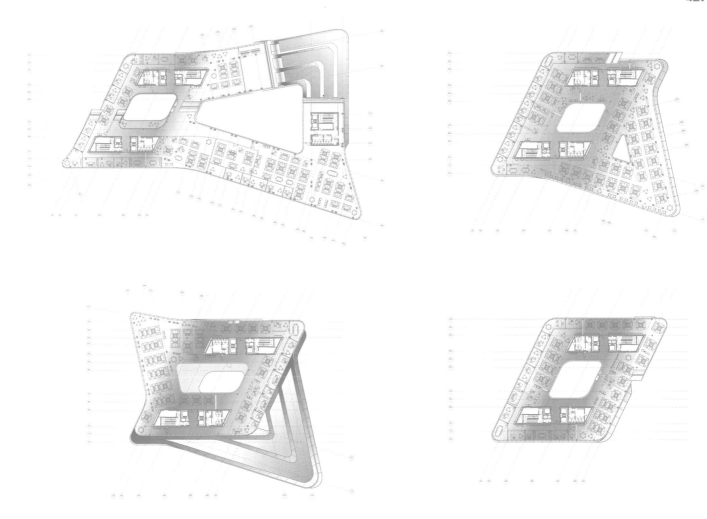

The spiraling appearance of the building results from the displacement of the floor blocks, creating large overhangs and outdoor terraces. More than a simple rotation of a given form, the displacement involved also plays on different floor plans on each group of levels.

Die spiralförmige Optik des Gebäudes ergibt sich aus der Verschiebung der Etagenblöcke, wodurch erhebliche Auskragungen und Terrassen entstehen. Mehr jedoch als die simple Verschiebung einer gegebenen Form, wurde hier bei den einzelnen Etagengruppen mit verschiedenen Grundrissen gespielt.

L'aspect en spirale de l'immeuble résulte du déplacement des niveaux qui génère de grands porte-à-faux et l'apparition de terrasses. Plus que la simple rotation d'une forme, ce déplacement entraîne également des variations entre les sols de chaque groupe de niveaux.

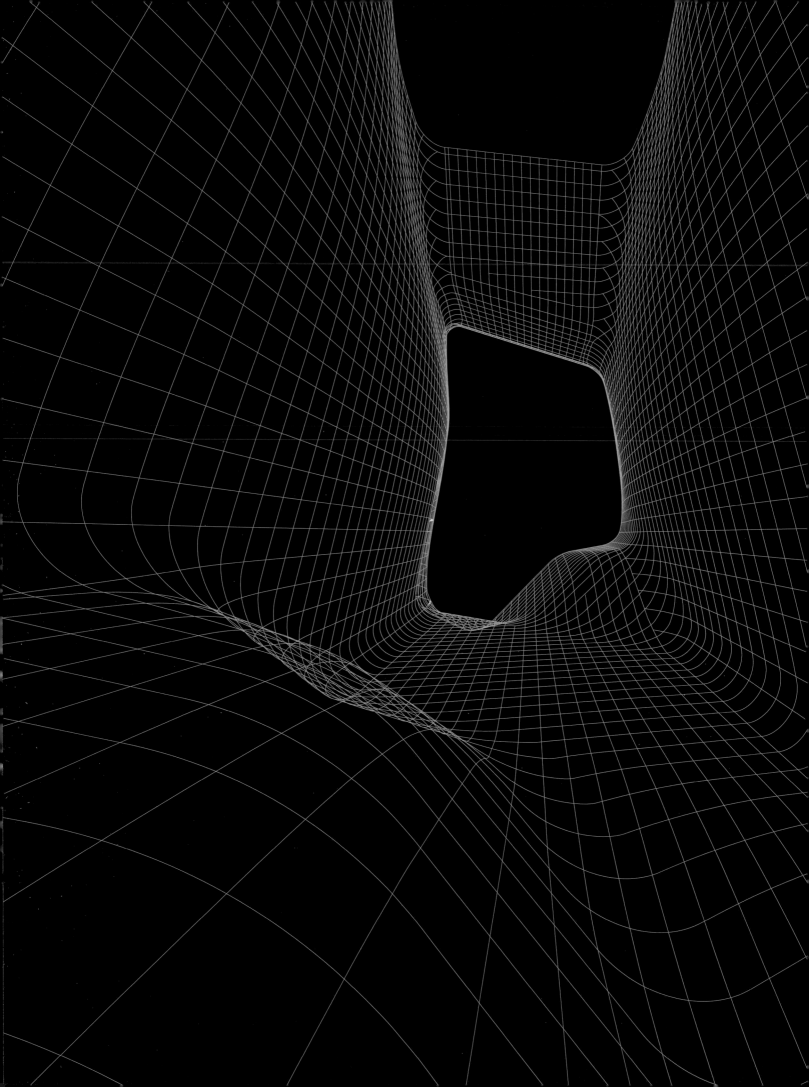

OPUS
OFFICE TOWER

Dubai, UAE. 2007–

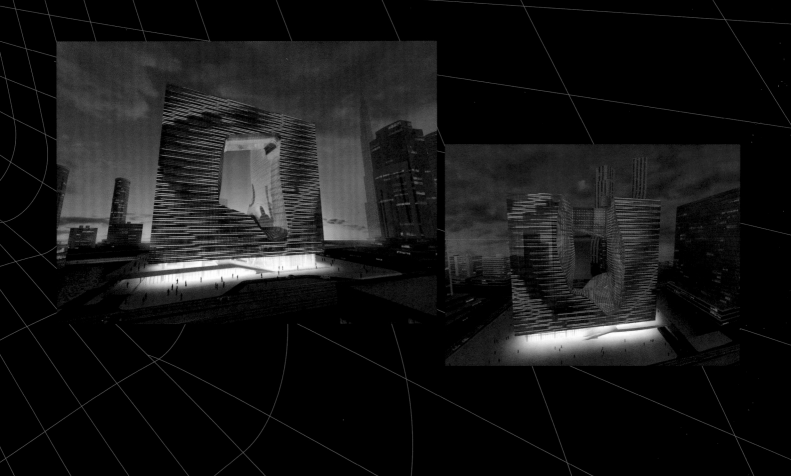

OPUS
OFFICE TOWER

Project

Location
DUBAI, UAE

Client
OMNIYAT PROPERTIES

Area/Size
84 345 m²

In the forest of towers slated for Dubai's enormous Business Bay development area, Zaha Hadid's Opus Office Tower, with its dramatic and irregular central void, stands out, making it readily identifiable and thus attractive to clients.

Im Wald der Hochhäuser in Dubais riesigem Bauerschließungsgebiet Business Bay fällt Hadids Opus Office Tower mit seiner dramatischen, unregelmäßigen zentralen Aussparung auf. Dieser hohe Wiedererkennungswert macht es zugleich attraktiv für Kunden.

Dans la forêt de tours prévue pour l'énorme zone de développement urbain de Business Bay à Dubaï, l'Opus Office Tower de Zaha Hadid se distingue par son spectaculaire vide central de forme libre. Il lui assure une forte identité qui peut attirer des clients.

Located in the Business Bay development area of Dubai, this new mixed-use commercial and retail complex will be set close to the area of the Burj Dubai tower and Hadid's own Signature Towers (2006–; see page 462). Designed for Omniyat Properties, the project carries an estimated construction cost of £235 million for a gross area of 84 345 square meters. The visible form is that of a large cube that appears to "hover off the ground," although the design in fact consists of three separate towers 93-meters high. A freely formed void cuts into these volumes, while the ground floor "is developed as a transparent open field with multiple pathways that are drawn into the interior of the plan areas within the two separate lobbies." The void is lit from within at night, in a sense reversing the volumetric appearance of the building. Pixelated striations are to be applied to the glass façade, reducing solar gain and giving it "a degree of reflectivity and materiality." The architect explains: "It is clear that from its inception, this concept seeks interconnectedness and uniqueness. By applying these two qualities to our design repertoire, our research allowed us to provide unique, variable, and fluid spaces within the project." And Hadid concludes: "This is a building that challenges traditional concepts of office space. Not only will it be visually stunning, it will also be a workable space, and a place that allows every occupant to experience a better quality working environment, using the very latest technological advances."

Der neue Gewerbe- und Einkaufskomplex mit gemischter Nutzung liegt in der Business Bay, einem Neubaugebiet von Dubai, unweit des Burj Dubai und eines weiteren Entwurfs von Hadid, den Signature Towers (seit 2006; Seite 462). Das für Omniyat Properties entwickelte Projekt wird schätzungsweise 235 Millionen Pfund kosten und eine Bruttogeschossfläche von 84 345 m² haben. Nach außen wirkt der Bau wie ein monumentaler Kubus, der „über dem Boden zu schweben" scheint, obwohl der Entwurf im Grunde aus drei separaten, 93 m hohen Türmen besteht. Ein frei geformter Hohlraum zerschneidet die Volumina, während das Erdgeschoss „als transparentes, offenes Feld entwickelt wurde, das von zahlreichen Pfaden durchzogen wird, die in das Zentrum der Grundrisse innerhalb der zwei separaten Lobbys eingezeichnet sind". Nachts wird der Hohlraum von innen beleuchtet, was das volumetrische Erscheinungsbild des Baus von innen nach außen zu kehren scheint. Pixelförmige Streifenmuster werden auf die Glasfassade aufgebracht, was die Wärmeentwicklung im Gebäude reduziert und ihm „eine gewisse Reflexivität und Materialität verleiht". Die Architektin erklärt: „Bereits von der ersten Idee an war klar, dass das Konzept nach Durchlässigkeit und Einzigartigkeit strebt. Diese beiden Qualitäten wandten wir auf unser Designrepertoire an, wobei uns unsere Forschungen ermöglichten, unverwechselbare, variable und fließende Räume in diesem Bau zu realisieren." Hadid fasst zusammen: „Dies ist ein Gebäude, das traditionelle Vorstellungen von Büroräumen infrage stellt. Der Bau wird nicht nur optisch eindrucksvoll sein, er wird zudem ein Ort, an dem man arbeiten kann und an dem jeder Nutzer ein qualitativ besseres Arbeitsumfeld erleben kann, ein Ort, an dem neueste technische Errungenschaften zum Einsatz kommen."

Implanté dans la zone de développement urbain de la Business Bay à Dubaï, ce nouveau complexe mixte de bureaux et de commerces se dressera à proximité de la tour de Burj Dubaï et des Signature Towers également réalisées par Zaha Hadid (2006–, voir page 462). Conçu pour Omniyat Properties, ce projet devrait coûter 235 millions de Livres pour une surface totale de 84 345 m². Sa forme globale prend l'aspect d'un énorme cube qui « flotte au-dessus du sol », alors qu'elle se compose en fait de trois tours séparées de 93 m de haut chacune. Un vide aux contours libres se découpe entre ces volumes, tandis que le rez-de-chaussée est « traité selon un plan ouvert transparent à multiples cheminements aspirés vers l'intérieur par deux halls séparés ». Le volume en creux est éclairé de l'intérieur pendant la nuit, ce qui, d'une certaine façon, inverse la perception volumétrique du bâtiment. Des stries pixellisées seront appliquées sur les façades de verre pour réduire le gain solaire et créer « un certain niveau de réflectivité et de matérialité ». Pour Zaha Hadid : « Il est clair que, dès le départ, ce concept est une quête d'interconnexion et d'unicité. En assignant ces deux objectifs à notre expression conceptuelle, nos recherches nous ont permis de créer des espaces uniques, fluides et variables à l'intérieur du projet… C'est un projet qui remet en cause les concepts traditionnels d'immeubles de bureaux. Non seulement il sera visuellement étonnant, mais il offrira à chaque occupant de bénéficier de conditions de travail d'une meilleure qualité grâce au recours aux dernières avancées technologiques. »

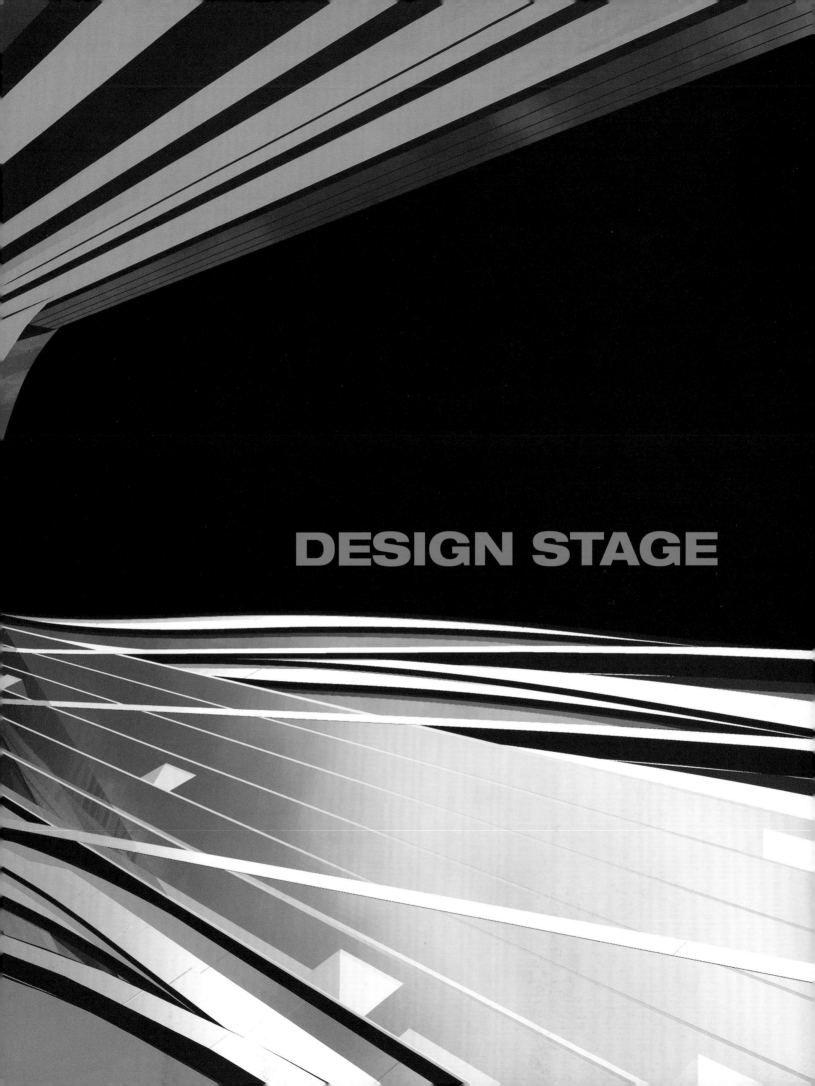

DESIGN STAGE

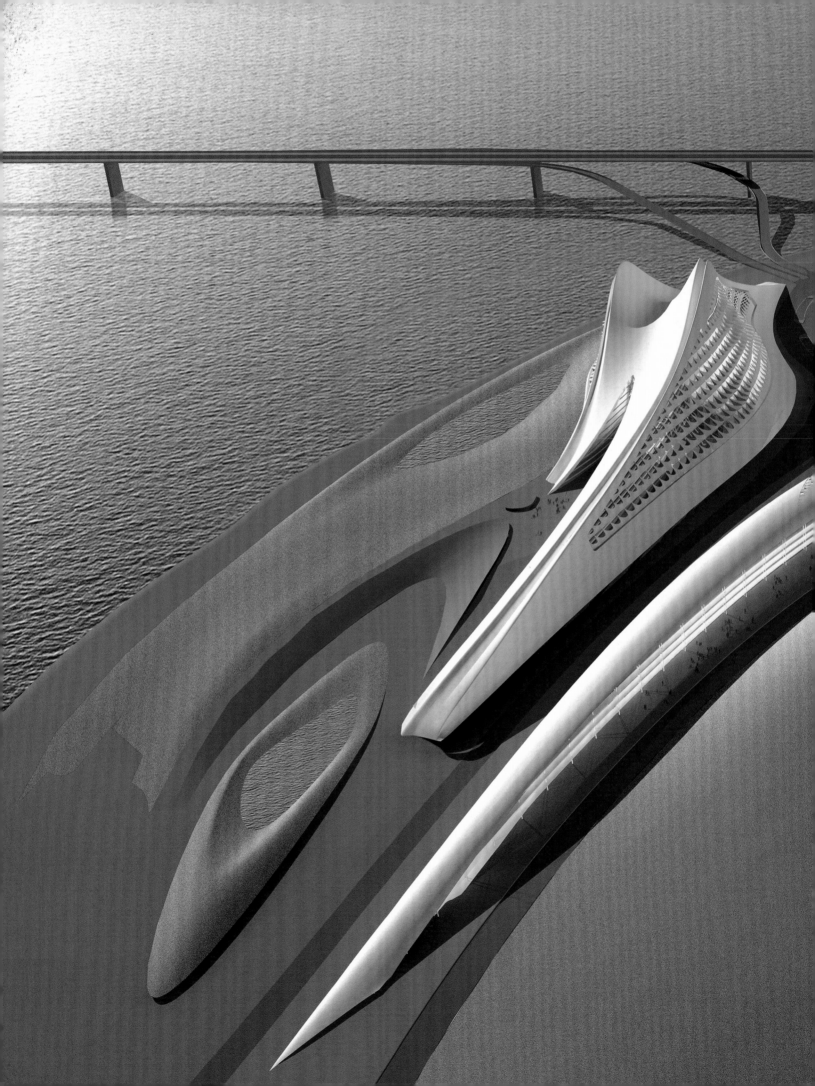

DUBAI OPERA HOUSE AND CULTURAL CENTER

Dubai, UAE. 2006–

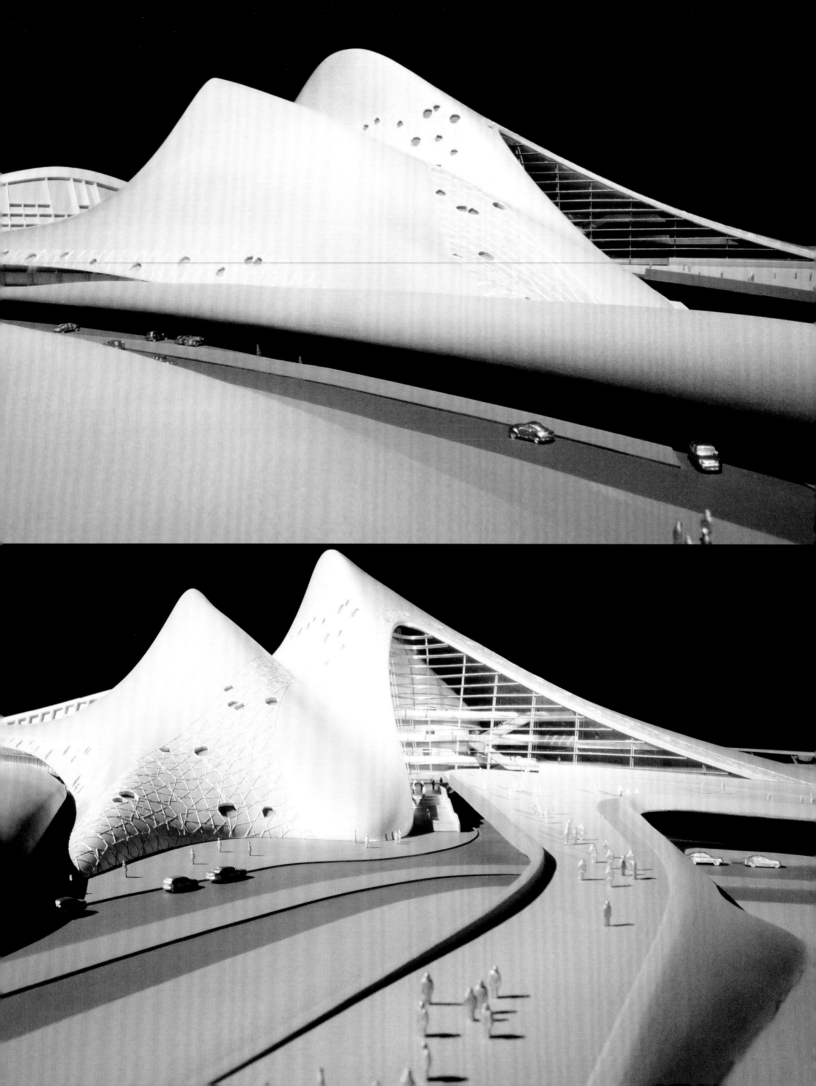

Project
DUBAI OPERA HOUSE AND CULTURAL CENTER

Location
DUBAI, UAE

Client
SAMA DUBAI

Area/Size
MAXIMUM BUILDING HEIGHT 97.5 m

In a city now dominated by towers, this cultural facility had to be more horizontal because of its function. Zaha Hadid has called on the imagery of sand dunes, also seen in her furniture, for example, blending the height of contemporary design with the age-old shifting forms of the landscape.

Inmitten einer von Hochhausbauten dominierten Stadt musste die Kultureinrichtung aus funktionalen Gründen horizontaler gestaltet werden. Hadid nimmt hier Bezug auf das Dünenmotiv, das auch bei ihren Möbeln auftaucht, und versteht es, neueste Designtendenzen und uralte, sich ändernde Landschaftsformationen zu verknüpfen.

Dans une ville aujourd'hui dominée par des tours, cet équipement culturel se devait d'être plus horizontal, ne serait-ce que par sa fonction. Zaha Hadid s'est inspirée de l'imagerie de dunes, que l'on retrouve parfois dans son mobilier, en harmonisant son œuvre d'architecture contemporaine aux formes millénaires du paysage.

The program for this project calls for a 2500-seat opera house, 800-seat playhouse, 5000-square-meter arts gallery, performing arts school, and a "six-star" themed hotel on an island in Dubai Creek connected by road to the mainland. All of these facilities are housed together in forms that clearly recall the ongoing interest of Zaha Hadid in sand dunes, or perhaps mountains. The entire design appears to rise up out of the landscape, which in Dubai is in fact constituted in good part by sand. Parking facilities and a monorail station are located in the land formations that rise up toward the actual, visible structure. There are two "peaks" in the design, marking the location of the opera house and playhouse. A single large foyer serves both main performance facilities and includes an entry to the exhibition zone. The architect explains: "The auditoria are contained in flowing shapes that seem to emerge from the underside of the main shell. This inner shell, however, does not quite touch the main shell. Instead, the two surfaces disappear into a light gap between them. Supporting functions found off the foyer are defined by walls that merge into the underside of the main shell."

Das Programm dieses Projekts sieht ein Opernhaus mit 2500 Plätzen vor, ein Theater mit 800 Plätzen, eine 5000 m² große Ausstellungshalle, eine Schauspielschule und ein Sechssterne-Erlebnishotel. Der Komplex liegt auf einer Insel im Fluss Dubai und ist über eine Straße mit dem Festland verbunden. Alle Einrichtungen sind zusammen in Bauformen untergebracht, die von Zaha Hadids andauerndem Interesse an Dünen oder Bergen zeugen. Der Entwurf scheint aus der Landschaft zu wachsen, die in Dubai zu einem Großteil aus Sand besteht. In den Landschaftsformationen, die sich zum zentralen sichtbaren Bau hin auftürmen, sind Parkmöglichkeiten und ein Monorailbahnhof untergebracht. Der Komplex

hat zwei „Gipfel", die das Opernhaus und das Theater markieren. Die beiden Einrichtungen teilen sich ein großes Foyer, das zudem Zugang zum Ausstellungsbereich bietet. Die Architektin führt aus: „Die Auditorien sind in fließenden Formationen untergebracht, die sich aus der Unterseite der Hauptschale herauszuwölben scheinen. Die innere Schale jedoch berührt die Hauptschale nicht wirklich. Vielmehr scheinen sich die beiden Oberflächen in dem hellen Spalt zwischen beiden aufzulösen. Zusätzliche Einrichtungen grenzen an das Foyer und werden durch Wände gegliedert, die mit der Unterseite der Schale verschmelzen."

Le programme de cette opération sur une île de la crique de Dubaï, reliée par une route au continent, comprend un opéra de 2500 places, un théâtre de 800, une galerie d'art de 5000 m², une école pour les arts du spectacle et un hôtel à thème « six étoiles ». L'ensemble de ces installations est logé dans des formes qui confirment l'intérêt de longue date porté par Zaha Hadid aux dunes ou aux montagnes. Le projet tout entier semble jaillir du paysage, qui, à Dubaï, est en grande partie constitué de sable. Les parkings et une gare de monorail sont implantés dans un modelé du terrain qui s'élève autour de la structure prévue. Le projet comporte deux « pics » qui marquent l'emplacement de l'opéra et du théâtre. Les deux salles sont desservies par un foyer commun qui donne également accès aux expositions. Selon la présentation de Zaha Hadid : « Les auditoriums sont inclus dans deux formes fluides qui semblent émerger du dessous de la coque principale. La coque intérieure, cependant, ne touche pas vraiment la coquille principale. Les deux plans disparaissent dans le petit creux qui les sépare. Les fonctions techniques et de support à l'écart du foyer sont délimitées par des murs qui se fondent dans la partie inférieure de la coque principale. »

KARTAL PENDIK MASTER PLAN

Istanbul, Turkey. 2006–

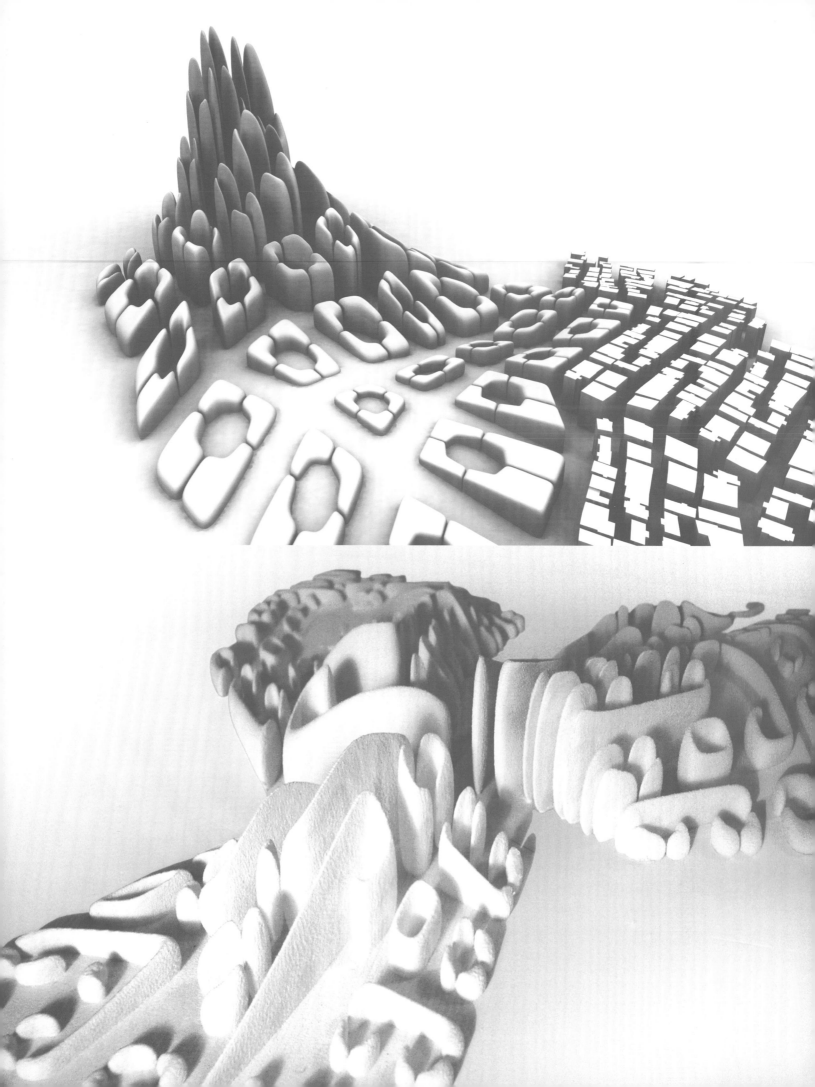

Project
KARTAL PENDIK MASTER PLAN

Location
ISTANBUL, TURKEY

Client
GREATER ISTANBUL MUNICIPALITY AND KARTAL URBAN REGENERATION ASSOCIATION

Area/Size
555 HECTARES

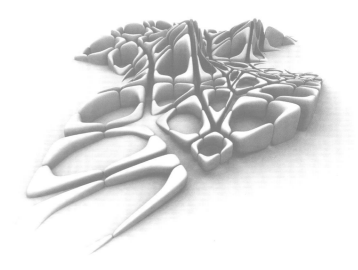

Hadid's drawings for this project bring to mind natural organisms, but the logic employed is an urban one on a large scale, with taller buildings grouped together in a progression leading up from lower structures.

Hadids Zeichnungen für dieses Projekt erinnern an natürliche Organismen. Dabei ist die hier im weitaus größeren Maßstab angewandte Logik durchaus eine urbane. Niedrigere Strukturen entwickeln sich progressiv zu höheren Gebäudegruppen.

Les dessins de Hadid pour ce projet évoquent des organismes naturels, mais sa logique reste celle d'une approche de l'urbanisme à grande échelle à travers une progression entre des constructions basses et des immeubles de grande hauteur.

This is a winning competition proposal for a new city center, to be located in a former industrial zone on the east bank of Istanbul. The Greater Istanbul Municipality wishes to occupy the area with a "central business district, high-end residential development, cultural facilities such as concert halls, museums, and theaters, and leisure programs, including a marina and tourist hotels." Public transportation infrastructure, including the highway that connects Istanbul to Europe and Asia, passes through the area, and Hadid's plan calls for "stitching" together the urban structure of the existing and new areas. The architect states: "The fabric is further articulated by an urban script that generates different typologies of buildings that respond to the different demands of each district. This calligraphic script creates open conditions that can transform from detached buildings to perimeter blocks, and ultimately into hybrid systems that can create a porous, interconnected network of open spaces that meanders throughout the city." Hadid here applies her ideas about the seamless integration of architectural forms to an entire urban district. The rising and falling forms of the district create a rhythm both in plan and section that is quite untypical of most contemporary urban design schemes.

Hadids Entwurf für ein neues Istanbuler Stadtzentrum in einem ehemaligen Industriegebiet am östlichen Ufer des Bosporus konnte sich in einem Wettbewerb durchsetzen. Nach Wunsch der Istanbuler Stadtverwaltung sollen in dem Gebiet ein „zentrales Geschäftsviertel, ein hochwertiges Wohngebiet, kulturelle Einrichtungen wie Konzerthallen, Museen und Theater sowie Freizeitanlagen, einschließlich eines Jachthafens und eines Touristenhotels" angesiedelt werden. Öffentliche Verkehrswege, darunter auch die Schnellstraße, die Istanbul an Europa bzw. Asien anbindet, verlaufen durch das Gebiet, und Hadids Entwurf sieht vor, die urbane Struktur der bestehenden und neuen Stadtviertel „zusammenzufügen". Die Architektin führt aus: „Genauer ausgearbeitet wird die Bausubstanz mithilfe eines urbanen Skripts, das unterschiedliche bauliche Typologien erzeugt, die den verschiedenen Anforderungen der einzelnen Bezirke entsprechen. Dieses kalligrafische Skript erzeugt offene Systeme, die sich zu frei stehenden Bauten oder Blockbebauungen und letztendlich zu hybriden Systemen transformieren lassen, dank derer sich ein durchlässiges, verwobenes Netzwerk offener Räume gestalten lässt, das sich durch die gesamte Stadt zieht." Hier wendet Hadid

ihre Vorstellungen von der nahtlosen Integration architektonischer Formen auf ein ganzes Stadtviertel an. Die aufsteigenden und fallenden Formen erzeugen einen Rhythmus in Grund- und Aufriss, der für die meisten zeitgenössischen Stadtplanungsentwürfe höchst untypisch ist.

Cette proposition de plan directeur a remporté le concours organisé pour un nouveau centre urbain construit sur une ancienne zone industrielle de la rive orientale d'Istanbul. La municipalité du Grand Istanbul souhaite créer à cet endroit « un quartier d'affaires au centre, une zone résidentielle de haut standing, des équipements culturels comme salles de concerts, musées, théâtres, installations de loisirs, une marina et des hôtels touristiques ». L'infrastructure de transports publics, y compris l'autoroute qui relie Istanbul à l'Europe et à l'Asie, traverse cette zone. Le plan Hadid se propose de « coudre » ensemble les constructions des quartiers existants et à venir : « Le tissu trouve son articulation dans un scénario urbain qui génère différentes typologies d'immeubles répondant aux divers besoins de chaque quartier. Ce scénario d'esprit calligraphique crée de multiples possibilités qui peuvent aller d'immeubles indépendants à des blocs fermés et même à des systèmes hybrides créant un réseau poreux et interconnecté d'espaces ouverts qui serpenteront à travers la ville. » Hadid applique ici ses concepts d'intégration sans rupture des formes architecturales à un quartier urbain tout entier. Les formes ascendantes et descendantes créent, aussi bien en plan qu'en coupe, un rythme assez atypique dans l'urbanisme contemporain.

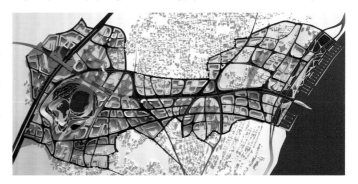

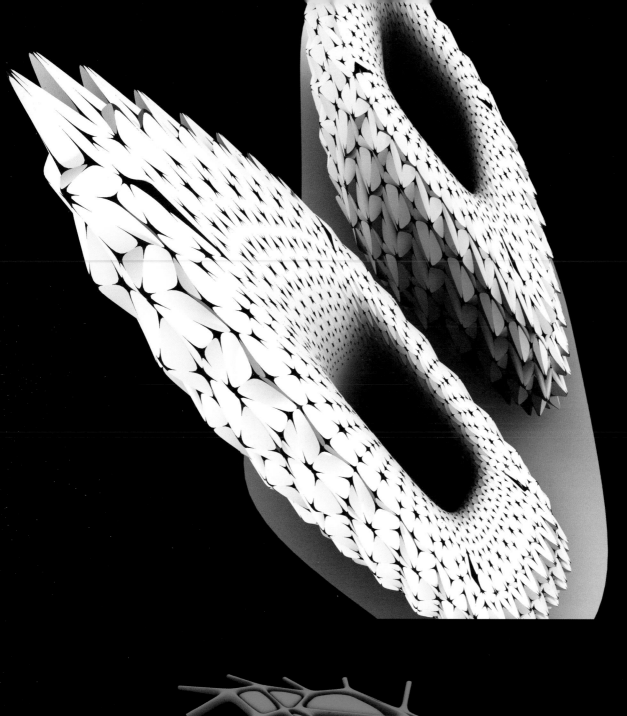

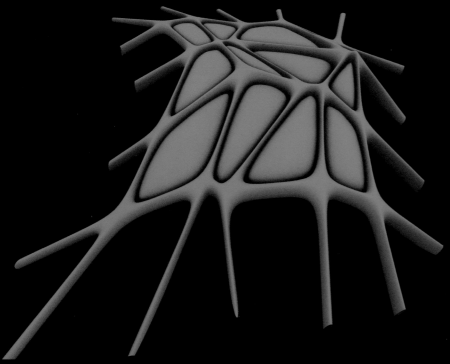

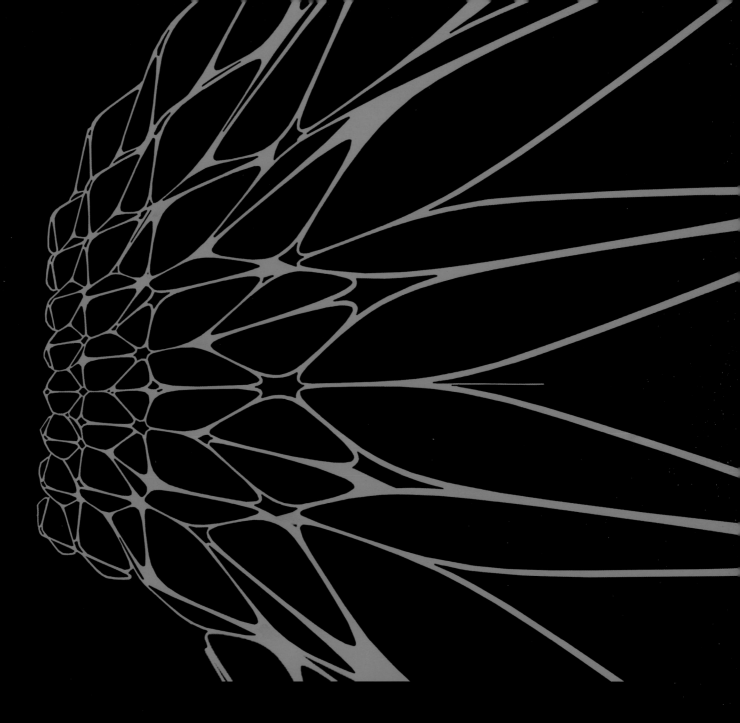

Perhaps informed by microphotography or sea-bound growth patterns, these images suggest a strong connection to nature without any precise, identifiable source. They are examples of progressive organization that varies in scale.

Die möglicherweise von der Mikrofotografie oder Wachstumsmustern von Meereskreaturen inspirierten Motive lassen eine enge Verbindung zur Natur vermuten, ohne dabei spezifische, erkennbare Inspirationsquellen preiszugeben. Sie stehen für eine progressive Organisation in unterschiedlicher Maßstäblichkeit.

Inspirées peut-être de la microphotographie ou de processus de croissance de plantes marines, ces images suggèrent une forte connexion avec la nature sans que leur source ne soit précise ni identifiable. Ce sont des exemples d'une organisation en progression qui évolue aussi en échelle.

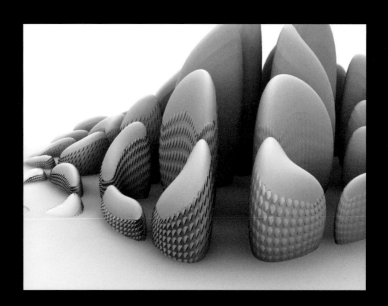

Hadid's concept of lines of force works well in this urban development plan, since the curving axes and delineated forms inevitably flow together to create a coherent whole, a very rare occurrence in modern urbanism.

Hadids Konzept der Feldlinien funktioniert bei diesem Stadtentwicklungsplan besonders gut. Die geschwungenen Achsen und umrissenen Objekte erzeugen im Zusammenspiel ein kohärentes Gesamtbild, was in der modernen Stadtplanung allzu selten vorkommt.

Le concept de Hadid de lignes de force opère bien dans ce plan d'urbanisme. Les axes incurvés et les formes délinéées œuvrent concurremment pour créer un tout cohérent, ce que l'on ne trouve que rarement dans l'urbanisme moderne.

NURAGIC AND CONTEMPORARY ART MUSEUM

Cagliari, Italy. 2006–

Project
NURAGIC AND CONTEMPORARY ART MUSEUM

Location
CAGLIARI, ITALY

Client
REGIONE AUTONOMA DELLA SARDEGNA ASSESSORATO PUBBLICA ISTRUZIONE

Floor area
12 000 m²

Even more than some earlier projects, this flowing design evokes a continuity of space also developed actively in Zaha Hadid's lines of furniture. The straight line may exist here, but it is by no means dominant, giving way to the sweeping curve.

Noch stärker als einige frühere Projekte lässt dieser Entwurf ein räumliches Kontinuum ahnen, das Zaha Hadid auch in ihren Möbelserien weiterentwickelte. Hier mag es wohl gerade Linien geben, doch dominieren sie keinesfalls, sondern weichen dramatischen Kurven.

Plus encore que dans certains de ses projets antérieurs, ce dessin tout en fluidité évoque la continuité de l'espace que recherche également activement Zaha Hadid dans ses travaux sur le mobilier. Les lignes droites existent mais ne dominent pas, laissant toute leur place aux courbes enveloppantes.

The client of this 12 000-square-meter project is the Autonomous Region of Sardinia. Its purpose is to be a "node of cultural exchanges that simultaneously serve as a landmark announcing the arrival to Cagliari from the sea." Aligned along the axis of the sea and extending toward the Sant' Elia Stadium, the structure seeks to assimilate itself to the site. Hadid compares the design to the structure of coral: "Hard and porous on the external surface, able to accommodate, in a continuous osmotic exchange with the external atmosphere, cultural activities in a lively and changing environment." In an unusual combination, this facility is intended for both Nuragic and contemporary art. The *nuraghe* is the main type of megalithic edifice found in Sardinia, dating from before 1000 BC. It is considered to be the symbol of Sardinia and its distinctive culture. The shape of the edifice, described by the architect as "open and dynamic," is continued in the interior design, where open spaces encourage a comparison or confrontation between the different types of art displayed. This is a "fluid" design in the sense of the seamless continuity willfully sought by Zaha Hadid. Public paths allow visitors or others to cross the building parallel to a path along the sea. Specific paths are devoted within the museum to the two types of art displayed. The design allows for an intentionally phased construction, according to demand and economic conditions, ending with the third phase research laboratories in a separate yet connected building.

Bauherr dieses 12 000 m² großen Projekts ist die autonome Region Sardinien. Der Bau soll als „Knotenpunkt des kulturellen Austauschs dienen und zugleich ein Wahrzeichen sein, das die Ankunft in Cagliari signalisiert, wenn man sich von der See aus nähert". Der Bau erstreckt sich der Küste entlang bis zum Sant'-Elia-Stadion. Hadid vergleicht den Entwurf mit einer Koralle: „Hart und porös an der Außenseite [ist er] fähig, durch unablässigen osmotischen Austausch mit der äußeren Atmosphäre Raum zu bieten für kulturelle Aktivitäten in einem lebendigen und wandelbaren Umfeld." In einer ungewöhnlichen Kombination ist das Museum sowohl auf zeitgenössische Kunst als auch die Kunst der Nuraghen ausgerichtet. Nuraghen sind sardische Turmbauten, die vor 1000 v. Chr. entstanden. Sie gelten als Symbol Sardiniens und seiner einzigartigen Kultur. Die Gestaltung

des Museums von der Architektin als „offen und dynamisch" beschrieben, setzt sich innen fort, wo offene Räume dazu anregen, die verschiedenen Formen der präsentierten Kunst miteinander zu vergleichen. Es ist ein „fließender" Entwurf im Sinne jenes nahtlosen Kontinuums, nach dem Zaha Hadid strebt. Museumsbesucher und andere Passanten können parallel zum Ufer auf öffentlichen Wegen durch das Gebäude hindurchlaufen. Im Museum selbst leitet ein Wegesystem zu den beiden dort ausgestellten Kunstformen. Der Entwurf sieht bewusst verschiedene Bauphasen vor, die sich nach Bedarf und Verfügbarkeit der wirtschaftlichen Mittel richten. Die dritte Phase wird mit dem Bau von Forschungslabors in einem eigenen, jedoch an das Museum angeschlossenen Gebäude abschließen.

Le commanditaire de ce projet de 12 000 m² est la Région autonome de Sardaigne. L'objectif est de créer un « nœud d'échanges culturels qui soit également un monument annonçant l'arrivée à Cagliari par la mer ». Aligné le long de la rive et s'allongeant vers le stade Sant' Elia, le bâtiment tend à s'intégrer dans le site. Hadid compare ce projet à une structure corallienne : « Dure et poreuse pour sa surface extérieure, en mesure d'accueillir dans un échange osmotique continu avec l'atmosphère extérieure, les activités culturelles d'un environnement vivant et changeant. » Dans une combinaison inhabituelle, le musée est destiné à la fois à l'art contemporain et à l'art nuragique. Le *nuraghe* est un type d'édifice mégalithique sarde datant de 1000 avant J.-C., considéré comme un symbole de l'île et de sa culture spécifique. La forme du bâtiment, décrite par l'architecte comme « ouverte et dynamique », se retrouve dans l'aménagement intérieur, où des espaces ouverts encouragent les comparaisons ou les confrontations entre les différents types d'art exposés. C'est une conception « fluide » dans le sens où Zaha Hadid recherche une continuité sans rupture. Des passages permettent aux visiteurs ou aux piétons de traverser le bâtiment parallèlement à un chemin côtier. Des circulations spécifiques sont prévues dans le musée pour les deux formes d'art exposées. Les plans, réalisés en plusieurs temps en fonction de besoins et de la situation économique, se termineront par une troisième phase qui verra la construction de laboratoires de recherche dans un bâtiment autonome mais relié au musée.

The large scale of the composition is indicated by the figures in the perspective seen above. Below, the complex fits into the waterside site, extending its own presence beyond the strict volumes of the architecture.

Die Größe des Komplexes wird durch die Figuren in der Ansicht oben angedeutet. Unten schmiegt sich der Komplex in sein Grundstück am Ufer. Seine Präsenz geht weit über die physischen Grenzen der eigentlichen Architektur hinaus.

L'importante échelle de la composition est donnée par les personnages figurant dans la perspective ci-dessus. Ci-dessous, le complexe s'intègre dans son site du bord de mer et étend sa présence au-delà du strict volume de l'architecture.

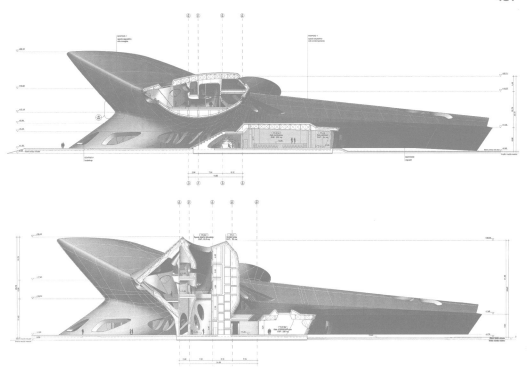

Rising up and falling back to the earth, the building undoubtedly has an organic inspiration, but it is not, strictly speaking, one that can be traced to any living creature. Rather, it is the logic of the building itself that generates an impression of organic unity.

Das aufsteigende und wieder abfallende Gebäude ist organisch inspiriert, geht jedoch nicht im strengen Sinn auf ein konkretes Lebewesen zurück. Vielmehr ist es die Logik des Baus selbst, durch die der Eindruck einer organischen Einheit entsteht.

S'élevant du sol, puis retombant, le bâtiment est certainement d'inspiration organique mais sans que l'on puisse le relier à aucune créature vivante. C'est plutôt sa logique qui génère une impression d'unité organique.

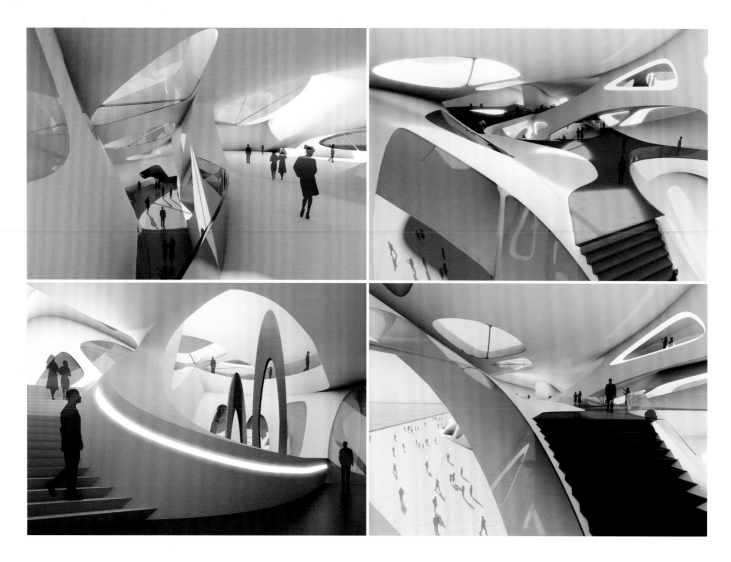

These interior perspectives might well recall the temporary exhibition design conceived by Zaha Hadid for the Deutsche Guggenheim, albeit on a much larger scale and in a more permanent mode.

Die Innenansichten erinnern an Zaha Hadids temporäre Ausstellungsarchitektur im Deutschen Guggenheim, wenn auch in erheblich größerem Maßstab und in diesem Fall auf Dauer angelegt.

Ces perspectives intérieures peuvent rappeler le projet d'exposition temporaire de Zaha Hadid pour le Deutsche Guggenheim, mais à une beaucoup plus vaste échelle et dans une esprit de permanence.

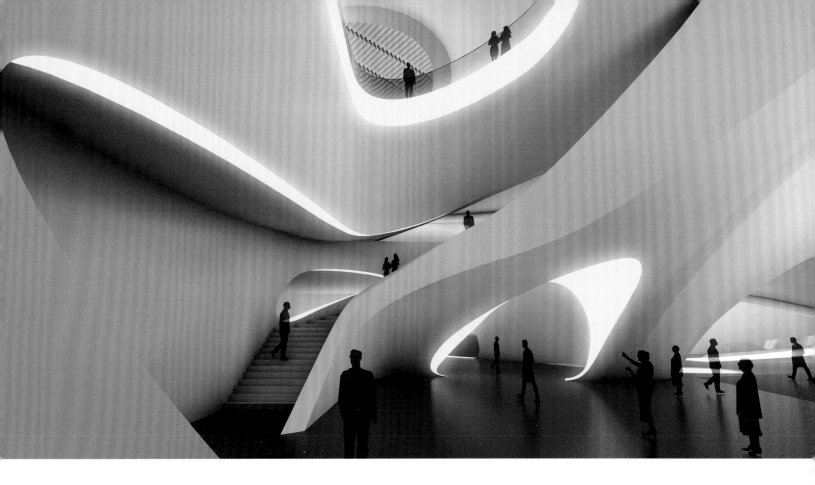

Alveolar openings between spaces or toward the sky give a sense of continuity but also hint at activity just beyond the sight of visitors, creating a living space.

Alveolare Wandöffnungen zwischen den einzelnen Räumen oder zum Himmel hin erwecken den Eindruck eines Kontinuums und lassen zugleich Aktivität ahnen, die sich außerhalb der Sicht der Besucher abspielt. Es entsteht ein lebendiger Raum.

Les ouvertures en alvéoles entre les espaces ou vers le ciel créent un sentiment de continuité mais ouvrent également des perspectives sur les activités du musée en créant ainsi un espace vivant.

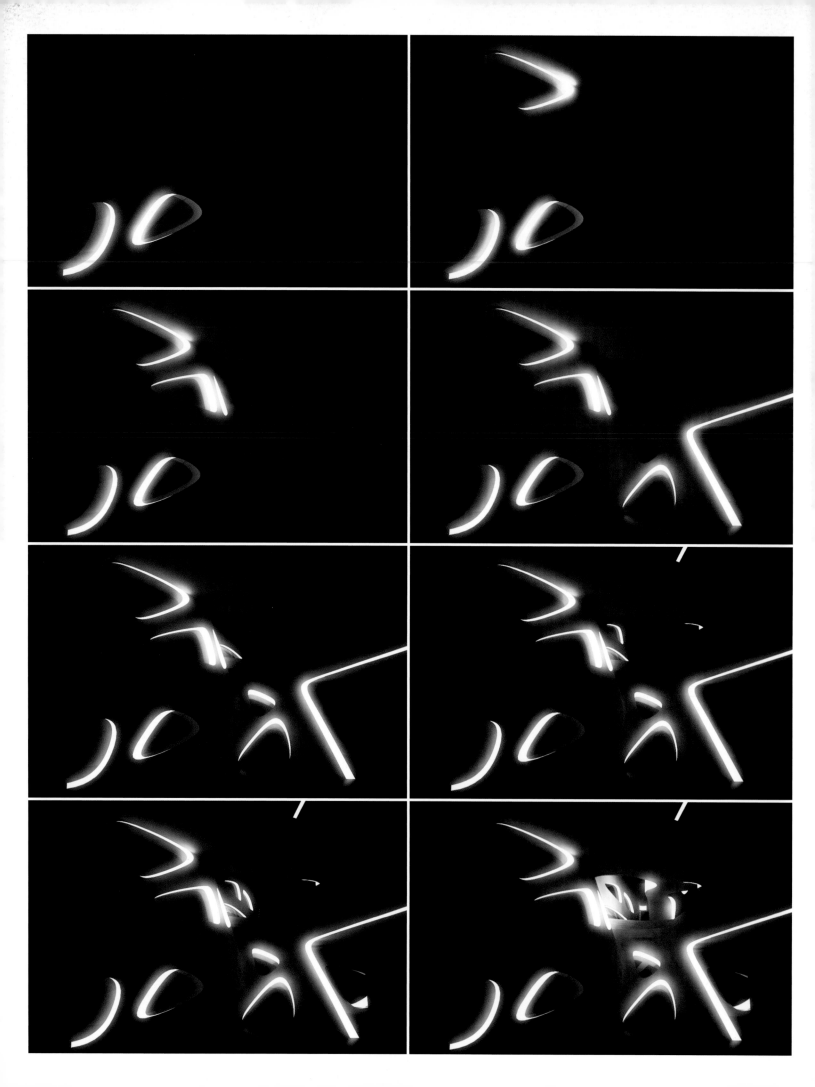

Studies of the complex openings between spaces and in the shell of the structure—seen below in section drawings that again emphasize the organic unity of the whole.

Studien der komplexen Wandöffnungen zwischen den Räumen und in der Außenhaut der Konstruktion – unten auch in Schnittzeichnungen zu sehen, die wiederum die organische Gesamtwirkung des Ganzen unterstreichen.

Études sur les ouvertures complexes entre les espaces et dans la coque de la structure, vues ci-dessous dans des dessins de coupe qui soulignent l'unité organique de l'ensemble.

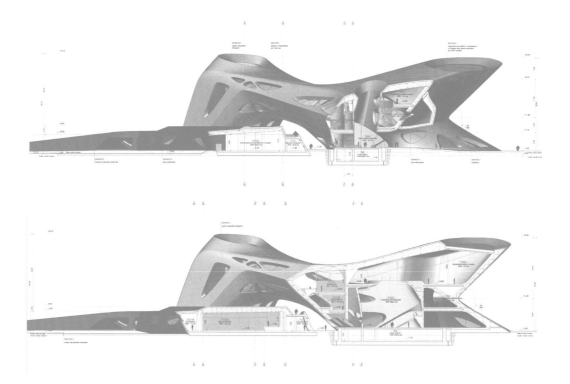

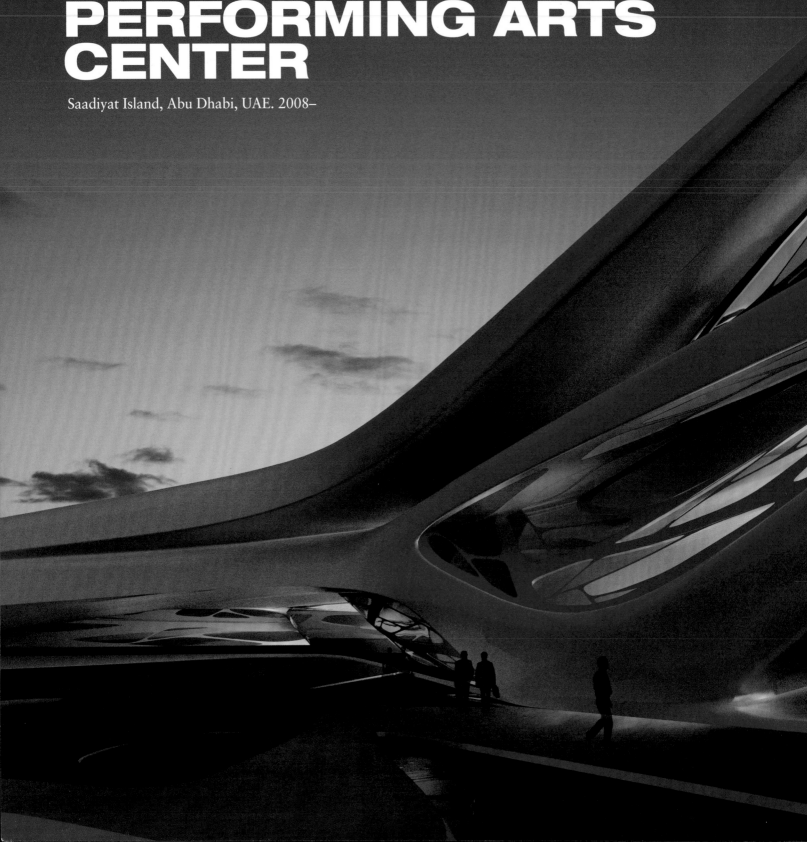

ABU DHABI PERFORMING ARTS CENTER

Saadiyat Island, Abu Dhabi, UAE. 2008–

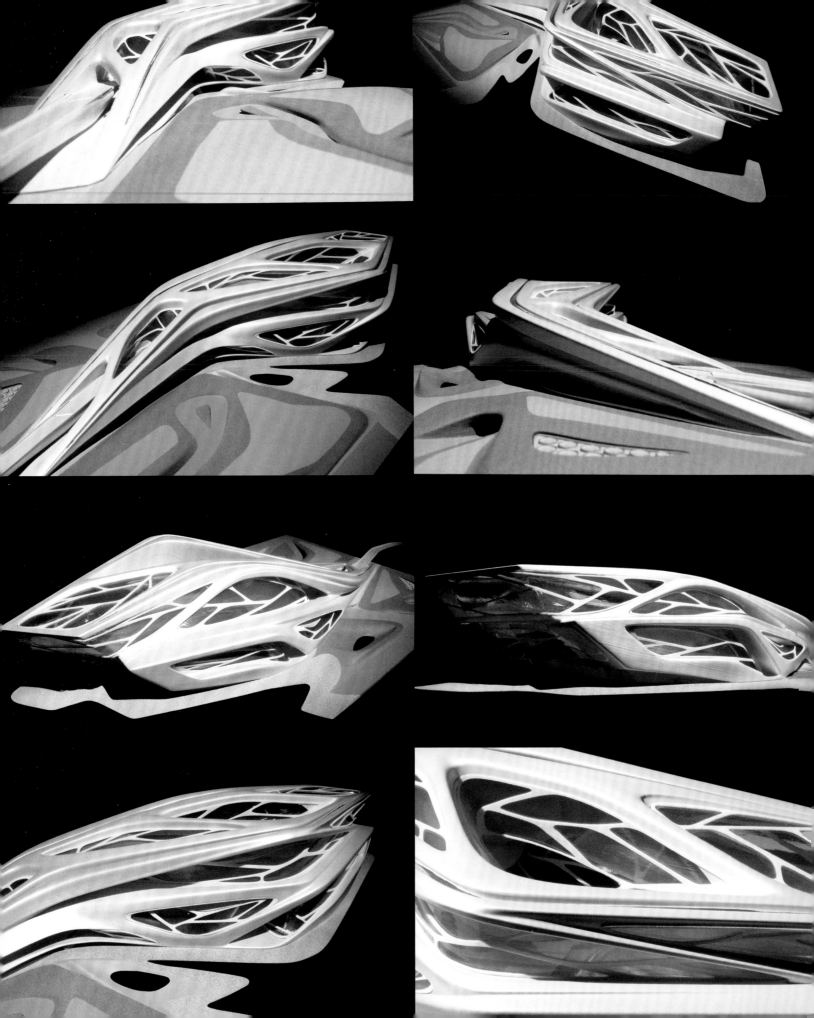

Project
ABU DHABI PERFORMING ARTS CENTER

Location
SAADIYAT ISLAND, ABU DHABI, UAE

Client
THE TOURISM DEVELOPMENT AND INVESTMENT COMPANY OF ABU DHABI (TDIC)

Ares/Size
62 770 m²

Drawings show the lavalike flow of the layers of the building, advancing as they form pockets of space, and openings within and without.

Zeichnungen veranschaulichen den lavaähnlichen Fluss der verschiedenen Gebäudeschichten, der sich ausbreitet und dabei Raumtaschen sowie Öffnungen innen und außen bildet.

Ces dessins montrent le flux des strates du bâtiment qui progressent comme des coulées de lave en formant des poches d'espace et des ouvertures sur l'intérieur ou vers l'extérieur.

This 62-meter-high building is intended to house a music hall, concert hall, opera house, drama theater, and a flexible theater. The combined seating capacity of the facility will be 6300 people. This is one of the five cultural institutions being created by the Tourism Development and Investment Company of Abu Dhabi (TDIC), assisted by the Solomon R. Guggenheim Foundation. In 2004, the Abu Dhabi Tourism Authority (ADTA) asked Gensler to create a master plan for Saadiyat Island (Island of Happiness), a 27-square-kilometer natural island, into a "world-class, environmentally sensitive tourist destination." The centerpiece of this scheme is the 270-hectare cultural district, master planned by Skidmore, Owings & Merrill (SOM), where Tadao Ando, Jean Nouvel, and Frank Gehry also have buildings planned. Zaha Hadid described the design of the Performing Arts Center as "a sculptural form that emerges from a linear intersection of pedestrian paths within the cultural district, gradually developing into a growing organism that sprouts a network of successive branches. As it winds through the site, the architecture increases in complexity, building up height and depth and achieving multiple summits in the bodies housing the performance spaces, which spring from the structure like fruits on a vine and face westward, toward the water." In fact, Zaha Hadid would seem to be justifiably enthusiastic about the development of the new cultural projects in Abu Dhabi. She states: "The plans for Saadiyat Island and the cultural district, envisioned and developed by the Abu Dhabi Government, are, quite simply, extraordinary. When this comprehensive and inclusive vision is realized, it will set a standard for global culture that will resonate for decades to come."

Das 62 m hohe Gebäude wird Raum für eine Konzerthalle, eine Oper, ein Theater und eine Mehrzweckbühne bieten. Der Komplex wird über insgesamt 6300 Plätze verfügen und ist eine von fünf Kultureinrichtungen, die mit Unterstützung der Solomon R. Guggenheim Foundation für die Tourism Development and Investment Company of Abu Dhabi (TDIC) realisiert wird. 2004 beauftragte die Tourismusbehörde von Abu Dhabi (ADTA) das Büro Gensler mit der Erstellung eines Masterplans für die 27 km² große Insel Saadiyat (Insel des Glücks) als „umweltbewusstes Reiseziel von Weltrang". Herzstück des Bauprojekts ist das 270 ha große Kulturviertel nach einem Masterplan von Skidmore, Owings & Merrill (SOM), für das auch Tadao Ando, Jean Nouvel und Frank Gehry Bauten planen. Zaha Hadid beschreibt den Entwurf für das Performing Arts Center als „skulptu-

rale Form, die aus einer geradlinig angelegten Kreuzung von Fußgängerwegen mitten im Kulturviertel aufzusteigen scheint und sich mehr und mehr zu einem wachsenden Organismus entwickelt, aus dem ein Netz von Verzweigungen entspringt. Die Architektur windet sich durch das Terrain und nimmt an Komplexität, an Höhe und Tiefe zu. Die Abschnitte, in denen die Bühnenräume untergebracht sind, bilden mehrere ‚Gipfel' aus, die aus dem Bau wie Trauben an einem Weinstock zu wachsen scheinen und sich nach Westen, zum Wasser hin orientieren." Zaha Hadid scheint zu Recht von den geplanten Kulturprojekten in Abu Dhabi begeistert zu sein. Sie meint: „Die Pläne für die Insel Saadiyat und das Kulturviertel, von Abu Dhabis Regierung konzipiert und entwickelt, sind ganz einfach außergewöhnlich. Ist diese großangelegte und umfassende Vision erst einmal realisiert, wird sie Maßstäbe für die globale Kulturwelt der kommenden Jahrzehnte setzen."

Ce bâtiment de 62 m de haut devrait abriter une salle de variétés, un théâtre, une salle de concerts, un opéra et une salle polyvalente, ensemble qui comptera 6300 places. C'est l'une des cinq institutions culturelles prévues par la Tourism Development Investment Company d'Abu Dhabi (TDIC), assistée par la Solomon R. Guggenheim Foundation. En 2004, l'Abu Dhabi Tourism Authority (ADTA) a demandé à Gensler d'établir un plan directeur pour faire des 27 km² de l'île naturelle de Saadiyat (île du Bonheur), une « destination touristique de classe internationale appliquant les principes du développement durable ». Le principal élément de ce projet est un quartier culturel de 270 ha, dont le plan directeur est dû à Skidmore, Owings & Merrill (SOM), et où devraient intervenir Tadao Ando, Jean Nouvel et Frank Gehry. Zaha Hadid décrit son projet de Centre des arts du spectacle comme « une forme sculpturale qui émerge à l'intersection de cheminements piétonniers du quartier culturel, se transformant graduellement en un organisme qui projette un réseau de branches les unes après les autres. En se déployant sur le site, l'architecture gagne en complexité, en hauteur et en profondeur, et projette de multiples pics dans les volumes abritant les salles orientées vers l'Ouest et la mer, qui jaillissent de la structure comme les fruits d'une vigne. » Zaha Hadid semble pleine d'enthousiasme pour les projets culturels d'Abu Dhabi : « Les plans pour l'île de Saadiyat et le quartier culturel prévus et développés par le gouvernement d'Abu Dhabi sont tout simplement extraordinaires. Ce grand projet visionnaire, une fois réalisé, fondera un nouveau standard de la culture globale qui fera parler de lui pendant les décennies à venir. »

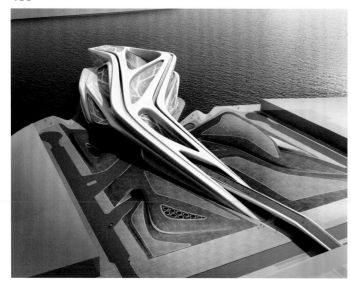

The irregularity of the building, at least as expressed in more traditionally modern terms, is visible in perspectives, plan, and section, showing that Zaha Hadid has gone far beyond the kind of superficial break with the past seen in some current computer-driven designs.

Die Unregelmäßigkeit des Gebäudes, zumindest aus traditioneller Sicht, wird in Ansichten, Grundrissen und im Schnitt deutlich und beweist, dass Zaha Hadid weit über vergleichsweise oberflächliche Brüche mit der Vergangenheit hinausgeht, die man häufig in zeitgenössischen computergestützten Entwürfen sieht.

L'irrégularité de la forme du bâtiment, du moins si on l'exprime en termes traditionnels modernes, est visible dans les perspectives, le plan et les coupes qui montrent que Zaha Hadid va bien au-delà de ces ruptures superficielles avec le passé que l'on voit dans certaines images conçues par ordinateur.

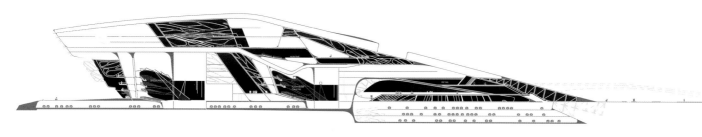

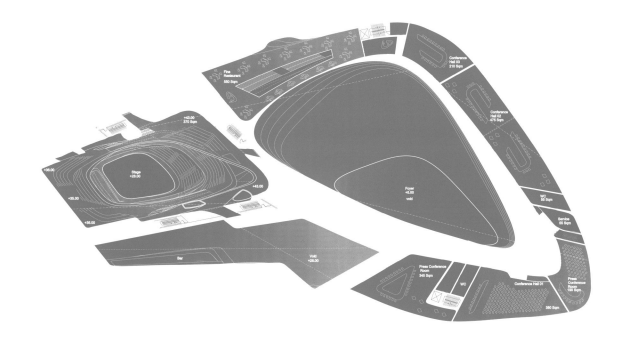

Drawings of the building and its plans suggest an organic form, and certainly do not follow what might be called an expected pattern; rather, they are the result of continual layering and a study of movement and use of space.

Zeichnungen und Grundrisse erinnern an organische Formen und folgen ganz offensichtlich keinem üblichen Muster. Vielmehr entstehen sie aus kontinuierlichen Schichtungen und als Ergebnis von Bewegungs- und Raumnutzungsstudien.

Les dessins et les plans du bâtiment suggèrent une forme organique, loin de tout modèle prévisible. Ils dérivent d'une stratification continue et de l'étude du mouvement et de l'utilisation de l'espace.

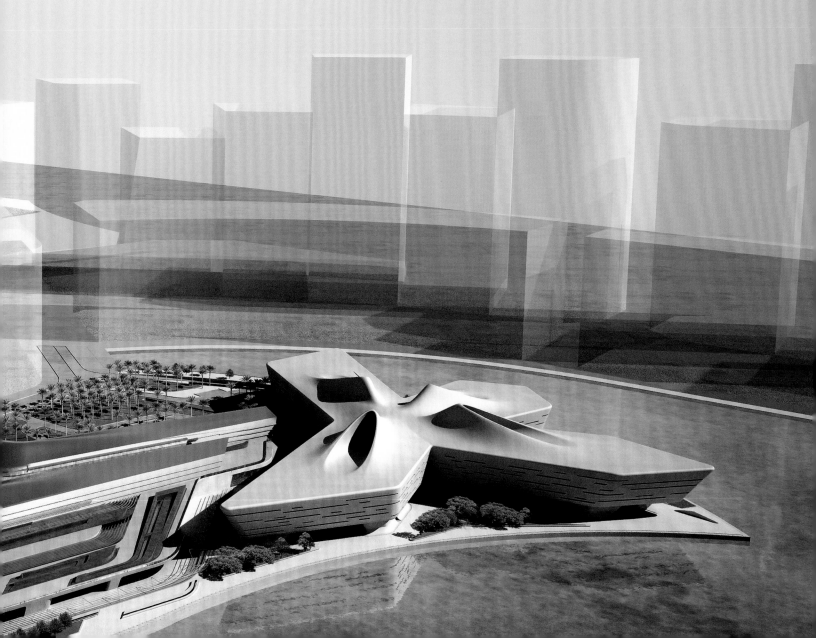

SIGNATURE TOWERS

Dubai, UAE. 2006–

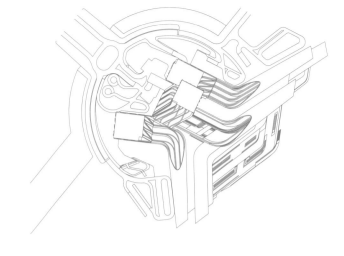

Project
SIGNATURE TOWERS

Location
DUBAI, UAE

Client
DUBAI PROPERTIES

Area/Size
1 000 000 m²

Located just behind Hadid's Dubai Financial Market, the Signature Towers stand out in the city of rising skyscrapers, not far from the tallest building in the world, the Burj Dubai. Related and rising in a series of orchestrated curves, the buildings indeed offer a signature presence to the area.

Die unmittelbar hinter Hadids Financial Market gelegenen Signature Towers fallen in der Stadt aufstrebender Wolkenkratzer auf und stehen unweit des höchsten Gebäudes des Welt, des Burj Dubai. Die aufeinander bezogenen Türme erheben sich in orchestrierten Schwüngen und prägen das Stadtviertel buchstäblich mit ihrer Signatur.

Situées juste derrière le Dubai Financial Market de Hadid, les Signature Towers se détachent sur le fond du panorama de cette ville de gratte-ciels, à proximité du plus haut immeuble du monde, le Burj Dubaï. S'élevant concurremment en une suite de courbes orchestrées, les immeubles imposent leur « signature » sur ce quartier.

Designed by Zaha Hadid with Patrik Schumacher, this 1 000 000-square-meter complex confirms the ongoing presence of the architects in the United Arab Emirates, and in Dubai and Abu Dhabi in particular. Set to be a central element of the rapidly developing Business Bay area near the Burj Dubai tower, the Signature Towers are designed for mixed-use, including offices, hotel, residential, and retail space. The complex includes two link bridges, Waterfront Park and promenade. The triple-tower design is extremely unusual insofar as its fluid lines are concerned. The architect writes: "The three towers rise above the creek and project themselves as an icon for the surrounding developments and for the Gulf region. The towers' striking design creates a new presence that punctures the skyline with a powerful recognizable silhouette. The fluid character of the towers is generated through an intrinsically dynamic composition of volumes. The towers are intertwined to share programmatic elements and rotate to maximize the views from the site toward the creek and neighboring developments." Plans call for direct connections to main thoroughfares such as Sheikh Zayed Road. The site is composed of four elements, leading to the idea of a "woven" combination of connections and linking public spaces, and the tripartite tower configuration was developed as a result of the requirement to provide hotel, residential, and office space. A shared base or podium underlines the connectivity of the towers and suggests a continual movement of activities and users within the complex. Large multiuse complexes such as this one are numerous in the planned architecture of Dubai, but often they tend to create an image of disconnection or disembodiment, while Hadid has, on the contrary, sought an inviting movement, sure to remain "iconic" no matter what odd shapes may be looming on the horizon, but also deliberately and effectively connected to the emerging city.

Der von Zaha Hadid und Patrik Schumacher entworfene, 1 000 000 m² große Komplex bekräftigt die anhaltende Präsenz der Architekten in den Vereinigten Arabischen Emiraten und insbesondere in Dubai und Abu Dhabi. Zweifellos werden sich die Signature Towers als zentrales Element des rapide wachsenden Business-Bay-Bezirks durchsetzen. Unweit des Burj Dubai gelegen, ist der Neubau für verschiedene Nutzungen vorgesehen und soll Büros, ein Hotel, Wohn- und Einkaufsflächen beherbergen. Zu dem Komplex zählen auch zwei Verbindungsbrücken, der Waterfront Park und eine Promenade. Der Entwurf mit seinen drei Türmen ist gerade wegen seiner fließenden Linienführung höchst ungewöhnlich. Die Architektin schreibt: „Die drei Türme erheben sich über dem Fluss und manifestieren sich als Wahrzeichen für die angrenzenden Bauprojekte und die Golfregion. Die auffällige Gestaltung verleiht den Türmen eine neuartige Präsenz, die die Skyline um eine kraftvolle, wiedererkennbare Silhouette bereichert. Die fließende Formensprache der Türme ergibt sich aus einer dynamischen Komposition der Volumina. Die Türme sind miteinander verbunden, um Elemente des Pro-

gramms gemeinsam nutzen zu können, und gedreht, um eine maximale Aussicht auf den Fluss und auf die angrenzenden Bauten zu bieten." Die Pläne sehen eine direkte Anbindung an Hauptverkehrsadern wie die Scheich-Zayed-Straße vor. Das Grundstück setzt sich aus vier Elementen zusammen, was konzeptuell zu einem „Geflecht" von Verbindungen und miteinander verknüpften öffentlichen Plätzen führt, während die Dreifach-Turmkombination die Antwort auf die Anforderung ist, Hotel-, Wohn- und Büroflächen zu schaffen. Ein gemeinsam genutzter Sockel- oder Podiumsbau betont die Verbundenheit der Türme und verweist auf den ständigen Fluss innerhalb des Komplexes. Großkomplexe mit gemischter Nutzung wie dieser gehören zu den häufigen Bauvorhaben in Dubai. Allerdings neigen sie oft zu Trennung und Ausgliederung, Hadid dagegen hat versucht, eine einladende Geste zu schaffen. Ganz gleich, was für merkwürdige Formen noch am Horizont auftauchen werden, dieses Projekt wird seine Zeichenhaftigkeit bewahren und ist dabei bewusst und wirkungsvoll mit dem entstehenden Stadtteil verbunden.

Conçu par Zaha Hadid et Patrik Schumacher, ce complexe de 1 000 000 m² confirme la présence grandissante de ces architectes dans les Émirats arabes unis, à Dubaï et Abu Dhabi en particulier. Futur élément central de la zone de développement de la Business Bay, non loin de la tour du Burj Dubaï, les Signature Towers sont de type mixte : bureaux, hôtel, appartements et commerces. Le complexe comprend également deux ponts, un parc en front de mer et une promenade. Ce projet de triple tour est extrêmement original par sa fluidité. Zaha Hadid le présente ainsi : « Les trois tours s'élèvent au-dessus d'une crique et se projettent en une forme iconique qui marquera aussi bien leur environnement immédiat que la région du golfe. Leur dessin surprend et crée une présence nouvelle qui ponctue le panorama d'une silhouette puissante et originale. Le caractère fluide des tours est généré par la composition intrinsèquement dynamique de leur volume. Elles s'imbriquent dans un partage de leurs éléments programmatiques et pivotent pour optimiser les vues vers la crique et les réalisations voisines. » Ca imagine les connexions directes à venir avec les principaux axes de circulation comme la route du Cheikh Zayed. Le site se compose de quatre éléments, dans un « tissage » de connexions et de liens avec les espaces publics. La configuration tripartite provient de la mixité du programme. Une base ou podium commun renforce la connectivité entre les tours et suggère des échanges et des mouvements permanents d'activités et d'usagers à l'intérieur du complexe. Les vastes ensembles mixtes de ce type sont nombreux dans les plans de Dubaï, mais tendent souvent à donner une image de déconnexion ou de désincarnation alors que Zaha Hadid, au contraire a cherché à créer un mouvement chaleureux, certaine de la valeur « iconique » de cette tour effectivement reliée à cette ville nouvelle quelles que soient les formes étranges pouvant encore surgir à l'horizon.

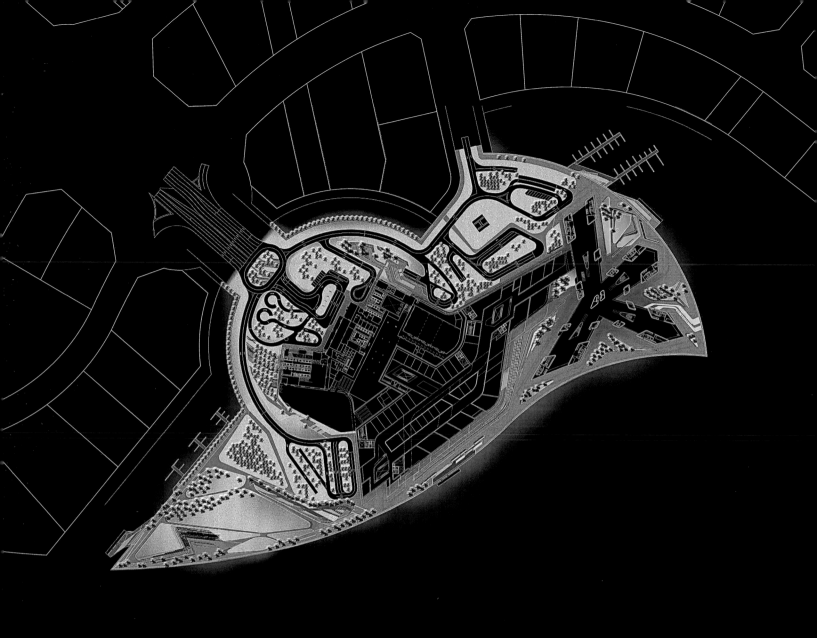

A plan of the entire project shows the shared base or podium and the manner in which the different elements are drawn together into a complex whole.

Ein Grundriss der Gesamtanlage zeigt die gemeinsame Basis bzw. Plattform und veranschaulicht, wie die verschiedenen Elemente zu einem komplexen Ganzen zusammengefügt werden.

Un plan d'ensemble du projet montre la base ou podium que les tours se partagent et la façon dont les différents éléments se rejoignent dans un tout global et complexe.

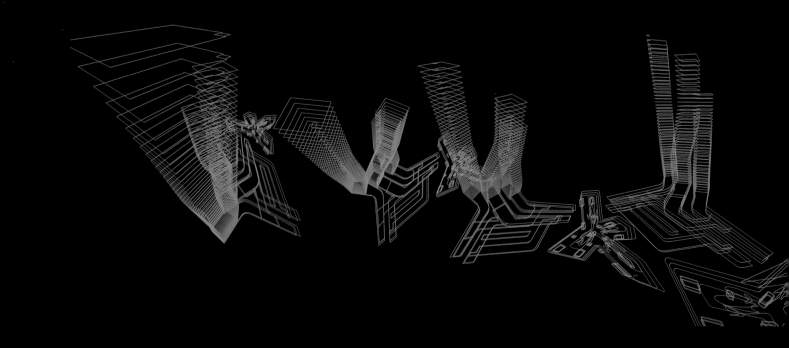

The drawing below expresses the project in three dimensions, relating to the plan to which it can be compared on the opposite page. The bending and twisting of the towers give them an iconic form but also improves views and affirms the unconventional nature of the whole.

Die Zeichnung unten zeigt eine dreidimensionale Ansicht des Projekts und stellt es in Bezug zum Grundriss auf der gegenüberliegenden Seite. Das Biegen und Verdrehen der Türme lässt sie nicht nur formal unverwechselbar werden, sondern optimiert auch die Ausblicke und unterstreicht die Unkonventionalität des gesamten Baus.

Le dessin ci-dessous exprime le projet en trois dimensions, que l'on peut relier au plan de la page ci-contre. La torsion et la courbure des tours génèrent une forme iconique qui optimise les vues et affirme la nature non-conventionnelle de l'ensemble.

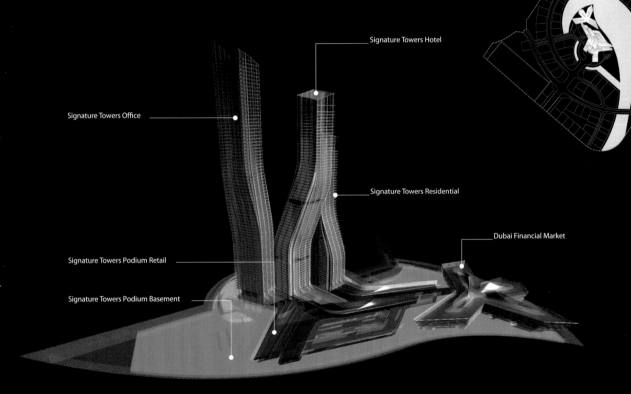

Signature Towers Hotel

Signature Towers Office

Signature Towers Residential

Dubai Financial Market

Signature Towers Podium Retail

Signature Towers Podium Basement

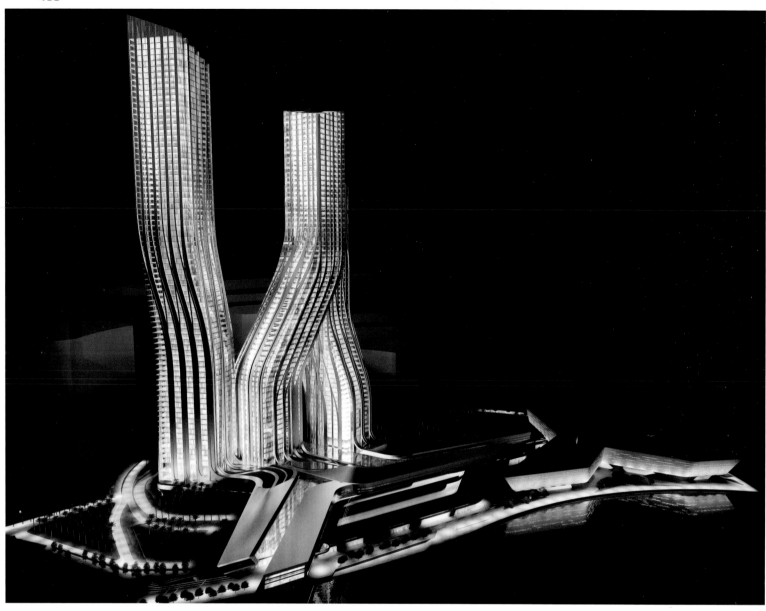

Banded together, the towers show a different profile from each angle, nonetheless remaining recognizable because of their dramatic curving volumes.

Als Gruppe zeigen die Türme aus jeder Perspektive ein anderes Profil, bleiben wegen ihrer dramatisch geschwungenen Form aber stets wiedererkennbar.

Reliées entre elles, les tours présentent un profil différent selon l'angle de vision mais restent identifiables par leurs volumes incurvés spectaculaires.

Seen from below, as in the perspective on this page, the towers seem to come together like banyan trees, intertwining to the point of symbiosis. Drawings show the building from other angles.

Aus der Froschperspektive gesehen (unten) scheinen sich die Türme wie Banyan-Feigen aufeinander zu zu bewegen und geradezu symbiotisch zu umwinden. Zeichnungen zeigen den Bau aus verschiedenen Blickwinkeln.

Vues en contre-plongée, comme dans la perspective figurant sur cette page, les tours semblent pousser comme un banian et s'entrelacent presque jusqu'a la symbiose. Les dessins montrent l'immeuble sous d'autres angles.

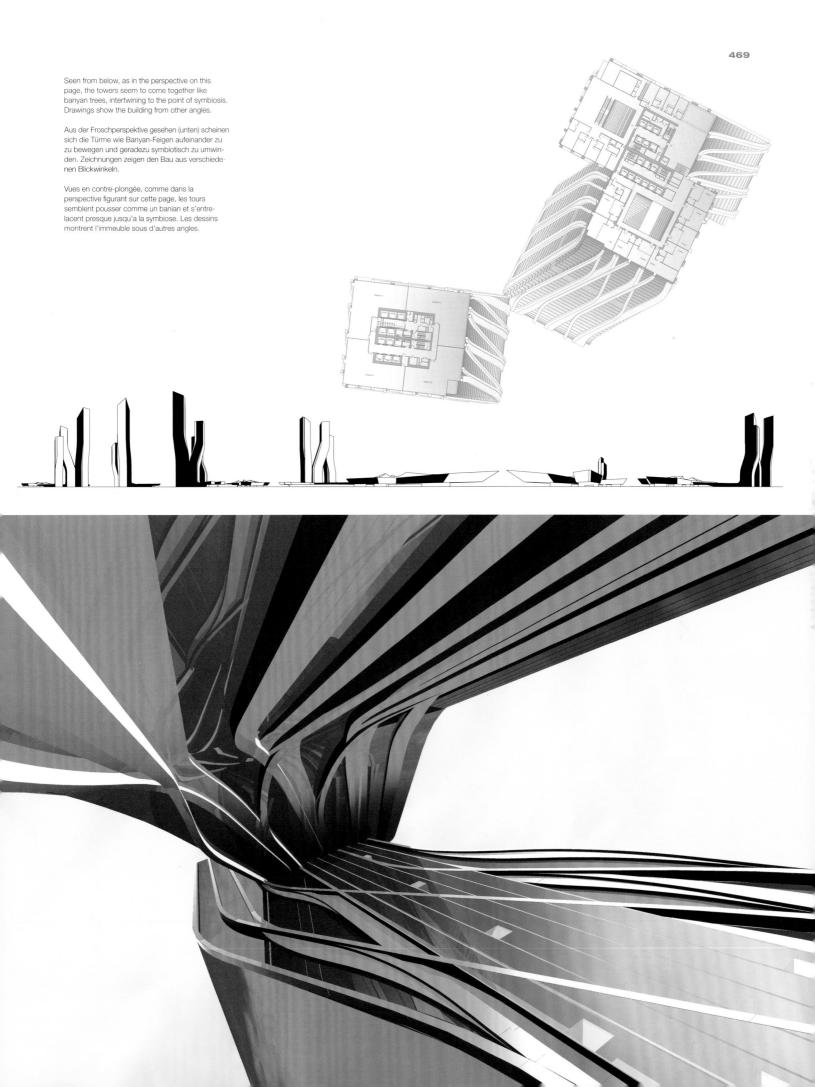

DUBAI FINANCIAL MARKET

Dubai, UAE: 2007–

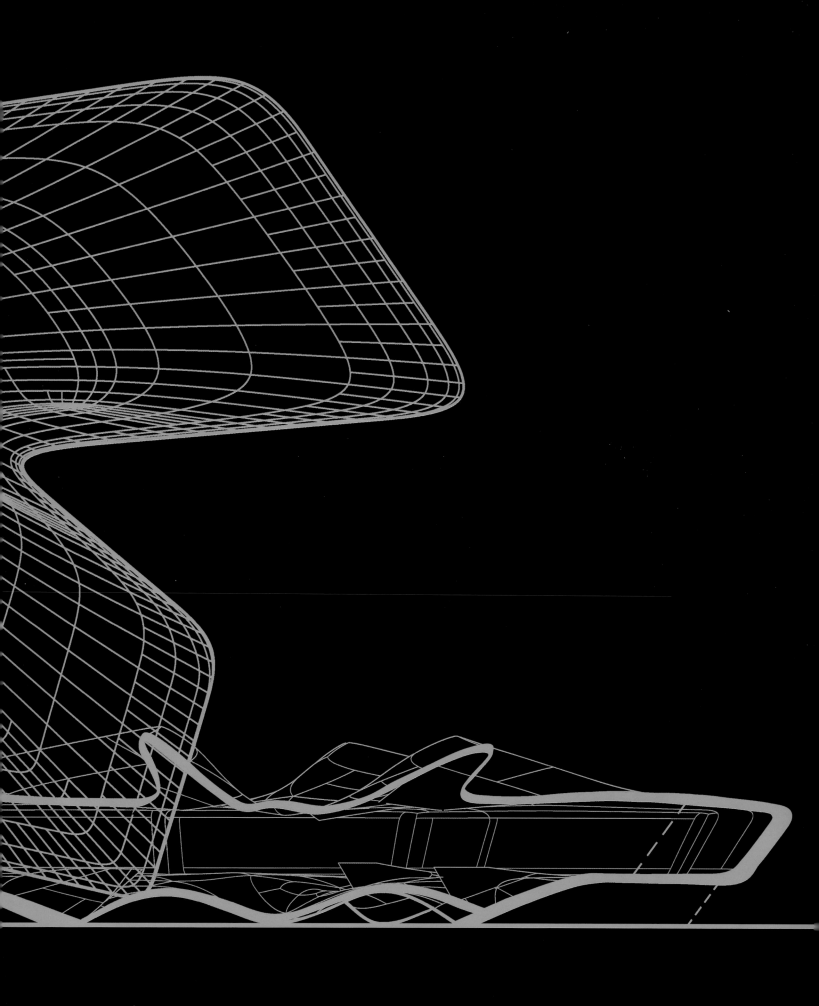

Project
DUBAI FINANCIAL MARKET

Location
DUBAI, UAE

Client
DUBAI PROPERTIES,
A MEMBER OF DUBAI HOLDING

Area/Size
42 000 m²

In a highly stylized leaf pattern, the Dubai Financial Market extends outward in four directions, rising up off the ground, with dramatic cantilevers and long slit windows, standing just beyond the Signature Towers also by Hadid.

Der Dubai Financial Market breitet sich in Form eines äußerst stilisierten Blattmusters in vier Richtungen aus. Mit seinen dramatischen Auskragungen und schlitzförmigen Fenstern scheint er über dem Boden zu schweben und liegt direkt unter den ebenfalls von Hadid entworfenen Signature Towers.

En forme de feuille très stylisée, le Dubai Financial Market s'étend dans les quatre directions, se soulevant du sol en multipliant les porte-à-faux spectaculaires et les longues baies en bandeau. Il se trouve juste devant les Signature Towers également de Hadid.

Located in the Business Bay development area of Dubai, this scheme calls for a floor area of 42 000 square meters. The architects explain: "The aim of the design is to create a strong sculptural element that will be prominent from the waterfront but also has a distinctive roof form when viewed from the adjacent dancing towers and from the high-rise developments around Business Bay." A "heavier sculptural solid" placed above a glazed base is cantilevered over the water and it is in this volume that offices or "shop fronts" for stockbrokers are placed in the context of a large trading floor, a challenge met by the architects with a petal-like design. The difficulty was to provide more private spaces for the brokers without breaking up the continuity of the main areas. Balconies and bridges on the first and second levels connect shop areas and form "a continuous ribbon skimming the perimeter of the trading floor." A series of domed skylights are used to bring natural light into the trading areas, especially at the beginning and end of the trading day.

Der in der Erschließungszone Business Bay von Dubai gelegene Komplex erforderte eine Geschossfläche von 42 000 m². Die Architektin führt aus: „Ziel des Entwurfs ist es, ein ausdrucksstarkes skulpturales Element zu schaffen, das zum Ufer hin prominent in Erscheinung tritt, aber auch ein unverwechselbares Dach zeigt, wenn man von den nahe gelegenen ‚tanzenden Türmen' oder anderen Hochhausprojekten an der Business Bay auf den Bau hinabblickt." Über dem verglasten Sockelgeschoss kragt ein „schwererer, skulpturaler Baukörper" über das Wasser aus. Hier sind die Büros bzw. „Ladenfronten" der Börsenmakler untergebracht, die dennoch im größeren Gesamtkontext des Börsenparketts

bleiben – eine Herausforderung, der die Architektin mit ihrem vierpassartigen Entwurf begegnete. Die Schwierigkeit war, private Räume für die Börsenmakler zu schaffen, ohne dabei die Kontinuität der Kernbereiche aufzubrechen. Balkone und Brücken im ersten und zweiten Stock verbinden die Ladenzonen und bilden zugleich ein „durchgängiges Band, das das gesamte Börsenparkett umspannt". Eine Reihe kuppelförmiger Oberlichter lässt natürliches Licht in die Börsenbereiche einfallen, besonders zu Beginn und Ende des Handelstags.

Situé dans la zone de développement urbain de la Business Bay à Dubaï, ce projet devrait représenter une surface de 42 000 m². Comme l'expliquent ses architectes : « L'objectif du projet est de créer un élément sculptural fort qui soit très visible du front de mer, tout en offrant une forme de toiture originale qui sera vue des tours "dansantes" adjacentes et des immeubles de grande hauteur de la Business Bay. » Une « masse sculpturale plus lourde » implantée au-dessus d'une base vitrée s'avance en porte-à-faux au-dessus de l'eau et c'est dans ce volume que sont implantés les bureaux ou *shop-fronts* des opérateurs dans le contexte d'une vaste salle des marchés, défi auquel les architectes ont répondu par un plan en pétales. La difficulté était d'offrir des espaces plus privatifs aux courtiers sans rompre la continuité de l'ensemble principal. Au premier et second niveau, des balcons et des passerelles relient les zones de travail et forment « un ruban continu balayant le périmètre de la salle des marchés ». Une succession de verrières en forme de coupoles apporte la lumière dans les salles, en particulier au début et à la fin de la journée de travail.

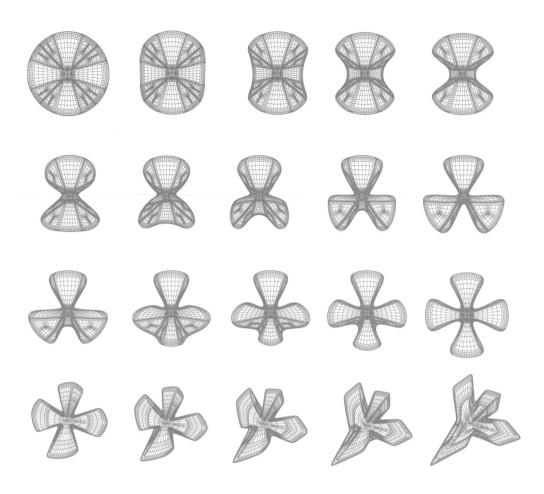

A series of iterations originally based on a circle progressively give rise to the quatrefoil shape of the Market.

Aus einer Reihe von Varianten, die ursprünglich auf einem Kreis basieren, kristallisiert sich nach und nach die vierblättrige Erscheinungsform des Komplexes heraus.

Une série d'itérations partant d'un cercle ont donné naissance à la forme en trèfle du centre.

Although the Business Bay itself did not yet offer a real urban landscape that the architect could work with, she based the development of the project and its volumes on those of the neighboring Signature Towers, which by contrast rise high and intertwine.

Obwohl die Business Bay noch keine wirkliche urbane Landschaft ist, an die die Architektin hätte anknüpfen können, orientiert sich die Entwicklung des Projekts und seiner Baukörper an den nahe gelegenen Signature Towers, die im Gegensatz dazu in die Höhe steigen und einander umwinden.

Bien que la zone de la Business Bay ne soit pas encore un véritable paysage urbain sur lequel s'appuyer, Zaha Hadid a tenu compte dans le développement du projet des volumes des Signature Towers à proximité immédiate, qui, par contraste, s'élèvent à la verticale.

Within the complex, office volumes are housed under the main space, providing space for individual firms while maintaining the coherence of the whole.

Im zentralen Baukörper des Komplexes sind Büros untergebracht. Der Platz ist ausreichend für verschiedene Firmen – dennoch wird die Kohärenz des Ganzen gewahrt.

Les volumes des bureaux s'organisent dans l'espace principal intérieur. Les entreprises peuvent s'exprimer tout en participant à la cohérence de l'ensemble.

Above, an interior perspective emphasizes the continuity of the design, linking exterior and interior in a recognizable whole. Below, the dynamic quatrefoil plan of the Market with its arms converging on the central space.

Eine Innenansicht (oben) unterstreicht die Kontinuität des Entwurfs, in dem Außen- und Innenbau zu einem erkennbaren Gesamtbild verschmelzen. Der dynamische Vierpassgrundriss des Komplexes, dessen Arme im zentralen Innenraum zusammenfließen.

Ci-dessus, une perspective intérieure met en valeur la continuité du plan qui lie l'extérieur et l'intérieur en un tout identifiable. Ci-dessous, plan dynamique en trèfle dont les « feuilles » convergent vers l'espace central.

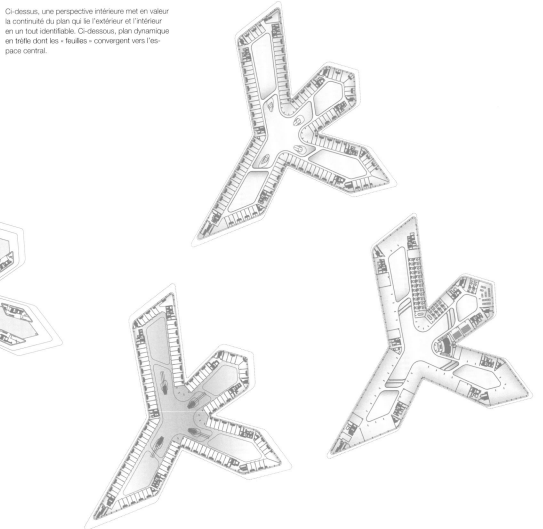

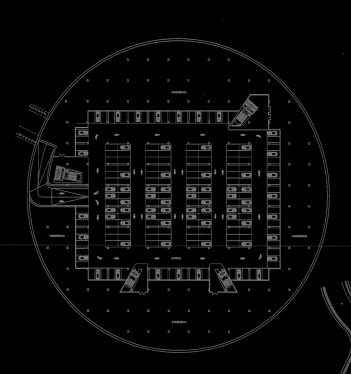

CIVIL COURTS MADRID

Madrid, Spain. 2007–

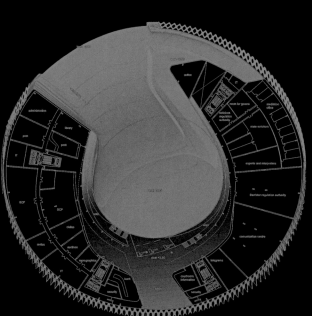

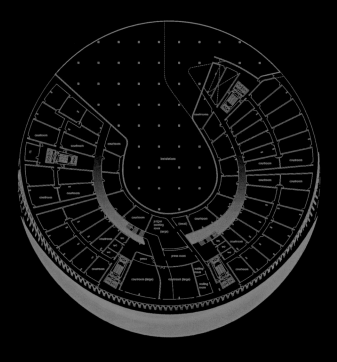

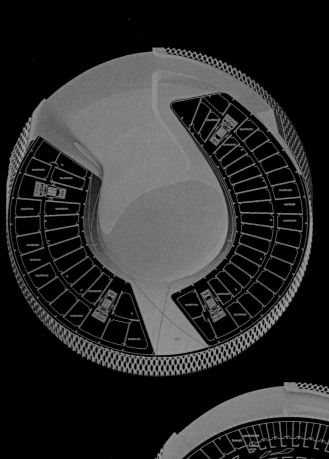

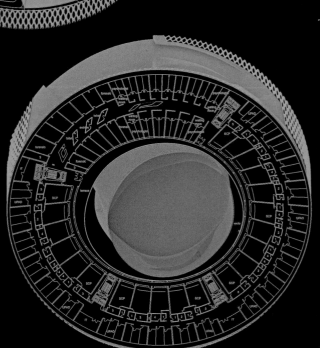

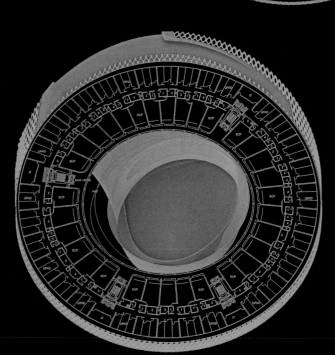

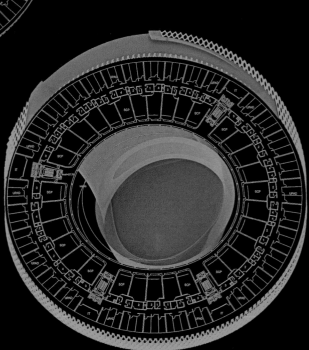

Project
CIVIL COURTS MADRID

Location
MADRID, SPAIN

Client
CAMPUS DE LA JUSTICIA DE MADRID

Area/Size
74 448 m²

The master plan of the City of Justice calls for all the buildings to be essentially circular, but Zaha Hadid succeeds in making this constraint into a virtue, bending and shaping the basic circle at will.

Der Masterplan für den Justizcampus sieht vor, dass alle Bauten im Grunde rund zu sein haben. Zaha Hadid gelingt es, diese Einschränkung zur Tugend werden zu lassen, indem sie den Kreis nach ihren eigenen Vorstellungen biegt und formt.

Le plan directeur de la Cité de la Justice voulait que tous les bâtiments soient circulaires. Zaha Hadid a réussi de faire de cette contrainte une vertu en déformant et modifiant la forme basique du cercle.

Part of an ambitious master plan for a new City of Justice on a large site near Barajas Airport, the Courts of Law designed by Zaha Hadid will measure 74 448 square meters (24 415 square meters below grade). The master plan conceived by Spanish designers provides for a series of essentially round buildings designed by the likes of Norman Foster, Rafael de La-Hoz, and Alejandro Zaera Polo (Foreign Office Architects). Hadid's scheme calls for her project to be more than "a mere component of the overall system to becoming its pivoting point, serving as a reference that provides structure and organizes the entire urban master plan complex." She speaks in terms of the "static configuration of the surrounding buildings" without designating any colleague in particular—and it is true, in this instance, that a complex constituted only of round buildings might risk being static. Hadid's solution is to create horizontal shifts in the building's mass—generating an "elasticity" that would draw visitors in and permit the structure to appear to float above the ground. A focus of the interior is a spiraling semicircular atrium overlooking a courtyard and allowing natural light into the heart of the building. The double façades would consist on the exterior layer of metallic panels that can shift to open or close, while the roof of the structure will have arrays of photovoltaic panels.

Das von Zaha Hadid entworfene Zivilgericht mit seinen 74 448 m² Geschossfläche (davon 24 415 m² unterirdisch) ist Teil eines ehrgeizigen Masterplans für ein neues Justizviertel auf einem großen Gelände in der Nähe des Flughafens Barajas. Der Masterplan eines spanischen Architektenteams sieht eine ganze Anzahl runder Bauten vor, die unter anderem von Norman Foster, Rafael de La-Hoz und Alejandro Zaera Polo (Foreign Office Architects) entworfen werden. Hadids Entwurf erhebt den Anspruch, „mehr als ein bloßer Bestandteil des Gesamtplans zu sein und vielmehr sein Dreh- und Angelpunkt zu werden, der den gesamten urbanen Masterplankomplex strukturiert und organisiert". Sie spricht von der „statischen Konfiguration der angrenzenden Bauten", ohne dabei Kollegen konkret zu benennen – und es ist hier sicherlich richtig, dass ein Komplex aus ausschließlich runden Bauten das Risiko birgt, statisch zu wirken. Hadids Lösungsansatz sind horizontale Verschiebungen innerhalb des Baukörpers, wodurch eine „Elastizität" entsteht, die einladend wirkt und den Eindruck erzeugt, als würde das Gebäude über dem Boden schweben. Blickpunkt im Innern des Baus ist ein spiralförmiges, halbrundes Atrium mit Blick auf einen Innenhof, das zugleich natürliches Licht in den Kern des Gebäudes lässt. Die Doppelfassade besteht aus einer Außenhaut aus verschiebbaren Metallsegmenten, die sich öffnen und schließen lassen. Auf dem Dach des Baus werden Solarzellen angebracht.

Appartenant à l'ambitieux plan directeur de la nouvelle Cité de la Justice en construction sur un vaste terrain près de l'aéroport de Barajas, les tribunaux conçus par Zaha Hadid totaliseront une surface de 74 448 m², dont 24 415 m² en sous-sol. Le plan directeur, conçu par des urbanistes espagnols, avait prévu une série de bâtiments de profil essentiellement arrondi à édifier par des architectes comme Norman Foster, Rafael de La-Hoz et Alejandro Zaera Polo (Foreign Office Architects). Le projet de Hadid n'est pas un simple composant du système prévu, mais son élément principal et de référence autour duquel s'organise le complexe urbain en son entier, tel que le prévoit le plan directeur. L'architecte parle de « configuration statique des bâtiments environnants », sans désigner aucun de ses confrères en particulier, et il est vrai, en fait, qu'un complexe uniquement constitué de bâtiments circulaires risquerait d'être statique. La solution de Zaha Hadid consiste à créer des glissements horizontaux dans la masse du bâtiment pour générer une « élasticité » qui attire les visiteurs et permette à la structure de paraître flotter au-dessus du sol. L'une des principales attractions intérieures est un atrium semi-circulaire en spirale qui domine une cour et laisse pénétrer la lumière naturelle jusqu'au cœur du bâtiment. Les doubles façades seront dotées d'une peau extérieure en panneaux métalliques qui pourront coulisser pour se fermer ou s'ouvrir tandis que la toiture supportera une installation de panneaux photovoltaïques.

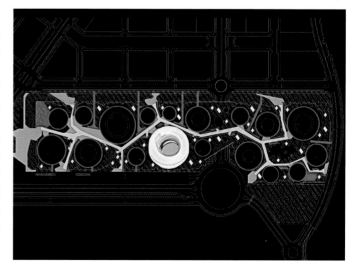

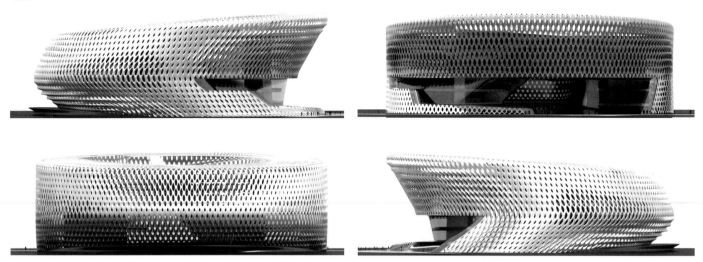

The building differs from every angle, as seen in the elevations above, despite adhering largely terms to the overall requirement to make a round building. Below, outward-leaning glazed walls look into the central courtyard.

Der Bau zeigt sich aus jeder Perspektive anders, wie die Aufrisse oben zeigen, obwohl man sich weitgehend an die allgemeine Vorgabe hielt, einen Rundbau zu gestalten. Nach außen geneigte Glaswände geben den Blick auf den zentralen Innenhof frei.

L'immeuble change d'aspects vu sous divers angles, comme le montrent les élévations ci-dessus, tout en se pliant à la contrainte d'un ensemble de constructions rondes. Ci-dessous, des parois vitrées inclinées vers la cour centrale.

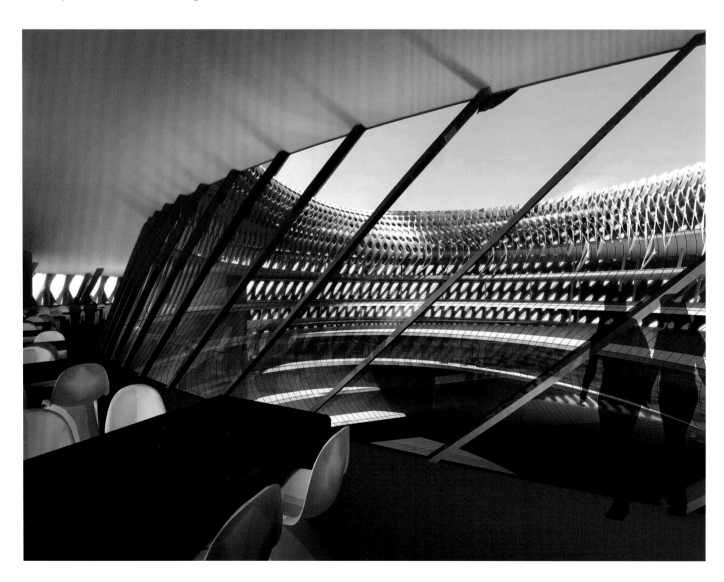

The dynamic spiraling shape of the building is orchestrated around a central void that also serves to bring light to the inner office spaces. The building opens and rises to create a generous entrance area.

Die dynamische Spiralform des Gebäudes wurde um einen zentralen Leerraum orchestriert, der zugleich Licht in die innen gelegenen Büros lässt. Der Bau öffnet sich und strebt nach oben, sodass ein großzügiger Eingangsbereich entsteht.

La forme dynamique en spirale du bâtiment s'orchestre autour d'un vide central qui sert également à amener la lumière naturelle à l'intérieur des bureaux. L'immeuble semble se soulever pour dégager une généreuse zone d'entrée.

BAHRAIN INTERNATIONAL CIRCUIT

Bahrain, Bahrain. 2007

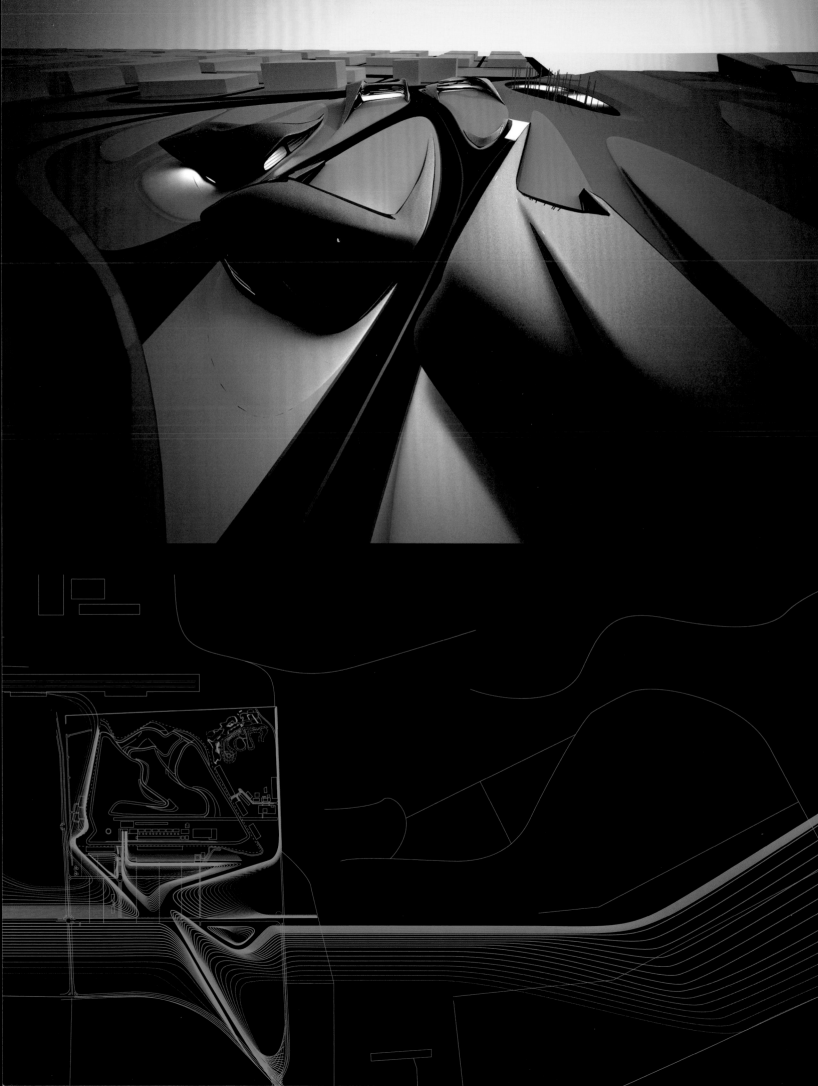

Project
BAHRAIN INTERNATIONAL CIRCUIT

Location
BAHRAIN, BAHRAIN

Client
THE BAHRAIN INTERNATIONAL CIRCUIT & MCC PROJECT PARTNERS

Area/Size
1000 HECTARES

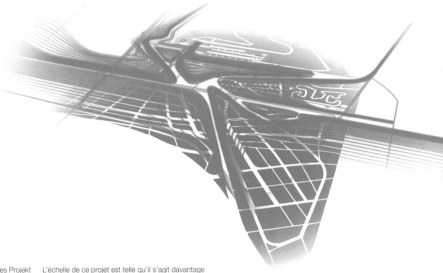

The scale of this project is such that it might almost be considered urban planning rather than the more traditional design of buildings. Hadid imposes an aesthetic continuity based on strong lines, as visible in the drawings above and bottom left.

Aufgrund seiner Größenordnung fällt dieses Projekt fast eher in die Kategorie Stadtplanung, statt ein traditioneller Gebäudeentwurf zu sein. Hadid schafft ästhetische Kontinuität, die auf ihrer klaren Linienführung beruht, wie an den Zeichnungen oben und unten links zu sehen.

L'échelle de ce projet est telle qu'il s'agit davantage d'urbanisme que de construction classique d'immeubles. Hadid a imposé une continuité esthétique qui repose sur des axes puissants, comme on le voit dans les dessins ci-dessus et en bas à gauche.

The program for this project, designed for the Bahrain International Circuit (BIC) and MCC Project Partners (MCCPP), includes a hotel, conference center, car showrooms, a master plan for a research center, high-end car manufacturing, and a university, the whole covering an area of no less than a thousand hectares, with an existing Formula One track carved out of yellow desert rock. Hadid seizes on the difference between the carefully calculated black tarmac of the racetrack and the rough stone that it is inserted into. Given the size of the site, her intervention here is architectural, but at the level of the overall landscape—emphasizing the impressions of driving and speed associated with the entire complex. Her firm description of the project affirms: "As one approaches the car experience development with its hotels, showcases, and the car and activity-oriented programs, additional roads bring one into close interaction with the architecture. Flitting above the architecture and diving below it, ramping past the iconic new buildings and coming into and out of view, the cars on the site dance through the landscape, interact with the buildings, and add to the visual drama of movement on the site." The idea of "oases" and "jewels" carved out of the landscape, integrated with each other and flowing from one construction phase into the next, dominates the program. The overall aesthetic of the complex, recognizably that imagined by Hadid, is "high-tech and streamlined," as might be expected of architecture associated with a prestigious annual Formula One race. She rightfully calls this project "a new choreography of automobiles, architecture, and landscape."

Das Programm dieses Projekts für den Bahrain International Circuit (BIC) und MCC Project Partners (MCCPP) sieht ein Hotel, ein Konferenzzentrum, Ausstellungsräume für Autohersteller, einen Masterplan für ein Forschungszentrum, ein Werk für Luxusfahrzeuge sowie eine Universität vor. Die Gesamtfläche beträgt nicht weniger als 1000 ha und schließt auch die bereits realisierte Formel-1-Rennstrecke ein, die aus dem gelben Wüstenfels geschlagen wurde. Hadid greift den Kontrast zwischen dem präzise berechneten Teerbelag der Rennstrecke und dem rauen Felsen, aus dem sie herausgeschlagen wurde, auf. Angesichts der Größe des Terrains ist ihre Intervention zwar architektonischer Natur, jedoch zugleich vom Ausmaß einer Landschaft. Darüber hinaus betont sie die Assoziationen von Autofahren und Geschwindigkeit, die sich an den gesamten Komplex knüpfen. Ihre klare Projektbeschreibung bekräftigt dies: „Nähert man sich dem Autoerlebnispark mit seinen Hotels, Ausstellungsräumen und den vom Auto bestimmten Programmen und Aktivitäten, wird man durch zusätzliche Stra-

ßen zur Interaktion mit der Architektur eingeladen. Die Autos auf dem Gelände schießen über die Architektur hinweg, tauchen unter ihr hindurch, jagen auf Rampen an den neuen baulichen Wahrzeichen vorbei, geraten ins Blickfeld und verschwinden wieder, tanzen durch die Landschaft, interagieren mit den Bauten und tragen zur visuellen Dramatik des Komplexes bei." Aus dem Fels geschlagene „Oasen" oder „Juwelen", die ineinandergreifen und fließend von einem Bauabschnitt in den nächsten übergehen, sind eine Metapher, die das Programm prägen. Die gesamte Ästhetik des Komplexes, die erkennbar Hadids Handschrift trägt, ist „hightech- und stromlinienförmig", wie man es bei Architektur erwarten mag, die in Verbindung mit einem prestigeträchtigen, jährlich stattfindenden Formel-1-Rennen steht. Hadid bezeichnet das Projekt zu Recht als „eine neuartige Choreografie von Automobilen, Architektur und Landschaft".

Le programme de ce projet, conçu pour le Bahreïn International Circuit (BIC) et MCC Project Partners (MCCPP), comprend un hôtel, un centre de conférences, des halls d'expositions de voitures, un plan directeur pour un centre de recherche, une usine de voitures de luxe et une université, le tout ne recouvrant pas moins de 1000 ha, et intégrant un circuit existant de Formule 1 creusé dans la roche du désert. Zaha Hadid s'est accaparé la différence entre le tarmac noir de la piste et la texture brute de la pierre dans laquelle il a été tracé. Étant données les dimensions du site, son intervention qui est architecturale s'applique au niveau de la totalité du paysage, mettant en évidence les impressions de vitesse et de conduite associées au complexe. La description donnée par l'agence confirme cet esprit : « Dès l'approche des installations consacrées à la voiture avec ses hôtels, ses vitrines et ses programmes immobiliers axés sur l'automobile et les affaires, les routes vous placent en interaction étroite avec l'architecture. Filant au-dessus des constructions, plongeant en dessous, se glissant le long d'immeubles iconiques, apparaissant et disparaissant, les voitures dansent littéralement dans le paysage, interagissent avec le bâti et enrichissent le spectacle visuel d'un mouvement permanent. » L'idée d'« oasis » et de « joyaux » sculptés à partir du paysage, intégrés les uns aux autres d'une phase de construction à l'autre, domine ce programme. L'esthétique générale de ce complexe, qui ne pouvait être imaginé que par Hadid, est aussi « hi-tech et épuré » que ce que l'on pouvait attendre d'une architecture associée à une prestigieuse course annuelle de Formule 1. L'architecte parle à juste titre de « nouvelle chorégraphie d'automobiles, d'architecture et de paysage ».

Though the metaphor of the tent may be present in the reviewing stands (below), the overall lines of the project recall Zaha Hadid's interest in continuous space and dynamic forms, well suited to car racing in this instance.

Auch wenn sich die Zuschauertribünen (unten) als Zeltmetapher deuten lassen, belegt die gesamte Linienführung des Projekts wieder einmal Hadids Interesse an einem räumlichen Kontinuum und dynamischen Formen, was im Kontext des Autorennens sicher sehr passend ist.

Bien que la métaphore de la tente soit peut-être identifiable dans les stands (ci-dessous), les lignes générales du projet rappellent le goût de Zaha Hadid pour les espaces continus et les formes dynamiques, particulièrement bien adaptées à un projet portant sur des courses automobiles.

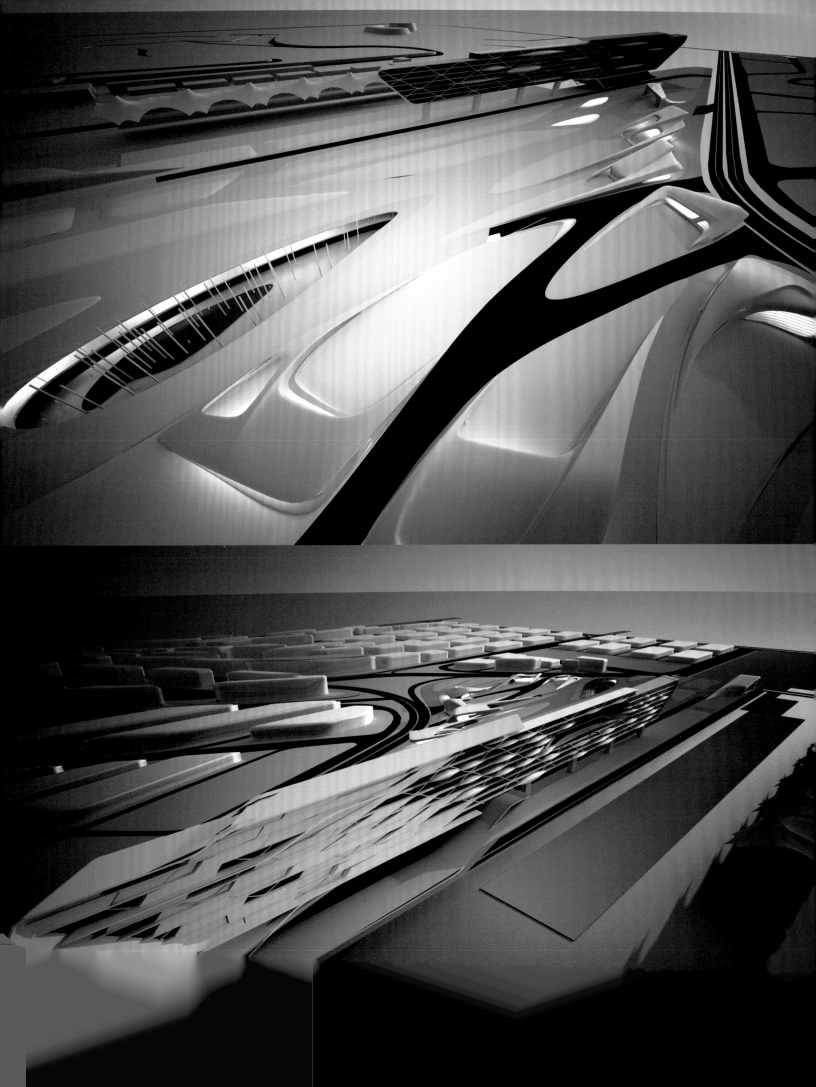

A plan of the site shows the relatively simple and elegant way that the volumes fit into the allotted space, assuming its irregularity and making the most of it. Below, an interior perspective suggests architecture that appears to be in a perpetual state of movement.

Ein Lageplan macht deutlich, wie leicht und elegant sich die Baukörper in den vorgesehenen Raum fügen, dessen Unregelmäßigkeit aufgreifen und optimal nutzen. Eine Innenansicht (unten) zeigt eine Architektur, die ständig in Bewegung zu sein scheint.

Le plan du site montre la façon élégante et relativement simple avec laquelle les volumes s'adaptent à l'espace disponible en assumant pour le meilleur leur irrégularité. Ci-dessous, une perspective intérieure suggère une architecture en état de mouvement perpétuel.

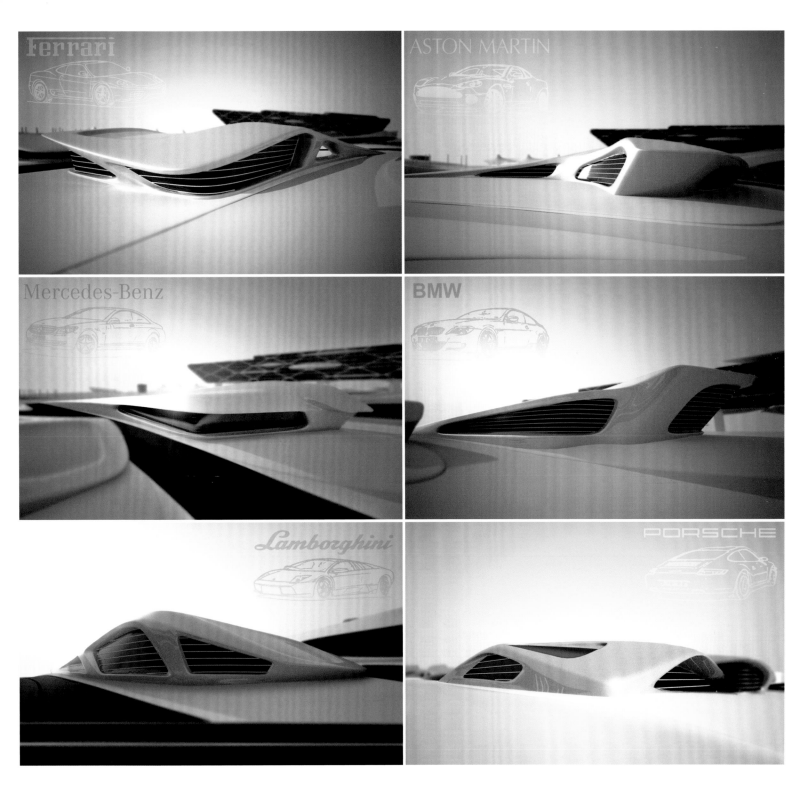

Building forms are placed in juxtaposition here with drawings of cars and their brand names, although Hadid's vocabulary does no more to suggest that each shape is indeed a literal interpretation of a car's design.

Den Gebäudeformen sind Zeichnungen von Autos und ihren jeweiligen Markennamen gegenübergestellt. Dennoch lässt Hadids Formensprache nicht den Schluss zu, die einzelnen Formen seien tatsächlich eine wörtliche Interpretation eines konkreten Fahrzeugdesigns.

Les formes des constructions sont rapprochées de dessins de voitures et de marques de constructeurs, même si le vocabulaire de Hadid ne suggère pas que chaque forme est une interprétation littérale du design d'une automobile.

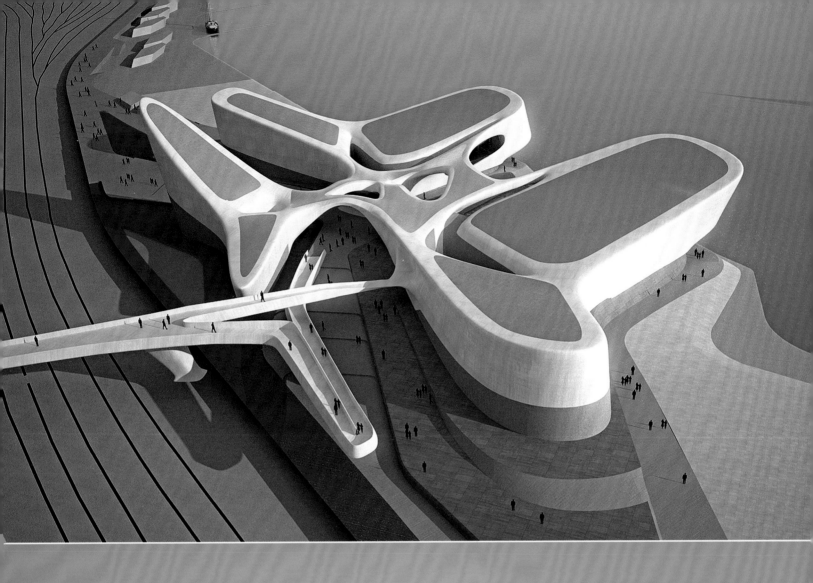

REGIUM
WATERFRONT

Reggio Calabria, Italy. 2007–

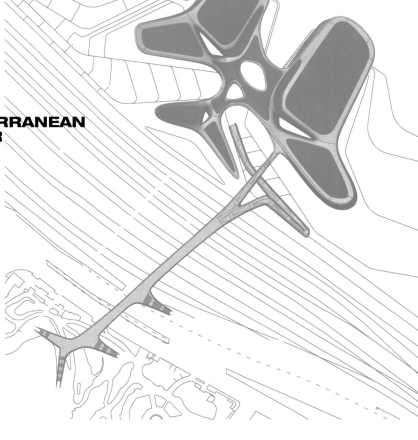

Project
REGIUM WATERFRONT

Location
REGGIO CALABRIA, ITALY

Client
COMUNE DI REGGIO CALABRIA

Area/Size
**8375 m² MUSEUM OF THE MEDITERRANEAN
13 000 m² MULTIPURPOSE CENTER**

Zaha Hadid herself speaks of "organic morphology" in describing this project, although as usual no specific creature or landscape form can be identified as a source. Very large scale openings and sweeping curves characterize both the plan above and the perspectives on the left page.

Zaha Hadid selbst spricht in ihrer Projektbeschreibung von „organischer Morphologie", obwohl auch hier, wie üblich, keine spezifische Kreatur oder Landschaftsformation als Inspirationsquelle erkennbar sind. Monumentale Wandöffnungen und ausgreifende Schwünge prägen sowohl den Grundriss oben als auch die Ansichten links.

Zaha Hadid parle de « morphologie organique » pour décrire ce projet même si, comme d'habitude, on ne peut identifier aucune source animale ou naturelle précise. D'immenses ouvertures et des courbes enveloppantes caractérisent à la fois le plan ci-dessus et les perspectives de la page de gauche.

Zaha Hadid was the winner of a 2007 competition for the realization of a Museum of Mediterranean History and a multifunctional block in the city of Reggio di Calabria on a site situated on the strait separating the continent from Sicily. As the architect's statement confirms: "The shape of the Museum is vaguely inspired by a starfish and a coherent continuation of Zaha Hadid Architects' exploration of organic morphology." The architect insists on the "movement and openness" of the project, and it is clear that its dramatic lines fit in closely with other projects that seek a "seamless" continuity between site and architecture. The planned Museum will include exhibition spaces, an archive, a restoration lab, an aquarium, and a library. The rest of the complex consists of three buildings around a covered square with administrative offices for the Museum in the southern section and a gym, craft laboratories, shops, and a cinema in the northern block. Also to the south, the third block contains three flexible auditoriums that can be converted into a single space for important events.

2007 gewann Zaha Hadid einen Wettbewerb für die Realisierung eines Museums für Mittelmeergeschichte und einen Multifunktionsbau in Reggio di Calabria auf einem Grundstück an der Meeresenge zwischen Sizilien und dem italienischen Festland. Dem Architekturbüro zufolge „orientiert sich die Form des Museums frei an einem Seestern; sie ist die konsequente Fortführung der Beschäftigung Zaha Hadids mit organischen Morphologien". Die Architektin betont die „Dynamik und Offenheit" des Projekts. Es wird deutlich, dass die dramatische Formgebung eng an andere Projekte anknüpft, die nach „nahtloser" Kontinuität zwischen Standort und Architektur streben. Das geplante Museum wird Ausstellungsräume, ein Archiv, eine Restaurationswerkstatt, ein Aquarium und eine Bibliothek umfassen. Der übrige Teil des Komplexes besteht aus drei Gebäuden, die um einen überdachten Platz herum angeordnet sind. Hier befinden sich im südlichen Abschnitt Verwaltungsbüros für das Museum, im nördlichen Block ein Fitnesscenter, Kreativwerkstätten, Geschäfte und ein Kino. Ebenfalls nach Süden liegt ein dritter Block mit drei flexiblen Auditorien, die sich für größere Veranstaltungen zu einem großen Saal zusammenschließen lassen.

Zaha Hadid a remporté en 2007 le concours pour la construction d'un musée de l'histoire méditerranéenne et d'un immeuble polyvalent à Reggio di Calabria, en bordure du détroit entre le continent et la Sicile. Comme le mentionne l'un de ses communiqués : « La forme du musée est en partie inspirée de celle d'une étoile de mer et de l'état actuel de l'exploration permanente de la morphologie organique par l'agence Zaha Hadid Architects. » L'architecte insiste sur le « mouvement et l'ouverture » du projet dont les lignes spectaculaires sont, dans l'esprit de ses projets, à la recherche d'une « continuité sans rupture » entre le site et l'architecture. Le musée comprendra des salles d'expositions, des archives, un laboratoire de restauration, un aquarium et une bibliothèque. Le reste du complexe se compose de trois immeubles réunis autour d'une place couverte contenant des bureaux administratifs pour le musée au sud, des laboratoires d'artisanat, un gymnase, des boutiques et un cinéma au nord. Le troisième élément contiendra trois salles polyvalentes qui pourront être réunies en un espace unique pour de grandes manifestations.

The building occupies a long green band along the waterfront, seen in the aerial perspective (left). Below, four elevations confirm that aside from rising and falling forms, no one view of the building gives a complete understanding of its "morphology."

Der Bau liegt auf einem lang gestreckten Grünstreifen am Ufer, wie links in der Luftansicht zu sehen. Vier Aufrisse (unten) bestätigen, dass außer den aufstrebenden und abfallenden Formen keine Ansicht des Komplexes einen vollständigen Gesamteindruck seiner Morphologie vermittelt.

Le bâtiment occupe un long espace vert au bord de la mer, comme le montre la perspective aérienne (à gauche). Ci-dessous, quatre élévations confirment qu'en dehors de formes ascendantes et descendantes, aucune vue simple ne permet d'appréhender entièrement la morphologie de l'immeuble.

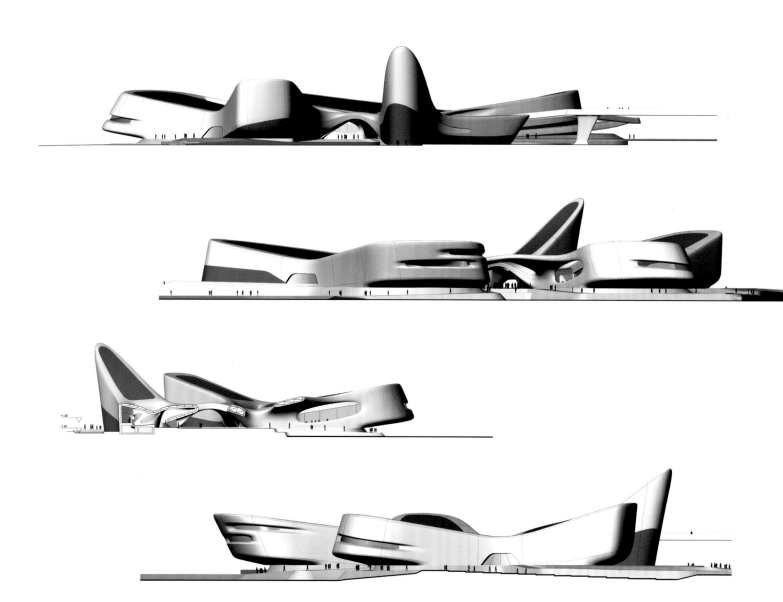

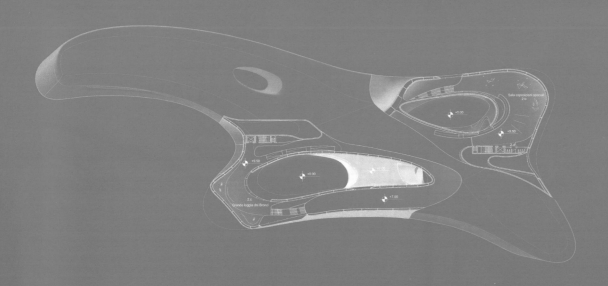

Plans for the building show a disposition that corresponds closely to the elevations or perspectives, showing that the design is far more than skin-deep; it is rather an "organic" whole.

Grundrisse des Baus zeugen von der engen Verwandtschaft mit seinen Aufrissen und perspektivischen Ansichten und belegen, dass der Entwurf keineswegs oberflächlich bleibt. Vielmehr erweist er sich als „organisches" Ganzes.

Les plans montrent une organisation qui correspond précisément aux élévations et aux perspectives. Le projet n'a rien de superficiel, il est un tout « organique ».

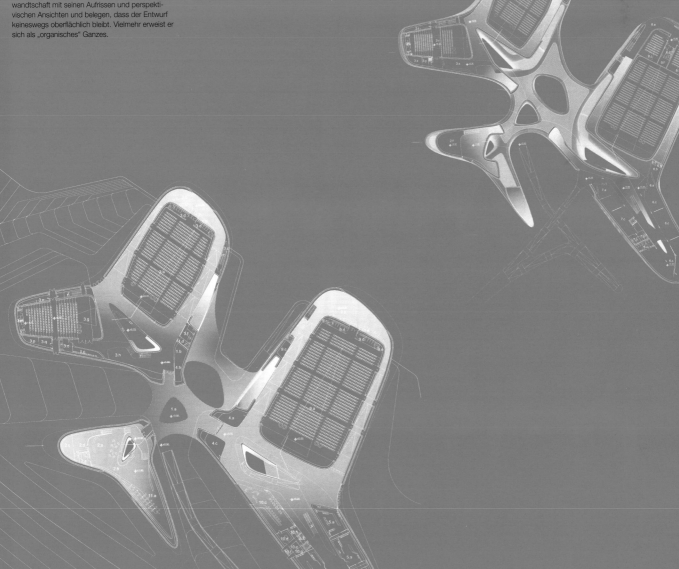

A series of interior perspectives (left page) suggests a continuity and interpenetration of spaces that corresponds well to the rising and falling volumes seen in the perspectives here. Though fish do come to mind, these are by no means the figurative fish of a Frank Gehry.

Eine Reihe von Innenansichten (linke Seite) veranschaulicht die Kontinuität und Durchdringung der Räume, die ideal mit den aufstrebenden und abfallenden Baukörpern auf den Perspektivzeichnungen korrespondieren. Obwohl man hier an Fische denken mag, ist diese Anspielung keineswegs so figurativ wie etwa bei Frank Gehry.

Une série de perspectives intérieures (page de gauche) indique une continuité et une interpénétration des espaces qui correspond aux volumes ascendants et descendants vus dans les perspectives de cette page. Si l'on peut penser à un poisson, ce n'est en rien un poisson figuratif à la Frank Gehry.

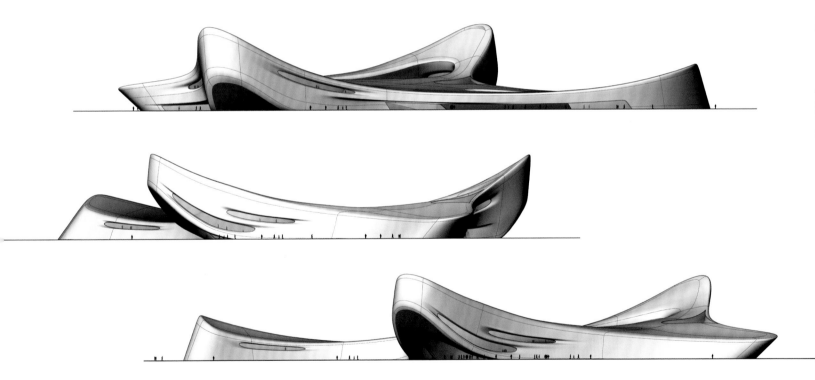

LILIUM TOWER

Warsaw, Poland. 2007–

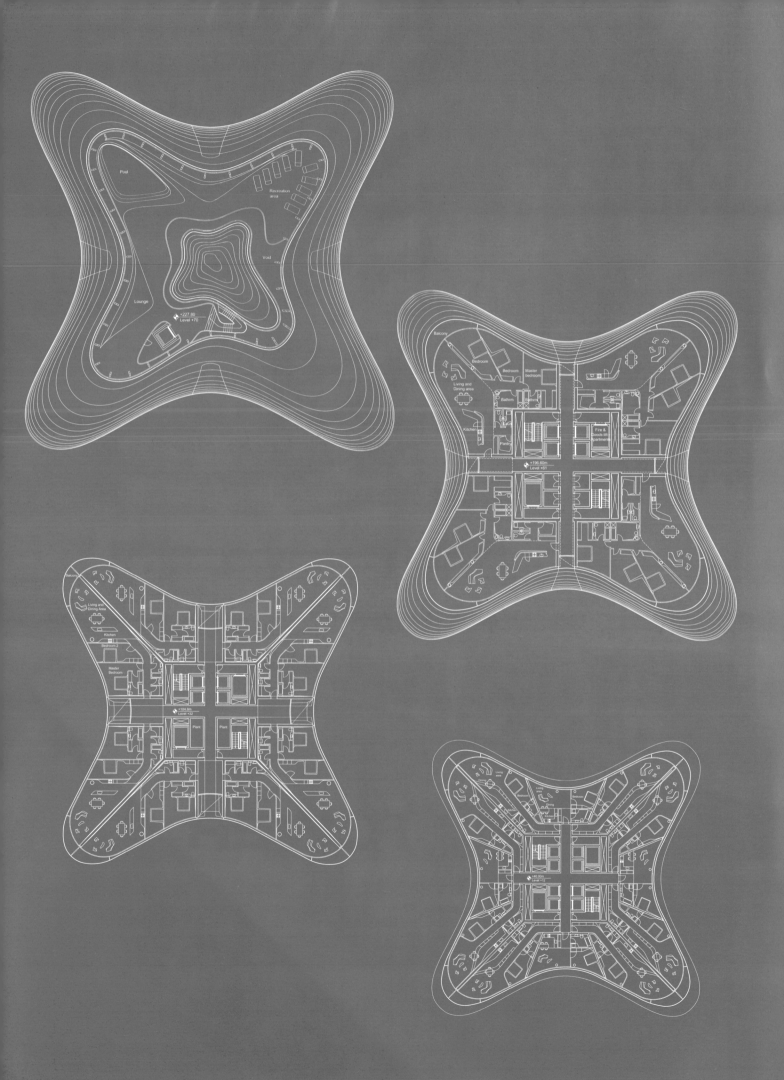

Project
LILIUM TOWER

Location
WARSAW, POLAND

Client
LILIUM POLSKA SP. ZO. O.

Area/Size
GROSS FLOOR AREA 130 000 m²

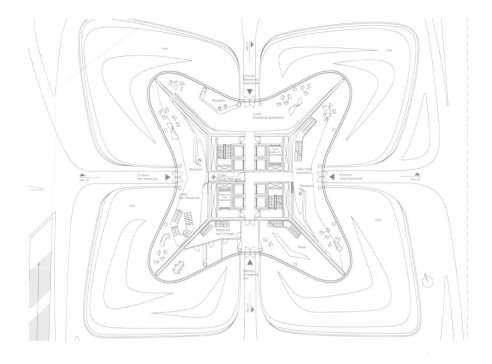

In this instance, the quatrefoil design chosen by the architect is regular, and not as intentionally unexpected as in her other buildings. The very floor plan does, however, express originality, even if the tower will look the same from each angle.

Hier ist das Vierpassmotiv regelmäßig und nicht ganz so eigenwillig gestaltet wie bei anderen Bauten Hadids. Der Grundriss jedoch zeugt von Originalität, auch wenn der Turm aus jedem Blickwinkel gleich aussieht.

Ici, la forme en trèfle est régulière, et non aussi volontairement surprenante que dans ses autres réalisations. Le plan au sol exprime cependant une grande originalité, même si la tour aura le même aspect vue sous ses divers angles.

Located in central Warsaw, this 101 000-square-meter, 240-meter-high, 71-story luxury residential and mixed-use project will be adjacent to the Marriott Tower and opposite the central train station. Though other tall buildings are rising in the area, the Lilium Tower will have a distinctive, smooth, double-façade transparent design with a changing appearance according to the angle under which it is viewed. A central hollow spine, or core with diagonal walls that run to the edges of the floor plates, provides the solidity required for any conceivable wind load for this building, due to be the tallest in Poland, just next to the 237-meter Palace of Science and Culture. The complex will include an apartment hotel, a spa, and an underground retail space with an adjacent exterior mall. Separate access is offered to each of these functions at ground level. A great deal of attention has been paid to issues of sustainability and access, providing for vehicular and pedestrian entrances, bridges, and passages wherever they are useful. Optional natural ventilation, as well as efficient mechanical systems, is used, as is a reversible-cycle ground-water heat pump.

Das zentral in Warschau gelegene, 101 000 m² große, 240 m hohe 71-stöckige Luxusgebäude mit gemischter Nutzung, unter anderem Wohnen, liegt neben dem Marriott Tower und gegenüber dem Hauptbahnhof. Obwohl sich in der Gegend auch andere Hochhausbauten erheben, wird der Lilium Tower durch sein unverwechselbares, glattes Design und seine transparente Doppelfassade auffallen, die je nach Blickwinkel stets anders wirkt. Ein zentrales, hohles „Rückgrat" und diagonal angeordnete Wände, die strahlenförmig zu den Außenkanten der Geschossplatten verlaufen, verleihen dem Gebäude die erforderliche Stabilität, um selbst stärksten Windlasten standzuhalten. Der Bau liegt in unmittelbarer Nach-

barschaft des 237 m hohen Kulturpalasts und wird das höchste Gebäude Polens sein. Im Komplex sind ein Apartmenthotel, ein Spa sowie unterirdische Einkaufszonen untergebracht, die an ein angrenzendes Einkaufszentrum anschließen. Alle Einrichtungen sind vom Erdgeschoss aus separat zugänglich. Besondere Aufmerksamkeit wurde auf die Nachhaltigkeit und die Erschließung des Baus gerichtet, weshalb Fahrzeug- und Fußgängerzugänge, Brücken und Passagen eingeplant wurden, wo immer möglich. Neben einem mechanischen kommen auch ein optionales natürliches Belüftungssystem und eine Wärmepumpe zum Einsatz.

Implantée en plein centre de Varsovie, près de la tour Marriott et face à la gare centrale, cette tour mixte comptera 71 niveaux sur 240 m de haut et une surface de 101 000 m². Par rapport aux autres immeubles de grande hauteur qui s'élèvent dans ce quartier, la tour Lilium présentera une façade double lisse et originale dont l'aspect évoluera selon l'angle d'observation. Elle sera l'immeuble le plus haut édifié en Pologne, se rapprochant des 237 m du Palais de la science et de la culture. Un noyau central creux, à murs de refend se projetant en diagonale jusqu'aux limites des plateaux, offre la résistance nécessaire à la force des vents. Le complexe comprendra un hôtel résidentiel, un spa, un ensemble souterrain de boutiques commerciales, ainsi qu'un centre commercial en surface. Chacune de ces fonctions bénéficiera d'un accès séparé en rez-de-chaussée. Une attention particulière a été portée aux aspects écologiques et d'accès, aussi bien pour les piétons que pour les voitures, en positionnant de façon utile des passerelles et des passages. Une ventilation naturelle optionnelle, aussi efficace que les systèmes mécaniques, sera mise en place, ainsi qu'un système de pompes à chaleur réversible utilisant les eaux souterraines.

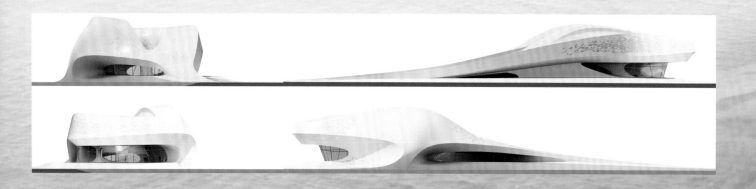

BAHRAIN MUSEUM
OF CONTEMPORARY ART

Al Muharraq, Bahrain. 2007–

Project
BAHRAIN MUSEUM OF CONTEMPORARY ART

Location
AL MUHARRAQ, BAHRAIN

Client
H. H. SHAIKHA MAI MOHAMMED AL KHALIFA
CULTURE & NATIONAL HERITAGE SECTOR

Area/Size
10 000 m²

More than other Hadid buildings, this one comprises what is essentially a single volume, albeit a curved rising one, rather than the assemblies of related components, which she has favored in other instances.

Stärker als andere Hadid-Bauten besteht dieses im Grunde aus einem einzigen Baukörper, wenn auch aus einem geschwungenen und aufwärts strebenden Volumen und nicht aus aufeinander bezogenen Kompositformen, die Hadid in anderen Fällen bevorzugte.

Plus que d'autres réalisations de Hadid, celle-ci assume sa composition de volume unique, même incurvé, et non la formule d'assemblage d'éléments reliés entre eux qu'elle avait préférée à d'autres occasions.

This project is described by the architect as an "enigmatic volume," or a "gentle curve," on a coastal site on the Gulf of Bahrain, "mystically floating" and reaching out over the water toward Manama. Dynamism and fluidity are again the key words in a structure that lifts near its entrance in a cantilevered volume containing museum elements that also serve, below, as a canopy. Though Hadid often refers to specific site elements in her projects, here she also brings in references to Islamic architectural tradition, for example in geometric patterns and ornamentation that can be used to control the desert light. Intended to show traveling exhibitions, the Museum has interior space that is conceived as a path through a series of galleries "with distinct characters to enhance the visitor's art experience as well as the artists creating and exhibiting their work." Self-contained "exhibition capsules" are inserted into the skin of the building. Views of other parts of the structure and sometimes the coastal setting create variety in the exhibition and museum sequence. As is most often the case with Zaha Hadid's buildings, the Bahrain Museum will be a "visually arresting landmark" located on reclaimed land between the rising contemporary city and the water—representing, as she says, the two sides of Bahraini culture, modern and traditionally linked to the sea.

Die Architektin beschreibt das Projekt als „rätselhaften Baukörper" oder „sanfte Wölbung" auf einem Ufergrundstück am Golf von Bahrain, der „mystisch zu schweben" und über das Wasser hinweg nach Manama zu greifen scheint. Auch hier sind Dynamik und Fluss wieder die Schlüsselbegriffe eines Bauwerks, das sich zur Eingangsseite hin mit einem auskragenden Baukörper erhebt, in dem Museumsräume untergebracht sind und der zugleich als Baldachindach dient. Während Hadid in ihren Projektbeschreibungen oft Bezüge zu speziellen Eigenheiten des baulichen Umfelds herstellt, verweist sie hier außerdem auf die islamische Architekturtradition, etwa durch die geometrischen Muster und dekorativen Elemente, die zur Regulierung des Lichteinfalls dienen. Der Innenraum des Museums, in dem Wanderausstellungen zu sehen sein werden, ist als Wegeführung durch verschiedene Galerien konzipiert, „deren einzigartiger Charakter das Kunsterlebnis der Besucher, das kreative Schaffen der Künstler und die Präsentation ihrer Arbeiten steigern wird". Eigenständige „Ausstellungskapseln" wurden in die Haut des Baus integriert. Ausblicke auf andere Bereiche des Gebäudes und vereinzelt auf die Küstenlandschaft lockern die Sequenz der Ausstellungsund Museumsräume auf. Wie meistens bei Zaha Hadids Bauten, so wird sich auch das Museum in Bahrain zweifellos als „Wahrzeichen, das alle Blicke auf sich zieht", behaupten. Auf einem dem Meer abgewonnenen Bauplatz zwischen der wachsenden modernen Stadt und dem Wasser gelegen, symbolisiert es die zwei Seiten der bahrainischen Kultur, die gestern wie heute mit der See verbunden ist, wie Hadid betont.

Ce projet est présenté par Zaha Hadid comme un « volume énigmatique » ou « une courbe douce » qui devrait trouver place en bordure de la côte du golfe de Bahreïn, « flottant de manière mystérieuse », et se projetant même au-dessus de l'eau vers Manama. Le dynamisme et la fluidité sont là encore les mots-clés d'une structure qui se redresse au niveau de son entrée par un volume en porte-à-faux contenant le musée et faisant office d'auvent. Si Hadid se réfère souvent aux éléments spécifiques au site dans ses projets, elle prend ici pour référence la tradition architecturale islamique, comme on le voit par exemple dans les motifs géométriques et ornementaux déployés pour filtrer la lumière du désert. Conçu pour des expositions itinérantes, l'espace muséal s'organise autour d'un cheminement à travers une succession de galeries « aux caractères différents, pour stimuler la découverte de l'art par les visiteurs, comme celle des artistes créateurs et exposants ». Des « capsules d'exposition » indépendantes sont insérées dans la peau du bâtiment. Des perspectives ouvertes sur les autres parties de la construction, ou parfois sur la côte, apportent un élément de variété dans le parcours. Comme très souvent chez Zaha Hadid, le Musée de Bahreïn sera un « monument visuellement surprenant » implanté sur un terrain conquis sur la mer, situé entre la ville nouvelle en cours de construction et l'eau, et représentant, comme elle l'explique, les deux faces de la culture bahreïnite : la modernité et la tradition liées au Golfe.

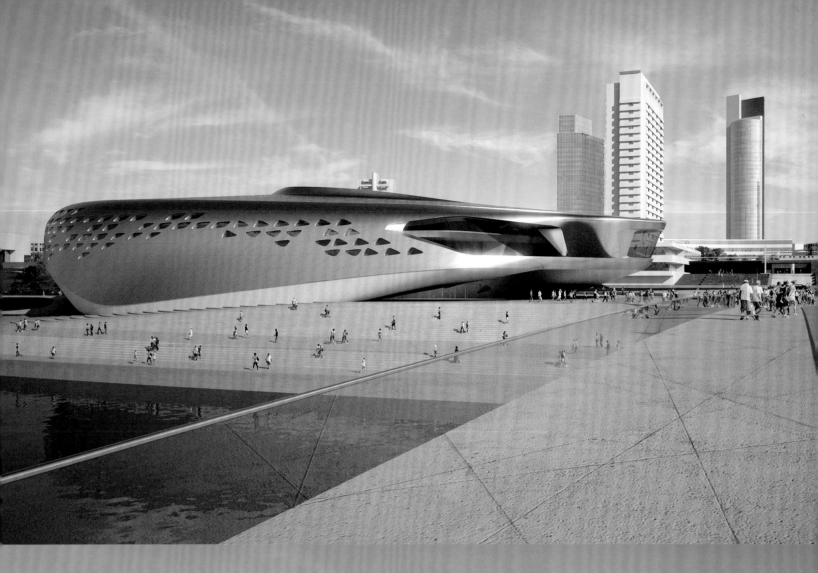

VILNIUS MUSEUM

Vilnius, Lithuania. 2007–

Project
VILNIUS MUSEUM

Location
VILNIUS, LITHUANIA

Client
CITY OF VILNIUS, LITHUANIA

Area/Size
13 000 m²

These interior renderings demonstrate how the overall design of the proposed museum in Vilnius, seen on the previous double-page spread, is related to its exhibition spaces, creating a curvilinear unity that envelops the visitor.

Die Darstellungen des Innenraums veranschaulichen die Beziehung des Gesamtentwurfs für das Museum in Vilnius (vorige Doppelseite) zu seinen Ausstellungsräumen, deren geschwungene Geschlossenheit die Besucher umfängt.

Ces perspectives intérieures montrent comment la conception d'ensemble de ce musée destiné à Vilnius (double-page précédente), est défini par ses espaces d'exposition au service d'un univers curviligne et unifié qui enveloppe le visiteur.

The concepts of "fluidity, velocity and lightness" are further explored in this recent project. According to the official description: "The building appears like a mystical object floating above the extensive artificial landscape strip, seemingly defying gravity by exposing dramatic undercuts towards the surrounding entrance plazas." Intended to contrast with the largely vertical and rectilinear forms of the business district of the Lithuanian capital, the building is described as "sculptural" or "enigmatic" with an emphasis on its curvilinear form. Folds or protrusions in the overall "glossy metallic" structure house programmatic units inlaid into the overall shape. The architect's comparison of the interior space to a "canyon" confirms the impression that there is a clear reference, albeit in indirect ways, to nature—a kind of artificial nature. The project description also refers to the "Fluxus spirit of informality and vivacity surrounding art." The Lithuanian artist George Maciunas (1931–78) organized the first events of the Fluxus art movement in 1961 and 1962. Vilnius is located at the confluence of the Vilnia and Neris Rivers and the project aims to intensify public life along the river. Advanced digital design and fabrication methods are part of this project, allowing the creation of the building's fluid shapes without undue cost increases. Zaha Hadid won the competition for this 13 000-square-meter facility over Studio Daniel Libeskind and Studio Fuksas.

Im Zuge dieses neuen Projekts werden die Prinzipien „Fließen, Geschwindigkeit und Leichtigkeit" weiter vertieft. Der offiziellen Projektbeschreibung zufolge „wirkt der Bau wie ein mystisches Objekt, das über dem weitläufigen, künstlichen Landschaftsstreifen zu schweben scheint, und das dank der dramatischen Unterschneidungen, die es den umliegenden Vorplätzen präsentiert, der Schwerkraft zu trotzen scheint." Der Bau wurde, im Gegensatz zu den überwiegend vertikalen und geradlinigen Formen des Geschäftsviertels der litauischen Hauptstadt, als „skulptural" oder „enigmatisch" beschrieben und fällt mit seiner geschwungenen Formgebung auf. In den Falten und Ausbuchtungen der rundum „glänzend metallischen" baulichen Struktur, die in die Gesamtform integriert wurden, sind einzelne Bereiche des Programms untergebracht. Dass die Architektin den Innenraum mit einem „Canyon" vergleicht, bestätigt die klaren, wenn auch indirekten Bezüge zur Natur – eine Art künstliche Natur. Darüber hinaus nimmt die Projektbeschreibung auf den „Geist des Fluxus" Bezug, „mit seiner kunstspezifischen Informalität und Lebendigkeit". Der litauische Künstler George Maciunas (1931–78) hatte 1961 und 1962 die ersten Veranstaltungen der Fluxus-Bewegung initiiert. Vilnius liegt an der Flusseinmündung von Vilnia und Neris; Ziel des Projekts ist es, das öffentliche Leben verstärkt an den Fluss zu holen. Neue digitale Entwurfstechniken und Fertigungsmethoden kamen zum Einsatz und ermöglichten die Realisierung der fließenden Bauformen ohne unzumutbare Kostenzuwächse. Im Wettbewerb um diese 13 000 m² große Einrichtung konnte sich Zaha Hadid gegen Studio Daniel Libeskind und Studio Fuksas durchsetzen.

Ce récent projet explore encore plus avant les concepts hadidiens de « fluidité, de vélocité et de légèreté ». Selon le descriptif officiel : « Le bâtiment évoque un objet mystique flottant au-dessus d'une longue bande de paysage artificiel, semblant défier la gravité en exposant de spectaculaires découpes qui s'ouvrent sur les plazzas d'entrées environnantes. » Dans un contraste voulu avec les formes en grande partie verticales et orthogonales du quartier des affaires de la capitale lituanienne, ce musée qui met l'accent sur les formes curvilignes attire les qualificatifs de « sculptural » ou « d'énigmatique ». Les plis ou les protubérances pris dans la structure « métallique brillante » abritent des éléments du programme. La comparaison proposée par l'architecte de l'espace intérieur qui serait un « canyon » confirme l'impression d'une référence claire, bien qu'indirecte, à la nature, en l'occurrence à une sorte de nature artificielle. Le descriptif du projet se réfère également à « l'esprit Fluxus d'un art d'environnement informel et vivace ». L'artiste lituanien George Maciunas (1931–78) avait organisé les premières manifestations du mouvement artistique Fluxus en 1961 et 1962. Vilnius étant située au confluent de la Vilnia et la Neris, le projet se propose d'intensifier l'animation le long de la rive. Il fait appel à des méthodes de conception et de fabrication par ordinateur sans pour cela entraîner une augmentation de prix injustifiée. Zaha Hadid a remporté le concours pour cet équipement culturel de 13 000 m² devant le Studio Daniel Libeskind et le Studio Fuksas.

An aerial perspective rendering shows how the form of the museum, much freer than that of nearby buildings, relates to the riverbank and to the proposed green spaces that continue and emphasize the natural lines of the site.

Eine Ansicht aus der Luft macht deutlich, wie die im Vergleich zu den Nachbarbauten viel freiere Form des Museums Bezug auf das Flussufer und auf die geplanten Grünflächen nimmt, die die natürliche Linienführung des Geländes aufgreifen und unterstreichen.

Cette perspective aérienne montre comment la forme du musée, beaucoup plus libre que celle des immeubles voisins, est en relation avec la rive du fleuve et les espaces verts prévus qui reprennent et mettent en valeur les courbes naturelles du site.

A vaulting internal space and bridge clearly relate to the scale of visitors but also creates an impression of a larger, holistic entity that wraps and warps around those who enter.

Der überwölbte Innenraum und die Brücke nehmen zwar deutlich Bezug auf die Maßstäblichkeit der Besucher; dennoch zeugen sie auch von einer übergeordneten, umfassenderen Instanz, die all jene umfängt und umschwingt, die hier eintreten.

Un espace intérieur sous voûte et une passerelle donnent l'échelle par rapport aux visiteurs mais créent également une impression d'entité holistique plus vaste qui enveloppe de ceux qui la pénètrent.

In this night view, the structure takes on an almost biomorphic appearance, although, as is almost always the case with the work of Hadid, there is no specific reference to any creature or natural formation. It is rather a form born of this place.

Auf dieser Nachtansicht wirkt der Bau fast wie eine biomorphe Gestalt, obwohl hier, wie fast immer im Werk Hadids, keine spezifischen Bezüge zu irgendwelchen Geschöpfen oder natürlichen Formationen hergestellt werden. Vielmehr wird die Form aus ihrem räumlichen Kontext geboren.

Dans cette vue nocturne, la structure prend un aspect quasi biomorphique, bien que, comme presque toujours chez Hadid, on ne puisse identifier de référence précise à quelque créature ou formation naturelle. C'est plutôt une forme née du lieu, inspirée par lui.

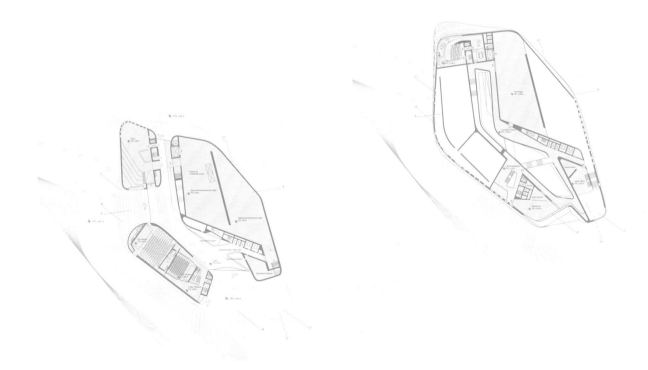

KING ABDULLAH II
HOUSE OF CULTURE & ART

Amman, Jordan. 2008–

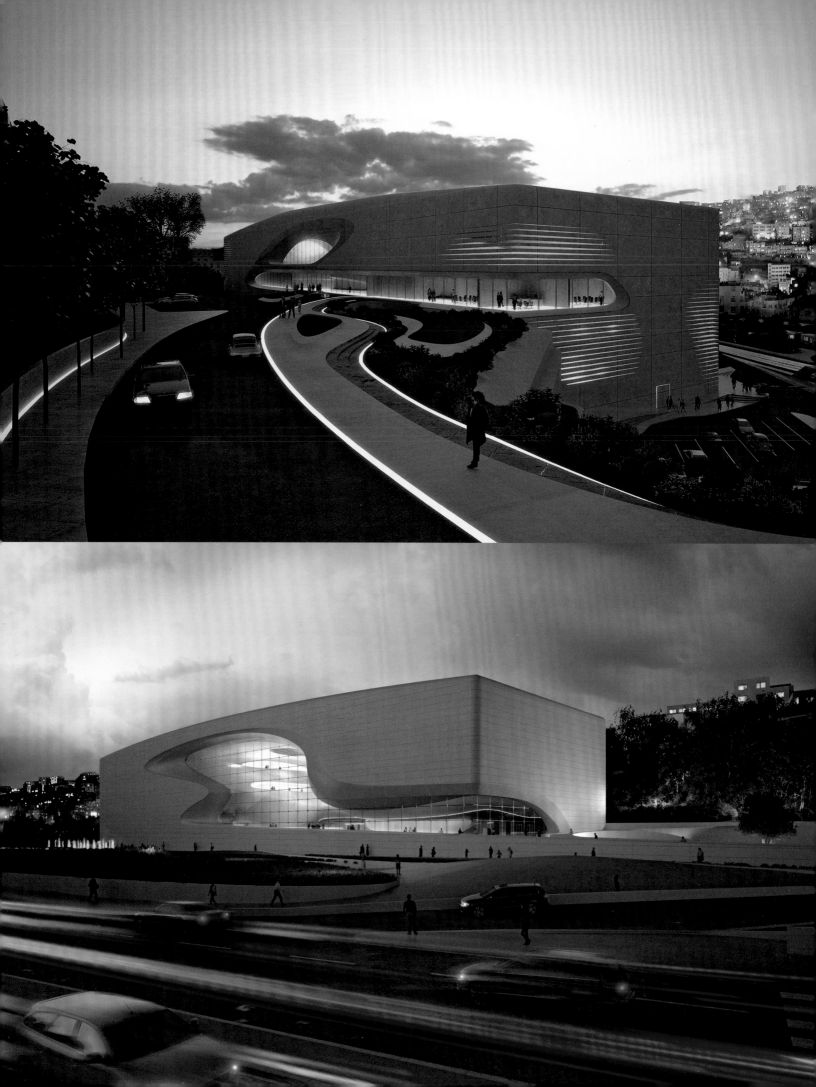

Project
KING ABDULLAH II HOUSE OF CULTURE & ART

Location
AMMAN, JORDAN

Client
THE GREATER AMMAN MUNICIPALITY

Area/Size
24 000 m²

The theme of erosion or dune-like movement defined by the exterior volumes of the structure is carried through to interior spaces, like the one seen bottom left.

Das Motiv der Erosion und die an Dünen erinnernde Bewegtheit, die sich am Außenbau zeigen, werden in den Innenräumen weitergeführt, wie links unten im Bild zu sehen ist.

Les thèmes de l'érosion ou du mouvement de dunes définis par les volumes extérieurs du bâtiment se retrouvent dans les espaces intérieurs, comme celui illustré en bas à gauche.

Being designed for the Greater Amman Municipality, this is a 1600-seat concert theater together with a smaller 400-seat facility, an education center, rehearsal room, and galleries. The project emphasizes public space on the western side of the site, meaning that the larger part of its mass is to the east, freeing space for a plaza. The building opens in a generous way toward the plaza and has an interior plaza and gathering space. Service and support spaces are located in a spine on the south side of the building. Citing the monument at Petra as a source of inspiration for the architecture, the architect states: "Petra is also a fantastic example of the interplay between architecture and nature. Contemporary architecture is striving to emulate nature and imbue architecture with the intricate complexity and elegance of natural forms. In Petra we admire the way the rose-colored mountain walls have been fissured, eroded, carved and polished to reveal the strata of sedimentation along the fluid lines of the fluvial erosions." The concept of fluidity and natural forms seen throughout Hadid's work is thus expressed here in comparison to an ancient monument. The interior performance spaces are therefore conceived as "eroded" forms. Indeed, the basically block-like exterior outline of the building expresses this idea of erosion clearly. This is also the case at the ground levels in the approaches to the building.

Der im Auftrag der Stadtverwaltung von Amman entworfene Bau umfasst ein Konzerthaus mit 1600 Plätzen und eine kleinere Bühne mit 400 Plätzen sowie ein Bildungszentrum, Probenraum und Galerien. Das besondere Augenmerk des Projekts liegt auf dem öffentlichen Raum an der Westseite des Grundstücks, weshalb der größte Teil der Gebäudemasse in den östlichen Bereich verlegt wurde. So entstand zugleich Raum für einen Vorplatz. Der Bau öffnet sich großzügig zum Vorplatz hin, umfasst eine weitere Plaza und offene Plätze im Innern. Tragende Elemente und Versorgungseinrichtungen wurden in einen Kern an der Südseite des Gebäudes verlegt. Die Architektin verweist auf die Stadt Petra als Inspiration für die Architektur: „Petra ist zudem ein fantastisches Beispiel für das Zusammenspiel von Architektur und Natur. Die zeitgenössische Architektur versucht, die

Natur nachzubilden und der Architektur eine ebenso aufwendige Komplexität und Eleganz zu verleihen, wie wir sie in der Natur finden. An Petra bewundern wir die rosagetönten Felswände mit ihren Rissen, Erosionsspuren, Schnitzereien und glatt geschliffenen Stellen, an denen die Sedimentschichten dort zu erkennen sind, wo die fluviale Erosion ihre fließenden Spuren hinterlassen hat." Hier wird das gestalterische Prinzip des Fließens und natürlicher Formen also anhand eines Vergleichs mit einem antiken Monument zum Ausdruck gebracht. Entsprechend wurden die Konzerträume im Innern des Baus wie „erodierte" Formen gestaltet. Tatsächlich vermittelt das im Grunde kubische Profil des Außenbaus den Eindruck von Erosion sehr deutlich. Im Eingangsbereich trifft dies auch auf die unteren Gebäudeebenen zu.

Conçu pour la municipalité du Grand Amman, cette salle de concert de 1600 places s'accompagne d'une seconde de 400 places, d'un centre éducatif, d'une salle de répétition et de galeries. Le projet met en valeur les espaces d'accueil à l'ouest, ce qui reporte la plus grande partie de sa masse vers l'est et dégage de l'espace pour une place. Le bâtiment s'ouvre généreusement vers celle-ci et possède également une place intérieure et un hall de réunion. Les volumes réservés aux services sont situés au sud dans un volume structurant. Citant Pétra comme la source de l'inspiration de cette architecture, Zaha Hadid a déclaré : « Pétra est aussi un fantastique exemple de jeu entre l'architecture et la nature. L'architecture contemporaine s'efforce d'émuler la nature et de se pénétrer de la complexité intriquée et de l'élégance des formes naturelles. À Pétra, nous admirons la façon dont les parois naturelles roses se sont fissurées, ont été érodées, creusées et polies, révélant des strates de sédimentation le long de lignes fluides ou des traces de l'érosion fluviale. » Le concept de fluidité et de formes naturelles que l'on observe dans toute l'œuvre d'Hadid s'exprime ainsi dans une comparaison avec un monument antique. Les salles de spectacle sont conçues comme des formes « érodées ». La silhouette extérieure du bâtiment et sa découpe expriment clairement cette idée d'érosion, reprise également dans les niveaux inférieurs.

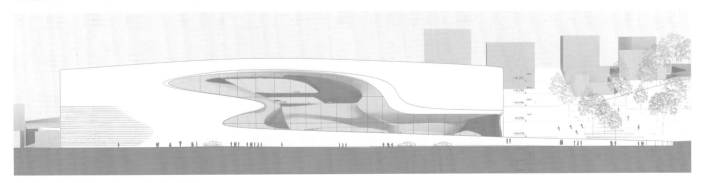

A concert hall (below) and interior spaces show the broad, generous lines that characterize the building, within and without. A sense of movement is imparted to all the spaces. A site plan (bottom right) shows how the building itself is related to its environment with curvilinear park zones.

Im Konzertsaal (unten) und anderen Innenräumen sind die ausgreifenden, großzügigen Linien zu sehen, die den Bau innen wie außen prägen. Alle Räume wirken wie bewegt. Ein Lageplan (unten rechts) veranschaulicht, wie sich der Bau in seine Umgebung mit den geschwungenen Linien der Parkanlagen einfügt.

Une salle de concert (ci-dessous) et des espaces intérieurs illustrent l'ampleur et la générosité des formes qui caractérisent le bâtiment aussi bien à l'intérieur qu'à l'extérieur. Une impression de mouvement se retrouve dans tous les volumes. Le plan de l'ensemble (en bas à droite) montre comment le bâtiment est relié à son environnement à travers des zones vertes curvilignes.

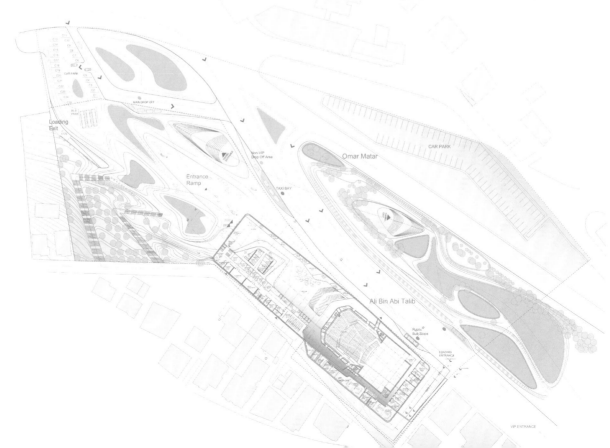

NEW PASSENGER TERMINAL AND MASTER PLAN ZAGREB AIRPORT

Zagreb, Croatia. 2008–

Project

NEW PASSENGER TERMINAL AND MASTER PLAN ZAGREB AIRPORT

Location
ZAGREB, CROATIA

Client
ZRAČNA LUKA ZAGREB – ZAGREB AIRPORT

Area/Size
75 000 m²

The airport takes on the shape of an organic but relatively regular progression from the entrance sequence to the broader band of the boarding gates for the aligned aircraft.

Der Flughafenkomplex präsentiert sich als organische, wenn auch relativ regelmäßige Sequenz – vom Eingangsbereich bis hin zum breiteren Band der Flugsteige für die aufgereihten Maschinen.

L'aéroport suit une progression organique relativement régulière de la séquence d'entrée jusqu'aux portes d'embarquement pour les avions.

This 2008 competition involved a new terminal building for Zagreb Airport, a 75 000-square-meter facility with a capacity for five million passengers per year, with a possible further 150 000-square-meter expansion for ten million passengers, and a 500 000-square-meter mixed-use "Airport City" development project. Viewed as a strategic stop for international traffic, the Zagreb facility adds to the existing airport and "engages the natural landscape setting" with an emphasis on local ecology. The mixed-use development around the terminal area employs a "tapestry-like" landscape strategy that connects the different parts of the site and adds a large urban park. Even the multistory car-parking facilities have green roofs, tying them into the overall landscape strategy and "blurring the lines" between landscape and architecture. An airport development of this nature, with its medium-density clusters, seems ideally suited to Zaha Hadid's concepts of fluidity and continuity, and this project takes those concepts to their logical high point, since, where the architecture is concerned, floors, walls, and ceilings are rendered continuous and indistinguishable. Ease of access to the terminal facilities has been emphasized in this project, where arrivals and departures are situated on the same level and rail and road transport are within short distances. The planning of these flows is fully conceptualized for future expansions. Careful control of daylight, solar gain, and artificial lighting is part of the ambitious energy strategy of the design.

In dem 2008 ausgelobten Wettbewerb ging es um ein neues Terminalgebäude für den Flughafen Zagreb, einen 75 000 m² großen Komplex mit einer Kapazität für jährlich fünf Millionen Passagiere, einschließlich einer möglichen 150 000 m² großen Erweiterung für zehn Millionen Passagiere sowie ein 500 000 m² großes Bauvorhaben mit gemischter Nutzung, die „Airport City". Als strategischer Haltepunkt im internationalen Verkehr ergänzt das Terminal den bestehenden Flughafen in Zagreb, „lässt sich auf das landschaftliche Umfeld ein" und legt besonderen Wert auf Ökologie. Das an das Terminal angrenzende, gemischt genutzte Bauvorhaben zeichnet sich durch eine „flickenteppichartige" Landschaftsgestaltung aus und lässt die „Grenzen" zwischen Landschaft und Architektur „verschwimmen". Ein Flughafenprojekt dieser Art mit mitteldichten Clustern scheint ideal auf Zaha Hadids Konzept von Fluss und Kontinuität zugeschnitten zu sein. Der Komplex treibt diese Konzepte, zumindest im Hinblick auf die Architektur, logisch auf die Spitze: Böden, Wände und Decken wurden als nicht abgrenzbare, kontinuierliche Formen gestaltet. Besonderer Wert wurde auf die leichte Zugänglichkeit des Terminals gelegt, weshalb Ankunft und Abflug auf derselben Ebene liegen und Schiene und Straße nicht weit entfernt sind. Die

Planung der Verkehrsflüsse wurde bereits im Hinblick auf mögliche zukünftige Erweiterungen durchkalkuliert. Die sorgfältige Steuerung von Tageslichteinfall, Solargewinn und künstlicher Beleuchtung ist Teil der ehrgeizigen Energiestrategie des Entwurfs.

Ce concours organisé en 2008 portait sur un nouveau terminal pour l'aéroport de Zagreb (75 000 m², 5 millions de passagers par an, avec possibilité d'extension à 150 000 m² pour 10 millions de passagers) et le projet d'une « Airport-City » à fonction mixte de 500 000 m². Ces projets d'accroissement de la capacité de l'aéroport actuel, étape stratégique du trafic aérien international, « mettent en jeu le paysage naturel existant » et s'attachent en particulier à l'écologie locale. Les constructions mixtes prévues autour du terminal développent une stratégie paysagère « en tapisserie » qui unifie les différentes parties du site et fait apparaître un vaste parc urbain. Même l'immeuble des parkings à plusieurs niveaux est doté de toits végétalisés, qui participent à la stratégie du paysage et « brouillent les limites » entre le paysage et l'architecture. Un aéroport de cette nature, à groupes de bâtiments de densité moyenne, semble idéalement adapté aux concepts de fluidité et de continuité de Zaha Hadid. Ils sont ici portés à leur aboutissement logique puisque, sur le plan architectural, les sols, les murs et les plafonds forment un tout continu. L'accent a également été mis sur les facilités d'accès au terminal dans lequel les zones de départ et d'arrivée sont situées au même niveau tandis que les liaisons avec le rail et les autoroutes sont à proximité immédiate. Le contrôle très étudié de l'éclairage naturel, de l'éclairage artificiel et du gain solaire participe à une ambitieuse stratégie énergétique.

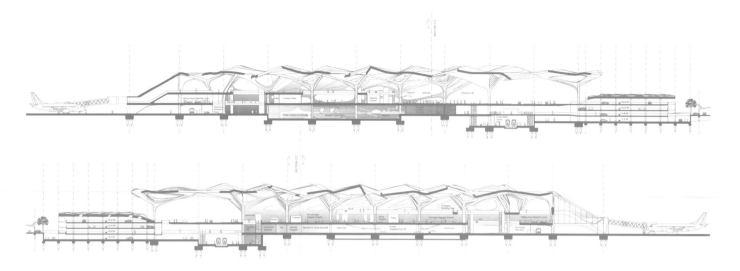

The treelike structures of the airport continue inside the building, providing an unexpected orchestration of leaning columns and broad, irregular glazed openings.

Die baumähnlichen Strukturen, aus denen das Terminal.besteht, ziehen sich im Innern des Gebäudes fort und erzeugen ein überraschendes Zusammenspiel von geneigten Stützen und großflächigen, unregelmäßigen Glasfronten.

Les structures en forme d'arbre qui constituent le terminal se poursuivent à l'intérieur du bâtiment et offrent au regard une orchestration inattendue de colonnes inclinées et de vastes ouvertures vitrées aux contours irréguliers.

Above, a perspective of the automobile entrance zone. The entire airport, as seen in the plan below, is made up of continuous horizontal and vertical bands, connected by the overriding canopy system.

Oben eine Ansicht der Pkw-Zufahrtszone. Wie am Plan unten zu sehen, besteht der gesamte Flughafen aus durchgängig verlaufenden horizontalen und vertikalen Bändern, die durch das Dachsystem miteinander verbunden sind.

Ci-dessus, une perspective de la zone d'accès des voitures. L'aéroport tout entier, comme le montre le plan ci-dessous, se compose de bandeaux continus horizontaux et verticaux, reliés par un système d'auvents.

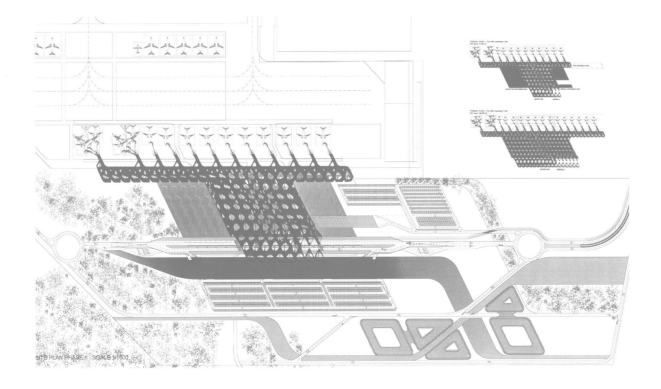

PRODUCTS
EXHIBITIONS
INSTALLATIONS

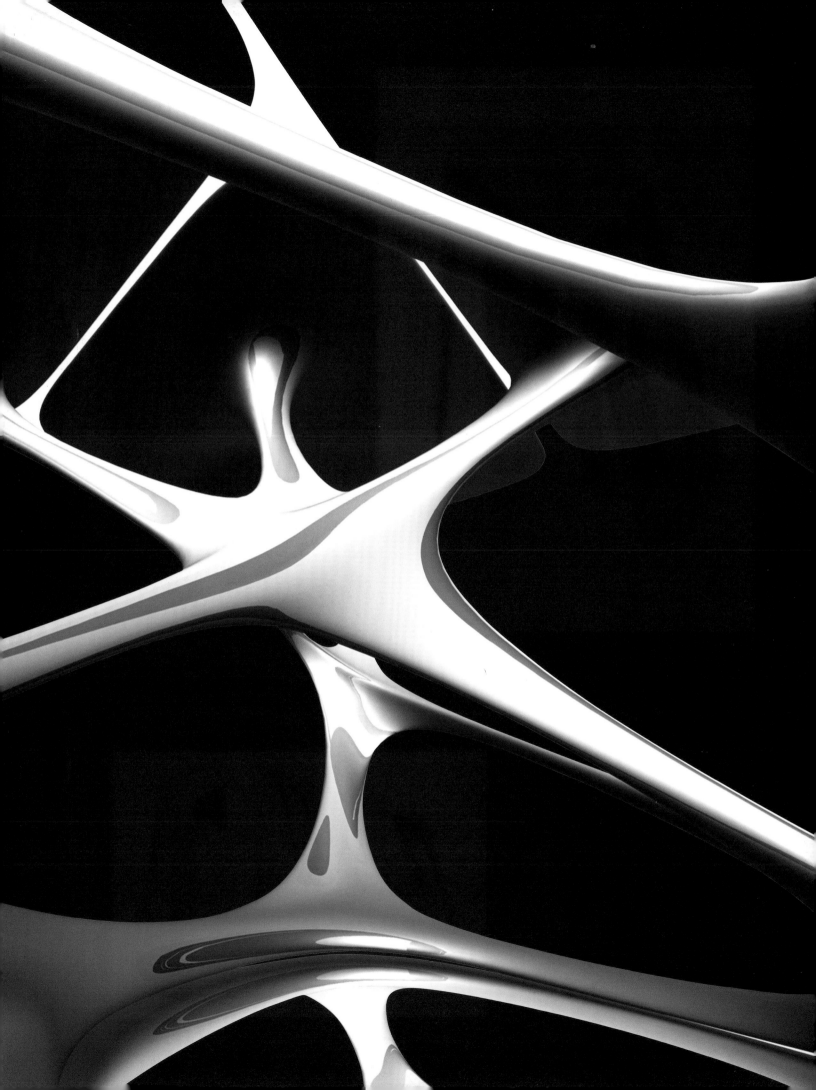

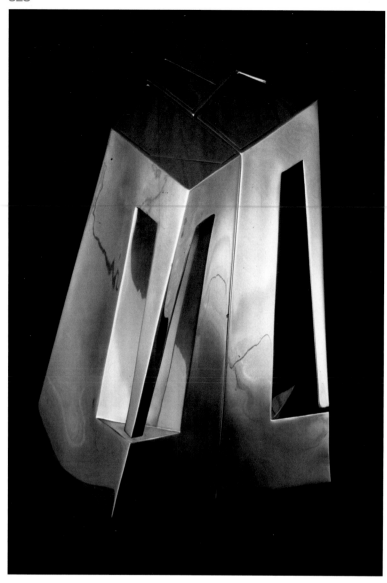

Project
TEA AND COFFEE SET

Client
SAWAYA & MORONI, MILAN, ITALY

Date
1995–96

The architect refers to this work as a "table sculpture" that is made up of four elements—tea- and coffeepots, milk jar, and sugar pot. The parts can be placed in a "representative mode" and carried easily, or in the functional mode for actual use.

Die Architektin bezeichnet das Objekt als „Tischskulptur" aus vier Elementen – Tee- und Kaffeekanne, Milchkännchen und Zuckerdose. Die Einzelteile lassen sich „repräsentativ" arrangieren und leicht tragen oder auch „funktional" nutzen.

L'architecte parle de cette œuvre comme d'une « sculpture de table » composée de quatre éléments : une théière, une cafetière, un pot à lait et un sucrier. Ils peuvent être configurés en « mode de représentation » et facilement transportés ou en « mode fonctionnel » pour être utilisés.

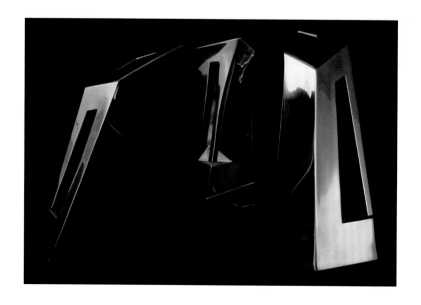

Project
Z-PLAY

Client
SAWAYA & MORONI, MILAN, ITALY

Date
2000

The elements of the system fit together or complement each other in patterns that can be determined by the user, always tending to create their own landscape within any chosen interior volume.

Die Systemelemente lassen sich vom Nutzer nach Belieben zusammenrücken oder zu Gruppen arrangieren. Dabei bilden sie im jeweiligen Interieur stets eine eigene Landschaft.

Les éléments du système s'adaptent entre eux ou se complètent selon des configurations qui peuvent être déterminées par l'usager, pour créer son propre paysage spatial à l'intérieur d'un volume donné.

STALACTITE

STALAGMITE

Though the names chosen for the object lines are quite specific, their precise connection to the appellation is not figurative or literal, it is rather an evocation, much as Zaha Hadid uses the landscape as inspiration for her architecture.

Obwohl die Namensgebung der Objekte durchaus spezifisch ist, ist sie weder figurativ noch wörtlich zu verstehen, sondern vielmehr als Assoziationsfeld, ähnlich wie die Landschaftsformen, von denen sich Hadid für ihre Architektur inspirieren lässt.

Si les noms choisis pour ces meubles sont assez spécifiques, leur lien avec leur appellation n'est ni figurative ni littérale. Il s'agit plutôt d'une évocation, de même que Zaha Hadid s'inspire du paysage dans son architecture.

Project
Z-SCAPE
Client
**SAWAYA & MORONI,
MILAN, ITALY**
Date
2000

MORAINE

GLACIER

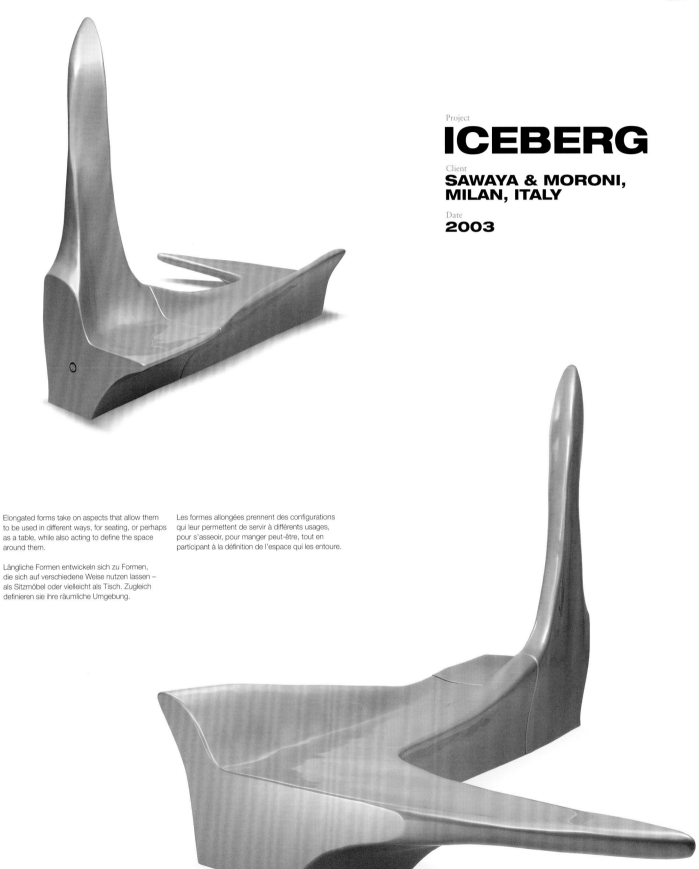

Project
ICEBERG
Client
SAWAYA & MORONI, MILAN, ITALY
Date
2003

Elongated forms take on aspects that allow them to be used in different ways, for seating, or perhaps as a table, while also acting to define the space around them.

Längliche Formen entwickeln sich zu Formen, die sich auf verschiedene Weise nutzen lassen – als Sitzmöbel oder vielleicht als Tisch. Zugleich definieren sie ihre räumliche Umgebung.

Les formes allongées prennent des configurations qui leur permettent de servir à différents usages, pour s'asseoir, pour manger peut-être, tout en participant à la définition de l'espace qui les entoure.

ICEBERG

ZAHA HADID
ARCHITECTURE/
ARCHITEKTUR
AT THE MAK

Vienna, Austria. 2003

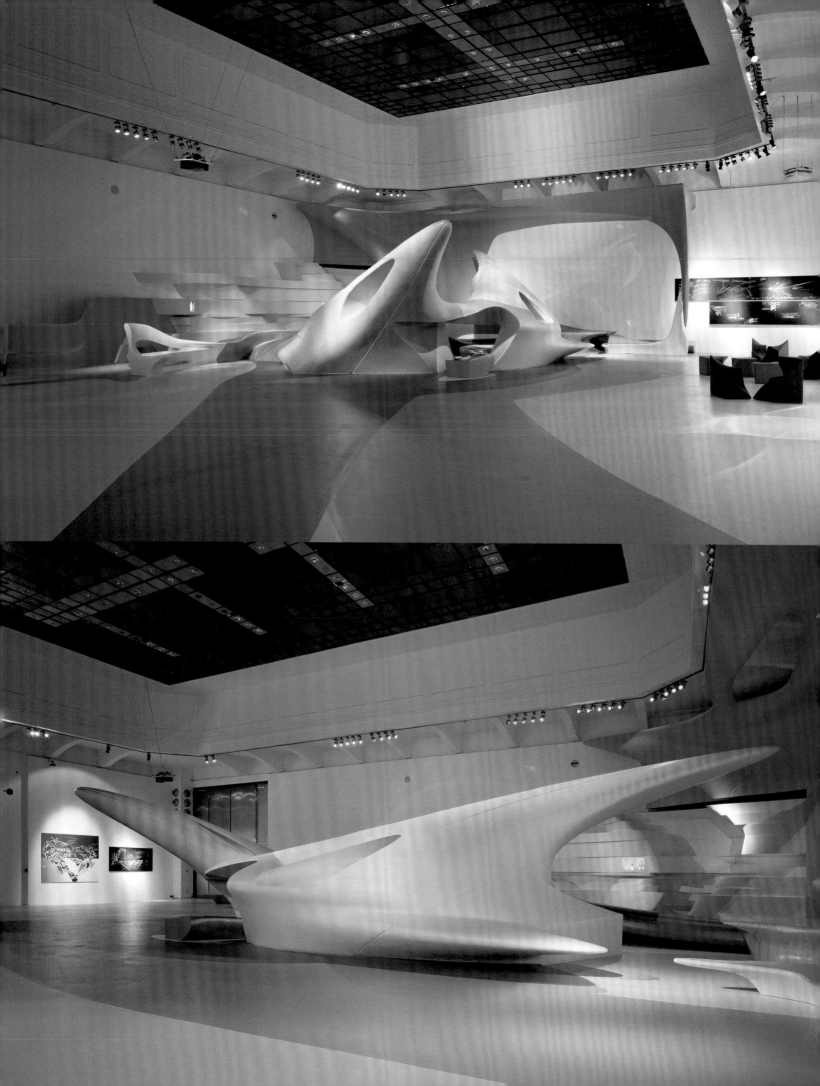

Project
ZAHA HADID ARCHITECTURE/ ARCHITEKTUR AT THE MAK

Location
VIENNA, AUSTRIA

Client
MAK, AUSTRIAN MUSEUM OF APPLIED ARTS AND CONTEMPORARY ART

The MAK (Österreichisches Museum für angewandte Kunst), the Museum of Applied Arts in Vienna, under the leadership of its Director Peter Noever has taken a leading role in exhibiting and encouraging the leading lights of contemporary architecture. In this show of the work of Zaha Hadid Architects, held at the MAK from May 14 to August 17, 2003, a central installation, or "built manifesto," called *Ice Storm* occupied the MAK exhibition hall. As described in the presentation of the installation: "The semi-abstract shape can be read as an apartment carved from a single continuous mass. Suggestive of a new type of living/lounging environments, it is a latent environment whose morphology is not yet associated with familiar typologies or codes of conduct." The show also made use of models, photos, sketches, and drawings, as well as renderings and computer animations. A number of Hadid's large paintings were also part of the exhibition, and it was asserted that: "These paintings are less to be understood as concrete representations of architecture; rather, they explore perspective, space, color, light, and shade through 'multiperspective projection,' reflecting the spatial imagery and ambiance of the respective project."

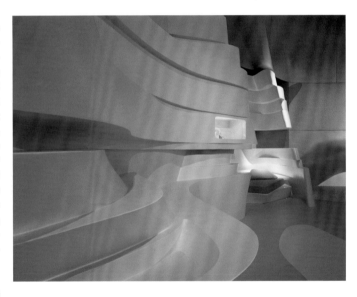

Das MAK (Österreichisches Museum für angewandte Kunst) wurde unter der Leitung seines Direktors Peter Noever zu einer führenden Institution, in der Koryphäen der zeitgenössischen Architektur präsentiert und gefördert werden. Bei dieser Ausstellung zum Werk Zaha Hadids im MAK (14. Mai bis 17. August 2003) stand in der Haupthalle des Museums eine Installation an zentraler Stelle. Der sog. *Ice Storm* war ein „bauliches Manifest". Die Beschreibung der Installation lautete: „Die semi-abstrakte Form lässt sich als Wohnung interpretieren, die aus einer geschlossenen Masse herausgearbeitet wurde. Sie ist ein in sich geschlossenes Umfeld, das auf einen neuen Wohnmilieu-Typus vorausweist und deren Morphologie mit bislang nicht bekannten Typologien oder Verhaltensformen assoziiert ist." Die Ausstellung umfasste zudem Modelle, Fotografien, Skizzen und Zeichnungen sowie Renderings und Computeranimationen. Gezeigt wurden auch einige großformatige Gemälde von Zaha Hadid, die mit einem expliziten Hinweis versehen waren: „Diese Gemälde sind weniger als konkrete Darstellungen von Architektur zu verstehen; vielmehr erkunden sie Perspektive, Raum, Farbe, Licht und Schatten mithilfe einer ‚multiperspektivischen Projektion' und spiegeln die räumliche Bildsprache und Atmosphäre des jeweiligen Projekts wider."

Le MAK, Musée des arts appliqués de Vienne, dirigé par Peter Noever joue un rôle éminent dans la connaissance des célébrités de l'architecture contemporaine par l'exposition de leurs travaux et l'appui qu'il leur apporte. Dans cette exposition consacrée à l'œuvre de Zaha Hadid Architects, organisée du 14 mai au 17 août 2003, un installation centrale ou « manifeste bâti » intitulée *Ice Storm* occupait le hall d'exposition du musée. L'installation était ainsi présentée : « La forme semi-abstraite peut se comprendre comme un appartement sculpté dans une masse unique et continue. Suggérant un nouveau type d'espace environnemental séjour/salon, c'est un environnement latent dont la morphologie n'est pas encore associée à des typologies ou codes de conduite familiers. » La manifestation mettait également en scène des maquettes, des photos, des croquis et des dessins ainsi que des rendus et des animations virtuelles. Un certain nombre des grandes peintures d'Hadid étaient également présentées et ainsi commentées : « Ces peintures doivent moins être comprises comme des représentations concrètes d'architecture mais plutôt comme des explorations de la perspective, de l'espace, de la couleur, de la lumière et de l'ombre par des "projections en multiperspective" reflétant l'imagerie spatiale et l'ambiance respective des projets. »

Hadid's installation at the MAK seen in these images clearly expresses her will to integrate the normally distinct areas of design and architecture into a coherent whole, in this case dedicated to explaining her own approach.

Hadids Installation im MAK, auf diesen Bildern zu sehen, bringt deutlich ihre Absicht zum Ausdruck, die üblicherweise klar getrennten Bereiche von Design und Architektur zu einem schlüssigen Ganzen zu verknüpfen – in diesem Fall, um ihren persönlichen Ansatz zu illustrieren.

L'installation d'Hadid au MAK présentée ici exprime clairement sa volonté d'intégrer les domaines normalement distincts du dessin et de l'architecture en un tout cohérent, consacré ici à l'explication de son approche.

Making use of her dynamic and flowing forms, the architect immediately immerses the visitor in a world of her own creation. Though the installation itself was ephemeral, it bears the seeds of her creative drive in a clear and coherent way.

Die Architektin greift auf dynamische und fließende Formen zurück und lässt den Besucher in ihre schöpferische Welt eintauchen. Obwohl die Installation temporär war, zeugte sie auf besonders klare und präsente Art von Hadids kreativer Energie.

Mettant en œuvre ses flux de formes dynamiques, l'architecte plonge le visiteur dans un univers de sa propre création. Si l'installation était bien éphémère, elle exprimait pourtant les racines de sa pulsion créative d'un façon claire et très présente.

25 YEARS
OF DEUTSCHE BANK
COLLECTION AT THE
DEUTSCHE GUGGENHEIM

Berlin, Germany. 2005

Project

25 YEARS OF DEUTSCHE BANK COLLECTION AT THE DEUTSCHE GUGGENHEIM

Location

BERLIN, GERMANY

Client

DEUTSCHE BANK ART

In this installation, Hadid verges very clearly on a sculptural presence: the forms suspended in the atrium of the Deutsche Bank connect to the exhibition pods, emphasizing the continuity of the presentation.

Mit dieser Installation kommt Hadid einer skulpturalen Präsenz sehr nahe: Die im Atrium der Deutschen Bank abgehängten Formen knüpfen an die „Gehäuse" an, in denen die Exponate ausgestellt sind, was die Kontinuität der Präsentation unterstreicht.

Dans cette installation, Hadid opte clairement pour une présence sculpturale : les formes suspendues dans l'atrium de la Deutsche Bank sont liées aux « cosses » mises au point pour l'exposition, ce qui renforce l'impression de continuité de la présentation.

Zaha Hadid was responsible for the exhibition design for the show held from April to June 2005 in the Deutsche Guggenheim to celebrate the 25th anniversary of the Deutsche Bank art collection. Located on the ground floor of the Deutsche Bank in Berlin, a 1920 sandstone building, the Deutsche Guggenheim is based on a 510-square-meter art gallery designed by the New York architect Richard Gluckman. The 300 works displayed ranged from German Expressionism to more recent works by such artists as Thomas Struth, Bill Viola, and Hiroshi Sugimoto. The exhibition's curator invited 25 friends of the collection and personalities with close ties to it (godfathers/godmothers) to choose their favorite pieces of art from the collection, as well as the most important. On this occasion, the Deutsche Guggenheim extended its exhibition space into the adjacent premises of the Deutsche Bank. The show was thus housed in the existing gallery plus a tall glass-roofed atrium. As Hadid's office describes the installation: "The intervention designed for the exhibition hall of the Berlin Guggenheim Museum is a carved-out solid. As a result, the visitor walks through a series of carved ellipsoid voids reflecting the curatorial concept and forming niches containing aspects of the individual 'collections' of the godfathers/godmothers. The spatial interrelation of the ellipsoids was developed using the size and amount of selected works. In the progression of the visitor route through the exhibition the ellipsoids become more dynamic and turn into solids as they enter the atrium hall. In the atrium hall the ellipsoids are dramatic, shell-like, horizontal and vertical structures that rise up to the glass." In fact, it is Hadid's installation itself that dominated the atrium, morphing in space from the exhibition shells into the floating, pure forms rising to the atrium ceiling.

Zaha Hadid zeichnete verantwortlich für die Ausstellungsarchitektur im Deutschen Guggenheim (April bis Juni 2005) anlässlich des 25-jährigen Jubiläums der Kunstsammlung Deutsche Bank. Das Deutsche Guggenheim, ein 510 m² großer Ausstellungsraum nach Entwürfen des New Yorker Architekten Richard Gluckman, befindet sich im Erdgeschoss der Deutschen-Bank-Niederlassung in Berlin, einem 1920 erbauten Sandsteingebäude. Die 300 Exponate der Ausstellung reichten vom deutschen Expressionismus bis hin zu jüngeren Werken von Thomas Struth, Bill Viola, Hiroshi Sugimoto und anderen. Die Kuratorin der Ausstellung hatte 25 sog. Paten – Freunde und Persönlichkeiten mit engen Bindungen zur Sammlung – eingeladen, Lieblings- und Schlüsselwerke der Kunstsammlung auszuwählen. Zu diesem Anlass erweiterte das Deutsche Guggenheim seinen Ausstellungsraum in die angrenzenden Räumlichkeiten der Deutschen Bank hinein, sodass die Schau sowohl in der bestehenden Galerie als auch im hohen, glasüberdachten Atrium des Baus zu sehen war. Hadids Büro beschreibt die Installation wie folgt: „Die für die Ausstellungshalle des Berliner Guggenheim entworfene Intervention ist ein ausgehöhlter massiver Körper. Entsprechend laufen die Besucher durch ellipsenförmige Hohlräume, die das kuratorische Konzept reflektieren, indem sie Nischen bilden, in denen die individuelle Auswahl der Paten präsentiert wird. Die räumlichen Beziehungen der ellipsoiden Räume zueinander ergab sich aus den Formaten und der Anzahl der jeweils ausgewählten Werke. Im Verlauf des Ausstellungsparcours werden die geschwungenen Formen zunehmend dynamischer und schließlich, je näher sie dem Atrium kommen, zu massiven Körpern.

Im Atrium selbst werden sie zu dramatischen, schalenähnlichen, horizontalen oder vertikalen Gebilden, die bis zum Glasdach hinaufragen." Tatsächlich war es Hadids Installation selbst, die das Atrium dominierte und sich allmählich von einem „Gehäuse" für die Exponate zu schwebenden, reinen Formen entwickelte, die sich bis zur Decke hinaufschwangen.

Zaha Hadid a été chargée du projet d'exposition organisée à Berlin d'avril à juin 2005 au Deutsche Guggenheim pour célébrer le 25e anniversaire de la collection d'art de la Deutsche Bank. Installé au rez-de-chaussée de la DB à Berlin dans un immeuble de grès des années 1920, le Deutsche Guggenheim consiste en une galerie de 510 m² aménagée par l'architecte new-yorkais Richard Gluckman. Les trois cents œuvres exposées vont de l'expressionnisme allemand à des œuvres plus récentes d'artistes comme Thomas Struth, Bill Viola ou Hiroshi Sugimoto. La commissaire de l'exposition avait invité vingt-cinq amis de la collection et des personnalités (parrains ou marraines d'œuvres) qui lui sont étroitement liées à choisir leurs œuvres d'art favorites ou les plus importantes. À cette occasion, le musée a étendu son espace d'exposition dans l'atrium à toiture de verre de la banque. Selon le descriptif de l'agence : « L'intervention conçue pour la salle d'expositions du Guggenheim Museum de Berlin est un solide creusé. Le visiteur se déplace à travers une série de vides ellipsoïdaux creusés dans la masse, reflétant le concept de l'exposition, et formant des niches contenant divers exemples tirés des collections des parrains/marraines. L'interrelation entre les ellipsoïdes a été mise au point en fonction de la quantité et des dimensions des œuvres présentées. En progressant

à travers l'exposition, le visiteur voit ces ellipsoïdes devenir de plus en plus dynamiques et se transformer en masses pleines lorsqu'elles envahissent l'atrium. Dans celui-ci, elles prennent des formes spectaculaires de coques et de structures verticales ou horizontales qui s'élèvent vers le plafond de verre. » En fait, l'installation de Z. Hadid dominait cet atrium, transformant l'espace d'exposition en formes pures et suspendues qui s'élevaient vers la lumière.

The elongated white volumes suspended in the atrium echo the curvilinear exhibition areas with their nearly organic profile.

Die im Atrium abgehängten, länglichen weißen Volumina wirken wie ein Echo der geschwungenen Ausstellungsarchitektur mit ihrer fast organischen Anmutung.

Les volumes blancs allongés en suspension dans l'atrium font écho aux zones d'exposition curvilignes et de profil quasi organique.

Project
VORTEXX CHANDELIER

Client
SAWAYA & MORONI, MILAN, ITALY

Date
2005

Made of fiberglass, car paint, acrylic, and LED lighting, the chandelier is 1.8 meters wide and 0.8 meters high, and has an opaque surface with two transparent acrylic light spirals and a programmable recessed LED light strip.

Der 1,8 m breite und 0,8 m hohe Leuchter ist aus Glasfaser, Autolack, Acryl und LED-Elementen gefertigt. Durch die opake Außenhaut verlaufen zwei Lichtspiralen aus transparentem Acryl und ein programmierbarer, versenkter LED-Leuchtstreifen.

Réalisé en fibre de verre, acrylique, peinture pour voiture et éclairage à base de Leds, ce lustre de 1,80 mètre de large et 0,80 mètre de haut se présente sous la forme d'une surface opaque avec deux spirales lumineuses en acrylique transparent et un bandeau programmable de Leds encastrés.

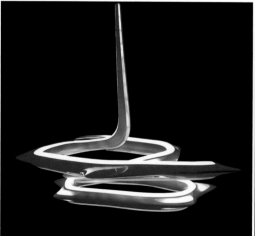
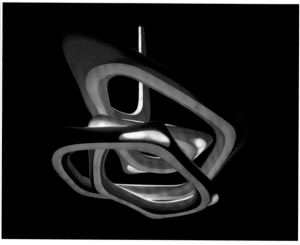

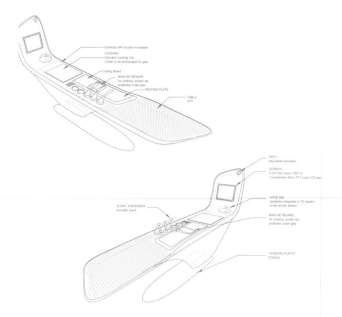

The precise function of the different elements of the kitchen is subsumed in the overall design, emphasizing continuity within the "island" form that even includes an unexpected TV screen.

Die spezifische Funktion der verschiedenen Küchenelemente ordnet sich dem Designkonzept unter, das mit der „Insel"-Form, in die überraschenderweise sogar ein TV-Bildschirm integriert ist, Kontinuität betont.

La fonction précise de ces différents éléments de cuisine est subsumée dans le projet d'ensemble et fait ressortir la continuité de l'îlot qui comprend même un écran de TV inattendu.

Project

Z-ISLAND KITCHEN

Client

ERNESTOMEDA S. P. A., MONTELABBATE, ITALY, AND DUPONT™ CORIAN® SOLID SURFACE, MARGARITELLI, ITALY

Date

2005–06

Project
AQUA TABLE

Client
ESTABLISHED & SONS,
LONDON, UK

Date
2005

Taking on as fundamental a furniture type as the table is just the kind of challenge that Zaha Hadid enjoys. Here she creates continuity between the surface of the table and its supports, no longer condemned to the traditional pattern of a plane supported by four legs.

Sich mit einer so fundamentalen Möbelgattung wie dem Tisch auseinanderzusetzen, ist genau die Art von Herausforderung, der sich Hadid gern stellt. Hier definiert sie ein Kontinuum aus Tischoberfläche und -basis, das sich nicht mehr auf das traditionelle Muster einer Platte mit vier Beinen reduzieren lässt.

S'emparer d'un type de meuble aussi basique que la table est un de ces défis qu'apprécie Zaha Hadid. Ici, elle crée une continuité entre les surfaces de la table et ses supports et se libère de la configuration traditionnelle du plateau soutenu par quatre pieds.

Z-CAR I AND II

Client
KENNY SCHACHTER, ROVE LLP, LONDON, UK

Date
2005-08

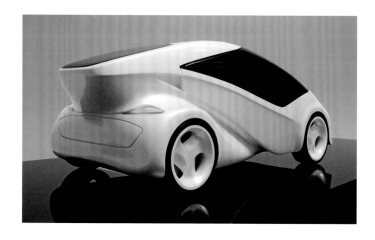

The automobile (above Z-Car II, below Z-Car I), perhaps even more than the table, has functional requirements that condition its form. Zaha Hadid succeeds here in imposing her own design while respecting the mechanical and spatial needs of the car.

Das Auto (oben Z-Car II, unten Z-Car I) muss funktionalen Anforderungen, die seine Form bedingen, vielleicht noch stärker gerecht werden als ein Tisch. Hier gelingt es Hadid, ihr eigenes Design zu verwirklichen und zugleich die mechanischen und räumlichen Erfordernisse eines Autos zu berücksichtigen.

L'automobile (ci-dessus : Z-Car II, ci-dessous : Z-Car I), plus encore que la table, présente des contraintes fonctionnelles qui conditionnent sa forme. Zaha Hadid a réussi à imposer son propre design tout en respectant les exigences mécaniques et spatiales d'une voiture.

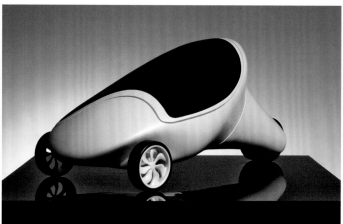

Rising up in the air, the Belu Bench acts to define space more than a purely sculptural object
might. It is at once abstract and usable, no small
accomplishment.

Die aufwärts strebende Belu Bench definiert den
Raum eher wie ein skulpturales Objekt. Sie ist ab-
strakt und funktional zugleich, was keine geringe
Leistung ist.

S'élevant dans les airs, le banc Belu définit l'espace
plus qu'un objet purement sculptural ne pourrait
le faire. Il est à la fois abstrait et utilisable, ce qui
n'est pas une petite réussite.

Project
BELU BENCH
Client
**KENNY SCHACHTER, ROVE LLP,
LONDON, UK**
Date
2005

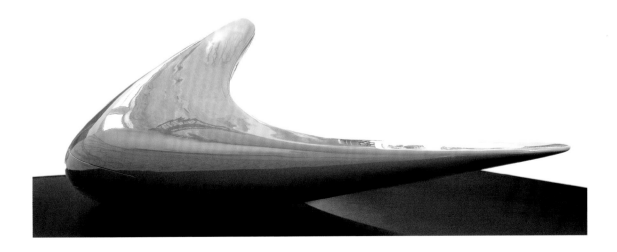

ZAHA HADID AT THE SOLOMON R. GUGGENHEIM MUSEUM

New York, NY, USA. 2006

Project
ZAHA HADID AT THE SOLOMON R. GUGGENHEIM MUSEUM

Location
NEW YORK, NY, USA

Client
SOLOMON R. GUGGENHEIM MUSEUM

Under Frank Lloyd Wright's celebrated rotunda, the work of Zaha Hadid takes on a particular aura, relating her work for the time of the exhibition to that of another great architect who did not fear curves nor even the idea of a spiraling museum ramp.

Unter Frank Lloyd Wrights berühmter Rotunde gewinnt Zaha Hadids Werk eine besondere Aura. Es tritt in Dialog mit dem eines anderen großen Architekten, der nicht vor geschwungenen Formen oder gar der Idee eines Museums mit spiralförmiger Rampe zurückschreckte.

Sous la fameuse rotonde de Frank Lloyd Wright, le travail de Zaha Hadid prend une aura particulière. Son œuvre est ainsi reliée à celle d'un autre grand architecte qui ne craignait ni les courbes ni l'idée d'un musée organisé autour d'une rampe en spirale.

Held between June 3 and October 25, 2006, this was retrospective exhibiton of Zaha Hadid's works, over the preceding 30 years. The show was organized by Germano Celant (Senior Curator, Contemporary Art) and Monica Ramirez-Montagut (Assistant Curator, Architecture & Design) together with the ZHA team led in this instance by Woody Yao. Zaha Hadid's interdisciplinary approach with "a wide range of mediums on display including painting, drawing, large-scale urban plans, proposals for international design competitions, building designs for contemporary cultural and sports facilities, documentation of current projects under construction, and a site-specific work created especially for the Solomon R. Guggenheim Museum rotunda" formed the show. The exhibition also included Hadid's 1992 design for *The Great Utopia* exhibition, also held in Frank Lloyd Wright's rotunda at the Guggenheim.

Diese Ausstellung im New Yorker Guggenheim-Museum vom 3. Juni bis 25. Oktober 2006 war eine Retrospektive des in den vergangenen 30 Jahren entstandenen Werks Zaha Hadids. Organisiert wurde die Schau von Germano Celant (Chefkurator für zeitgenössische Kunst) und Monica Ramirez-Montagut (Assistenzkuratorin für Architektur und Design) in Zusammenarbeit mit einem Team aus dem Büro von Zaha Hadid, in diesem Fall unter der Leitung von Woody Yao. Im Mittelpunkt der Ausstellung stand Zaha Hadids interdisziplinärer Ansatz. Gezeigt wurde „eine große Bandbreite verschiedener Medien, darunter Gemälde, Zeichnungen, großformatige Stadtplanungsentwürfe, Beiträge zu internationalen Architekturwettbewerben, Bauentwürfe für zeitgenössische Kultur- und Sporteinrichtungen, Dokumentationen aktueller, im Bau befindlicher Projekte sowie eine ortsspezifische, speziell für die Rotunde des Guggenheim-Museums entworfene Arbeit". Darüber hinaus präsentierte das Guggenheim auch Hadids Ausstellungsdesign für die Schau *The Great Utopia,* die im Jahr 1992 ebenfalls in der Rotunde des Guggenheim-Museums von Frank Lloyd Wright zu sehen gewesen war.

Du 3 juin au 25 octobre 2006, cette exposition rétrospective fut consacrée aux trente années précédentes de la carrière de Zaha Hadid. Son commissaire était Germano Celant (Senior curat, Contemporary art) assisté de Monica Ramirez-Montagut (Assistant-curator, Architecture et design), et en collaboration avec l'équipe de ZHA menée pour ce projet par Woody Yao. L'exposition retraçait l'approche interdisciplinaire de Zaha Hadid, « à partir d'une vaste gamme de médias, dont des peintures, des dessins, des plans d'urbanisme à grande échelle, des propositions pour des concours internationaux, des projets d'installations culturelles ou sportives, une documentations sur les projets en cours de construction et une œuvre spécifiquement conçue pour le lieu, la rotonde du musée Solomon R. Guggenheim. » L'exposition comprenait également le projet de Hadid pour « The Great Utopia », manifestation qui s'était également déroulée dans la rotonde du Guggenheim en 1992.

Project
SEAMLESS COLLECTION

Client
ESTABLISHED & SONS, LONDON, UK

Date
2006

By "Seamless," one might conclude that the architect means not so much objects that are joined together without a seam, but that can and do form a spatial continuity when placed together, or even when disposed separately in a given architectural volume.

Mit „Seamless" (dt. nahtlos) meint die Architektin vermutlich nicht nur nahtlos gefertigte Objekte, sondern deren Fähigkeit, ein räumliches Kontinuum zu erzeugen, sobald man sie zu Gruppen arrangiert oder in einem architektonischen Raum auch nur einzeln platziert.

Par le nom de « Seamless », on peut comprendre que l'architecte ne s'intéresse pas tant à des objets que l'on peut réunir sans joint, qu'à d'autres intégrables dans une continuité spatiale lorsqu'ils sont rapprochés ou même disposés séparément dans un volume architectural donné.

Zaha Hadid's own press release for this group of objects leaves no doubt about its intentions: "The 'Seamless' furniture collection for Established & Sons represents the result of Zaha Hadid Architects' exploration into a world of seamless fluidity. It is a built manifesto toward the potential for a new language of design and architecture, which is driven by the latest in digital design processes and the most cutting-edge manufacturing techniques." Intended to be employed together and to literally redefine the space they inhabit, these objects rely on the complex curvilinear geometry that has become a familiar element of Zaha Hadid's architecture. She relates this collection to the interiors of the Hotel Puerta América in Madrid (see page 214), to the Z-Scape (see page 530), or to the Aqua Table (see page 547). The smooth transition between the different parts of objects as opposed to the visible joints or right angles so typical of furniture mark Hadid's originality. The collection was exhibited at the auctioneers Phillips de Pury & Company in New York in 2006, in limited editions, shortly after the Guggenheim *Zaha Hadid* exhibition, a confirmation that these objects, presented as her "first ever collection of furniture," are decidedly to be placed at the juncture between art, architecture, and design. The firm Established & Sons, created by Angad Paul and Alasdhair Willis, was first seen at the Milan Fair in 2005. Hadid's Aqua Table was presented with their first collection and a prototype of the table sold at Phillips de Pury in December 2005 for $296 000.

Zaha Hadids Presseerklärung zu dieser Objektserie lässt keinen Zweifel an deren Zielsetzung: „Die Seamless-Möbelserie für Established & Sons ist das Ergebnis der Erkundungen Zaha Hadids in einer Welt nahtloser, fließender Übergänge. Sie ist ein materielles Manifest, ein Plädoyer für das Potenzial einer neuen Formensprache in Design und Architektur, angeregt von den neuesten digitalen Entwurfsprozessen und zukunftsweisenden Fertigungstechniken." Die Objekte sind dazu gedacht, als Gruppe zum Einsatz zu kommen und den Raum, den sie besetzen, buchstäblich neu zu definieren. Sie zeichnen sich durch jene komplexen, gerundeten Geometrien aus, die inzwischen zu einem so vertrauten Element in Zaha Hadids Architektur geworden sind. Hadid stellt die Kollektion in Zusammenhang mit dem Hotel Puerta América in Madrid (siehe Seite 214), der Z-Scape-Serie (siehe Seite 530) oder dem Tisch Aqua (siehe Seite 547). Die sanften Übergänge der verschiedenen Objektteile – statt der für Möbel so typischen

sichtbaren Verbindungsstücke oder rechten Winkel – zeugen von Hadids Originalität. Präsentiert wurde die Kollektion 2006 in limitierter Auflage im Auktionshaus Phillips de Pury & Company in New York. Kurze Zeit später fand im Guggenheim-Museum die Ausstellung *Zaha Hadid* statt, eine weitere Bestätigung, dass diese Objekte, präsentiert als ihre „erste Möbelkollektion überhaupt", definitiv an der Schittstelle von Kunst, Architektur und Design anzusiedeln sind. Established & Sons, gegründet von Angad Paul und Alasdhair Willis, hatten ihren ersten Auftritt 2005 auf der Mailänder Möbelmesse. Hadids Tisch Aqua war Teil ihrer ersten Kollektion; ein Prototyp des Tischs wurde im Dezember 2005 bei Phillips de Pury für 296 000 Dollar verkauft.

Le communiqué de presse sur ce groupe d'objets envoyés par Zaha Hadid ne laisse aucun doute sur ses intentions : « La collection de mobilier "Seamless" pour Established & Sons est l'aboutissement de l'exploration d'un univers conceptuel de fluidité sans rupture par Zaha Hadid Architects. C'est un manifeste en faveur du potentiel d'un nouveau langage en design et architecture, que permettent les processus de conception par ordinateur les plus avancés et des techniques de fabrication d'avant-garde. » Prévus pour être utilisés ensemble et littéralement redéfinir l'espace qu'ils occupent, ces objets illustrent la géométrie curviligne complexe qui est devenue un composant familier de l'architecture de Zaha Hadid. Elle relie cette collection aux aménagements intérieurs de l'Hotel Puerta América à Madrid (voir page 214), au Z-Scape (voir page 530) et à la table « Aqua » (voir page 547). C'est la transition sans la moindre rupture entre les différentes parties de ces objets mobiliers, par opposition aux joints visibles ou aux angles droits typiques des meubles habituels, qui marque l'originalité de Zaha Hadid. Cette collection a été exposée dans la maison de vente aux enchères Phillips de Pury & Company à New York en 2006, et proposée en édition limitée lors de l'exposition « Zaha Hadid » au Guggenheim Museum, confirmation que ces objets, présentés comme sa « première collection de meubles jamais réalisée », occupent décidément une place à la croisée de l'art, de l'architecture et du design. La société Established & Sons, créée par Angad Paul et Alasdhair Willis, est apparue pour la première fois à la Foire de Milan en 2005 où elle présentait la table « Aqua » de Zaha Hadid dans sa première collection. Un prototype de la table a été vendu par Phillips de Pury en décembre 2005 pour 296 000 dollars.

Zaha Hadid's objects are willfully placed at the frontier between abstraction and the domestic object. They look like nothing one ever normally sits on and yet they are designed to be sat on, or eaten on, in the case of a table. They are also the agents of alchemy of space, agents provocateurs in a certain sense.

Zaha Hadids Objekte stehen bewusst an der Grenze zwischen Abstraktion und Wohnobjekt. Sie ähneln nichts, worauf wir normalerweise sitzen und doch wurden sie zum Sitzen entworfen oder – im Fall eines Tisches –, um von ihnen zu essen. Sie sind Agenten einer räumlichen Alchemie, erweisen sich in gewisser Weise als Agents Provocateurs.

Les créations de Zaha Hadid franchissent volontairement la frontière entre l'abstraction et l'objet domestique. Elles ne ressemblent à aucun siège connu, mais en même temps sont conçues pour s'asseoir, ou pour manger comme dans le cas des tables. Ce sont également les agents d'une alchimie de l'espace, des agents provocateurs en un certain sens.

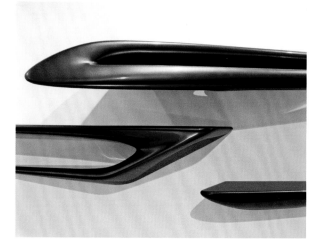

Location/Date
Area/Size
Type of Building/Object
Client

**ELASTIKA,
MIAMI ART BASEL**
Miami, FL, USA. 2005

Installation
design.05 Miami

SKI TOURING TUNNEL
Oberhof, Germany. 10/2005–02/2006
10 000 m² site /6513 m² building
Cross-country skiing tunnel
Stadt Oberhof

**CHENNAI
TECHNOLOGICAL PARK**
Chennai, India. 2005–08
140 000 m²
Mixed-use development
India Land and Properties Ltd.

I TOWER
Business Bay, Dubai, UAE. 2006
23 360 m²
Residential development
Omniyat Properties

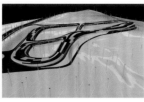

Location/Date
Area/Size
Type of Building/Object
Client

**ZAHA HADID,
GUGGENHEIM MUSEUM**
New York, NY, USA. 2006

Exhibition
Solomon R. Guggenheim Museum

33-35 HOXTON SQUARE
London, UK. 2006
3000 m²
Art gallery, offices and apartments
ROVE Developments LLP

**ARCHITECTURE
FOUNDATION**
London, UK. 2006
640 m²
Exhibition space, cafe, offices
Architecture Foundation

**TAIPEI HIGH-SPEED
AIRPORT RAIL LINK**
Taipei, Taiwan. 2006
Master plan 30 hectares
Residential tower
Department of Rapid Transit Systems

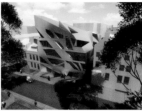

Location/Date
Area/Size
Type of Building/Object
Client

**GUGGENHEIM
SINGAPORE**
Singapore, Singapore. 2006

Art museum
Guggenheim-Hermitage

**CAPITAL HILL
RESIDENCE**
Moscow, Russia. 2006–14
2650 m²
Private residence
Private client

**METROPOLITAN OPERA
HOUSE TAICHUNG**
Taichung, Taiwan. 2006

Central metropolitan opera house
Taichung Municipal Government

**DUBAI OPERA HOUSE
AND CULTURAL CENTER**
Dubai, UAE. 2006–
36 000 m²
Opera house, cultural center, and hotel
Sama Dubai

Location/Date
Area/Size
Type of Building/Object
Client

**EVELYN GRACE
ACADEMY**
London, UK. 2006–10
10 745 m²
Secondary school for 1200 pupils
ARK Schools

EDIFICI CAMPUS
Barcelona, Spain. 2006–
27 650 m²
Offices, university, exhibition hall, retail
El Consorci / Consorci El Campus
Interuniversitari del Besòs

CMA CGM TOWER
Marseille, France. 2006–11
93 200 m²
Head offices and parking
CMA CGM

**ISSAM FARES
INSTITUTE, AUB, BEIRUT**
Beirut, Lebanon. 2006–13
5500 m²
University institute building
AUB American University of Beirut

Location/Date
Area/Size
Type of Building/Object
Client

**KARTAL PENDIK
MASTER PLAN**
Istanbul, Turkey. 2006–
555 hectares (5.5 million m²)
Proposal for a new city center
Greater Istanbul Municipality and Kartal
Urban Regeneration Association

**PEOPLE'S
CONFERENCE HALL**
Tripoli, Libya. 2006
45 000 m² + 40 000 m² parking
Conference center
Eng. Consult. Off. for Utilities Org. for
Development of Administrative Centers

**NURAGIC AND
CONT. ART MUSEUM**
Cagliari, Italy. 2006–
12 000 m²
Art museum
Regione Autonoma della Sardegna,
Assessorato Pubblica Istruzione

SCJ PROJECT HONOR

Racine, WI, USA. 2006

Johnson Campus
SC Johnson Wax

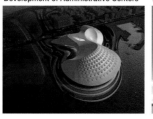

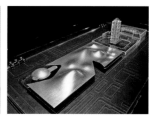

SWARM CHANDELIER

Location/Date: 2006
Area/Size:
Type of Building/Object: Chandelier
Client: Established & Sons

LOUIS VUITTON ICONE BAG

2006

Bag
Louis Vuitton Malletier

ONE-NORTH BUILDING

Singapore, Singapore. 2006

Rock Productions

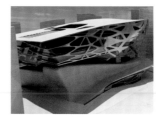

SZERVITA SQUARE

Budapest, Hungary. 2006–
ca. 32 000 m²
Office and retail
Orco Property Group

HEIDSIECK HEADQUARTERS

Location/Date: Reims, France. 2006
Area/Size: 1600 m²
Type of Building/Object: Corporate headquarters
Client: Charles & Piper Heidsieck Champagne

VALENCIA MASTER PLAN

Valencia, Spain. 2006

Master plan
City of Valencia

E.ON ENERGY RESEARCH DEPT. – RWTH AACHEN

Aachen, Germany. 2006
Gross floor area 6900 m²

Building and Real Estate NRW

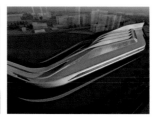

SEAMLESS COLLECTION

2006

Furniture collection
Established & Sons

EXPOCENTER EXHIBITION HALLS

Location/Date: Moscow, Russia. 2006–
Area/Size:
Type of Building/Object: Office, retail, and residential towers
Client: BCI Construction Limited

GLOBUS PLAZA

Baku, Azerbaijan. 2006
109 343 m²
Hotel and residential development
Taher Gozel

SIGNATURE TOWERS

Dubai, UAE. 2006–
1 000 000 m²
Mixed-use development
Dubai Properties

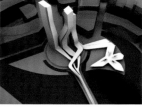

DUBAI BUSINESS BAY SIGNATURE BRIDGE

Dubai, UAE. 2006–
360 000 m²
Mixed-use development
Dubai Properties

CULTURAL CENTER

Location/Date: Dubai, UAE. 2006
Area/Size:
Type of Building/Object: Cultural center
Client: Dubai Properties

THYSSENKRUPP HEADQUARTERS

Essen, Germany. 2006
146 100 m²
Corporate headquarters
ThyssenKrupp AG

MIDDLE EAST CENTRE ST ANTONY'S COLLEGE

Oxford, UK. 2006–14
1200 m²
Academic building
St Antony's College University of Oxford

MIAMI ART BASEL

Miami, FL, USA. 2006

Installation
Kenny Schachter ROVE

GARMISCH SKI JUMP

Location/Date: Bavaria, Germany. 2006
Area/Size:
Type of Building/Object: Ski jump
Client: Markt Garmisch-Partenkirchen

HAMBURG RIVER PROMENADE

Hamburg, Germany. 2006–
750 m
Promenade walk and facilities
Landesbetrieb Straßen, Brücken u. Gewässer

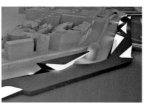

REPUBLIC SQUARE

Almaty, Republic of Kazakstan. 2006–
150 000 m²
Mixed-use development
TS Engineering

ATELIER NOTIFY

Paris, France. 2006–
670 m²
Atelier concept
CRYSTAL DENIM SAS

Location/Date	
Area/Size	
Type of Building/Object	
Client	

FOREST OF TOWERS, ROVE GALLERY
London, UK. 2006
50 m²
Exhibition
Kenny Schachter ROVE

FLOW VASE
2006–07

Vase
Serralunga

SOCAR TOWER
Baku, Azerbaijan. 2006
Gross area 42 242 m²
Offices
Socar, State oil company of Azerbaijan Republic

OFFICE BUILDING
Innsbruck, Germany. 2006–08
7000 m²
Offices
Malojer

MUSEUM FOLKWANG
Essen, Germany. 2006

Museum
Neubau Museum Folkwang Essen GmbH

VALENTINSKAMP COMPETITION
Hamburg, Germany. 2006

Office and housing
Union Investment Real Estate AG

ADIDAS MARKETING
Herzogenaurach, Germany. 10/2006–04/07
53 400 m² 1st phase; 80 600 m² 2nd phase
Office building development
Adidas AG

U2 TOWER
Dublin, Ireland. 2006

Mixed-use development
Treasury Holdings Ireland

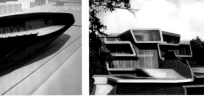

ADMINISTRATION COMPLEX TRIPOLI
Tripoli, Libya. 2006
Mixed-use development
Great Socialist People's Libyan Arab Jamahiriya, Organization for Development of Administrative Centers

FRANKFURT WESELER WERFT EXHIBIT. SPACE
Frankfurt, Germany. 2006

Temporary exhibition space
Deutsche Bank

KUSNACHT 1
Zurich, Switzerland. 2006–
Each villa 1000 m²
Two exclusive villas
Private Client

NATIONAL ART GALLERY SINGAPORE
Singapore, Singapore. 2006
GFA 40 600 m²
Museum
Singapore Ministry of Information, Communications and the Arts [MICA]

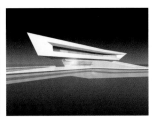

MUNANDHUA ISLAND RESORT
Maldives, Maldives. 2006

High-end luxury resort
Confidential

VILLA HILLINGER
Lake Neusiedl, Austria. 2007–09
Gross floor area 700 m²
Residential villa
Private Client

PRIVATE VILLA
Austria. 2007–09
800 m²
Residential
Private Client

VILNIUS MUSEUM
Vilnius, Lithuania. 2007–
13 000 m²
Museum, cultural center
City of Vilnius

SILVER BOWL
2007

Bowl in sterling silver
Sawaya & Moroni

OPUS OFFICE TOWER
Dubai, UAE. 2007–
84 345 m²
Office tower
Omniyat Properties

MOBILE ART, CHANEL CONT. ART CONTAINER
Hong Kong, Tokyo, New York. 2007–08
29 m x 45 m / total of 700 m²
Traveling exhibition pavilion
Chanel

DUBAI FINANCIAL MARKET
Dubai, UAE. 2007–
42 000 m²
Mixed-use development
Dubai Properties

IDEAL HOUSE, 07 CO-LOGNE FURNITURE FAIR

Cologne, Germany. 2007

Installation
German Design Council

HEYDAR ALIYEV CULTURAL CENTER

Baku, Azerbaijan. 2007–13
52 417 m²
Mixed-use cultural center
The Republic of Azerbaijan

CIVIL COURTS MADRID

Madrid, Spain. 2007–
74 448 m²
Courts of law
Campus de la Justicia de Madrid

GRONINGER FORUM

Groningen, The Netherlands. 2007

Forum
City of Groningen

Location/Date
Area/Size
Type of Building/Object
Client

MOON SYSTEM

2007

Seating
B&B Italia

NK PERFORMING ARTS CENTER

Kaohsiung, Taiwan. 2007
Building area 20 500 m²; floor area 103 400 m²
National performing arts center
Taiwan Council for Cultural Affairs

GLOBUS PLAZA

Baku, Azerbaijan. 2007
Site area 38 892 m²; project area 109 343 m²
Hotel and residential development
Taher Gozel

BAHRAIN INTERNATIONAL CIRCUIT

Bahrain, Bahrain. 2007
100 hectares
Car manufacturing master plan
BIC & MCC Project Partners

Location/Date
Area/Size
Type of Building/Object
Client

ZAHA HADID, ARCH. AND DESIGN, DESIGN MUSEUM

London, UK. 2007
1300 m²
Exhibition
Design Museum

MAJAN PARK TOWER

Dubai, UAE. 2007–
27 000 m², 30 stories
Office and mixed-use tower
Hamshari-Dahleh Property Mgmt Ltd

SALLE PHILARMONIQUE

Paris, France. 2007
Total net area 35 500 m²
Concert hall, exhibition space, educational center, restaurant, offices
Philharmonie De Paris

UNIVERSITY COLLEGE DUBLIN GATEWAY

Dublin, Ireland. 2007

University College Dublin Gateway
University College Dublin

Location/Date
Area/Size
Type of Building/Object
Client

REGIUM WATERFRONT

Reggio Calabria, Italy. 2007–
Museum 8375 m² + center 13 000 m²
Museum and multifunctional center
Comune di Reggio Calabria

NILE TOWER

Cairo, Egypt. 2007–
10 000 m²
Hotel and apartment tower
Living in Interiors

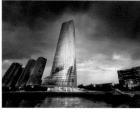

MESA TABLE

2007

Table
Vitra AG

CENTRO URVASCO

Vitoria, Spain. 2007–
10 000 m²
Office and expo centers
Centro Urvasco

Location/Date
Area/Size
Type of Building/Object
Client

URBAN VOIDS, LISBON TRIENNALE

Lisbon, Portugal. 2007

Installation
Lisbon Triennale

BERNIA HOTEL, MIRAGOLF

Alicante, Spain. 2007
29 000 m²
7-star hotel & wellness center
Miragolf Playa, S.A

WINTERFESTSPIELHAUS

Erl, Austria. 2007
Gross floor area 6000 m²
Festival hall extension
Passionsspielverein Erl

SALOBREÑA

Salobreña, Spain. 2007

Lift station and viewing platform
Salobreña Town Council

Location/Date
Area/Size
Type of Building/Object
Client

DUNE FORMATIONS, VENICE BIENNALE 2007

Location/Date Scuola dei Mercanti, Venice, Italy. 2007
Area/Size
Type of Building/Object 20 furniture pieces
Client David Gill Galleries

DONGDAEMUN WORLD DESIGN PARK AND PLAZA

Seoul, Korea. 2007–14
83 000 m² + 30 000 m² park
Park and design complex
Seoul Metropolitan Government

WONDERWALL, SELFRIDGES

London, UK. 2007

Exhibition
Selfridges

PEOPLE'S ASSEMBLY

Damascus, Syria. 2007
Gross area 42 500 m²
Public building
The People's Assembly in the Syrian
Arab Republic

NATIONAL HOLDING HEADQUARTERS

Location/Date Abu Dhabi, UAE. 2007
Area/Size 34 286 m²
Type of Building/Object Headquarters building
Client Emirates Int. Investment Company L.L.C.

CRATER

2007

Table
David Gill Galleries

WMF CUTLERY

2007

Cutlery
WMF-AG

33 WAITANYAUN

Shanghai, China. 2007
Total area 40 000 m²
Museum and boutique hotel
Handel Lee

GLOBAL CITIES, TATE MODERN

Location/Date London, UK. 2007
Area/Size
Type of Building/Object Exhibition
Client Tate Modern

LILAS INSTALLATION, SERPENTINE GALLERY

London, UK. 2007
310 m²
Temporary tensile fabric installation
Serpentine Gallery

ELI & EDYTHE BROAD ART MUSEUM

East Lansing, MI, USA. 2007–12
4274 m²
Museum for university campus
Michigan State University

NASSIM ROAD VILLAS

Singapore, Singapore. 2007–12

Two villas
Satinder Garcha

SURFERS PARADISE TRANSIT CENTRE

Location/Date Surfers Paradise, Qld., Australia. 2007
Area/Size 119 100 m², height: 346.60 m
Type of Building/Object Redevelopment of transit center
Client Sunland Group

URBAN NEBULA, SIZE & MATTER

Royal Festival Hall, London, UK. 2007
2.4 m x 11.3 m x 4.6 m
Installation for the London Design Festival
London Design Festival 2007

LILIUM TOWER

Warsaw, Poland. 2007–
Gross floor area 130 000 m²
Housing and mixed-use development
Lilium Polska Sp. z o.o.

INNOVATION TOWER

Hong Kong, China. 2007–13
15 000 m²
School of Design development
Hong Kong Polytechnic University

BAHRAIN MUSEUM OF CONTEMPORARY ART

Location/Date Al Muharraq, Bahrain. 2007–
Area/Size 10 000 m²
Type of Building/Object Museum of Contemporary Art
Client H. H. Shaikha Mai Mohammed Al Khalifa,
Culture & National Heritage Sector

D'LEEDON

Singapore, Singapore. Master plan 2007
220 000 m² towers + 70 000 m² basement
Residential towers and landscape deck
CapitaLand

PORT HOUSE

Antwerp, Belgium. 2008–15
12 800 m²
Port headquarters
Antwerp Port Authority

AVILION TRIFLOW TAPS

2008

Tap
Avilion

D-VILLA

Location/Date — Dellis Cay, Turks & Caicos Islands. 2008
Area/Size — 585 m²
Type of Building/Object — Ocean-view villa
Client — The O Property Collection

MELISSA

2008

Footwear
Grendene S/A

ABU DHABI PERFORMING ARTS CENTER

Abu Dhabi, UAE. 2008–
62 770 m²
Performing arts center
The Tourism Development and Investment Company of Abu Dhabi

HOME HOUSE

London, UK. 2008
158 m²
Private members club interior
Home House Ltd

NEIL BARRETT FLAGSHIP STORE

Location/Date — Tokyo, Japan. 2008
Area/Size — 400 m²
Type of Building/Object — Interior design, flagship store
Client — Neil Barrett

LAZAAR FOUNDATION

Tunis, Tunisia. 2008
6000 m²
Foundation building
Mr. Kamel Lazaar

PERM MUSEUM

Perm, Russia. 2008
22 550 m²
Art museum
Perm Administration and Ministry of Culture

BBVA BANK

Madrid, Spain. 2008
100 000 m²
Corporate headquarters
BBVA Bank

TORUS BAR

Location/Date — 2008
Area/Size —
Type of Building/Object — Bar, lounge
Client — Kenny Schachter ROVE

CITADEL CAPITAL OFFICE BUILDINGS

Cairo, Egypt. 2008–
26 000 m² (+12 000 m² undergr. parking)
Office buildings
Citadel Capital

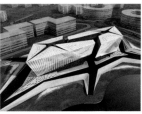

ZAHA HADID CHANDELIER

Swarowski Crystal Palace, Milan, Italy. 2008

Chandelier
Swarovski Crystal Palace

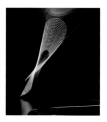

NEXT GENE ARCHITECTURE MUSEUM

Taipei, Taiwan. 2008–
700 m²
Museum
De-Nian International Company, Inc.

SMART VILLAGE LANDMARK PAVILION

Location/Date — Cairo, Egypt. 2008–
Area/Size — 4000 m²
Type of Building/Object — Conference and exhibition center
Client — The Egyptian Government

CELESTE NECKLACE AND CUFF

2008

Showpiece jewelry
Swarovski Gem Couture, Runway Rocks

VIENNA TOWER

Vienna, Austria. 2008–
100 000 m²
Mixed-use development
Confidential

CIRRUS

2008

Furniture
L & R Rosenthal Center for Cont. Art

KING ABDULLAH II HOUSE OF CULTURE & ART

Location/Date — Amman, Jordan. 2008–
Area/Size — 26 800 m²
Type of Building/Object — Performing arts center
Client — The Greater Amman Municipality

DOROBANTI TOWER

Bucharest, Romania. 2008–
100 000 m²
5-star hotel/apartments
Smartown Investments

MAISON & OBJET

Paris, France. 2008
100 m²
Exhibition/installation
Maison & Objet

WIRL

Hong Kong, China. 2008
Inscribed from 3 m x 3 m cube
Seating, sculpture
Sun Hung Kai Properties Ltd

Location/Date
Area/Size
Type of Building/Object
Client

Z-STREAM, SUDELEY CASTLE
Gloucestershire, UK. 2008

Slide
Kenny Schachter, Elliot McDonald, Mollie Dent-Brocklehurst

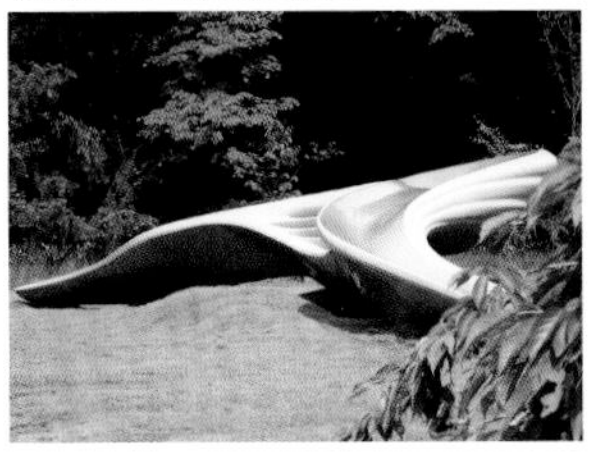

LOTUS, VENICE BIENNALE 2008
Corderie, Venice, Italy. 2008
85 m^2
Furniture/installation
ROVE

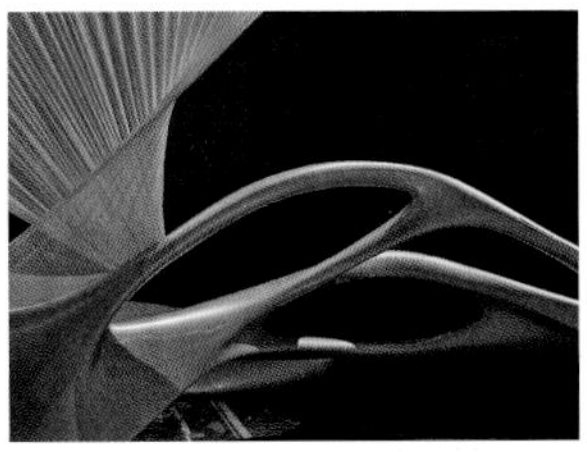

EXPERIMENTATION WITHIN A LONG WAVE OF INNOVATION
Venice, Italy. 2008
Exhibition
La Biennale di Venezia

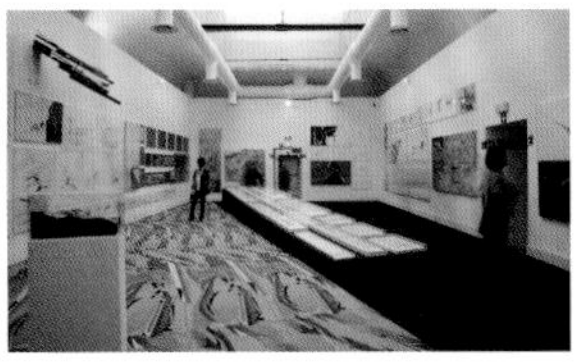

LACOSTE
2008–09

Footwear
Lacoste, Pentland

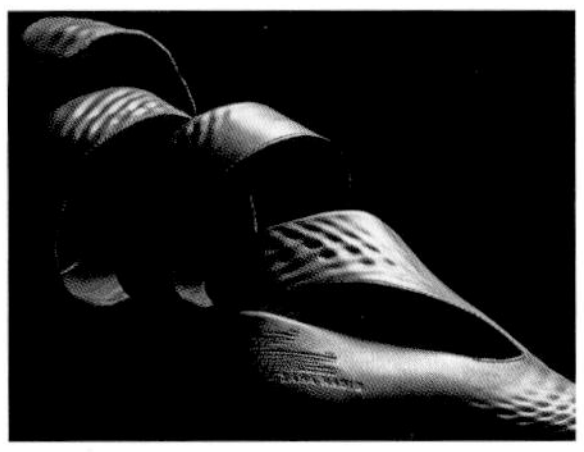

Location/Date
Area/Size
Type of Building/Object
Client

SCOOP SOFA
2008

Seating
Sawaya & Moroni and Kenny Schachter ROVE

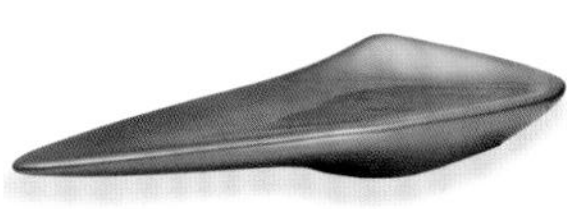

AURA L AND *AURA S* VILLA LA MALCONTENTA
Mira, Venice, Italy. 2008

Furniture
Venice Biennale, Fondazione La Malcontenta

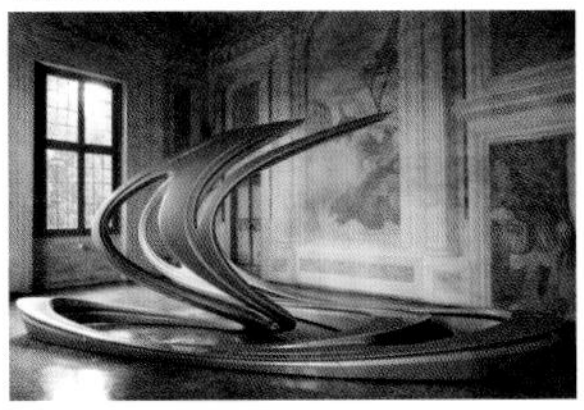

KLORIS, CHATSWORTH
Derbyshire, UK. 2008
6500 x 5100 x 80 mm
Outdoor seating
Julian Treger and Kenny Schachter ROVE

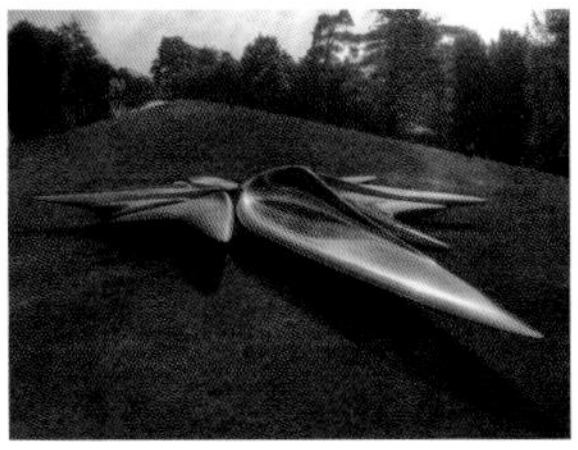

NEW PASSENGER TERMINAL AND MASTER PLAN
Zagreb Airport, Zagreb, Croatia. 2008–
75 000 m^2 airport + 500 000 m^2 master plan
Airport
Zraãna Luka Zagreb, Zagreb Airport

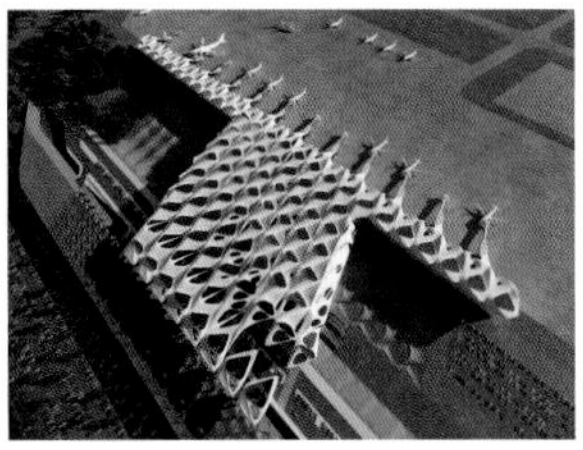

Location/Date
Area/Size
Type of Building/Object
Client

HAUSER & WIRTH TABLE HENRY MOORE EXHIBIT.
London, UK. 2008

Table, shelf, and exhibition design
Hauser and Wirth

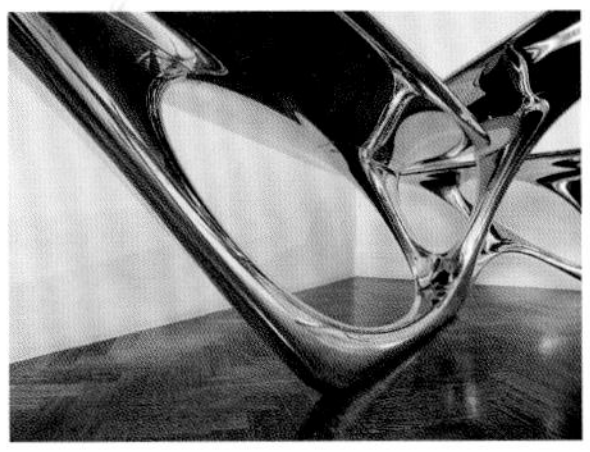

SEOUL TABLE AND YUNG HEE DESK
2008

Table and desk
NY Projects

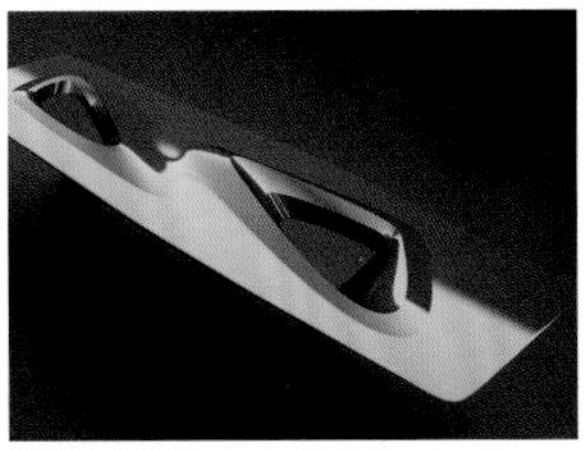

GALAXY SOHO
Beijing, China. 2008–12
332 857 m^2
Mixed-use development
Soho China

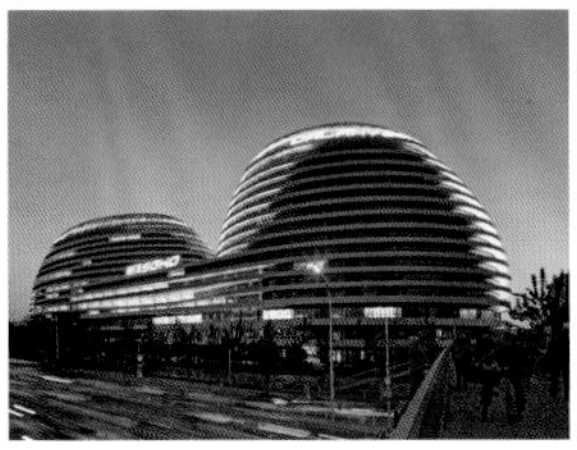

SYMBIOTIC VILLA
Taipei, Taiwan. 2008–10
700 m^2
Villa
De-Nian International Company, Inc.

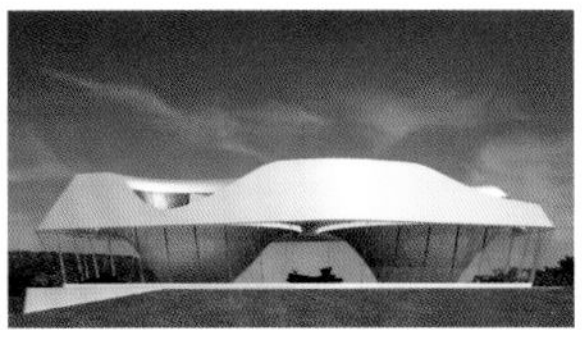

Location/Date
Area/Size
Type of Building/Object
Client

LIBRARY AND LEARNING CENTER, WU WIEN
Vienna, Austria. 2008–13
28 000 m^2
Library and learning center
University of Economics Vienna

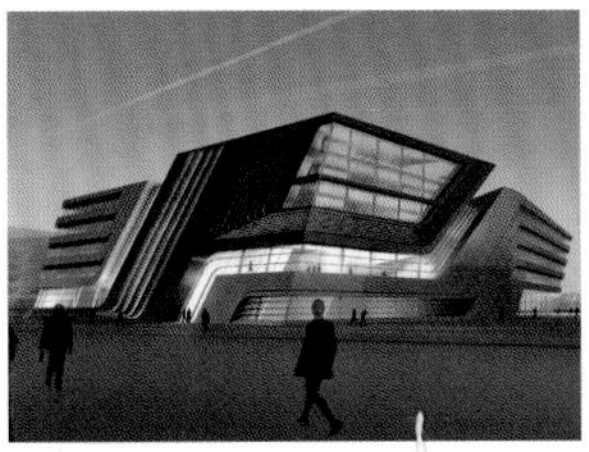

ZAHA HADID, SONNABEND/ROVE GALLERIES
New York, NY, USA. 2008

Exhibition
Julian Treger and Kenny Schachter

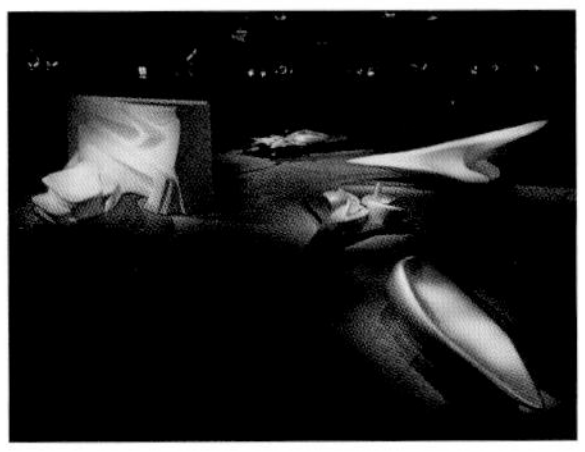

STONE TOWERS
Cairo, Egypt. 2008–
525 000 m^2
Business park, hotel and retail
Rooya Group

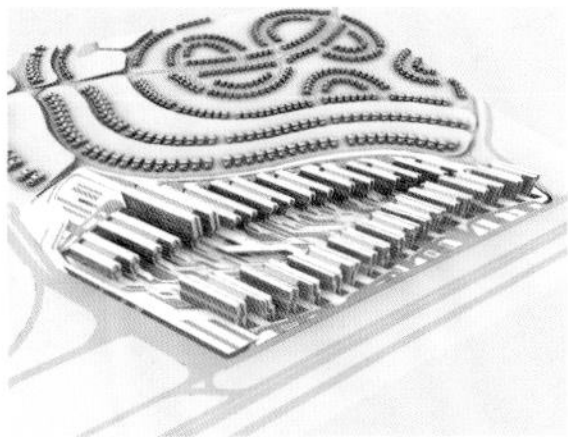

DESIGNER'S CHRISTMAS TREE
2008

Christmas tree for charity auction
Les Sapins de Noël des Créateurs

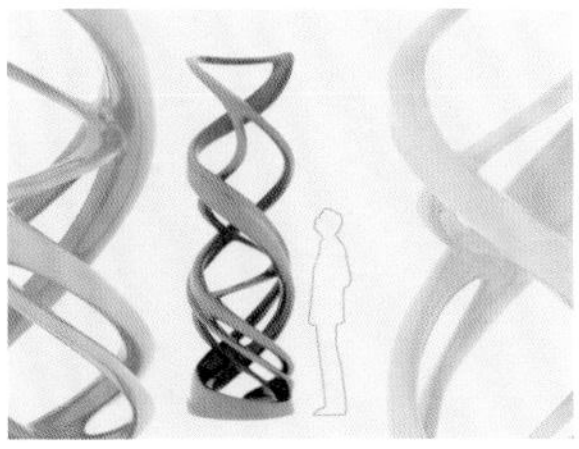

Location/Date
Area/Size
Type of Building/Object
Client

NEW BEETHOVEN CONCERT HALL
Bonn, Germany. 2008–09
Total floor area 12 800 m^2
Concert hall
Deutsche Post AG, Dt. Telekom, Dt. Postbank

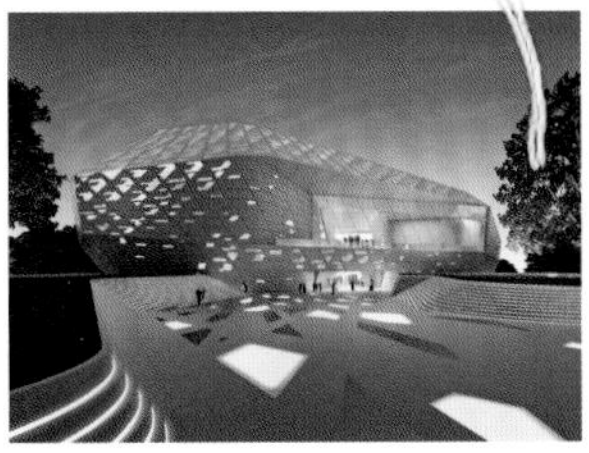

ROCA LONDON GALLERY
London, UK. 2009–11
1100 m^2
Conference and exhibition center
Roca

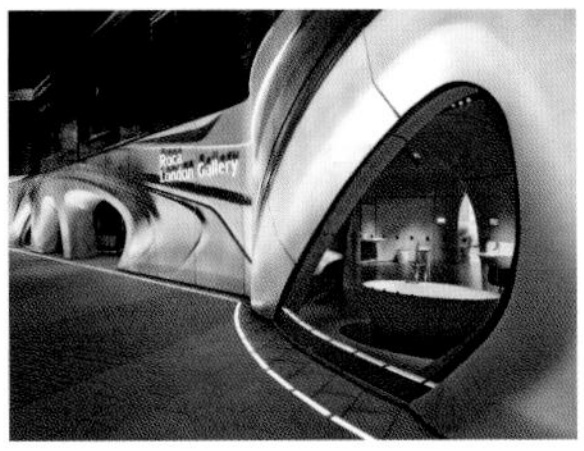

FRAUNHOFER-INSTITUT FÜR SILICATFORSCHUNG
Würzburg, Germany. 2009–
5775 m^2
Academic building
Fraunhofer-Institut für Silicatforschung

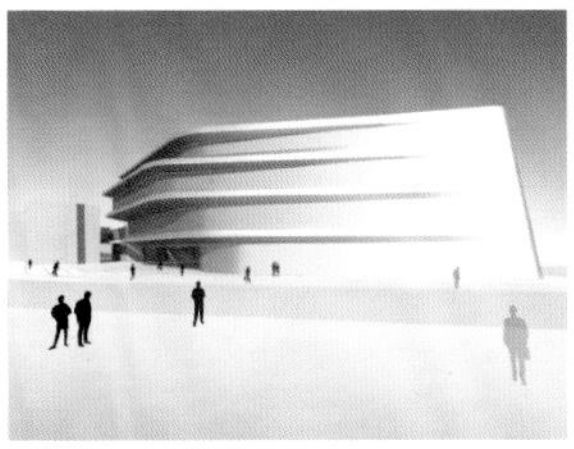

JESOLO RETAIL CENTER
Jesolo, Italy. 2009–14

Mixed-use development
Jesolo 3000 Home Group

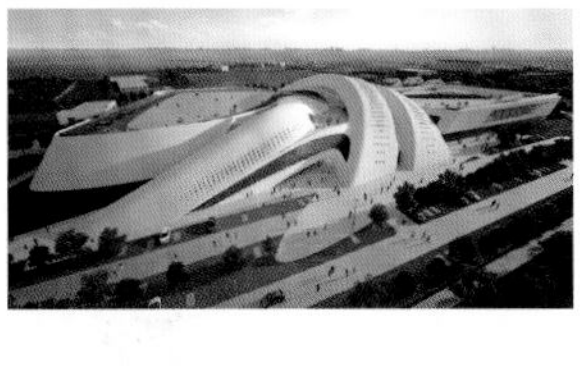

SOHO PEAKS

Beijing, China. 2009–14
Gross floor area 521 265 m²
Office and retail complex
SOHO China Ltd.

SERPENTINE SACKLER GALLERY

London, UK. 2010–2013
900 m²
Exhibition space renovation
The Serpentine Trust

FORM IN MOTION

Philadelphia, USA. 2011–12
395 m²
Exhibition
Philadelphia Museum of Art

Z-CHAIR

Milan, Italy. 2011
920 x 880 x 610 mm
Seating
Sawaya & Moroni

LIQUID GLACIAL TABLE

London, UK. 2012

Dining table
David Gill Galleries

ARUM, VENICE BIENNALE 2012

Corderie dell'Arsenale, Italy. 2012

Installation and exhibition
La Biennale di Venezia

KING ABDULLAH FINANCIAL DISTRICT

Riyadh, Saudi Arabia. 2012–17
20 434 m²
Metro station
Arriyadh Development Authority

NEW NATIONAL STADIUM OF JAPAN

Tokyo, Japan. 2012–19
290 000 m²
Stadium
Japan Sports Council

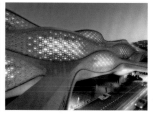
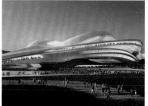

FUDGE POP-UP HAIR SALON

London, UK. 2012

Hair salon, showroom
Fudge Hair

AQUA AT DOVER STREET MARKET

London, UK. 2012

Window installation
Dover Street Market

PARAMETRIC TOWER RESEARCH

Cologne, Germany. 2012
300 m²
Exhibition
AIT-ArchitekturSalons

TWIRL

State University of Milan, Italy. 2012
800 m²
Installation
Lea Ceramiche and Interni

ESFERA CITY CENTER

Monterrey, Mexico. 2012–15

City center
Citelis, Organización Ramírez

SERAC BENCH

Salone del Mobile, Milan, Italy. 2013

Seating
LAB 23

KUKI CHAIR

Salone del Mobile, Milan, Italy. 2013

Seating
Sawaya & Moroni

ARIA & AVIA LAMPS

Salone del Mobile, Milan, Italy. 2013

Lighting
Slamp

ARRAY

Salone del Mobile, Milan, Italy. 2013

Auditorium seating
Poltrona Frau Contract

NOVA

Paris Fashion Week, France. 2013

Shoe
United Nude

PRIMA INSTALLATION

Weil am Rhein, Germany. 2013

Installation
Swarovski & Vitra

520 WEST 28TH STREET

New York, NY, USA. 2013–

Residential development
Related

ZAHA HADID ARCHITECTS STAFF CREDIT LIST FOR ALL FEATURED PROJECTS

IRISH PRIME MINISTER'S RESIDENCE
Design Team Zaha Hadid with K. Ahari, Jonathan Dunn

THE PEAK
Design Team Zaha Hadid with Michael Wolfson, Jonathan Dunn, Marianne van der Waals, N. Ayoubi
Presentation Michael Wolfson, Alistair Standing, Nan Lee, Wendy Galway

24 CATHCART ROAD
Design Team Zaha Hadid with Michael Wolfson, Brett Steele, Nan Lee, Brenda MacKneson

ZOLLHOF 3 MEDIA PARK
Design Zaha Hadid
Project Architects Brett Steele, Brian Ma Siy
Project Team Paul Brislin, Cathleen Chua, John Comparelli, Elden Croy, Craig Kiner, Graeme Little, Yousif Albustani, Daniel R. Oakley, Patrik Schumacher, Alistair Standing, Tuta Barbosa, David Gomersall, C. J. Lim
Competition Team Michael Wolfson, Anthony Owen, Signy Svalastoga, Craig Kiner, Edgar González, Patrik Schumacher, Ursula Gonsior, Bryan Langlands, Ed Gaskin, Yuko Moriyama, Graeme Little, Cristina Verissimo, Maria Rossi, Yousif Albustani

RHEINAUHAFEN REDEVELOPMENT
Design Zaha Hadid
Design Team Patrik Schumacher, Daniel R. Oakley, Craig Kiner, Yousif Albustani, Cathleen Chua, David Gomersall, John Stuart, Simon Koumijan
Model Tim Price

CARDIFF BAY OPERA HOUSE
Design Zaha Hadid
Project Architect Brian Ma Siy
Design Team Patrik Schumacher, Ljiljana Blagojevic, Graham Modlen, Paul Brislin, Edgar González, Paul Karakusevic, David Gomersall, Tomás Amat Guarinos, Wendy Ing, Paola Sanguinetti, Nunu Luan, Douglas Grieco, Woody K. T. Yao, Voon Yee-Wong, Anne Save de Beaurecueil, Simon Koumjian, Bijan Ganjei, Nicola Cousins
Models Ademir Volic, Michael Kennedy, James Wink

EXTENSION OF THE REINA SOFIA MUSEUM
Design Zaha Hadid with Patrik Schumacher
Design Team Sonia Villaseca, Christos Passas, Jorge Ortega, Eddie Can, Paola Cattarin, Chris Dopheide, Bergendy Cooke, Jee-Eun Lee, Caroline Voet, Oliver Domeisen, David Gomersall, Electra Mikelides

MUSEUM FOR THE ROYAL COLLECTION
Design Zaha Hadid with Patrik Schumacher
Design Team Sonia Villaseca, Christos Passas, Caroline Voet, Jorge Ortega, Eddie Can, Paola Cattarin, Jee-Eun Lee, David Gomersall, Chris Dopheide, Silvia Forlati, J. R. Kim

ART MUSEUM IN GRAZ
Design Zaha Hadid with Patrik Schumacher
Design Team Sonia Villaseca, Stanley Lau, Paola Cattarin, David Gerber, Eddie Can, Gianluca Racana, Yoash Oster, Janne Westermann

NATIONAL LIBRARY OF QUEBEC
Design Zaha Hadid with Patrik Schumacher
Project Team Stéphane Hof, Sonia Villaseca, Christos Passas, Chris Dopheide, Sara Klomps, Djorde Stojanovic, Dillon Lin, Lida Charsouli, Garin O'Aivazian, David Gerber, Andreas Durkin, Liam Young
Competition Model Ademir Volic

MOONSOON RESTAURANT
Design Zaha Hadid
Project Team Bill Goodwin, Shin Egashira, Kar Hwa Ho, Edgar González, Bryan Langlands, Ed Gaskin, Yuko Moriyama, Urit Luden, Craig Kiner, Dianne Hunter-Gorman, Patrik Schumacher

VITRA FIRE STATION
Design Zaha Hadid
Project Architect Patrik Schumacher
Design Team Simon Koumjian, Edgar González, Kar Wha Ho, Voon Yee-Wong, Craig Kiner, Cristina Verissimo, Maria Rossi, Daniel R. Oakley, Nicola Cousins, David Gomersall, Olaf Weishaupt
Local Architect Roland Mayer (Lörrach, Germany)

LANDSCAPE FORMATION ONE (LF ONE)
Design Zaha Hadid with Patrik Schumacher
Project Architect Markus Dochantschi
Project Director Patrik Schumacher
Project Team Oliver Domeisen, Wassim Halabi, Garin O'Aivazian, Barbara Pfenningstorff, James Lim
Local Architect Mayer Bahrle Freie Architeken DBA (Lörrach, Germany)

MIND ZONE, MILLENNIUM DOME
Design Zaha Hadid
Project Architect Jim Heverin
Project Team Barbara Kuit, Ana Sotrel, Graham Modlen, Patrik Schumacher

HOENHEIM-NORD TERMINUS
Design Zaha Hadid Architects
Local Firm Albert Grandadam (Strasbourg, France)
Project Architect Stéphane Hof
Project Team Silvia Forlati, Patrik Schumacher, Markus Dochantschi, David Salazar, Caroline Voet, Eddie Can, Stanley Lau, David Gerber, Chris Dopheide, Edgar Gonzáles

BERGISEL SKI JUMP
Design Zaha Hadid Architects
Local Firm Baumeister Ing. Georg Malojer (Innsbruck, Austria)
Project Architect Jan Hübener
Project Manager Markus Dochantschi
Design Team Matthias Frei, Cedric Libert, Silvia Forlati, Jim Heverin, Garin O'Aivazian, Sara Noel Costa de Araujo
Competition Team Ed Gaskin, Eddie Can, Yoash Oster, Stanley Lau, Janne Westermann

LOIS AND RICHARD ROSENTHAL CENTER OF CONTEMPORARY ART
Design Zaha Hadid Architects
Local Firm KZF incorporated (Cincinnati, USA)
Project Architect Markus Dochantschi

Assistant Project Architect Ed Gaskin
Project Team Ana Sotrel, Jan Hübener, David Gerber, Christos Passas,
Sonia Villaseca, James Lim, Jee-Eun Lee, Oliver Domeisen, Helmut Kinzler,
Patrik Schumacher, Michael Wolfson, David Gomersall
Competition Team Shumon Basar, Oliver Domeisen, Jee-Eun Lee, Terence Koh,
Marco Guarinieri, Stéphane Hof, Woody K. T. Yao, Ivan Pajares, Wassim Halabi,
Nan Atichapong, Graham Modlen
Models Chris Dopheide, Thomas Knüvener, Sara Klomps, Bergendy Cooke,
Florian Migsch, Sandra Oppermann, Ademir Volic

ORDRUPGAARD MUSEUM EXTENSION
Design Zaha Hadid
Project Architect Ken Bostock
Design Team Caroline Krogh Andersen
Competition Team Patrik Schumacher, Ken Bostock, Adriano De Gioannis,
Sara Noel Costa de Araujo, Lars Teichmann, Vivek Shankar, Cedric Libert,
Tiago Correia
Model Riann Steenkamp

PHAENO SCIENCE CENTER
Design Zaha Hadid with Christos Passas
Project Architect Christos Passas
Assistant Project Architect Sara Klomps
Special Contributor Patrik Schumacher
Project Team Sara Klomps, Gernot Finselbach, David Salazar, Helmut Kinzler
Competition Team Christos Passas, Janne Westermann, Chris Dopheide,
Stanley Lau, Eddie Can, Yoash Oster, Jan Hübener, Caroline Voet

BMW CENTRAL BUILDING
Design Zaha Hadid with Patrik Schumacher
Project Architects Jim Heverin, Lars Teichmann
Project Team Matthias Frei, Jan Hübener, Annette Bresinsky, Manuela Gatto, Fabian
Hecker, Cornelius Schlotthauer, Wolfgang Sunder, Anneka Wegener, Markus Planteu,
Robert Neumayr, Christina Beaumont, Achim Gergen, Caroline Anderson
Competition Team Lars Teichmann, Eva Pfannes, Ken Bostock, Stéphane Hof,
Djordje Stojanovic, Leyre Villoria, Liam Young, Christiane Fashek, Manuela Gatto,
Tina Gregoric, Cesare Griffa, Yasha Jacob Grobman, Filippo Innocenti, Zetta Kotsioni,
Debora Laub, Sarah Manning, Maurizio Meossi, Robert Sedlak, Niki Neerpasch,
Eric Tong, Tiago Correia

HOTEL PUERTA AMÉRICA
Design Zaha Hadid
Project Architect Woody K. T. Yao
Project Design Thomas Vietzke, Yael Brosilovski, Patrik Schumacher
Design Team Ken Bostock, Mirco Becker

MAGGIE'S CANCER CARE CENTRE FIFE
Design Zaha Hadid Architects
Project Architects Jim Heverin, Tiago Correia

NORDPARK RAILWAY STATIONS
Design Zaha Hadid with Patrik Schumacher
Project Architect Thomas Vietzke
Design Team Jens Borstelmann, Markus Planteu
Production Team Caroline Andersen, Makakrai Suthadarat, Marcela Spadaro,
Anneka Wagener, Adriano De Gioannis, Peter Pichler, Susann Berggren

MOBILE ART, CHANEL CONTEMPORARY ART CONTAINER
Design Zaha Hadid with Patrik Schumacher
Project Architects Thomas Vietzke, Jens Borstelmann
Project Team Helen Lee, Claudia Wulf, Erhan Patat, Tetsuya Yamasaki, Daniel Fiser

ZARAGOZA BRIDGE PAVILION
Design Zaha Hadid with Patrik Schumacher
Project Architect Manuela Gatto
Project Team Fabian Hecker, Matthias Baer, Soohyun Chang, Ignacio Choliz,
Federico Dunkelberg, Maria José Mendoza, José M. Monfa, Marta Rodriguez,
Diego Rosales, Guillermo Ruiz, Lucio Santos, Hala Sheikh, Marcela Spadaro,
Anat Stern, Jay Suthadarat
Competition Team Feng Chen, Atrey Chhaya, Dipal Kothari

MAXXI: NATIONAL MUSEUM OF XXI CENTURY ARTS
Design Zaha Hadid with Patrik Schumacher
Project Architect Gianluca Racana
Site Supervision Team Paolo Matteuzzi, Anja Simons, Mario Mattia
Project Team Anja Simons, Paolo Matteuzzi, Fabio Ceci, Mario Mattia, Maurizio
Meossi, Paolo Zilli, Luca Peralta, Maria Velceva, Matteo Grimaldi, Ana M. Cajiao,
Barbara Pfenningstorff, Dillon Lin, Ken Bostock, Raza Zahid, Lars Teichmann,
Adriano De Gioannis, Amin Taha, Caroline Voet, Gianluca Ruggeri, Luca Segarelli

SHEIKH ZAYED BRIDGE
Design Zaha Hadid
Project Architect Graham Modlen
Project Team Garin O'Aivazian, Christos Passas, Patrik Schumacher,
Sara Klomps, Zahira Nazer, Steve Power

GUANGZHOU OPERA HOUSE
Design Zaha Hadid
Project Directors Woody K. T. Yao, Patrik Schumacher
Project Leader Simon Yu
Project Team Jason Guo, Yang Jingwen, Long Jiang, Ta-Kang Hsu, Yi-Ching Liu,
Zhi Wang, Christine Chow, Cyril Shing, Filippo Innocenti, Lourdes Sánchez,
Hinki Kwong, Junkai Jian
Competition Team (1st stage) Filippo Innocenti, Matias Musacchio, Jenny Huang, Hon
Kong Chee, Markus Planteu, Paola Cattarin, Tamar Jacobs, Yael Brosilovski, Viggo Haremst,
Christian Ludwig, Christina Beaumont, Lorenzo Grifantini, Flavio La Gioia, Nina Safainia,
Fernando Pérez Vera, Martin Henn, Achim Gergen, Graham Modlen, Imran Mahmood
Competition Team (2nd stage) Cyril Shing, Yan Song Ma, Yosuke Hayano,
Adriano De Gioannis, Barbara Pfenningstorff

GLASGOW RIVERSIDE MUSEUM
Design Zaha Hadid Architects
Project Director Jim Heverin
Project Architect Johannes Hoffmann
Project Team Matthias Frei, Agnes Koltay, Malca Mizrahi, Tyen Masten,
Gemma Douglas, Daniel Baerlecken, Achim Gergen, Christina Beaumont,
Markus Planteu, Claudia Wulf, Alasdair Graham, Rebecca Haines-Gadd,
Brandon Buck, Naomi Fritz, Liat Muller, Elke Presser, Hinki Kwon, Michael Mader,
Ming Cheong, Mikel Bennett, Jieun Lee, Chun Chiu, Aris Giorgiadis, Lole Mate,
Thomas Hale, Andreas Helgesson, Andrew Summers, Des Fagan, Laymon Thaung,
Johannes Hoffmann, Electra Mikelides
Competition Team Jim Heverin, Malca Mizrahi, Michele Pasca di Magliano,
Viviana R. Muscettola, Mariana Ibanez, Larissa Henke

LONDON AQUATICS CENTRE
Design Zaha Hadid
Project Director Jim Heverin
Project Architects Glenn Moorley, Sara Klomps
Project Leader Saffet Kaya Bekiroglu
Project Team Alex Bilton, Alex Marcoulides, Barbara Bochnak, Carlos Carijo, Clay Shorthall, Ertu Erbay, Giorgia Cannici, Hannes Schafelner, Hee Seung Lee, Kasia Townend, Nannette Jackowski, Nicholas Gdalewitch, Seth Handley, Thomas Soo, Tom Locke, Torsten Broeder, Tristan Job, Yamac Korfali, Yeena Yoon, George King
Competition Team Mariana Ibanez, Karim Muallem, Marco Vanucci, Agnes Koltay, Feng Chen, Gemma Douglas, Kakakrai Suthadarat, Sujit Nair

CMA CGM TOWER
Design Zaha Hadid
Project Director Jim Heverin
Project Architect Stephane Vallotton
Project Team Karim Muallem, Simone Contasta, Leonie Heinrich, Alvin Triestanto, Muriel Boselli, Eugene Leung, Bhushan Mantri, Jerome Michel, Nerea Feliz, Prashanth Sridharan, Birgit Eistert, Evelyn Gono, Marian Ripoll, Andres Flores
Competition Team Jim Heverin, Simon Kim, Michele Pasca di Magliano, Viviana R. Muscettola

ROCA LONDON GALLERY
Design Zaha Hadid with Patrik Schumacher
Project Directors Woody K. T. Yao, Maha Kutay
Project Architect Margarita Yordanova Valova
Design Team Gerhild Orthacker, Hannes Schafelner, Jimena Araiza, Mireia Sala Font, Erhan Patat, Yuxi Fu, Michal Treder, Torsten Broeder

PIERRESVIVES
Design Zaha Hadid
Project Architect Stéphane Hof
Project Team Joris Pauwels, Philipp Vogt, Rafael Portillo, Melissa Fukumoto, Jens Borstelmann, Jaime Serra, Kane Yanegawa, Loreto Flores, Edgar Payan, Lisamarie Villegas Ambia, Stella Nikolakaki, Karouko Ogawa, Hon Kong Chee, Caroline Andersen, Judith Reitz, Olivier Ottevaere, Achim Gergen, Daniel Baerlecken, Yosuke Hayano, Martin Henn, Rafael Schmidt, Daniel Gospodinov, Kia Larsdotter, Jasmina Malanovic, Ahmad Sukkar, Ghita Skalli, Elena Perez, Andrea B. Caste, Lisa Cholmondeley, Douglas Chew, Larissa Henke, Steven Hatzellis, Jesse Chima, Adriano De Gioannis, Simon Kim, Stéphane Carnuccini, Samer Chamoun, Ram Ahronov, Ross Langdon, Renata Paim Tourinho Dantas, Yacira Blanco, Marta Rodriguez, Ivan Valdez, Leonardo Garcia, Sevil Yazici, Hussam Chakouf, Thomas Vietzke, Marie-Perrine Placais, Monica Noguero, Naomi Fritz, Stephanie Chaltiel

**ELI & EDYTHE BROAD ART MUSEUM,
MICHIGAN STATE UNIVERSITY**
Design Zaha Hadid with Patrik Schumacher
Project Director Craig Kiner
Project Architect Alberto Barba
Project Team Michael Hargens, Edgar Payan Pacheco, Sophia Razzaque, Arturo Revilla, Charles Walker
Project Director (Competition) Nils-Peter Fischer
Project Architects (Competition) Britta Knobel, Fulvio Wirz
Competition Team Daniel Widrig, Melike Altinisik, Mariagrazia Lanza, Rojia Forouhar

GALAXY SOHO
Design Zaha Hadid with Patrik Schumacher
Project Director, Associate Satoshi Ohashi
Associate Cristiano Ceccato
Project Architect Yoshi Uchiyama
Project Team Kelly Lee, Rita Lee, Eugene Leung, Rolando Rodriguez-Leal, Lillie Liu, Seung-ho Yeo
Project Team (Design Development) Dorian Bybee, Michael Grau, Shu Hashimoto, Shao-Wei Huang, Chikara Inamura, Lydia Kim, Christoph Klemmt, Yasuko Kobayashi, Raymond Lau, Wang Lin, Yereem Park, Tao Wen, Stephan Wurster
Project Team (Schematic Design) Samer Chamoun, Tom Wuenschmann, Michael Hill, Shuojiong Zhang

HEYDAR ALIYEV CULTURAL CENTER
Design Zaha Hadid with Patrik Schumacher
Project and Design Architect Saffet Kaya Bekiroglu
Design Team Liat Muller, Sara Sheikh Akbari, Deniz Manisali, Lillie Liu, Marc Boles, Shiqi Li, Jose Lemos, Jose Ramon Tramoyeres, Phil Soo Kim, Yelda Gin, Yu Du, Josef Glas, Michael Grau, Erhan Patat, Simone Fuchs, Deepti Zachariah, Fadi Mansour, Jaime Bartolome, Tahmina Parvin, Ceyhun Baskin, Daniel Widrig, Helen Lee, Murat Mutlu

SALERNO MARITIME TERMINAL
Design Zaha Hadid
Project Architect Paola Cattarin
Design Team Andrea Parenti, Giovanna Sylos Labini, Cedric Libert, Filippo Innocenti, Paolo Zilli, Eric Tong
Competition Team Paola Cattarin, Sonia Villaseca, Chris Dopheide

INNOVATION TOWER
Design Zaha Hadid with Patrik Schumacher
Project Director Woody K. T. Yao
Project Leader Simon Yu
Project Team Hinki Kwong, Jinqi Huang, Juan Liu, Bianca Cheung, Charles Kwan, Zhenjiang Guo, Junkai Jian, Uli Blum
Competition Team Hinki Kwong, Melodie Leung, Long Jiang, Zhenjiang Guo, Yang Jingwen, Miron Mutyaba, Pavlos Xanthopoulus, Margarita Yordanova Valova

SERPENTINE SACKLER GALLERY
Design Zaha Hadid with Patrik Schumacher
Project Director Charles Walker
Project Leader (First Phase) Thomas Vietzke, Jens Borstelmann
Project Leader (Second Phase) Fabian Hecker
Project Team Ceyhun Baskin, Torsten Broeder, David Campos, Suryansh Chandra, Inanc Eray, Matthew Hardcastle, Dillon Lin, Elke Presser, Marina Duran Sancho, Timothy Schreiber, Jianghai Shen, Marcela Spadaro, Anat Stern, Laymon Thaung, Claudia Wulf

CAPITAL HILL RESIDENCE
Design Zaha Hadid with Patrik Schumacher
Project Architect Helmut Kinzler
Project Designer Daniel Fiser
Design Team Anat Stern, Thomas Sonder, Kristina Simkeviciute, Erhan Patat, Talenia Phua Gajardo, Tetsuya Yamazaki, Mariana Ibanez, Marco Vanucci, Lourdes Sánchez, Ebru Simsek, Daniel Santos, Muthahar Khan

DONGDAEMUN WORLD DESIGN PARK AND PLAZA

Design Zaha Hadid with Patrik Schumacher
Project Leader Eddie Can
Project Manager Craig Kiner
Project Team Kaloyan Erevinov, Martin Self, Hooman Talebi, Carlos S. Martinez, Camiel Weijenberg, Florian Goscheff, Maaike Hawinkels, Aditya Chandra, Andy Chang, Arianna Russo, Ayat Fadaifard, Josias Hamid, Shuojiong Zhang, Natalie Koerner, Jae Yoon Lee
Competition Team Kaloyan Erevinov, Paloma Gormley, Hee Seung Lee, Kelly Lee, Andres Madrid, Deniz Manisali, Kevin McClellan, Claus Voigtmann, Maurits Fennis

SOHO PEAKS

Design Zaha Hadid with Patrik Schumacher
Project Director Satoshi Ohashi
Associate Cristiano Ceccato
Project Manager Raymond Lau
Project Architect Armando Solano
Project Team Bianca Cheung, Yu Du, Ed Gaskin, Sally Harris, Chao-Ching Wang, Feng Lin, Yikai Lin, Oliver Malm, Rashiq Muhamadali, Matthew Richardson, Yichi Zhang, Yan Guangyuan, Ma Xinyue, Zhang Zhe

CITYLIFE

Design Zaha Hadid with Patrik Schumacher
Project Director Gianluca Racana
Tower Project Architects Paolo Zilli (Tower) Maurizio Meossi (Residential)
Tower Design Team H. Goswin Rothenthal, Gianluca Barone, Marco Amoroso, Alvin Triestanto, Letizia Simoni, Subharthi Guha, Marina Martinez, Luis Miguel Samanez, Santiago F. Achury, Massimo Napoleoni, Massimiliano Piccinini, Annarita Papeschi, Martha Read, Peter McCarthy
Residential Design Team Paola Bettinsoli, Gianluca Bilotta, Fabio Ceci, Veronica Erspamer, Stefano Iacopini, Serena Pietrantonj, Florindo Ricciuti, Giulia Scaglietta, Giovanna Sylos Labini, Anja Simons, Marta Suarez, Tamara Tancorre, Giuseppe Vultaggio
Competition Team Simon Kim, Yael Brosilovski, Adriano De Gioannis, Graham Modlen, Karim Muellem, Daniel Li, Yang Jingwen, Tiago Correia, Ana Cajiao, Daniel Baerlecken, Judith Reitz

NEW NATIONAL STADIUM OF JAPAN

Design Zaha Hadid with Patrik Schumacher
Project Director Jim Heverin, Cristiano Ceccato
Project Architect Paulo Flores
Design Team Rafael Contreras, Antonio Monserrat, Fernando Poucell, Irene Guerra, Junyi Wang, Karoly Markos, Tokyo Support Team, Yoshi Uchiyama, Ben Kikkawa
Tokyo Support Team Yoshi Uchiyama, Ben Kikkawa

ONE-NORTH MASTER PLAN

Design Zaha Hadid with Patrik Schumacher
Project Director Markus Dochantschi
Project Architects (Master Plan Phase) David Gerber, Dillon Lin, Silvia Forlati
Project Team (Master Plan Phase) David Mah, Gunther Koppelhuber, Rodrigo O'Malley, Kim Thornton, Markus Dochantschi
Project Architect (Rochester Detail Planning Phase) Gunther Koppelhuber
Project Team (Rochester Detail Planning Phase) Kim Thornton, Hon Kong Chee, Yael Brosilovski, Fernando Pérez Vera
Competition Team David Gerber, Edgar González, Chris Dopheide, David Salazar, Tiago Correia, Ken Bostock, Patrik Schumacher, Paola Cattarin, Dillon Lin, Barbara Kuit, Woody K. T. Yao

HIGH-SPEED TRAIN STATION NAPOLI-AFRAGOLA

Design Zaha Hadid with Patrik Schumacher
Project Architect Filippo Innocenti
Project Managers Filippo Innocenti, Paola Cattarin
Design Team Cesare Griffa, Federico Bistolfi, Mario Mattia, Paolo Zilli, Tobias Hegemann, Michele Salvi, Roberto Vangeli, Chiara Beccarini, Alessandra Belia, Luciano Letteriello, Domenico Di Francesco, Marco Guardincerri, Serena Pietrantonj, Roberto Cavallaro, Karim Muallem
Competition Team Fernando Pérez Vera, Ergian Alberg, Hon Kong Chee, Cesare Griffa, Karim Muallem, Steven Hatzellis, Thomas Vietzke, Jens Borstelmann, Robert Neumayr, Elena Perez, Adriano De Gioannis, Simon Kim, Selim Mimita

EUSKOTREN HEADQUARTERS AND URBAN PLANNING

Design Zaha Hadid with Patrik Schumacher
Project Architect Juan Ignacio Aranguren
Project Team Jimena Araiza, Andrés Arias, Muriel Boselli, Daniel Dendra, Alejandro Díaz, Elena García, John D. Goater, DaeWha Kang, Kia Larsdotter, Sophie Le Bienvenu, Murat Mutlu, Mónica Noguero, Markus Nonn, Benjamin Pohlers, Aurora Santana, Guillermo Álvarez
Competition Team Alvin Huang, Yang Jingwen, Simon Kim, Graham Modlen, Sujit Nair, Annabelle Perdomo, Makakrai Suthadarat, Philipp Vogt

EDIFICI CAMPUS

Design Zaha Hadid with Patrik Schumacher
Project Director Tiago Correia
Project Architects Alejandro Diaz, Aurora Santana
Project Team Fabiano Continanza, Rafael González, Víctor Orive, Oihane Santiuste, Mónica Bartolomé, Raquel Gallego, Esther Rivas, Jessica Knobloch, Hooman Talebi, Maria Araya, Ebru Simsek

OPUS OFFICE TOWER

Design Zaha Hadid
Project Director Christos Passas
Project Architect Vincent Nowack
Project Team Javier Ernesto Lebie, Dimitris Akritopoulos, Paul Peyrer-Heimstaett, Phivos Skroumbelos, Jesus Garate, Thomas Frings, Chiara Ferrari, Wenyuan Peng, Sylvia Georgiadou, Marilena Sophocleous
Competition Team Daniel Baerlecken, Alvin Huang, Paul Peyrer-Heimstaett, Gemma Douglas, Saleem Abdel-Jalil

DUBAI OPERA HOUSE AND CULTURAL CENTER

Design Zaha Hadid with Patrik Schumacher
Project Director Charles Walker
Project Architect Nils-Peter Fischer
Project Team Melike Altinisik, Alexia Anastasopoulou, Dylan Baker-Rice, Domen Bergoc, Shajay Bhooshan, Monika Bilska, Alex Bilton, Elizabeth Bishop, Torsten Broeder, Cristiano Ceccato, Alessio Constantino, Mario Coppola, Brian Dale, Ana Valeria Emiliano, Elif Erdine, Camilla Galli, Brandon Gehrke, Aris Georgiadis, Pia Habekost, Michael Hill, Shao-Wei Huang, Chikara Inamura, Alexander Janowsky, DaeWha Kang, Tariq Khayyat, Maren Klasing, Britta Knobel, Martin Krcha, Effie Kuan, Mariagrazia Lanza, Tyen Masten, Jwalant Mahadevwala, Rashiq Muhamadali, Monica Noguero, Diogo Brito Pereira, Rafael Portillo, Michael Powers, Rolando Rodriguez-Leal, Federico Rossi, Mireia Sala Font, Elke Scheier, Rooshad Shroff, William Tan, Michal Treder, Daniel Widrig, Fulvio Wirz, Susu Xu, Ting Ting Zhang

Project Director (Competition) Graham Modlen
Project Architect (Competition) Dillon Lin
Competition Team Christine Chow, Daniel Dendra, Yiching Liu, Simone Fuchs, Larissa Henke, Tyen Masten, Lourdes Sánchez, Johannes Schafelner, Swati Sharma, Hooman Talebi, Komal Talreja, Claudia Wulf, Simon Yu

KARTAL PENDIK MASTER PLAN
Design Zaha Hadid with Patrik Schumacher
Overall Project Architect Bozana Komljenovic
Project Team (Second stage) Amit Gupta, Marie-Perrine Placais, Susanne Lettau, Elif Erdine, Jimena Araiza, Oznur Erboga
Project Team (First stage) Leaders Bozana Komljenovic, DaeWha Kang
Project Team (First stage) Sevil Yazici, Vigneswaran Ramaraju, Brian Dale, Jordan Darnell
Competition Leaders DaeWha Kang, Saffet Kaya Bekiroglu
Competition Team Sevil Yazici, Daniel Widrig, Elif Erdine, Melike Altinisik, Ceyhun Baskin, Inanc Eray, Fulvio Wirz, Gonzalo Carbajo, Miya Ushida

NURAGIC AND CONTEMPORARY ART MUSEUM
Design Zaha Hadid with Patrik Schumacher
Project Architect Paola Cattarin
Team Leader Paolo Matteuzzi
Project Team Federico Bistolfi, Michele Salvi, Serena Pietrantonj, Alessandra Belia, Cristina Capanna, Giuseppe Vultaggio, Tamara Tancorre
Competition Team Paola Cattarin, Paolo Matteuzzi, Federico Bistolfi, Michele Salvi, Serena Pietrantonj, Vincenzo Barilari, Samuele Sordi

ABU DHABI PERFORMING ARTS CENTER
Design Zaha Hadid with Patrik Schumacher
Project Director Nils-Peter Fischer
Project Architects Britta Knobel, Daniel Widrig
Project Team Jeandonne Schijlen, Melike Altinisik, Arnoldo Rabago, Zhi Wang, Rojia Forouhar, Jaime Serra Avila, Diego Rosales, Erhan Patat, Samer Chamoun, Philipp Vogt, Rafael Portillo

SIGNATURE TOWERS
Design Zaha Hadid with Patrik Schumacher
Project Director Lars Teichmann
Project Architects Chris Lepine (Towers), Tyen Masten (Master Plan and Podiums), Tiago Correia (Competition)
Project Team (Towers) Chris Lepine, Stephan Wurster, Eren Ciraci, David Campos, Alessio Constantini, Hoda Nobakhti, Chryssanthi Perpatidou, Daniel Norell, Nahed Jawad, Don Burusphat, Bowornwan May Noradee, Hussam Chakouf, Bassam Al Shiekh, Tomas Rabl, Chiara Ferrari, Erhan Patat, Inanc Eray, Jose Lemos, Ceyhun Baskin, Josias Hamid, Chris Lepine, Arianna Russo, Carlos S. Martinez, Judith Wahle, Vincenzo Cocomero, Agata Kurzela
Project Team (Master Plan and Podiums) Tyen Masten, Michael Hill, Pia Habekost, Miron Mutyaba, Amalthea Leung, Rodrigo Baretto Brandon Gehrke, Judith Wahle, Vincenzo Cocomero, Agata Kurzela
Competition Team Ana Cajiao, Saleem Abdel-Jalil, Sophie Le Bienvenu, Hooman Talebi, Mathias Reisigl, Diego Rosales, Tyen Masten, DaeWha Kang, Renos Constantino, Graham Modlen

DUBAI FINANCIAL MARKET
Design Zaha Hadid with Patrik Schumacher
Project Director Lars Teichmann
Project Architect Raymond Lau
Project Team Raymond Lau, Arturo Lyon, Arturo Revilla, Chikara Inamura, Bessy Tam, Renato Pimenta, Amalthea Leung, Judith Wahle, Vincenzo Cocomero, Agata Kurzela
Project Leader (Concept Design) DaeWha Kang
Design Team DaeWha Kang, Simone Fuchs, Andrea Caste, Chiara Ferrari, Tariq Khayyat, Maria Eva Contesti, Jesse Chima

CIVIL COURTS MADRID
Design Zaha Hadid with Patrik Schumacher
Project Architect Juan Ignacio Aranguren
Competition Team Andrés Arias Madrid, Jimena Araiza Olivera Toro, Brian Dale, Amit Gupta, Ho-Ping Hsia, Sara Sheikh Akbari, Tomas Rabl, Paulo E. Flores

BAHRAIN INTERNATIONAL CIRCUIT
Design Zaha Hadid with Patrik Schumacher
Project Leader DaeWha Kang
Project Team Ceyhun Baskin, Andrea B. Caste, Jordan Darnell, Inanc Eray, Simone Fuchs, Tariq Khayyat, Mariagrazia Lanza, Fadi Mansour, Liat Muller, Daniel Widrig, Fulvio Wirz

REGIUM WATERFRONT
Design Zaha Hadid with Patrik Schumacher
Project Architect Filippo Innocenti
Design Team (Competition) Roberto Vangeli, Michele Salvi, Luciano Letteriello, Fabio Forconi, Andrea Balducci Castè, Giuseppe Morando, Johannes Weikert, Deepti Zachariah, Gonzalo Carbajo

LILIUM TOWER
Design Zaha Hadid with Patrik Schumacher
Project Architect Markus Planteu
Competition Team Thomas Mathoy, Sophia Razzaque, Naomi Fritz, Daniel Widrig, Fulvio Wirz, Mariagrazia Lanza, Dennis Brezina, Seda Zirek

BAHRAIN MUSEUM OF CONTEMPORARY ART
Design Zaha Hadid with Patrik Schumacher
Project Architect Elke Scheier
Project Team Gerhild Orthacker, Jimena Araiza, Susanne Lettau, Hee Seung Lee, Alexander Janowsky

VILNIUS MUSEUM
Design Zaha Hadid with Patrik Schumacher
Project Architects Thomas Vietzke, Jens Borstelmann
Project Team Kristof Crolla, Julian Breinersdorfer, Melodie Leung, Claudia Wulf, David Seeland

KING ABDULLAH II HOUSE OF CULTURE & ART
Design Zaha Hadid with Patrik Schumacher
Project Director Charles Walker
Project Architect Tariq Khayyat
Project Team Jalal El-Ali, Matteo Melioli, Eren Ciraci, Diego Rossel, Akif Cinar
Competition Team Maria Araya, Melike Altinisik, Dominiki Dadatsi, Renata Dantas, Sylvia Georgiadou, Britta Knobel, Rashiq Muhamadali, Bence Pap, Eleni Pavlidou, Daniel Santos, Daniel Widrig, Sevil Yazici

NEW PASSENGER TERMINAL AND MASTER PLAN, ZAGREB AIRPORT
Design Zaha Hadid with Patrik Schumacher
Project Architect Tiago Correia
Project Team Victor Orive, Fabiano Continanza, Alejandro Diaz, Goswin Rothenthal, Oihane Santiuste, Rafael Gonzalez, Monica Noguero, Irene Mennini, Maren Klasing, Martin Krcha, Andres Schenker, David Seeland

TEA AND COFFEE SET
Design Zaha Hadid
Design Team Maha Kutay, Anne Save de Beaurecueil

Z-PLAY / Z-SCAPE FURNITURE
Design Zaha Hadid
Design Team Caroline Voet, Woody K. T. Yao, Chris Dopheide, Eddie Can

ICEBERG
Design Zaha Hadid with Patrik Schumacher
Design Team Thomas Vietzke, Woody K. T. Yao

ZAHA HADID ARCHITECTURE/ARCHITEKTUR AT THE MAK
Design Zaha Hadid with Patrik Schumacher
Design Team Woody K. T. Yao, Thomas Vietzke, Rocio Paz, Adriano de Gioiannis, Tiago Correia

25 YEARS OF DEUTSCHE BANK COLLECTION AT THE DEUTSCHE GUGGENHEIM
Design Zaha Hadid with Patrik Schumacher
Project Architect Helmut Kinzler
Design Team Tetsuya Yamazaki, Yael Brosilovski, Saleem A Jalil, Joris Pauwels, Manuela Gatto, Fabian Hecker, Gernot Finselbach, Judith Reitz, Daniel Baerlecken, Setsuko Nakamura

VORTEXX CHANDELIER
Design Zaha Hadid with Patrik Schumacher
Design Team Thomas Vietzke

Z-ISLAND KITCHEN
Design Zaha Hadid with Patrik Schumacher
Project Architect Thomas Vietzke
Design Team Georgios Maillis, Maurice Martel, Katharina Neuhaus, Ariane Stracke

AQUA TABLE
Design Zaha Hadid with Patrik Schumacher
Project Designer Saffet Kaya Bekiroglu

Z-CAR I AND II
Design Zaha Hadid with Patrik Schumacher
Project Designer Jens Borstelmann
Design Team David Seeland

BELU BENCH
Design Zaha Hadid with Patrik Schumacher
Project Designer Saffet Kaya Bekiroglu
Design Team Maha Kutay, Tarek Shamma, Melissa Woolford

ZAHA HADID AT THE SOLOMON R. GUGGENHEIM MUSEUM
Design Zaha Hadid with Patrik Schumacher
Project Architect Woody K. T. Yao
Design Team Ana Cajiao, Melodie Leung, Thomas Vietzke, Helmut Kinzler, Tiago Correia, Ken Bostock
Support Team Muthahar Khan, Miya Ushida, Jevin Dornic, Andrea B. Caste, Josefina del Rio
Artist Consultant Antonio de Campos

SEAMLESS COLLECTION
Design Zaha Hadid with Patrik Schumacher
Design Team Saffet Kaya Bekiroglu, Melodie Leung, Helen Lee, Alvin Huang, Hannes Schafelner

MOON SYSTEM
Design Zaha Hadid with Patrik Schumacher
Project Designer Viviana Muscettola
Design Team Michele Pasca di Magliano, Viviana Muscettola

FLOW VASE
Design Zaha Hadid with Patrik Schumacher
Lead Designers Michele Pasca di Magliano, Viviana R. Muscettola

MESA TABLE
Design Zaha Hadid with Patrik Schumacher
Project Designer Saffet Kaya Bekiroglu
Design Team Chikara Inamura, Melike Altinisik, Saffet Kaya Bekiroglu

DUNE FORMATIONS AT THE SCUOLA DEI MERCANTI, VENICE BIENNALE 2007
Design Zaha Hadid with Patrik Schumacher
Design Team Michele Pasca di Magliano, Viviana R. Muscettola

CRATER
Design Zaha Hadid with Patrik Schumacher
Project Designer Saffet Kaya Bekiroglu
Design Team Chrysostomos Tsimourdagkas, Chikara Inamura

LILAS INSTALLATION AT THE SERPENTINE GALLERY
Design Zaha Hadid with Patrik Schumacher
Project Architect Kevin McClellan

AURA L AND AURA S AT THE VILLA LA MALCONTENTA
Design Zaha Hadid with Patrik Schumacher
Design Team Fulvio Wirz, Mariagrazia Lanza

SEOUL TABLE AND YUNG HEE DESK
Design Zaha Hadid with Patrik Schumacher
Design Team Daniel Widrig

ZAHA HADID AT THE SONNABEND & ROVE GALLERIES
Design Zaha Hadid with Patrik Schumacher
Project Architect Melodie Leung
Exhibition Team Tom Wuenschmann, Emily Chang, Maha Kutay, Filipa Gomes, Gerhild Orthacker

ZAHA HADID ARCHITECTS STAFF OVER 30 YEARS

Directors: Zaha Hadid, Patrik Schumacher, Jim Heverin, and Gianluca Racana
Associate Directors: Christos Passas, Woody K. T. Yao

Abdellatif El Alami, Abel Pinheiro Caval Cante, Achim Gergen, Adam Atraktzi, Adam Walker, Aditya Chandra, Adrian Aguirre Herrera, Adrian Krezlik, Adrian Muller, Adriano De Gioannis, Adriano De Gioannis, Agata Kurzela, Agnes Koltay, Agnieszka Jablonska, Ai Sato, Aida Mofakham, Akhil Laddha, Alasdair Graham, Alberto Barba-Guerrero, Alberto Moletto, Alejandro Diaz, Alejandro Nieto, Alessio Costantino, Alexander Bilton, Alexander Janowsky, Alexander Robles Palacio, Alexandra Andrews, Alexandra Fisher, Alexandre Kuroda, Alexandria Beckett, Alexandros Kallegias, Alexandros Marcoulides, Alexia Anastasopoulou, Alia Zayani, Alicia Nahmad, Alissa Dumitru, Alvin Huang, Alvin Triestanto, Amalthea Leung, Amanda Leat, Amelia Ward, Amina Hussein, Amit Gupta, Amita Kulkarni, Amrita Deshpande, Ana Cajiao, Ana Gonzalez, Ana Margarita Wang Zuniga, Ana Varela Emilliano, Anakkottil Sujit Nair, Anas Younes, Anastasia Lianou, Anat Stern, Andrea Antonucci, Andrea Balducci Caste, Andrea D'Imperio, Andrea Vincenti, Andreas Helgesson, Andreas Urff, Andres Arias Madrid, Andres Cesar Moroni, Andres Flores, Andres Schenker, Andrew P. Coles, Andrew Paul, Andri Shalou, Andy Summers, Aneta Bednarowicz, Angelica Castro, Angelique Wright, Anita Patel, Anna Papachristoforou, Anna Wilson, Annabelle Perdomo, Annarita Papeschi, Anne Marie Campbell, Anneka Wegener, Annette Bresinsky, Annie Ah Tee Li, Annie Johnson, Antonio Monserrat, Aram Gimbot, Arianna Russo, Aris Georgiadis, Aritz Moriones, Arlene Samuel, Arnold Lole Mate, Arturo Lyon Gottlieb, Arturo Revilla Perez, Ashwin Ravindra Shah, Atrey Chhaya, Aurora Santana, Ayat Fadaeifard, Ayca Vural Cutts, Aylishia Chiffers

Babar Latif, Barbara Pfenningstorff, Barbara Bochnak, Barida Lekara Daanwi, Bassam Al Sheikh, Ben Kikkawa, Bence Pap, Bentolhoda Nobakhti, Berenice Motais de Narbonne, Bianca Cheung, Bidisha Sinha, Birgit Eistert, Blas Revilla Gorka, Bowornwan May Noradee, Bozana Komljenovic, Brandon Gehrke, Brandon Scott Buck, Brian Dale, Brian Mulhall, Britta Knobel, Brunella Velardi, Bryan Scheib, Bushan Mantri

Caitlin May Murray, Camiel Weijenberg, Camilla Galli, Camille Sherrod, Can Cakmak, Capucine Lasen, Carine Posner, Carine Tshishimbi, Carla-Maria Baz, Carlos Garjo Vidal, Carlos Luna Pimienta, Carlos Michael-Medina, Carlos Parraga Botero, Carlos Piles Puig, Carlos Vera, Carmen Morris, Carolina Lopez-Blanco, Caroline Anderson, Caroline Poloni, Catalina Pollak, Catherine Hennessy, Cedric Libert, Celina Auterio, Celine Dalcher Da Silva, Ceyhun Baskin, Chantavudh Burusphat, Chantelle Lue-Elton, Chao Ching Wang, Chao Wei, Charbal Chagoury, Charity Osei-Tutu, Chee Beng Koh, Chiara Ferrari, Chikara Inamura, Chiu Fai Can, Christian Gibbon, Christian Ludwig, Christina Beaumont, Christine Chow, Christoph Eppacher, Christoph Klemmt, Christopher Daley, Christopher Lepine, Christos Sazos, Chrysi Fradellou, Chryssanthi Perpatidou, Chrystomos Tsimourdagkas, Chun Chieh Fang, Chun Fatt Lee, Chun Xia, Chun Yeu Chiu, Chung Wang, Chung-Shun Chang, Claire Cahill, Clara Martins, Claudia Fruianu, Claudia Glas-Dorner, Claudia Wulf, Claus Voigtmann, Constanze Stinnes, Cordelia Barker, Corinne Roberts, Cornelius Schlotthauer, Craig Kiner, Cristiano Ceccato, Cynthia J. Ottchen, Cyril Owen Manyara, Cyril Wing Y. Shing, Cyril Wing Yin

Dachun Lin, Daewha Kang, Daghan Cam, Dana Kathleen Blaker, Daniel Baerlecken, Daniel Dendra, Daniel Domingo, Daniel Fiser, Daniel N. Parker, Daniel Piccinelli, Daniel Santos, Daniel Toumine, Daniel Widrig, Danilo Arsic, David Campos, David Doody, David Gerber, David Mah, David McDowell, David Salazar, David Seeland, David Wolthers, Davide Del Giudice, Davide Giordano, Dawna J. E. Houchin, Deepti Anna Zachariah, Demetris Alexiou, Deniz Manisali, Dennis Brezina, Derick Johnson, Des Fagan, Di Yuan, Diane Amanda Unwin, Diego Perez-Espitia, Diego Rosales, Diego Rossel, Dimitrios-Achillefs Kolonis, Dimitris

Akritopoulos, Diogo Brito Pereira, Dipal Kothari, Domen Bergoc, Domenico Di Francesco, Dominiki Datatsi, Duarte Cabral Reino, Dylan Davies, Dylan Rice

Ebru Simsek, Edgar Payan Pacheco, Edward Calver, Edward Sorgeloose, Effie Kuan, Efthalia Chatzichronoglou, Eirini Fountoulaki, Eleanor Bloomfield, Eleanor Kate Bloomfield, Electra Mikelides, Elena Garcia Perez, Elena Scripelliti, Eleni Pavlidou, Elif Erdine, Elin Tiberg, Elizabeth Batula, Elizabeth Bishop, Elizabeth Choroszczuk, Elizabeth Hennessy Jones, Elizabeth Jenny Keenan, Elizabeth Westgarth, Elke Frotscher, Elke Presser, Ellen Jane Arnold, Elsa Karin Susanne Berggren, Enrico Kleinke, Enzio Michael Cocomero, Eren Ciraci, Ergian Alberianti, Ergin Birinci, Erhan Patat, Eric Tong, Erik Norell, Ertu Erbay, Erwan Gallou, Esther Rivas Adrover, Eugene Leung, Eva Pfannes, Eva Tiedemann, Evan Erlebacher, Evelyn Gono, Evgeniya Yatsyuk, Ewelina Owsiana, Ezhil Vigneswaran

Fabian Hecker, Fabiano Continanza, Fadi Mansour, Federico D'Angelo, Federico Dunkelberg, Federico Rossi, Fei Wang, Felicity Khoo, Feng Lin, Feng Xu, Fernando Poucell, Fernando Sanchez, Filipa Gomes, Filipa Valente, Filippo Innocenti, Filis Jovesic, Flavio La Gioia, Florian Goscheff, Francesca Venturoni, Francis Mike Hill, Frenji Koshy, Frida Sofia Sjodin, Fulvio Wirz

Gabriela Jimenez, Gabriella Blasi, Ganesh Nimmala, Garin O'Aivazian, Gary Power, Gayle Markovitz, Gemma Douglas, Genevieve Harrison, George Giokalas, George King, Georgia Kotsioni, Georgios Ermis Chalvatzis, Georgios Maillis, Gerhild Orthacker, Gernot Finselback, Gianluca Barone, Gianni Giuffrida, Giorgia Cannici, Giorgio Radojkovic, Giorgio Realeza, Giuseppe Morando, Glenn Adams, Glenn Moorley, Gonzalo Carbajo, Gordana Jakimovska, Graham Modlen, Gregory Unsworth, Guillermo Alvarez, Gunter Koppelhuber

Hala Sheikh, Harriet Warden, Hassan Ali, Hee Seung Lee, Heinrich Goswin Rothenthal, Heinrich Goswin Rothenthal, Helen Aaron, Helena Farrington, Helmut Kinzler, Hendrik Rupp, Henning Hansen, Henriette Helstrup, Henry J. E. Virgin, Hilal Kabbara, Hinki Kwong, Ho-Ping Hsia, Hon Kong Chee, Hooman Talebi, Hussam Chakouf, Hussein Ali, Hyoun Hee Na, Hyunbai Jun

Ibraheem Ammash, Ifeanyi Anthony Oganwu, Igor Pantic, Ilana Brilovich, Inanc Eray, Ioannis Schinis, Irena Predalic, Irene Guerra Gomez, Irene Mennini, Irene Pabustan, Isik Troy Hawkins, Itzhak Balfur Samun, Ivan Felipe Ucros Polley, Ivan Valdez-Torrico

Jaime Bartolome, Jaime Serra Avila, Jaimie-Lee Haggerty, Jakub Klaska, Jalal El-Ali, James Gayed, James Thomas, Jamie Mann, Jan Hubener, January Poitras, Javier Lebie, Javier Rueda, Jee Seon Lim, Jen Hwang Ho, Jennifer Hamil-Kiehn, Jenny Huang, Jens Borstelmann, Jeong Hoon Lee, Jeremy Tymms, Jerome Michel, Jesus M Garate, Jia Yue Zhu, Jiali Zhou, Jianghai Shen, Jieun Lee, Jimena Araiza Olivera Toro, Jin Mi Lee, Jin Yong Helen Lee, Jing Wen Yang, Jingqi Qin, Jinqi Huang, JinSoo Kim, Joann Hong, Joanne F Gold, Johanna Huang, Johannes Elias, Johannes Hoffmann, Johannes Jack Byron, Johannes Schafelner, Johannes T. H. Schijlen, John Archdale Clegg, John Bloomfield, John Martin Randle, John Simpson, John Szlachta, Jolien Osborn, Jordan Darnell, Jorge Xavier Mendez-Caceres, Joris Pauwels, Jose Cadilhe, Jose Gerardo Cruz Galvez, Jose L Da Silva Neto, Jose Manuel Arnaud, Jose Monfa, José Ramon Tramoyeres, Josef Glas, Joshua Daniel Noad, Josias Hamid, Juan Aranguren, Juan Camilo Mogollon, Juan Carlos Estrada Gomez, Juan Gilsanz Saez, Juan Liu, Judith Reitz, Judith Schafelner, Judith Wahle, Julian Jones, Julian Sauer, Jules Davies Marriott, Julien Breinersdorfer, Jun Yi Wang, Junkai Jian, Junyi Wang, Justin Kelly, Jwalant Mahadevwala

Kalimba Culverwell, Kaloyan Erevinov, Kane Yanagawa, Kanop Mangklapruk, Karen Sherman, Karim Muallem, Karin Malm, Karine Yassine, Karoly Markos, Katarzyna D Towend, Kate Pointon, Katharina Gudrun Hieger, Katharina Hernadez, Katrina King Yee Wong, Katrina Larsdotter, Kay Kulinna, Kelly Sedge, Kenneth Bostock, Kevin M. d'Assalenaux Sheppard, Kevin McClellan, Kevin Sheppard, Kimberley Thornton, Kirsti Perera, Klein John Joseph, Konstantinos

Mouratidis, Krishna Hindocha, Kristina Simkeviciute, Kristof Crolla, Kutbuddin Nadiadi, Kwanphil Cho, Kyla Farrell, Kyungeun Lee

L. N. Smith, Lana Rose Palumbo, Larissa Henke, Lars Teichmann, Laura Aquili, Lauren Barclay, Lauren Mishkind, Laurence Dudenley, Lay-Mon Thaung, Le Ha Hoang, Leonardo Alves, Leonid Krykhtin, Leonie Heinrich, Letizia Simoni, Leyre Asensio Villoria, Li Hongdi, Li Zou, Liat Muller, Lillie Liu, Linda McChesney Martin, Line Rahbek, Lisa Ingrid Cholmondeley, Lisa Kinnerud, Lisa-Astrid Curran, Lisamarie Ambia, Long Jiang, Lorena Camiuli Delgado, Lorenzo Grifantini, Loulwa Bohsali, Lourdes Sanchez, Luca Ruggeri, Luciano Letteriello, Lucio Dos Santos, Ludovico Lombardi, Luis Miguel Samanez, Luisa Daniela Alves, Luke Bowler, Lydia Kim

M. Dillon Lin, M. I. Fontoura A Toledo, Maaike Anne Hawinkels, Magda Cernia Milla, Maha Kutay, Mahmoud Riad, Makakrai Jay Suthadarat, Malca Mizrahi, Malgorzata Kowalczyk, Manon Janssens, Manpreet Singh, Manuela Gatto, Manya Uppal, Marc Boles, Marc Fornes, Marcela Spadaro, Marco Amoroso, Marco Guardincerri, Marco Paolo Cuomo, Marco Vanucci, Maren Klasing, Margarita Valova, Maria Antonia Ripoll, Maria Araya Pereira, Maria Elena Popovici, Maria Jose Cardona, Maria Jose Rodero, Maria L Flores Reyes, Maria Tsironi, Mariagrazia Lanza, Mariana Beatriz Ibanez, Marie-Noelle Janssens, Marie-Perrine Placais, Marilena Sophocleous, Marina Martinez, Mario Coppola, Mario Mattia, Marisa Carvajal, Mariya Ilieva, Markus Nonn, Markus Planteu, Marlon Rueberg, Marta Rodriguez Tabernero, Martha Read, Martin Henn, Martin Krcha, Martin Pfleger, Martin Self, Massimiliano Piccinini, Massimo Napoleoni, Mathais Frei, Mathias Paul Reisigl, Matias Musacchio, Matteo Bigliardi, Matteo Melioli, Matteo Pierotti, Matthew C. G. Hardcastle, Matthew Carapiet, Matthew Donkersley, Matthew Engele, Matthew Johnston, Matthew Lai Wong, Matthew Richardson, Matthias Baer, Mattia Gambardella, Maurits Fennis, Maurizio Meossi, May Benbady, Meheret Hamid, Mehmet Cinar, Mei-Ling Lin, Melika Aljukic, Melike Altinisik, Melissa Fukumoto, Melissa Woolford, Melodie Leung, Meng Chen Tang, Mey Yee Cheng, Michael Grau, Michael Hargens, Michael Harris, Michael Mader, Michael McCall, Michael McNamara, Michael Melmoe, Michael Powers, Michael Rissbacher, Michael Sims Jr, Michael Tyrrell, Michail Desyllas, Michail Roidis, Michal Treder, Michal Wojtkiewicz, Michele Pasca Di Magliano, Michele Salvi, Michelle O'Neill, Michelle Thompson, Michelle Wu, Mikel S Bennett, Ming Ken Cheong, Miranda Savva, Mirco Becker, Mireia Sala Font, Miron Mutyaba, Mirren Rosie, Miya Ushida, Moa Carlsoon, Mohammad Rashdan, Mohammadali Mirzaeikouchaksaraei, Mohammed Ali Hussein, Monia De Marchi, Monica B Noguero, Monica Jarpa, Monica Jarpa Martinez, Monika Bilska, Montserrat Gili-Mari, Mostafa El Sayed, Moufid Banna, Mu Ren, Mubarak Al Faheem, Muriel Sofia Boselli Masana, Muthahar Khan, Myung Ho Lee

Nabil Shehada, Nadia Aldoukhi, Nadja Salihbegovic, Nahed Jawad, Nannette Jackowski, Naomi Fritz, Nassif Faour, Nassim Eshaghi, Natacha Viveiros, Natalia Marianna Wrzask, Natalie Popik, Natalie Rosenberg, Navvab Taylor, Neda Mostafavi, Nerea Feliz, Nicholas Armitage, Nicholas Puckett, Nicholette Chan, Nick Ceulemans, Nicky Walker, Nicola Berkowski, Nicola Jane Alger, Nicola McConnell, Nicolas Gdalewitch, Nicole Berry, Nils-Peter Fischer, Nina Safainia, Niran Buyukkoz, Nisrit Bahleby, Nupur Shah

Odilo Weiss, Oihane S Cardano, Olga Banchikova, Olga Yatsyuk, Oliver Von Malm, Olivier Ottevaere, Olutobi Adamolekun, Osbert So, Osita Jason Nwachukwu, Otto Schade

Paola Cattarin, Paola Domenica Salcedo Bacigalupo, Paolo Gamba, Paolo Matteuzzi, Paolo Succo, Paolo Zilli, Patryk Ruszkowski, Paul Crosby, Paul Kilpatrick, Paul Peyrer-Heimstatt, Pauline Morgan, Pauline-Anne Rolla, Paulo Flores, Pavlos Xanthopoulos, Pedja Pantovic, Pedro Sanchez Reche, Penny Cook, Peter Eriemo, Peter McCarthy, Petra Palumbo, Phil Soo Kim, Philipp Nikolaus Vogt, Philipp Ostermaier, Phivos Skroumbelos, Pia Habekost,

Pierandrea Angius, Pierre Alexander De Looz, Pierre Gilles Forissier, Prashanth Sridharan, Priti Joshi, Prudence Sanders, Puja Shah

Rachel Anne Alderman, Rafael Cabello, Rafael Contreras, Rafael Portillo, Rafael Schmidt, Ralph Andrew Merkle, Rand Abdul Jabbar, Raquel Gallego Lorenzo, Rashiq Muhamad Ali, Raul Forsoni, Raymond Lau, Raza Zahid, Rebecca Greaves, Rebecca Moldenhauer, Regina Geier, Renata Paim Dantas, Renato Pimenta, Reza Esmaeeli, Rhian Dixon, Ricardo Sosa Mejia, Richard Wasenegger, Rita Yen-Chun Lee, Robert May, Robert Neumayer, Roberto Sforza, Roberto Vangeli, Rochana Chaugule, Rocio Paz, Rodolfo Cordoves Jr, Roger K. W. Howie, Roger Turner, Rojia F. Abadeh, Rokhsana Rakhshani, Rolando Rodriguez-Leal, Romeo Realeza, Ronie Duro, Rooshad Shroff, Rory Michael MacTague, Rosalina Pulido

Saahil Parikh, Sabi Dau, Sabrina Summer, Saffet Kaya Bekiroglu, Saleem A Jalil, Sally North, Saman Saffarian, Samantha Rodrigues-Mactague, Samar Rizkallah, Samer Chamoun, Samir Mhamdi Alaoui, Sandra Riess, Sang Hoon Oh, Santiago Fernandez Achury, Sara Criscenti, Sara Klomps, Sara Saleh, Sara Sheikh Akbari, Sarah Ladkani, Sarah Schuster, Sarah Thurow, Sarah Wesson, Scott Taylor, Sean Burton, Sebastien Delagrance, Sebastian Andia, Sebastian Carlos, Seda Zirek, Selahattin Tuysuz, Selina Johnson, Seth Handley, Sevil Yazici, Shajay Bhooshan, Shaju Nanukuttan, Shameel Muhammed, Shankara Kothapuram Sriram, Shao Wei Huang, Sharansundar Sundar, Shaun Farrell, Shereen Doummar, Shih-Chin Wu, Shiqi Li, Shirley Hottier, Shivani Naidoo, Shukura Jackson, Shuojiong Zhang, Shyamala Duraisingam, Si Chen, Silvia Forlati, Silvia Lucchetta, Simon Kim, Simon Martin Johns, Simon Yu, Simone Contasta, Simone Fuchs, Sina Davari, Sobitha Ravichandran, Sofia Amodio Bernal, Sofia Danilidou, Sofia Danilidou, Sofia Hagen, Soomeen Hahm, Sophia Razzaque, Sophie Davison, Sophie Le Bienvenu, Spyridon Kaprinis, Stefan Brabetz, Stefan Pateman, Stefan Rinnebach, Stefano Iacopini, Stella Dourtme, Stella Nikolakaki, Stephan Bohne, Stephan Wurster, Stéphane Carnuccini, Stéphane Hof, Stephane Vallotton, Stephanie Chaltiel, Stephen John Arnold, Stephen P Webb, Steve Hatzellis, Stuart Huggan, Subharthi Guha, Suryansh Chandra, Susan Altinok, Susan Maharaj, Susanne Lettau, Susu Xu, Suzie Rendle, Swati Sharma, Sylvia Georgiadou

Ta-kang Hsu, Taekjin Kim, Tahmina Parvin, Talenia Phua Gajardo, Talia Paboudjian, Tam Shun Yee, Tamar Jacobs, Tamara Vincent, Tania Sequeira, Tariq Z. Khayyat, Tea Agbaba, Teoman Ayas, Teresa Alana Zumtobel, Teresa Golloy, Tetsuya Yamazaki, Theodor Wender, Theodora Ntatsopoulou, Theodore Spyropoulos, Thomas Caldwell, Thomas Clayton Shortall, Thomas Freiherr von Buseck, Thomas Frings, Thomas Hale, Thomas Jensen, Thomas Mathoy, Thomas Seng Chin Soo, Thomas Sonder, Thomas Vietzke, Tiago Correia, Timothy Schreiber, Tina Pintev, Ting Na Chen, Ting-Ting Zhang, Tom Locke, Tom Wunschmann, Tomas Rabl, Tomasz Starczewski, Torsten Broeder, Tracey Morgans, Tristan C. H. Job, Tristan John De Las Alas, Tsigay Tesfay, Tunisha Kapadia, Tyen Masten

Ujjal Roy, Ulrich Arno Schifferdecker, Ulrich Blum

Valerie Thanh Thuy Dao, Verena Hoch, Veronika Ilinskaya, Victor Martins, Victor Orive, Victoria Goldstein, Victoria Lampkin, Viggo Hjort Haremst, Vincent Nowak, Vincenzo Barilari, Vincenzo Reale, Virginia Cayzer, Vishu Bhooshan, Vivian-Varvara Pashiali, Viviana Rosanna Muscettola, Vladimir Tchaly

Wai Shing Chang, Wandy Mulia, Wen Yuan Peng, Wen-Kai Li, William Tan, Wolfgang Sunder

Xiao Long Rui, Xiaosheng Li, Xiejing Yin, Xin Du

Yacira Blanco, Yael Brosilovski, Yamac Ugur Kurfalu, Yamesha Korte, Yan Song Mar, Yassin Kulifa Idris, Yeena Yoon, Yelda Gin, Yevgeniy Beylkin, Yevgeniya Matusova, Yevgeniya Pozigun, Yi Ching Liu, Yi-Wen Chen, Yifan Zhang, Yikai Lin, Yosuke Hayano, Yu Du, Yuchen Zhang, Yue Shi, Yueying Cathy Liang, Yun Zhang, Yung-Chieh Huang, Yusef Ali, Yuxi Fu

Zhenjiang Guo, Zhi Wang, Zhihong Lin, Zhong Tian

BIBLIOGRAPHY CREDITS ACKNOWLEDGEMENTS

BIBLIOGRAPHY

Hadid's work is widely published in periodicals and monographs, which include

ZAHA HADID: PLANETARY ARCHITECTURE II *AA files* (no. 6, 1984)

ZAHA HADID *GA Architect* (no. 5, 1986, Japan)

ZAHA HADID 1983–1991 *El Croquis* (no. 52, 1991, Madrid)

ZAHA M HADID *GA Document Extra* (no. 3, 1995, Japan)

ZAHA HADID 1992–1995 *El Croquis* (no. 73, 1995, Madrid)

ZAHA HADID: THE COMPLETE BUILDINGS AND PROJECTS (London, UK, 1998)

ZAHA HADID: LF ONE (Basel, Switzerland, 1999)

ARCHITECTURE OF ZAHA HADID IN PHOTOGRAPHS BY HELENE BINET (Baden, Switzerland, 2000)

ZAHA HADID 1996–2001 *El Croquis* (no. 103, 2001, Madrid)

SCIENCE CENTRE, WOLFSBURG / ZAHA HADID *GA Document International* (no. 65, 2001, Japan)

ZAHA M HADID: CAR PARK AND TERMINUS HOENHEIM-NORD, STRASBOURG, FRANCE *GA Document* (no. 66, 2001, Japan)

ZAHA HADID, OPERE E PROGETTI (Turin, 2002)

ZAHA HADID ARCHITEKTUR (MAK, Vienna, Austria, 2003)

ZAHA HADID SPACE FOR ART (Baden, Switzerland, 2004)

ZAHA HADID 1983–2004 *El Croquis* (2004, Madrid)

DIGITAL HADID (Basel, Switzerland, 2004)

CAR PARK AND TERMINUS STRASBOURG (Baden, Switzerland, 2004)

ZAHA HADID COMPLETE WORKS (London, UK, 2004)

BMW CENTRAL BUILDING (Princeton, USA, 2006)

ZAHA HADID Catalog for the Solomon R. Guggenheim Museum (2006)

ZAHA HADID *GA Document, Special Issue* (no. 99, 2007, Japan)

ZAHA HADID (Milan, Italy, 2007)

TOTAL FLUIDITY Catalog for Seoul Design Olympiad Exhibition (2008)

ZAHA HADID Catalog of the Architecture Biennale Barbara Cappochin (2010)

MAXXI: ZAHA HADID ARCHITECTS (Skira-Rizzoli, New York, 2010)

BEING ZAHA HADID *ABITARE* Monographic issue (no. 511, 2011, Milan)

ZAHA HADID: UNE ARCHITECTURE Catalog (Paris, 2011)

I PROTAGONISTI DEL DESIGN – ZAHA HADID (Hachette, Milan, 2011)

ZAHA HADID: INSPIRATION AND PROCESS IN ARCHITECTURE (Moleskine SpA, Milan, 2011)

FORM IN MOTION Catalog, Yale Univ. Press (USA, 2012)

ZAHA HADID AND SUPREMATISM (Hatje Cantz, Germany, 2012)

ZAHA HADID: PIERRESVIVES (Skira-Rizzoli, New York, 2013)

CREDITS

All sketches, paintings and drawings are by Zaha Hadid Architects. The renderings are by Zaha Hadid Architects, Neutral, Stack Studios, Front Top and Smoothe. The model photographs are by David Grandorge, Edward Woodman. Unless otherwise stated, the photographs are by Zaha Hadid Architects.

The photographers/copyright owners:
© **Iwan Baan** 242 top, 243 top, 262/263, 266, 270, 271 top and bottom left, 278/279, 281, 285, 302/303, 310 top, 311, 322/323, 326, 327 top, 328, 329, 335 top, 336 top, 338 top, 339, 341 bottom, 343, 344/345, 346, 351 bottom, 353 © **Courtesy of B&B Italia, photography by Fabrizio Bergamo** 562 © **Virgile Simon Bertrand** 249 top left and bottom, 250, 251 bottom left, 282/283 © **Hélène Binet** 125 top right, 130/131, 137–141, 142/143, 146, 147 bottom, 150, 152, 153 top right, 154 bottom, 155 top right and bottom, 161–162, 163 top right, 164/165, 169 top left and right, 170, 171 bottom, 172 top left and right, 173, 184 top left and right, 199 bottom, 202/203, 206 bottom left and right, 208 top and middle, 210, 211, 214/215, 216, 218 top left, 220 top and bottom left, 224, 227 middle, 228 top, 238, 239 middle, 324, 327 bottom, 536 bottom © **BMW AG, photography by Erik Chmil** 213 top © **Henry Bourne** 2 © **Richard Bryant/Arcaid** 62/63, 66 top, 67–69 © **Jack Coble** 554, 556–557 © **Gautier Deblonde** 584 © **Courtesy of Deutsche Guggenheim, Berlin, photography by Mathias Schormann** 538–543 © **Courtesy of DuPont™ Corian ®, photography by Leo Torri** 550 © **Courtesy of Established & Sons, photography by Dan Tobin Smith** 551 top © **GA Photographers, Katsumasa Tanaka** 244/245 © **Chris Gascoigne/VIEW** 226 top, 229 © **Marc Gerritsen** 249 top right © **Courtesy David Gill Galleries, photography by Michael Molloy** 568/569 © **David Grandorge** 548 © **FS GUERRA** 178, 179 top left and right, 180/181, 185, 252/253, 256 top, 257–259, 260 top right, 261 © **Courtesy of Guggenheim New York, photography by David M. Heald** 550–553 © **Roland Halbe** 148/149, 154 top, 156/157, 166, 174/175, 176, 184 bottom, 209, 232, 240/241, 243 bottom left, 267 bottom, 268/269 © **Hawkeye Aerial Photography** 288 top © **Luke Hayes** 254, 260 bottom, 374/375, 376, 559 top, 564, 570–572, 574–577 © **Hufton + Crow/VIEW** 158, 160 bottom, 163 bottom left, 280, 288 bottom, 292/293, 294, 298–301, 304, 306, 307 top left and bottom, 308, 309, 316–320, 321 bottom, 348–350, 351 top, 352 © **Werner Huthmacher** 186–188, 190 bottom, 191 top, 192–201, 204, 206 top, 208 bottom, 212, 213 top, 222/223, 227 top right and bottom, 230/231, 234 top left, 235–237, 239 top, 242 bottom © **Toshio Kaneko** 248 top, 251 top and bottom © **Farid Khayrulin** 354/355, 358 bottom, 360, 361 © **John Linden** 246, 248 bottom © **Alan McAteer** 286/287, 290, 291 © **ORCH** 562/563, 566, 567 © **Klemens Ortmeyer/fabpics** 190 top © **Cristóbal Palma** 182/183 bottom © **Christian Richters** 116/117, 122 top, 123, 125 top left and bottom, 126–129, 160 middle left, 168, 169 bottom right, 272/273, 274, 276 top, 284 top, 307 top right, 310 bottom © **Courtesy of Roca** 312/313, 314, 321 top © **Airdiasol.Rothan** 153 bottom © **Courtesy of Sawaya & Moroni** 528–531 © **Jason Schmidt** 586 © **Courtesy of Serralunga** 563 middle right © **Courtesy of Silken Hotel** 218 bottom, 219, 221 © **Barbara Sorg** 549 © **Morley von Sternberg** 31 © **David Sykes** 547 bottom © **Courtesy of Vitra, photography by Eduardo Perez** 560/561 © **Paul Warchol** 112, 113, 115 bottom, 330/331, 332, 334/335 bottom, 336 bottom, 337 top, 338 bottom right, 340, 342 top © **Isa Wipfli** 580/581, 582, 583 © **Gerald Zugmann** 532–535, 536 top left and right, 537 © **Courtesy of Zumtobel Lighting** 544, 545.

ACKNOWLEDGEMENTS

The author wishes to thank Zaha Hadid, Patrik Schumacher, Woody K. T. Yao, Roger Howie, Corinne Roberts, Davide Giordano, and Manon Janssens for their kind support and help throughout the work on this project.

IMPRINT

© 2013 TASCHEN GmbH
Hohenzollernring 53, D–50672 Köln
www.taschen.com

Design: Sense/Net, Andy Disl and Birgit Eichwede, Cologne
Project management: Florian Kobler and Inga Hallsson, Berlin
Production: Ute Wachendorf, Cologne
German translation: Kristina Brigitta Köper, Berlin
French translation: Jacques Bosser, Montesquiou

Printed in Italy
ISBN 978–3–8365–4283–8